The Advice Business

Essential Tools and Models for Management Consulting

Charles J. Fombrun
Mark D. Nevins

PEARSON

Prentice
Hall

Upper Saddle River, New Jersey 07458

Library of Congress Cataloging-in-Publication Data

Fombrun, Charles J.
 The advice business : essential tools and models for management consulting / by Charles
J. Fombrun and Mark D. Nevins.
  p. cm.
 Includes bibliographical references and index.
 ISBN 0-13-030373-9
  1. Business consultants. 2. Management. I. Nevins, Mark D. II. Title.

HD69.C6F66 2003
001´.68–dc21

2003042922

Acquisitions Editor: David Parker
Editor-in-Chief: Jeff Shelstad
Assistant Editor: Ashley Keim
Editorial Assistant: Melissa Yu
Executive Marketing Manager: Shannon Moore
Marketing Assistant: Amanda Fisher
Managing Editor (Production): John Roberts
Production Editor: Kelly Warsak
Production Assistant: Joe DeProspero
Permissions Supervisor: Suzanne Grappi
Manufacturing Buyer: Michelle Klein
Cover Design: Kiwi Design
Cover Illustration/Photo: Getty Images/Jeff Venier
Composition/Full-Service Project Management: Rainbow Graphics/Linda Begley
Printer/Binder: Hamilton Printing Company
Cover Printer: Coral Graphics

Credits and acknowledgments borrowed from other sources and reproduced, with permission, in this
textbook appear on appropriate page within text.

10 9 8 7 6 5 4 3 2 1
ISBN 0-13-030373-9

For the colleagues, clients, students, and friends who taught us the ins and outs of consulting. We hope this book rings true.

Contents

Introduction:
Of Doctors and Witch Doctors

Charles J. Fombrun and Mark D. Nevins

The film begins as darkness falls. The scene: a remote village in a thick jungle; a small, straw-covered hut; a red-dirt floor. A visibly ill, half-naked young woman lies prone on a tattered mat surrounded by concerned relatives and friends. Hovering over her is a colorfully dressed old man, face marked with paint, wearing elaborate headgear, and clutching at a plumed wand that he waves over the sobbing woman as he chants. The group follows the song; heavy drumbeats mark the rhythm of their chant, which they match by pounding their feet on the dirt. Dust flies, arms wave, the patient moans. Suddenly, her eyes open and spasms shake her body. She rises in fits and starts, her head jerking wildly from side to side. Within minutes, she stands and rocks to-and-fro with the music as the rhythmic chants envelop her. A rumbling sound comes from deep within her . . . she sways, then collapses. The chanting stops, and the woman looks up, her previously cloudy eyes wide open and now clear—she's cured!

We know these clichéd ceremonial rites all too well from movies depicting the tribal practices of ancient peoples. These rituals are just as apt to describe people today as they consult medical specialists, anticipating cure-alls to solve their health problems. They're also just as apt to describe savvy business executives when they approach management consultants: They pose as sick clients coming to a consultant for assistance, anticipating a wave of the magic wand, and poof! a cure. To the outside observer (and the client), the consultant very much resembles a witch doctor capable of redressing ills by conjuring spirits, dispelling demons, and applying magical potions to physical and emotional wounds.

In truth, practitioners of Western medicine and witch doctors have things in common—characteristics they also share with consultants. In remarkably similar ways:

- Doctors and witch doctors rely on specialized knowledge and replicable practices to address a specific client problem—as do consultants;
- Doctors and witch doctors rely on patients' cooperation and belief that the treatment will work—as do consultants;
- Doctors and witch doctors are well compensated for their work—as are consultants (often very well indeed).

So, what exactly is the value proposition consultants proffer to their clients? Why do consulting firms pay young, often inexperienced MBA students fabulous starting salaries and bonuses for their hard work and brain power? Why the consulting mystique? The answer is actually fairly simple: managers, engrossed as they are in their daily grind, are caught up in the tactical demands of their work, and often blinded to underlying strategic issues of their business. There are times—times of crisis as well as moments of opportunity—when these managers can benefit from an external perspective, unbiased advice, technical expertise and active coaching that consultants can provide—the kind of advice that can help them improve their company's profitability, ratchet up its competitiveness, unlock innovation, or drive transformational change through thick layers of bureaucracy.

The dramatic growth of the consulting industry in the last 20 years can also be traced to rapid advances in technology, which have provoked fundamental changes in the ways companies compete. Consultants provide companies facing such rapidly changing environments with important means of developing, acquiring, and processing much-needed know-how. In challenging environments, consultants can be a vital strategic weapon that companies can rely on to improve their competitiveness in a world characterized by technological convergences, strategic consolidations, growing interdependence, and a changing social contract between employer and employee.

Rapid growth has increased specialization and diversity in the consulting industry itself. Consultants today provide wide-ranging advice to managers at all levels and across most functions, including strategic planning, information systems, marketing, organization, finance, human resources, and change implementation. Indeed, consulting is big business today. Vast numbers of professional consultants work as independent specialists and entrepreneurs in solo practices or small boutiques. Many of the most prominent corporate advisors work either with large consulting firms like McKinsey & Company or as in-house staff in public companies. Whatever their business cards say, all consultants have as their compelling core purpose the imperative to help a company improve its performance.

The purpose of *The Advice Business* is to introduce readers to the art, the practice, and the problems that consultants face. We try to shed light on the complex roles that consultants and consulting firms play in enhancing the effectiveness of their clients. *The Advice Business* draws heavily on pragmatic contributions that practitioners are making in this profession. It also relies on the increasingly intertwined literatures of strategic management and organizational analysis to frame discussions and analyze problems. We hope you are inspired by the profession, and perhaps bewitched.

THE STRUCTURE OF THE BOOK

The book consists of five parts. Part I introduces the reader to the consulting industry and profiles some of the major changes taking place as the industry converges and clashes with complementary professional services offered by accounting firms and software producers. Part II examines how consultants think, and introduces readers to the approaches consultants take when they frame client situations and conceive and execute a client engagement from start to finish. Part III addresses questions of implementation: how consultants create value by helping companies implement solutions. In Part IV, we call on the expertise of specific consultants to describe representative engagements carried out with "real-world" clients; these case studies provide concrete evidence of the dialogue that takes place between concepts and practice as an engagement unfolds. Finally, Part V raises questions (and meta-questions) about the profession and professionalism: What does it mean to "be a consultant," and what key ethical, marketing, and career issues should readers keep in mind as they consider becoming advisors to corporate clients?

Figure I–1 describes the architecture of the book. You'll find much sound advice and pragmatic wisdom in these chapters—we hope you'll learn from it, whether you're a student contemplating a career in consulting or a seasoned professional looking for renewal and new ideas.

FIGURE I–1   The Advice Business

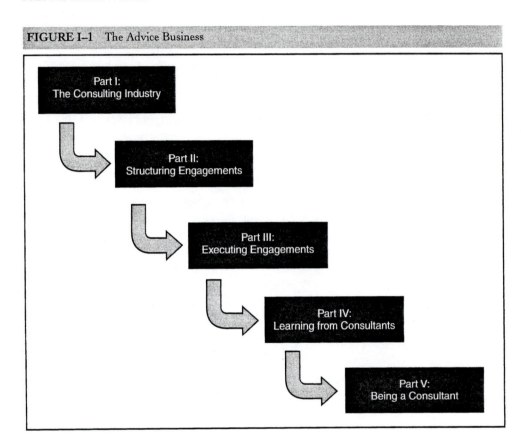

About the Authors

Charles J. Fombrun is Executive Director of the Reputation Institute and Professor Emeritus of Management at the Stern School of Business of New York University. Before discovering the social sciences, he earned a B.S. in Physics from Queen's University (Canada) and did his early research on magnetic levitation. Tired of staring at oscilloscopes in lonely labs, he turned first to mathematical economics before edging closer to the social sciences at the University of California (Berkeley) and then at Columbia University where he completed a Ph.D. in organizational theory in 1980. He was the youngest professor at the Wharton School (University of Pennsylvania) when he taught there from 1979 to 1984.

Dr. Fombrun is the author of *Strategic Human Resource Management* (1984), *Turning Points: Creating Strategic Change in Corporations* (1992), and the best-seller *Reputation: Realizing Value from the Corporate Image* (1996). He has published over 100 articles in leading research and professional journals, where he writes principally about how companies build and sustain valuable reputations, and how they should manage their resources strategically.

Dr. Fombrun's perspective on corporate reputations has made him an invited speaker at many corporate or industry gatherings and international conferences, as well as an advisor to such companies as Royal Dutch/Shell, Interpublic Group, and Amway. He has served on numerous editorial boards, including *Administrative Science Quarterly, Strategic Management Journal, Academy of Management Review, Academy of Management Journal, Human Resource Management*, and *Human Resource Planning*. In 1996, he ran into Cees van Riel, a professor at Erasmus University in the Netherlands, from which a fruitful collaboration started that has fostered executive programs, annual conferences, a quarterly journal (the *Corporate Reputation Review*), and the Reputation Institute, a private organization devoted to research, measurement, valuation, and consulting about corporate reputations.

Mark David Nevins is the President of Nevins Consulting; he is an organizational advisor and coach, and consults in the areas of organizational design and development, curriculum creation, leadership and management development, change management, and sales and client-facing effectiveness.

Prior to starting his own firm, Dr. Nevins was Global Vice President of Human Resources and Organizational Development for Korn/Ferry International, the world's leading retained executive search firm, where he drove organizational and cultural change to help the firm migrate from a private sales-focused partnership to a publicly held professional services firm. Previously, he was for many years the head of professional development and training worldwide for Booz Allen Hamilton, one of the world's leading strategy and management consulting firms, where he had responsibility for all of the firm's formal and informal training and development programs for all levels of professional staff, and was one of the drivers of the firm's HR strategy and people programs as well as primary architect of the Booz Allen Curriculum.

Dr. Nevins has consulted with large and small organizations, both public and private, for more than 15 years; he has studied leadership, management, and organizational development extensively, with a special focus in professional services firms. He is a moderator for The Aspen Institute's Executive Seminar on Values-Based Leadership, and regularly guest lectures on major business school campuses.

Prior to his career in the private sector Dr. Nevins taught at Harvard University, where he also held several administrative positions. He was graduated with honors from the College of the Holy Cross, where he studied sciences, philosophy, and literature. He took his Ph.D. in English Literature from Harvard University, during which time he received awards for his teaching, as well as scholarships for research and study in the United States and abroad. He has worked, traveled, and taught in more than 60 countries on 5 continents, and in his free time he enjoys film, wine, reading, snowboarding, and scuba diving.

Kristina Alterson is Manager of Organizational Development for DoubleClick, based in New York, with global responsibilities. Her primary focus is on the design, development, and implementation/facilitation of all new internal "people programs" for DoubleClick, including management and leadership training, performance management, and culture building and change management initiatives. She was previously Global Manager of Professional Development for Korn/Ferry International. Prior to joining Korn/Ferry, Ms. Alterson was a Consultant in the Strategic Change Practice at PricewaterhouseCoopers LLP, based in Fairfax, Virginia, and specializing in organization and change strategy. Before PwC, Ms. Alterson was a member of the Professional Development team at the strategy and management consulting firm of Booz Allen Hamilton. Ms. Alterson holds a B.S. in Human Development and Family Studies from Cornell University, and has completed course work toward an M.A. in Organizational Psychology at Columbia University. When not working, she enjoys reading good books and traveling to interesting places.

Carol Ballock is a Managing Director in Burson-Marsteller's Corporate Practice in New York, where she specializes in corporate and employer reputation, new CEO positioning, thought leadership, and corporate change communications. Prior to joining Burson in May 2000, she was a director of global thought leadership at PricewaterhouseCoopers, one of the world's largest professional services firms, responsible for driving initiatives that demonstrated the firm's command of issues that "keep CEOs awake at night." For more than a decade, Carol has worked with CEOs to help them craft the messages that create their strategies for the future. She started her executive communications career at Westinghouse headquarters in Pittsburgh. She then joined GE Capital Services, where she was responsible for planning and executing internal communications to the company's 34,000 employees in 24 businesses around the globe. Prior to the merger of PricewaterhouseCoopers, she was Global Communications Director for the Office of the Chairman of Coopers & Lybrand, one of the predecessor firms. Carol graduated *summa cum laude* from the University of Pittsburgh and received a master's degree in management from Carnegie-Mellon University. She also studied law at Duquesne University. Ever curious, consulting is the best career choice Carol has made to date: "Consulting is a license to get inside of people's minds, which is where the future of business resides," she says. Making sense of the golden nuggets of wisdom, Carol finds there is where she believes she contributes the most value to her clients. It fits with her personal and professional motto, "Give up the search, you die."

Deborah Baxley is a Managing Principal and leader in the Banking Strategy and Change practice within IBM Business Innovation Services. She specializes in applying information technologies for strategic competitive advantage and has in-depth experience in credit cards, retail financial services and customer relationship management.

Ms. Baxley leads IBM's 200-strong "Credit Card Virtual Team" of services, sales, development, and research professionals from 12 countries around the world who continuously collaborate on issues and insights of interest to the credit card industry.

Ms. Baxley is well known and sought after globally as IBM's top credit card expert and is well versed in both business and technology issues and trends. She regularly speaks with top executives in the world's largest credit card firms and is part of IBM's solution definition team for the payments and credit card business and a leader in defining IBM's credit card strategy for IBM China.

When IBM entered the consulting field, Ms. Baxley developed its curriculum for consulting education and taught over 1,000 IBMers from 15 countries. She is a leader among the IBM "Thought Leadership" team for retail banking, credit cards, and customer loyalty. She has addressed the CEOs and top executives of dozens of major North and South American and Asian banks and financial services firms on which business models will emerge, particularly in retail banking, credit cards, and customer loyalty.

She authored several articles and book chapters, including "The Great Divide: Loyal Customers Will Determine the Winners from the Losers in Tomorrow's Financial Services Industry" in *World Markets*, and "Mastering the Networked Economy," in IBM's *Thought Starter*." She has addressed the American Bankers Association on topics including Customer Loyalty best practices and readiness for electronic commerce.

Ms. Baxley received a B.S. degree in mathematics from the University of Oklahoma, and studied for a master of applied science in computer science at Florida Atlantic University.

In her spare time, Ms. Baxley likes to use her frequent flyer miles on exotic vacations with her husband, who is a full-time politician.

Deon Binneman is Managing Partner of Repucomm. He has a strong commitment to raising awareness of reputation as a business asset. He is an expert on how corporate and individual reputations are created, maintained, and enhanced. At Repucomm, he has spoken to numerous management audiences and counseled CEOs on the impact of their reputation on corporate image, financial performance, and employee and stakeholder loyalty.

Mr. Binneman has extensive experience in the areas of training and development, communications, public affairs, public relations, organizational development, and entrepreneurial development consulting and marketing.

Prior to starting Repucomm in 1994, Mr. Binneman was an Internal Organization Development Consultant where he was responsible for advising and consulting to six business units on external and internal communications, human capital development and management of change. Mr. Binneman was also a principal architect of the Small Business Development Training Services (South Africa's pioneer SBA). He was instrumental in the development and facilitation of the "How to Run a Small Business" program, now in its sixth edition, which has been attended by more than 15,000 entrepreneurs.

Mr. Binneman is a graduate of Henley Management College and the Graduate Institute of Management and Technology and the Port Elizabeth Technikon and holds qualifications in Public Relations, General Management, Strategic Human Resources Development, and Occupational Health and Safety. He is professionally registered as a Chartered Public Relations Practitioner with the Public Relations Institute of Southern Africa and as a Specialist Practitioner in Training and Development. He is a Certified Small Business trainer, and an instructor and facilitator for numerous organizations, including QMS Scott-Safe—an occupational health and safety consultancy. The

Chartered Institute of Management Accountants, the Public Relations Institute of Southern Africa, the National Electronic Media Institute of Southern Africa, and Marcus Evans (Ex-International Communications in Management, a division of the international THG Worldwide Group, one of the world's largest players in event management and business strategy creation). He serves on the Executive Advisory Panel of PR Management Education for the Wits Technikon and regularly lectures at local universities on Organizational Development and Communication topics. He is widely sought by conference organizers as a chairperson or keynote speaker for large international or local business conferences on issues relating to reputation and strategic management.

Not only is he a management and public relations consultant, he is also a professional trainer who has developed and facilitated more than 50 types of training products and change interventions, ranging from programs on how to run your own business and strategic planning sessions to coaching skills and integrated communications programs.

Mr. Binneman's consultancy business, Repucomm, operates out of Johannesburg, South Africa. It provides reputational risk consulting services; strategic PR and communications counseling; and speaking, training, and facilitation services that aid strategic communication and PR interventions. Repucomm is one of the South African Government's GCIS (Government Communication Information System) preferred service providers. He has trained and counseled government ministers on media relations. He is well known for his "Marketing Your Practice" workshops that teach consultants how to market and promote their professional consulting services.

Mr. Binneman has provided management and corporate communication consulting and training for many corporations and nonprofit organizations in both South Africa and abroad over the past 20 years. The workshops that he provides range from Managing Reputation to Media Survival Skills to Writing Effective Business Plans. He has written many published articles, and is the author of various articles for both academic and managerial journals. His electronic newsletter, *Powerlines*, is read by readers from Canada to India.

Mikelle A. Calhoun is an Assistant Professor at Valparaiso University while also working on her dissertation to complete the requirements for a Ph.D. from the Stern School of Business, New York University. Her areas of concentration are Management and International Business. Before entering the academic field, Ms. Calhoun was a commercial litigation attorney and, briefly, a Civil District Court Master in Dallas, Texas. She received her B.A. in Communications Studies from Pennsylvania State University and an M.A. in Speech Communications from the University of Minnesota. She later received a joint J.D./M.B.A. degree from the University of North Carolina. As an attorney, Ms. Calhoun worked with senior executives of international firms and *Fortune* 500 companies on a variety of litigation matters that exposed her to technical and often sensitive internal issues. In the courtroom, she worked to present her company clients in the most effective light possible—thus allowing their side of the story to be delivered and accepted. As a Civil District Court Master, she presided over many corporate disputes—adding to her experience with and understanding of the impact of a variety of corporate decisions and events.

Ron Carucci is a Partner with Mercer-Delta Consulting, LLC, a management consulting firm that provides services related to the management of strategic organizational change to major corporations. He works in the areas of executive leadership, building executive teams, strategy formulation and implementation, and large-scale organizational and culture change.

Prior to working at Mercer-Delta, Mr. Carucci previously managed his own consulting practice specializing in aligning and implementing organizational change initiatives in the financial services, consumer products, and information technology industries. He worked on several large-scale merger integrations and subsequent culture change initiatives in the pharmaceutical industry. He has also held executive positions in several *Fortune* 100 organizations leading internal human resource consulting and change management functions.

Most recently, Mr. Carucci has been working with CEOs of both large enterprises as well as start-up organizations on the challenges of managing rapid growth in consolidating industries, as well as on how to swiftly move into e-business space. He has helped organizations rearchitect themselves for global scale-up, e-commerce, and to build appropriate talent-pipeline strategies to ensure the effective selection, development, retention, and reward of key leaders of major growth businesses. He is a faculty member at Fordham University Graduate School, serving as an associate professor of organizational behavior in the Human Resource Education program.

He is co-author of the book, *The Value Creating Consultant: How to Build and Sustain Lasting Client Relationships* (2000), as well as the book *Relationships that Enable Enterprise Change: Leveraging the Client–Consultant Connection* (2002).

Kevin P. Cone is a director in McKinsey's Atlanta office.

Chuck Durrant has 30 years of business experience with 22 years of being behind the business desk and 8 years of providing consulting services. As a business leader, he has been responsible for building and leading marketing teams primarily supporting the financial services industry in their planning and use of information technology. In his last marketing position, he created a financial services office for IBM that resulted in over a quarter billion dollars in revenue annually. This business perspective helped to create a solid understanding of business opportunities and challenges, and the value that information technology may provide.

For the past 8 years, Mr. Durrant has been working with both senior business leadership and chief information officers creating ways to unlock the power of information technology. Senior business leaders still struggle with ensuring that they receive a high return on investment from the promise of technology. It is in this context that information technology strategic planning can bring the alignment of business strategy and information technology strategic plans. Over the last two years, Mr. Durrant has further extended his consulting reach by focusing on merger and acquisition information technology integration planning on a global basis. The result has been a broadening of his client base to include several major European financial services companies. However, the lessons from information technology strategic planning have remained constant.

Mr. Durrant received a B.S. degree from Ohio State University and an M.B.A. from Capital University and has been a regular speaker at business planning seminars.

Soam Goel, a member of PA Consulting Management Group has consulted to energy companies in eight different countries. He has conceived, designed, and led a variety of consulting assignments, including strategy development, restructuring, planning and implementation, mergers and acquisitions, breakup/spin-off value analysis, organization design, and operations improvement. He leads the firm's e-commerce efforts in the energy industry. He also leads the PA venture dedicated to developing a digital marketplace for the utility industry. Prior to joining PA Consulting, Mr. Goel worked for UMS Group, Inc. and the Unilever Group of Companies. He has a B.S. in Chemical

Engineering and an MBA from the University of Texas at Austin. His role with Unilever as an internal consultant got him started in a consulting career with a strong focus on tangible value creation. When not consulting, his primary interests are reading, travel, photography, cricket, and golf.

A. Cowpland Harris is Robert D. Lilien's partner in Lilien Communications. Based in Boston, her particular areas of expertise include the consulting, biotech, and high-tech industries. Her background as president and cofounder of an international mail order business informs much of her teaching. She has presented to audiences of all sizes; appeared on national U.S. and French television; and was featured in *BusinessWeek* and the *Wall Street Journal* and in syndicated columns in newspapers all over the United States. She attended Tufts, UMass/Boston and the University of Missouri, where she majored in Speech and Drama, English, and French.

Ms. Harris and Mr. Lilien have taught worldwide: Europe, the Middle East, Asia, South America and throughout the United States.

Craig Hart is a consultant in PA Consulting Group's Energy Practice. Prior to consulting, he worked in the environmental industry before returning to Yale University, where he graduated with an M.B.A. from the Yale School of Management and an M.E.S. from the Yale School of Forestry and Environmental Studies. With an interest in environmental strategy, he was drawn to consulting to the energy industry given the numerous environmental issues faced by energy clients. Mr. Hart has worked on a variety of projects in the industry ranging from strategy development for an unregulated subsidiary of a major utility holding company to competitive analysis for an e-commerce start-up. He has also worked on several distributed generation projects, where he assisted the client with financial analysis and strategic planning. Outside of work, Mr. Hart enjoys mountaineering, running, kayaking, and windsurfing.

Daniel R. Idzik joined Booz Allen Hamilton, Inc. in 1967. He served as General Counsel, working with four Booz Allen chairmen, from 1972 until his retirement in 1998. During this time, he oversaw numerous corporate reorganizations, acquisitions and divestitures, executive compensation plans, international transactions, and other issues common to global management consulting firms. He is the principal author of the Booz Allen "Statement of Professional Policies and Practices," as well as the firm's Statement of Governance, and had a leadership role in the development of all the firm's corporate policies. Mr. Idzik has lectured extensively and conducted seminars related to corporate and professional ethics and responsibilities. Prior to joining Booz Allen, and after graduating from Harvard Law School, Mr. Idzik was a corporate attorney in a Buffalo, New York, law firm. He has balanced his professional life by serving in leadership positions with several regional and national arts organizations.

Timothy M. Laseter, a Vice President at Booz Allen Hamilton, founded the firm's global network of sourcing practitioners. Additionally, he serves on the firm's e-Business Core Team, providing thought leadership in e-Business Operations. Mr. Laseter has helped companies build organizational capabilities in a wide range of operational areas. His extensive experience covers the United States, Europe, South America, and the Pacific Rim, plus industries ranging from aerospace, automotive, consumer goods, communications, electronics, financial services, industrial equipment, natural resources, retail to textiles.

Mr. Laseter authored the book *Balanced Sourcing: Cooperation & Competition in Supplier Relationships.* He is also a regular contributor to *strategy + business,*

Purchasing Today, and *Purchasing* magazines and quoted in a host of periodicals rang-ing from the *Wall Street Journal, Industry Standard, Progressive Grocer*, and *Advertising Age* to *The New Yorker*.

Prior to joining Booz Allen, Mr. Laseter worked for Siecor Corporation, a manu-facturer of fiber-optic cable for the communications industry. He received his M.B.A. from the Darden School at the University of Virginia and earned the Faculty Award for Academic Excellence. He graduated with high honors from the Georgia Institute of Technology with a B.S. in Industrial Management. Currently, he is pursuing a doctorate in Operations Management at the Darden School on a part-time basis.

Mr. Laseter was certified at the Fellow level by the American Production and Inventory Control Society and has been certified as a Quality Engineer by the American Society for Quality Control. Also, Mr. Laseter received Booz Allen Hamilton's 1990 Professional Excellence Award.

Robert L. Laud is currently affiliated with Deloitte Consulting. Previously, he was Global Managing Partner, Center for Innovation at Andersen, where he was respon-sible for creating the Center and directing solution development, intelligence, research, commercialization, and building brand through thought leadership. He brings an uncommon blend of entrepreneurial, consulting, and academic experience to both his clients and innovation activities. Mr. Laud also served as Chief Performance Officer and VP Business Development for a Silicon Valley technology-based spin-off of SRI (Stanford Research Institute). Prior to this, he was a partner at Andersen Consulting (now Accenture) where he served as Worldwide Director for Organization Change services, was the lead Change Management partner on five of the firm's largest accounts, served as an advisor during the firm's 1998 restructuring, and authored the firm's signature program in IT Transformation. His initial interest in consulting was developed when he served on the business faculty of two universi-ties early in his career. He is a frequent contributor to professional journals, maga-zines, and books, and served on the Editorial Advisory Board for the *OD Practitioner*. Mr. Laud received his Ph.D. from Columbia University, M.B.A. from Adelphi University, and B.A. from Colgate University. He enjoys spending time with his family and their Alaskan malamutes, and is involved in wildlife preservation and predator reintroduction.

Robert D. Lilien founded Lilien Communications in 1995. He had been Senior Vice President at Communispond, Inc., an international training company, where he helped develop many of their top training programs. He also taught thousands of business exec-utives and developed an unparalleled expertise in helping companies to launch initial public offerings.

Mr. Lilien's business career started at Procter & Gamble, and continued at American Home Products and J. Walter Thompson, where as Vice President he man-aged the Media Department and then the Corporate Communications Group. A gradu-ate of Andover and Princeton, he holds an A.B. in English literature. He works for New York City.

David Maister has been a consultant to prominent firms in a broad spectrum of profes-sions for two decades, covering all strategic and managerial issues. Even though he is a solo practitioner, he has a global practice, working in over 15 countries in any given year. All of his books, *Managing the Professional Service Firm* (1993), *True Professionalism* (1997), *The Trusted Advisor* (2000), and *Practice What You Preach*

(2001), are written for and about consulting firms and other professional firms, and have been translated into 10 languages. His books (or portions thereof) are widely used as training materials in major consulting firms around the world. A native of Great Britain, Mr. Maister holds degrees from the University of Birmingham, the London School of Economics, and the Harvard Business School, where he was a professor for seven years. He is still amazed that people sometimes actually listen to him and take his advice, and that it is really possible to get paid for doing what you truly love to do.

Pedro Masetto is a consultant with Ernst & Young. Until 2002 he was an experienced risk-consulting manager working for Arthur Andersen's Financial and Commodity Risk Consulting practice out of Chicago. Mr. Masetto is recognized as an expert in the structural design of trading activities, including front-, middle-, and back-office operations. He has helped global financial institutions and major energy and utilities companies improve their risk management capabilities, including risk measurement methods, policies, oversight structures, and various market risk management processes. Before joining Arthur Andersen, Mr. Masetto had a leading role in various initiatives to develop and enrich various financial systems, including the creation of the Mexican Derivatives Exchange (MexDer) and the negotiation of strategic agreements between the Chicago Mercantile Exchange and the Chicago Board Options Exchange with Mexico's BMV. Mr. Masetto obtained his M.P.P. in Finance and Regulation from the University of Chicago and his B.S. in Management from El Colegio de Mexico. He has been a Teaching Fellow of Finance and Applied Microeconomics at the Center for Economic Research (CIDE) in Mexico and has presented various risk management topics at international conferences. Mr. Masetto is a certified derivatives trader.

Douglas M. McCracken, Chief Executive Officer of Deloitte Consulting, has been a leader of the consulting industry for more than 20 years. In addition to the many leadership roles he has played within Deloitte Consulting and its predecessor firms, he has served a wide variety of clients in industries ranging from manufacturing to information technology, focusing on improving competitiveness and effectiveness. In 1999, Mr. McCracken was named by *Consulting* magazine to its list of "Top Ten Most Influential Consultants." In the same year, the *Larry King Cardiac Foundation* named him "Man of the Year."

Mr. McCracken joined the consulting practice of Touche Ross in 1977 in Detroit. He was promoted to partner in 1982 and five years later, he became leader of the Detroit consulting practice. In 1991, he was appointed managing partner of the firm's Boston consulting practice and for the next several years he played a key role in the development and implementation of the globalization strategy for Deloitte Consulting. In 1996, Mr. McCracken assumed the role as Managing Director–Americas, and in 1999, he was elected Chairman of the Board of Deloitte & Touche USA. In February 2000, he was elected Chief Executive Officer of Deloitte Consulting and assumed that role on June 1.

Mr. McCracken has been a member of the Board of Directors of Deloitte & Touche since 1995 and a member of the Board of Directors of Deloitte Consulting since its inception in 1996. He also is a member of Deloitte Touche Tohmatsu Board of Directors.

Mr. McCracken is a board member of the Lincoln Center Consolidated Corporate Fund. He has been active in many cultural and community organizations, serving on a number of boards of directors. He is a Certified Management Consultant and a member of the Institute of Management Consultants.

Mr. McCracken holds a bachelor of arts degree in economics from Norwich University. He also holds a master of arts degree in Economics from Northeastern University and a master of science degree in Management from Rensselaer Polytechnic Institute.

Mr. McCracken and his wife, Naomi, have a son and a daughter, Doug and Kristi. They reside in Wellesley, Massachusetts.

Scott Meyer, is former Chief Strategic Officer of Weber Shandwick Worldwide, where he led the strategic planning efforts for the world's leading public relations firm and its expanding portfolio of global clients. He also is the architect of WSW's suite of reputation-based programs. With more than 30 years in communications, he is viewed as one of the top strategic thinkers in the public relations industry. He is a strong believer in values-based, community-involved, and people-centered organizations.

Mr. Meyer's background includes corporate experience with Piper Jaffray Companies, International Multifoods, US Bank, and Control Data Corporation. He was a founder of the highly respected Minneapolis-based public relations firm, Mona Meyer McGrath & Gavin. The firm was sold to Shandwick International in 1989. Meyer went on to assume several management positions with Shandwick before being named Chief Executive Officer in 1999. He guided the firm to the number two ranking worldwide, before it merged with its sister company, The Weber Group, in January 2001, to form Weber Shandwick Worldwide.

A journalism graduate of the University of Minnesota, Meyer is a strong believer in education, having taught on the adjunct journalism faculties at both the University of Minnesota and the University of St. Thomas. A dedicated grandfather who enjoys the outdoors, politics, reading, film, and the theater, Meyer divides his time among residences in New York City and Saint Paul and Ely, Minnesota.

José E. Molina is now a partner at Ernst & Young. Before that, he was Arthur Andersen's Financial and Commodity Risk Consulting (FCRC) Managing Partner for Latin America. Mr. Molina has had significant international experience in financial and risk management engineering, including energy risk management consulting and price/financial risk management. Mr. Molina has led numerous engagements in risk management finance function restructuring and business process improvement in the United States, Europe, and Latin America. Mr. Molina is currently advising some of the top Latin American corporations and financial institutions in the implementation of Enterprise-Wide Risk Management infrastructures, which includes putting into action how Internal Audit interacts with Compliance and Chief Risk Officer functions. Mr. Molina has conducted seminars and conferences on the financial services industry and risk management themes in the United States and internationally. Mr. Molina has published several articles in specialized international publications on financial risk management design and related implementation issues. Mr. Molina holds a master's degree in Business and Economics from the University of Sevilla (Spain). He is a member of Spain's ICAC (Certified Public Accountants of Spain), REA (Economics and Audit Institute of Spain), and GARP (Global Association of Risk Professionals).

Gloria Moon has several years of broad management consulting experience. Her specialty is the energy industry, although she has served clients across several industries. Gloria became particularly interested in the energy sector because of the dynamic atmosphere created by industry deregulation. In dealing with challenging restructuring issues, she has leveraged her background in economics and public policy. Gloria holds a bachelor's degree in economics and government from Cornell University and a master's degree in Public Administration from the Cornell Institute of Public Affairs.

Robert A. Neiman began his career as a mechanical engineer. After several years in industry he found himself getting into management, but without knowing much about it. Curious, he took a leave of absence and went to the Harvard Business School to see if there was anything new to be learned. There, as the saying goes, his life changed forever.

Getting a good introduction to the social sciences as well as management, he saw a great opportunity—putting together some of the ideas of the social scientists with the very practical challenges of running businesses.

He took some of this new learning back to his old employer and, despite a lot of skepticism at first, created a new goal-setting process, which generated a raft of operations improvements and payoff and got a lot of people excited. He didn't know it at the time, but that was his first consulting engagement.

At the same time, he met Bob Schaffer, an ambitious Ph.D. in Industrial Psychology, who wanted to start a new kind of consulting firm. And there began a collaboration that continues to this day—over 30 years later.

The firm, Robert H. Schaffer & Associates, is headquartered in Stamford, Connecticut, with offices in Toronto and Montreal as well. There are 17 Senior Consultants, working with corporations such as Citicorp, GE, Johnson & Johnson, Zurich Financial Services; government agencies such as the state of Washington, the World Bank, and the State of Connecticut; and many others. The firm is well known for its success helping leadership companies and consultants create bottom-line "breakthrough" payoff and building high-performance organizations and management. Bob Neiman himself has led performance improvement and strategic change efforts in electronics, chemicals, public utilities and financial services industries, hospitals, education institutions, and government agencies, as well as working with both consulting firms and internal consultants.

Charles A. ("Terry") Nichols, III is a manager of Professional Development in the commercial consulting business of Booz Allen Hamilton. He designs, develops, and delivers programs for the worldwide consulting staff at all levels in the firm in topics ranging from core consulting skills to leadership. Before joining Booz Allen, Mr. Nichols did graduate work in philosophy at Harvard University, and was a Graduate Fellow in the Harvard Program in Ethics and the Professions. While a graduate student, he was also a Research Associate at Harvard Business School, where he wrote numerous business cases and teaching notes in business ethics and finance. Before his graduate studies, he worked as an actuarial consultant for Ernst & Young, where his work included designing and delivering seminars in actuarial concepts and GAAP accounting for insurance companies. He has qualified both as a certified public accountant and as a Fellow in the Society of Actuaries. He received his undergraduate degree in philosophy from Harvard College.

Mr. Nichols lives with his wife Donna, an attorney, and their two cats, Ellery and Dana, in Cambridge. In his spare time, he is an omnivorous reader, and he and his wife enjoy traveling together.

Daniel F. Oriesek is an Associate with Booz Allen Hamilton in Zurich, Switzerland. Prior to joining Booz Allen Hamilton, Mr. Oriesek was a financial analyst with UBS Brinson in New York, and prior to that he worked in several functions for the former

Union Bank of Switzerland in Zurich. Mr. Oriesek holds a B.S. degree in Management from City University in Zurich and an M.B.A. from the Stern School of Business at New York University, where he majored in Management and Marketing with a specialization in Consulting and the Digital Economy. Mr. Oriesek's project work at Booz Allen Hamilton included a large-scale change program for a high-tech company, designing a risk management methodology for an insurance company, blueprinting new reporting structures for a telecommunications company, and the development of an incentive system to support the transition from old to new organizational structures.

John C. Scott is an international business consultant currently at IBM. He has worked for NCR, IBM, Intel, Saudi Arabian Airlines, Pepsi, Morrison-Knudsen, Ralph E. Parsons, Daniel International, Reza Investments, and a number of other companies throughout the world. These locations include Saudi Arabia, Holland, Thailand, India, the Philippines, Argentina, Uruguay, Canada, and all points of the United States from Anchorage, Alaska, to Brownsville, Texas. His specialty is software development and software development management, but he has recently delved into business modeling and business architecture. This resulted from a strong conviction that project managers will not be measured by "on-time, in-budget" projects, but will also be measured by the degree to which an application meets its business goals. His best products to-date are his son, Harrison Potter Scott, and two daughters, Gabriella Esther Scott and Mathilda Rose Scott. His greatest accomplishment has been to keep his wife Katie happy enough not to leave during long and remote consulting engagements. His home is in Easton, Pennsylvania.

Mr. Scott's formal credentials include B.B.A. International Business, American University of Beirut (1971) and A.A.S. Data Processing, Kansas (1985). His consulting experience includes IBM Charlotte–Banking Products Division; Morrison-Knudsen, MKSAC, in Project Management Systems for the world's largest construction project; Parsons-Daniel, in Predictive Preventative Maintenance; Boston Company, Institution Brokerage Estimation; Home Savings Bank, Mortgage Backed Securities Analysis; PepsiCo, Year 2000; Saudi Arabian Airlines, Software Quality Assurance; and Reza Investments, Competitive Government Contracting.

Mr. Scott's interests include reading, writing, discovery of new ways of doing things, business model and business proposal evaluation, and merger and acquisition technical due diligence. His family has sponsored 13 Bosnian refugees over the last year.

Somu Subramaniam is a director in McKinsey's New York office.

Toby J. Tetenbaum is President of Toby Tetenbaum Associates, a consulting firm specializing in organizational behavior. Her clients include DuPont, Ethicon (J&J), Exxon, Forbes, Gartner Group, Merrill Lynch, Sun Microsystems, and UBS Paine Webber. A licensed psychologist, she is a professor at Fordham University where she directs the Human Resource Education Master's Degree Program. She was also an Adjunct Professor in the Human Performance Technology doctoral program at the University of Southern California. Dr. Tetenbaum received her doctorate from New York University in Educational Psychology. Her postdoctoral studies at Harvard University focused on the interface between organizational behavior and management. She is co-author of *The Value-Creating Consultant* (2000) and author of numerous articles in professional journals.

Peter Thies is a Partner with Mercer Delta Consulting, a management consulting firm offering strategic change services to CEOs and senior executives in major corporations.

His client work has spanned a number of areas, including organizational design/architecture, executive team development, governance design, succession planning, and merger/acquisition integration. He has worked with CEOs and senior executives in global *Fortune* 500 corporations, particularly those in the consumer products, high-technology, and professional services industries.

Dr. Thies has published numerous articles on the topics of CEO effectiveness, culture change, executive team effectiveness, and change implementation.

Before joining Mercer Delta in 1994, Dr. Thies worked in the Change Management Practice of Andersen Consulting's New York office. Prior to that, he was an Adjunct Professor of Organizational Behavior at Rensselaer Polytechnic Institute's School of Management and managed an independent organization development practice.

Peter holds a Ph.D. and an M.B.A. in Organizational Behavior from Rensselaer Polytechnic Institute, an M.S. in Educational Psychology from the University of Pennsylvania, and a B.A. in Psychology from SUNY Albany.

When not working with clients in North America, Europe, and Latin America, he enjoys spending time with his wife and three children. He enjoys coaching soccer, playing golf (badly), and drumming in a local rock band.

Elise Walton is a partner at the Mercer Delta Consulting Group, specializing in the practice areas of change management, executive teams, global strategy, organization design, and quality. Her recent projects include: identifying the strategic global design choices for a *Fortune* 100 company; realigning a $25 billion business unit around changed market needs; design and implementation of a new activist corporate center for a *Fortune* 100 oil company; design and deployment of the new ventures unit of a top-tier oil company; realignment of the executive team of a major brokerage firm around a new industry strategies; restructuring a *Fortune* 100 corporation, from functional to business units; and realignment of a professional services firm around a new set of offerings and new clients.

Dr. Walton has authored several books and book chapters on the topics of discontinuous change and increasing executive team effectiveness. She has taught in the executive M.B.A. programs of Columbia University and the NYU Stern School. She has an active speaking practice including talks for the Conference Board, the Planning Forum, the Human Resource Planning Society, and individual companies.

Prior to joining Mercer Delta, Dr. Walton was an independent consultant working with clients such as Merrill Lynch, Becton Dickinson, BBDO, and Citibank. Dr. Walton also has experience in Russia and Eastern European countries, and participated in a joint venture between Harvard Business School and the Soviet Institute for International Economics to assess and compare management practices. She also worked for the Yugoslav Investment Bank and the Yugoslav Foreign Trade Research Institute.

Dr. Walton holds a B.A. from Bowdoin College, an M.A. from Columbia University, and a Ph.D. from Harvard Business School.

PART

I

The Consulting Industry

The consulting industry enjoyed extraordinary growth between 1980 and 2000, riding a wave of technological developments brought on by computerization, Internet penetration, and the ripple effects they provoked throughout the economy. When the Internet bubble burst in 2000, consulting firms entered a new era of uncertainty and slowdown. Since then, many boutique firms have come and gone, some venerable firms have disappeared, and most of the remaining firms have had to make drastic changes to weather the economic downturn. Although overall spending on consulting has declined since 2000, the profession has been resilient enough to survive, and no one doubts that it will pick up again as the economy picks up.

The story of the growth of the consulting industry is a fascinating one, and it is the subject of Chapter 1, written by Charles Fombrun and Daniel Oriesek. That growth has been fueled by a generation of newly minted MBAs, as well as by a series of restructurings in the private sector over the last 20 years that produced large numbers of senior managers who found themselves courted by consulting firms for their industry expertise. The growth was also aided by consolidations among various professional service firms, particularly accounting firms and software developers. The top-end firms today are those able to generate the highest revenues per consultant—not coincidentally, these are the strategy firms (led by McKinsey & Company) whose work is heavily customized.

Consulting guru David Maister takes up where Chapter 1 leaves off. He explains the differences among consulting firms by examining those factors that build profitability for a consulting firm. Drawing on his early work in this area, David shows how successful consulting firms rely on "leverage" to build profits: They hire platoons of junior consultants that they bill out at hefty rates to do visionary work shaped by senior partners. He describes different types of consulting practice and draws valuable inferences about the way each firm is structured, the kind of work they do, and the cultures likely to develop in firms that emphasize diagnosis over execution, or favor low versus high contact with clients.

How do consulting firms survive? By developing a base of applied knowledge in a specialized field and building reputation for it. In Chapter 3, Carol Ballock examines the "thought leadership" function via which consulting firms achieve distinctiveness in the marketplace. What is it that a consulting firm wants to be known for, and how does that firm get there? Carol's chapter raises the bar by asking how a consulting firm, driven as it is by pressures to minimize overhead costs (and hence research) as well as by the need to leverage junior staff, can continue to renew itself with new ideas and create knowledge capital.

Thought leadership is very much on Bob Laud's mind as well: In Chapter 4, he describes how innovation acts as a growth engine for consulting firms. Bob explores how consultants and consulting firms codify new knowledge and methodologies; how they manage that intellectual capital; how they work with their clients to add value; and how positive results create brand and reputation that are often of more value to the consultants than their fees. How should consulting firms drive and accommodate innovation? How should markets value it? These are some of the key questions Bob addresses, and that consultants will have to address in the future.

We conclude Part I with a forward-looking chapter by Douglas McCracken, who offers a bird's-eye view of the consulting business and speculates about what's likely to happen to the industry in the coming years. Particularly fascinating are his views on the increasing importance for consulting firms of stakeholder relationship management, "speed learning" and agility, and strong corporate cultures. Whatever happens in the future—and the last few years make guessing quite difficult—the victors in any "consulting wars" will be those most capable of building strategy from chaos, identifying and attracting hard-to-find talent, and capitalizing on "relationship portfolios."

CHAPTER 1

The Advice Business:
The Industry of Consulting

Charles J. Fombrun and Daniel F. Oriesek

When polled, business school graduates generally say they most want to work for a consulting firm. While dot-coms had their day and the elite investment banks always place high, it's the major consulting firms that typically dominate the "most desired employers" list among business schools—and the firms themselves are quite competitive about their "share of mind" on business school campuses. A recent survey of employment preferences conducted among MBA students showed:

- Consulting ranked number 1, with five of the top ten favorite employers being McKinsey, Bain, Boston Consulting Group, Booz Allen Hamilton, and Accenture.
- Investment banking came in second, with perennial favorites Goldman Sachs and MorganStanleyDeanWitter at the top of the list.
- A few "traditional" companies and technology companies (such as Cisco Systems, Hewlett-Packard, and Intel) known for their cultures of training and rapid promotion rounded out the top ten.

The favored status of consulting among MBA students has held true for years, since it replaced investment banking in the late 1980s. True, the consulting sector briefly lost ground in the late 1990s as the dot-com craze attracted many to the entrepreneurial environments of initial public offering (IPO)-bound high-tech start-ups. But back it came in early 2000 as the Internet bubble burst, leaving all too many high flyers in the lurch, coveting the job security and steady incomes of the old economy.

In one way or another, all of the top firms favored by MBA students are in "The Advice Business": They provide counsel to corporate clients about best management practices, about technology choices, and about investment strategies. They require advisors skilled at diagnosing a client's situation, solving problems, and implementing solutions—the very heart and soul of "consulting to management."

Charles J. Fombrun is Executive Director of the Reputation Institute and Professor of Management at the Stern School of Business of New York University. Mr. Fombrun earned a B.S. in Physics from Queen's University (Canada) and completed a Ph.D. in organizational theory at Columbia University in 1980.

Daniel F. Oriesek is an Associate with Booz Allen Hamilton in Zurich Switzerland. Mr. Oriesek holds a Bachelor of Science Degree in Management from City University in Zurich and an MBA from the Stern School of Business at New York University, where he majored in Management and Marketing with a specialization in Consulting and the Digital Economy.

WHY IS THE ADVICE BUSINESS SO HOT?

Four kinds of strategic issues have been forcing companies to rethink how they operate and increasing demand for external advisors, particularly for management consultants:

1. *Technological Forces:* Companies are experiencing the effects of increased connectivity among employees, directly with customers, and all along the value chain. Increased connectivity is made possible by the widespread availability of the Internet, by developments in wireless communications, and by the multiplicative effects of miniaturization on computing power.

2. *Economic Forces:* Companies are struggling to compete with ever more sophisticated and aggressive rivals. The removal of trade barriers has created vast open markets in North America, Europe, and the East — giving substance to companies' demands for global strategies, global operations, and the organization structures they imply.

3. *Social Forces:* With growth and globalization have come diversity, personal choice, and the need to tailor corporate practices to the demands of a diversified workforce. Dual-career families, home offices, and virtual workplaces are changing corporate cultures in dramatic ways, with vast implications for the design of benefit plans, compensation practices, and the internal systems to support them.

4. *Political Forces:* With diversity has come a multiplicity of demands on companies from the diverse stakeholders with which they interact. Accountability requires corporate responsiveness, not only to the requirements of customers, investors, and employees, but also to the expectations of governments, regulators, activists, and the general public. Stakeholder pressure induces companies to adopt agendas that often take them far afield from their core competencies, be it in addressing environmental issues or societal issues.

Jointly, these converging forces have put significant pressure on companies to change — pressures that often stretch the abilities of incumbent managers to carry them out. Hence the need for strategic and tactical advisors who can help managers understand the ways in which these forces apply to their unique business situations by examining:

a. *Strategic Implications:* How should companies position their offerings, businesses, and corporate portfolios to take advantage of marketplace developments?

b. *Operational Implications:* What organizational structures, systems, and practices are appropriate to carry out these strategies?

c. *Change Implications:* What developmental processes are needed for companies to get from here to there?

To address these implications, managers regularly turn to top consulting firms — the leaders in the advice business.

THE WORLD'S TOP ADVISORS

The boundaries of the advice business are not well defined. The terms *advisor* and *consultant* are in widespread use, yet mean little in terms of formal qualifications. Numerous self-employed and specialized practitioners from all industry sectors often refer to themselves as "consultants," in which roles they share knowledge and proffer advice to clients. Despite ad-hoc attempts to form associations among consultants, there are still today no universally recognized accreditation bodies to license consultants, nor is there an examining body or professional association that actively governs the industry's activities. The facts may explain why the major consulting firms have largely canonized the MBA degree as the rite of passage and the MBA curriculum as the body of knowledge vital to the success of professional management consultants.

By *management consulting* we mean advice-giving to companies provided by trained professionals who help managers solve operational and strategic problems through application of knowledge and systematic analysis of facts. Many of these professionals work in one of the top-tier firms that constitute the "management consulting industry" (see Figure 1–1).

The management consulting industry has grown rapidly in the last two decades. In 1980, total revenues for the global management consulting industry were estimated at $5 billion. In 1996, the market had grown to $60 billion, and it surpassed the $100 billion mark in 2000. More than 100,000 professionals work full time in management consulting firms worldwide. Since 1990, the industry has grown at an average rate of 10 percent per year with top firms growing at astonishing rates of 20 to 30 percent.[1]

One reason growth has been so tremendous is that growth creates opportunities, and top firms in the consulting industry today offer some of the most attractive starting salaries and career opportunities to newly minted business school graduates. Figure 1–2 shows the results of a salary survey in 1999 for strategy consulting jobs.

In May 2000, the average starting salaries of top business school graduates with 3 to 4 years of prior work experience hovered around $95,000[2]; while this number has dropped a bit in recent years as a number of firms have slowed their hiring and supply

FIGURE 1–1   The Top 16 Management Consulting Firms in 2002

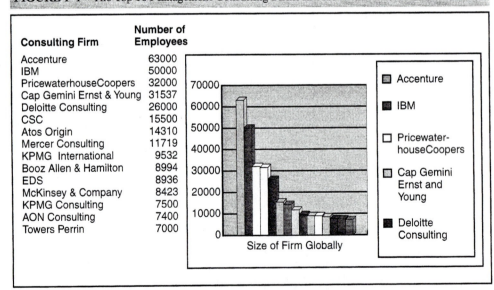

Consulting Firm	Number of Employees
Accenture	63000
IBM	50000
PricewaterhouseCoopers	32000
Cap Gemini Ernst & Young	31537
Deloitte Consulting	26000
CSC	15500
Atos Origin	14310
Mercer Consulting	11719
KPMG International	9532
Booz Allen & Hamilton	8994
EDS	8936
McKinsey & Company	8423
KPMG Consulting	7500
AON Consulting	7400
Towers Perrin	7000

SOURCE: Consultant News, Kennedy Information Research Group, June 2002.

---

[1]*Source:* Tom Rodenhauser, analyst at Consultant News.

[2]*Consultant News*, Kennedy Information Research Group, 1998–2000.

FIGURE 1-2 Consulting Salary Survey 1999

1999 Strategy Consulting Firms Salary Summary - August 1999				
Position	**Average Experience**	**Salary**	**Bonus**	**Sign-on Bonus**
Partner/VP/Director	11 years	$400K - $600K	50% - 107%	Variable
Director/Associate Principal/ Principal/Manager	9 years	$170K - $350K	25% - 65%	Variable
Sr. Manager/Manager/ Sr. Associate/Case Leader	6 years	$120K - $160K	10% - 45%	Variable
Consultant/Associate	0.5 years	$90K - $100K	15% - 30%	$15K - $25K
Analyst/Associate (pre-MBA)	1.5 years	$50K - $52K	5% - 20%	$3K - $8K

SOURCE: The Ransford Group, Houston, TX (713-722-7281).

has outstripped demand, a first-year consultant at a "brand name" firm can still expect to earn at least $70k-plus in his or her first year. (Much of the difference in compensation is due to smaller "signing bonuses"; during the days of heady competition, top firms were adding signing bonuses of up to $40,000 for the most desirable candidates). Many consulting firms have also recruited top undergraduates as research assistants; in 1999–2000, undergrads were being offered base salaries of around $40,000, with signing bonuses estimated at about $5,000.

Some consulting firms also offer opportunities to seasoned business professionals looking to make a career change. As companies merge or experience downturns in their core businesses, they often downsize, thereby freeing up pools of experienced managers. Large consulting firms welcome the hands-on experiences of these managers and often recruit them into project teams in those industries; those that add business development and engagement management skills to their technical and industry knowledge find fulfilling second careers in consulting.

KEY SEGMENTS IN THE ADVICE BUSINESS

There are millions of self-employed professionals—CPAs, engineers, and university-based academics—who sell their services as consultants. They are typically specialists in a particular industry or functional area, and tend to provide a limited array of services to a narrow group of clients. We focus here not on these solo practitioners, but on the professionals who work for consulting firms.[3]

---

[3]Solo practitioners can build credibility by becoming Certified Management Consultants (CMCs). Contact the Institute of Management Consultants, 230 Park Ave., Suite 544, New York, NY 10169, (212) 697-9693.

Size and Structure

Consulting firms vary widely in size, ranging from independent entrepreneurial shops (often set up by academic "gurus") to large companies with thousands of employees. Some are specialized groups that claim consulting as their sole focus. Others are outgrowths of firms that operate in related domains, for instance, the consulting groups of the "Big Four" public accounting firms or the consulting groups of technology giants like IBM, EDS, or Hewlett-Packard.

Most consulting firms operate in one of three segments: the giants of consulting, the consulting divisions, and the specialty firms.

1. *Consulting Generalists:* These are the genuine consulting firms, pursuing no other business. They typically employ more than 50 consultants, with the largest of them employing several thousand. These large firms often have several divisions, each with their distinct specialty. Examples include McKinsey & Company, Booz Allen Hamilton, and The Boston Consulting Group.

2. *Consulting Divisions:* Many consultants work for companies that have diversified into consulting. Chief among these are accounting firms (PricewaterhouseCoopers, KPMG, Ernst & Young) and the technology firms (IBM, EDS) whose consulting groups have grown dramatically in recent years. Their consulting services focus heavily on information systems, electronic data processing (EDP), financial management, and strategic planning. When their consulting billings are tabulated, these divisions rank among the largest of all consulting firms.

3. *Specialty Firms:* Some 20 to 30 percent of all consultants work in specialized small or medium-sized consulting firms. They normally offer a limited range of services or target only a specific type of client, and typically employ less than 50 full-time consultants.

Consulting firms are typically organized around three axes: functional specialties, geographies, and industries. Each axis is normally governed by a director, with multiple "managing consultants" reporting to him or her. Managers supervise the activities of senior and junior consultants, and work with them on client project teams. These teams typically represent a cross-section of hierarchical levels in the firm.

Industry Sectors and Practice Areas

Consulting firms are of two sorts: generalists and specialists. Top consulting firms like McKinsey & Company, The Boston Consulting Group, or Booz Allen Hamilton are pure generalists and work broadly with clients across industries. Others specialize in serving particular types of clients and industries. For instance, The Wilkerson Group and Hamilton KSA are both consultants that specialize in the health care industry; in contrast, Gemini Consulting and The Boston Consulting Group have engagements in the health care industry but do not specialize in that sector. Among the more popular specialty segments are communications, financial services, health care, insurance, manufacturing, media and entertainment, oil and gas, and retail and transportation.

Consulting firms can also be distinguished by the type of work they do. Although they define their functional areas differently, most include practices specialized in Corporate Strategy, Operations Management, Information Technology, Reengineering, and Human Resources. Among the best-known strategy firms are McKinsey & Company, Booz Allen Hamilton, The Boston Consulting Group, and Bain & Company. A. T. Kearney and Accenture are best known for their operations management and information technology capabilities, while Gemini Consulting is recognized for its pioneering efforts in reengineering.

Although all consulting firms focus on the well-paying private sector, some also have public-sector practices from which they derive sizeable billings. The most attractive nonprofit assignments involve advice-giving to municipal, state, national, and international governments. Governments have deeper pockets than nonprofits, and savvy consulting firms can often generate lucrative multiyear engagements that are comparable to those of the private sector. For example, Booz Allen Hamilton has long had a successful Worldwide Technology Business, doing primarily military industrial assignments, which runs at equal or greater annual revenues with its Worldwide Commercial Business, more familiar to MBAs.

Internal versus External Consulting

To reduce their expenditures on external consultants, some companies hire "internal consultants." These in-house consultants are permanent employees who are expected to build deep knowledge about the company and serve internal units in comparable ways to external consultants. Generally, they are part of a corporate staff, and so are considered "overhead." To overcome the stigma of treating internal consultants as an overhead expense, many value-driven companies such as American Express, General Electric, Sara Lee, Pepsico, Sony, and Chase Manhattan compel their internal consultants to market their services both internally and externally. By competing for clients against outside consulting firms, they justify their billings, and so behave like internal profit centers. The engagements that internal consultants take on therefore come to look very much like those of external consultants and are structured in similar ways. The distinctive advantage they have over external bidders is their familiarity with the internal cultures and political systems of the company, and thus the relative ease with which they can help a company to change.

HISTORICAL BACKGROUND OF CONSULTING

The Advice Business is as old as mankind. However, most experts trace the roots of "management consulting" to the industrial revolution and to the rise of the era of "scientific management." Engineers such as Frederick W. Taylor largely developed the analysis of production management systems around 1895 and identified how to improve the efficiency of assembly-line processes. Engineers also explored how we might standardize the size and shape of frequently used products to ensure compatibility. Most of the large consulting firms were founded in the late 1800s and early 1900s. They were started by engineers and accountants who saw market potential in offering their services to clients for a fee. Figure 1–3 shows the founding dates of many recognizable firms.

The early development of the advice business is closely tied to the evolution of American industry in the early part of the twentieth century. A booming chemical industry induced the founding of Arthur D. Little in 1886. In parallel, the challenges of ever-larger plants and buildings led to the founding of Stone & Webster in 1889. As client companies grew larger, they came to face unprecedented managerial challenges. Edwin Booz founded Booz Surveys in 1914 to help companies assess the health of their

FIGURE 1-3	Founding Years of Selected Management Consulting Firms

Arthur D. Little	1886
Stone & Webster	1889
Arthur Andersen	1913
Booz Allen Hamilton	1914
McKinsey & Company	1926*
Towers Perrin	1934
The Hay Group	1943
A. T. Kearney	(1926)1946*
The Boston Consulting Group	1963
The Wilkerson Group (IBM Consulting)	1967
Cap Gemini Sogeti	1968
Mercer Management Consulting	1970
William M. Mercer	1975
Bain & Company	1973
Monitor Company	1983

*The original James O. McKinsey & Company was founded in 1926 in Chicago. The company was split in two in 1937 following the death of founder James McKinsey, and the New York branch was christened McKinsey & Company, whereas the Chicago branch was named McKinsey, Kearney (after Tom Kearney, First Partner). The latter was renamed A. T. Kearney in 1946.

SOURCE: The Global Management Consulting Marketplace: Key Data, Forecasts & Trends, 1997 Edition. Kennedy Information Research Group, 1998. Individual firm information.

businesses; his business remained fairly humble until he was asked by the U.S. Navy to assess its preparedness for World War II. A. D. Little was an early advisor to General Motors as it struggled with developing a technical laboratory and building an efficient organization structure. McKinsey & Company was an early advisor to U.S. Steel and Royal Dutch Shell on dynamics in their internal organizations.

Over time, consulting firms therefore reached far beyond their accounting and engineering roots to proffer advice on strategic, organizational, and managerial matters. They brought in experienced professionals from industry who could provide expert advice rooted in their past experience. They also sought out freshly minted college and graduate students whom they could train in the use of consulting "tools" and methodologies.

In the postwar era, demand for consulting services far outpaced supply as companies spread their operations around the world in an effort to capitalize on economies of scale and labor productivity. Client growth fueled the rapid growth of the largest consulting firms, and top firms like McKinsey & Company, Booz Allen Hamilton, A. T. Kearney, and Arthur D. Little grew in parallel, first in major urban centers around the United States, and then on a global scale. During this time many of them also experimented in adding affiliated services such as compensation consulting and executive search.

As with most professional service firms, knowledge and expertise are core competencies and are largely enshrined in people. Over the years, new firms were born as experienced partners left an established firm to start one of their own. For example, Bruce Henderson left Arthur D. Little to found The Boston Consulting Group (BCG). Bill Bain left BCG with a number of colleagues and founded Bain & Company. The financial services specialist Mitchell Madison Group was started as an offshoot of A. T. Kearney.

In the early 1980s, established auditors Arthur Andersen, PricewaterhouseCoopers, Deloitte & Touche, Ernst & Young, and KPMG Peat Marwick fueled significant growth by opening their own consulting practices. They did so to capture what they saw as attractive cross-selling opportunities that would capitalize on their familiarity and knowledge of audit clients, all of which are among *Fortune* 1000 companies. After all, accounting firms were in a natural position to spot a client's problems and so to help them develop strategies to address those issues. Over the next 15 years, the consulting groups grew at astounding rates. Figure 1–4 shows the amazing growth rates that the consulting groups attained in 1998, and foreshadows the problems they would soon confront with their parent companies.

The strategy worked so well that by the late 1990s, Andersen Consulting alone had become the world's largest management consulting firm, with consulting revenues of over $6.6 billion in 1997 and about 59,000 professionals. So profitable were the consulting groups of the audit firms that they created unprecedented tensions over partnership distributions among audit partners and consulting partners within the firms—a factor that contributed heavily to the divestiture of their consulting groups by Arthur Andersen and Ernst & Young in 2000–2001. Andersen Consulting was reborn as Accenture in 2001, and immediately took the top ranking in the industry.

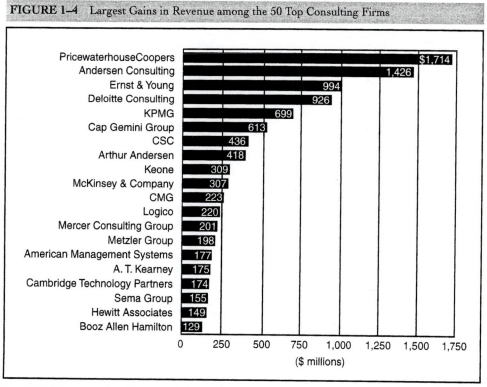

FIGURE 1–4   Largest Gains in Revenue among the 50 Top Consulting Firms

SOURCE: Firm reports and Kennedy Research Group estimates.

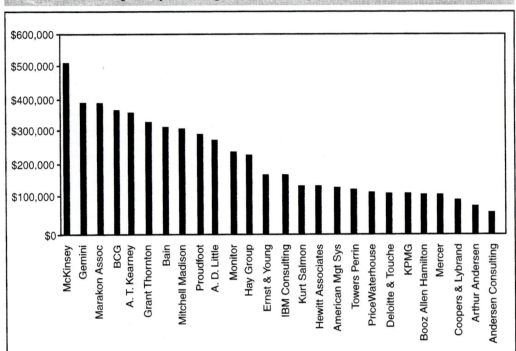

FIGURE 1–5 Leverage of Top Consulting Firms: Revenues per Consultant, 1998

Leverage is the degree to which a consulting firm relies on less costly junior consultants to staff assignments and generate revenues. Calculating the ratio of revenues per consultant provides a rough indicator of leverage and suggests how firms are likely to differ internally. Figure 1–5 shows the ratio for selected firms in 1998.

As the leverage ratios indicate, the strategy firms earn higher revenues per consultant than most firms in the consulting industry. In part, this results from their reputation for providing high-value-added work. Their ability to do so is itself a function of having highly paid consultants ("better brains") with which to staff assignments—reinforcing the mystique associated with their names. In contrast, Accenture (named Andersen Consulting at the time) claims lower revenues per consultant, due in part to their strength in technology and systems consulting that relies on selling "productized" services, and draws on an army of lower-paid associates (what used to be called the "Andersen androids") with which engagements are staffed.

RECENT DEVELOPMENTS IN MANAGEMENT CONSULTING

Just as consultants help companies respond to the changing environments in which they operate, so have consulting firms found themselves forced to reorganize their service delivery in recent years to respond to new circumstances, emerging technology, and an overall quickening of the pace of business and change. Changes experienced by consulting firms in recent years include:

- Acquisitions across specialty areas
- Increased demand for accountability
- Public sale of corporate shares to enlarge capital access

Growth Through Acquisition

Throughout the 1990s, firms decided that the key to sustained success would lie in diversification. They therefore aggressively sought ways to expand their consulting capabilities, and to become global one-stop shops for strategy, operations, information technology (IT), and implementation solutions.

Diversification can be achieved in one of two ways: either from in-house organic growth, or through strategic acquisitions. Eager to move quickly, most consulting firms pursued aggressive acquisition strategies. Figure 1–6 summarizes key merger and acquisition (M&A) activity in the consulting industry since 1990. It is by no means an exhaustive list, but indicates the kinds of diversification and consolidations the firms have sought.

Public Sale of Corporate Shares to Enlarge Capital Access

Global expansion and broadening portfolio offerings created major capital needs. To address their capital needs, many consulting firms dissolved their crusty partnership structures, incorporated, and went public. In 1999, the former Metzger Group became Navigant Consulting and went public. A. D. Little added to its staff in the fall of 2000 in preparation to spin off a stake in its IT consulting unit C-Quential (Boston), but early in 2001 withdrew the IPO due to poor market conditions, and has since folded. In 2001, Ernst & Young merged with France's Cap Gemini to become a public company. None were more visible than the 2001 IPOs of KPMG and Accenture.

Much of the IPO push in 2000–2001 was born in accounting firms and resulted (1) from pressure by the Securities and Exchange Commission on accounting firms to set their consultants free, arguing that having auditors and consultants under the same corporate roof posed serious conflicts of interest, (2) from growth strategies that demanded a larger capital base to finance expansion, and (3) from tensions between accounting partners and consulting partners for their fair shares of net incomes generated.

KPMG raised $2 billion in an IPO in February 2001. Accenture—Arthur Andersen's former offspring consulting group, Andersen Consulting—went public in April 2001, with a mission to compete head-to-head against IBM and EDS by offering IT integration and outsourcing as well as traditional management consulting services. Despite a depressed stock market, Accenture succeeded in selling 115 million shares to the public at $14.50 a share, for a $1.67 billion IPO.

The jury is very much still out on consulting firms going public. A look at history—and at business school case studies—suggests that there is rarely a strong business case for a professional services firm going public, since they can't usually grow at a rate that will satisfy shareholders, and since they are so affected by economic cyclicality. Booz Allen Hamilton went public in the early 1970s, and then in the mid-1970s thought better of it and bought themselves back; some would say that the firm suffered a real setback in the process. Yet there have been some success stories among recent consulting IPOs and, in private, some of their senior management teams assert that going public has been as good for the firms and for their clients as it has been for the senior equity holders.

Year	Buyer	Acquired Firm	Acquired Capability
1989	McKinsey & Company	Information Consulting	Information Technology
1991	Cap Gemini Sogeti	MAC Group	Strategy
1993	The Boston Consulting Group	Canada Consulting Group	Strategy and Organization with focus on Canada
1995	EDS	A. T. Kearney	General Management Strategy in the manufacturing sector
1995	IBM Consulting	The Wilkerson Group	Pharmaceuticals & Medical Strategy
1996	Gartner Group	Productivity Management Group	Measurement and evaluation for information Technology (IT) project management
1996	A. T. Kearney	Cannon Associates	Russia's leading strategy firm
1997	Mercer Management Consulting	Corporate Decisions, Inc.	Customer-Driven Growth Strategy
1997	Kurt Salmon Associates	Levy, Kerson, Aronson & Assoc.	Consulting arm of recruiting specialists in the retail industry
1997	Renaissance Solutions	International Systems Service Corp.	IT Strategy and Implementation
1997	PriceWaterhouse	LVS	Russia's leading IT integrator
1997	Coopers & Lybrand	Mecrastor, Ltd.	Finland's leading management consultancy
1997	A. T. Kearney	Aarso Nielsen & Partners	Leading Scandinavian management consulting firm
1997	Technology Solutions Company	HRM Resources	NY-based specialist in implementing financial and HR software packages
1997	Answerthink	Hackett Group	Technology enabled transformation solutions created by former KPMG partners
1997	Hagler Bailly	Apogee Research	Economic and financial analysis of infrastructure (environment and transportation)
1997	Metzler Group	Resource Management International	Specialist in strategic management, resource mgt, and engineering consulting in electric, gas, and water industries, telecom, and government
1997	A. D. Little	Compagnie de Service et Conseil	Specialist in finance, trading, and investment banking
1998	Hagler Bailly	Putnam Hayes Bartlett Inc.	Economic and management consulting in network and energy industries
1998	Nextera Enterprises	Sigma Consulting Pyramid Consulting Sibson & Company	IT & operations consulting Back office and IT Solutions HR & strategy consulting
1998	Metzler Group	Peterson Consulting	Information management and data processing
1998	KPMG	Ambrose Consulting	ERP Consulting
1998	PriceWaterhouse	Coopers & Lybrand	Consolidation of practices
1999-2000	MarchFIRST	WhittmanHart USWeb/CKS Mitchell Madison Group	Integrated strategy, marketing, creative, and technology capabilities
2000	PA Consulting	Hagler Bailly	Specialist in energy and transportation
2001	Scient	iXL	e-Consulting

Increasing Accountability

Accountability actually took center stage in 1997 as firms faced numerous challenges in court and in the media. For one, Towers Perrin was sued by a client for allegedly selling generic work as a unique analysis. A subsequent investigation revealed striking similarities in work that had been delivered to different clients. Club Med alleged that Bain & Company had provided unsatisfactory work as well as inappropriate feedback on personnel and took them to court. The Boston Consulting Group was among a group of firms sued by the Cleveland-based conglomerate Figgie International for alleged overbilling in the United Kingdom. Andersen Consulting was ordered by the government to pay $18 million for not delivering a computer system on time. In April 1999, Ernst & Young agreed to pay a whopping $185 million to its former client Merry-Go-Round Enterprises. The settlement resolved a $3.8 billion lawsuit in which Merry-Go-Round charged Ernst & Young with providing incompetent and fraudulent turn-around-strategy advice.

Incidents such as these raised enormous client concerns around the consulting industry, threatening the relationship of trust and integrity necessary for success in the advice business. As a result, consulting firms have become far more active in specifying deliverables and managing client relationships. Some firms go as far as to postpone billing until the client reports satisfaction with the work. Other firms routinely follow up with clients after projects and offer additional guidance at no charge where necessary.

The Brain Drain to the E-Sector—and Back Again

In the late 1990s, rising competition for talent came from the new e-business sector, and was concretized by the brain drain into newly minted e-consulting firms such as Scient, Sapient, iXL, and Razorfish. Traditional consulting firms suddenly found themselves scrambling not only to recruit new hires, but to keep their own in-house talent as well. How to compete against stock-option offers from the e-sector that promised to turn smart entrepreneurs into multi-millionaires in a flash? How to keep a disciplined army of consultants on client jobs when the alternative was working on vanguard offerings for the new world order? The go-public decisions of KPMG, Accenture, and Cap Gemini were partly fueled by concern over employee retention, which had become a widespread industry problem for consulting firms competing against Internet start-ups offering stock options as well as lofty salaries.

Leading consulting firms sought quickly to adjust their financial packages by looking for incentives for their consultants. The IPOs of KPMG and Accenture enabled them to offer new investment vehicles (including employee stock options) that they couldn't before. Andersen and PricewaterhouseCoopers created investment portfolios consisting of funds invested in upstart firms they had advised, and offering shares in those funds to its consultants. In this way, consultants could participate in the booming new economy without leaving the consulting world.

By early 2001, of course, the collapse of the e-sector had everyone singing a different tune. Freshly minted MBAs were no longer talking independence and entrepreneurship, and were eagerly seeking out consulting jobs once again. To their dismay, the stalling U.S. economy had taken its toll on the consulting firms as well—and most were in a hold pattern at best, if not in cutback mode. By the time early 2002 rolled around, the dramatic collapse of Enron was all the talk, and was followed soon thereafter by a guilty verdict against Enron's auditor Arthur Andersen: The firm admitted members of its staff had circumvented the law by shredding documents relating to the company's dealings with Enron. The year 2002 would be a low point for the accounting industry, with critics charging that the lack of separation between the firm's auditing practice and its more lucrative consulting business was a root cause that explained its lack of independence from the client's business affairs. Irreparably damaged by the guilty finding, Arthur Andersen's fate was virtually sealed as clients left in droves and its consultants moved into rival firms.

Despite all that, the advice business lives on, and will surely continue to survive as long as there are people and enterprises. Which firms will be most successful in the new world order, and which ones will be the most desired employers? What will be the next areas from which innovation and added value will come? What kinds of people will prosper as the next generation of gurus, witch doctors, and change agents? The following chapters hint at possible answers to these questions, but for the most part, only time will tell.

CHAPTER 2

The Anatomy
of a Consulting Firm

David H. Maister

The structure and management of consulting firms are driven primarily by two key factors: the degree of customization in the firm's work activities, and the extent of face-to-face interaction with the client. Both of these characteristics (customization and client contact) imply that the value of the firm is often embedded less in the properties of the firm and more in the specific talents of highly skilled individuals. The consulting firm must therefore compete actively in two markets simultaneously: the "output" market for its services and the "input" market for its productive resources, the professional workforce. It is the need to balance the often conflicting demands and constraints imposed by these two markets that creates the special challenge of structuring and managing the consulting firm.

LEVERAGE STRUCTURE

The consulting firm may be viewed as the modern embodiment of the medieval craftsman's shop, with its apprentices, journeymen, and master craftsmen. The early years of an individual's association with a consulting firm are, indeed, usually viewed as an apprenticeship, and the relation between juniors and seniors the same: The senior craftsmen repay the hard work and assistance of the juniors by teaching them their craft.

Every consulting project (and hence every consulting firm) has its own appropriate mix of three kinds of people. By tradition, these are called "Finders, Minders, and Grinders." This refers to the three main activities that make up consulting work. Finders (usually the most senior level) are responsible for bringing in the business, scoping and designing the projects, and engaging in the high-level client relations necessary during the work. The main responsibility of Minders is to manage the projects and the team of people working on it. Grinders (the lowest level) perform the analytical tasks. Naturally, this is an idealized structure and, depending on the firm, all may participate in analysis and junior people may be delegated tasks associated in the ideal model with higher levels.

The required shape of the organization (the relative mix of juniors, middle-level staff, and seniors) is usually described as its leverage structure and is primarily determined by the (aggregate) skill requirements of its work: the mix of senior-level, middle-level, and junior-level tasks involved in the projects that the firm undertakes.

Getting the leverage structure right is key to the consulting firm's success. If a firm brings in a mix of client work that requires more juniors and fewer seniors than the

For two decades, David Maister has been a consultant to prominent firms in a broad spectrum of professions, covering all strategic and managerial issues. A native of Great Britain, David holds degrees from the University of Birmingham, the London School of Economics and the Harvard Business School, where he was a professor for seven years.

firm has in place, higher-priced people will end up performing lower-value tasks (probably at lower fees), and there will be an underutilization of senior personnel. The firm will make less money than it should be making. The opposite problem is no less real. If a firm brings in work that has skill requirements of a higher percentage of seniors and a lesser percentage of juniors, the consequences will be (at least) equally adverse: a shortfall of qualified staff to perform the tasks and a consequent quality risk. Matching the skills required by the work to the skills available in the firm (i.e., managing the leverage structure) is central to keeping the firm in balance.

LEVERAGE AND THE PEOPLE MARKETPLACE

The connection between a firm's leverage structure and the people marketplace can be captured in a single sentence: People do not join consulting for *jobs*, but for *careers*. They have strong expectations of progressing through the organization, from Grinder to Minder to Finder, at some pace agreed to (explicitly or implicitly) in advance.

While the pace of progress may not be a rigid one ("up or out in X years"), both the individual and the organization usually share strong expectations about what constitutes a reasonable period of time for each stage of the career path. Individuals who are not promoted within this period will seek greener pastures elsewhere, either by their own choice or career ambitions, or at the strong suggestion of the firm.

Few firms offer career positions at the middle level or junior ranks. Partnership or ownership is usually restricted to those who attain the highest levels. In recent years, however, which have seen a people shortage or "war for talent," some firms have experimented with offering profit sharing, stock options, or other financial incentives to allow those who are not at the highest levels to share in the firm's overall success. This has not removed the expectation that most staff will continue to strive for promotion to the highest levels.

This promotion system serves an essential screening function for the firm. Not all young professionals hired subsequently develop the project management and client relations skills required at the higher levels. While good initial recruiting procedures may serve to reduce the degree of screening required through the promotion process, it can rarely eliminate the need for the promotion process to serve this important function. The existence of a "risk of not making it" also serves the firm in that it constitutes a degree of pressure on junior personnel to work hard and succeed.

The promotion incentive is directly influenced by two key dimensions: the normal amount of time spent at each level before being considered for promotion, and the "odds of making it" (the proportion promoted). For any given rate of growth, a highly leveraged firm (one with a high ratio of juniors to seniors) will offer a lower probability of "making it" to the top, since there are many juniors seeking to rise and relatively few senior slots opening up. A less leveraged firm at the same rate of growth will need to "bring along" a higher percentage of its juniors, thus providing a greater promotion incentive.

LEVERAGE AND PROFITABILITY

A consulting firm's leverage is also central to its economics. The rewards of partnership or ownership (the high levels of compensation attained by vice presidents or senior partners) come only in part from the high hourly (or daily) rates that the top professionals can charge for their own time. A significant portion of profits derives from the surplus generated from hiring staff at a given salary and billing them out at multiples of that salary. By leveraging its high-cost seniors with low-cost juniors, the professional firm can lower its effective hourly rate and thus reduce its cost to clients while simultaneously generating additional profit for the partners.

The market for the firm's services will determine the fees it can command for a given project; its costs will be determined by the firm's abilities to deliver the service with a cost-effective mix of junior, manager, and senior time. If the firm can find a way to deliver its services at the same quality with a higher proportion of juniors to seniors, it will be able to achieve lower service delivery costs. (Note that this is true whether the firm bills by the hour or on a fixed-fee basis.) The project team structure of the firm is therefore an important component of firm profitability.

THE CLIENT MARKETPLACE

Degrees of client contact and customization vary from firm to firm, or even practice area to practice area. Some differences between types of practice are shown in Figure 2–1, which defines four kinds of professional practice to which we will refer as Pharmacist, Nurse, Brain Surgeon, and Psychotherapist.

The Pharmacist

A Pharmacist practice is one in which the client is trying to buy a relatively familiar service and does not require very much counseling, consultation, or contact. The client wants the service performed to strict technical standards at a minimal cost. Notice that this type of practice is defined as a standardized *process*, conducted with little, if any, client contact. This does not mean that the *result* cannot be highly customized, merely that the process to be followed in producing the result is well specified. While this type of work is common in systems installation and other information technology (IT) firms, it can also be found in high-end strategy firms, in which component analyses of cost structures, market shares, competitive positioning, and many other studies, as valuable as they can be, have been highly proceduralized and can be conducted with thoroughness and accuracy by junior staff. The method of conducting these analyses does not vary from job to job.

Quality standards, in the sense of "conformance to specifications" must be high for this work, since the client will be "swallowing the pills." However, the client does not require that the pill be specifically designed for him (or her). The client wants to buy well-established methodologies and procedures, not innovation and creativity.

The client is, in effect, saying "I have a headache, and I know that you, along with many others, are licensed to make aspirin. Don't waste your time and mine trying to convince me that it's brain surgery that I need. I've done this before, and I can tell for myself the difference between the need for aspirin and brain surgery. I want aspirin! What's your best price?"

The Nurse

The Nursing practice also delivers relatively familiar (or "mature") services that do not require high levels of innovation. However, it differs from the Pharmacist practice in

FIGURE 2–1   The Different Types of Consulting Practice

	STANDARDIZED PROCESS	CUSTOMIZED PROCESS
	EMPHASIS ON EXECUTION	EMPHASIS ON DIAGNOSIS
HIGH DEGREE OF CLIENT CONTACT VALUE IS RENDERED IN THE "FRONT ROOM," I.E., DURING INTERACTIONS WITH THE CLIENT	NURSE 	PSYCHOTHERAPIST (or Family Doctor) 
LOW DEGREE OF CLIENT CONTACT VALUE IS RENDERED IN THE PROFESSIONAL'S "BACK ROOM." CLIENT FOCUS IS ON RESULT ONLY	PHARMACIST 	BRAIN SURGEON 

that the emphasis is not only on the ability to make the pill (which still may be required), but also the ability to counsel and guide the client through the process. This time, the client wants to be nurtured and nursed: "Help me understand what's going on; explain to me what you're doing and why; involve me in the decision making; help me understand my options. Be with me and interact with me throughout the process, until this is all over. I need a front-room advisor, not a back-room technician." (The nursing practice can be distinguished from the pharmacy practice by the proportion of total project time that is spent in contact with the client.) Practices that work in this area are those in which the consultant's approach is to help the client (and the client's organization) arrive at its own decisions and conclusions, rather than performing independent studies and presenting the consultant's recommendations. This requires interpersonal and consultation skills, in addition to analytical skills.

The Brain Surgeon

The Brain Surgeon combines high levels of customization, creativity, and innovation with a low degree of client interaction. The client is searching for a practitioner who is at the leading edge of his or her discipline, and who can bring innovative thinking to bear on a unique assignment. Here, the client says: "I have a bet-your-company problem. Save me! I don't want to know the details, just find the right answer! If I wake up in the morning, I'll pay your outrageous bill! I'm not shopping on price, I'm trying to find the most creative provider I can." Consulting firms positioned here tend to be regarded as leading thinkers, and as tackling unique, one-of-a-kind problems, whether they are in the areas of strategy, technology, or organization.

The Psychotherapist (or Family Doctor)

Finally, the Psychotherapist (or Family Doctor) practice is one in which the client says: "Again I have a bet-your-company problem. This time, I don't want you to give me the anesthetic and leave me out of the process. I want to be intimately involved in the problem-solving process. What I'm really trying to buy is someone who can sit down with me, help me understand why my company is falling apart, how I differentiate between a symptom and a cause, what I *must* deal with, and what I can afford to postpone. Sit down with me and my executive team, and help us understand our problem and our options."

As with the Brain Surgeon, the emphasis in being a Psychotherapist is as much about creative diagnosis as it is about execution. When buying the services of a Nurse or Pharmacist, clients know what they want done: They are hiring someone to execute it. But with Brain Surgeons and Psychotherapists, the clients are seeking help on what needs to be done as well as on how to do it.

Psychotherapy practitioners can be found in most high-end consulting firms, since many client projects contain an initial diagnostic component. Except for solo practitioners and some small firms, few consulting firms spend all their billable hours in this activity.

DIFFERENCES BETWEEN PRACTICES

There is a market for all four of these kinds of providers, and they all represent "honorable" ways of being of value to clients. However, the four services described represent four profoundly different businesses. Virtually everything, from marketing to hiring, from managerial styles to economics, from key skills and career paths to performance appraisal criteria, all vary significantly depending on which service the firm is trying to provide.

Consider, for example, how each of these providers makes money. The Pharmacist is in a fee-sensitive business in which the key to economic success lies in finding ways to "make the aspirin" at a very low cost (without compromising quality). This means getting the work done with a minimum of high-priced senior professional time, and extensive use of either low-cost (junior) time or time-saving tools such as methodologies, systems, templates, and procedures. The Pharmacist is in a low-fee, high-leverage business.

The Nurse also needs to have well-established procedures, methodologies and tools, but if the Nurse has superior counseling skills, then he or she can command higher fees than the aspirin maker. Since the client is buying a relationship with the "primary care" provider, he or she will be less inclined to shop on price and more likely to pay a premium for an advisor they can work well with and trust.

However, since much of the work is likely to involve client contact, there is probably a little less chance to leverage (by using low-priced junior professionals) for the "front-room" portion of the work. The Nurse thus makes money by charging higher fees than the aspirin maker, but probably employs lower leverage.

The Brain Surgeon is paid for innovation, creativity, and frontier technical skills. Accordingly, the Brain Surgeon has even less ability to get projects done by leveraging junior resources or established methodologies. Instead, the Brain Surgeon makes money if (and only if) he or she is truly recognized by the market as being a frontier, leading practitioner who can then charge premium fees. Brain Surgeons make money through high fees and low-to-modest leverage.

The Psychotherapist (or Family Doctor) has the most unleveraged business of all. Since most of the work is face-to-face counseling at the highest level of the client organization, little use can be made of junior staff (except for background analytical work in support of the Psychotherapist's efforts).

The Psychotherapist makes money in one of two ways: Either high fees are charged or work results from his (or her) diagnosis that can be referred to other parts of the "hospital." In other words, the Psychotherapist may not be very profitable on a stand-alone basis but makes money by being a "relationship manager" and generating work for others.

THE NEED TO FOCUS

The categorization scheme used here does not define whole disciplines, but rather different market segments. For example, some clients for a service like market research may (historically) seek out a Pharmacist (the work, in their view, being mostly programmatic and performed with little need for ongoing client contact). However, other market research clients may want pioneering work and require (and request) extensive diagnosis, and also want a great deal of ongoing client interaction. They may seek a provider with demonstrated Nursing or Psychotherapy skills and methodologies. Which box a firm is in is determined less by the profession it practices than by the market segments it is trying to serve.

And therein lies the problem! Suppose that you are a highly skilled tax practitioner who handles complex, frontier tax problems through creative, innovative thinking (i.e., you are a Brain Surgeon). A client comes along who wants to get their basic tax forms completed to ensure compliance with all tax laws. Since this is your client, and it's a tax problem, and you're a tax provider, it is tempting to conclude that you're the perfect person to help the client.

Wrong! As a Brain Surgeon, you are probably high priced, and your key talent is creativity and complex problem solving. However, completing tax forms and ensuring compliance is a Pharmacy job; it is not work for a Brain Surgeon. A Brain Surgeon may have the tendency to treat all problems "as if" they required Brain Surgery: The client says, "I'd like to buy some aspirin," and the Brain Surgeon replies, "Sure! But first, get on the operating table so we can investigate and find out whether it's aspirin you really need!" (Of course, the opposite problem is equally unacceptable. If a client says, "I have a unique bet-your-company problem," it is not very sensible to respond by saying "Let us show you our established methodology based on years of solving identical problems!")

Even if the Brain Surgeon recognizes the need to treat a problem as an "aspirin job," it would still be a misallocation of resources for the Brain Surgeon to do it, since low-cost, methodology-driven activities are not the Brain Surgeon's key talents. In fact, everyone will lose if you, the Brain Surgeon, do it yourself: The client will not get low cost, you will be underutilizing your talents (and will probably find the work dull), and your junior staff will be denied the opportunity to perform work that, while old hat for you, might be interesting and skill-building for them.

What this analysis points out is that while it may be acceptable for a *firm* to be a "full-service hospital" with capabilities to meet a broad range of client needs, it is not acceptable for individual professionals to try to do so. It is highly unlikely that any one individual will excel simultaneously at *all* the virtues of efficiency, creativity, counseling, and diagnosis.

While Brain Surgery is the traditional self-image of many professions, the harsh reality is that it probably represents a very small percentage of the total fees paid in any profession. It is also true in "real" health care, wherein surgeons may be the most "glamorous" providers, yet they represent a tiny fraction of the health care needs of society.

OWNERSHIP AND GOVERNANCE

Among the many things that are affected by the market positioning (i.e., mix of services) of the firm are ownership and governance. The traditional model in consulting has been a privately held partnership, with all significant decisions being made after extensive consultation with the senior group. This model matches well with a Brain Surgery or Psychotherapy practice, which requires significant power and autonomy to be left in the hands of the senior practitioners. A related, but different, part of the partnership tradition is that senior people are rewarded by the income they derive during their time at the firm, and not from the increase in the value of the firm itself. (Many firms transfer their ownership between generations through an "in and out at book value" system.) Ownership is restricted to those currently practicing within the firm.

However, recent years have seen the emergence of publicly held consulting firms. Theoretically, there is nothing in the corporate form, or in public ownership, that would prevent the preservation of a "partnership ethos," with decision making through extensive consultation and the retention of significant autonomy for senior practitioners. However, when a firm has gone public, the value of the shares (and hence of the company) takes on a greater significance, and this inevitably affects the process of decision making. A greater emphasis is given to building the systems of the firm to embed value in the firm, rather than just in the individuals who belong to it, and this often leads to greater codification. It is easier to "own" a chain of pharmacies than a rambunctious group of brain surgeons and psychotherapists

STRUCTURAL TRENDS

Two trends suggest where the bulk of the market lies. First, clients are buying fewer services as if their problem is totally unique. Rather, they more frequently want to tap into a firm's accumulated experience and methodologies, in order to benefit from the efficiencies that come from dealing with providers who have done it before. Accordingly, they are buying less brain surgery and more aspirin. (The widespread use of technology also has the effect of allowing complex analyses formerly performed by Brain Surgeons to be conducted by junior staff, thus reinforcing this trend.)

Second, clients are increasingly reluctant to say to their professionals, "You take care of things and report back when it is done." More and more, clients want to be involved in the process or, at a minimum, be kept informed of their options, be kept up-to-date on progress, and assisted in understanding what is going on and why.

From these two trends, we can hypothesize that the bulk of the market is moving toward Nursing (established, proven procedures with high client contact), and away from Brain Surgery. As reflected by the amount of price competition in most professions, the Pharmacy also represents a high percentage of fees. While critical, the role of Psychotherapist is not a high-volume area. It is filled with those few individuals who have sufficiently earned their clients' trust and confidence so that, whenever the client has a problem, the Psychotherapist is called in to diagnose what is needed.

Most professional firms put new entry-level people to work in the Pharmacy first, so they can learn the key technical skills of their profession. As time progresses, people have historically moved in one of two directions, following either the technical career path to Brain Surgeon or the client contact career path to Nurse.

Psychotherapists have tended to evolve from the more creative Nurses, although not all Nurses can make the transition to being accepted as the client's prime diagnostician. While it is possible for Brain Surgeons to become Psychotherapists, it is more rare. Unless a professional learns the basic client contact skills early in his or her career, they are difficult to develop later.

This traditional approach to career development (often called "paying your dues") is, increasingly, under attack. Consider the Pharmacy service. Under the traditional career model, the aspirin is being made by professionals "temporarily" working in the Pharmacy, serving their time until they are "promoted" to a "higher-level" service. This method of having the aspirin made by "Brain-Surgeons-in-training" is not entirely aligned with the clients' interests.

Unlike the Brain Surgeon firm, which can only afford to hire the "best and brightest" from the top schools, a focused Pharmacy practice would, appropriately, view these as the wrong people to bring in. Not only do they command higher salaries, but their "superior intellect" may be inappropriate for the service the Pharmacy is trying to provide. If a firm's business is making hamburgers, it will not want to hire people who are dreaming of the day they can leave and become "cordon bleu" chefs. It will want and need people who are excited about hamburgers.

A focused Pharmacy practice would be able to hire people without a formal education in its *specific* area, since smart people can learn to apply well-defined methodologies and tools. Training and development would be structured and formal; to ensure that new people can learn quickly to apply the firm's established methodologies. (This is exactly what is happening in some management consulting firms that now hire people with degrees in such diverse fields such as biology and liberal arts.)

Employees in the Pharmacy would not be promised a fast-track promotion and career path. In fact, there would be no traditional "up-or-out" policy. (This is one reason why the big accounting firms, increasingly realizing that much of their business is Pharmacy, have recently moved away from such policies.)

The Nursing practice requires capable people who are not only able to apply methodologies, but who are also able to work well with clients. One common approach is to hire individuals who have prior industry experience working in client environments, in order to maximize the chance that these individuals can "empathize" with the client situation.

GURU ASSOCIATES: A NUMERICAL EXAMPLE

Let's consider a numerical example (Figure 2–2) to see how the forces at work in a consulting firm interrelate. Guru Associates, which engages in a variety of projects, nevertheless has a "typical" project that requires 50 percent of a senior's time, 100 percent of a middle-level person's time, and the full-time efforts of three juniors. In order for the firm to meet its economic goals, it requires that seniors and managers are engaged in billable work for 75 percent of their time, and juniors 90 percent.

Guru Associates currently has four seniors. If it is to meet its target of 75 percent billed senior time, its available senior time will be 4 × 75 percent, or the equivalent of three seniors working full time. This implies six projects, if the typical project requires 50 percent of a senior's time.

With six projects, the firm needs the equivalent of six full-time middle-level staff, according to the project team structure. (Each project requires 100 percent of a middle-level person). At 75 percent target utilization (billed hours divided by available hours), this means that the firm must have 6/0.75 or eight middle-level staff. Similarly, at three juniors per project, the firm needs 18 full-time juniors, or at 90 percent billability, 20 juniors.

Simple calculations such as these show that, with eight seniors, the firm would need 16 managers and 40 juniors. The proportions remain constant: one senior to every two managers, to every five juniors. Unless there is a change in either the project team structure (i.e., the types of projects the firm undertakes) or the target utilization (matters that will be discussed below), the firm must keep these ratios constant as it grows.

This seemingly simple-minded calculation, relating the staffing mix requirements of the work to the staffing levels existing in the firm, is in fact of extreme importance.

If we know the salaries of the staff members and their billing rates, we can construct the pro forma income statement of this firm at full utilization (Figure 2–3).

FIGURE 2–2 Guru Associates Utilization Overview

Level	Requirements for Average Project (By Number of Partners)	Target Utilization	Required Staffing for 6 Projects at Target Utilization	Required Staffing for 12 Projects at Target Utilization
Senior	50% of 1 person	75%	4	8
Middle	1 person	75%	8	16
Junior	3 people	90%	20	40

FIGURE 2–3 The Economics of Guru Associates

Level	No.	Target Utilization	Target Billable Hours at 2000 Hours per Person, per Year	Billing Rate	Fees	Salary per Individual	Total Salaries
Senior	4	75%	6,000	$200	$1,200,000		
Middle	8	75%	12,000	$100	$1,200,000	$75,000	$600,000
Junior	20	90%	36,000	$50	$1,800,000	$32,000	$640,000
TOTALS					$4,200,000		$1,240,000

Fees	$4,200,000
Salaries	(1,240,000)
Contribution	$2,960,000
Overhead*	$1,280,000
Partner Profits	$1,680,000
Per Partner	$420,000

* *Assume overhead costs of $40,000 per professional.*

The role of leverage is amply illustrated by Guru Associates. The four seniors (partners) personally bill a total of $1,200,000, or $300,000 apiece. At per–professional overhead costs of $40,000 (including the costs of all secretaries, administrative staff, space, supplies, etc.), this would result in a per-partner profit of $260,000 if these seniors were totally unleveraged.

With a healthy seven staff members per senior, partner profits now total $420,000 apiece. About 60 percent of each partner's profit comes not from what he or she bills, but from the profit generated by the nonpartner group—thus, the benefits of leverage!

It should be immediately stressed that high leverage is not *always* good. As we have already observed, having high leverage is completely inappropriate if the firm has a high level of Brain Surgery or Psychotherapy work. What we can say is that leverage should be as high as the requirements of the work allow.

We now turn to Guru Associates' position in the market for staff. Guru Associates has the following promotion policies: It considers that it requires four years for a junior to acquire the expertise and experience to perform the middle-level function, and it expects to promote 80 percent of its candidates to this position. A lower percentage would be insufficient to attract new juniors, and a higher percentage would imply that insufficient "screening" was taking place (i.e., that there was no room for "hiring mistakes"). From middle-level to senior is also expected to take four years; but because fewer candidates develop the critical client relations skills that Guru Associates requires, on average only 50 percent of candidates make it.

We shall now trace the evolution of Guru Associates over time. Among the eight middle-level staff, we may assume that, since it takes four years to make senior, there are one quarter (i.e., two) in their final year as middle-level staff. If Guru Associates is to abide by its promotion policies, then it can expect to promote 50 percent (i.e., one candidate). Whether by firm policy or by the personal decision of the individual, the nonpromoted candidate will leave the firm. (Note that this result tends to happen in most consulting firms regardless of whether the firm has an up-or-out policy. Middle-level staff may, if allowed, hang on for another year or two, but most eventually leave if not promoted. As we shall see, there is a strong incentive for the firm to encourage them to leave, since they are occupying a slot eagerly being sought by the juniors coming up behind them.)

Counting both those promoted and those leaving, we have reduced the number of middle-level staff by two and increased the number of seniors by one. Since we now have five seniors, we require 10 middle-level staff (unless the mix of project types changes), and have six remaining. We must seek out four new middle-level staff from among our juniors. Of the 20 in the firm, we assume one quarter (five) will be in their final year as juniors. Since our expectation (or policy) is to promote 80 percent at this level, we will, indeed, promote four out of the five to fill our four available slots. (The fact that these figures match is not, of course, fortuitous. The percentage that can be promoted at a lower level is determined by the shape of the professional pyramid.) Like the "passed over" middle-level staff person, the fifth junior may reasonably be assumed to leave the firm.

We now have 15 juniors left. However, with five seniors and 10 managers, the firm requires 25 juniors: it must hire 10. These changes are summarized in Figure 2–4, which follows the same logic for years 1 through 9.

In year 5, the first batch of middle-level staff that were promoted from junior in year 1 will be ready to be considered for promotion to senior. It will be recalled that there are four of them. If promotion opportunities are to be maintained, then 50 percent will be promoted (i.e., two) and two will leave. This creates a total of 10 seniors. With a total of 10 seniors in year 5, twenty middle-level staff are required. Of the 16 in the firm the previous year, four have been promoted or have left, meaning that a total of eight juniors must be promoted. Fortunately (but not fortuitously), there are 10 juniors who were hired in year 1 and are to be considered for promotion. The expected 80 percent target may be maintained!

What must be stressed at this point is that we have arrived at these staffing levels solely by considering the interaction of the firm's leverage structure with the promotion incentives (career opportunities) that the firm promises. What we have discovered by performing these calculations is that the interaction of these two forces determines a target (or required) growth rate for the firm. As Figure 2–4 shows, Guru Associates must double in size every four years solely to preserve its promotion incentives. If it grows at a lower rate than this, then it either will remove much of the incentive in the firm or will end up with an "unbalanced factory" (too many seniors and not enough juniors), with a consequent deleterious effect on the firm's economics.

If the firm attempts to grow faster than target rate, it will be placed in the position of either having to promote a higher proportion of juniors or to promote them in a shorter period of time. Without corresponding adjustments, this could have a significant impact on the quality of services that the firm provides.

FIGURE 2–4 The Consequences of Guru Associates' Promotion Policies

	STAFF NUMBERS									
	0	1	2	3	4	5	6	7	8	9
Senior	4	5	6	7	8	10	12	14	16	20
Middle	8	10	12	14	16	20	24	28	32	40
Junior	20	25	30	35	40	50	60	70	80	100
TOTAL	32	40	48	56	64	80	96	112	128	160
New Hires		10	10	10	10	20	20	20	20	40
Resignations		2	2	2	2	4	4	4	4	8
Annual % Growth in Staff		25	20	17	14	25	20	17	14	25

We have seen that the leverage structure and the promotion policies together determine a target (required) growth rate. It should be acknowledged, however, that there is another way of looking at the relationship between these variables. An equivalent way of stating the relationship would be to observe that, if given a growth rate and a leverage structure, the promotion incentives that result can be specified. We may see this by examining Figure 2–4 once more. Suppose that we had constructed this by specifying the growth rate and the project team structure. We would then have discovered that we could afford to promote only four out of five juniors and one out of two managers. We would also have discovered that we would have a "built-in," or target, turnover rate averaging over 4 percent (two resignations per year for the first four years, while the average number of nonsenior staff was 45.5).

In this example, Guru Associates can achieve what would be considered an extremely low target turnover rate if it achieves its optimal growth. However, the norm in many consulting firms is a much higher rate than this, often reaching as high as 20 to 25 percent or even 30 percent. The key point to note here is that, given a growth rate and an organizational structure, the target turnover rate of the firm can be specified. (This does not, of course, tell us what the actual turnover experience of the firm will be.

We are considering here the turnover that the firm requires to keep itself in balance. While it may be able, through its promotion system, to ensure that the actual rate does not get too low, it may have to use other devices to ensure that the actual turnover rate does not get too high through too many people quitting.)

In most professions, one or more firms can be identified that have clearly chosen a high target rate of turnover. Partners (or shareholders) can routinely earn a surplus value from the juniors without having to "repay" them in the form of promotion. This high turnover rate also allows a significant degree of screening so that only the "best" stay in the organization. Not surprisingly, firms following this strategy tend to be among the most prestigious in their industry.

This last comment gives us the clue as to why such firms are able to maintain this strategy over time. Individuals continue to join these organizations, knowing that the odds of "making it" are very low. In the eyes of many potential recruits, the experience, training, and association with the prestigious firms in the industry make the poor promotion opportunities at such firms worthwhile.

Young professionals view a short period of time at such firms as a form of "post-post-graduate" degree, and often leave for prime positions they could not have achieved (as quickly) by another route. Indeed, most of the prestigious firms following this strategy not only encourage this but provide active "outplacement" assistance. Apart from the beneficial effects that such activities provide in recruiting the next generation of juniors, such alumni are often the source of future business for the firm when they recommend to their corporate employers hiring their old firm (which they know and understand) over other competitors.

The ability to place ex-staff in prestigious positions is thus one of the prerequisites of a successful churning strategy. (An exception might be provided by those professions in which legal requirements such as professional certification necessitate that juniors spend time in a firm. However, even here, the prestige firms provide active outplacement assistance.)

GROWTH AND PROFITABILITY

Before we leave the topic of growth, we should take a quick peek back at Guru Associates. How did its growth contribute to its profitability? Let us perform our analysis on the basis of constant (year 0) dollars, to remove the effect of inflation. By implication, this means that the salaries and billing rates at each staff level remain the same. What does the firms Profit and Loss Statement now look like? Figure 2–5 repeats the analysis of Figure 2–3, using year 5 staffing levels instead of year 0.

The result? Per-partner profits have not increased! In fact, they have remained *precisely* the same!

What this simple example shows is that there is no necessary relationship between growth and profits. As we have seen, growth in a professional firm is driven primarily by the need to attract and retain staff, and is critical for that reason, but is not a guarantee of higher per-partner profits.

Why is this so? We shall explore the reasoning in greater detail in subsequent chapters, but the basic fact is this. If a firm grows subject to two conditions, as Guru Associates has, whereby (a) the mix of client projects (and hence fee levels) remains the same, and (b) the project staffing (or leverage) is such that the same *proportion* of

FIGURE 2–5   The Economics of Guru Associates (Year 5 in constant dollars)

Level	No.	Target Utilization	Target Billable Hours at 2000 Hours per Person, per Year	Billing Rate	Fees	Salary per Individual	Total Salaries
Senior	10	75%	15,000	$200	$3,000,000		
Middle	20	75%	30,000	$100	$3,000,000	$75,000	$1,500,000
Junior	50	90%	90,000	$50	$4,500,000	$32,000	$1,600,000
TOTALS					$10,500,000		$3,100,000

Fees	$10,500,000
Salaries	(3,100,000)
Contribution	$7,400,000
Overhead*	$3,200,000
Partner Profits	$4,200,000
Per Partner	$420,000

* Assume overhead costs of $40,000 per professional.

senior or partner time is required to handle each project, then the number of seniors or partners that the firm requires will correspond *exactly* to the growth rate. In consequence of this, the profit pool may increase because of the higher volume, but it must be shared among a correspondingly increased number of partners.

If per-partner profits are to increase, then one of the two conditions must be broken. Either the firm must bring in a different mix of business commanding higher billing rates (i.e., find higher-value work for its people to do), or it must find ways to serve the same kinds of work with an ever-increasing proportion of junior time and a declining proportion of senior time.

It is interesting to note that few prominent consulting firms act as if growth were profit neutral. Indeed, rapid growth is often listed as a primary goal of the firm, and advances in top-line growth used as a primary internal and external measure of success. If justified in the name of providing career opportunities for staff, this indeed makes sense. However, if desired on profitability grounds, it would appear as if many consulting firms are fooling themselves!

SUMMARY

Perhaps the most significant management variable to be disclosed by the previous analysis is the choice of the mix of projects undertaken, and the implications this has for the (average) project team (i.e., leverage) structure. As we have seen, this latter variable is a significant force in influencing the economics of the firm, its organizational structure, and its positioning in the client and people markets. The leverage structure, in the sense used in this book (i.e., as the average or typical proportion of time required from professionals at different levels) has not been a variable that is routinely monitored by firm management. However, as we have shown, its role in balancing the firm is critical.

It is possible, and not uncommon, for the firm's project team structure to change over time. If it is possible to deliver the firm's services with a greater proportion of juniors, this will (in general) reduce the costs of the project. Competition in the market for the firm's services will, over time, require the firm to seek out lower costs for projects of a particular type, and there will often be opportunities for an increasing proportion of juniors to be used on projects that, in the past, required a high proportion of senior time. What, in past years, had the characteristics of a Brain Surgeon project may, in future years, be accomplishable as a procedural or Pharmacy project.

When considering new projects to undertake, it is usually more profitable for the firm to engage in one similar to that recently performed for a previous client. The knowledge, expertise, and basic approaches to the problem that were developed (often through a significant personal and financial investment) can be capitalized on by bringing them to bear on a similar or related problem. Frequently, the second project can be billed out to the client at a similar (or only slightly lower) cost, since the client perceives (and receives) something equally custom-tailored: the solution to his problem. However, the savings in costs incurred by the firm in delivering this customization are not all shared with the client (if, indeed, any are). The firm thus makes its most money by "leading the market": being able to sell as a fully customized service (at a fully customized price) what increasingly becomes a service with reproducible, standardized elements.

While it is in the best interests of the firm that similar or repetitive engagements be undertaken, this is often not in accord with the desires of the individuals involved. Most individuals that join consulting do so out of the desire for professional challenge and variety and the avoidance of routine and repetition. While they may be content to undertake a similar project for the second or third time, they will not be for the fourth or sixth or eighth.

The solution, of course, is to convert the past experience and expertise of the individual into the expertise of the firm by accepting the similar project, but utilizing a greater proportion of juniors on "second- or third-time" projects. Apart from requiring a lesser commitment of time from the experienced seniors, this device serves the admirable purpose of training the juniors.

For all these reasons, we might suspect that, over time, the proportion of juniors to seniors required by the firm in a particular practice area will tend to increase. If this is allowed to proceed without corresponding adjustments in the range of practice areas, the basic project team structure of the firm will alter, with significant impacts on the economics and organization of the firm. The dangers of failing to monitor the leverage structure are thus clearly revealed.

CHAPTER

Thought Leadership: Making Sense of What Consultants Do

Carol Ballock[1]

In a May 2000 editorial entitled "Thought Followership," *The Economist* suggested that "management consultants appear to have been inspired by [a] sort of untruth-in-advertising. The buzziest among them now claim not just to be consultants, advisers, or even experts. They are 'thought leaders.'" It goes on to say: "These two words are, to be sure, among the finest in the language. One of the few certainties in business, or economics, or life in general is that thought is in short supply and high demand (at least among those who have thought about it)."[2]

The Economist got us to *rethinking* what we do for a living, which, in large part, involves making sense of "thought leadership" for ourselves and our clients. Yes, we are among the management consultants whose work *The Economist* appears to be "labeling a commonsense process with a baffling phrase," so we do have a professional stake in the debate. Even if we admit the term is among the most overused and underdefined in our industry, is it really "untruth-in-advertising"?

Our colleagues at Burson-Marsteller are excited by what many consultants and our clients are calling "thought leadership"—and, we think, for good reason. It is widely accepted that ideas and knowledge form the basic capital of any consulting firm. In an idea economy, it is a competitive advantage to have more of the better ideas. Firms rich in idea capital grow and prosper. *But how do consultants differentiate themselves when one consultant can look very much like another?*

Our answer, in short, is a reputation for having more of the better ideas. Of course, how one arrives at that reputation, develops the ideas, and delivers them to the marketplace in a way that creates sustained economic value, requires more than a short explanation. Hence, this chapter.

Our opinions are based on our research and ongoing work in helping Burson-Marsteller clients develop and disseminate "thought leadership" initiatives, as well as

---

Carol Ballock is a Managing Director in Burson-Marsteller's Corporate Practice in New York where she specializes in corporate and employer reputation, new CEO positioning, thought leadership, and corporate change communications. Carol graduated summa cum laude from the University of Pittsburgh and received a master's degree in management from Carnegie-Mellon University. She also studied law at Duquesne University.

[1]Enormous appreciation goes to Bobby Schrott, formerly Manager, Knowledge Center, Burson-Marsteller New York, a brilliant researcher whose insights on the topic gave this chapter the kind of rigor and credibility that could only have resulted from our collaboration.

[2]"Thought Followership," *The Economist*, May 20, 2000, U.S. edition.

on my own prior experience as a director of global thought leadership at one of the world's largest professional services firms.

We are glad to report that we have moved beyond being annoyed at *The Economist* for poking fun at our livelihood. Rather, our objective in writing this chapter is to contribute to what little published literature exists on a process for creating thought leadership and executing as thought leaders in the marketplace for ideas.

As we start, we are reminded of a novel set in the late nineteenth-century in New York City. The book, *Martin Dressler, The Tale of an American Dreamer,* is a Pulitzer prize winner by Steven Millhauser. In it, Dressler, a cigar maker's son, has the audacity to make his dreams come true and the ability to do so on such a grand scale that other people want to dream them too. Dressler always had a sense that "a different future awaited him, a future that, once he saw it rising in the distance, would be as deeply familiar to him as his own childhood." In the book, we watch young Dressler make the ascent from a hotel bellhop to a builder of hotels on his own. Of note, Dressler's passion is not so much for the new buildings he creates; but, rather, for "working things out, bringing things together, arranging the unarrangeable, making combinations." This, in a nutshell, is what thought leaders do at their best: They see the future rising in the distance and make sense of that future so clearly that others want to come along.

It is in the spirit of *Martin Dressler* that we begin our attempt at making sense of thought leadership. Our chapter is written in five "commonsense" steps. Steps 1 and 2 focus on developing clarity about what is meant by thought leadership and what it means to become a thought leader. Steps 3, 4, and 5 address the more practical aspects of creating the organizational mindset and aligning resources to deliver thought leadership to create sustained economic value into the future.

STEP 1: DEFINE WHAT YOU MEAN BY THOUGHT LEADERSHIP

A lot of confusion exists about what thought leadership is and isn't. As an applied discipline, the term does not appear as a robust concept in the general, business, or academic literature. Instead, it is applied to "thinking about leadership" or "leadership thinking." For more clarity, we interviewed two leading thinkers on the topic from the two organizations we work with day to day: Accenture is one of our firm's largest and most successful clients. Burson-Marsteller is where we make our professional homes.

According to Michael May, the lead partner for global thought leadership at Accenture: "Thought leadership is the creation of new ideas that, when packaged in some form, create extraordinary levels of value in the economy—that's the content piece. The second piece is the distribution piece—that is, when delivered to clients and/or venture opportunities allows you to realize that economic value. Allows your clients to realize it, and allows you as a firm to realize it as the provider of the idea."

May explains thought leadership content as follows: "Most thinking by consultants is what I call 'thought leadership on the margin,' or forwarding an existing idea. The consultants have worked on something for a client or an industry and developed new insights that push an existing idea forward, make it better. That kind of thought leadership is very valuable, but it is not 'break-the-mold' new thinking. The very, very real thought leadership creates a completely new idea that is going to be meaningful to society, meaningful to business into the future. This is the sort of thought leadership needed to get out in front of clients with fresh ideas beyond what they are thinking."

May uses the simple chart in Figure 3–1 to illustrate the many definitions of thought leadership that exist in the marketplace. They include: smart ideas, the process of creating smart ideas, the process of disseminating smart ideas, structured internal studies, leveraged client insights, distinct points of view, marketplace visibility and acceptance, and market offerings. "The point is to have clarity about what you mean by thought leadership as a company, or as an individual. So often, the term is used without defining it."

Dr. Leslie Gaines-Ross, Chief Knowledge and Research Officer at Burson-Marsteller, agrees: "Thought leadership is what you define it to be for your organiza-

FIGURE 3–1   Accenture's Views on Thought Leadership

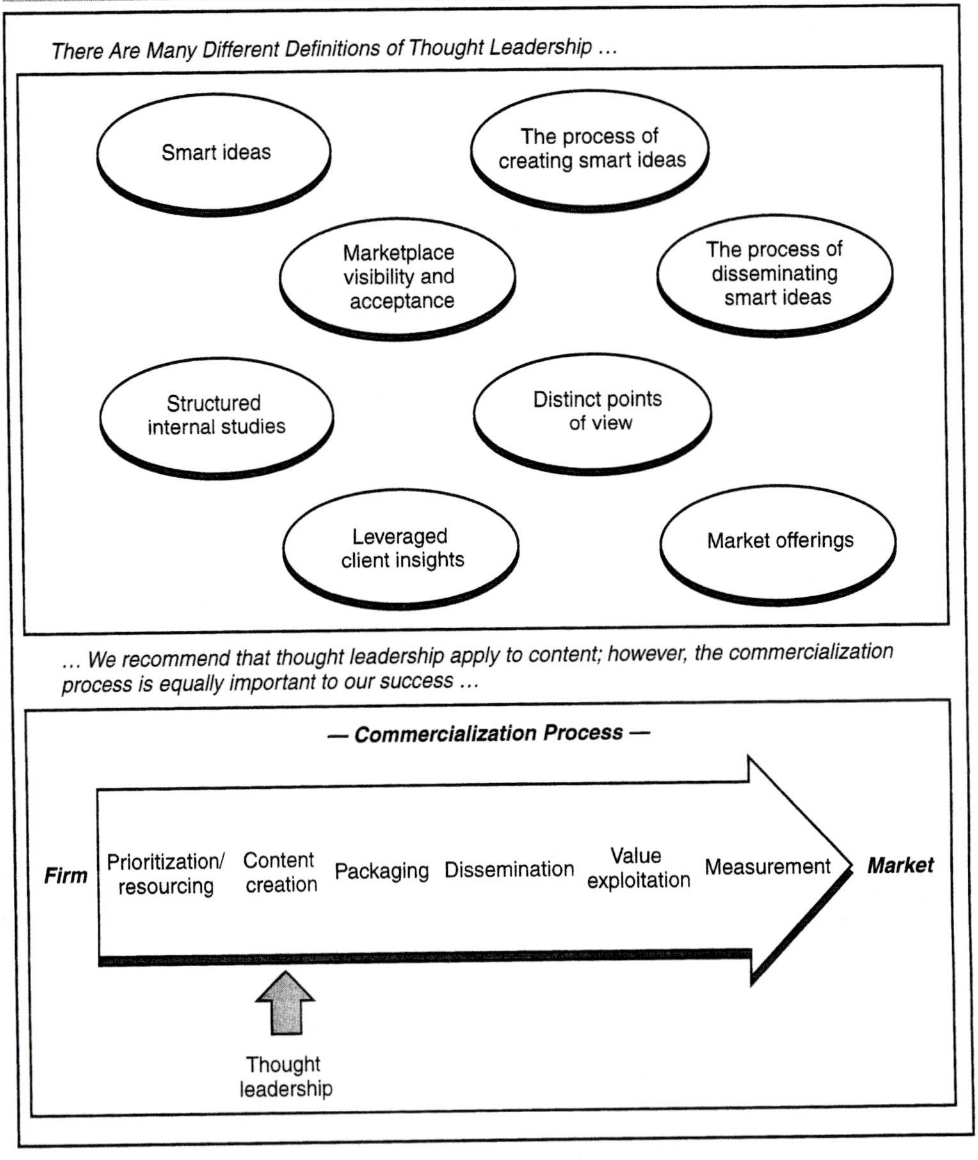

There Are Many Different Definitions of Thought Leadership ...

Smart ideas

The process of creating smart ideas

Marketplace visibility and acceptance

The process of disseminating smart ideas

Structured internal studies

Distinct points of view

Leveraged client insights

Market offerings

... We recommend that thought leadership apply to content; however, the commercialization process is equally important to our success ...

— Commercialization Process —

Firm | Prioritization/ resourcing | Content creation | Packaging | Dissemination | Value exploitation | Measurement | Market

Thought leadership

tion. It's your point of differentiation, a point of departure. You don't have to have it. But it makes a difference; if it attracts the right people, the right clients—that matters."

What is clear is that the competition for thought leadership and for thought leaders is incredibly intense. The ongoing "buzz" about thought leadership is a direct result of the increasingly frenetic pace of change and of the desperate search for new ideas. The technological revolution is doing two things," says May. "First, it is causing the relevant life cycle of products and services to be shorter and shorter, and, second, it is converting new products and services into commodities much faster. That dual linkage is forcing companies in many industries to think about new ways of doing things and to become much more creative in defining new spaces in which to compete."

Idea capital has replaced economic capital as the value driver in business. "Our concern used to be where to get the new capital to fund a business," says May. "Now, it's where to get the new ideas and how to create the new spaces in which to make money. That shift has pushed every single industry into thinking about thought leadership."

STEP 2: KNOW WHAT YOU WANT TO ACCOMPLISH BY BECOMING A THOUGHT LEADER

How you define thought leadership is inextricably linked to what you want to accomplish by becoming a thought leader. The stronger the link, the greater your potential for building a reputation for having more of the better ideas. Again, we look to our client, Accenture, and inside of our own organization, Burson-Marsteller. For each, we include a sidebar that features the kinds of new ideas and breakthrough results that can only enhance their reputations for thought leadership.

"At Accenture, we want to be known for the quality of our ideas, not just our ability to execute," says May. "That was a very deliberate choice. So one of our reasons for creating thought leadership is to drive the image of our firm. Another is the creation of economic value over some reasonable period of time. The ultimate objective is to create something completely new that is going to be meaningful to society, meaningful to business—a well-formulated idea, concept, or model that gives incredible insight into the future and allows clients to gain significant strategic advantage around that insight. What would be on the Chief Executive's agenda five years from now, ten years from now, is one way to approach it," says May.

One of the firm's reports, "Fault Lines," looks to the future for the financial services industry. An excerpt is presented in Figure 3–2 and was featured on the front page of the September 22, 2000, issue of *American Banker:*

> Seven years from now people will not go to the branch or log on to the Internet to do their banking. Rather, electronic assistants in the form of personal financial ' 'bots'—short for robots—will scoot around the Internet, balancing checkbooks, allocating excess funds to various accounts, paying bills, and even shopping.[3]

"What do you do for your clients today if that's the future?" asks May.

Is there a relationship between thought leadership and knowledge management. The effort to generate new ideas starts within the organization itself. As a result, many

---

[3]"Traditional Banking's Next Nemesis ... 'Bots?," *American Banker,* September 22, 2000.

FIGURE 3-2   Accenture's View of the Future of Financial Services

---

January 7, 2007.

Your personal electronic financial 'bot—a software robot that acts as an intelligent search engine—receives your pay for the day (bimonthly paychecks are obsolete in this real-time worlds) and immediately allocates the funds among various financial instruments as determined by the amount of risk with which you are comfortable and your particular lifestyle. A portion of the funds moves to a transaction account, where it is securely stored until you need to buy lunch or pay the electric bill. The financial 'bot distributes the rest of the funds to accounts whose providers offer to pay the highest rates. If the financial 'bot detects a better deal, it will move the money to another provider immediately.

On your lunch break, you decide to do something different—you actually go to a store to shop. You see a watch you like, ask to try it on, then point your wireless phone at the bar code on the watch case. Your financial 'bot takes the information to the Internet, searching for a better deal. By the time you've taken off the watch and handed it back to the sales clerk, the 'bot has obtained several price, warranty and financing altlernatives—including insurance—and recommends the best ones. In fact, the 'bot has found a credit provider who has offered to finance the purchase for a little less than what you're currently receiving in interest on your transaction account. You show the offer to the clerk, who agrees to match the sale price and consult the manager about an even more attractive financing package. The store has a special program in place for people who actually walk in—so few do—and you leave with watch on your wrist.

Science fiction? Hardly.

SOURCE: Excerpted from "Fault Lines: The Future of Financial Services," Global Thought Leadership Special Report by Accenture.

firms have appointed "knowledge officers" to ensure that learning circulates freely across organizational boundaries.

It is generally accepted that knowledge is the DNA of any creative company in the idea economy. The primary goal for knowledge managers is to leverage that knowledge across the organization and to spin it into client-winning innovations.

"The way we come up with ideas," says Gaines-Ross, "is to think about what clients don't know that they need to know. You have to know as much as you can to find the missing piece. You can't come up with an idea if you don't know what's missing."

That's how Burson-Marsteller developed its research study on maximizing the value of a CEO's reputation. It fits with our business—managing perceptions. It comes from our company's mission—creating superior value for clients. And it comes from asking the question: How can our approach to leveraging intangibles be furthered in a way that no one has thought of before? Figures 3–3 and 3–4 demonstrate key points from Burson's thought leadership on CEO reputations. They describe the value and the payoffs that a company can expect from having a well-regarded CEO.

One head of global thought leadership. One chief knowledge officer. Two distinctly different vantage points, yet of one like mind when it comes to getting to *"What's missing?"* And then asking: *"Why not do it today?"*

Jack Welch, longtime chairman and chief executive of General Electric, thinks similarly: "It's like a dinner party with 12 people," he told the *New York Times*. "You bring as many intellects together as you can and then take the best ideas out of each. The leader who gets the most ideas from the most sources will have the most success."

A great definition of—or great aspirations for—thought leadership will mean nothing without people who can turn them into reality. Aligning your organization to

FIGURE 3-3   Thought Leadership at Burson-Marsteller: The Impact of CEO Reputation

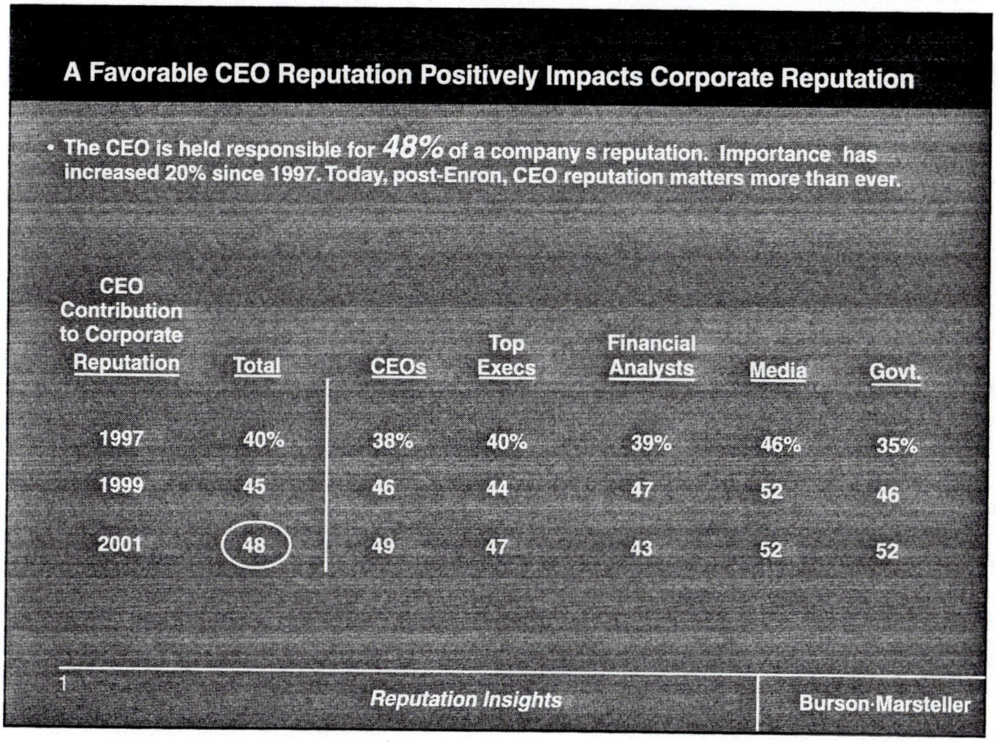

A Favorable CEO Reputation Positively Impacts Corporate Reputation

- The CEO is held responsible for *48%* of a company's reputation. Importance has increased 20% since 1997. Today, post-Enron, CEO reputation matters more than ever.

CEO Contribution to Corporate Reputation	Total	CEOs	Top Execs	Financial Analysts	Media	Govt.
1997	40%	38%	40%	39%	46%	35%
1999	45	46	44	47	52	46
2001	(48)	49	47	43	52	52

1   *Reputation Insights*   Burson-Marsteller

An Example of the Payoff of CEO Reputation.

deliver your thought leadership in a way that creates sustained value into the future is the focus of the remainder of our chapter.

STEP 3: CREATE THE RIGHT ORGANIZATIONAL MINDSET

"You clearly cannot become a thought leader without the right organizational mind-set," says May. "At Accenture, we made a deliberate change in culture. We told people: *'You can make a mistake.'* That is a whole new way of thinking, especially for management consultants."

"It takes a tremendous commitment from the top or it's not going to happen," says Gaines-Ross. "The other part of the process is channeling ideas up to the top."

May agrees: "Where you get the seeds for ideas is not just a top-down thing; you also need a process to extract ideas from the bottom up. Our entry-level people off campus, on the ground, working at clients, have so many new thoughts on their minds. As they work their way up the organization, their creativity can dissipate without the right organizational mindset. We have 75,000 people, hundreds and hundreds of client

FIGURE 3–4   Thought Leadership at Burson-Marsteller: The Payoffs of CEO Reputation

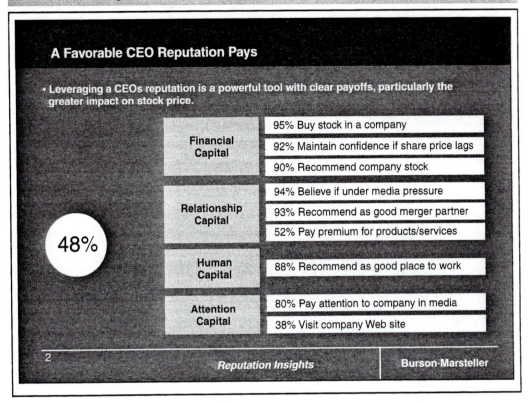

A Favorable CEO Reputation Pays

• Leveraging a CEOs reputation is a powerful tool with clear payoffs, particularly the greater impact on stock price.

48%

Financial Capital	95% Buy stock in a company
	92% Maintain confidence if share price lags
	90% Recommend company stock

Relationship Capital	94% Believe if under media pressure
	93% Recommend as good merger partner
	52% Pay premium for products/services

| Human Capital | 88% Recommend as good place to work |

| Attention Capital | 80% Pay attention to company in media |
| | 38% Visit company Web site |

2   *Reputation Insights*   **Burson-Marsteller**

relationships. If we're going to be relevant around the world, we need more than a dozen partners sitting in a room creating ideas."

"The question is," says May, "if you don't have the right mindset can you migrate yourself as an organization to get it? That answer is 100% dependent on your top 5-to-10 people in leadership positions."

What does it take to infect an organization with a craving for thought leadership?

- Setting an environment in which a mistake is allowed
- Engaging your most creative people
- Making sure that thought leadership is tied to the performance metrics
- Making sure your leadership understands and communicates its importance
- Aligning your resources to deliver thought leadership

"Thought leadership is the commitment you make about what matters. And it is a value to say what matters," says Gaines-Ross. "If you don't put the budget aside, if you don't allocate the time, if your leadership doesn't value it, if it gets done after hours, that speaks to your organizational values," says May, "and what it says is that it's not going to happen."

Thought leadership defines your point of view about the world—and your values about how you are going to operate in the world as an entity. "Values are an attractive proposition for people who choose to work with your company," says Gaines-Ross. "It's our biggest recruiting draw," says May.

STEP 4: ALIGN YOUR RESOURCES TO DELIVER THOUGHT LEADERSHIP

Nobody "sells" thought leadership; the insights are bought into. "Commercialization is equally important to our success," says May, although he doesn't believe that thought leadership is ever "productized." "We can attach projects or programs to our ideas, but the arsenal of solutions we pull together depends upon the unique client situation. It takes a very creative individual to be able to have those conversations."

In the words of an old philosophical puzzle, "If a tree falls in the forest, does it make a sound?" In the case of thought leadership, one might ask, "If your company has it but no one else knows it, does it exist?" Thought leadership is like a diamond in the rough. Until it is cut, polished, and displayed, its economic value is strictly latent. Realizing its full potential requires communication.

So what do thought leaders do?

Thought leaders write articles, white papers, and books. They give speeches and seminars to make their ideas accessible to large audiences. Gaines-Ross has spoken on CEO and corporate reputation at conferences and forums around the world and has been quoted in dozens of publications as "the expert" on the topic. She recently published *CEO Capital: A Guide to Building CEO Reputation and Company Success* (John Wiley & Sons, 2003).

In fact, much of the business book market has been taken over by the thought leadership competition. In the year 2000 alone, more than 2,000 books on leadership were published, some even repackaging Machiavelli and Shakespeare as leadership gurus. We caught up with one of New York's most sought-after business book publicists, Barbara Monteiro, at an event at the Plaza Hotel celebrating the book *Elizabeth I CEO, Strategic Lessons from the Leader Who Built an Empire.*

In a subsequent interview with Monteiro, we asked: "Why *Elizabeth I*?" Monteiro had built her reputation handling "high-brow" books. Her clients include authors such as Paul Krugman, Warren Bennis, Adrian Slywotzky, Burton Malkiel, Michael Bloomberg, and publications like *BusinessWeek* and *The Harvard Business Review.*

"The lesson of *Elizabeth I* is simple," says Monteiro—and one that, we think, is important for thought leaders: "Create your self image—or others will create one for you." Elizabeth understood that as a woman, and as a leader, she could give the people a cultural icon that would satisfy a need. (On becoming queen, Elizabeth worked quickly to transform her image from a bastard child to a Virgin Queen at a time when virginity was a highly regarded societal "*value*" [*our emphasis*].) In total, the book dispenses 136 such bite-size pronouncements. "It's written in snippets," says Monteiro, "so you can read one and think about it, which makes it more accessible to the person going to their job in Boston, or in Idaho, or in Los Angeles."

How does Monteiro select projects given her demand? "I read the first chapter of everything," she says, "and from there I decide. I've been reading business books for more than ten years now. If I don't learn something new, if I don't see a reason to change my mind about something, I move on to the next opportunity."

Monteiro reviews at least 50 business books a year in what she defines as three distinct categories. The first are "high-brow," or very high-level books. A second, or mid-level, are the books written by consulting firms. The third are historical and/or biographical. "The books are related, but different," says Monteiro. "The 'high-brows' are by gurus looking to push the envelope in their fields. Too often, the consulting books are written by a committee and there isn't really a voice. Having a voice makes a big difference in getting publicity. Histories and biographies are colorful, easy to remember. They stick with people."

Business books don't have to read like 300-page business-school cases, but they do have to educate. "Thought leadership is what you bring to the table," says Monteiro. "It's not just branding, or marketing, it teaches something. The content can be complex, as long as it's understandable." Gaines-Ross uses a three-part diagnostic to ensure a "teachable point of view" in her work. First, it has to be simple. Second, it has to make sense to the outside world. And third, it has to be meaningful inside the organization.

What does an author have to do to capture attention?

"Have what we call a 'green' personality," says Monteiro. "People who can be at ease talking to anyone, and who are very outgoing. They talk from the heart. They believe in their ideas. And when you hear them, you believe in their ideas too."

And to market the book, "It takes an integrated campaign," says Monteiro. "Advertising is expensive, but it makes an impression like nothing else. Add in book publicity, public relations, marketing, retail, an Internet component—you have to have all of these buttons pushed at once. Otherwise, it's very hard to make a book happen."

What could possibly have made Welch's book worth $7.1 million?[4] "Books are related to the entertainment business," says Monteiro. "A book representative doesn't sell just one book, but a whole line-up of books. It's like a billboard and he's at the top of the list, and other acts follow."

STEP 5: DELIVER SUSTAINED ECONOMIC VALUE FOR YOUR CLIENTS AND YOUR FIRM

How do you know when an idea catches fire? "First, you know by virtue of your short-term profit," says May, "but in today's world it doesn't take long for competitors to duplicate the idea and drive margins down. So you also know by the disintegration of your intermediate-term profit by new competitors. That's why sustaining profitability over the long term requires increasing levels of thought leadership."

The ability to generate a continuous flow of marketable ideas separates true thought leaders from the rest of the crowd. A big idea on its own is not enough; what is needed is a constant stream of ideas.

What's next on our contributors' agendas?

In December 2001, Burson-Marsteller launched the findings of its *e*-fluentials survey. The research identifies a group of online movers and shakers—the *e*-fluentials—who are shaping the opinions and attitudes of the Internet community. Representing 10 percent of the U.S. adult Internet population—about 11 million users—this group influences more people on more topics than other online users.

---

[4]"The $7 Million Man," *The New York Times*, July 16, 2000.

The effort has opened a rich vein of information about how ideas spread among the community of online users under their influence. Now, Gaines-Ross is working with practitioners to develop innovative ways for clients to reach these influencers and engage them in meaningful dialogues.

And, at Accenture, May is at work creating an industrial-strength capability to produce 10 new ideas a day—every day. The firm's new name and identity proclaim what it is as an organization and what it wants to become: a market maker, architect, and builder of the new economy.

As we near conclusion, our initial line of query bears repeating: What will be on the CEO's agenda five years from now, ten years from now? Will there even be a CEO? Your point of view in answer to these kinds of questions will begin to define your thought leadership. Thought leadership starts with your unique response to the question: "What's missing?" And what you do to fill that need—today, and every day—builds your reputation for having more of the better ideas.

So what is the "truth-in-advertising" tag line for thought leadership? "It's all about sustained value creation—it's always been that way. But the economy is moving so rapidly that the need to do it repetitively makes thought leadership a requirement now," says May. And Gaines-Ross: "There is no silver bullet. We're all trying to make sense of our work and thought leadership is a way of trying to make sense." And ours: Like young Martin Dressler, you want to make sense of the future so clearly that others want to come along. Ultimately, the truth of thought leadership lies in thought followership.

Had *The Economist* only stopped with its title!

CHAPTER

Innovation: The Growth Engine of Consulting

Robert L. Laud

Innovation is hard work. Innovation has a bottom line, demands discipline, and requires creative thinking, insight, extensive experience, and yes, luck and timing. And it can be, and often is, quite exhilarating, grand, and noble. For consulting firms, it is the lifeblood of both positioning and of new revenue sources in a very competitive space. Consulting firms need to be at the epicenter of new and commercially useful ideas. The days of implementing someone else's safe ideas for the client are over, and new structures and models of innovation are emerging. Among these, I have found that the more robust, integrated, and purposeful innovation centers have proven extremely useful in an economic climate in which applied research has become synonymous with solution development and, hence, value added for the client, and new revenue for the consulting firm. Yet developing this new vision of strategic innovation is far from a simple linear process. It requires a cross-functional leadership mindset that can help drive today's complex firms with a new level of integration and competitiveness.

THE IMPORTANCE OF THOUGHT LEADERSHIP IN MEETING CLIENT NEEDS

Clients have a variety of needs that must be attended to and balanced by consulting suitors. Buyer values have dramatically changed over time reflecting the rapid pace of competitive upheaval influenced by the dynamic breakthroughs of technology, social change, globalization, and regulatory shifts. Whereas clients not long ago were complacent and likely to accept an "industry standard" from implementers, now they often look for a return on their substantial investments that includes some form of competitive advantage. Without a component of thought leadership or differentiation, a consulting firm is relegated to competing on price or speed or some other component that directly cuts into its ability to charge a premium for its services. On the other hand, those firms that can develop and defend proprietary service offerings that keep pace and push the evolution of client preferences are clearly in the best position to command strong margins.

In today's environment, clients want to be apprised of new thinking and are often fairly current themselves as they go through the process of exploration before investments are made. Their own internal functions may also be fairly sophisticated and

Bob Laud is currently affiliated with Deloitte Consulting. Bob received his Ph.D. from Columbia University, MBA from Adelphi University, and BA from Colgate University.

often come with a set of advisors drawn from boutiques, university settings, or professional groups. For this reason, major consulting firms today experience even stronger pressure to stay "on top" of their fields, and the consulting business has clearly moved from repeat implementation to the successful application of innovative thinking—regardless of its originating source. If a consulting firm cannot differentiate itself on the basis of thought leadership, it has to play in a "commodity space" with ever decreasing margins. And given the ever-shrinking half-life of new knowledge, the replacement effort has to be that much more formidable and rigorous.

To be sure, not every potential client is ready to be the beta site for cutting-edge ideas. However, as one managing partner for a major consulting firm noted, "Clients want to talk about tomorrow, but they buy for today." It means that in order to get to the finals in a consulting selection process, you need to be invited to the table to begin with. Most major firms are structured by industry verticals and pride themselves on deep industry knowledge. In a recent study on buyer values (see Figure 4–1), "knowing our business" is the highest-ranking client buyer value. However, in today's market, industry knowledge is a credential that only gets you into the game and is usually not sufficient to create any notable differentiation that by itself will entice a client to select your firm over another.

Those consulting firms that have demonstrated innovation and more advanced knowledge are simply invited more often to compete, are more favored by industry analysts, and consequently win more contracts. Apparently, firms that have invested in next generation concepts and strategies also receive the added benefit of higher levels

FIGURE 4–1   Ranking of Client Buyer Values

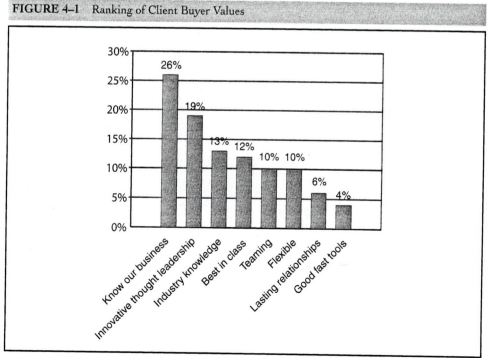

SOURCE: Big Five Research 2000–2001.

of trust or recognized competency to deliver "today's solutions" and become the preferred provider over more traditional implementers.

NO SCARCITY OF IDEAS

The amount of "new ideas" has grown geometrically over the last decade. Thought leadership volume has increased tenfold from what it was just five years ago. Approximately 500 thought leadership items are produced by the consulting industry every quarter. Volume is high, but so is noise and the growing competition to reap the benefits of reputational capital. Strategy firms, which dominated thought leadership publication for years, now rank behind the major systems implementers in publishing volume. The new Big 3 firms, however, have not yet captured top reputational rankings, but their volume of strategy work is steadily encroaching on the once sacred ground of the elite strategy firms. Simultaneously, the recent reconfiguring of the consulting industry and its larger "constellation" of nontraditional competitors has created a new paradigm wherein idea generation and innovation now also come from sources well beyond the scope and expertise found in most consulting firms. Figure 4–2 describes the new constellation of players in the management consulting industry.

Many new and nontraditional innovation breeders have entered the consulting marketplace as the level of sophistication and complexity in science, technology, business, and globalization have demanded skills that only very deep and specialized orga-

FIGURE 4-2   Constellation of Thought Leaders

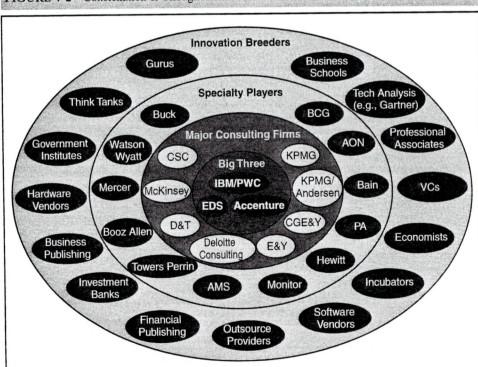

nizations can offer. These organizations, however, often lack the commercialization process, client network, project management, and implementation skills that are the backbone of most consulting firms. The pragmatic drive that underlies most consulting firms' operations and culture is quite antithetical to the norms found in think tanks, universities, and research institutes. Hence, combining these two disparate entities through various business models creates the possibility to exploit the core competencies of each entity. Although easy to understand in theory, the ability to "work" this model has been exceedingly challenging.

First, most consulting firms are better prepared to deliver "repeatable" solutions through a proven methodology. The more times the process is repeated, the more efficient it becomes and marginal revenue increases. Thus, incremental growth becomes the norm as the methodology is rolled out across other practices, all contributing to the bottom line. However, when a new service is introduced, it will lack efficiency and experienced personnel, thus increasing risk and costs. For this reason, it is rare to find even a few consulting firms who reward for innovation and its rollout. Those few firms, however, who have managed by whatever means to be the first to introduce the "blockbuster" ideas such as reengineering or Business Process Redesign, have received returns that far out exceed their competition.

Second, there is considerable complexity surrounding the legal ownership of intellectual property. Universities are often reluctant to "sell" wholesale the rights to their faculty's research, although individual researchers and departments may hold a different opinion. Patent searches may uncover numerous royalty complications, time sensitive ownership issues, constraints on applications and new risks or liability issues. Nonetheless, if consulting firms and research groups can come to terms with these issues, the rewards for each party can be considerable.

The challenges for the consulting firms in terms of making thought leadership produce a return on investment are several:

- How will a firm gain intelligence and insight on market trends and possibilities that are ever expanding and becoming more complex?
- How will the next solution area be determined? What are the risks? How will a firm know with whom to align? How will the process of solution development function?
- How will the commercialization and rollout programs work? How will consultants learn, gain experience, conduct sales, and contribute to excellence in delivery?
- How will the firm brand the innovation concepts and increase the reputational capital of the firm?

All of these issues are significant and complex hurdles that must be overcome in order to successfully compete in today's competitive consulting market. Thus, it is not just having a good idea that counts, but having a good idea that can be successfully commercialized. By combining the core delivery competencies of consulting firms with the research and ideation capacity of various "think tanks," new models of collaboration can be formed playing to each other's exceptional strengths.

A CLUSTERED MARKETPLACE OF INNOVATION LEADERSHIP

It is clear even to the most conservative of consulting firms that they can no longer rely on their legacy services to maintain their market position and growth rates. The traditional "repeatable" implementations of the big information technology (IT) shops have proven to become commodities with smaller marginal returns year by year. Large human resource (HR) firms have realized the need to aggressively move into the largely untapped world of outsourcing, although their product lines are still limited. And strategy firms are struggling to be the first to determine the "next strategy." Clearly, the age-old proverb of being "the best darn buggy whip manufacturer" has reached the consulting community. The elite world of consulting has long avoided the strict discipline and investment required for formal science and research, instead relying on extremely bright business minds working their way through what appeared to be an endless market of cash-rich clients. Now, however, the pace of change and the level of sophistication of both competitors and clients have raised the bar in demanding more ideas, greater differentiation, faster installations, and quicker and larger returns. Clients are no longer content, nor should they be, to simply have a consulting firm implement the client's own idea at a premium price.

The response from the consulting community has been very positive. Strategies to manage the complexity of innovation have evolved to cover the gamut from highly pragmatic investigation and application to highly theoretical and future oriented. Some firms have focused almost exclusively on pure thought leadership, advanced research, and theoretical possibilities. Others have focused much more on incremental advances, practical solution applications, and the leveraging of outsourced development services. Either way, firms have sought to bolster their reputation as definitive thought leaders realizing that without this edge they will be viewed as little more than commodity traders and certainly will not be able to command any price differential, other than low price provider. This has been a major factor in contributing to the lower margins of the least differentiated firms.

A recent study of market leadership found a positive correlation between market leadership (revenue, growth, reputation) and high-quality thought leadership (research, solution innovation, outreach) (see Figure 4–3). One can easily see that the brand strength of a consulting firm is enhanced through strategic innovation, but it must be remembered that one-time breakthroughs will not sustain a brand indefinitely. Continuous innovation is needed for sustained reputational capital to accrue.

Figure 4–3 demonstrates a clustering of the major consulting firms and segments with generally little distinction for most of the firms. The challenge then for each of the firms is to break away from the pack as they attempt to position for thought leadership dominance. Those few firms which have already begun developing an innovation capability appear to be at an advantage, at least for the time being. The next phase on the evolutionary ladder of innovation, however, will go well beyond thought leadership and sound science, as important as that may be. Deep scientific capability in a wide range of disciplines will be the basis of the initial foray, but an equally deep understanding and ability to lead and integrate organization architecture and commercialization will play an equally important role.

DISCIPLINED APPROACH TO STRATEGIC INNOVATION

There is a good deal of debate relative to innovation at consulting firms. How does innovation come about? Is it something structured or free flowing? Should a firm look for low-risk incremental innovation or out-of-the-box breakthrough? What is more

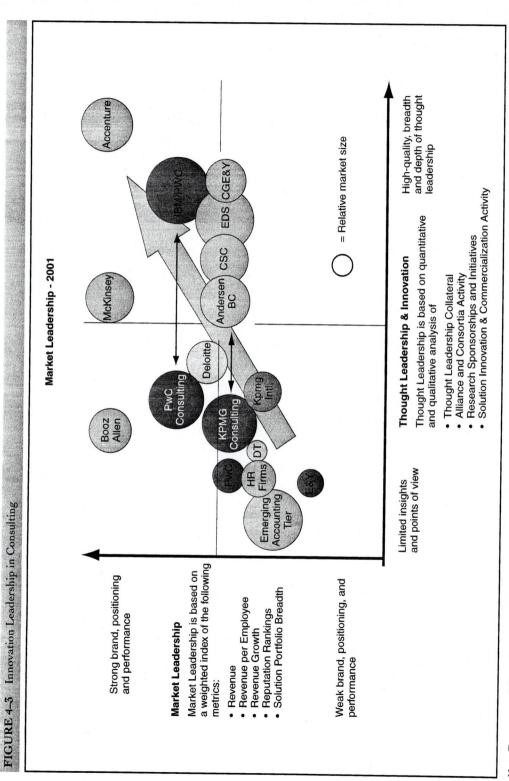

FIGURE 4–5 Innovation Leadership in Consulting

Market Leadership - 2001

Strong brand, positioning and performance

Market Leadership

Market Leadership is based on a weighted index of the following metrics:

• Revenue
• Revenue per Employee
• Revenue Growth
• Reputation Rankings
• Solution Portfolio Breadth

Weak brand, positioning, and performance

Limited insights and points of view

Thought Leadership & Innovation

Thought Leadership is based on quantitative and qualitative analysis of

• Thought Leadership Collateral
• Alliance and Consortia Activity
• Research Sponsorships and Initiatives
• Solution Innovation & Commercialization Activity

High-quality, breadth and depth of thought leadership

◯ = Relative market size

Accenture
McKinsey
Booz Allen
IBM/PwC
EDS CGE&Y
CSC
Andersen BC
Deloitte
PwC Consulting
Kpmg Intl
KPMG Consulting
PwC
HR Firms
DT
E&Y
Emerging Accounting Tier

Note: For comparability, all revenue numbers have been adjusted to align with calender year 2001 and 2000 for revenue growth
SOURCE: Fortune; Vault.com; Company Web sites; Andersen analysis.

profitable: continuous innovation or radical step-wise innovation? Is being a fast follower financially safer than being a cutting-edge leader? Can firms lead incremental innovation in-house while effectively outsourcing the Big Idea breakthroughs? What is "safe" to collaborate on with competitors and clients, and what isn't? And, can research and development (R&D) models from other industries apply equally as well to consulting firms?

In the 20 years that I have engaged in innovation and solution development at a variety of consulting firms (professional services, technology, and HR), I have found that the most important factor in successful introduction of innovation and profitability has more to do with the consulting firm's organizational architecture than with the quality and overwhelming value attributable to any single innovation. Put another way, it doesn't much matter how good the idea is—it matters extensively how good a commercialization engine it has.

So how does organization architecture affect innovation? Let's begin with a simple truth: Innovators are pressured, punished, and pushed out of organizations that seek conformity. That's why creativity abounds in diverse cultures and is strangled by the social ties found in very strong cultures. I am also amazed at the large number of excellent ideas generated in some cultures that eventually become bogged down in some bureaucratic quagmire. By the same token, I am perhaps even more amazed by the even larger volume of bad ideas that are extensively funded and receive top level executive support at these same organizations. On the positive side, this suggests management's general willingness and inclination to support innovation. But it also highlights a general misunderstanding of the "science of innovation" and the deep relationship that innovation must share with the organization's commercialization capability. (*Side comment:* The challenge lies in having a deep understanding of science, research, organization architecture, finance, and marketing and being able to orchestrate all the components at once—and better than the competition.)

A simple solution that many firms have chosen is to "decentralize" or isolate the innovation function and create a separate R&D world where the creative types can flourish. To a degree that is a workable model, but case after case has shown that to the extent the R&D function is a stand-alone entity, it will produce less relevant products than if it is integrated. Hence, we start down the path to conformity again.

The business innovation model in Figure 4–4 is based on a comprehensive review of leading practices in industrial and pharmaceutical R&D functions, private and public think tanks, major research universities, and leading consulting firms. I have implemented this model keeping one point uppermost: it must fit and leverage the organization architecture. It is not a stand-alone unit, and it is not so integrated as to lose its identity and integrity. It combines a delicate balance between the tension and discipline needed to produce high-quality pragmatic ideas regularly, and the degree of freedom required to feel independent, explore, and hope for serendipitous breakthrough. No easy task.

Key to the innovation model is an overall capability for the center to "own" the entire end-to-end value chain including intelligence, solution development, commercialization and branding. Each of these components is essential for a strategic well-integrated innovation process and is quite different than "pure business research" centers that focus almost exclusively on scientific theory, intellectual interests, or personal research areas. The Strategic Innovation Model ensures that the right "product" is

FIGURE 4-4   A Model for Strategic Innovation

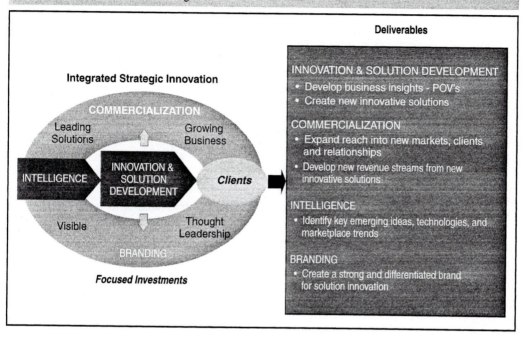

developed, brought to market in a timely manner, is delivered with quality and profitability, and builds or enhances the consulting firm brand. If any one of these components is missing, the whole model becomes suboptimized. On the flip side, when all components are synchronized together, and with the firm strategy, the investment return is maximized.

INNOVATION DRIVES STRATEGY AND MARKET EXECUTION

Traditionally, and even today many innovation centers in consulting firms have been stand-alone entities. They are purposefully designed to operate from distant locations, have little relationship with line activities, and focus primarily on thought leadership as a reputation builder. In addition, they seek to conduct original research in an atmosphere that promotes unbiased activity without the influence of profit and loss pressures. In fact, the staff of some of these functions may represent more of an academic research model that places little value on the client experience that ultimately drives the business and revenue generation. Depending on the specific goals of management and the needs of the consulting firm, this more traditional model of pure research needs to be evaluated in juxtaposition to more pragmatic research models in which accountability for solution development is paramount, and becoming more standard in the industry. Some firms might even argue that unless research has a short-term application and a somewhat predictable return on investment (ROI), they may not be willing to make significant research investments. In fact, those firms who avoid innovation and solution development for the most part have focused almost exclusively on acquiring software alliances, thus relegating the firm to being a systems implementer. These firms will be valued for their implementation capability, but will probably not be invited to compete on more strategic levels at the beginning of engagements. At the other end of the spectrum are the more strategic innovators who look for ownership of thought leadership and the premium prices the brand can command. As long as either theoretical research or pragmatic research is conducted, these firms will benefit through brand building and marketplace recognition. Ideally, firms should balance both short and long-term research in an attempt to build an innovation portfolio that has a regular pipeline of new solutions emerging over time, as well as differentiated investments that support both solution development and separate brand building activities.

A model that is becoming more prevalent today ensures that the innovation function becomes highly integrated with the other major corporate functions and also with the typical consulting firm matrix (see Figure 4–5).

This model demonstrates that the innovation function has now been recognized by top management as an activity with strong strategic importance. It is no longer stand-alone, but exists on par with all other major functions, and is very closely tied to firm

FIGURE 4–5 Innovation: From Stand-Alone to Center Stage

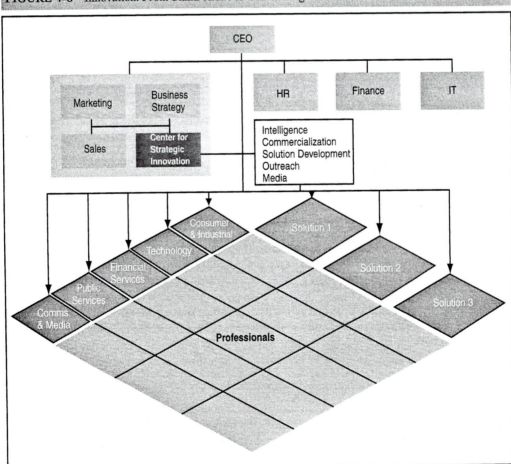

strategy, marketing, and sales. In turn, it also becomes specifically accountable both to help define and advance the firm on a particular path. Innovation is a direct feeder into corporate strategy since it is responsible for identifying trend data and early warnings, and preparing the organization to understand the future. It plays a key role in marketing and helping line management with client relationship development through seminars, briefings, and joint projects. It supports sales with upfront presentation support, sales materials, and delivery services.

The structure of the innovation entity will most likely reflect the overall organization matrix in terms of the balance between industry verticals and solutions or lines of business. Different consulting firms will have varying degrees of decentralization of their industries. Also, firms will vary on the degree of independence between stand-alone versus integrated solution development and delivery. Accordingly, the innovation function may take varying designs, which should reflect the overall focus and strategy of the firm.

The return on innovation investment is optimized when solutions are developed within one industry with the expectation that the solution will then be modified to apply across industries. This provides deep support in the initial stages of development and helps to defray costs in the long run. The challenge of this model is the accuracy in which projects can be selected so that cross-industry application is possible. Further, because this model is cross-industry in design, it focuses more on large and emerging trends, which by definition are hardest to anticipate and plan for. Incremental advances may be more predictable, but they will not have the returns and break-through insights that clients are expecting to hear from their high-priced consultants.

SOLUTION LIFE CYCLES: INNOVATION AS THE GROWTH ENGINE

There is a great deal of economic research on the importance of innovation in sustaining and driving a free-market economy. This is especially true in the twenty-first century, wherein the pace of change and the explosion of disruptive technologies has added even more fuel to the theoretical economic models that have proven true in predicting the inevitability of long-term free-market growth over planned socialist models. In particular, it is the competition that stems from new technology, new processes, and the inevitable transformation from differentiated product/service to commodity that now moves organizations to compete in a new arena. Innovation has replaced those business models that relied on price cutting and diminishing marginal revenue gains that were more appropriate for eras in which things were stable and change was slow. The new competition strikes at the foundations of corporate existence, not at the margins of incremental gain. Thus, the ever-growing specter of corporate stagnation and speedy meltdown becomes a stimulus for expanding the business model and extending the competitive thinking. Innovation now takes center stage as it couples itself to new research portfolios, associated marketing and profitable commercialization. In turn, the demonstrated profitability and brand enhancement will draw other competitors into the new space, stimulate further innovation development, increase new competition, and provide clients with alternative choices.

The impact of innovation in terms of profitability, competitive advantage, and market image is forcing consulting firms to make innovation development formal and routine. A review of solution life cycles in Figure 4–6 demonstrates that new services are

FIGURE 4–6   Solution Life Cycles: Innovation as the Growth Engine

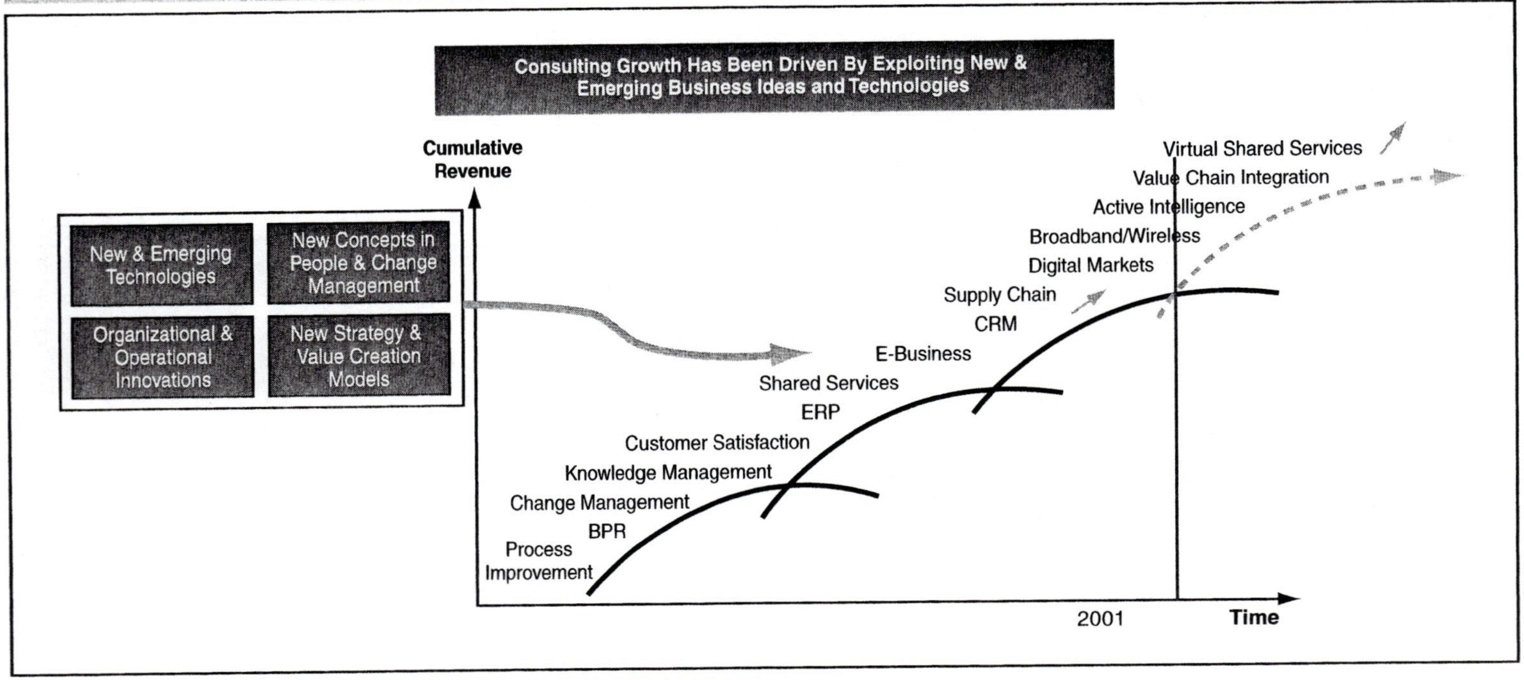

Consulting Growth Has Been Driven By Exploiting New & Emerging Business Ideas and Technologies

Cumulative Revenue

New & Emerging Technologies

Organizational & Operational Innovations

New Concepts in People & Change Management

New Strategy & Value Creation Models

Process Improvement
BPR
Change Management
Knowledge Management
Customer Satisfaction
ERP
Shared Services
E-Business
CRM
Supply Chain
Digital Markets
Broadband/Wireless
Active Intelligence
Value Chain Integration
Virtual Shared Services

2001

Time

being added to the consulting firm's repertoire on a regular basis. In fact, there is a more extensive proliferation of potential services that haven't made this list.

Figure 4–6 notes a series of new innovations that have been selected, launched, and successful, but does not include the large number of innovations that have either been marginal in terms of uptake or have been eliminated altogether. What is important to keep in mind is that there is no way of knowing how many other innovations could have been wildly successful, but were vetted out along the way. Some of these innovations might have been eliminated intentionally, by oversight, or have simply lacked meaningful commercialization. Even superlative concepts without a strong and aggressive commercialization plan will not go very far. Thus, it is not just a powerful new idea and research funding that is required for innovation success, but execution of the entire innovation value chain that also includes marketing and commercialization excellence.

A GLANCE AT THE FUTURE

Placing the right investments on the innovation process is a difficult and complex process. Consideration must be given to a series of decisions, including the amount of investment money required over time, potential barriers to competition that can be created, whether follow-on products are likely to be forthcoming, how the competition will respond, strategic fit, client demand, and the expected probability of success and the return on investment. In addition, most consulting firms have not historically been known for cultures and reward systems that place a high value on original R&D. Partners or senior executives have more likely moved into the senior ranks through excellence in sales and delivery against specific monetary targets, not through solution creation regardless of how successfully it was leveraged. Those who spent the time needed for solution development activity were probably more likely to be penalized for taking time away from the most valued contribution (i.e., sales and revenue generation). Today, however, firms have realized that the half-life of solutions is diminishing steadily and that customers are demanding more original thinking from high-priced firms. The longer a firm tries to hold on to static solutions, the more likely they will face margin erosion as solutions become commodities and differential pricing is lost.

Many consulting firms are realizing the need to stay in front of the "innovation curve" today either through original research or through some form of multiple alliances where they can gain access and license to apply new knowledge. In either case, the firm must decide what innovation investments will support their strategy and business model. The first major step in the process is to understand at a detailed level the direction of innovation in the marketplace. Although this is a routinized activity for most major industries and may even be considered a core competency in some, such as pharmaceutical firms, scientific research and market intelligence in consulting firms is mostly at its infancy except in a few major firms.

The options for strategic firm direction and innovation investment are quite extensive. As we look at the proliferation of scientific discovery in technology and process advancements (see Figure 4–7), it becomes apparent that predicting future revenue streams has lots of variables that need to be analyzed. Firms must have a thorough understanding not only of the science involved in the innovation, but also its commercialization potential and client readiness to invest in something that may not have

FIGURE 4-7 Cutting-Edge Concept and Technology Evolution

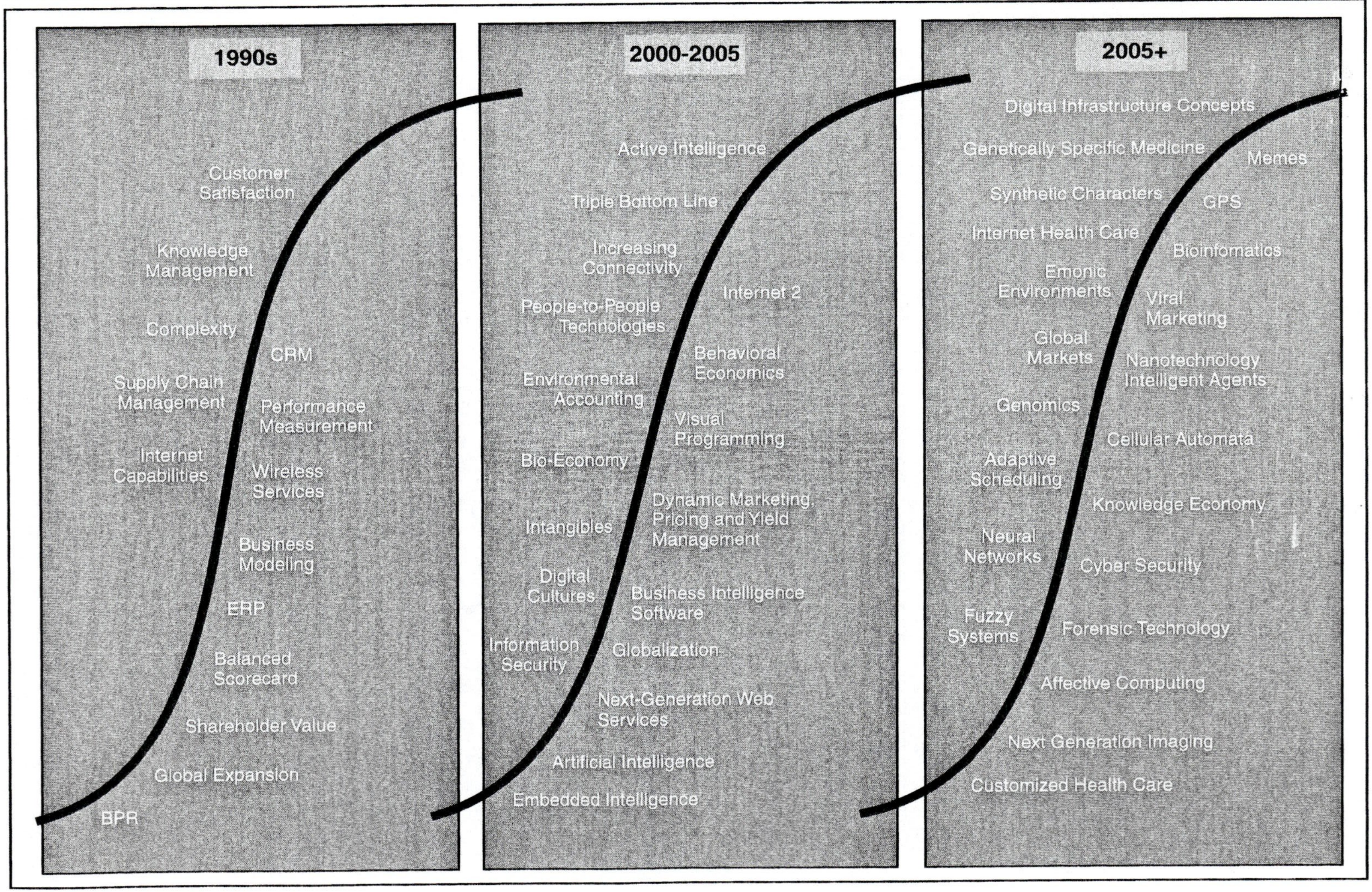

1990s

Customer Satisfaction
Knowledge Management
Complexity
CRM
Supply Chain Management
Performance Measurement
Internet Capabilities
Wireless Services
Business Modeling
ERP
Balanced Scorecard
Shareholder Value
Global Expansion
BPR

2000-2005

Active Intelligence
Triple Bottom Line
Increasing Connectivity
People-to-People Technologies
Internet 2
Environmental Accounting
Behavioral Economics
Bio-Economy
Visual Programming
Intangibles
Dynamic Marketing, Pricing and Yield Management
Digital Cultures
Business Intelligence Software
Information Security
Globalization
Next-Generation Web Services
Artificial Intelligence
Embedded Intelligence

2005+

Digital Infrastructure Concepts
Memes
Genetically Specific Medicine
GPS
Synthetic Characters
Bioinformatics
Internet Health Care
Emonic Environments
Viral Marketing
Global Markets
Nanotechnology
Intelligent Agents
Genomics
Cellular Automata
Adaptive Scheduling
Knowledge Economy
Neural Networks
Cyber Security
Fuzzy Systems
Forensic Technology
Affective Computing
Next Generation Imaging
Customized Health Care

extensive testing. Some client organizations pride themselves on breakthrough applications, but others shun anything that is not proven.

In developing an innovation agenda it should be understood that not all "bets" will come to fruition. Projects should be reviewed on regular schedule and decisions need to be made as to which solution development projects are viable and deserve further investment, and which should be culled. With so many exciting and enticing opportunities, these decisions will not be easy.

SUMMARY

Consulting firms are being held to a higher level of accountability by their clients. Economists are now arguing that the driving force behind growth is not price competition and cost cutting, although these are requirements of the game, but routinized innovation that promotes customer excitement, creates new demand and increases market share. Simply put, systematic innovation is now essential for every company within any innovating industry. Without innovation and a formal system to regularly produce new ideas, processes, and services, companies are left unprotected to compete at this level.

Consulting firms, in particular, are being driven by clients to provide new insights, breakthroughs, differentiated solutions, and competitive advantage. Although many consulting firms have been driven by repeatable delivery methodology to widen their own margins and provide clients with proven processes, this strategy eventually produces a commodity "service" and does not provide an impetus for growth. At the heart of free-market growth is the competitive pressure to create, explore, build, and innovate. The consulting firm that can develop its own internal innovation engine and collaborative alliances, and bring this edge to its clients will create its own competitive advantage. And those firms and organizations that fail to innovate in today's market will surely pay an alternative price. Finally, routinization will reduce the sawtooth aspects of innovation, while innovation success will further advance this new engine of growth.

CHAPTER

The Future of Management Consulting

5

Douglas M. McCracken

Assessing any future market is an iterative process: Trends change, client needs change, and technology changes, as do values, visions, and cultures within the enterprises and countries that consultants serve. This chapter presents Deloitte Consulting's current view of the consulting marketplace from the vantage point of the early twenty-first century. We will continue to revisit our trends and assumptions in this rapidly changing world on an ongoing basis to assist our clients as well as our own internal planning efforts.

There is no universal definition of the consulting market. For our purposes, we define "consulting" as providing advice, systems building, creating or reengineering processes, operations management, and training that assist a client in solving its business problems. There is an implicit assumption in the client-consultant relationship: That the client knows his or her business inside-out, but that the consultant knows more about the issues at hand than the client, and is capable of bringing those issues to bear in a more effective manner than the client is on his or her own.

By the term *enterprise* we mean "a group of people legally and politically bound together for a common business goal." We use the word as a synonym for organization, business, or company.

This chapter addresses broad global trends in consulting in the early twenty-first century; outlining the impact that the forces of business change will have on both enterprises and the consulting firms that serve them.

CONSULTING IN FLUX

The consulting industry is in a state of unprecedented flux, and mirrors the state of markets practically everywhere. The same forces of change that are reshaping enterprises are also reshaping consultancies and the way they do business. These forces include: globalization, information ubiquity, "always on" operations, and the shortage of top-shelf talent.

To meet client needs in the future, consulting firms must embrace the real effects of these factors, which include:

Douglas M. McCracken, Chief Executive Officer of Deloitte Consulting, has been a leader of the consulting industry for more than 20 years. Mr. McCracken holds a Bachelor of Arts degree in Economics from Norwich University. He also holds a Master of Arts degree in Economics from Northeastern University and a Master of Science degree in Management from Rensselaer Polytechnic Institute.

- Ability to handle more complexity (options, solutions, variables, changes) in managing for business success
- Creation of new business strategies
- Further refinement of reinvention skills

These factors, in turn, are changing the way consultants operate. Consequently, some consulting models in the future will resemble traditional areas in consulting, while others will be new. The consulting firms that survive will be the ones that find the elusive formula of scale, consistency, globalization, and recruitment and retention of the best people. Financial performance will be a necessary yet challenging end result.

A BRIEF HISTORY OF THE CONSULTING MARKET

The future of consulting, although it will be quite different from its past, will neverthe-less be shaped by it. Consultants of one type or another have been around since the advent of modern business. What we call the *consulting market*, however, has been a more recent phenomenon—one that has evolved significantly in the last 30 years.

The 1970s marked the heyday of consultancies that earned their fees by advising clients on strategy. In those days, leaders in the field (e.g., Booz Allen, McKinsey, Boston Consulting Group, Bain) commonly devoted several months or more to look-ing at the workings of a company before determining how its management could improve market and operating performance.

Major changes in business and constant advances in technology during the 1980s and early 1990s led to an ever-increasing need for advice on, as well as assistance with, the development and implementation of technology-based systems. This was the era of reengineering and client-server consulting. This period also marked the expansion of the Big Five Accounting Firms (originally the Big Eight) into the consulting market. Arthur Andersen, Deloitte & Touche, Ernst & Young, KPMG, and PricewaterhouseCoopers, developed consulting branches to offer their skill in professional services, competing with the traditional strategy firms noted above. The Big Five drew on their strengths in opera-tions and information technology (IT). During this period, large, established hardware vendors such as IBM also dramatically expanded their consulting presence. So too did the traditional outsourcing firms such as EDS and CSC. For most consultancies, revenue grew rapidly, and the prospect of gaining ever-increasing business led to an expanding field of newcomers (e.g., American Management Systems, Lante Corporation, Technology Solutions Corp.) and non-U.S. players (e.g., Cap Gemini Sogeti, Sema Group, Logica). These firms that provided a plethora of consulting offerings now evolved to become the new "traditional" consulting firm.

During this era the primary manner of assessing consultants was by "skill buckets." Firms too were generally organized around one or more of these competencies: strat-egy, reengineering, IT, and operations or outsourcing (OS) (see Figure 5–1). Helping employees deal with change (change management) generally occurred within each cat-egory, although only recently has it been treated as a true competency in its own right. Over time, the competency groupings had increasingly overlapping boundaries.

The latest era of consulting began in the mid-1990s and continues today: It is marked by sudden market changes that underscore the consultancies' need to foresee their clients' changing requirements and help them transform themselves to meet their

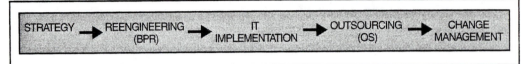

FIGURE 5-1   1980–1990 Consulting Market Overview of Capabilities

newer competitive requirements. It is also a time of consolidation, "speed," and an increase in competition for talented men and women. Consultants know that without scale in geography and a range of services for clients, they will have a hard time prospering.

Many companies and the consulting firms that served them were generally caught off-balance by the Internet revolution. In the mid-1990s, many viewed the Internet merely as means of marketing through the construction of a corporate Web page. It seemed little more than an electronic advertisement venue and fulfillment mechanism. Consultants were largely unenthusiastic about Web-design because the exercise did not bring in much revenue. Nor did it attract the attention of influential senior management among clients. Some consultancies, furthermore, lacked in-house skills for the work. In 1997 and 1998, however, matters changed as new boutique consultancies positioned themselves as e-business experts, increasing competition for traditional consultants.

Business-to-business (B2B) applications helped enterprises function more efficiently. Business-to-consumer (B2C) enterprises also gathered steam as viable operations. The Internet was a sudden dramatic threat to the status quo. Technology became an issue that worried chief executive officers. Any CEO who lacked a strategy for using the Internet, or who did not sound comfortable talking about e-business, was at risk. Clients needed help in strategizing a viable e-business strategy and implementation. Few consulting firms could address these complex client needs, thus leading to major shifts in how they organized themselves to pursue these market upheavals.

As the "Internet bubble" came and went and we assess its legacy while we await "the new new thing," the consulting industry has never been more turbulent than today. This environment has created significant new opportunities and challenges. The changes are drastically impacting the consulting market and will necessitate redefining consulting skills and organizational structures to successfully address evolving unique client needs. The forces that are shaping these changes are discussed in the next section.

MEGA FORCES AFFECTING ENTERPRISES

Changing conditions affect the way in which consultants deliver value to their clients. The nature of a consulting firm's work reflects the business conditions affecting their clients. Before we can address the direction of consulting, we must look at the reasons for the great changes that have and are affecting business, nationally and globally, their effect on enterprises, and the responses that successful enterprises are making (see Figure 5–2).

FIGURE 5–2   Framework for Understanding Enterprise Success

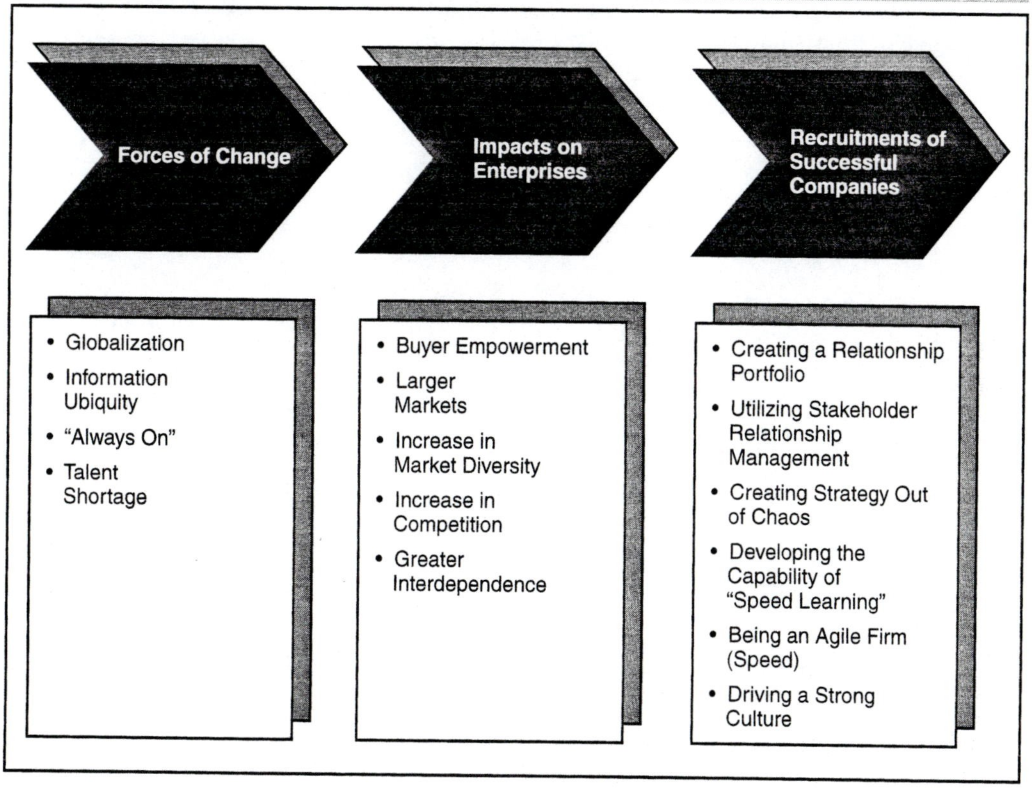

Forces of Change	Impacts on Enterprises	Recruitments of Successful Companies
• Globalization	• Buyer Empowerment	• Creating a Relationship Portfolio
• Information Ubiquity	• Larger Markets	• Utilizing Stakeholder Relationship Management
• "Always On"	• Increase in Market Diversity	• Creating Strategy Out of Chaos
• Talent Shortage	• Increase in Competition	• Developing the Capability of "Speed Learning"
	• Greater Interdependence	• Being an Agile Firm (Speed)
		• Driving a Strong Culture

The magnitude of change experienced in the recent past will continue. In fact, much of it will intensify as enterprises, communities, and individuals all confront these four major forces of change: globalization, information ubiquity, "always on" operations, and talent shortage. We are already feeling the impact of these four forces of change. What is new is their increasing interaction. These four forces, in turn, are impacted by big demographic, political, and economic changes, as well as accelerated and intensified by technology developments.

All four forces of change are under way now, but their intensity is increasing. Dealing with these forces is a necessity for all enterprises to simply survive, let alone create some competitive differentiator.

Globalization

A simple definition of globalization is the increasingly free movement of goods, services, capital, and labor between countries. However, this force of change is underpinned and accelerated by new, technology-induced routes to market, improving global communications, expanded risk management controls, and reduction of traditional trade barriers in some regions of the world.

Globally successful firms will show flexibility in attracting and retaining professionals to work for them, while stressing the common goal of serving clients anywhere and anytime. Consequently, the enterprise, as well as consulting firm, that stresses the importance of recognizing, respecting, and capitalizing on differences stands a better chance of flourishing internationally.

Globalization will force enterprises to drive revenues in new markets versus simply using other countries as low-cost manufacturing facilities. It will force the effective management of multicultural workforces. It also will bring much consolidation as well as specialization, as organizations look to exploit competitive advantage by geography.

Expected Path of Globalization
Trade blocs continue
Trade barriers continue to fall
Industry deregulation continues
Laissez-faire expands unevenly

Expected paths (directions) of globalization:

Trade blocs expand. The European Union (EU), North American Free Trade Agreement (NAFTA), and Association of South East Asian Nations (ASEAN) are increasing in membership and beginning to overlap as trading relationships increase through events such as the World Trade Talks.

Trade barriers continue to fall. While a key trade barrier continues to be exchange rate risk, this is being mitigated by common currencies (U.S. dollar and euro) and improvement in economic management as central banks become more independent.

Industry deregulation continues. Key industries currently affected are: energy, telecommunications, financial services, and health care. Deregulation creates the opportunity to consolidate and create scale economies. It also brings increased risk of market turmoil, both short and long term.

Laissez-faire expands unevenly. Although free trade will continue to increase, there will be increased regulation in areas such as privacy, competition (antitrust), independence, and copyright.

Information Ubiquity

The next three to five years will focus on leveraging the still largely untapped power in information. Primarily via technology, which can now deliver information ubiquity, information is becoming universally available and accessible. Management's focus will be driving competitive advantage through leveraging information, combining it with the historically major emphasis on cost savings via more efficient processes.

Expected Path of Information Ubiquity
Increase in choices
Increased demand for value
Increase in use of exchanges
Technology pervasiveness
Increase in information quality

Expected paths of information ubiquity include:

Increase in choices. The increased availability of information, particularly through the Internet, provides the buyer (business or consumer) with more informed choices.

Increased demand for value. The developed economies represent the bulk of the world's market. In that market the increasingly better educated and knowledgeable consumer base will become more selective in its purchase decisions. Buyers will acquire more power because they will be able to exchange information among themselves with greater ease. This leads to more emphasis on true, consumer-perceived value as the basis for purchasing decisions.

Increase in use of exchanges. Information aggregators and exchanges (or digital marketplaces) will grow in importance as the volume of accessible information increases. While the use of exchanges by enterprises will increase, the absolute number of exchanges will decrease over time as market consolidation and shakeout occurs.

Technology pervasiveness. The effect of ubiquitous information outside the developed economies of the world is less certain in our timeframe. Although technology is becoming pervasive in developing economies, these countries lack infrastructure that is essential to expand the use of new technology on any great scale. In some parts of the world, for example, any talk of being wired makes little sense when so few people have regular access to electricity.

Increase in information quality. Information quality will reduce transaction costs and facilitate and ultimately force organizational consolidation. For example, in any given market or industry as the cost of information discovery and usage is brought down, market consolidation will occur as marginal players who relied on or exploited information inefficiencies become non-competitive.

"Always On" Operations

The Internet is never switched off. Enterprises in the new economy are required to meet customer and employee needs by providing services which transcend normal working hours across time and space—the "always on" phenomenon is becoming a primary business challenge. The "always on" Internet is both a cause and a solution to this problem.

These expectations are pushing enterprises to provide a $24 \times 7 \times 365$ operating environment globally. Market leaders investing today will enjoy major competitive advantages. But ultimately (over the next five years), this "always on" capability will become a necessity (i.e., the ante) for enterprises to be successful.

The next three to five years will require enterprises to put in place the infrastructure to support an "always on" environment. This is *not* just a $24 \times 7 \times 365$ infrastructure for data centers; the entire business infrastructure of the enterprise in the near future will also need to function "always on." This business infrastructure will decrease product development cycles and drive the need for universal standards as well as dramatically change the way people work.

Expected Path of "Always On"
Increasing need to understand the buyer
Access devices increase "always on" demand
Customer support and relationship management constant
Increase in active marketing

Expected paths of "always on" include:

Increasing need to understand the buyer. Understanding how the buyer enters and uses the "always on" service is crucial to understanding the support required to assure the purchase decision, particularly in a global environment.

Access devices will increase "always on" demand. Access devices, to include wireless communication devices such as phones and personal digital assistants, will begin to converge and increase the demand for "always on services" with immediate delivery expectations.

Highly refined customer support and relationship management. Both must be done exceedingly well when 24 × 7 × 365 and real-time availability is demanded. Customer expectations will be very high. Customer-facing people must be more knowledgeable and personable.

More pro-active marketing. Standards will be rationalized to a push model where access to buyers requires active, rather than passive, marketing.

Talent Shortage

Enterprises will face unprecedented shortage of talent driven by (see Figure 5–3):

- An older population
- Gaps between new economy skill requirements and the output of educational, training, and retraining institutions
- Unprecedented demand for qualified men and women.

According to Information Technology Association of America (ITAA), the current demand for skilled IT people is 1.6 million persons, far exceeding the supply, with half of these positions likely going unfilled. According to a Kelly Services Study, over 60 percent of respondents expect job changes, which has given rise to a volatile job market that favors employees over employers. The survey also found that respondents

FIGURE 5–3   The Talent Shortage Gets Worse

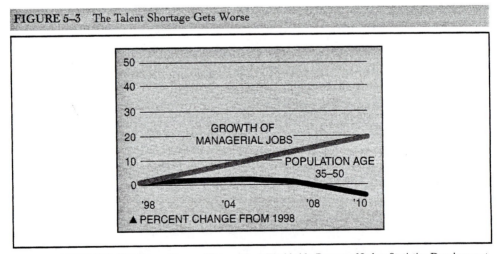

SOURCE: ©BW DATA: U. S. Census Bureau, Watson Wyatt Worldwide, Bureau of Labor Statistics, Development Dimensions International.

identify with their profession more than their employer, validating the strong trend toward "free agents" in the IT industry.

Today, more then ever, the pursuit of talent is on executives' mind. A recent report by Hewitt Associates LLC states that:

- 75 percent of corporate officers say they are critically short of talent.
- 85 percent of IT companies report the shortage of talent has hurt their business.
- 65 percent of growth company CEOs view the talent shortage as a major constraint.

Organizations will focus more attention on identifying, recruiting, retaining, and retraining the intellectual capital components of their organization. This challenge is borne out by the "2000 Human Resources Practices Survey" conducted by the Human Resources Strategies Group of Deloitte & Touche LLP. Nearly all studied companies (*Fortune* 1000) report that the retention continues to be a central concern of HR leaders (67 percent). Perhaps more telling is the fact that over one out of three respondents identifies recruiting as the major challenge, while nearly one in five attaches that label to retention. This trend is driven by demographics, skill needs, and the competitive advantage of harnessing information. To do so requires a more skilled labor force than most organizations have invested in historically. Capabilities such as more flexible hiring, better retention philosophies, and improved training effectiveness will become crucial.

Expected Path of "Talent Shortage"
More aged work population
Uneven access to education
Limited access to talent
Lack of corporate "people skills"

Expected path of talent shortage includes:

More aged work population. The demographic profile of developed nations is aging as the bulge of baby boomers move toward retirement, leading to a shortage of talent in the core employment ages of 25–45.

Uneven access to education. Although the population of developing countries is growing younger, uneven access to education will prevent these future workers from fully meeting the needs of the new economy.

Limited access to talent. Access to potential talent in developing countries will remain limited. The recruiting processes will continue to be less than needed.

Corporate "people skills" lacking. Many firms will continue to struggle with effectively identifying, recruiting, and retaining skilled people.

For example, corporate guidelines for job descriptions and titles must do a better job of reflecting the reality of changing job responsibilities. Difficulties exist in "labeling," categorizing and communicating skills required for a role, such as: what is a team leader?" and "how should that role be measured?"

IMPACT ON ENTERPRISES

The forces of change outlined above greatly influence what an enterprise (and the consultants who serve it) must do to be successful in the future. This section discusses the anticipated impact of each of these forces on organizations.

Buyer Empowerment

Globalization will help empower buyers by giving them more options from which to choose. This increase in options, in turn, will create more competition among suppliers/vendors.

Information ubiquity will empower buyers because they will be able to more easily access information on all competitors for specific product/service, and thus quickly and inexpensively compare and assess features, functions, service, and price.

"Always on" empowers buyers in that they will be able to get what they want, anytime and from anywhere. As buyers become more insistent on this "always on" requirement, they will severely penalize those suppliers that are slow to provide it.

The talent shortage will empower buyers in that they will gravitate more quickly to those enterprises/suppliers who *do not* have a talent shortage and who can serve their product and support needs quickly and with quality.

Larger Markets

Globalization will create larger markets because it provides easier access to and ready acceptance by buyers of "foreign" enterprises and their goods. Globalization will also make it easier to get into those markets via alliance partners from other countries.

Information ubiquity will provide vendors with more market intelligence faster and easier, making new opportunities more visible.

"Always on" impacts larger markets in that if a firm has the "always on" capability it will aid the firm in expanding into larger markets. Conversely, if a firm lacks the "always on" capability, it is at a competitive disadvantage.

The talent shortage will slow down the opportunity to take advantage of larger markets because ultimately nothing can be done by an enterprise without the talent to execute.

Increase in Market Diversity

Globalization will help increase market diversity by identifying and driving new opportunities in markets not previously addressed, due to either country, cultural, and/or regional differences.

Information ubiquity will help increase market diversity in that if an enterprise wants to penetrate diverse markets, using the raft of information available especially via the Internet, it can research diverse markets more quickly and effectively and therefore increase its chance of market success.

"Always on" will increase market diversity since it can be such a key requirement for buyers that they may be willing to overlook some feature or functional weaknesses in a supplier's offering, just for the sake of an "always on" capability (e.g., 24-hour customer service).

The talent shortage will slow down the opportunity for market diversity for those who cannot overcome this challenge.

Increase in Competition

Globalization will increase competition because it will result in the entrance of firms to markets previously outside of their core (to include regional) market areas.

Information ubiquity will increase competition because it levels the playing field. Competitors will know more information about each other, which will enable each to respond faster and better to the other's strategy.

"Always on" impacts an increase in competition due to the popularity by users of an "always on" environment. This popularity (demand) moves all competitors closer to having this type of environment. A firm that is an "early adopter" will be more competitively successful; a laggard will fall farther behind.

Talent shortage impacts market competition in that those enterprises that are successful in acquiring and retaining difficult to find talent will have an even greater competitive advantage than before.

Greater Interdependence

Globalization will help increase interdependence because it will provide more partnership and alliance opportunities to firms in various countries to address global market needs quickly. Essentially it provides a bigger supply for alliance partners as well as a larger demand.

Information ubiquity will help create greater interdependence by revealing partnership and alliance opportunities more quickly.

"Always on" will help increase interdependence by allowing an enterprise to get needed technical infrastructure support and the like to make "always on" happen from alliances as opposed to developing it internally.

The talent shortage will help drive the use of more interdependent alliances as a possible solution to the talent shortage problem.

REQUIREMENTS FOR SUCCESSFUL ENTERPRISES

In response to these impacts, the winning enterprises will be those that master a number of critical success factors, such as Relationship Portfolio Creation, Stakeholder Relationship Management, Creating Strategy from Chaos and Speed Learning, Being an Agile Firm, and Driving a Strong Culture.

Portfolio Management

To compete in the future firms will make more use of *partnering, joint ventures*, and *alliances* with a much broader array of enterprises. In effect, enterprises will create a portfolio of relationships so that each enterprise becomes more focused on its true competencies. Firms will be viewed as a collection of core capabilities coupled with a portfolio of relationships with other providers.

In moving to this relationship portfolio model, firms will have to:

- Identify their core competencies
- Determine which parts of the value creation process can be supplied by other entities

- Find the best partners (or create "pods") to provide the other parts of the value creation process
- In the process, optimize systems and processes to more rapidly and effectively enable all of these activities

Some typical functions of external relationships are: providing access to new markets or capital, offering specific technologies, and/or physical assets and processes, and supplying knowledge and/or talent. Figure 5–4 highlights the similarities between a relationship portfolio and a financial portfolio.

Client Success Story 1: Hanes/Sara Lee & Portfolio Management

In 1999, Hanes (whose parent is Sara Lee), a major player in the innerwear market, had succeeded in capturing 30+ percent market share, radically transformed itself, and was relying more on partners than its historical vertically integrated business model. In contrast, Fruit of the Loom, its major competitor, had stayed with traditional business models and was bankrupt by that same year.

FIGURE 5–4 The "Portfolio" Metaphor: How a Relationship Portfolio Is Like a Financial Portfolio

Just as financial portfolio management helps hedge against market unknowns, a Relationship Portfolio helps reduce the risks and increase the opportunities of potential relationships. For instance:

Assets
By definition, a portfolio is a set of holdings, or "assets." The financial portfolio contains various financial instruments such as stocks, bonds, or derivatives, each with unique characteristics. The Relationship Portfolio is a collection of assets as well–the assets are the relationships and the underlying capabilities they provide the enterprise.

Diversification
In both portfolio concepts, one organizing principle is "diversification": many different equities in one, many different relationships in the other. A financial portfolio is diversified to the risk/return profiles of individual securities, the goal being to maximize the portfolio's overall return, given a certain risk level. In the Relationship Portfolio approach, relationships are diversified along company-relevant dimensions.

Goal
In both the financial and relationship model, there is also the notion of a "goal," meaning the desired outcome. In the financial portfolio, the goal issue might be whether the investor seeks income or capital gains. In the Relationship Portfolio, it might be whether the most sensible goal is profitability or growth.

Asset Allocation
Both relationship models also include the concept of "asset allocation." In the financial model, this means allocating assets in accordance with investment objectives. In the Relationship Portfolio, it means investing management time and other resources in ways consistent with the relationship's value to the firm.

Connection
In both financial and Relationship portfolios there is a "connection" between assets—one asset is dependent on the performance of other assets in the portfolio.

SOURCE: Deloitte Consulting.

Hanes saw the future and changed accordingly. In 1995, the firm was a classic vertically integrated company with a highly diverse product line: men's innerwear, intimates, sportswear, and accessories. That year, however, the traditional business model began to unravel. The passage of NAFTA and other global forces (e.g., mergers in the retail industry, consumer desire for "designer brands," and the technology innovation) created revenue and profit challenges which in turn led the firm to rethink its fundamental way of doing business.

At the same time that it saw increased competition, the forces of globalization produced a pool of potential partners ready to provide complementary first-class capabilities—capabilities that many firm's at that time considered ancillary to its primary value proposition.

Hanes saw that its old business model was doomed. Spinning, finishing, cutting, and sewing—the traditional drivers of success—were no longer creating value. Hanes decided to respond to the handwriting on the wall: It was time to get out of manufacturing.

Over a three-year period, Hanes sold off 13 North American yarn and textile manufacturing operations (during its "De-verticalization Program"), thus raising $3 billion in cash. It also shifted employees to other operations, and outsourced almost all production. Its goal was to retain the ability to focus on its core strengths: building and managing leadership brands.

Hanes became more flexible by building what amounted to a Relationship Portfolio—creating relationships with partners better able to do all those things that they wanted to shed. The ultimate result was that Hanes saved tens of millions in operations it no longer had to run, it increased its market share in the men's innerwear, intimates, sportswear, and accessories market and even expanded into women's innerwear and gained 8 percent of that market.

Stakeholder Relationship Management

Stakeholder relationship management is related to "creating a relationship portfolio" but is centered on a wider range of participants than just partners. Stakeholder relationship management is an extension of customer relationship management, which looks to *optimize all relationships* of an enterprise to include: clients, employee, partners, and investors.

One of the key contributors to this type of relationship will be better integrated and more powerful information management tools, such as "employee experience" systems that manage crucial activities from hire to fire.

Client Success Story 2: JP Morgan and Stakeholder Relationship Management[1]

An undisputed giant of global finance, JP Morgan offers investment banking, asset management, and financial market services to clients around the world. In an age of constant change and accelerating e-innovation, Morgan maintains an unerring focus on the heart of its business—its clients—and consistently strives to innovate and lever-

---

[1]On September 14, 2000, Chase Manhattan Bank acquired JP Morgan and the combined company became JP Morgan-Chase.

age its deep customer relationships and branding to maximize revenues. Today in financial services, almost more than in any other industry, being truly client-centric can yield increased profits and customer loyalty.

As Joe MacHale, the head of JP Morgan-Europe recognized, the path to client-centricity lies in effective cross-marketing. In principle, this is as simple as presenting a single face to the client and selling complementary products. In practice, it is staggeringly complex.

The natural tendency of any culture like JP Morgan is to focus on the "mega deals"—the big rewards—and to sustain the practices that have historically served them well. So cross-marketing is a huge opportunity—and a challenge for the company to orchestrate, for the business units to implement, and for individuals to execute. It calls for an enormous effort and cultural shift to manage relationships from a client's point of view rather than from a business unit or geographical perspective.

In just eight months, the cross-marketing initiative helped JP Morgan where it matters most—in relationships with its clients. Besides extending the company's profile as an innovator in financial services, the initiative has caught the attention of the company's U.S. leadership since it brought real, incremental revenue and positive client feedback. Within a remarkably short time, cross-marketing was no longer viewed as just an add-on. It is simply the model of how JP Morgan does business.

CREATING STRATEGY OUT OF CHAOS

Rapid technological change has resulted in a multitude of new isolated systems and an abundance of information, much of which is still hard to access and use. Enterprises haven't even begun to leverage all the IT investments they have made over the last three to five years.

To remain competitive enterprises must:

- Coordinate IT and business strategies in a more frequent and tightly integrated planning cycle.
- Understand the increasingly complex information technology environment, its components and interrelationships.
- Realize the promised benefits from IT investments, both past and pending (such as enterprise resource planning [ERP] and CRM).
- Develop processes and techniques to aggregate and synthesize the new abundance of information.
- Integrate systems both vertically through the supply chain and horizontally across different partner relationships.

"Speed Learning"

Organizations will need to learn a lot more and in a much faster and continuous time frame than ever before due to the complexities, business relationships, and globalization previously mentioned. The real plus here is that technology will make it possible to do this.

Business strategy is increasingly derived from the customer/consumer experience. Thus, enterprises will need deeper knowledge of suppliers, partners, customers, and consumers by industry to create client confidence and reduce risk.

Client Success Story 3: Vodafone and "Speed Learning"

In February 2000, British-based Vodafone sent shock waves through the world by acquiring German cellular giant and competitor Mannesman AG for US$186 billion. Coming on the heels of other rapid-fire global acquisitions, the merger established Vodafone as not just the world's largest mobile telecommunications company but one of the world's largest companies. Vodafone is now a truly global operation with a presence in 25 countries.

The firm however has dual challenges. While it keeps growing at a phenomenal pace, it is continually launching new services that are shaping the wireless industry, such as wireless Internet and m-commerce. In the meantime, Vodafone is helping shape other sectors such as banking and consumer business as wireless technology begins to change the way we all live and do business.

The frenzy of activities in the wireless arena means that companies must be agile and quick to market—yet with well-calculated moves based on sound business analysis. Consequently, learning quickly about new markets and services and acting on that learning is a key to the firm's continued growth.

Vodafone has in place processes that help them learn about the hidden costs and the true value of products, services, and individual customers. This helps them identify which products and services to invest in, what their costs will be, and what their pricing models should be. In this way, Vodafone is well informed and well armed for the wireless revolution.

Agility and Speed

An agile firm has in place a culture, business strategies, processes, organized and accessible knowledge, and technology to assist the enterprise in recognizing early and responding quickly (via deploying resources) to market shifts. It also has the ability to quickly integrate diverse talents, perspectives, and experiences into high-performance teams that can be created and disbanded quickly.

Driving a Strong Culture

Focusing on "culture" is often overlooked as a requirement of the successful enterprise. However, without formally establishing a firm's culture and following through with it in all aspects of daily business activities (such as hiring, sales, marketing, and operations), an enterprise will slowly but surely lessen its effectiveness. Organizational focus on common goals is the essence of why an enterprise exists. The sum is greater than the parts. Culture is a key way by which such common goals are selected, communicated, and measured.

Corporate culture is distinct for all firms and is created through an unrelenting adherence to an enterprise's core values and goals. No one corporate culture is inherently right and the other wrong. For some firms it includes creating an environment that provides superior intellectual challenge and personal growth opportunities for attracting and retaining exceptional people (such as our own firm, Deloitte Consulting). For others, it includes focus on people and processes for creating sustainable, repeatable, dependable, low cost consumer experiences (such as McDonalds, the global fast food chain).

Selection and strengthening of a strong culture will become even more important in the future as organizations strive to prosper in the face of almost overwhelming change. Culture is the glue that helps organizations execute in unison on their chosen business model.

WHAT DOES IT IMPLY?

Thus far, this chapter has focused on market forces driving change, how these forces impact enterprises and in light of these impacts, what enterprises need to do to be successful. In the remainder of the chapter, we examine how these forces, their impacts, and the ensuing client needs will drive how consulting firms will execute their business going into the future.

New Skills Needed by Consultants

All enterprises want to possess the aforementioned "requirements" for market success. However, many firms lack the necessary skills and experience to complete strategic initiatives in a timely manner. This gives rise to the essence of the market for consulting firms. But do consulting firms of today have the skills necessary to help their clients succeed tomorrow?

Changing Client Needs

There will be a number of newer project types and consultant delivery mechanisms (addressing newer client needs) that consulting firms will encounter over the next three to five years.

Examples include:

- Source, select, and connect potential business partners for the client.
- Develop a deep understanding of consumer requirements (by industry) in the economy of the future; advise the client on future products and services and create systems and processes to address future customer needs.
- Outsource noncore business functions (e.g., finance).
- Obtain injections of capital or resources in lieu of capital.
- Use creative contracting (value-based pricing, equity for service).
- Integrate not just information but knowledge, and create systems and processes to extract appropriate knowledge from the plethora of data.
- Provide guidance, processes, and systems for hiring, training/retraining, and retaining talent.
- Create infrastructures to underpin past and future technology investments.
- Assist clients in realizing value from past and pending investments in technology solutions such as ERP.
- Integrate technology vertically through the supply chain and horizontally across different partner relationships.
- Assist CEOs with creating and sustaining corporate culture.

Future consulting projects, such as the ones listed above, are more focused on the five requirements of successful firms outlined in the previous section than consulting projects of the recent past.

Future Consultant Skills

Historically consultants provided more generic advice (strategy), build (implementation), and run (outsourcing) capabilities—along with workforce change management (as mentioned earlier). These generic skills will still be relevant for the future. However, to successfully address the future projects listed above, these same skills will need to be: (1) enhanced in breadth, (2) increased in depth, and (3) new skills will need to be added.

Thus, consulting firms of the future will need skills, programs, and initiatives to strengthen the following key business components:

ORGANIZATIONAL EFFECTIVENESS

- Larger and more formalized R&D groups (and relationships with "think tanks" and academic institutions) to develop expertise in multiple business and technical areas to include: new hiring models, customer segmentation strategies, industry trends, future markets (vertical and horizontal).
- Ability to create new HR policies (used within as well as for clients) with the goal of more effectively acquiring and retaining talent. This would include: new reward systems, employee development resources, processes and systems for "talent mining," and so on.
- Deeper business case and project management talent, which is utilized on *each* engagement.

KNOWLEDGE MANAGEMENT

- Thought leadership to help support credibility with clients/prospects.
- Deeper knowledge management skills to: find available knowledge, determine additional knowledge that is needed by the enterprise, create processes to make knowledge more readily available to decision makers, as well as to create a better culture for sharing of such information.

VALUE NETWORKS

- Expanded relationship portfolio (or value networks) creation skills to assist the client in doing what it does best and partnering for the rest.
- Stakeholder relationship management creation skills (to include strategy, processes, and technology solutions) for understanding and managing not just client customers but also their employees and investors.
- Efficient access to capital and creative funding options (this includes venture capital and investment management skills).
- Possess and/or partner for deep infrastructure creation skills.
- Possess and/or partner for cultural skills to include: executive coaching, team building, and diversity coaching.

SOLUTIONS

- Replicable solutions or components of solutions that can be pieced together, and then customized to quickly solve client's problems.
- Turnkey methods and tools for engagements that can be utilized by partners and clients as well as in-house practitioners.
- Consulting firms also will need to undertake internally many of the client consulting projects that we discussed above in order to remain competitive.

FUTURE CRITICAL SUCCESS FACTORS
FOR CONSULTING FIRMS

A number of consultant business models will evolve to address the aforementioned client needs. Some consulting models in the future will resemble traditional areas in consulting, while others will be new. Some of the models will be more "full-service based" while others will be more focused on a particular industry or competency (e.g., business process outsourcing). These models will not be mutually exclusive, but successful consulting firms will generally gravitate towards one of the models in order to sharpen their focus and differentiate their offerings. Marketing and branding of firms will be critically important and increasingly be based on the business model chosen. All models will likely include IT and strategy skills.

In the recent past the largest consulting firms tended to be those that managed to reinvent themselves successfully through new generations of technology and management disciplines. Smaller firms tended to flourish and then falter when the wind shifted and either fell by the wayside or were acquired. Obsolescence risk is high in consulting firms that are narrowly focused. We believe, to be successful, large firms will have to embrace the following critical success factors:

RELATIONSHIP PORTFOLIO MANAGEMENT
- Develop a relationship management culture for both developing individuals and operating programs.
- Have a stable of quality alliances to offer clients.

CREATING STRATEGY OUT OF CHAOS
- Have strong seasoned management that understands the business will have multiple changing cycles and has the ability to navigate through change, create a strategy, and lead his/her people in attaining that strategy in a timely manner.
- Have the ability to create a "virtual firm" to deliver full services to clients when needed. To succeed with this type of firm (virtual) a large investment must first be made in: creating a stable of quality alliances and relationship management processes, methodologies, and standard operating procedures.

SPEED LEARNING
- Develop deep industry expertise in a select number of industries to include:
  - Industry variations of applications
  - A greater number of people who have worked their whole lives or were executives in that industry
  - Industry centers of competency (including showcasing "the industry of the future") for speeding engagement delivery as well as adding credibility to depth of expertise

SPEED AND AGILITY
- Demonstrate an ability to transform themselves, rapidly, in response to new technologies and management disciplines.
- Take advantage of alternatives to reducing costs. One example is moving more development as well as analysis (to include financial analysis) services to markets with lower relative labor costs. Another is using temporary staffing agencies to add and then prune skills that may be needed for one client engagement but not the next.
- Have access to adequate levels of capital.

DRIVING A STRONG CULTURE

- Demonstrate an ability to create and operate a global consultancy, to include:
  - Worldwide as opposed to country-level strategy
  - Common processes (education, hiring, training)
  - Offices in multiple countries and teams from many
  - Common culture
  - Knowledge networks
  - Common global infrastructure

WHAT LIES AHEAD?

The consulting industry will continue to change, and continue to thrive. Consolidation will be prominent—the big will get bigger, and the mid-sized will be acquired or fall by the wayside. Yet there will continue to be rafts of smaller specialized firms for skill partnering. More than ever in the past, consulting firms will be identifiable to a client by the combination of alliances, partnerships, and networks that they develop as the situation demands.

To offset the great capital costs inherent in devising client solutions, consultancies will explore novel forms of partnerships. In confronting the increasing complexity of knowledge acquisition, many consultancies will lower costs by collaborating with clients on creating training courses for both consultants and clients. Creating replicable or scaleable solutions will continue. Time to market and economies of scale lead as the market drivers.

In the future, the advice driven (strategy) consulting market will be impaired due to client-centralized R&D (economists, statisticians, brand experts). These internal client experts will have the ability to create almost the entire case that a strategy firm used to build. What, however, will continue to be necessary is "outside" objective insight and advice or assessment on internally created plans.

Most of the major consultancies have developed joint venture arms to enable start-ups within their firm. This trend will continue. The new entities incubate thought leadership in new areas, in order to help the parent firm to more quickly respond to client needs. Such ventures also have the potential of bringing additional revenue to a consultant coffer should a new entity "go public."

The "public" (publicly traded) owned consultancy model is not yet a proven one. Yes, there are mega services firms that are public (e.g., IBM, Computer Sciences Corp.), but the primary focus of their business is not consulting. Until consulting firms can produce margin expansion with scale, which is difficult in an intellectual capital, nonproduct, or patent business, in the long term, public investors will not likely award very high valuations. The speculative bubble that existed in the late 1990s and into 2000, particularly for Internet consultants, was not rational and was therefore unsustainable. The key questions now are how capital-intensive is consulting becoming, and how do firms best meet that challenge? Over the long term, need for capital resources will increase in proportion to how quickly changes such as global scale, industry expertise, training and retraining, and relationship teams become critical to consulting firm success. The quicker these changes, the more capital-intensive the business will need to be. We suspect there will be multiple ownership models in the future, with one not necessarily being defined as optimal.

Consulting firms that survive and prosper will be the ones that find and embrace the elusive formula of scale, consistency, globalization, recruitment, and people retention, all in the context of maintaining good financial performance with their partners, staff, and shareholders.

SUMMARY

Markets of all types are in a state of constant flux. Major forces such as globalization, information ubiquity, always on operations, and talent shortage will continue to crash upon enterprises' once safe shores. Those firms will thrive that effectively protect themselves against and even ride the waves via newer competencies such as relationship portfolio management, developing rapid strategies for chaos, speed learning, agility, and driving a strong culture.

Assisting enterprises in quickly creating these solutions will be one consulting firm's forte and another less agile firm's downfall. The determining factors will include a number of newer technical, business, and people skills.

One thing is certain—consulting will continue to be a viable business and a huge marketplace. Enterprises will need all the support they can find to stay afloat in the turbulent early years of this new millennium. As a result, consulting will offer a rewarding and challenging environment for the world's best minds.

PART II

Structuring Engagements

"What do consultants do?" As we began teaching the art and science of consulting in business schools and in consulting firms in the mid-1990s, we sought an answer to that question in books that purported to deal with the topic. We were disappointed by what we found: Most descriptions focused on the relatively mundane aspects of what consultants do and didn't explain the true contribution a good consultant makes to a client situation: an ability to articulate and solve problems. In preparing this book, we therefore felt we had to place problem solving at the heart of the consultant's job.

The purpose of Part II is to provide readers with an architectural rendering of what consultants do: The major conceptual tools they bring to bear on client problems, the actual "thought processes" that take place, and how they use frameworks to communicate with a client, to formulate a project proposal, to build a team, and to carry out a project from beginning to end. In our view, the real infrastructure of consulting lies in these areas: they differentiate the consultant from the manager, and they are the beating heart of "the advice business."

In Chapter 6, Charles Fombrun introduces a basic "toolkit" of generalist frameworks or "models" that all consultants draw on as they work with clients. These models are both the jargon and the worldview of consultants—they have become common parlance throughout the profession. Most of these models derive from an understanding of the client company as an organization operating in an environment. The models provide frameworks for thinking about a company's strategic positioning compared to rivals, and the effectiveness levels it achieves.

However, a toolkit is just that: a set of tools that can help a consultant to think about a client problem. In many instances the tool has to be modified or adapted to the specific client or situation, or a unique tool built. In Chapter 7, Charles Fombrun and Mark Nevins discuss how consultants use causal and systemic analysis to think about problems, and how they develop unique models that represent their understanding. In doing so, consultants act somewhat like scientists: they formulate deductive hypotheses which they then put to the test with as much research and data support as they can find.

Mark Nevins extends this perspective in Chapter 8 by explaining the vital role that communications between consultants and clients play in driving clients to change. After all, the best consultants are not those who have the theoretically "perfect" answers—they are those who are best able to help the client make meaningful change. Knowing the cause of a problem is not enough: the client must also appreciate and agree with the consultant's assessment, and feel willing and able to make the necessary changes to see positive results. Getting the client to that position requires a mix of thoughtful framing and persuasive communication. Good consultants work closely with their clients throughout the engagement so that their recommendations are packaged in narratives and presold to clients—the most effective kind of persuasion.

In Chapter 9, John Scott shows how the thinking process gets embedded in the proposal. As he points out, a proposal builds on the consulting firm's stock of know-how and expresses the value-add in a reasonably standardized format. At the heart of the proposal is an effort to convey to the prospective client how the firm typically "thinks" about problems, how it typically approaches the problems, and the kinds of staffing, financial, and operational commitments that the engagement will require.

In Chapter 10, Terry Nichols links the thinking process to the actual execution of the engagement. Specifically, he begins by showing us how to relate the "engagement letter" which starts off a client project to the project work plan, the issue diagram, and the storyboard. He then turns our attention to some of the pragmatic tools consultants rely on to carry out complex engagements, particularly the organization of the project team, the use of Gantt charts and PERT charts, and time and cost tools to gauge progress along the way.

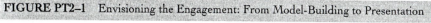

FIGURE PT2–1   Envisioning the Engagement: From Model-Building to Presentation

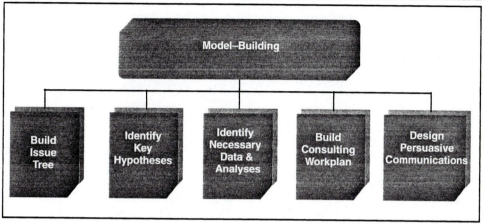

Throughout Part 2, the emphasis is on the three key roles that consultants perform:

1. Helping clients get to the core of a problem by articulating key issues and conducting rigorous analysis
2. Communicating in ways that help clients understand, value, and mobilize behind the consultant's thinking process
3. Designing proposals and managing the project in ways that capitalize on insights gained throughout the engagement and energize execution of appropriate solutions

Figure PT2–1 illustrates a sequence that will help the consultant go from data analysis to recommendation, or "from insight to impact."

CHAPTER

6

The Consultant's Toolkit

Charles J. Fombrun

Consultants offer clients their deep and specialized knowledge of a particular discipline: typically strategy, technology, marketing, finance, or change. Clients rely on consultants to gain exposure to a rich and often esoteric set of concepts married with industry experience. If you talk to enough consultants, however, you'll soon recognize that most of them draw on a common repertoire of concepts, frameworks, and models—a shared language, as it were—when they work with clients. These core models constitute a frame of reference that consultants use to diagnose client problems and which they often customize to the circumstances at hand. The models are the heart and soul of MBA programs the world over—and constitute the consultant's essential "toolkit."

In this chapter, I provide a brief overview of a set of key models and frameworks that constitute the generalist consultant's basic toolkit. Figure 6–1 classifies these models into six groupings whose principal focus is identifying and understanding key business drivers from the different perspectives of context, strategy, marketing, organization, change, and performance.

There are many other models not covered here, of course, and I do not dwell on those in any real depth—that has been better done in more specialized publications. My purpose is to remind you about these generalist "hammers" that consultants rely on and, if they appear unfamiliar, to dig a little deeper to add them to your repertoire. They'll serve you well.

GENERALIST MODELS

In thinking about companies, consultants invariably rely on metaphors of one kind or another. Metaphors affect what you see and how you describe what you see, and so influence the kinds of problems and solutions a consultant will propose. Some time ago, Gareth Morgan, a professor at Canada's York University, wrote a notable book in which he described the key "images" that most people rely on to talk about companies. Among the two most influential were images of organizations as "machines" and images of organizations as "organisms." These two views remain central to most descriptions consultants make today. On the one hand, consultants who rely on machine imagery tend to diagnose corporate problems as rooted in nonfunctioning parts, broken

Charles J. Fombrun is Executive Director of the Reputation Institute and Professor of Management at the Stern School of Business of New York University. Mr. Fombrun earned a B.S. in Physics from Queen's University (Canada) and completed a Ph.D. in organizational theory at Columbia University in 1980.

FIGURE 6–1 The Consultant's Toolkit — Selected Models

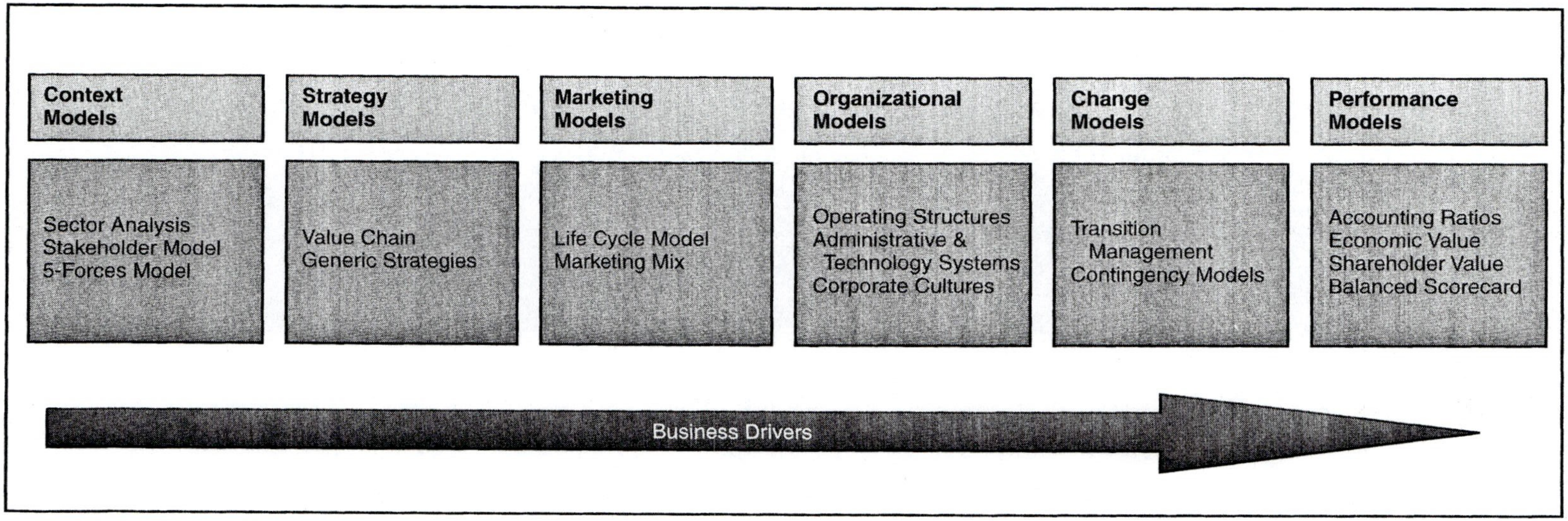

Context Models	Strategy Models	Marketing Models	Organizational Models	Change Models	Performance Models
Sector Analysis Stakeholder Model 5-Forces Model	Value Chain Generic Strategies	Life Cycle Model Marketing Mix	Operating Structures Administrative & Technology Systems Corporate Cultures	Transition Management Contingency Models	Accounting Ratios Economic Value Shareholder Value Balanced Scorecard

Business Drivers

mechanisms, misalignments of parts, and the need to "grease the wheels" or "oil the joints" to "get the ball rolling" and to "make things work." On the other hand, those who rely on organismic thinking tend to diagnose corporate problems as manifestations of pain, illness, and disease, rooted in "poor adaptation" to the environment. They call attention to "flows of resources" in and out of the organization, or the degree of "equilibrium" a company has achieved. Some take the metaphor toward the medical end of the continuum and focus on the pathologies of client companies they work with. Others see companies as integral members of larger groupings of similar organisms, striving to acquire scarce resources like labor and capital, constantly pressured in their "habitats" by "population density," "congestion," and "resource scarcity," much as herds of animals compete for food and drink in a larger ecosystem of predators and prey, whose members feed on each other, and whose numbers fluctuate as a result.

These two views characterize the dominant paradigms that guide most consultants as they formulate diagnoses and interpretations of what "ails" a company and what should be done about it. More advanced versions have been proposed, of course, and you might define the stock-in-trade of consulting firms as the development, refinement, and elaboration of unique images capable of galvanizing attention and generating revenues. In his dissertation work at NYU, Eric Abrahamson, now a professor at Columbia University, described the popularity of specific consulting models as similar to "fads and fashions." He showed that the tools that consultants create periodically to attract clients rise and fall in popularity with cyclical regularity, much like the hemlines of dresses or the width of men's ties and lapels.

The ebb and flow of consultant tools like "quality circles," "management by objectives," "reengineering," "value-based management," or other techniques does not belie the underlying constant in the images that consultants hold of companies as machines and organisms. "Machine consultants" are generally the ones with standard products and solutions to sell, quick to offer a packaged "fix" for a client's problem. The "organic consultants" may also have products to sell, but generally are more likely to invite clients to "partner" in a change process that will be necessary to address the problems. Whereas the former may offer arm's-length pills and panaceas, the latter tend to proffer treatments and cures that intimately involve the client.

It's valuable to understand in which of these models consultants root their analyses in order to appreciate the remedies they propose. The two paradigms underlie many of the models in Figure 6–1. I turn first to context models, then describe the principal strategy models, marketing models, organization models, change models, and performance models in the toolkit.

CONTEXT MODELS

All context models are rooted in "organism" metaphors, and suggest that companies must adapt to environmental circumstances in order to function properly. Any client problem is therefore a result of a mismatch between the company's internal arrangements and external conditions—identifying the root cause of the misalignments is crucial for effecting a proper diagnosis and proposing a remedy or cure. The sectors model, the stakeholder model, and the 5-forces model are the three most popular context models that consultants routinely rely on to identify whether a company is more or less adapted to its environment. In all cases, strong financial profitability, growing market share, and high employee morale are key indicators that the company is operating effectively in the short run and is therefore "well-adapted"; ability to innovate and grow are indicators of the company's adaptability in the long run.

The Sectors Model

Figure 6–2 portrays the sectors model. In this view, companies operate in a stratified external environment that heavily constrains what they can and should do. The company itself is described as having an internal environment that influences how people work, what they feel, and how well they can individually contribute to the company's performance. All analyses of a company begin by apprehending the nature of the environment itself—the economic, social, political, and technological forces that are acting on the company. Client problems are thought to be rooted in part in a company's failure to "see" these effects of the environment, or in terms of inappropriate responses managers make that limit the company's ability to perform.

> *Economic sector.* Every company faces macro and micro economic conditions that affect profitability. Prevailing interest rates, growth rates, business cycles, and disposable income, as well as trend forecasts, constrain a company's actions, influence the competitive conditions it will face, and so affect the company's ability to generate future profits.

FIGURE 6–2 The Sector Analysis Model

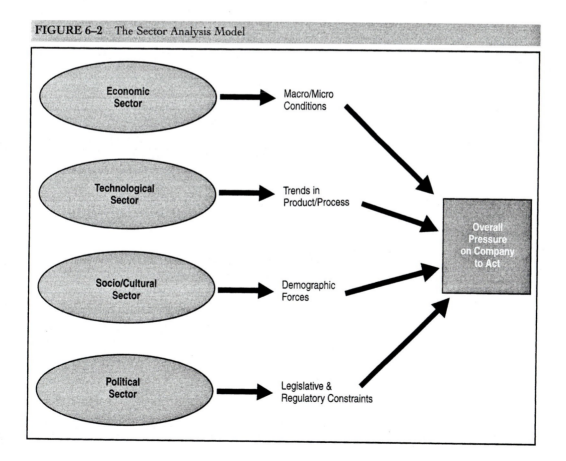

Technological sector. Developments in the realm of technology constantly influence a company's ability to develop, produce, and market its products and services. Examining trends in technology can enable improved understanding of emerging challenges to the company's future performance, as well as suggest ways the company can capitalize on opportunities to develop new products or to improve the efficiency of its operations.

Social sector. People matter to companies as both employees (the labor market) and as customers (the product market). As employees, they are central to the operations of most companies. Trends affecting recruitment and retention of personnel, their motivation, satisfaction, and productivity can therefore influence corporate performance and profitability. At the same time, trends affecting customers—their ability and interest in purchasing the company's products and services—have a direct effect on sales and therefore on the company's profitability.

Political sector. Companies operate in a political environment of appointed and elected officials, legislators, regulators, and other monitoring agencies. Profits can be heavily affected by the actions of the political sector because of the formal clout they carry and their ability to enforce rules of conduct.

Overall, the sectors model calls attention to the general influence of the environment on the performance of a company. Consultants use a sectors model as an organic mental framework for cataloging the likely effects of the environment on a client company's current and future performance.

The Stakeholder Model

The stakeholder model complements the sectors model by describing the environment of the company in terms of specific groups of actors that have a "stake" in what the company does because they control important resources the company needs. *Primary stakeholders* have the greatest influence on the company's performance and include employees, investors, and customers. *Secondary stakeholders* also influence performance and include regulators, activists, and the public at large. By providing or withdrawing support from the company, they enable or limit performance. A client problem may therefore be rooted in its insensitivity to one or more stakeholder groups, and the need to strengthen those direct and indirect relationships. Figure 6–3 describes the stakeholder model and the way stakeholders affect a company's responsiveness and performance.

The 5-Forces Model

Popularized by Harvard Business School professor Michael Porter, the 5-forces model roots a client company's performance problems in its structural position in an industry. As Figure 6–4 shows, the 5-forces model suggests that a company's profits are limited by the extent to which it is pressured to keep prices low by powerful customers and suppliers, as well as aggressive rivals—and threatened by potential substitute products and new entrants. Companies in weak structural positions have low profit potential.

- *Customers and suppliers:* Companies that have few customers or suppliers are at their mercy—those customers and suppliers can dictate higher prices and thereby undermine a client's margins.
- *Substitutes:* Companies whose products and services are easily substituted for others have limited ability to raise their prices for fear of losing customers to others, and so have lower profit margins.

FIGURE 6–3 The Stakeholder Model

Employees
Investors
Customers
THE COMPANY
Regulators
Pressure Groups

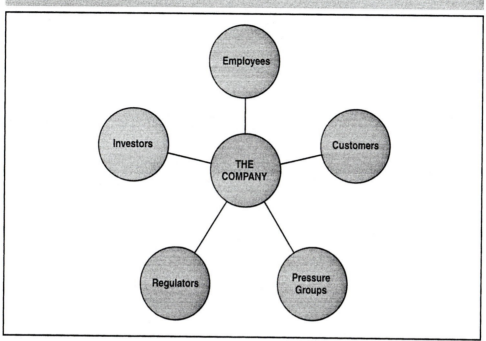

FIGURE 6–4 The 5-Forces Model

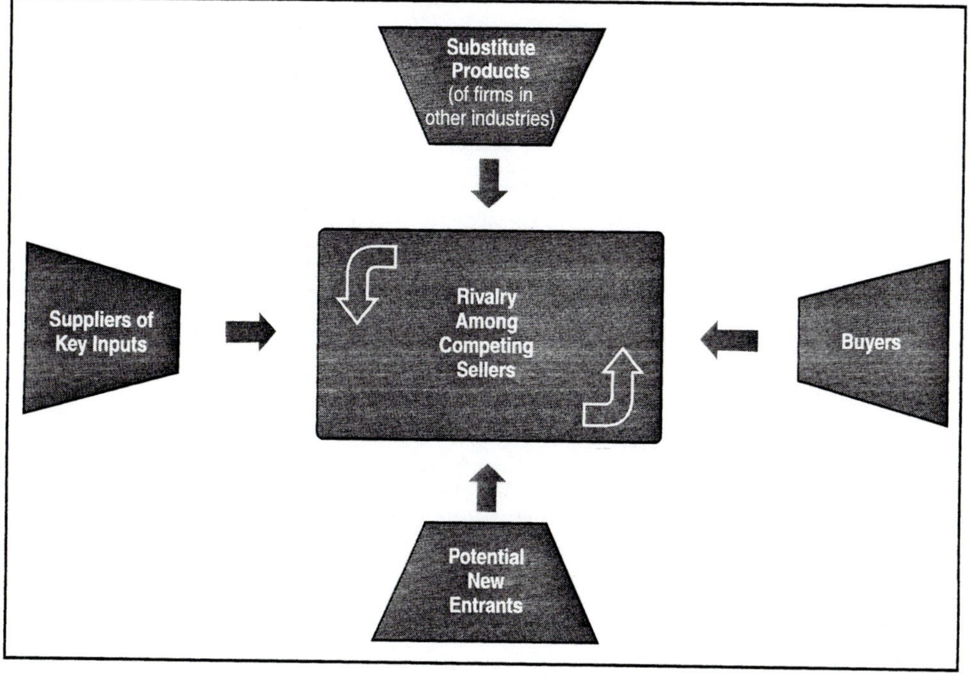

Substitute Products (of firms in other industries)
Suppliers of Key Inputs
Rivalry Among Competing Sellers
Buyers
Potential New Entrants

- *Rivalry:* Companies competing in very contentious markets are forced to offer their products and services at relatively low prices to avoid losing customers to aggressive rivals.
- *Entry barriers:* Finally, companies that operate in industries with high entry barriers due, for instance, to prohibitive research and development (R&D) costs or high production set-up costs, are less threatened with new rivals, and so better able to charge high prices and build attractive profit margins.

Consultants typically use the 5-forces model as a subset of the sector and stakeholder models. It provides a more focused understanding of the direct economic forces that constrain a company's financial performance within an industry.

STRATEGY MODELS

Consultants use strategy models to recommend actions that companies should take to improve their performance. The metaphor is that of companies vying for scarce resources and hampered by competitiveness from other companies in the population. In the words of strategy consultants Gary Hamel and C. K. Prahalad, "The essence of strategy lies in creating tomorrow's competitive advantages faster than competitors mimic the ones you possess today."

Strategy prescriptions follow immediately from diagnoses provided by context models. For instance, the sector model suggests what forces companies must address to improve performance; the stakeholder model suggests which groups clients are most sensitive to and with which they should negotiate better relationships; the 5-forces model tells a company that to improve performance it should strengthen its structural position by finding ways to thwart the power of rivals, buyers, and suppliers, and by raising barriers to entry in the industry.

In addition to drawing strategy implications from context models, consultants also frequently rely on two key strategy models to identify specific steps that a client company can take to improve its performance: the value chain model and the generic strategies model.

The Value Chain Model

Also widely diffused by Harvard's Michael Porter, the value chain decomposes a company's margins along a chain of value-creating activities. It suggests that a client's performance problems are rooted in processes or activities that don't add value, and so create an overhead burden on the company that hampers competitiveness. Figure 6–5 describes a standard value chain. Consultants draw on the value chain model to help clients identify the specific elements of the chain to improve, and the costly activities to prune, outsource, or eliminate entirely.

Generic Strategies Model

There are no unique strategies. Companies draw from a limited menu of major strategic alternatives their preferred way to compete in an industry and across industries. Corporate-level strategies describe the choice of markets and industries that companies make. Business-level strategies describe how companies choose to compete in each of those markets. The strategy question involves uncovering whether a company's

---

[1]Gary Hamel & C. K. Prahalad, *Competing for the Future,* Cambridge: Harvard Business School Press, 1994.

FIGURE 6–5   The Value Chain Model

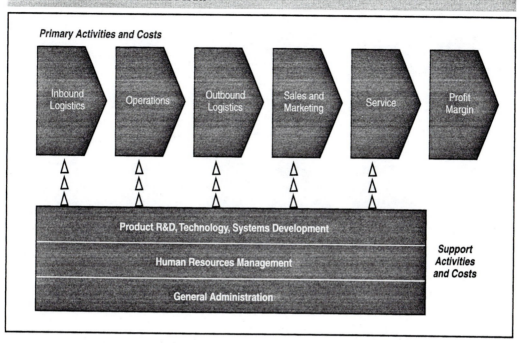

Primary Activities and Costs

Inbound Logistics · Operations · Outbound Logistics · Sales and Marketing · Service · Profit Margin

Product R&D, Technology, Systems Development

Human Resources Management

General Administration

Support Activities and Costs

performance problems are rooted in poor selection or poor implementation of its corporate and business strategies.

At the corporate level, a company can be more or less diversified. There's a fair bit of evidence that high diversification limits returns, and that more focused strategies are advisable. A corporate-level analysis, therefore, involves close examination of the degree of realized synergy between the diversified products, markets, technologies, and personnel across a company's divisions. What are the potential synergies? Are they achieved? Can barriers to achieving synergy be removed?

At the business-level, the consultant examines the way in which the company is positioned against rivals in the industry. Two generic strategies are possible: competing on the basis of price or competing through differentiation of the company's products through quality and image. The diagnostic query from the consultant is the degree to which the company has adopted a viable business-level strategy given industry conditions, and if it's executing the strategy well. Pursuing a low-price strategy requires a company to be more efficient and have lower costs than rivals if it is to be equally profitable. In contrast, a differentiation strategy requires an ability to sustain premium prices since the company has to carry the costly burden of generating innovative product features, quality production, and advertising those strengths. Figure 6–6 contrasts the principal types of generic corporate-level and business-level strategies.

MARKETING MODELS

Two marketing models with high currency among consultants are the life cycle model and the marketing mix model. The first explicitly draws on an organic analogy in rec-

FIGURE 6–6   The Generic Strategies Model

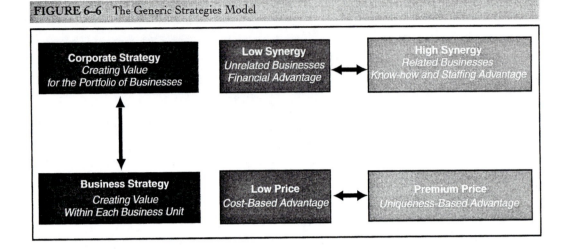

ognizing that products, industries, and technologies tend to develop in a sequence of life stages from birth to growth, to maturity, and decline. The second calls attention to the four interrelated factors that characterize the marketing mix: product features, pricing, place, and promotion.

Life Cycle Models

Like humans, products are born, nurtured, developed, and exploited before being replaced by new products. Life cycle models suggest that products and businesses move in evolutionary terms much like natural living systems. Empirical studies show that many markets do demonstrate evolutionary development of this sort, even though these stages are far from inevitable and the actual length of time a company's products spend in any one stage is indefinite. Though often stretched, the analogy is useful because it forces examination of the typical marketing issues a company faces with its products. It suggests, in particular, that demand for most products resemble an S-curve: Early exponential growth is followed by a period of steady growth that gives way to a declining rate of expansion, which ends as the growth rate drops (see Figure 6–7). Applied to a new product or business, the stages unfold as follows:

Stage 1: Birth. To successfully introduce a new product, companies must pave the way by examining the market's likely receptivity to the product's attributes, and creating favorable conditions for its introduction. The model forces examination of the infrastructure surrounding product development, and the related portfolio of activities through which a company identifies a market opportunity, develops alternative products that will enable it to capitalize on that opportunity, conducts market tests to select the most attractive combination of product features, conveys those features to targeted customers through ads and promotions, and actually introduces the product to the market.

Stage 2: Growth. Once the product finds a target market, the company's challenge is to grow sales. The life cycle model invites close examination of the mechanisms through which the company can reach even more customers by advertising existing features, building brand equity, adding options, or otherwise adapting new features to the product in order to reach even more customers and fuel growth.

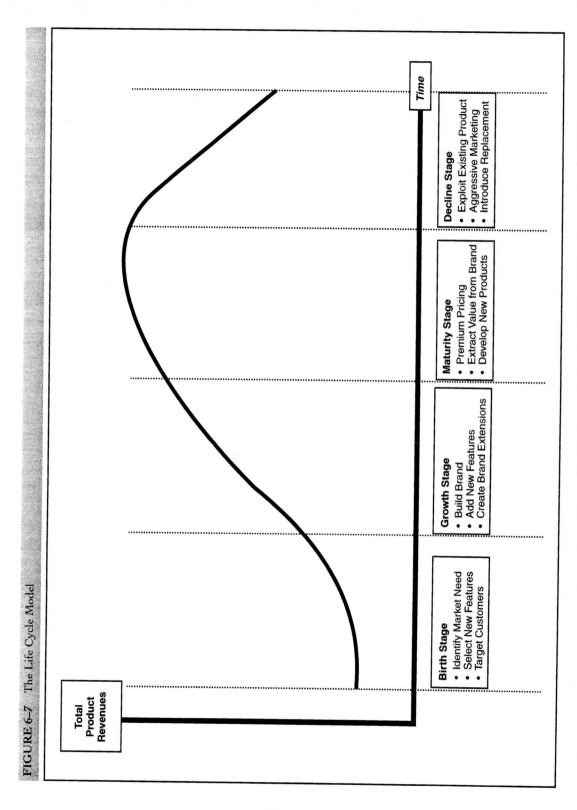

FIGURE 6–7 The Life Cycle Model

Total Product Revenues

Time

Birth Stage
- Identify Market Need
- Select New Features
- Target Customers

Growth Stage
- Build Brand
- Add New Features
- Create Brand Extensions

Maturity Stage
- Premium Pricing
- Extract Value from Brand
- Develop New Products

Decline Stage
- Exploit Existing Product
- Aggressive Marketing
- Introduce Replacement

Stage 3: Maturity. At some point, growth normally slows, demand for the product stabilizes, and the market becomes saturated—the market for the product is said to be "mature." Although not inevitable, sooner or later most markets reach saturation levels. The life cycle model calls attention to the kinds of actions companies should initiate to maintain revenues from this product. They include premium pricing to capitalize on the company's first mover advantage and extract value from the brand; actions designed to increase relative market share if competitors have already introduced rival products; and most importantly investments in creating new products capable to secure customer retention in anticipation of the existing product's coming decline.

Stage 4: Decline. Here the model recognizes the anticipated decline in sales and forces clients to examine ways to draw maximum value from the product's current market through discount pricing, promotions, and "active neglect" while introducing a replacement product that can ride aggressively the next S-curve.

The life cycle model can be applied not only to products but to the evolutionary development of whole industries and technologies as well. A similar plot of total industry sales or of the number of companies in an industry shows a similar S-curve form, suggesting that whole industries go through a sequence of stages in which a few companies account for limited sales at the dawn of an industry. Quickly, a flood of imitators comes into the industry, and industry sales skyrocket. In time, the industry stabilizes as companies come to control their own niches. Some industries take years and decades to reach maturity. Others mature more quickly. In time, industry sales can drop, players consolidate, and the industry as a whole can even vanish, only to be replaced by another industry to which customers turn.

Consultants use the life cycle model to help them situate the client, its products, and the industry as a whole. Like a diagnostic test, it suggests that different marketing strategies are appropriate at different points in the product and industry life cycle.

Marketing Mix Model (4P's)

All consultants know their 4P's—a model that suggests four key marketing variables clients must attend to in order to build sales: product features, pricing, promotion, and place (distribution). Different combinations of variables are possible in particular circumstances, and the model merely guides the consultant to assess the particular combination the client relies on to reach its target customer segment.

Product: The company's revenues derive from the products (and services) it supplies. The product's features are the customer's first point of contact. The 4P's model calls attention to the crucial features of the company's products and the extent to which they are recognized by customers as different from those of rivals.

Pricing: A crucial way products differentiate is on price. Some companies charge premium prices, others discount radically. Pricing communicates information to customers and heavily influences sales. The 4P's model forces the consultant to consider carefully the company's pricing policy and its effectiveness with the targeted customer segment.

Promotion: Advertising is a powerful tool that companies can use to inform customers about product features and build brand recognition. Companies can also conduct various types of promotions to activate sluggish sales and remind customers of the company's products. The 4P's model suggests close examination of how the company is managing its promotions and whether they are effective in sustaining or renewing interest in specific products.

Place: Finally, where are the products sold? An analysis of "place" draws the consultant's attention to questions of distribution: How are the company's products distributed? Where are they displayed or delivered? Are distributors motivated to make the company's products more salient than those of rivals?

Taken altogether, the 4P's model encourages the complementary analysis of all four factors of product, price, promotion, and place—the marketing mix. It suggests that the marketing mix must be understood in its totality to assess how effectively the company is reaching the customers it targets.

ORGANIZATION MODELS

Seldom do consultants have the luxury of working with clients *de novo.* Most of the time, they are called upon to diagnose problems whose roots are intertwined and difficult to untangle from the inner workings of the client's organization. They therefore need tools that can help them deconstruct those organizations and recognize how particular facets of a company can affect the company's performance and limit the effectiveness of any proposed solutions.

Companies vary widely: Some are formal, others informal; some are hierarchical, others not; some are collaborative, others competitive. In this section, I review three organizational models that consultants find useful when diagnosing a company's performance problems or recommending new client initiatives. They address a company's operating structure, its administrative and technological systems, and its corporate culture.

Operating Structures

Companies develop quite unique operating structures over time—that is, the blueprints through which work gets done, products are developed, made and sold. Nonetheless, consultants can understand much about a company's operating structure from assessing two key dimensions:

- *Centralization:* The degree to which top managers control key decisions that are made throughout the organization, as well as the types of strategic and operational decisions. Standard functional structures tend to foster centralization, whereas companies that organize around products or geographies tend to decentralize decision making.
- *Fragmentation:* The degree to which a company operates with distinct fiefdoms, having little interaction across boundaries. Standard functional structures tend to encourage fragmentation around specialty groups. Product structures and geographies encourage cooperation across specialties, but solidify boundaries across those groups.

A vast literature in organization behavior confirms these trade-offs between more or less centralization and more or less fragmentation. In other words, there is no universal panacea, and the consultant's job is to identify the trade-offs the company has elected to make and ensure that they are appropriate given competitive circumstances.

For instance, we know that centralized companies can make quick decisions once they recognize a problem. However, they are often slow to respond to a problem that is not immediately apparent or agreed upon by the company's top managers. Centralization can also discourage innovation by limiting participation. Creative people expect more involvement, and so favor decentralized companies where their contributions are valued.

Fragmentation also has its pros and cons. On the one hand, fragmented companies tend to duplicate activities throughout the company and so have higher administrative costs. Since boundaries act as obstacles, they tend to limit the ability to coordinate across departments, groups, and operating units. On the other hand, fragmentation results from efforts to place responsibility squarely in the hands of identifiable units to facilitate monitoring. Companies that operate with distinct subsidiaries or as holding companies, for instance, often do so in order to localize responsibility for results in a specific team.

Understanding a client company's operating structure is an important aspect of a consultant's diagnostic process. It helps build a more thorough understanding of a company's performance problems, and anticipate possible barriers to change.

Administrative and Technological Systems

Companies develop complementary administrative and technological systems in order to manage flows of resources through their operating structures. These systems are generally designed to help a company manage flows of people, products, and money. When management consultants are asked to assess a company, they generally examine closely the effects these systems have on the motivation and satisfaction of people who work with them. Loss of productivity and alienation are often the unintended result of systems that were created to achieve other ends.

- *Human resources systems:* Employees are hired, compensated, trained, and assessed. On what criteria are they recruited? What skills are they trained to acquire over time? And what kinds of incentives does the company offer them—and do those incentives motivate higher levels of performance?
- *Production systems:* Products (and services) are developed, made, and sold. What systematic processes are used to guide effective delivery to customers? How is technology working to facilitate these processes or acting as a hindrance?
- *Financial systems:* Costs accumulate; revenues are generated. Companies use various accounting and control systems to monitor costs, recognize revenues, and manage their cash flows. Perversely, applying these control systems to monitor financial flows can sometimes contradict what top managers intend to achieve through the human resource systems.

Management consultants normally examine closely these three sets of systems in order to develop a solid grasp of existing organizational processes and their effects on the company's current performance, and may limit the company's ability to implement a solution to its performance problems.

Corporate Cultures

Finally, consultants recognize that companies are also like human "tribes" with a more or less developed sense of identity, shared beliefs, adherence to norms and values, and that participate in various rituals on a regular basis. Developing cultural insight is a crucial skill that good consultants find invaluable in building robust diagnostics about a client's situation. Few are the consultants who can survive in the client's world without that level of sensitivity.

A cultural view calls attention to two key aspects of the company:

- *Shared values and beliefs:* Do top managers claim adherence to particular values? Are those merely espoused or are they actually lived throughout the company? Are the values in line with the company's strategic and operational objectives? How widely shared are those values and beliefs?

- *Rites and Rituals:* How does the company celebrate its achievements? Are there regular meetings of all employees, or are these few and far between? Do top managers encounter lower level employees in the cafeteria for lunch, or is there limited interaction across levels and among operating units? What occasions bring people together?

Examining the client company's cultural make-up can help consultants better understand the roots of the client's situation and recommend appropriate steps.

CHANGE MODELS

Ultimately, all consulting comes down to changing management: Getting a client to implement a set of recommendations that will address and remedy the problem the client faced initially. I suggest here two widely used frameworks for thinking about change.

Transition Management Model

MIT's Dick Beckhard long ago suggested that change involves moving a company from a "current state" to a desired "future state." Doing so, therefore, requires that the consultant and the client manage and orchestrate an orderly "transition state." A consultant's diagnosis of the current state (the "From" state) is therefore only a third of the "change equation." The other two thirds require defining the ideal "future state" (the "To" state) to which the client should move, as well as the host of activities that are required to get there (the "How" processes). Figure 6–8 diagrams the transition management model and its dynamic implications.

Contingency Model

Organizations are complex systems of interdependent parts. Contingency models recognize companies as systems, and suggest that the degree of "alignment" or "fit" among those parts explains human and financial performance. Originally developed by organizational psychologist Harold Leavitt, contingency models are in widespread use today. Two contingency models are in widespread use among consultants: The 7-S model and the congruence model.

The 7-S model was developed by McKinsey & Company consultants and popularized in various best-selling books. The model is shown in Figure 6–9. It suggests that the key business drivers in any company can be decomposed into seven categories: strategies, structures, systems, staff, superordinate goals, supervision, and shared values. The degree to which a company builds consistency among these elements, the better it performs.

In similar ways, the congruence model was developed by David Nadler and Michael Tushman, then at Columbia University. It's employed systematically with clients of the Delta Consulting Group (which has since merged with Mercer) that Nadler founded in the late 1970s. Figure 6–10 diagrams the Congruence Model. Key elements of the model are that:

- Top manager formulates strategies that are designed to adapt organizations to their environments.

FIGURE 6–8 Transition Management Model

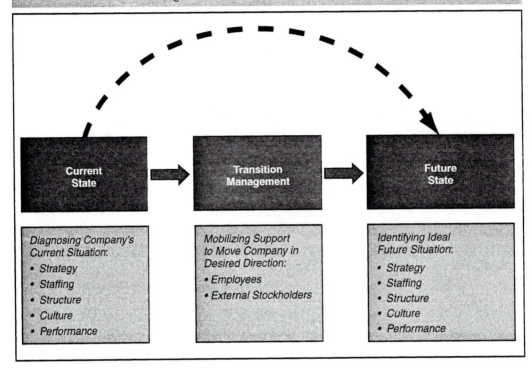

FIGURE 6–9 McKinsey's 7-S Model

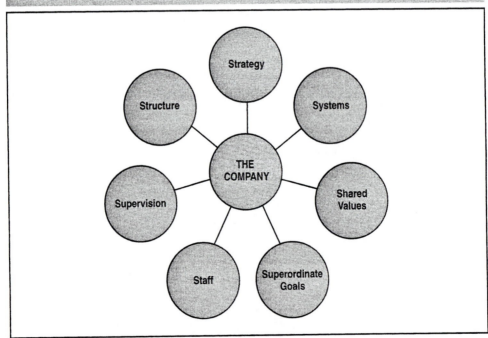

FIGURE 6–10   Mercer-Delta's Congruence Model

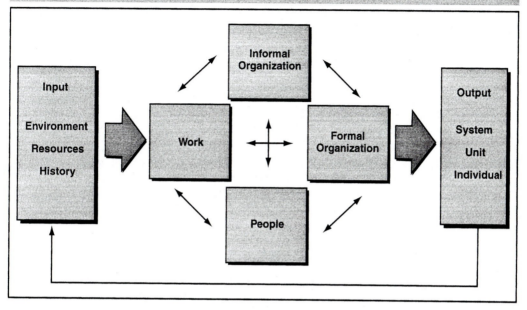

FIGURE 6–10   Mercer-Delta's Congruence Model

- Organizations can be described by four key elements: people, work processes, formal structures, and cultures.
- The overall degree of alignment or fit between these elements explains how well the organization is performing on both social and economic criteria.

Consultants use the congruence model to examine whether top managers have designed systems and processes that are consistent across the company's disparate units. A diagnosis that uncovers mismatches induces consultants to suggest interventions designed to improve the degree of fit across the system.

Contingency models remind the consultant of the impossibility of effecting change in any one element in isolation: Resistance will result since elements that already align well together will tend to favor the status quo. So change must be patterned if it is to be effective—change must simultaneously be carried out in multiple components of the model if it is to take hold.

PERFORMANCE MODELS

Since performance is the endgame of all consulting, it's only natural that consultants pay attention to measurement. What are the performance indicators the client attends to? Are they the right ones? Do they motivate employees to higher levels of productivity? How much control do individuals, groups, departments, and business units have over those performance indicators? The selection of appropriate measures requires an understanding of the causal drivers that underlie the performance of the organization—the "performance model."

There are many performance models consultants use. Most organic models of strategy, organization, and change are, in fact, high-level performance models. We review briefly four of the most popular models used to actually *measure* corporate performance: accounting models; shareholder value models; economic value-added models; and the balanced scorecard.

Accounting Ratios

The operating and financial statements of the company are among the most widely used measures of performance. They focus on the firm's success at managing the aggregate flows of financial resources through its departments, processes, structures, and over time. The most prevalent sources of macro-level financial data are probably the quarterly and annual balance and income statements. From these statements, consultants typically extract one or more of the performance indicators described in Figure 6–11.

Aggregate ratios are generally too broad to provide useful information that can lead consultants to recommend changes. Standard cost accounting data generally fail to monitor financial flows at the necessary level of detail. Once inside a company, consul-

---

FIGURE 6–11   Accounting Models: Aggregate Ratios

Category	Ratio	Description	Formula
Liquidity Measures	Current Ratio	A measure of the short-term safety of the firm	$\text{current ratio} = \dfrac{\text{current assets}}{\text{current liabilities}}$
	Quick Ratio	Adjusts for non-liquidity of equity	$\text{quick ratio} = \dfrac{\text{current assets} - \text{stocks}}{\text{current liabilities}}$
Leverage Measures	Debt-Equity Ratio	A measure of relative indebtedness and probability of short term pressures on cash flows	$\text{debt to equity ratio} = \dfrac{\text{total debt}}{\text{equity}}$
	Interest Coverage	Ability to cover short term cash needs	$\text{times interest earned} = \dfrac{\text{operating profit}}{\text{interest payments}}$
Efficiency Measures	Turnover Ratio	Measures relative inventory turnover	$\text{stock turnover ratio} = \dfrac{\text{cost of goods sold}}{\text{stock}}$
	Asset Turnover Ratio	Measures efficiency in use of assets to generate revenues	$\text{fixed asset turnover ratio} = \dfrac{\text{sales}}{\text{fixed assets}}$
Profitability Measures	Net Profit Margin	Proportion of sales revenues that create profits	$\dfrac{\text{net profit}}{\text{margin}} = \dfrac{\text{profit before interest and tax}}{\text{sales}}$
	Return of Assets	Economic rate of return from use of all corporate assets	$\text{return on total assets} = \dfrac{\text{operating profit}}{\text{total assets}}$
	Return on Capital Employed	Adjusts returns to recognize long-term capital funding	$\dfrac{\text{return on capital employed}}{} = \dfrac{\text{operating profit}}{\text{total assets} - \text{current liabilities}}$
	Return on Shareholders' Equity	Economic rate of return to shareholders for invested capital	$\dfrac{\text{return on shareholders' funds}}{} = \dfrac{\text{profit after tax}}{\text{equity}}$

tants therefore typically create more detailed breakdowns. Activity-based costing (ABC) is a popular consulting tool through which consultants break down the company's value chain into a comprehensive set of detailed activities involved in different organizational processes (such as parts purchasing, inventory management, or customer service), and identify the direct and indirect costs associated with each activity. The ABC process then compares the company's costs and yields with those of best-in-class rivals to identify redundant activities and areas to target for performance improvement. Finally, having redesigned the business processes there needs to be a means of tracking costs by measuring the impact of the cost and value drivers on a small number of key performance indicators. In so doing, ABC integrates a number of different activities including value analysis, process analysis, Total Quality Management (TQM), and cost control.

Economic Value

Accounting models are often criticized. As Sir Brian Pitman, Chairman of Lloyds, once put it: "Accounting profit is of limited use as a measure of performance as it ignores the cost of equity capital that had to be invested to generate the profit. We choose economic profit as a measure of performance because it captures both growth in investment and return."[2]

A widely used performance model marketed by the consulting firm of Stern Stewart & Company relies on a measure of performance termed *economic value added* (EVA). Developed by founder Bennett Stewart, the EVA model proposes that, to create value, a company's operations must earn more than the cost of capital. At its simplest, EVA is the amount a company earns less the cost of the capital required to produce these returns. It therefore improves on accounting measures of performance by recognizing the opportunity costs of the capital already invested to generate those returns.

In practice, to calculate EVA a company's accounts are reconstructed to identify "economic" profits. Doing so requires various adjustments. For instance, in cost accounting, expenditures on marketing or research and development are expensed; in EVA accounting, they are recognized on the balance sheet because they build brand value and reputation. Similarly, goodwill on acquisitions that is normally written off should be retrieved. The resulting measure of "operating profit" should then be divided by the company's "economic capital" to produce an economic (instead of an accounting) return on capital.

The next task is to calculate the cost of capital. According to the capital asset pricing model (CAPM), the cost of a company's equity can be divided into an available rate of return on risk-free assets and a risk premium. Add these two together, adjust by beta to take account of the risk specific to the company in question, and then weight the figure to take account of the split between equity capital and debt. Subtract this from the economic return on capital and you have an indication of whether or not value has been created. Multiply the ratio by the stock of economic capital and you can put a figure on the amount of value created—or, more pertinently, the "economic" value of the company.

---

[2]Quoted in *European Banker*, March 11, 1997, p. 7.

EVA models are now in widespread use in the United States and international companies, and many business units tie their managers' bonus incentives to EVA measures.

Shareholder Value

To paraphrase economist Milton Friedman, the business of business is profits. From this perspective, shareholder value is the only lens through which a client company's performance should be gauged. For a public company, value creation is judged on the basis of market data—how well is the stock price doing? Is it growing relative to competitors? How does it fare when compared to market indexes like the NYSE's Dow Jones Index, the S&P 500, the Japanese Nikkei Index, the French CAC, or the British FTSE100?

For privately held companies, and for examining subunits of larger public companies, shareholder value creation is more difficult to assess. Consultants therefore turn to other measures that enable tracking internal processes more clearly. A study by McKinsey consultants examined companies widely known for having high quality planning practices and found they had six features in common—all of which are crucial to the implementation of shareholder value management:

- A strong focus on strategic planning at both the business unit and corporate levels with corporate strategy evolving from business unit strategies.
- Integrated performance measurement driven down to the grass roots level of front line management.
- Planning led by those responsible for implementation.
- Excellent flow of information and facts used to provide benchmarking and fact-based decision making.
- Genuine dialogue—two-way communication—between layers of management.
- Planning ingrained in the culture of the organization.

The framework links these common sense features of excellent strategic planning to the process of value creation, not only at the corporate level, but also at the business unit level and below. At the corporate level, value drivers translate into economic value added or discounted cash flows that are generic: The spread between the return on invested capital and the weighted average cost of capital applies to all companies.

At the business unit level, however, value drivers are more specific to the activity set, and depend on the economics of the customer mix, on sales force productivity, capacity management, labor productivity per hour worked, and working capital management.

Below the business unit level there are often incomplete income statements or balance sheets, and the discussion between operating heads of business units and their direct reports centers on continuous improvement of operating value drivers. These are specific to the business unit, but traceable to value creation in the unit, and in the company as a whole. When value-based management is carried to this level, business unit managers learn to rank order activities according to their impact on value.

Balanced Scorecard

Performance models rooted in accounting and economic data provide a valuable assessment of the financial health of a client's company and business units—and so recognize the shareholder/investor as the crucial stakeholder to please. In doing so, however, they ignore other indicators of the company's "health"—considerations affecting nonfinancial stakeholders, particularly employees and customers.

The Balanced Scorecard is a model and associated methodology developed by former Harvard professors Robert Kaplan and David Norton, founders of Renaissance Consulting, and most recently of The Balanced Scorecard Collaborative, a professional services firm created to "facilitate worldwide awareness, use, enhancement, and integrity of the Balanced Scorecard as a value-added management process." Their approach relies on both financial and nonfinancial measures of performance, and links these measures to the strategies and goals of the client companies. Many companies have implemented the Balanced Scorecard in the last few years, and have found it to be an effective strategic tool.

The Balanced Scorecard defines corporate performance from the point of view of shareholders, customers, and employees, and relies on metrics in each of the following categories:

- Financial
- Customer Service and Satisfaction
- Performance of Internal Business Functions
- Innovation, Growth, and Position Relative to Competitors

Applying the Balanced Scorecard involves selecting relevant metrics for a particular company and its industry, and implementing a process to capture and measure those metrics. Especially challenging is developing measures of innovation and competitive position that require reliable information about the external environment as well as determining what key measures provide the best feedback to understand the client's strategic performance, and linking those measures to key success factors for the company.

The Balanced Scorecard is not just a measurement tool; it is a strategic management system. Its purpose is to get people to make the right decisions. It is intended to enable and empower employees to focus on the key drivers of the business. The process also creates a powerful communication tool for a business that gives all members of an organization a consistent message about the key drivers of success. Incentive compensation plans based on scorecard measures further align employees' and managers' business goals.

SUMMARY

Models help consultants analyze problems and diagnose situations. Like blueprints of the mind, they guide how we think about the client company's situation, and so the kinds of problems we see, as well as the solutions we are likely to propose. This chapter reviewed a set of key models in widespread use that constitute a "generalist toolkit"—the set of tools most consultants use, more or less formally, more or less explicitly, as they encounter clients, to develop diagnostic insights of the situation, and to recommend solutions. In the next chapter, we show how consultants can build their own "unique" models of the situation and thereby further provide value to clients by framing the way problems are defined and addressed.

CHAPTER 7

Thinking Like a Consultant

Charles J. Fombrun and Mark D. Nevins

The real magic of discovery lies not in seeking new landscapes but in having new eyes.

— Marcel Proust

Geneneral managers often face challenges that lie outside their direct experience or that are beyond their ability to address without the collaboration of peers in far-flung parts of the company. Among them might be pressure on a manager's department to improve performance quickly, with minimal capital; to respond to new competitor initiatives that compel a new long-term vision or strategy for the business unit; or to reengineer the organization's structure or core processes to address escalating coordination costs. In these situations, consultants are often useful collaborators because they can help a client articulate the roots of problems and identify suitable responses.

In working with a client, the consultant's most powerful skill is the ability to build credible models of the situation. Models are cognitive maps: They describe a set of variables the client needs to address, and demonstrate how these variables relate to each other. Models frame a situation: They guide how the client and the consultant "see" the issues.

Beyond diagnostics, models are also critical for communicating the value of the proposed solution and for motivating the client company to change. Once adopted, a model is normally used to structure and communicate analyses and findings in reports and presentations—and thus the model acts as an analytical framework, a project management tool, and a facilitator for the change process, all in one. Models inextricably link the twin processes of thinking and communicating throughout the consulting engagement.

Charles J. Fombrun is Executive Director of the Reputation Institute and Professor of Management at the Stern School of Business of New York University. Dr. Fombrun earned a B.S. in Physics from Queen's University (Canada) and completed a Ph.D. in organizational networks at Columbia University in 1980.

Mark D. Nevins is President of Nevins Consulting. Dr. Nevins has been global head of organizational development and training for both Booz Allen Hamilton and Korn/Ferry International. He received a Ph.D. in English Literature from Harvard University.

This chapter argues that a consultant's added value derives from an ability to structure and visualize a problem, to articulate key issues, and to create a framework for understanding cause–effect relationships, which facilitates identifying the best solutions to the problem. Models are central to what consultants do—let's examine how they work.

MODEL BUILDING: ASKING THE FIVE WHYS

Consider a simplified version of a common consulting scenario: You receive a call from a prospective client, and the person on the other end of the line tells you that she is the CEO of a consumer products company that has been logging losses for the last 3 years. She's heard that you've helped other companies turn things around and is curious to know how you would approach working with her company.

Consultants regularly face situations like this one. Your reply—and the ensuing conversation—should demonstrate how you think about problems and how you frame situations. In fact, the basic methodology and approach are fundamentally the same whether you're discussing the challenges facing a major company with its CEO or whether you're simply trying to "crack a case" during a consulting interview. In either case, success depends on employing a structured and inquisitive approach to assess the situation, develop an understanding of the key issues the client should address, and identify the action to improve the company's performance.

A very good first step is for the consultant to take the client through a process called "The Five Whys," which has been described by Peter Senge. This process may seem simplistic, but it's a powerful tool for identifying the major issues and avoiding getting lost in the morass of trivia and extraneous details that often obscure a situation. The conversation goes something like this:

CLIENT: Our company is losing money badly.

CONSULTANT: Why do you think the company has been losing money?

CLIENT: Because competitors are killing us on price.

CONSULTANT: Why can't you match their prices?

CLIENT: Because we've got low margins.

CONSULTANT: Why are your margins so low?

CLIENT: Because we have high overheads.

CONSULTANT: Why do you have such high overheads?

CLIENT: Because we carry high inventories and pay our people better than anyone else.

CONSULTANT: Why are your inventories so high, and why do you pay your staff so much?

CLIENT: Because distributors won't stock in bulk, and want us to carry them. As for the staff, we're a one-company town, and our people work for us from cradle to tomb.

If you pay attention to this conversation, you'll recognize that the only thing the consultant did was ask "Why?" five times—and then listen carefully to the answers to

frame the next question. The resulting discussion was a series of ever-focusing asser-
tions that enabled the consultant to "dig down," to identify, and to list four factors that
are related to the company's core problem of mounting losses:

- Inventory levels
- Employment policy
- Pricing level
- Competition

From that list the consultant can deduce a key "issue" that the company appears to be
facing, which considers the mounting losses as resulting from increasing costs:

Issue 1: Is the company facing increasing costs?

From this issue and the client's replies, the consultant is then able to formulate a
group of three tentative "hypotheses" about factors that might explain the company's
current situation:

**Hypothesis 1: Losses are occurring because this company's lifetime employment pol-
icy creates high fixed costs.**

**Hypothesis 2: Losses are occurring because this company has no leverage over its dis-
tributors to carry its products.**

**Hypothesis 3: Losses are occurring because this company faces intensifying competi-
tion from more cost-effective rivals.**

These three preliminary hypotheses are thought provoking, and can help the consultant through the initial conversation as she works to understand the situation. The
savvy reader, however, may recognize that missing from this preliminary analysis is a
serious omission: the failure to recognize that losses can result not only from the "cost
side" but also from the "revenue side" of the equation:

$$\text{Profits} = \text{Revenues} - \text{Costs}$$

The short conversation with the client did not address a whole field of inquiry:
whether or not revenue considerations might be an essential cause of the problem.
Therefore, it's up to the consultant to "enrich" the conversation with that insight. Such
a path might come about by the consultant reminding the client that profits (and
losses) are a function of both costs and revenues, and suggesting a second issue to consider:

Issue #2: Is the company suffering from declining revenues?

Following the "Five Whys," the consultant might therefore probe with queries such
as the following:

- "Are your company's sales growing as fast as the industry?"
- "Has your company boosted its advertising spending as fast as industry rivals?"

Such queries, and the answers obtained, will suggest related hypotheses the consultant might want to explore, such as:

Hypothesis 4: *Losses are occurring because of industry-wide decline in sales.*

Hypothesis 5: *Losses are occurring because this company is not advertising and promoting its products as much as its competitors.*

Hypothesis 6: *Losses are occurring because this company's sales incentives are too low.*

We might diagram the result of the consultant's conversation with the client by means of an "issue tree" (Figure 7–1). For the client, the issue tree formalizes in an easily grasped visual manner how the consultant is thinking about the situation, and therefore how the consulting firm might help address the problems. For the consultant, the preliminary issue tree maps out possible avenues to pursue in an engagement with the client: the "hypotheses" that should be tested, and therefore the kinds of information that will have to be collected and the manner in which it should be analyzed. Thus, by means of a simple "structuring" tool in an initial conversation—asking the "Five Whys"—the consultant can already envisage the kind of work that will have to be done on behalf of the client and, to some extent, the way the results will be shared with the client in the form of a presentation or report. (For example, a specific section of the report might be devoted to each of the hypotheses identified in the issue tree.)

In this example, the issue tree was built around a simple model of financial profitability. It's an approach the consultant could use to understand and analyze this situ-

FIGURE 7–1   An Issue Tree

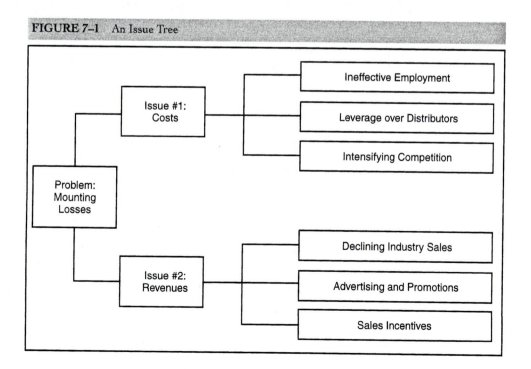

ation, to gather data, and to communicate results and recommendations. The issue tree is a simple visual description of the consultant's underlying framework for approaching the client's problem.

Chapter 6 described some "prepackaged" models that consultants regularly draw on to explain a company's performance. These models constitute a generalist "toolkit" that the skilled consultant can also use to structure a preliminary issue tree. Picking the right one is part art and part intuition—in most client situations there is no single "best" model to use *a priori*. The right framework for assessing a specific client's problem or situation can be tailored through conversations with the clients and with those around them who are most familiar with the situation. Skillful consultants are those who have lots of these "tools" in their toolkits, and minds agile enough to assess which tool to use in a given situation—but when necessary, can also think "out of the box."[1]

In many cases, it's not immediately obvious which of the prepackaged models in the toolkit might be most appropriate to use in constructing an issue tree. Following below, we suggest a systematic process for building a *unique, emergent* model of the client's situation that can lend structure to an ambiguous and complex situation. The tailor-made model that results can help the consultant configure the most appropriate issue tree for the client, and better conceive the design of the ensuing engagement.

FRAMING PROBLEMS: CONSTRUCTING UNIQUE MODELS OF THE SITUATION

When you begin discussions with a client, your primary role as a consultant is to ask effective questions and to listen as the client describes the situation, problem, and related issues, and then to structure what you hear into a model of the situation. In essence, constructing a model is a process of dialogue through which you frame the underlying problems and its component issues from the discussion and your preliminary observation of the client's situation.

In his best-selling book *The Fifth Discipline*, Peter Senge describes how all of us climb a "ladder of inference" as we observe the world around us (see Figure 7–2). Sometimes our inferences are off the mark; sometimes they are remarkably accurate. Skillful consultants are careful to build "robust inferences" as they climb the ladder.

In essence, models are mental images we hold about ourselves, other people, and how the world works. They embody both our formal knowledge and our "intuition"—a form of insight that derives either from past experience or from vicarious knowledge about similar situations but can be difficult to capture in explicit terms. A model is therefore a mental tool that we use to simplify the world by structuring:

- What we *observe:* It limits the data and events around us to which we pay attention.
- How we *interpret* what we see: It clarifies what we identify as "meaningful" in relating one observation to another.

---

[1]Philosopher Thomas Kuhn's influential theory of scientific progress suggests that models are a double-edged sword—powerful and necessary for representing complex reality and allowing human minds to assess and analyze, but also capable of trapping the model builder in a single way of seeing things, and blinding him or her from seeing other, perhaps better, paths of inquiry. (See *The Structure of Scientific Revolutions.*) To return to the "toolbox" metaphor, remember the old saying "If your only tool is a hammer, every problem looks like a nail." The best consultants will develop (through experience and creativity) as many tools as possible and, most of all, carefully assess and consider the problem before reaching for a tool.

FIGURE 7–2   Senge's Ladder of Inference

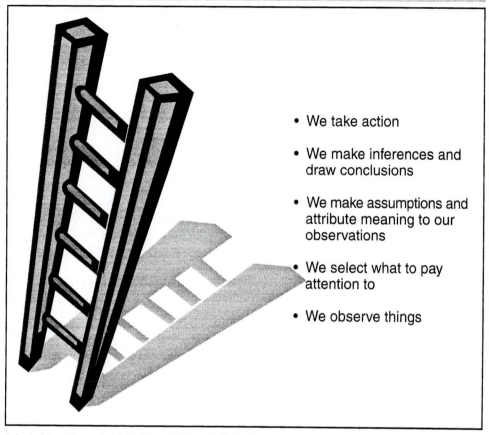

- We take action

- We make inferences and draw conclusions

- We make assumptions and attribute meaning to our observations

- We select what to pay attention to

- We observe things

Adapted from Senge, P. M., Roberts, C., Ross, R. B., Smith, B. J., & Kleiner, A. (1994). *The Fifth Discipline Fieldbook*. New York: Doubleday Currency.

- How we *act:* It guides the steps we take as a result of those interpretations (our actions and reactions).

In everyday life, all of us rely on intuitive models that lie below our level of awareness. These models guide our daily behavior. Consider the common situation in which you come suddenly face to face with someone who thrusts a hand toward you. The ladder of inference suggests that you will do the following:

- You'll *observe* the hand as it comes toward you.

- You'll *observe* other factors around you: whether the hand is open or closed into a fist; whether you know this person or not.

- Based on your observations and your prior experience with this person or other similar situations you've lived through in the past, you'll *interpret* the situation as one in which the person is about to either strike you or greet you.

- You'll then *act and react* according to the interpretation you made: You'll either dodge the closed fist or shake the outstretched open hand.

This is a simple case of the kind of intuitive model-building that we do constantly and that guides our everyday interactions and behaviors. In this sense, every human being is an expert model builder. The differences between each person—the differences that may in part determine which of us succeed as scientists, consultants, critics, lawyers, that is, people who rely on disciplined thinking for their work—lies in the *degree of attention* we pay to the process of making inferences and in the *repertoire of experiences* on which we rely to make those inferences. Unlike everyday intuitive modelers, scientists are trained to pay close attention to the inferential process by which they make inferences: the "scientific method" requires a rigorous process through which one observation is related to another in the form of a hypothesis; multiple observations are made to ensure that the relationship is not accidental; and other influences are eliminated wherever possible.

Skillful consultants are like scientists: They apply a deductive approach through which they identify key issues involved in a problem and specify causal hypotheses about the situation that they observe. They then look for information that will enable them to verify or reject those hypotheses. A key role the consultant plays is therefore to help clients construct a valid model of the company's situation in order to identify tentative hypotheses about the nature of the problems that they face.

In fact, when working with companies, consultants rely heavily on two types of models: causal models and systemic models.

Causal Models

A machine fails. The consultant asks why, and is told that it has been poorly maintained and breaks down regularly. A causal model of the situation suggests that the machine's breakdown is a *result* of poor maintenance. Further observation of the situation might also reveal that the maintenance department is overworked and unmotivated, and has been repairing the machine with cheap parts. Asking "why?" again could lead the consultant to discover that top management initiated a lowest-bidder purchase policy six months earlier.

A backwards chain of cause–event relationships (shown in Figure 7–3) can therefore be constructed to explain the observed breakdown of the machine: Breakdowns occur for multiple reasons, many of which can be traced to management's top-down low-cost purchasing policy. The diagram also points out that relationships are positive: The more cheap parts are used, the more the consultant expects machines to break down; the more committed top managers are to the low-cost purchasing policy, the more likely workers are to use cheap parts, the more demoralized the staff, and the more frequently machines will break down. By a *positive* relationship, we mean that an increase in one variable is matched by an increase in another. Two variables are said to have a *negative* relationship when an increase in one variable results in a decrease in the other variable.

Clearly, this example is limited: for one, it highlights the presence of *positive* relationships between variables. Yet, there are surely many negative relationships. One might include for instance a variable such as the "average age of the maintenance staff." A hypothesis might be: The higher the average age of the maintenance workers, the lower the number of machine breakdowns—a negative relationship.

A second reason the example is limited is that all of the observed problems are rooted in one underlying cause. Rarely will a set of observed problems ever converge

FIGURE 7–3   A Causal Model

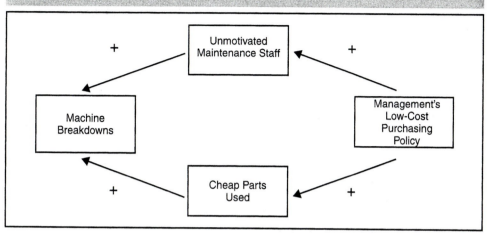

on a single underlying cause. In our example, multiple causes are probably acting in concert to influence the breakdown rate of machines in the plant. An overworked and undertrained maintenance staff is another factor that could also contribute to the observed breakdowns, as might the temperature in the room, or quality problems in the supplier's manufacturing process. All models will limit the number of variables examined: Articulating a good causal model means specifying a sufficiently realistic and comprehensive set of variables that can help the consultant to pinpoint the primary drivers of the observed problem.

Cause–effect maps are powerful tools by means of which consultants construct models of the situation. These maps force clients to examine the chains of relationships that lead from an observed symptom back to its roots in other actions, initiatives, and policies in the company. Both positive and negative relationships arise as consultants search out root causes with which to explain the observed outcomes, symptoms, or effects.

Systemic Models

We drew the model in Figure 7–3 as a causal model, but it clearly hints at a deeper set of interactions between the elements. A *system* consists of interdependent elements that act on each other in ways that produce more than a linear chain of actions and reactions, and so generates outcomes that are difficult to anticipate from simple cause–effect reasoning.

Consider the natural world. A farmer uses a fertilizer to kill insects that would otherwise destroy his crop. In Year 1, it increases his yield. By Year 2, the chemical gets into the aquifer that he relies on to water his crop. His neighbor's cows also drink from the same water, from which they develop chemical poisoning. The supermarket buys milk from the farmer's poisoned cows—which the farmer himself purchases, and which damages his health.

This is a not-so-farfetched example of a systemic interaction that terrifies ecologists. Europe's considerable concern about "mad cow disease" in the United Kingdom throughout the 1990s was born of just such a systemic model that related chemical consumption to livestock poisoning to human meat consumption and human death.

Consultants regularly find themselves faced with complex situations in which simple causal thinking is unacceptable—there are too many interdependencies, time lags, and interactions among variables. Systemic models enable more complete descriptions of the situation. They call attention to:

- Unanticipated effects of actions
- Hidden or latent variables
- Time lags between causes and effects
- Mutual interdependencies in which a variable is both a cause and an effect of the other (e.g., the relationship between productivity, morale, and pay levels: Low pay reduces productivity and morale, but low morale reduces productivity and pay)
- *Virtuous cycles* through which small changes in some variables dampen an effect, and *vicious cycles*, through which small changes in one variable are amplified across the system

Figure 7–4 presents a systemic model that relates the effects of changes in environmental conditions on a company's strategic initiatives and performance. In the model, changes in technology and increased globalization are increasing competition in the industry and reducing the company's financial performance. In turn, declining performance has negative effects on the company's advertising, research, and human resource investments (because of the positive relationships between the variables and financial

FIGURE 7–4   A Systemic Model Relating Environmental Effects to a Company's Strategic Initiatives

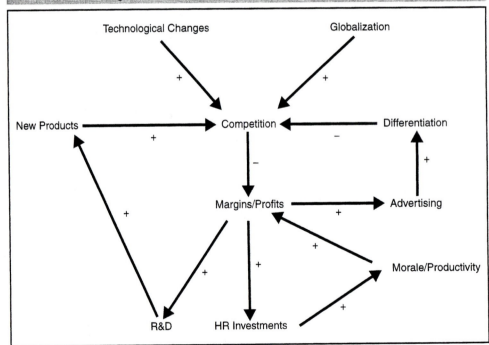

performance). The resulting decline in these variables acts, perversely, to increase competition in the industry, fueling a vicious cycle by propelling further decline in the company's performance. Systems models focus heavily on identifying these kinds of cyclical chains of causality that can lead to spiraling effects in companies. Systemic models are more elaborate than causal models, although not necessarily "better." They are, however, often more useful than causal models in circumstances wherein mutual interdependencies are high or time lags between causes and effects vary.

Building a Unique Model

Let's play for a bit. Consider the following situation:

> You receive a call from the newly appointed dean of a large business school. He is concerned about the standing of the business school (relative to major rivals) in a recent survey of alumni and recruiters that was published by *BusinessWeek*. In particular, he points to the following trends of the last four years:
>
> • The school's ranking in the survey has steadily dropped from 17th to 24th.
> • Applications have dropped by 20 percent.
> • Enrollment (percentage of accepted applicants who enroll) has dropped by 18 percent.
> • Faculty are well regarded in their fields, but the school's success with new hires is low.
> • Students complain about the school's antiquated and crowded facilities.
> • Alumni donations have declined by 10 percent, and are low compared to other schools.
>
> The dean asks for your assistance. How do you build him a model that can help him understand the drivers of a business school's performance and so the issues he should consider as he embarks on his new job?

One way to begin this process is to start by identifying the "effect or outcome variable" that is of particular interest to the dean—in this case, the school's relative reputation. Write this down on a Post-It note and stick it on a wall. Now create a laundry list of all the "facts" you know about the situation your client is in. Put them on individual Post-It notes as well. If you are working with others in a team, each of you should conduct the exercise individually. Once done, stick all of the Post-It notes up on the wall at random, around the words *Business School Reputation*. Have everyone look at the wall. Are there any factors that could also affect the school's reputation missing from those stuck on the wall that might be important to know about? List these on individual Post-It notes as well, and put them on the wall. At this point, you should have anywhere from 20 to 30 notes stuck on the wall around the words *Business School Reputation*.

Now push them apart. Move them around. Cluster together those that are similar, and remove those that are redundant; separate those that have little in common into another area; write new notes for larger categories that seem to be simpler ways to explain the ideas on different notes, and remove the previous notes. Try to reduce the set of notes left on the wall to no more than 10 key factors.

Now look at those factors. See if you can establish a causal relationship between any two of them. Draw a line with a one-directional arrow where you believe there is probably a strong relationship. See if the relationship can be described as positive or negative, and if it can, then put a + or − sign on the arrow. Don't stop until all your factors are connected in some way. Try to arrive at a "clean" representation by avoiding crossed lines and multiple arrows between the same two factors, and by moving them around.

If you continue this process for a time, you'll arrive at a model that describes how you (and your team) collectively "think" about the dean's problem. It might look something like Figure 7–5 (or in fact it might look completely different—there is rarely a single "right" systemic model).

The major factors in the model are the topics you would examine at greater length if you embarked on an engagement with the dean and his school to improve its reputational standing in the *BusinessWeek* rankings. We reiterate, however: There's no "right" answer here. You've simply created a model that is grounded in how you and your team think—that is, your model is grounded in your intuitive understanding of the situation. It's entirely possible (and probable) that you're not entirely on target. It's also probably true that you could enrich this mental model with other insights drawn from deep knowledge you or others have about how business schools operate, how they compete, and the trends that affect them—or from further interviews with the dean, faculty, students, and alumni. The point is this: The mental model you developed provides you with a *preliminary* model for examining the factors that drive a business school's reputation, and to explore with the dean how you might proceed with an engagement.

FIGURE 7–5 An Example of a Systemic Model for Explaining a Business School's Reputation

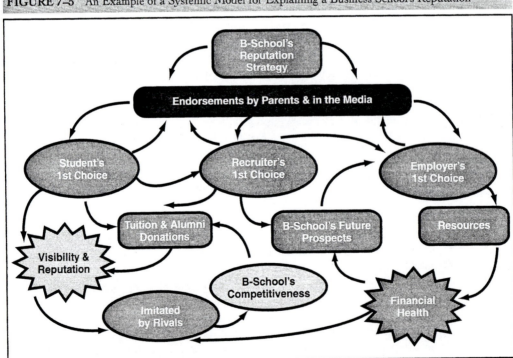

In fact, the example we provided for building a model of the situation using Post-It notes derives from a systematic process that treats every problem as an "effect" or "outcome," and involves four steps:

1. *Listing:* Identifying all issues that are seemingly related to the "effect."
2. *Pruning:* Eliminating issues that are too highly related or unmeasurable.
3. *Clustering:* Grouping related issues together into larger categories and factors and eliminating duplicate issues.
4. *Linking:* Connecting related issues through directed, causal links.

The elements of this general approach to model-building are diagrammed as a jigsaw puzzle in Figure 7–6. In general, you should use this approach in problem situations that lack clarity, in which many factors are relevant, and where there is little agreement about the key issues. The picture the model paints is a personal model of the situation.

If you work through the same model-building activity with a team of colleagues, you create a group model. To do so, let everyone brainstorm individual factors associated with the problem. Combine them when they are identical, eliminate duplicates, and continue through the process. After much back and forth, you'll end up with a

FIGURE 7–6   The Model-Building Process

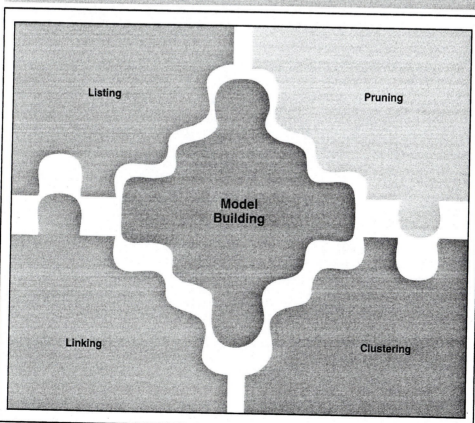

shared model of the situation that describes how the team sees things, what it pays attention to, and implies how an engagement with this team might unfold.

MCKINSEY & COMPANY: AN EXAMPLE

Figure 7–7 captures various paragraphs taken from a reporter's description of McKinsey & Company. If you were asked to build a model that might explain how McKinsey operates, you would begin by listing the factors highlighted in the text. After eliminating duplicates and clustering similar variables, you would then identify possible linkages between them. How are these variables related? Which factors cause the others? Are there vicious or virtuous cycles operating that link these variables?

A possible model of McKinsey is presented in Figure 7–8. It suggests that McKinsey is a complex system that can be described in terms of five virtuous cycles:

- **Cycle 1:** The quality of training McKinsey provides its consultants creates external opportunities for them with clients who hire away those that the firm elects not to keep. Outplacement enlarges McKinsey's networks of "alumni" who speak well of the firm. This enables . . .
- **Cycle 2:** The hiring of more smart people—of "brains and talent"—brought together through a culture that stimulates knowledge sharing, and creates a "one-firm" environment, encourages learning, and further attracts smart people, enabling . . .
- **Cycle 3:** Getting better results for clients, which justifies charging high fees, and compensates consultants accordingly, further attracting smart people to the firm, and generates . . .
- **Cycle 4:** Good word of mouth, which builds reputation and further attracts smart people, with positive results for the client, high fees, and . . .
- **Cycle 5:** Fuels the firm's growth, expands its network, and builds its reputation.

If you were asked by McKinsey's top management team to examine the firm's overall well-being, this model suggests key points of departure for exploring questions of employee morale, recruiting success, "one-firm" culture, outplacement success, strength of its alumni network, client satisfaction with its services, and firm profitability.

FIGURE 7–7   McKinsey & Company

McKinsey's sterling reputation is based on a long history of providing strategic advice to the top management of the world's largest corporations. That means it knows more CEOs on a first-name basis than just about any other organization around. In fact, many of those CEOs (including more than 70 leaders of the *Fortune* 500, such as Lou Gerstner of IBM, Philip Purcell of Morgan Stanley, Leo Mullin of Delta Air Lines, Kevin Sharer of Amgen, and the infamous Jeffrey Skilling of Enron) once worked for McKinsey. The firm also has an unrivaled depth of experience. Given the sheer number of engagements the firm takes, there is a good chance that McKinsey has prior experience in any given situation. Critics charge that this can lead to a cookie-cutter approach to solving business problems, but even competitors acknowledge the formidable intellectual capital of the firm. And the numbers don't lie. McKinsey's clients have been happy to pony up for a premium that has traditionally been 25 percent higher than any of their competitors. McKinsey's worldwide revenues totaled $3.3 billion in 2001, more than any other pure strategy firm, and more than 80 percent of the firm's clients are repeat customers.

SOURCE: http://www.wetfeet.com/asp/insiderguide_detail.asp?insiderguide pk=17&px ID=3201.

FIGURE 7–8 The McKinsey System

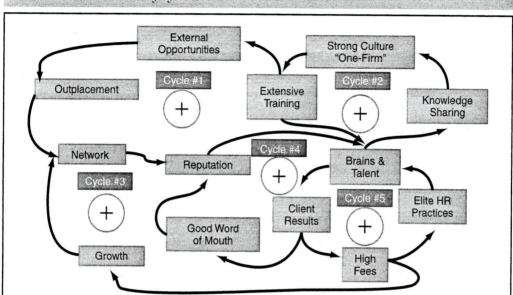

FROM MODEL TO WORK PLAN

We've indicated in this chapter that a good consulting model lays out critical issues that the client will want to examine closely. The model therefore provides a preliminary framework for deducing key *hypotheses* that the consultant will need to test, and the kinds of *data* that will be needed to test those hypotheses. It also suggests the way the consultant will ultimately communicate a set of recommendations to a client.

Ultimately, management consultants are in the business not merely of providing "good answers" but of bringing about positive change. Therefore, knowing the cause of a problem is not enough: The client must also appreciate and agree with the assessment, and feel willing and able to make the necessary changes to see positive results. Since human beings are generally uncomfortable with change—and managers are especially so (after all, why "rock the boat"?)—consulting advice can sometimes have less of an impact than it should. Many a brilliant client report has sat unimplemented on a senior manager's desk. The most insidious aspect of this problem is that sometimes the "right" answer, intellectually speaking, may not in fact be the *best* course of action for a client and his company. (In our opinion, it's better to see a good recommendation that gets 80% implemented than a very good recommendation that's only 20% implemented.) Building clear models is an essential part of the change process, but it's still only one part. Avoid becoming that unhappy consultant who "falls in love with the model" and never helps drive real improvement for the client.

CHAPTER

From Insight to Impact: Communicating to Influence

Mark D. Nevins

After a consultant has built a robust model of the client's situation, formulated key hypotheses, and gathered and analyzed the necessary data to verify or refute the hypotheses, the time has come to make a recommendation to the client. The recommendation can take many forms: an interim report designed to demonstrate progress and gain "buy-in" that the project is proceeding on track and in scope; a final presentation to the senior clients who contracted the engagement; or a detailed free-standing report that the company's managers will use to implement change.

Consulting presentations are generally documents created in a structured format that are given to the client in hardcopy or projected on a screen for purposes of facilitating a discussion. Contrary to much general practice, the best consultant presentations are not written from scratch in the days and nights immediately preceding the meeting. They are actually written along the way during the engagement, and writing and persuasion should play important roles throughout the consulting assignment, from structuring the problem to communicating the recommendation.

A number of "best practices" apply to the way that writing and presentations are used over the course of an engagement:

1. The consulting report or presentation should be used as a *thinking* tool to help work through the problem and check the logic of what's being done.
2. Reports or presentations should be the basis on which the project is managed, tasks are allocated across the team, and progress is checked.
3. A strong framework or model should underlie the report—and the same basic model should be maintained over the course of the engagement.
4. From the beginning of the process, the consultant should work to create a "story": Narrative is the most powerful form of human communication and the surest means to ensure understanding.
5. Throughout the process, the consultant should strive to focus not on the consulting *process* ("what we did" or "what we found") but on the *impact of the analysis*—"what does this *mean*" and "what should be *done* as a result?"

Mark D. Nevins is President of Nevins Consulting. Dr. Nevins has been global head of organizational development and training for both Booz Allen Hamilton and Korn/Ferry International. He received a Ph.D. in English Literature from Harvard University.

6. In every case, the writer must make sure that the *audience* is kept firmly in mind; most consultants are ineffective when they focus too much on content, and not enough on the needs of the listeners/readers.

THE IMPORTANCE OF RHETORIC: BUILDING BRIDGES FOR YOUR AUDIENCE

Let's first consider issues related to audience, since these matters often prove most challenging for management consultants. In the Western intellectual tradition, beginning in the Classical world and up through early Modern times, *rhetoric* was a cornerstone of education. While in today's world "rhetoric" might have negative associations (calling to mind politicians with ulterior motives trying to slip something past their constituencies), in its original sense it was (and still is!) a skill critical for any public person.[1]

At its most basic, rhetoric is the art of communicating in order to persuade. (Interestingly, to ensure that this art was not misused, in the classical and medieval university rhetoric was taught together with *ethics*.) The principles of rhetoric are concerned with organizing an argument and understanding the audience—and both parts are of equal importance not only for classical orators, but for modern-day management consultants as well.

In simple terms, employing sound rhetorical principles means paying as much attention to *whom* you are addressing as you pay to *what* you are saying. Consultants sometimes spend endless hours crafting the content of their arguments, and too little time considering the important details of their audience, such as:

- Who is my audience?
- What do they want to hear—and *not* want to hear?
- Why are they listening to me?
- What is their knowledge base, political bias, agenda?
- What do I want them to understand or do differently based on what I tell them?
- How can I best get them to "hear" or understand me?

If I ask someone to give a presentation, I hope that person will immediately ask two questions:

1. What is the topic?
2. Who is the audience?

While the first question is critical for developing the subject matter, the second can actually have a much bigger impact on the *form* of the presentation or report. For example, imagine giving a presentation on the topic of "Uses of Power in Shakespeare's *King Lear*" to a number of different audiences: college students studying the play; a general audience about to see the play in a theater; a group of schoolchildren first encountering the playwright; a seminar of corporate executives (for whom, incidentally, this play would

---

[1]For various reasons the evolution of the modern university at the beginning of the twentieth century resulted in rhetoric being dropped from the curriculum—surely one of the grossest injustices ever foisted on students, since the basics of rhetoric are the foundations of effective communication, and effective communication is a skill critical for every academic discipline, not to mention any leadership role in the business world.

contain some very powerful messages about responsibility and decision making); or even (to allude to a famous anthropological experiment) a group of African Bushmen who have never heard of England, never mind this legendary monarch. In each case the *subject matter* of the presentation would be exactly the same, but the *form* of the presentation, and the nature of the argument and how it is made, would have to vary dramatically. Consultants, then, would be wise to think carefully about the audiences to whom they are presenting in order to increase impact, influence, and subsequent action: a presentation to a board of directors on the redesign of a business unit would and *should* look very different from a presentation to that business unit's line managers.

Most of the mistakes consultants make as writers are a result of failing to pay attention to audience and the basic rules of storytelling. Remember that human beings have from time immemorial passed on knowledge and wisdom by means of stories—even before writing itself was invented. Homer's *Iliad*, recited orally for generations before the Greeks had even adopted the technology of writing, is as much a catalog of that society's values as it is a tale of a war fought on foreign shores. Consultants, then, need to learn the art of *telling stories* appropriate for business audiences. (By "telling stories" I don't mean fabricating fictions, but rather creating effective narratives for communicating, understanding, and motivating changes of belief and action.)

As Chapter 7 described, the consulting process has a basic form or methodology: It begins by articulating key issues and hypotheses, after which the consultant gathers and analyzes data in order to test those hypotheses and reach a conclusion. One challenge in communicating a conclusion is that in most cases the audience has, in fact, *not* been involved in the consulting process itself—and they may not even be familiar or comfortable with the consulting methodology. The audience was likely "last seen" by the consultants at the point of proposal or progress report, and therefore it's critical that the recommendation be framed and communicated in the terms of that original proposal and the models that it embodied. Figure 8–1 illustrates a disconnect between

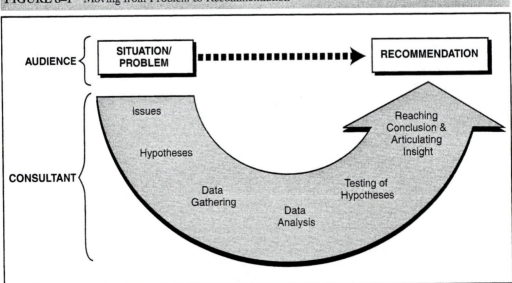

FIGURE 8–1 Moving from Problem to Recommendation

consultants and their client "audiences" that often develops during engagements and can limit the effectiveness of recommendations.

One way to explain how to address this potential disconnect is to make use of an instructional metaphor: Communicating can be thought of as **bridge-building** (see Figure 8–2). The audience is on one bank, the consultant on the other, and they are separated by a "Gulf of Lack of Understanding." In simple terms, you as the consultant would like your audience to understand or see things differently, accept an analysis, or be motivated to do something in a new way: You want to move them across the bridge to a new position, on "your" side.

In order to build that bridge effectively, the communicator must *begin* with the original framework or model—the one that the audience is already familiar with—and build an argument or narrative on that foundation. In essence, communicating is a *selling* process: As the author, I sell my argument to my listeners or readers, point by point, page by page. I build the bridge step by step.

The bridge metaphor introduces two of the key terms routinely used in consulting presentations: horizontal logic and vertical logic.[2] *Horizontal logic* refers to the overall

FIGURE 8–2   Communicating as Bridge Building

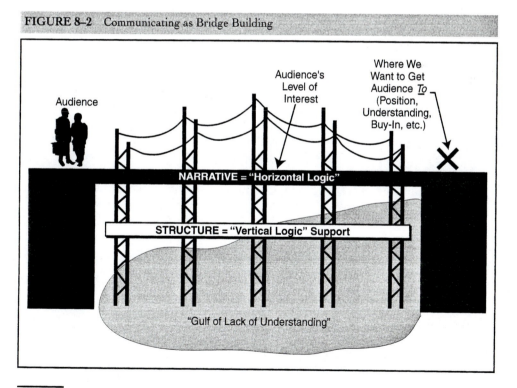

_____

[2]These terms were popularized by Barbara Minto in her book *The Pyramid Principle*. Originally created internally for McKinsey & Co., Minto's approach (which derives from classical rhetoric and logic) has become standard practice in many consulting firms. Consultants can benefit from the disciplined methodology but should adapt the approach to their own styles (e.g., Minto's didactic insistence on underlying pyramids for structuring all aspects of communication can sometimes lead to awkward results in the hands of inexperienced writers).

structure of the document, report, or presentation—what we might call its narrative trajectory, or its story. *Vertical logic* relates to each idea or point (or often each page in a traditional landscape-formatted report) as a discrete whole, with data arranged and organized in a compelling manner to support the central idea or point (often in a "pyramid" fashion wherein the supporting materials are subordinated and categorized in order to make the point in as clear and concise a manner as possible).

The key to good communication is to *balance* the horizontal and vertical logic, and learning to do so can be one of the biggest challenges for new consultants. To return again to the bridge metaphor: Your audience is primarily concerned with the story you are telling—they are curious to know where you are taking them and how they will get there. The horizontal logic of your report is like the path across the bridge: It should be clear of obstacles, the steps should come in logical sequence, and the audience should feel "safe" as you take them across the bridge—step by step. At some points, your audience may not feel that they are on entirely secure footing ("can we make that next step—will the logic hold?"), and it is here that you rely on your vertical logic to add support to the argument. As a good consultant, you have done sufficient and sound data gathering and analysis, and you know that you can fully demonstrate and argue any point you are making.

The vertical logic of the presentation is like the supporting structure of your bridge—when your audience is not sure of the next step, you can take them to the edge of the bridge, look over the side, and show them how well built the bridge (or the argument) is. Of course, most people who cross over bridges are not concerned with the architecture and the engineering—they simply want to get where they are going. Again, it's critical to know the needs and desires of your audience, because that will determine how you build your bridge (your report or presentation). Senior managers would like to zoom across the bridge quickly in their sports cars, and if they have a concern with a section of the bridge, they'll hit the brakes and let you know (and you'd better be able to show that it's solid in concise and compelling terms!). Line managers, however, are often as interested in the "architecture" as the consultants are—and they are very familiar with the terrain your bridge is being built on (their company, their business unit or function). These managers are "engineers" themselves, and they have a strong vested interest in seeing just exactly how all the pieces fit together. (They also have the technical acuity to question very specific details in your girders or joints!) A report or presentation for this sort of audience will likely spend more time on the details of the bridge—the specific pieces of its composition.

As you learn to write consulting reports (or "build bridges"), be as concerned about your audience as you are about your construction and the data that you are building from. Many consultants spend too much of their time on the intricacies of their analysis and the esoterica of their elegantly constructed arguments, and not enough time on the simple but important matters of audience and rhetoric. Remember that as a consultant you are a peculiar kind of bridge builder because you are not only an architect, but also a tour guide, leading your audience through the argument and ensuring that they arrive where they are going directly and comfortably. The satisfaction of the audience has a major effect on the satisfaction of the consultant—an audience that is led through a well-constructed argument will be less likely to ask difficult questions, and more likely to take the subsequent actions required to drive change.

THE CONSULTING REPORT: FORMAT AND LOGIC

Consultants create most of their reports and presentations in a standard format: They use "landscape" layout (the page is created horizontally rather than vertically), put large "headlines" at the top of each page, and lay out text (often in bullet points) and illustrations (graphs, charts, etc.) on the page to support a point as directly as possible. This format is not merely a cosmetic packaging device intended to impress clients; it is actually an analytical tool that makes use of its structure and graphical coherence to check logic, identify data needs, and manage deliverables of an engagement. Most often, consultants use a program like Microsoft PowerPoint to create their reports; while most everyone these days knows how to use PowerPoint, few people in fact know how to use it effectively as a communication tool. In "the old days," consultants had to create their presentations by adapting a word-processing program or, before the advent of the laptop, by means of elaborate mechanical paste-ups; an argument could be made that when creating reports was more laborious, the end results were often better because consultants had to think more carefully and plan ahead.

The format of the report drives the main argument. It indicates which ideas or data are of equivalent importance and which are subordinate, and how these data or ideas support the key points of the argument or analysis. Furthermore, a well-articulated report guards against chinks in the argument's intellectual armor: In a well-structured report it should be impossible to make an assertion that cannot be supported. Finally, if used as a means not only of communicating to the client but also for communicating among the consulting team, the consulting document can be a very effective project management tool to guide the consultants in selecting the data they need to obtain and analyze to make the argument, and to facilitate moving between the overall project objectives and specific data-intensive explications.

Figure 8–3 provides an overview of the key terms (as used in many major consulting firms—terminology will vary from firm to firm) for parts of a typical consulting report:

Page
Headline or Header
Dot Point (or Bullet Point) and Dash Point
Trailer or Footer
Facer Page

Horizontal logic relates to the overall argument and narrative—the progression of the report and the logic of the storyline. The most important aspects of the horizontal logic to manage are the steps in the argument (the "path" across the bridge) and the linguistic flow. There is no unwritten rule that business writing has to be poor or stilted, and every effort should be made to ensure that a report reads as smoothly and straightforwardly as possible. Special attention should also be paid to the headlines: These should be "punchy," making a strong impact, and if read in succession, the headlines of a report should represent the key steps in the argument, without gaps in the logic or the narrative progression. One useful standard to keep in mind is the "So What?" test, which means that if you suspect that a reader's or listener's reaction to the headline might be "So What?," it would be a good idea to rewrite the headline.

Vertical logic refers most usually to the internal logic of a discrete page of a report or presentation. Each page, much like a single paragraph in traditional expository

FIGURE 8–3   Structure of a Typical Page in a Consulting Report

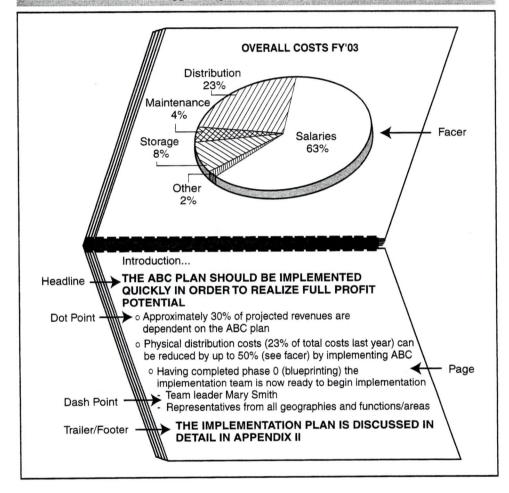

prose, should have a single key idea or topic. The topic should be expressed in the headline in a compelling way for the intended audience. That single point should be supported in the most direct way possible, either by text or with a graphic. If using text, a good way to present the text is in the form of dot points or bullet points and, if necessary, dash points under the dot points, which clearly show categorization and subordination of the supporting data. The consultant has only one chance to make the point—to "sell" this step of the argument—so care should be taken to ensure that the best support for the point is represented on the page as clearly as possible and that no extraneous information is cluttering the page. If you have information that is "related" or "interesting" but not critical, this information is best relegated to a facer page (which can be thought of as a footnote—providing further information that might be of interest to some readers) or to an appendix. In presentations to very senior executives, consider using appendices for backup and detail, and work to make the presentation itself lean and results-focused.

There is no magic to writing—and there are no "quick tips" to improve a consultant's writing. Improving comes from practice, hard work, and reading good examples of the genre. Young consultants should push their job managers to be given the chance to take a "first pass" at a document and ask for specific feedback on how to make it better. Again, much as we learn the basic structure of effective bedtime stories when we are children (who cannot instantly imagine the story that might follow if given a dwarf, a princess, a dragon, and a knight?), so must we learn how effective *business* stories are created. Consultants need to learn how to organize their analyses into stories that allow their clients to understand the problems and then be willing to make changes for improvement.

Just as writing takes time to learn, so does editing. The best means of editing is simply to create temporal distance from the document: Take a look at something you wrote six months ago and its weaknesses will be immediately evident. Unfortunately, the nature of consulting engagements rarely allows a consultant the luxury of putting a presentation away for a week to come back to it later with "fresh eyes." The best consultants proactively engage their superiors and peers to read and help edit reports, knowing that someone who has not been intimately involved in the engagement day to day will be in a better position to assess logic flow and adequate setting of context, and can also be helpful in applying the "So What?" test. (Some firms even maintain "editors" on staff to help with writing.) Strong editing is crucial: In spite of their best efforts, hard-working consultants are sometimes prone to "miss the forest for the trees"—and what's obvious to me if I've been deeply absorbed in the details of a project for the last week may not be obvious to you, client or fellow consultant, if you haven't been.

That said, there are some very useful tips for editing. First, always edit from the "top down"; that is, before you struggle with the wording of a specific bullet point, ensure that your overall narrative structure makes sense. There's no point working hard on a page now if later structural reorganization causes that page to be eliminated. To test the horizontal logic, concentrate mostly on the headlines: Are the headlines in an order that makes sense, and do they flow logically from page to page? Make sure the headers are powerful and drive insight or action—don't just describe the process of *what* was done as analysis; focus instead on what the analysis *means*. Also, be attentive to the audience's perspective: Is the story being told in the right way, and in the right level of detail, for the audience? To test the vertical logic, carefully examine the relationship between the headline and the rest of the page. Is the headline supported as directly and effectively as possible? Does the page have a single point, and is that point expressed efficiently and powerfully? Think carefully about whether the best support would be text or a graphic—what illustration would get the point across most cogently?

A few words should be said on graphics, though a whole chapter could easily be written on the subject.[3] Pay attention most of all to the effectiveness of the image or graphic (pie chart, bar chart, process flow diagram, whatever it might be) you have

---

[3]Those interested in the creation of effective graphics would be very well served by reading the truly fascinating series of books on the topic by Edward Tufte, especially his seminal *The Visual Display of Quantitative Information*. A more basic guide to the creation of graphics specifically for consulting reports is Gene Zelazny's *Say It with Charts: The Executive's Guide to Visual Communication*.

chosen: Does the graphic immediately relay the point you want to make? Does the graphic support a single message? Can it be explained easily? Many a consultant has been defeated by his or her overly complex graphics when faced with the challenge of explaining them to a live audience during a presentation. Remember, a picture may be worth a thousand words, but in a good consulting report you shouldn't have to use a thousand words to explain your picture! Also don't forget to attend to the more mundane details: Make sure your picture has a title, legends, a label, and (if appropriate) a source. Avoid visual clutter, and most of all avoid distortion of any kind. Your audience needs to feel that your consulting is objective, and a graphic distorted to underscore a point, if caught by the audience, may seriously undermine your credibility.

In his influential book *The Visual Display of Quantitative Information*, Edward Tufte provides a series of simple rules for making a graphic effective, and they are worth repeating here:

- Above all else, show the data.
- Maximize the data–ink ratio.
- Erase nondata ink.
- Erase redundant ink.
- Revise and edit.

Most new consultants will find that learning and writing in their firm's standard format is a significant challenge. Unfortunately, most business schools do not really stress the importance of writing and communicating, even though these skills are arguably a manager's or executive's most powerful tools. Furthermore, many people who go into consulting were not the kind who were drawn to humanities courses as undergraduates, and often don't have even rudimentary verbal communications skills, never mind an ear for effective writing.

While writing in format is not easy to learn, once you have begun to master it you will find it is very natural and powerful. Again, the best way to learn is by practicing and apprenticeship. If you're told that your document or report isn't good, ask the project manager what specifically can and should be done to improve it. Take the time to learn from more experienced consultants how to structure a good story. Finally, try to read well-written prose—the best way to improve one's writing is actually to read *good* writing on a regular basis. Most business books or best-sellers are not especially well written, so look elsewhere. Consider Jane Austen or Mark Twain for your next vacation rather than Tom Clancy or Danielle Steele. One admirable model for strong, persuasive prose is the English essayist and novelist George Orwell: His classic and widely reprinted essay "Politics and the English Language" is a manifesto on how to clean up ineffective business and technical writing as well as a brilliant illustration of clear and effective writing.

Finally, beware of one potential problem: The typical consulting presentation or report format can sometimes confuse or alienate clients. Unlike consultants, most general managers have not been taught disciplined methodologies for analyzing and communicating. You should always be sensitive to any cultural differences that might exist between you and your audience, and remember also that the best reports and presentations match the expectations of the audience. (Some consultants even adopt the format of their client organizations to improve the reception of the report.) Be careful that your report does not act at cross-purposes to your intentions or alienate your audience; remember that your presentation is not an end in itself, but rather a means to an end, and you should focus your efforts not on the final report as a "product" but rather on trying to ensure that your audience hears, understands, and is willing to act on your recommendations. Increasingly, the traditional final polished consulting report is not as effective for achieving that end as more informal presentations, collaboration with the client, and (if possible) engaging the client teams themselves to help write and present the findings and recommendations.

GOOD WRITING IS GOOD CONSULTING

Many of the best consultants have learned that few tools are as powerful for driving good thinking and good communication as the *storyboard*. If used well, a storyboard can help in generating ideas, crafting the essential storyline, identifying necessary data, and managing the project, by ensuring that all members of the consulting team have given their input and understand how their individual efforts contribute to the project as a whole.

First, some background: The term *storyboard* originated in the fields of filmmaking and advertising: Realizing that shooting film is expensive, directors began to employ illustrators or cartoonists to help block out the action they intended to film. Working quickly with pen and paper, the director works through an approach (a sequence of events, camera angles, cuts, etc.) until she is happy with it, and then uses that storyboard as a guide for the actors and camera crew to follow. The result is a more efficient use of film and less time spent in the editing room trying to patch together a final product that makes sense.

In much the same way, a consultant or consulting team can make use of a storyboard to ensure that the whole team is "on the same page," and that everyone understands the high-level project plan, the specific pieces of data gathering and analysis that will support the project, and, perhaps most important, the basic steps of the "story" that will be told to the client in the presentation or report. Use of storyboards is efficient: If the basic logic flow is laid out and agreed upon from the beginning, chances are good that time will not have to be spent later in "unwriting" or rewriting. The storyboard can also ensure that each consultant on the team knows exactly what information he or she needs to find to make the points—and if that information proves to be unavailable, then a different story can be created in response. Most important of all, a storyboard is a democratic process for ensuring that the entire team's input is collected and considered. Too many consulting projects suffer or fail because the "story" never exists except in some possibly inchoate and ever-evolving form in the project manager's head. By sitting down at the beginning of the project *with* the whole team and expressing the project in the form of a storyboard that will be developed and used *by* the whole team over the course of the engagement, the project manager can assure that the best thinking of each team member has been leveraged, and that each team member understands how what he or she is working on relates to the whole. Furthermore, by using a storyboard, the project manager is teaching the less experienced team members how to create and tell a story even while the project is moving ahead.

Storyboards for consulting projects exist in many forms and formats: pieces of paper or Post-It notes on the team room wall, a visual layout of the report pages as thumbnail sketches on a notepad, or even in documents created by software like PowerPoint. The specific physical form is less important than the fact that storyboards are *used* and used consistently. Figure 8–4 gives a very simple example of what a storyboard can look like, and suggests how the report is structured to make specific points and exhort the audience to accept and act on a recommendation. When the team has agreed on the basic "architecture" of the report, individual pieces can then be worked on by different team members. When closer to final form (all the data and analysis double-checked, graphics created, etc.), the report as a whole can be polished so that the language is effective and compelling.

Using storyboards vastly improves the consulting process, the quality of the deliverables, and the pleasure of the experience for all involved. Storyboards are also the best way to teach and coach junior staff, to build commitment and enthusiasm, and to ensure that the whole team from the beginning of the project is thinking not just about the details of the analysis but also about how to make the recommendations in the most elegant and effective manner.

SUMMARY

It should be clear by now that communicating effectively and cogently is a critical part of the consulting process and effective written communication is vital for the success of consulting engagements. Writing plays a role throughout the engagement—it is not just the "packaging" for the work created at the end of the assignment. Good consultants will use disciplined writing processes strategically at every phase of the engagement:

- Defining the problem (including in the proposal and by use of storyboards)
- Managing the work flow and checking deliverables
- Communicating progress (across the team as well as to the client)
- Gaining "buy-in"
- "Selling" the recommendation
- Effecting implementation
- Managing change
- Recognizing results
- Capturing insights gained during the engagement for future use

Unfortunately, experience proves that not all consulting projects employ the tools of effective writing in such an effective manner. Too often, consultants write reports that are fine documents for other consultants to read but very poor tools for teaching the client, explaining the nature of the problem, or influencing the client organization to undergo significant efforts to improve their processes or reorganize. MBA programs and internal training departments in consulting firms should appreciate how fundamental are the skills of truly good writing and communication. There may be no more powerful ability for any senior manager or senior advisor than adroitness at expressing ideas and influencing others to take actions based on those ideas.

One way to better appreciate the importance of writing as a driver of the problem-solving process in consulting is to rethink the idea of *editing*. Contrary to some opinions, editing does not simply mean hitting the spell-checker in the word-processing program before printing the final report. Rather, editing is a systematic process of test-

FIGURE 8–4   A Typical Storyboard

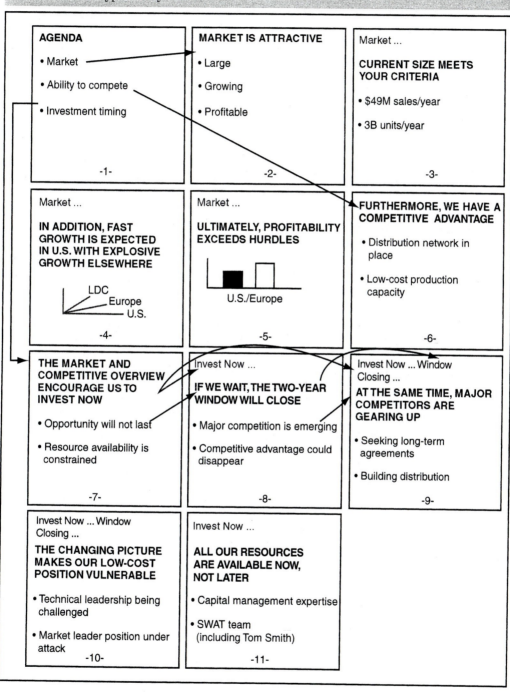

ing the logic of the argument, the way it is constructed, and the expected effect on the audience. If writing is employed from the beginning of the engagement, then strong editing is a means by which the engagement can move forward to completion. Good consultants will work together from the "top down" to test the overall rhetorical strategy of the report, the logic of individual sections, the vertical logic of the individual pages, and finally the clarity of individual sentences. If this process is followed faithfully from the beginning, the chances are good that the consulting team will not have to struggle with "all-nighters" to finish their presentation at the last minute.

As Figure 8–5 suggests, writing (W) is inextricably bound up in the thinking (T) process: Writing is in fact a thinking tool as much as it is a communications tool. Until you try to sit down and write out what you are thinking, you may be fooling yourself that you fully understand it. When you make the effort to write it down, the meaning and implications become clear. Just as writing (W) is a key part of the thinking process (T), so is editing (E) a critical part of the writing process (W). Once you've finished writing something down so that you understand it, you're only halfway to the conclusion. Unfortunately, too many consultants stop at this point: They use the writing process to clarify their own thinking, but don't take the next step to figure out the best way to make the insights they have reached clear to their audience. Remember that in most cases the audience has not been involved in the thinking process—they are coming to the presentation not having been immersed in the project for the last several weeks. Good consultants, then, will pay as much attention to the editing as they did to the writing, by asking the key question, "Now that I've worked to an answer, what's the best way to communicate this answer to my audience—to get them to understand the issues in a new way, or be willing to help make changes in the organization?"

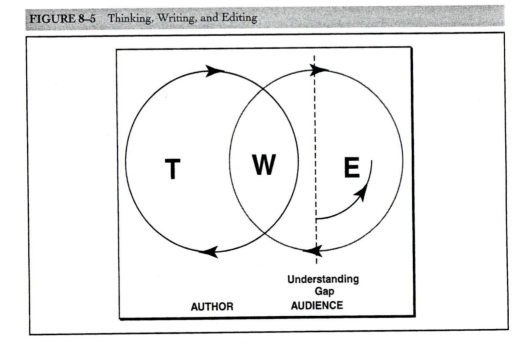

FIGURE 8–5 Thinking, Writing, and Editing

If the process of editing is reconceived as the way a consultant takes his or her insights and builds them into an argument that will have the most impact on the audience, then the result will be much more effective reports and presentations: reports that don't just encapsulate good ideas, but rather catalyze real improvement and change.

Finally, clear writing is a sign of clear thinking, and clear thinking is the consultant's most powerful tool. Remember, at the end of the day consultants are not researchers or authors—they are change agents. They are not hired and paid for good ideas alone—they are rewarded for improving processes and creating change that will have a demonstrable positive effect on the client organization. Consultants pay a lot of attention to data and to information, which is where the clues to solving the problems are to be found. But consultants should never forget that the client is not merely in need of good analysis: he wants knowledge and wisdom. Knowledge pertains to how to do things differently and better, and it has become a ubiquitous buzzword in today's business world (e.g., knowledge systems, chief knowledge officers). Wisdom, however, is a goal of an even higher level: it is the discretion and the vision of what to do differently, and why. The word *wisdom* comes from two Old English words—*wis* ("wise") and *dom* ("judgment," which survives today as "doom")—and it means most essentially the ability to make wise or good judgments or decisions. The pursuit of wisdom, then, should be the consultant's true goal, and wisdom is useless if it cannot be convincingly communicated so that others can benefit from it.

CHAPTER 9

Developing Proposals

John C. Scott

Most proposals look similar, whether developed by one consulting firm or another. At IBM, rarely do we get requests that are dissimilar from other work the firm has done, and we have a distinctive advantage in being able to draw on a large body of prior work to construct new proposals. So, rarely are any of our consulting proposals entirely new. Even when they address novel problems, they typically borrow from the firm's previous experience. For example, building a house for the first time draws from earlier experiences one has in carpentry, plumbing, glazier work, and electrical work. One may not have ever built a house before, but if one also has no experience in the basic craft disciplines, one probably shouldn't propose building a house for anyone else.

Having a core capability to do something can be defined as having a "method." Methods are blueprints or plans on how to do specific things. Over the years, IBM has found that one size does not fit all, and so has created a number of specific methods. Each method describes what the firm believes to be "best practice" for attacking a particular type of problem. It also describes a model for how the solution might be developed and implemented. Obviously, there are differences between methods used for an issue-based consulting engagement, a business transformation engagement, a package-enabled business transformation engagement, custom development, or strategic outsourcing.

Each method recommends an approach or plan of attack for doing the work. The project plan shows dependencies between work tasks, and shows intermediate work products. Each activity has an associated work product that is required input to a project deliverable, although the work products themselves are not generally considered deliverables. They allow a large project to be decomposed into smaller phases and tasks and managed more easily.

Past work products take their place in IBM's intellectual capital repository, in the hope that a subsequent team performing a similar project can reuse them. Because each work product is associated with a particular task or a particular method, they are already "classified" and in the same "reference domain." For instance, someone doing an e-business Net.commerce implementation should not have to go far to find a parameter table for Net.commerce on an AS/400 or UNIX box.

John C. Scott is an international business consultant currently at IBM. His specialty is software development and software development management.

Intellectual capital also benefits us in the same way that component integration does. Using prebuilt components or work products enables consultants to economize on the human and time-based capital associated with having to build them from scratch. It also reduces the degree of risk in the project by supplying "proven" components.

We call *offerings* types of projects that we expect to repeat from one customer to the next. They are typically complete solutions such as selling on the Web business to consumer (B2C) or data warehousing. The intellectual capital available to these particular practitioners is prepared specifically for reuse and incorporates best practices to date. The work products associated with offerings are supported through a managed model and are like standardized products in which the value proposition to the customer reflects the asset content as much as, if not more than, the professional services content.

Having set the stage, the rest of the chapter will discuss models, methods, managed models, and how we use the experience of previous engagements to create compelling proposals that win clients and turn into intellectual capital for subsequent proposals. In cyclical fashion, a proposal is the basis for the project that uses the model that draws on prior work products.

PROPOSAL INITIATION

A proposal is initiated when an opportunity comes along that the "opportunity management team" decides to pursue. Proposals are costly to prepare, and few consulting firms can afford to pursue every opportunity that comes along. Most firms also try to establish an identity by specializing in ways that differentiate them from the pack and give them some competitive advantage in engagements that align to their specialty.

Opportunity management is a function of a firm's capabilities and capacity. The capabilities of the firm must align with the proposed work—the work to be done should be something that the firm is good at doing. At the same time, the firm must have the necessary capacity—enough resources to complete the work in the expected time frame. After all, no one wants to wait a year and a half for an e-business solution. That said, a firm will initiate a proposal when it knows it has both the capability and the capacity to take on new work.

Unsolicited Proposals   Most unsolicited proposals involve offerings—products or standardized services that can be offered to multiple clients and that require very little change from one client to the next. For example, the world of e-business consulting is extremely broad and all-encompassing. However, "e-help desks" or "e-selling on the Web B2C" are fairly standard offerings. Up to 80 percent of what we do is very similar from one client to another in these projects. It therefore makes sense to bundle these projects and sell them as an offering. Since all companies in the B2C space share a common need for the offering, proposals can be constructed that require very little customization. In these unsolicited proposals, all work is predefined and standardized.

Solicited Proposals   Most proposals are solicited and, as such, are worded in the client's terms, and reply to specific requests. The degree to which they match a specific consulting firm's processes, capabilities, and capacity is the degree to which that firm should respond.

The City of New York, for example, may release a thousand requests for proposals (RFPs) a year, only a small number of which align with any single firm's capabilities.

The one thing common to all solicited proposals is that they are time boxed. When tendered, they present a short-lived opportunity. This rushed aspect of proposal development is probably responsible for more mistakes and lost business than any single part in preparing the proposal. One may not have time to gather the experts, or to really think about the problem, or to check out the cost of hot-skill labor in the market. Most consultants make heroic efforts to develop proposals and be "in the game" even though in some cases it would be wiser to forgo the attempt.

Receipt of an RFP

When received from a client, an RFP is typically time stamped and acknowledged. If the RFP aligns with an offering, it gets sent to the "owner" of the offering. Otherwise, it gets sent to the person who has responsibility for that client relationship. RFPs requiring bigger (more work) responses take longer than responding to simple RFPs. Complex RFPs typically need input from a number of different groups, which takes time. Complex RFP responses may also have to get reviewed by the legal department and by the quality assurance team or whoever controls pricing and profitability. That takes time.

Start-Up Response   The prerequisites for responding to a solicited proposal are having the request, making sure that the work required fits the firm's capabilities, and ensuring that the firm has sufficient capacity to perform the work within the terms of the request. The next major challenge is to determine the scope of work. Consultants have to put a fence around the goods and services in a proposal so that both the client and the consultant have a defined list of deliverables and a project plan. The client's goals must be satisfied by the proposed deliverables, and the deliverables must be defined in terms of work products, method to create the work products, and resources consumed. This further definition helps to ensure that the big-picture definition of a deliverable is qualified by its components to reduce ambiguity.

Determining Proposal Scope

In an offering, the scope is predetermined. Technology offerings often involve implementing a packaged solution, and the package itself determines the scope. Areas of ambiguity may include interfaces to other systems, interfaces to trading partners or conversions from older systems. When responding to an RFP, however, determining the scope is more difficult. Usually, the RFP is in "customer terminology" or may have terms that are specific to an industry. An example that comes to mind is from an engagement I worked on in the pharmaceutical industry. In my previous life as a software quality assurance person, we used the term *validate* or *validation* as part of the quality assurance VVT—Verification, Validation, and Test process. In the highly regulated world of pharmaceutical manufacturing, a validated process refers to a regulated method for manufacturing that is dictated by the Food and Drug Administration. Even though the information technology (IT) part of the business was quite separate from the manufacturing side, one was ill-advised to use the term as it caused all antennae to raise, and confused the audience.

Consultants from different firms sometimes collaborate on very large RFPs, in which case a specific firm can adopt a scope that is narrower than the RFP. For example, the U.S. Federal Aviation Administration (FAA) recently sent out an RFP for the complete overhaul of their major systems for air traffic control. Although it was a single RFP, it is unlikely any one company would want to take on the whole project. Therefore, two or more companies might bid on the project. Unless the client specifically dictates that bidders must bid on the entire work, it's possible to carve out part of the work and bid on just that portion. Flexibility allows you to synchronize your firm's capabilities and capacity with the part of the RFP that aligns with your service model. Most companies will not entertain such a model only because the management of two or more vendors is challenging. More typically, one firm will act as prime contractor for the whole project and assume responsibility for subcontracting the other work.

A critical determinant of proposal scope is the set of skills on the proposal team. Team members need expertise in both the technical domain and the problem domain. Failure to understand what is being asked in client terms necessarily leads to future problems. Unless the firm has done extremely similar projects in the same industry or problem area, creating the proposal is risky. The more eyes that see it, therefore, the better.

Early in my career I was asked to install two packages on a microcomputer and to provide training to the people who would be using the package. The first was a word-processing package and the second was an accounting system. Both packages had already been bought and as the organization was a nonprofit group I admired, I agreed to do it at considerably below what I would have charged a corporate client. Installation of the word-processing package and training went along as expected. The secretaries took to the package instantly and were able to use it almost immediately. The second application proved more challenging. Where I thought the scope of work was to teach accountants how to use a computerized accounting system, the real job was to teach secretaries double-entry bookkeeping, and once they understood bookkeeping, then teach them how to use the accounting system. They had no chart of accounts, and had been running everything out of a one write system, letting a real accountant figure it all out at the end of the year. Worse, as everything was "fund accounting" meaning that money could not be co-mingled and expenses against certain items had to be reported differently than money spent on other items, the accounting system purchased did not fit their needs and I had to go through a package selection process for a replacement.

Or consider Saudia or Saudi Arabian Airlines. They wanted to purchase a very specialized revenue accounting system for airlines. An RFP was sent out and two vendors were short-listed based primarily on their reputation in previous dealings with the airline. The first solution was mainframe-based IMS/DB and CICS/DC, which was also the technology currently supported by Saudia. The second solution was client–server— OS/2 workstations talking to a DB/2 server which connected to a mainframe via CICS. My interest in the offer was more to see what client–server was all about than revenue accounting or flight costing. With all the hype that client–server solutions were much cheaper than host-based systems, I expected the client–server model to be considerably cheaper than the host-based system, since the proposal involved solely software and training and did not include infrastructure upgrades or any hardware. I was completely surprised when the client–server version came in almost five times the cost of the host-based one.

Upon examination, the difference was in how one read the RFP. The host-based vendor read "install and train" to mean install on the mainframe and train operations how to run and support the application. The client–server vendor thought it also meant training users to do revenue-based accounting. They considered the training part to be the biggest challenge and had built in some 15 man-years of effort into training (starting with English). One of them was right, the other wrong, and the point is that one could not tell without knowing the environment, the organization you were selling to, and what the client actually expected to be done. It would have helped to have a team of experts look at it closely.

This is particularly sticky when one considers the measurements used to define project success subsequent to being awarded the work. In earlier days it might simply be meet the requirements, on time, in budget. Now it means that and completely satisfy the client. This latter metric is extremely hard to build into a project plan. Further, in the white paper on troubled projects produced by IBM, the major problem identified in troubled projects was always inability to manage scope or "scope creep." Based on my experience, I suggest that scope doesn't creep, at least not from the customer's view. Much more common is the mid-contract discussion in which the project manager is resisting scope creep and the client is insisting the requirement was always there, but missed or misunderstood. Although good software development and project management practice requires client participation and sign-off of requirements, specification, design, and implementation, I am always amazed how far into a project one can get before a major missing feature is identified. There are no easy answers for this problem, and the prescription is simply to be as thorough as time allows and to pull together the best team of consultants you can assemble.

As IBM's methodology is governed by work products and deliverables, the scope of the project and the scope of the proposal reflect the effort and intellectual capital required to create these work products and deliverables. Outside the software development arena and in IBM's pure issue-based consulting practices, the scope is bound in the same manner. The problem is defined by the customer. The proposal begins by demonstrating that the consultant understands the problem, demonstrates a logical method for arriving at a solution, and shows how use of the consulting firm's intellectual capital and new work products will satisfy the request. The proposal has to be a credible and compelling demonstration that the consultant has the capability to do the work within a certain time frame and budget.

Financial Structures

Proposals are financially structured in different ways, and vary mostly on the allocation of risk between the professional service firm and the client. In a fixed-price contract, the consulting firm assumes most of the risk; in an hourly service contract, the customer assumes most of the risk. When the solution is well known and the firm has considerable experience in performing similar work, the proposal can look very much like a sales contract for a product. These fixed-price agreements can be structured in a number of ways to protect both of the contracting parties. When the work is a known package like IBM's Websphere Internet Application Server, the proposal is an offer to sell a license to use. It is generally offered to all potential customers under the same terms and conditions and at the same price.

The next most common proposal is an hourly service contract in which the work is estimated, the types of labor are priced, the prices are extended, and the consultant provides the client with an overall estimate. These proposals are open-ended: There is typically a disclaimer in the proposal designed to protect the firm. The contract ends when the budget runs out without regard to whether the project has been completed.

A hybrid of these two is the hourly services proposal that specifies a certain amount not to be exceeded. These agreements are much more difficult to negotiate as they hold the risks associated with a fixed-price contract without offering the upside benefits one might expect in completing early. Going over the estimate in time and going into unbillable time either takes away from the profit or causes the contract to lose money. However, finishing the contract early provides no benefit to the performing group as they lose the opportunity to bill for the unused hours.

Another hybrid model comes from the move to asset-based consulting. In these proposals, up to 80% of the solution is prebuilt and sold as a product; the remaining 20% account for customization or additional professional services.

The happy medium seems to be one where the assets are valued and brought into a project similar to how one would bring in components in a component integration development project. Each component has a price, and inclusion of the component is added to the services price to come up with a total price. When one does this with real products like Windows/NT, Sybase, Oracle, or DB/2 charging for the asset seems reasonable and expected. When the asset is a work product such as a quality assurance plan, a security plan, a database model, or reference architecture for B2C commerce over the Internet, the picture is not so clear. Intuitively, one knows that reuse of intellectual capital provides benefit in labor and risk reduction, but there's little precision in estimating that benefit. In preparing the proposal, one can look at the inclusion of intellectual capital from a few different vantage points. If the client is a value shopper, it is possible to reduce the price based on the reduction in cost. Value pricing may not align with a firm's business model. Most hourly service–based firms hope for larger projects, and longer engagements with extended revenue streams. Reducing the length and value of a contract by using intellectual capital may not align with the earlier practice.

In many professional services firms, deployable resources are measured on utilization, or the percentage of time they are on assignment rather than available for assignment. Strategic outsource staff might be expected to have 90 to 92 percent utilization. Business consultants who do shorter-term consulting engagements might be expected to have 70 to 75 percent utilization. Some of the difference is due to opportunity, but much of it has to do with thrashing between engagements. It is extremely rare to transition directly from one engagement to another over the long term. This phenomenon explains why the same resources that could do a 100,000-hour job in a year cannot do ten 10,000-hour jobs in a year. At best, they can do nine.

As a consulting firm shortens the engagement cycle, it effectively lessens its revenue and profit potential. Instead, if the firm considers the asset to be part of the project work, and structures the charge by project, it takes on a different picture. If the overall project involves 100,000 hours of work done from scratch and the intellectual capital reuse allows doing the work in 50,000 hours, the intellectual capital is worth 50,000 hours. However, if we present that prospect to the client, most will not accept that premise under an hourly service–based contract. The only way they would except it is if we can then guarantee that the rest of the project will not exceed the other

50,000 hours. As this then becomes a fixed-price contract, it is risky. It does prove the old adage about not being able to have one's cake and eat it too.

Hourly Services

Hourly service proposals use a schedule of rates for different skills and different levels of skills to do the work. They typically have at least two different rates for each skill type that reflects the value of experience or technical competence held by the practitioner. Table 9–1 shows a sample rate table for technology consultants.

Once rates are established, we must again revert to the artifacts we built in the beginning of the proposal. The basic solution is outlined on a work breakdown structure, using a series of process decompositions.

Consider an RFP obtained from a client asking for assistance in creating an e-business. Obviously, this problem domain is too large to handle in one proposal, as you know little about the requesting firm's capabilities, their business, or what they are trying to accomplish. The proposal team might chunk the goal into a couple of different proposals, all tied together. This phased approach is rational and allows the client to commit to a series of smaller engagements, each with its own value proposition and risk. This approach has been so successful that IBM has constructed a standard offering for e-business Strategy and Assessment engagements. The goal of the engagement is to understand the business the client is in, to establish goals for subsequent e-business projects, and to establish the priorities and plans for executing implementation projects.

This is a fairly simple proposal that can be broken down into three phases: understanding the business context, establishing strategic intent and priorities, and planning the e-business portfolio and initiatives. Now, consider the deliverables. Obviously, there's a report or presentation defining the business context for e-business initiatives; there's a document that identifies the strategic intent of the organization and the priorities for addressing them. There is a prioritized list of e-business projects that align with the strategic intent. Finally, there is a set of project plans that define how each of the projects can be completed, with an identification of the required resources and time frame for implementation.

TABLE 9–1   Sample Cost and Billing Rates for Technology Consultants

Job Title/Skill Level	Cost	Billing Rate
Project Executive (Sr. Project Manager)	$200.00	$260.00
Project Manager (Jr. Project Manager)	160.00	220.00
Sr. Architect	215.00	275.00
Jr. Architect	160.00	220.00
Sr. Java Programmer	120.00	180.00
Jr. Java Programmer	60.00	120.00
Sr. Database Administrator	140.00	200.00
Jr. Database Administrator	80.00	140.00
Sr. TCP/IP SSL Programmer	150.00	210.00
Jr. TCP/IP SSL Programmer	100.00	160.00
ECommerce Specialist	150.00	210.00
Retail Distribution Specialist	140.00	200.00

Once we have the three phases, which by luck also align with the three big deliverables, we need to decompose these by understanding what we have to do to create the deliverable. Each deliverable requires a number of work products to be created that will become part of the deliverable. Each work product is the product of a task. So, our project then has three phases, each of which has one to many tasks each producing one or more work products. A problem domain expert can look at each task's work product and estimate both the skill set and skill level necessary to do the work. Typically, he or she can also size the task or estimate the number of hours it will take to complete.

Once we have the work effort in person-days we can look at our schedule of resource costs, and start applying cost to each work item. If the work item takes 20 hours of tier 1 labor, 40 hours of tier 2 labor, and 100 hours of tier 3 labor, and labor rates are $200 an hour for tier 1, $150 for tier 2, and $100 for tier 3, then it's simple arithmetic to estimate the cost of the work product at $4,000 + $6,000 + $2,000 or $12,000 for the work product. Add up all the work products and deliverables and one has the total cost for doing the work. If the project is considerably outside the previous experience of the firm, or if it involves radically new technologies, one must also consider a contingency in the estimate. Loss of a key architect, discontinuous infrastructure, and change in management direction can all contribute considerable risk to the project.

The first task then may be to understand the business context for which the solution will be built, and to document the project's goals. The method has three phases: understanding the business context, establishing strategic intent and priorities, and planning the portfolio and initiatives. Each phase is decomposed into activity and task if necessary, until there is a one-to-one relationship between the work item and a work product. The work product is defined (what is in it, how to make it, skills required, effort required).

> Understand business context—Business Analyst: 3 to 4 person-days
>
> Document project goals—Business Analyst: 3 to 4 person-days
>
> Develop work plans and procedures—Project Manager & Solution Architect: 2 person-weeks

Custom Services

Custom services usually refer to something that is one off, meaning that the model and artifacts developed are so specialized or proprietary they offer no opportunity for reuse. Typical examples of this might be the rocket and satellite work done for Goddard Space Center in Alabama. Most of the embedded systems designed for these space missions were used on single missions, and although one could argue that components and lessons learned went from one NASA project to the next, they did not go outside of NASA.

Most consulting firms do not like to provide custom services, although all of them do. In some instances, providing services is politically sensitive and market disruptive. For example, during the days of Y2K projects, most consulting firms offered Y2K services, and most were short on manpower. By necessity, much work was subcontracted to mutual benefit between consulting firms. However, when competing for work, it became very hard to differentiate companies as the bidders might be XYZ using ABC subcontractors, or ABC using XYZ subcontractors.

A professional services firm sometimes uses another to jump-start a practice. As the new practice is trying to establish itself in the marketplace, it could severely damage the business if it became generally known that the methods and processes were developed by a competitor. Therefore, when Accenture Consulting hires PricewaterhouseCoopers (PWC) for an engagement to develop process models for a new line of business, the engagement is considered to be a custom service as PWC gains nothing but a fee and is barred from using the engagement as a reference.

Much custom service work follows the OEM model (original equipment manufacturer). A client producing a high-speed wireless Internet connection capable of full-frame audio and video over the Net may require engineering, technical, or other services from a consulting firm. Obviously, the work done for the client belongs to the client. The intellectual capital developed is also the client's, and the client would be disheartened to find the same consulting firm working at a competitor's shop a month after the project. The client wants a custom service.

Custom service proposals recognize that there is very little collateral created by the project. All work products developed belong to the client. As this arrangement consumes valuable resources that might be used by the consulting firm on other projects that develop reusable intellectual capital, the cost is typically higher and reflects lost opportunities.

Consulting Services Letter

The consulting services letter is a derivative of the more common letter of understanding or letter of agreement. Although it is still a contract, it is less formal and usually less precise. It frames the work to be done in terms of work products and deliverables, but may be less precise than a formal proposal. As these usually are of short duration and relatively low value, the risks exposed by short-circuiting the more formal proposal preparation process are often warranted.

Although less precise, the letter format must make a statement that shows one understands the problem to be addressed, and must answer the same three or four questions required of a formal proposal—that is, provide a clear, precise definition of the problem, the proposed solution (or method that will be used to discern the solution), what will be delivered to the client, how much time and effort is involved, and how much the engagement will cost.

PROPOSAL CONSTRUCTION

Given that you have an appropriate proposal team, the next activity is to lock yourselves in a room away from distractions, have plenty of coffee and soda, be strategically located next to the comfort stations, and be prepared to work. To construct the proposal, the first task is to understand how the team plans to approach the problem. IBM has a family of available methods, such as issue-based consulting, business transformation, package-enabled business transformation, custom application development, e-business, strategic outsourcing, and others. Within each family type there are subsets, such as e-selling, e-procurement, e-billing, and such under e-business.

The proposal team takes a hard look at the RFP to determine which of the firm's available methods most closely approaches a solution. If the solution appears to be a study, then an issue-based consulting method may be most appropriate. On the other hand, if the goal is to enable B2C selling over the Internet, then an e-selling model is more appropriate.

The proposal team looks at the selected method to determine how it fits the problem and solution domain. Typically, IBM methods are overengineered. This is not a negative comment but an understanding that any established method usually attacks all possible angles of a problem, and most project teams recognize that many of the work products identified in the method are not needed on a particular project. A set of projects may perform all tasks and produce all work products, but few individual examples do. Hence, IBM conducts a Method Adoption Workshop (MAW). In the MAW, a prototype project plan is extracted from the catalog of methods and the proposal team evaluates each work product for its applicability to the proposed project. Tasks, activities, and work products deemed peripheral are discarded.

At this point, the consulting team typically extracts work product descriptions from the firm's intellectual capital database, which define, at the task level, the work to be done and the skill and time required to do the work. The team also identifies reusable intellectual capital to see if we can reduce the overall work and resource requirements. If so, we can also estimate the value of the intellectual capital we intend to reuse to fold it back into the pricing model.

The team now has a solution in mind, knows how it will tackle doing the work, and knows what resources will be needed. A quick check with human resources tells the team whether these resources are available, and if not, when they might be available. If the human resource constraint negatively affects the schedule, other approaches must be considered. For example, if the project calls for a certain skill set during weeks four and five, and no work can continue until that task has been completed, it makes little sense to start the project if the skill will not be available until week nine. Proposals have been written on speculation that resources will free up, but this is a risky way to do things as one can end up with an entire project team burning time while waiting for a specialized skill.

Building the Statement of Work

Much of a proposal is boilerplate material required by the legal or marketing departments (or both) but, typically, that part of the proposal is read only by the clients' counterparts in their legal and marketing departments. The actual client is interested in four things:

1. Do you understand the problem?
2. Do you have a solution?
3. How long is it going to take for us to get it?
4. How much will it cost?

A good proposal answers these four questions. The greater the precision with which consultants address these questions, the more likely they are to win the work. In more detail, a complete proposal typically has the following sections:

- Scope of Services
- Key Assumptions
- Responsibilities
- Estimated Schedule
- Estimated Charges
- Indirect Expenses

- Completion Criteria
- Reporting
- Deliverables
- Warranties
- Additional Terms and Conditions

Scope of Services

The scope of services defines the consultant's offering. It responds to the requirements of the RFP and should be written to reflect the benefits of the offering. The section should define each deliverable in terms of how it will satisfy the customer's requirements. It should be inclusive and exclusive at the same time, firmly establishing what work is in scope, and what work is out of scope.

As an example, consider the earlier e-business project. The scope was to: (1) understand the business context, (2) establish strategic intent and priorities, and (3) to plan the portfolio and initiatives. This clearly suggests that contracted work will produce three deliverables: a business context document, a strategic intent and priorities analysis document, and a plan for the e-business portfolio of initiatives. It clearly excludes high-level design, low-level design, implementation, and testing of any suggested applications.

The proposal scope should define what will be accomplished during the performance of the engagement. The analogy to putting a fence around the project is appropriate, as in many cases the proposed work is part of a network of other work in an ongoing business transformation. To be manageable, the proposal should clearly state the problem to be solved, the expected solution, the deliverables, time frame, and estimated cost.

Key Assumptions

Key assumptions in the proposal might include where the work is to be performed (who is supplying working space, equipment, etc.) and when dependent facilities will be ready. For example, a project to build an Internet sales application interfacing to SAP or BAAN may be dependent on the other application to be installed and available for test. Key assumptions should not be trivial, but should list possible dependencies that are assumed away.

Responsibilities

Consultant's Responsibilities   As it is quite common to split up activities and tasks between the professional services firm and the client firm, this section should clearly define your responsibilities under the contract. Although this is somewhat legalese, one should attempt to write this section of the proposal so that anyone can understand what work your firm is directly responsible for completing.

Client's Responsibilities   During negotiations, it is quite common for the client to agree to provide people, materials, computer time, or other valuable resources to reduce the cost of the work. It is prudent to enumerate those work items or resources that are the customer's responsibilities with a notation of the time frame in which they must be provided to avoid impacting the schedule.

Estimated Schedule

Estimating the schedule is a key part of the overall effort to develop the proposal. After assessing the work to be done and the methods that will be used to accomplish the work, the consultants develop the work-breakdown structure, from which they get the requirements for skills and staffing level of each unit of work. The optimum schedule and staffing plan are developed by examining tasks that can be done in parallel. The team then matches requirements for personnel against available personnel and shifts activities around to match workload to availability. The project plan and schedule follow.

Most proposals lay out the estimated schedule either through a Gantt chart or a timeline. This not only indicates the capability and capacity, but also puts an actual start and finish date to the work. Typically, this part of the proposal is an if–then proposition: If the proposal is accepted, it means the consultants can start within X days of notification and be finished Y days later.

In defining the amount of work to be done, the relationship between the tasks and the skill sets necessary to do the work, consultants typically rely on best of all possible scenarios and do not account for constraints in skill sets or key personnel. For example, the project plan might call for considerable interaction between an architect and a key member of the client's organization. If the client is unavailable when needed, the project may slip awaiting client input.

The schedule is therefore a best guess. It says, given the work, skill sets, and dependency between tasks, if we start on a particular day we can finish at some predictable later date. It is written as if there were no constraints, and some contingency time is put into it with the shared understanding that there will always be constraints. It's the old adage of sometimes the best laid plans of mice and men go astray. In most consulting firms, the assumption that one can staff a project immediately is seldom valid, especially if the project involves new, hot technologies.

The other major risk to the schedule comes from a growing trend to share project responsibilities between client and consulting staff. Increasingly, the desire to transfer skills to clients or to mitigate pricing induces consultants to create proposals that include work done by both parties. A major risk to the project is that one side or the other cannot do their part. How these issues are resolved is covered under risk, issues, and change management. In the scheduling, however, there must be assurances by both parties that they can mobilize the necessary resources in a timely manner.

Estimated Charges

All proposals include a section explaining the cost of the work and how the estimate was created. These are the direct costs of the project. Internal rates for people being supplied by the client, labor rate escalations for longer-term projects that may use contractors, and hardware and software costs may well be itemized to justify the bottom-line number.

In a product offering, one need not explain the components of price, but in service contracts this is expected. The client must feel that the price represents work and the level of work is appropriate for the solution proposed. Thus, an explanation of the estimate in the proposal reduces the chance that one will have to go recreate it when it's requested.

Estimating charges and identifying costs are not necessarily the same thing. Work is often shared between the client and the consultant. This is usually done to reduce costs and to transfer skills to clients. At IBM, as we determine which work items will be done by our firm and which by the client, we estimate the cost by simply applying the hourly rate for the skill against the number of hours they are expected to be used. Estimation of charges is generally for hourly service–type work, not a fixed-price contract. Typically, one has to estimate a little high to bring the project in on time and within budget. Unused estimated fees never get billed to the client.

The danger in estimating charges is that the ballpark figure you develop is considered the ceiling by the client despite disclaimer. And although the firm may judge a project manager by any number of other criteria, failure to stay within these numbers without a change order is a career-limiting experience due to its negative effect on customer satisfaction.

Direct expenses are often combined and estimated as a percentage of the total cost of the project. To develop reliable estimates, consultants must know the cost of labor (how much each person on the project will cost) and understand whether this is a burdened rate (one with embedded expenses) or whether these additional expenses must be funded by the project. If you plan to bring in talent from the other side of the country, you may figure that his or her travel and living expenses must be charged to the contract. There are pretty standard charts available to show average travel and entertainment costs in major cities of the world.

The proposal should also describe the burn rate for work being done and establish a schedule of periodic payments. Savvy consultants know that it is unwise to postpone billing until the end of any project, so the project plan should describe periodic billing and payment arrangements. These may be triggered by project milestones, time, or any other mutually agreed upon events.

Indirect Expenses

Indirect expenses are those that have nothing to do with labor, including office space, connectivity, telephone, fax, copiers, food and lodging, travel, and other incidentals.

Estimating equipment costs, network costs, infrastructure upgrade costs, and other similar expenses is a greater challenge. Typically, these are outside the scope of a project, unless the project is infrastructure focused. Nonetheless, they may be incurred during the course of the project.

Consider again the e-business solution we discussed above. Assume that after the application is built and moved into the test environment, the client runs acceptance tests against it and agrees that it meets all of the functional requirements in the specification. However, the client is not happy because the application exhibits canine-like qualities (it's a dog) with regard to performance. There are some things an application programmer can do to speed up Internet-based applications, but they are limited. True performance improvements usually involve better Internet Protocol (IP) management, load balancing, traffic management, broader bandwidth, and other such things that are outside the applications control. Thus, costs associated with general infrastructure upgrades may or may not be included in the estimate of expenses.

All projects also involve procurement. Whether hiring additional supplementary workers, buying toner and paper for the copiers and printers, getting another telephone line, or whatever. A software development project may require integrated development environments (like C/C++, Powerbuilder, etc.), specialized test tools, and test environments. The proposal should clearly state whether the client or the consultant will actually do the procurement, how it will be billed, when it will be paid, and what becomes of these assets at the end of the work.

Completion Criteria

Statements of work represent projects, and projects by definition are unique, have a defined beginning and a defined end, and consume resources, according to the Project Management Institute. Acceptance of a proposal defines the beginning—but what marks the end? Hourly service proposals usually can be considered complete due to any of three circumstances:

1. The work defined is complete.
2. The estimated and authorized expense fund is exhausted.
3. The client cancels further work.

Most engagements terminate due to either completion or cancellation. A proposal should state clearly when and how the agreement terminates. The professional services firm may incur considerable cost in mobilization, and may want to put a clause in the proposal that protects them in the event of a premature cancellation. For example, one might write an offer to set up a Web site for a firm in Saudi Arabia that would require hiring two language experts in Arabic to translate the user interface linguistically and culturally. These contractors may require 30 days' notice if their contract with you terminates prematurely. Prudent consultants will shift that risk to the client by adding special terms and conditions in the offer that protect them against such a contingency.

Reporting

The final part of the proposal must discuss reporting. Typically, an engagement will have both a client and a professional services project manager, who must report progress to upper management to justify the resources being spent on the project. The form and detail of these reports is sometimes termed the contract data requirements list. This list identifies what will be reported, its format, and its frequency.

Management typically wants to know how the project is going. In informal organizations, the "it's going okay" response works until the project starts to slip. Once project managers realize that their plan has slipped, however, they should inform management. Management wants to know how late it is now, how much later it will be, how much has been spent on it to date, how much more was allocated to complete it, and how much more it will likely take to complete it.

The metrics for project control and reporting must be clearly defined in the proposal. This is especially true if the proposal calls for periodic payments tied to work done or time passage. Tools like earned-value analysis help the project manager and sponsor understand the amount of work done for the burn rate, where the project currently stands, and the degree of commitment needed to complete the work. Tracking this precisely and reporting on it requires work that must be considered in the overall estimate of effort.

Deliverables

The proposal should clearly state what is to be delivered to the client. Unless the client has been supplied with examples of these materials or they follow an industry standard, it is always prudent to establish the quality and degree of detail that will be provided. Doing so reduces the chances for client dissatisfaction.

The final consideration on deliverables must be the method of delivery and acceptance criteria and process. The proposal outlines a linear process for doing the work, but many of the tasks are dependent on each other, and one task must finish before the next can begin. If the milestone is task completion of a work product, usually the project manager will authorize the team to go onto the next task. However, as deliverables are contractual requirements, there is typically a formal hand-over and acceptance process. This formality may be required to satisfy the legal wording of the agreement, but is typically a problem area in most contracts. If the deliverable must be accepted or approved, there must be some alternate way to go forward should the deliverable be delayed in the approval process. A common solution is to include wording that, in the absence of disapproval, the deliverable will be considered complete, accepted, and approved in X number of days after delivery by the project manager.

Warranties

In technology engagements, clients invariably pose questions about warranty on the work performed. Few consulting firms will warrant their work, as much of the work depends on the validity of information supplied by the client or by external sources. One might be able to warrant that database access will take no more than N nanoseconds, but one cannot guarantee sub–second response times over any TCP/IP network exposed to public traffic. Hardware and system software is usually warranted to the degree that they will be fixed or replaced with no protection against loss of business or consequential damages. The proposal must be quite clear to disclaim specific warranties that one is not prepared to address with corrective action and/or compensation.

Additional Terms and Conditions (if any)

The growing value attached to intellectual capital makes it a critical point to address in the proposal. Both consultants and clients should know who has ownership of the work products created during the engagement. Do they belong to the client or to the consultant? Is the client merely purchasing a license to use them? Can they be reused or other work derived from them?

Special conditions on licensed third-party products that are incorporated into the solution might also be defined in this section. Obviously, if a component is licensed to the development team to create a solution, the license must pass to the client as the solution moves from development to test and finally into production.

A final consideration might be a clause addressing extraordinary events. For example, the client may request your subcontractors to sign confidentiality agreements. Or your firm may be prohibited from producing a similar solution for the client's competitor for a period of time. Additional terms and conditions complicate the statement of work and require legal review on both sides.

Caution: Avoid Dangerous Words/Phrases

Finally, it is extremely dangerous to co-mingle proposed solutions with the hopes the client holds for the solution. If the proposed work, for example, were to build an e-commerce site, the proposal might well talk about time frame, capacity on the server for N number of catalog products, ability to handle N transactions an hour, and so on. Savvy consultants know that it's dangerous to use words or expressions like "user experience second to none," "increase sales by 25 percent," "increase gross profit by 15 percent," and "kill the competition." These goals, no matter how appealing from a purely sales point of view, require many stars to align and that is well beyond the control of the consultant. Consultants design proposals to maximize their control over a client engagement.

Appendix 9–1 shows a typical RFP letter. Appendix 9–2 presents a sample proposal for a portal development workshop designed to address part of the needs described in the RFP.

Sample RFP Letter

MissingTheDot.com
99 Avenue of the Americas
New York, NY 10011

Sirs:

Our company currently has 6 different Web entities, built to handle the e-commerce needs of our 6 divisions. We now wish to leverage our brand and bring these 6 into a common infrastructure and architecture. However, the content we put on our Web site comes from Apples at 2 of the sites, and from PCs at the other 4. Most of what we have now is static HTML, but we also publish some dynamic things from our databases.

With your experience in this area, we'd like you to help us organize our thoughts so that we could develop a common approach to content management, perhaps create a portal, and understand how to manage the production of things we'd like to put on the Web.

In talking to your sales representative, I guess the way we need to attack this is to develop a taxonomy, create a content management plan, and then a portal creation plan. Even though they are related, I'd like to see separate proposals for budget reasons.

Thanks and Regards,

J. Christopher Potter
CIO

Appendix 9-2

Sample Proposal for Portal Strategy Workshop

Prepared for: MissingTheDot.com
Date: xxx

The information in this proposal shall not be disclosed outside of MissingTheDot.com and shall not be duplicated, used, or disclosed in whole or in part for any purpose other than to evaluate the proposal, provided that if a contract is awarded to EBA as a result of or in connection with the submission of this proposal, MissingTheDot.com shall have the right to duplicate, use, or disclose the information to the extent provided by the contract. This restriction does not limit the right of MissingTheDot.com to use information contained in the proposal if it is obtained from another source without restriction. This proposal is valid for fifteen days from the above date.

Ebusiness Associates, Inc.

Table of Contents

1. INTRODUCTION

MissingTheDot.com has requested EBA to facilitate a workshop that will leverage its experience in the area of enterprise portals and the technology and processes to create and sustain them. The workshop is based on our experience across multiple clients and industries. At a high level, it is based on the following approach:

- **Quick but effective solution definition techniques** (1–2 day-studies), getting to the point very quickly but ensuring that the initial out-of-the-box approach will meet key business requirements. During these sessions we carefully sort out the requirements and corresponding implementation approach to allow the initial system to meet the most pressing business requirements in as little time and budget as possible, while simultaneously building the foundation for adding other features in the next release.
- **"Rapid prototyping" approach to defining an enterprise strategy,** quickly establishing the basics so that individual implementations can be rapidly converged into an umbrella strategy, while deferring less critical parts of the strategy to the next phase of development.
- **Quick implementations using primarily out-of-the-box features of commercial software,** satisfying all critical requirements but deferring more complex features until an enterprise strategy has been put into place. This ensures that the enterprise strategy does not impede progress, but minimizes the risk that early, complex implementations will diverge from the enterprise strategy.

Critical Success Factors

The critical success factors which MissingTheDot.com and EBA should keep focused on throughout this engagement are:

- A MissingTheDot.com and EBA team approach to executing the scope of this effort
- Commitment of the MissingTheDot.com management and staff to the workshop sessions
- Rapid decisions and resolution of issues to maintain schedule and focus
- Containing the scope of the engagement to meet EBA and MissingTheDot.com's requirements

2. STATEMENT OF WORK

This Statement of Work (SOW) defines the scope of work to be performed under the terms and conditions of the EBA Customer Agreement (the *Agreement*) between us. In the event of any contradiction, inconsistency or ambiguity between the terms and conditions of the two documents, this Statement of Work shall govern. This SOW and the EBA Customer Agreement (and any applicable attachments) represent the entire agreement between the parties regarding this subject matter and replace any prior oral or written communications.

The following are incorporated in and made part of this SOW:

Appendix A—Deliverable Guidelines
Appendix B—Project Change Control Procedure

Changes to this Statement of Work will be processed in accordance with the procedure described in "Appendix B—Project Change Control Procedure." The investigation and the implementation of changes may result in modifications to the Estimated Schedule, Charges, and/or other terms of this Statement of Work.

2.1 Project Scope

The purpose of this engagement is to provide a business and technical framework for designing and implementing the MissingTheDot.com Portal. The following are a summary of the major tasks to be performed under the SOW:

- Determine the business framework
- Establish measures of project success
- Describe current system
- Define high-level system capabilities
- Define high-level functional requirements
- Define benefits framework
- Prioritize requirements and validate benefit areas
- Model high-level solution
- Present Executive Summary findings

2.2 Key Assumptions

This Statement of Work and EBA's estimates to perform the Statement of Work are based on the following key assumptions. Any impact resulting from deviations to these assumptions will be assessed using the procedure described in "Appendix B—Project Change Control Procedure."

1. All participants will be available for, and fully engaged in, the applicable workshop sessions.
2. Workshop working sessions and interviews will not exceed 6 hours per day.
3. The facilitated workshop will not exceed three days.
4. Facilities for the workshop will be provided by MissingTheDot.com. Facilities includes: meeting room(s); flipcharts (stand and paper), markers and masking tape; dry-erase board and markers; overhead projector, screen, and power cords; PC screen projector, such as InFocus; place cards for participants.
5. MissingTheDot.com will provide a dedicated "team room" workspace for the EBA team's exclusive use for the duration of the engagement. Room furnishings include phone with dial-out capability, analog phone line for access to EBA's network, work table and adequate number of chairs, wall space to tape flip charts, lockable door.
6. Development work under this Statement of Work will be performed at appropriate EBA locations and at MissingTheDot.com's offices.
7. All deliverables will be provided in PowerPoint or Excel presentation format.
8. EBA may use subcontractors to perform a portion of the proposed work.

2.3 EBA Responsibilities

The tasks to be performed by EBA are listed below and will be performed by EBA personnel.

Perform Project Management

Description: The objective of this task is to provide direction and control of project personnel and to provide a framework for project communications and contractual activity. The subtasks include:

1. Resolve deviations from the Project Plan caused by EBA personnel.
2. Coordinate and manage the activities of project personnel.
3. With the MissingTheDot.com Project Manager, administer the Project Change Control Procedure in accordance with Appendix B.

Completion Criteria: This is a level of effort activity that continues for the duration of the engagement.

Deliverables: Project Change Requests, as appropriate.

Prepare for the Workshop

Description: The objective of this task is to prepare the MissingTheDot.com project team for the workshop sessions.

1. Review strategies and documentation related to the initiative
2. Identify participants for the workshop sessions
3. Conduct preparatory interviews with stakeholders
4. Prepare facilities and materials for workshop

Deliverable: None.

Conduct Jumpstart Workshop

Define Business Framework

Description: The objective of this task is to establish the goals, mission, and business issues for the MissingTheDot.com portal project. This framework is the basis for all other topics in the workshop. Key topics for discussion include:

1. Business Objectives (list 3–5)
2. Current Barriers to Meeting Those Objectives (list 3–5)
3. Desired Approach (review briefly)
4. How Success Will Be Measured (describe briefly)
5. Critical Success Factors (list 3–5)
6. Key Business Constraints (list 3–5)
7. Key Technical Constraints (list 3–5)

Completion Criteria: This task will be considered complete at the end of this 2–3-hour session.

Deliverable: None.

Describe Current System

Description: The objective of this task is to document the current system, including business organization and process and technical assets and data. Key topics for discussion include:

1. High-Level Information Flow—Contributors/Coordinators/Consumers (draw simple diagram)
2. Profile of Key Users—Administrators/Contributors/Consumers (describe briefly)
3. High-Level System Context (draw diagram showing all key interfaces with other systems/processes)
4. High-Level Process/Work Flow (draw diagram showing key users and processes)
5. Major Document Types (list 3–5) with Sizes/Volumes/Change Cycles/ Interrelationships
6. Location and Format of Repositories/Data (describe briefly)
7. Technical Infrastructure—Hardware/Software/Networking (draw simple diagram)
8. User Interface Approach (describe briefly)
9. Known Problems and Issues, Tied to the Business Framework

Completion Criteria: This task will be considered complete at the end of this 1–2-hour session.

Deliverable: None

Define High-Level System Capabilities

Description: The objective of this task is to identify the capabilities of a future system that satisfies the business objectives defined in the business framework. The future system is defined in terms of the flow of information, key systems, modified processes, and the objects in the future system. Key topics for discussion include:

1. Desired High-Level Information Flow — Contributors/Coordinators/Consumers (diagram changes)
2. Desired High-Level System Context/Interfaces (diagram changes from current system)
3. Desired High-Level Process/Work Flow (diagram changes from current system)
4. Required Major Object Types and Characteristics (describe changes from current system)

Completion Criteria: This task will be considered complete at the end of this 1–2-hour session.

Deliverable: None.

Define High-Level Requirements

Description: The objective of this task is to identify the major system functions, regulatory constraints, and technical issues of a future system that satisfies the business objectives defined in the business framework. Key topics for discussion include:

1. Key Features/Functions (list 10–20), covering:
   - Information delivery/publishing
   - Search and retrieval/reporting
   - Linking and reuse
   - Audit/archive
   - Fax and e-mail integration
   - Interfaces to other systems
2. Key Regulatory Requirements (list 3–5)
3. Key Security Issues (1–2)
4. Key User Interface/Usability Issues (1–2)
5. Key Data Validation Issues (list 1–2)
6. Key Data Conversion Issues (list 1–2)
7. Key Performance Issues (1–2)

Completion Criteria: This task will be considered complete at the end of this 2–3-hour session.

Deliverable: None.

Prioritize Requirements and Validate Benefit Areas

Description: The objective of this task is to set the requirements in the business context and to establish the anticipated benefits aligned with the business objectives defined in the business framework. Key topics for discussion include:

1. Identify key benefit areas to be realized by satisfying requirements
2. Categorize benefits into the three broad categories:
   - Tangible
   - Operational
   - Strategic

3. Map benefits onto requirements
4. Rank value of requirements based on business benefit
5. Identify issues and implications to be tracked in the implementation project(s)

Completion Criteria: This task will be considered complete at the end of this 2–3-hour session.

Deliverable: None.

Model High-Level Solution

Description: The objective of this task is to create and validate a working model of the solution that meets the business objectives. Key topics for discussion include:

1. Overall Approach (describe briefly)
2. Major Subsystems/Applications (draw diagram)
3. Preliminary List of Off-the-Shelf Products (list 3–5 per function)
4. Preliminary Location and Format of Repositories/Data (diagram locations and object/data types)
5. Preliminary High-Level Hardware/Software Architecture (physical architecture/repositories/products)
6. Probable Areas of Customization (list 10–20 with indication of approximate scope)
7. Phased Implementation Approach

Completion Criteria: This task will be considered complete at the end of this 3–4-hour session.

Deliverable: None.

Prepare Executive Summary of Workshop

Description: The objective of this task is to document the results of the workshop and deliver it to the key workshop participants. Key topics for discussion include:

1. Distill workshop notes into presentation format
2. Develop executive level scenario
3. Finalize sketches and drawings into consistent presentation form
4. Present dry-run of summary to MissingTheDot.com project manager
5. Conduct executive wrap-up session

Completion Criteria: This task will be considered complete when the 20–30 slide executive summary presentation has been delivered (in person and electronically) to the MissingTheDot.com executive team.

Deliverable: Executive Summary Presentation.

2.4 MissingTheDot.com Responsibilities

The responsibilities listed in this section are in addition to those responsibilities specified in the *Agreement* and the items listed in Assumptions, Section 2.2 herein, and are to be provided at no charge to EBA. EBA's performance is predicated upon the following responsibilities being fulfilled by MissingTheDot.com.

MissingTheDot.com Project Manager

Prior to the start of this Statement of Work, MissingTheDot.com will designate a person, called MissingTheDot.com Project Manager, to whom all EBA communications will be addressed and who has the authority to act for MissingTheDot.com in all aspects of the contract. This Project Manager will also ensure that MissingTheDot.com resources and personnel are available to provide the necessary information for this project. The responsibilities of the MissingTheDot.com Project Manager include:

1. Serve as the liaison between the EBA project team and all MissingTheDot.com departments participating in this project.
2. With the EBA Project Manager, administer Project Change Control.
3. Lead project status meetings.
4. Resolve deviations from project plans that may be caused by MissingTheDot.com.
5. Help resolve project issues and escalate issues within the MissingTheDot.com organization, as necessary.
6. Monitor and report project status on a regular basis to MissingTheDot.com as appropriate.
7. Provide and coordinate MissingTheDot.com technical resources as necessary.
8. Review intermediate work products and acknowledge acceptance within three business days. Review final deliverable and acknowledge acceptance within three business days. If intermediate work products or final deliverable provided are deemed not acceptable, the MissingTheDot.com Project Manager will notify EBA in writing and or in e-mail. Thereupon, EBA will assess the situation and recommend remedies to address the concern(s) raised.

Other MissingTheDot.com Personnel Responsibilities

1. Participate in meetings and interviews as necessary.
2. Provide any additional information as is necessary for the project, as mutually agreed upon by EBA and MissingTheDot.com.
3. Help schedule interview sessions and/or meetings with identified personnel and arrange conference rooms/meeting rooms for such interviews, as appropriate.
4. Review and provide input or changes to the documentation of the interview findings.
5. Conduct post-interview meetings with the management team to quantify identified tangible and strategic benefits and finalize input.
6. Provide the necessary interface and hardware/software infrastructure information required to facilitate the architecture and requirements definitions.
7. Provide subject matter experts who are knowledgeable in MissingTheDot.com's business processes and system architecture.

Security and Laws

MissingTheDot.com is responsible for the actual content of any data file, selection and implementation of controls on its access and use, and security of the stored data. MissingTheDot.com will identify and make the interpretation of any applicable federal, state, and local laws, regulations and statutes and ensure that products of the system meet those requirements.

Employment of EBA Personnel/No Hire Clause

From the execution date of this Agreement, to one year after the completion, termination, or expiration of this Agreement, whichever occurs first, MissingTheDot.com will not solicit for hire as an employee or independent contractor any employee of EBA who performs work under this Agreement.

2.5 Estimated Schedule

EBA shall deliver the work products on the following estimated dates:

Project Start Date:	1/22/01
Facilitated Workshop:	1/29/01
Executive Presentation:	2/02/01

2.6 Completion Criteria

EBA shall have fulfilled its obligations under this Statement of Work when any one of the following first occurs:

- EBA completes the work described in the "EBA Responsibilities" section, including delivery to MissingTheDot.com of the Deliverable Materials (ref. Section 2.8).
- EBA reaches the estimated end date of 2/2/01, or
- EBA or MissingTheDot.com terminates the Project in accordance with the provisions of the *Agreement*.

2.7 Estimated Charges

EBA will provide up to an estimated 100–300 hours of services for this Statement of Work at an hourly rate of $100–$150. The total estimated funding requirement is $10,000–$45,000 plus applicable taxes. MissingTheDot.com will be invoiced for the fixed amount in monthly payments over the period of performance. In addition, reimbursable expenses for travel, lodging, communications, report production, and other engagement expenses will be invoiced at actual cost and are estimated to be 10–15% of the professional fees. Invoices are payable upon receipt.

2.8 Deliverable Materials

EBA will deliver the following Materials, as defined by the *Agreement* (please see Appendix A—Deliverable Guidelines for details):

- Executive Summary Presentation

2.9 Additional Terms and Conditions

We are not providing any Year 2000 services under this SOW. EBA Product Specifications specify the Year 2000 readiness of the EBA Products. We do not make any representations regarding the Year 2000 readiness of the non-EBA Products.

Under the terms of this SOW we are not responsible for (1) MissingTheDot.com products, (2) a third party's products (including products MissingTheDot.com licenses from our subcontractors) or (3) EBA's previously installed Products ("Other Products"), to correctly process or properly exchange accurate date data with the Products or deliverables we provide. EBA will be relieved of our obligations under this SOW due to the inability of such Other Products to correctly process or properly exchange accurate date data with the Products or deliverables we provide to you. MissingTheDot.com acknowledges that it is your responsibility to assess your current systems and take appropriate action to migrate to Year 2000 ready systems.

MissingTheDot.com shall be responsible for promptly obtaining and providing to EBA all Required Consents necessary for EBA to access, use, and/or modify software, hardware, firmware, and other products used by MissingTheDot.com for which EBA shall provide services described hereunder. A Required Consent means any consents or approvals required to give EBA and its subcontractors the right or license to access, use, and/or modify (including creating derivative works) MissingTheDot.com's or a third party's software, hardware, firmware, or other products used by MissingTheDot.com without infringing the ownership or license rights (including patent and copyright) of the providers or owners of such products.

MissingTheDot.com agrees to indemnify, defend, and hold EBA and its affiliates harmless from and against any and all claims, losses, liabilities, and damages (including reasonable attorneys' fees and costs) arising from or in connection with any claims (including patent and copyright infringement) made against EBA alleged to have occurred as a result of MissingTheDot.com's failure to provide any Required Consents.

EBA shall be relieved of the performance of any obligations that may be affected by MissingTheDot.com's failure to promptly provide any Required Consents to EBA.

3. SIGNATURE PAGE

Customer Services Agreement

This document is a Statement of Work (SOW) to either the EBA Customer Agreement or the EBA Agreement for Services. If used with the EBA Agreement for Services, no machines or licensed program products may be acquired under this Statement of Work. Such items are available only under the terms of (1) the EBA Customer Agreement (or any equivalent agreement signed by both of us) or (2) the applicable third-party agreement.

Scope of Services, Completion Criteria, Charges, and other applicable terms: Refer to SOW Section 2.0.

Each of us agrees that the complete agreement between us about these Services consists of 1) this Statement of Work, and 2) the EBA Customer Agreement (or any equivalent agreement signed by both of us).

Agreed to:	*Agreed to:*
Customer name: **MissingTheDot.com** **<Location>**	**EBusiness Associated, Inc** **Easton, PA, 18040**
By	By

Authorized Signature	Authorized Signature

Name (type or print): _____   Name: _____

Date: _____   Date: _____

Reference
Agreement Number:

Customer Number:

Customer Address: Proposal Number:

Estimated Start Date: EBA Office Number:

Estimated End Date: EBA Office Address:

Appendix A. Deliverable Guidelines

Executive Summary Presentation

EBA will provide the Solution Outline Document (20–30 pages), in PowerPoint or Excel Presentation format, including the following information:

- Project Goals
- Business Framework Including:
  - Business Context Diagram
  - Business Event list
  - Business Process Model (as-is)
- Current Technology Environment
- Outline of Solution Requirements
  - System Context Diagram
  - Key Users
  - Document Inventory
- Solution Implications
- Action Plan

Appendix B. Project Change Control Procedure

The following provides a detailed process to follow if a change to this Statement of Work (SOW) is required.

- A Project Change Request (PCR) will be the vehicle for communicating change. The PCR must describe the change, the rationale for the change, and the effect the change will have on the project.
- The designated Project Manager of the requesting party will review the proposed change and determine whether to submit the request to the other party.
- Both Project Managers will review the proposed change and approve it for further investigation or reject it. EBA will specify any charges for such investigation. If the investigation is authorized, the Project Managers will sign the PCR, which will constitute approval for the investigation charges. EBA will invoice MissingTheDot.com for any such charges. The investigation will determine the effect that the implementation of the PCR will have on estimated charges, estimated schedule, and other terms and conditions of the Agreement.

A written Change Authorization and/or Project Change Request (PCR) must be signed by both parties to authorize implementation of the investigated changes.

CHAPTER

10
Managing Projects

Charles A. Nichols III

The advice business is carried out through work on projects. The managerial challenges of consulting work are significantly different from the typical challenges that line managers face in their daily activities. Corporate managers spend much of their time directing the activities of their people in the functions necessary for the economic health of their firms: their tasks are recurring, and there is no specific point that signals the end of their work. In contrast, consultants are engaged to help their clients define and solve specific business problems. Although the relationship between them may continue indefinitely, their collaboration takes place on discrete projects that begin and end.

This chapter overviews the basic principles of effective project management, from the initial agreement on the goals of a consulting project, through the various managerial challenges that must be met to bring it to a successful conclusion. A list of references is provided at the end where each of the topics of project management is covered at greater length. We will begin with a discussion of the document that governs the work of a consulting project: the engagement letter.

THE ENGAGEMENT LETTER

The start of any successful consulting project is an agreement between the consultant and the client on what they will do together. This agreement should be expressed in writing in an "engagement letter" that summarizes the work to be done on the consulting engagement. An engagement letter is typically prepared by the leader of the consulting team after initial discussions with the client executive, or "sponsor" who retains them.

The degree of formality of engagement letters can vary a great deal, depending on the size of the project, the nature of the existing relationship between the consultant and client, and the regulatory environment. An engagement letter for a small project with a client sponsor for whom the consultant has often worked in the past may be quite short and general in its description of the work to be done. On the other hand, the engagement letter for a very large project for a new client, especially a government

Charles A. Nichols III, is a manager of Professional Development in the commercial consulting business of Booz Allen Hamilton. He did graduate work in philosophy at Harvard University and was a Graduate Fellow in the Harvard Program in Ethics and the Professions.

client operating under regulatory requirements about the way it engages consultants, may be extensive and cover all aspects of the project in minute detail. Short or long, an engagement letter that expresses clearly the agreement between consultant and client is a prerequisite for a successful project, and all such letters should include the following information.

Objectives

What is the consultant here to do? If the stated objectives of the consulting project fail to answer this question, then they are inadequate. "Our objective is to help the XYZ Corporation improve its profitability" is much too vague to define the objective of a consulting engagement. "Our objective is to help the XYZ Corporation identify new markets for its products that will increase overall revenue and profitability" gives a clear sense of what the project is about.

Defining the objectives of a project also involves clearly stating its scope, as well as identifying any assumptions and constraints around the work.

Scope

Scope tells the client what aspects of the problem are included in the project, and even more importantly, what aspects are excluded. In the example of an objective described above, the following scope qualifications would be crucial for a proper understanding of the project: "Our investigations will be limited to products currently sold by XYZ Corporation, and to new markets in Asia only." Failure to agree upon scope definition and include it in the engagement letter can prove costly to consultants, either through disappointing client expectations or through doing additional work they had not planned on or been compensated for.

Assumptions and Constraints

Identifying assumptions and constraints is similar to specifying the scope of a project. The engagement letter should explicitly identify assumptions that will not be tested as a part of the consulting process; for example: "We will assume that XYZ Corporation will be able to scale up production to meet the demands of new markets without incurring higher unit costs." Similarly, constraints imposed upon the project work should be listed: "To ensure the confidentiality (*or:* To stay within the budget limits) of the project, we will not conduct benchmarking interviews with competitors in the industry."

It is important to realize that scope limitations, as well as assumptions and constraints placed on project work, can raise ethical issues for consultants, since they should not agree to work on a project when they do not believe that its objectives can be achieved under such conditions.

Work Products and Final Deliverables

What will the client receive from the consultant as a result of the engagement? Defining the work product and final deliverables of a project will answer this question. In our example, the client may be expecting a short report highlighting the new markets expected to be most profitable for its products; or else they may be looking for detailed projections of revenue for all markets reviewed during the project. The engagement letter should clearly indicate which product is to be delivered to the client.

Deadlines and Milestones

Once the client knows what objectives the project will achieve, and what they will receive as a result of it, the next question is: **When will we get the results?** The engagement letter should state both a completion date or deadline for the project as a whole, and also intermediate dates for deliverables that serve as milestones along the road to completion. In our example, the final report might be due at the end of three months, but at the end of the first month provide the client a "long list" of promising markets, and then at the end of the second month a preliminary "short list" of the likeliest ones.

Project deadlines and milestones are also closely related to two other timing issues that should be covered in the engagement letter: the status report cycle and the schedule for reviews and sign-offs on the project.

Status Report Cycle

The status report cycle tells the client when they should expect to receive updates on the progress of the project. These updates will include but are not necessarily limited to the intermediate deliverable milestones. The optimal status report cycle will depend on the degree of involvement that the client sponsor needs to have in the developing work of the project.

Reviews and Sign-Offs

A statement of the process by which the client will review and sign off on the project work is an important element in the consultant's project planning. The project manager must have a clear understanding of: the points at which the client wants to be involved in reviews or decisions affecting the project; who the decision maker at the client will be; and how long the client will need to make the decision. Without this information, it will be impossible to schedule the work to ensure on-time completion of the project.

Fees and Expenses

How much will it cost? Finally, the engagement letter needs to address this all-important client concern. Consulting projects can be priced many different ways: the two most common are fixed price, and time and materials. Under a fixed price contract, the client is quoted a set price for the entire project. If the consultant manages to complete the work for less than her team's cost in professional fees and expenses, the surplus is profit for her; if the team exceeds the price, the consultant sustains a loss. In contrast, a time and materials contract states that payment will be based on the fees for professional time and expenses incurred by the team in doing the work.

In practice, contracts can combine elements of both pricing methods; for example, the engagement letter might state that professional fees for the project would be billed based on the time incurred by consulting team members, but that expenses would be charged as a flat percentage of professional fees. Under this contract, the consultant will not be exposed to the risk that her team will need to work longer (or shorter) than originally estimated, but she can gain or lose to the extent that she is able to manage expenses on the project as a percentage of professional fees.

The fees and expenses section of the engagement letter should also describe how and when payments must be made by the client to the consultant, for example, every month in advance or in arrears, or in accordance with a specific schedule.

The engagement letter is the essential starting point for the manager of a consulting project, and provides the initial framework for planning the work of the engagement. This does not mean, of course, that project will exactly follow the path laid out in it: Client objectives might change during the course of the engagement, and events unforeseen by the consultant and the client might alter the situation. In these cases, any or all aspects of the engagement letter can be renegotiated, and the new agreement serve as a basis for managing the revised project. If the original agreement has not been fully documented in the engagement letter, though, it is much harder for the consultant to renegotiate terms when necessary, and therefore to manage the project in a way that meets client expectations within the budget of the engagement.

Assuming that the project is well described by its engagement letter, the consultant's first step in managing the project is to prepare a work plan.

THE PROJECT WORK PLAN

The project work plan is one of the most important tools that the manager of a consulting project will use to ensure on-time and within-budget delivery of results that meet client expectations. This section describes the elements of an effective work plan. However, we begin with a discussion of the thought process that connects both the engagement letter and the final deliverable report with the work plan, and thereby ensures that the work plan is focused and complete. Figure 10–1 provides an overview of the project management process.

The Project Thought Plan

Chapter 7 laid out a thought process used by consulting teams for maximum efficiency in solving problems that are initially large and ill-defined. This process requires consultants to begin with a clear statement of the problem to be solved, or project objective. The next step is to break this problem down into a set of questions, or issues, which, to the extent possible, are mutually exclusive and collectively exhaustive of the problem. An example of an issue, for the XYZ Corporation engagement discussed above, is "What is the potential for Internet-based marketing to increase revenues and profitability for XYZ Corporation?" The team knows they have a good set of issue questions when it is clear that if they are all answered, the solution to the problem will be apparent.

The work of the engagement then becomes answering the issue questions, which is accomplished through the scientific method, or "hypothesis-driven approach." The consulting team identifies hypothetical answers to the issue questions, and their data-gathering and analysis is driven by the attempt to support or disprove those hypotheses. A hypothesis falling underneath the issue question above is: "XYZ Corporation can significantly increase revenues and profits by forming a marketing alliance with an established Web portal." Data-gathering and analysis to test this hypothesis would include: performing a benchmarking study of Internet marketing alliances for companies in XYZ Corporation's industry; gathering cost data from the client; preparing a

FIGURE 10–1   Project Management Overview

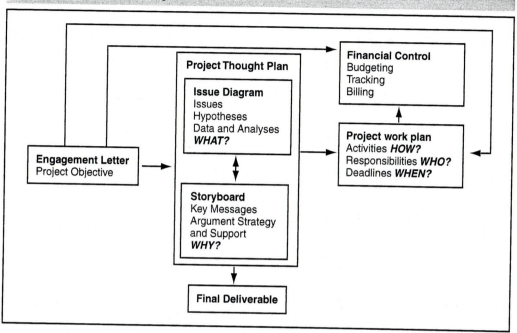

financial model to project revenues, costs, and profits from Internet marketing activities. Disproved hypotheses are replaced by new ones, and the work continues until a well-supported set of hypotheses emerges, from which the solution to the problem can be inferred and the engagement objective achieved.

The thought process described above provides the link between the high-level project objective as stated in the engagement letter, and the definition of the specific tasks that the manager of a consulting project must direct. This is one part of the "thought plan" ensuring that the project work plan stays focused on the tasks that need to be done. The other part of the thought plan links the project work plan to the ultimate deliverable, the report presented to the client at the end of an engagement. This part of the thought plan ensures that the work being done on the engagement is producing the information needed to support the story line in the final report that will persuade the client to adopt the consultant's recommendations.

The two parts of the thought plan are supported by two tools: the issue diagram and the storyboard.

The Issue Diagram

The issue diagram is a graphical arrangement, in a series of branching nodes, of the elements of the consulting thought process described above. The highest-level starting node is the problem statement, which then branches into the issue questions at the second level. Each issue question becomes a node that branches into the third level of hypotheses that are potential answers to it, and each hypothesis is a node that branches into a fourth level, the data and analysis necessary to test it.

Showing the thought process in graphical form underscores the need for specificity at each level, as well as tight logical linkages between levels; that is, issues must fully exhaust the problem, hypotheses must fully answer the issue questions, and data and analysis must provide a fully adequate test of the hypotheses. As explained below, it also turns the thought process into a visual document that can be shared among team members.

The Storyboard

The storyboard is a mock-up of the final deliverable, the report to the client. It lays out on a series of separate pages each step of the argument in support of the recommendations to the client. Laying out a final report mock-up allows the team to think through the key messages and the argument strategy, i.e. the optimal way to present recommendations and support for them to persuade the client. It also makes clear what data and analysis are needed to support the argument at its crucial points, and ensures that the team stays focused on the tasks that will produce them. Initially, the storyboard is based upon the first set of hypotheses generated by the consulting team. As the project work progresses, the argument in the storyboard gets revised to reflect the team's developing understanding, and support for the argument gets filled in. Ultimately, the storyboard becomes the final report.

The storyboard should be created in a medium that makes it easy to rearrange the flow of the argument: for example, on a set of Post-It sheets, or in a PowerPoint document, where the Slide Sorter view can be used to move pages around.

To ensure that these tools help the project manager keep the project running efficiently and on track, three rules apply:

1. Create an issue diagram and a storyboard at the beginning of a consulting engagement.
2. Keep both of them up to date as the engagement progresses.
3. Make them shared documents within the engagement team, so that everyone can see where the work stands, what still needs to be done, and how their part of the work fits into the overall project.

Once the consulting project manager has an initial version of the project thought plan, she can turn her attention to the creation of a project work plan.

Basic Elements of the Project Work Plan

The basic elements of a project work plan include the tasks and activities that need to be accomplished, time frame in which they must be completed, and assignments of responsibility for them to members of the team. Figure 10–2 gives a framework for the work plan development process.

Tasks and Activities

The tasks and activities to be accomplished during the consulting project derive from the issue diagram, and typically involve the testing of hypotheses. Tasks are the higher-level description of what needs to be done; for example, "Test the hypothesis that XYZ Corporation can significantly increase revenues and profits by forming a marketing alliance with an established Web portal." Tasks are decomposed into activities such as the benchmarking study, the gathering of cost data, and the preparation of a financial

FIGURE 10–2 Workplan Development Framework

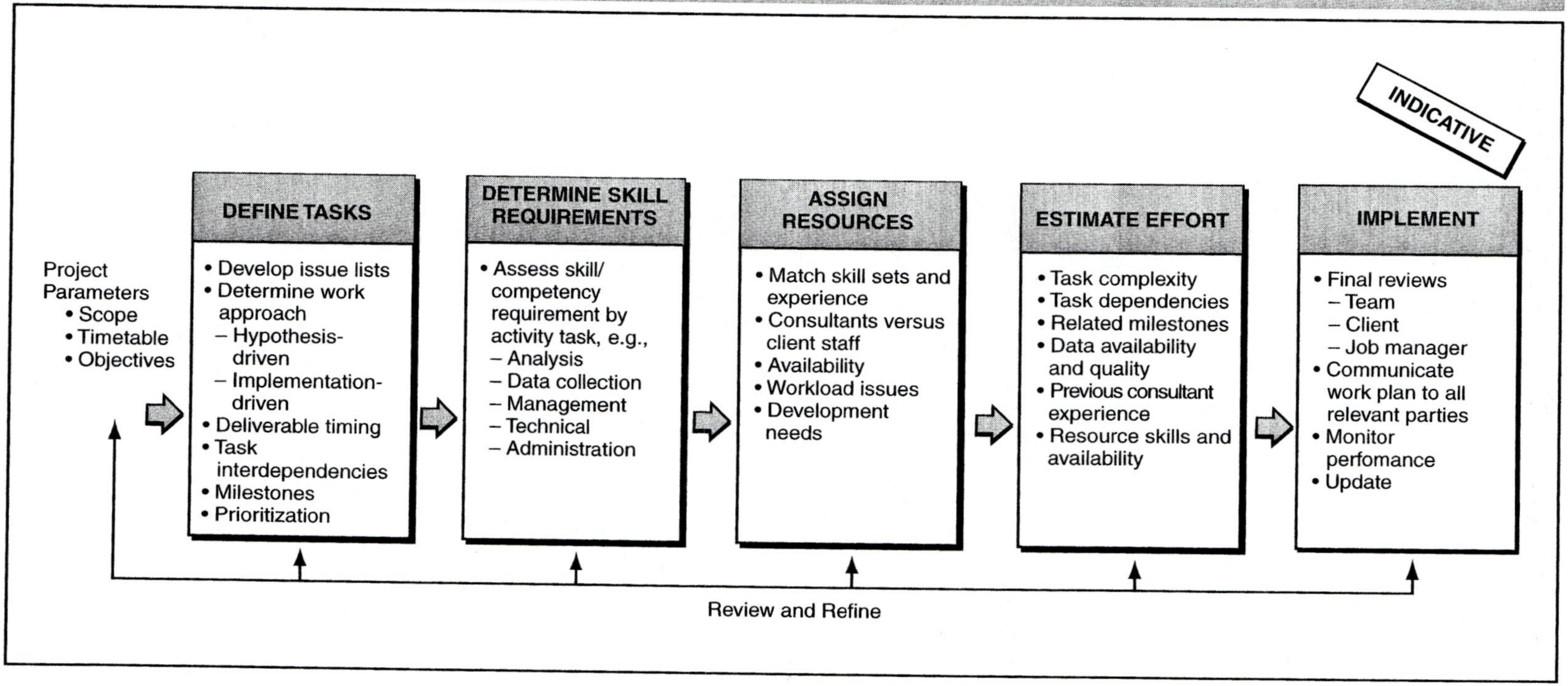

INDICATIVE

Project
Parameters
- Scope
- Timetable
- Objectives

DEFINE TASKS
- Develop issue lists
- Determine work
  approach
  – Hypothesis-
    driven
  – Implementation-
    driven
- Deliverable timing
- Task
  interdependencies
- Milestones
- Prioritization

DETERMINE SKILL REQUIREMENTS
- Assess skill/
  competency
  requirement by
  activity task, e.g.,
  – Analysis
  – Data collection
  – Management
  – Technical
  – Administration

ASSIGN RESOURCES
- Match skill sets and
  experience
- Consultants versus
  client staff
- Availability
- Workload issues
- Development
  needs

ESTIMATE EFFORT
- Task complexity
- Task dependencies
- Related milestones
- Data availability
  and quality
- Previous consultant
  experience
- Resource skills and
  availability

IMPLEMENT
- Final reviews
  – Team
  – Client
  – Job manager
- Communicate
  work plan to all
  relevant parties
- Monitor
  performance
- Update

Review and Refine

model described above. As necessary, these activities can be broken down even further. For example, the work on the financial model can be divided into phases of programming, testing and validation, and generation of results.

A complete list of activities constitutes the simplest form of a project work plan: a "to-do list." A "work breakdown structure" is a more formalized version of the to-do list, with activities organized into task categories. Many people maintain such lists to organize their own work, and they have the advantage of simplicity. However, a project that extends over weeks or months, involving a team of consultants doing the work, requires additional planning elements.

Time Frame

The time frame is, of course, the dates by which tasks and activities need to be completed. The overall project due date, as well as any agreed-upon intermediate deliverables and their due dates, provides the framework for assigning deadlines to the specific tasks, and in establishing these dates in the engagement letter the consulting project leaders must have made some broad estimates of the time it will take to accomplish the various pieces of the work. However, the project manager must work out the details of when the tasks and activities must be completed in order to meet the project due date. Figure 10–3 offers some tips on how to estimate time requirements and set deadlines.

Note that there can be a conflict between the project work plan need for predictability of tasks and due dates, and the open-ended nature of the hypothesis-driven approach that is the thought plan process for a consulting project. Both in the engagement letter and the initial work plan, the consultant needs to build in time for creating new sets of hypotheses and testing them, based on the results of the tests of the first set, even though she cannot know in advance what they will be or what tasks and activities will be necessary to test them. Thus, to be useful on an engagement, both the issue diagram and the work plan must be treated as dynamic documents that will be continuously updated as the work proceeds. In particular, a dynamic work plan will help the project manager to identify as early as possible any situation where it will be impossible to achieve the project objective in the time and with the resources available, and to open discussion with the client on how best to address this problem.

Responsibilities

The work plan should also include assignment of tasks and activities, with their associated deadlines, to individual team members on the project. The project manager typically has at her disposal a number of consultants with varying degrees of abilities and needs for skill development. The project manager's role in coaching and developing team members will be discussed later in this chapter, but part of it involves making assignments of work that allow team members to learn new skills, in addition to making use of the abilities that they already possess.

Sometimes project work will also be done by client employees, who may be assigned on a full- or part-time basis to the project. In assigning tasks, the project manager must take into account potentially lesser levels of motivation and commitment to the project by client employees—perhaps based on any continuing responsibility they may have for their ordinary duties at the client—as well as the fact that the consultants

FIGURE 10–3 Time Estimating Tips

TIP	COMMENT
Clearly define your deliverables (Do this first)	• Once defined, think through what is required to deliver against

Use effort drivers to determine work plan effort	• Potential drivers—diagnostic
	  – Number of interviews
	  – Number of hypotheses, data sources
	• Potential drivers—implementation work
	  – Number of processes to be changed
	  – Number of procedures to be re-written

Use multiple sources for guidelines	• Consulting firm intellectual capital • Consultant colleagues • Client experience
Allow for contingency	• Estimates can only blow out in one direction—things always go wrong • Double the time you think it takes to finalize analysis and make graphics production ready
Allow for management and administration	• Reporting, filing, work plan development, intellectual capital development

Plan for your own needs	• Allow time for
	  – Development planning
	  – Intellectual capital development
	  – Getting a life

Allow sufficient time for data collection, analysis, and documentation	• As the number of data points and data sources increases so does the analysis time
	• Allow time for
	  – Interview preparation (1/2 hr+)
	  – Interview documentation (1/2 hr+)
	  – Interview cancellations

will ultimately be responsible for the project results as a whole, regardless of the involvement of client employees.

The three elements of tasks and activities, time frames, and responsibility are combined in a commonly used project management tool, the Gantt chart.

The Gantt Chart

The Gantt chart was first developed and used by industrial engineer and management authority Harvey Gantt. Gantt worked with the Army Bureau of Ordnance during World War I, and was faced with the need to control daily scheduling of munitions production. He realized that the process could be broken down into precise phases and that many phases could be executed concurrently, in whole or in part. By organizing processes with this in mind, a schedule's efficiency could be maximized. He also realized that this would be most easily communicated with a visual representation of a process and its phases. With this in mind, the Gantt chart was developed.

Figure 10–4 gives a simplified example of a Gantt chart. Note the matrix structure, with activities and tasks listed along the vertical dimension and with the horizontal dimension as a timeline. Gantt charts can also include indications of critical milestones such as intermediate deliverables or interim project review meetings with the client sponsor.

Although a Gantt chart is usually sufficient to manage relatively short and simple projects, it fails to provide all the information a project manager might need for lengthier and more complicated ones. In particular, projects where carrying out some tasks or activities depends on having completed others requires tools that reflect these dependencies and isolate the "critical path" for on-time project completion, as described below.

Dependencies and the Critical Path

Let's make some assumptions about how long different tasks and activities will take for the XYZ Corporation engagement (time to completion shown in parentheses in what follows). The tasks required to test the hypothesis about marketing alliances with Web portals include:

- Gathering cost data from the client (three days)
- Performing a benchmarking study (five days)
- Building a financial model, which involves the activities of:
  Programming the model (two days)
  Testing and validating the model (one day)
  Generating results (one day)

While programming the model does not require input from any other task, testing and validation depends on the availability of cost and benchmarking data, as well as of the programmed model, and generating results depends on having already tested and validated the model. Therefore, ignoring all the other tasks required by the project, and assuming that there are enough team members to perform tasks simultaneously where possible, the XYZ Corporation engagement would at a minimum require seven days of work: five days to perform the benchmarking study (during which time cost data could be gathered and the financial model programmed), then one day to test and validate the model, and one day to generate results.

The benchmarking study, the testing and validating of the model, and the generating of results are on the critical path for the project, which means that delays in any one

FIGURE 10–4 Sample Project Work Plan - GANTT Chart Format

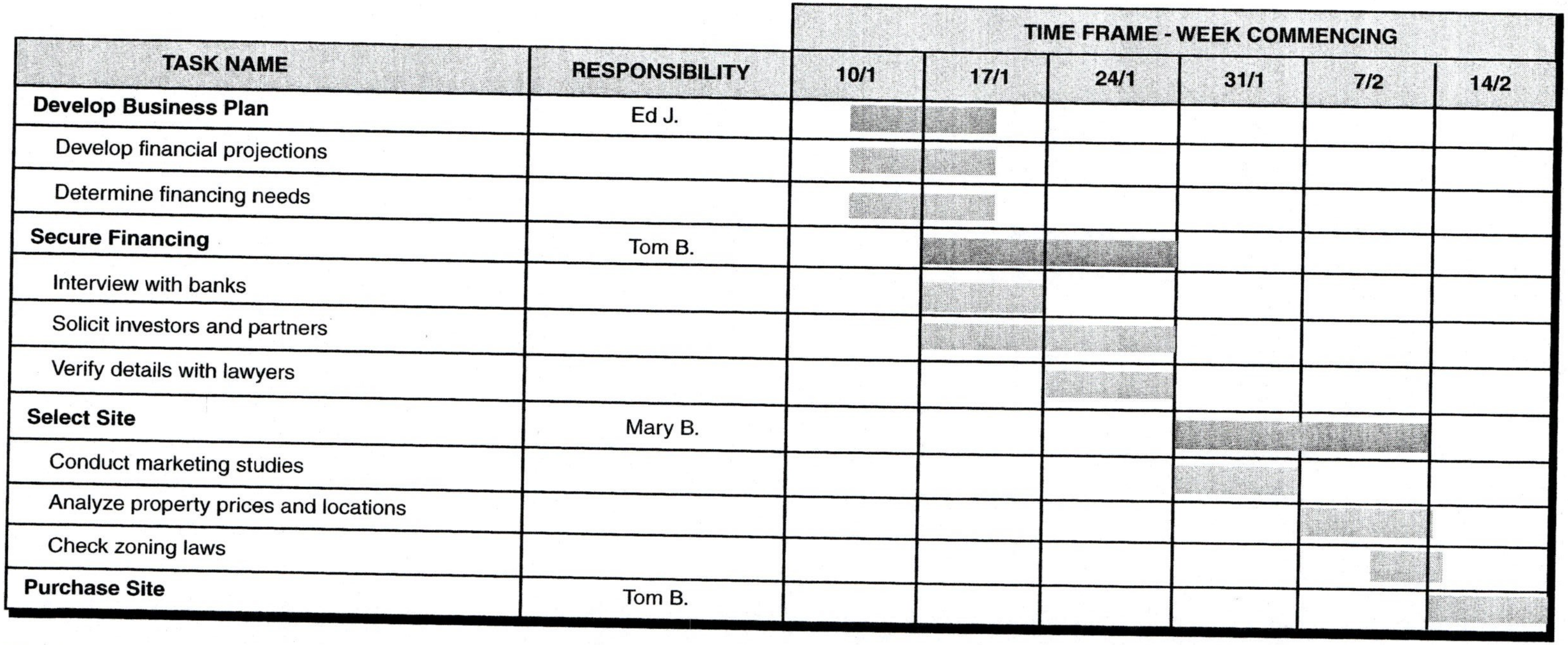

TASK

- Unambiguous, succinct statement of the work to be performed
- Structure and group tasks logically
- Consider your audience (consultant versus client staff)

RESPONSIBILITY

- Clear identification of the individual(s) assigned to perform the task
- Identify a lead responsibility if appropriate

TIMEFRAME

- Definite start and end dates
- Highlight interim checkpoints, meetings, or deliverables

of these activities will cause a similar delay in the completion of the overall project. In contrast, there is slack in the schedule for time overruns in gathering cost data (two days) and in programming the model (three days): they will not be on the critical path unless delays exceed their slack time.

The key to time management on a project lies in identifying the critical path and closely monitoring the activities and tasks on it to ensure that they do not produce delays in the overall completion date. On a simple project, identifying and monitoring the critical path is not too difficult with the help of a Gantt chart, but on a more complex one with multiple and interconnected streams of work dependencies the critical path cannot be easily managed.

Other Project Work Planning Tools

Program Evaluation and Review Technique (or PERT) is one tool that will help a project manager monitor the critical path in a project with complex dependencies. PERT was developed during the 1950s by consultants at the firm of Booz Allen Hamilton to assist the U.S. Department of Defense in managing a program to develop new military weapons. The PERT methodology involves flowcharting all the project activities and connecting together all those that are dependent on others. The connections are labeled with the amount of time it will take for the independent activity to be accomplished before the dependent activity can be started. The total time required is summed up for each of all possible paths through the flowchart, from start to finish, and the longest one is the critical path.

For very large projects, creating and keeping the PERT chart up to date is a significant task, and software has been developed to automate the process of creating and updating PERT charts and other project management tools. The trade-off in using PERT or computerized project management tools, compared to simpler methods such as Gantt charts, is the investment in learning and applying the more complex methods versus the benefits of greater control over a project. Figure 10–5 describes these key project management tools, and Figure 10–6 summarizes the pros and cons of each one.

ISSUES IN PROJECT MANAGEMENT

Kick-Off Meeting

The kick-off meeting is the formal beginning of the work of a consulting engagement. It brings together all members of the engagement team. The engagement leader or project manager outlines the objectives and scope of the engagement, as well as significant milestones in the process. Any special policies requested by the client for the engagement should also be explained, including unusual confidentiality requirements or guidelines for expenses (for example, the client may have discounted rates at certain hotels). The kick-off meeting can also be used as a brainstorming session to identify initial hypotheses for the team to test.

Team Structure and Role Definition

On any consulting project there are three broad roles required for accomplishing the work. First, every engagement must involve an officer or partner of the consulting firm, who bears the final responsibility for client service. Second, there must be a project

FIGURE 10–5 Work Planning Tools

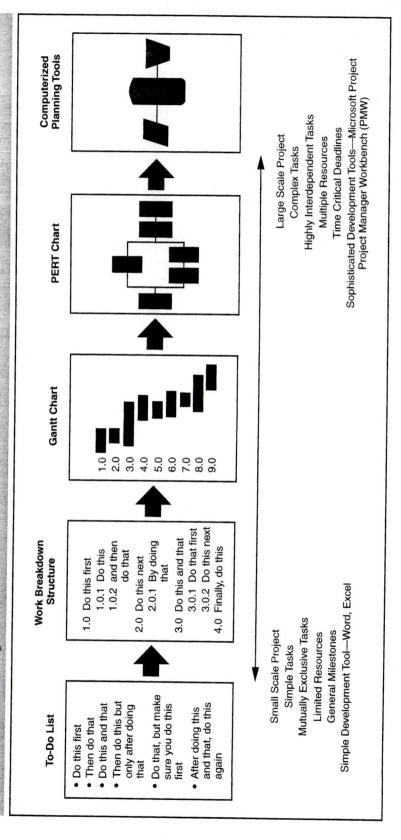

To-Do List

- Do this first
- Then do that
- Do this and that
- Then do this but only after doing that
- Do that, but make sure you do this first
- After doing this and that, do this again

Work Breakdown Structure

1.0 Do this first
   1.0.1 Do this
   1.0.2 and then do that
2.0 Do this next
   2.0.1 By doing that
3.0 Do this and that
   3.0.1 Do that first
   3.0.2 Do this next
4.0 Finally, do this

Gantt Chart

1.0
2.0
3.0
4.0
5.0
6.0
7.0
8.0
9.0

PERT Chart

Computerized Planning Tools

Small Scale Project
Simple Tasks
Mutually Exclusive Tasks
Limited Resources
General Milestones
Simple Development Tool—Word, Excel

Large Scale Project
Complex Tasks
Highly Interdependent Tasks
Multiple Resources
Time Critical Deadlines
Sophisticated Development Tools—Microsoft Project
Project Manager Workbench (PMW)

FIGURE 10–6 Pros and Cons of Work Planning Tools

TOOL	PROS	CONS
To-Do List	• Simple and quick to develop	• Difficult to visualize dependent tasks and milestones
Work Breakdown Structure	• Assists task organization and prioritization • Easy to maintain	• Difficult to visualize • Difficult to judge task lengths relative to other tasks
Gantt Chart	• Simple to create • Visual and intuitive • Assists basic performance tracking	• Does not show task dependencies or interconnections • Difficult to understand project wide scheduling issues
PERT Chart	• Emphasizes task interconnection • Defines project critical path	• More difficult to build with basic tools • Difficult to visualize task length
Computerized Tools, e.g.: — Microsoft Project, PMW	• Highly flexible • Highly visual • Sophisticated performance tracking tools and reports	• Initial learning curves and project set-up requirements • Requires frequent (e.g., weekly) input of quality project status information

manager who is responsible for planning out the steps of the project and managing the work. Third, there are team members, usually junior associates of the consulting firm, who perform the work.

On larger engagements, these roles can be elaborated and shared between several people. For example, the officer role may be shared among a senior partner of the consulting firm, who is responsible for maintaining the ongoing relationship with the client and who may have been involved in the selling of the project, and an "officer in charge," a more junior partner who oversees and provides quality control for the project. For projects with multiple teams and work streams, the project manager role may be shared between team leaders responsible for each team and a senior team leader who ensures coordination among the teams. Finally, on larger teams, there may also be some articulation in roles among the team, with more experienced members providing guidance and oversight for the junior members.

Consulting teams may also include client employees as team members. Figure 10–7 shows an example of the structure of a large team, and Figure 10–8 describes the typical roles and levels of involvement they have on a typical client engagement.

Securing the Workspace

The work on consulting projects is often performed in space provided by the client, so that the engagement team can easily access client information and collaborate with any client employees on the team. The project manager must make sure that the space is adequate for the team to work in, and includes sufficient lines for telephones and modem access for the team's computers. Because the work hours for the consulting team are often longer than the client's normal work hours, the project manager must also ensure that the team has access to the workspace at all times.

Data security is also an issue. The work consultants do for clients is often confidential, and information and documents used and created by the team may need to be kept secret from client employees as well as from outsiders. Therefore, the team's workspace should contain file cabinets that can be locked, and computers should have security software. The project manager must also ensure that team members observe procedures to secure documents and information when they are not working on them.

Project Team Communications

Meetings

Meetings are an essential tool for keeping project team members and also the client informed about the developing work of the engagement. The project manager has an important role in convening, leading, and facilitating many of these meetings: Farrell and Weaver's *The Practical Guide to Facilitation* offers a useful model and guidance in performing this role. Without facilitation, meetings can be inefficient and a drain on everyone's time. See Figure 10–9 for a list of best practices for conducting meetings.

Conference Calls

Conference calls are a specialized version of a meeting: They can be an efficient use of time and expense when meetings involve people who are in different locations. However, they present special difficulties, since most of the nonverbal signals that aid communication are unavailable over the telephone. The facilitator must ensure that all

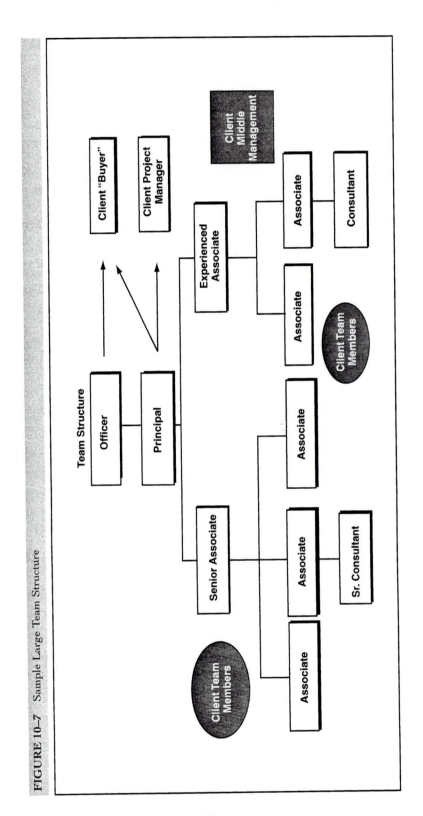

FIGURE 10–7 Sample Large Team Structure

FIGURE 10–8 Typical Levels of Involvement of Team Members

Client Team	Cohort Role	Average time on job
Client Service Officer	Partner who maintains ongoing client relationship	
Officer-in-Charge	Partner responsible for quality of work and building client relationship	4 days per month (20%)
Handling Officer (Partner or Principal)	Partner or Principal responsible for management of the project team	6–10 days per month (50%)
Job Manager (Principal or Sr. Associate)	Principal or Senior Associate who outlines work steps, manages team, and handles client day-to-day	10–20 days per month (50%–100%)
Associate Consultant	Responsible for getting the work done and working with client staff	Full time (100%)

Content Leadership

Thought Leadership

FIGURE 10–9 Best Practices for Meetings

Preparation	Conduct
• Identify purpose of meeting: what should it achieve?	• Ensure key roles are filled, e.g.: —Facilitator (to ensure that all participate productively) —Time keeper —Note taker
• Decide who needs to attend, based on the purpose	
• Draw up proposed agenda	• Use a "parking lot" to table matters not directly relevant to agenda (e.g., a flip chart to record them)
• Send out agenda and any prereading material to participants	
• At meeting, arrive early to check out any logistics —Audio-visual equipment —Handout materials —Arrangements for breaks	• Periodically provide summaries of decisions reached
Opening	**Closing and Follow-Up**
• Make introductions if necessary	• Summarize results of meeting, linking back to objectives
• Present objectives and agenda	• Outline next steps —Actions to be taken —Persons responsible —Deadlines
• Get feedback on objectives and agenda from participants	• After meeting, prepare summary of minutes, including next steps, and circulate to participants

participants are given a chance to contribute to the discussion, particularly if some are present together in the meeting room and others are calling in to it. Videoconferencing can come closer to reproducing the conditions of face-to-face meetings, although it still requires more facilitation.

Collaboration Tools

The most important collaboration tools in a consulting project are issue diagrams and storyboards, since they allow all members of the team to have a shared view of the project thought plan and the developing client report. Software tools such as shared data and document files can make the process of collaboration easier, although the project manager must set up procedures for "version control" to avoid a situation where everyone is working on slightly different versions of the shared documents. One way to do this is to give one team member the responsibility for keeping the most up-to-date version of key documents and numbering and archiving earlier versions.

Shared Storage

Because the engagement team will probably need to share documents and data and are working collaboratively on the final report, the best way to organize the files of the project is with shared storage. The issue diagram can serve as a structuring device for the filing system by organizing data and work papers according to issues and hypotheses being tested. Having common storage arrangements also simplifies the task of ensuring security for client data.

Coaching, Mentoring, and Project Leadership

In addition to planning and overseeing the work of an engagement, the project manager has an important role in coaching and mentoring the junior members of the team. These responsibilities include crafting and sharing expectations, tracking performance and giving feedback, and preparing evaluations of performance. Max Landsberg's book *The Tao of Coaching* offers excellent guidance on how to carry out these responsibilities.

Crafting and Sharing Expectations

At the beginning of an engagement, the project manager should meet with each of the junior team members individually to discuss their skill development goals for the project. Recent performance appraisals are an important source of information about development needs. The goal of the meeting is to create an action plan for the team member to achieve these goals through work assignments and coaching from other members of the team. In addition, the project manager and the team member should share expectations about the project work, including how to balance work commitments with other responsibilities. They should identify and plan for any commitments such as training classes, vacation, or need for personal time.

Tracking and Feedback

Once action plans have been agreed to with the junior team members, the project manager must monitor progress on them, as well as provide coaching and feedback on tasks the team members perform. The project manager should encourage everyone on the team to regard themselves as coaches for their fellow team members in areas where they have greater experience. This attitude is particularly important for teams that include client employees as members, and where one of the expectations of the client is that the consultants train their employees in the course of the engagement.

The ability to give productive feedback is an important skill for the job manager. Figure 10–10 lists some best practices for giving feedback, and *Difficult Conversations*, by Stone, Patton, and Heen, offers a very useful model for effective communication in difficult feedback situations.

Individual Evaluation

At the end of engagement, or periodically during a lengthy engagement, job managers must provide evaluations of team member performance. These assignment evaluations ensure that junior team members receive regular feedback, and they also provide data for more formal appraisals of performance.

Administrative Issues

Opening a Contract

Each consulting firm will have its own procedures for how to administer engagement contracts; the project manager should be sure to know them and follow them. In larger firms there will be a finance or administrative area responsible for keeping records, which will assign a job number to new engagements. This number is then used to report time worked and expenses incurred on a project.

Along with project thought and work plans, the project manager must also prepare a budget for the engagement. A high-level budget estimate may have been made during the selling of the engagement in order to arrive at any price quoted in the engagement letter, but the project manager needs to develop one based on more detailed knowledge of the team members and their billing rates. The budget should also include expenses to be billed to the client, typically estimated as a percentage of professional fees, as well as a contingency margin as a percentage of the total. Figure 10–11 presents an example of a budget calculation.

FIGURE 10–10   Best Practices for Giving Feedback

- If possible, give both positive (reinforcing) and negative (correcting) feedback

- Give feedback as soon as possible after the event

- Defer negative feedback until both you and the recipient are able to discuss the event calmly

- Focus on specific behaviors

- Explain the effects of the behaviors (on you and others)

- For negative feedback, offer specific alternative actions that could be taken

- Draw on your own experience, especially difficulties you have faced with the same subject

- Ask for a response from the recipient to ensure your message has been heard

- Encourage the recipient to seek others' views on the subject

FIGURE 10–11 Sample Budget Calculations

Person	Cohort	FTE%	Weeks	Hours (40/wk)	Billing Rate	Budget
Officer in charge	OFF-E	20	8	64	$520	$ 33,280
Handling Manager	P2	50	8	160	440	70,400
Job Manager	SA2	100	8	320	435	107,200
Team	A3	100	8	320	270	86,400
Team	A1	100	8	320	190	60,800
Team	A1	100	4	160	190	30,400
Team	C1	100	4	160	135	21,600

Subtotal Fees	$410,080
Contingency 10%	41,000
Total Budget Fees	$451,080
Expenses (% of Fees) 20%	90,000
Total Budget	$541,080

Time and Expense Tracking, Reporting, and Management

Throughout the engagement, the project manager should be tracking incurred professional time and expenses against the budget. Typically, project team members will file periodic time and expense reports in formats established by the consulting firm, and the finance and administrative function accumulates them and produces reports that the project manager can use to track them, and also to ensure that time and expenses were not charged in error to the project. The project manager should also ensure that team members file time and expense reports promptly, as late ones may hide the existence of a budget overrun. Figure 10–12 shows a sample reconciliation of actual to budget results, and illustrates the value of building a contingency reserve into the budget.

The project manager should report immediately to the engagement leader any significant deviations of actual time and expense charges from budget, which may require revisions to the work plan or renegotiations with the client on fees for the project.

Billing and Closing a Contract

Procedures for billing a client will be laid out in the engagement letter. If the engagement is a fixed-fee contract, the engagement letter may specify a payment schedule. Alternatively, the client might be billed monthly in advance for an estimate of time and expenses to be charged to project during that month.

All bills submitted to the client must typically be approved by the engagement leader, although the project manager may handle the details of assembling and delivering them. The bills usually contain very little detail, often only a single figure for professional fees and expenses, or a single breakdown between the two. However, clients have the right to audit bills and examine the detailed records supporting them. Payments by the client are generally sent to the consulting firm's finance and administrative function, which records the payments on the contract and reflects them on reports to the engagement leader and project manager.

At the end of an engagement, the contract must be closed. A final bill is submitted with a reconciliation of actual expenses to estimated, if the client has been billed for expenses as a percentage of fees. The project manager should follow whatever administrative procedures are laid down by the consulting firm for recording the contract as closed in the firm's records.

As the discussion in this chapter has shown, managing a consulting project is a complex task, involving many different kinds of responsibilities. The presence of a skilled project manager is a vital factor in the success of a consulting engagement.

FIGURE 10-12 Reconciliation of Budget to Actual Results

Person	Cohort	FTE%	Weeks	Hours (40/wk)	Billing Rate	Actual	Budget	Variance
Officer in charge	OFF-E	20	8	64	$520	$ 33,280	$ 33,280	$ 0
Handling Manager (Paris)	P2	50	8	160	**455**	72,800	70,400	2,400
Job Manager Postappraisal	SA3	100	4	160	365	58,400	53,600	4,800
Job Manager Preappraisal	SA2	100	4	160	335	53,600	53,600	0
Team	A3	100	8	320	270	86,400	86,400	0
Team	A1	100	8	320	190	60,800	60,800	0
Team	A1	100	6	240	190	45,600	30,400	15,200
Team	C1	100	6	240	135	32,400	21,600	10,800
Subtotal Fees						$443,280	$410,080	$33,200
Contingency					10%	0	41,000	(41,000)
Total Budget Fees						$443,280	$451,080	($ 7,800)
Expenses (% of Fees)					20%	96,000	90,000	6,000
Total Budget						$539,280	$541,080	($ 1,800)

175

PART

III

Executing Engagements

The previous section explored the ways that consultants structure problems and communicate results. A critical part of the consulting process centers on the collection and analysis of data: The causal and systemic hypotheses articulated in the initial conceptualization phase have to be tested against real data before credible recommendations to the client can be made. The treatment of data is important enough to warrant its own section, because gathering and analyzing data is a critical skill for consultants, not only for coming to conclusions but also for driving change.

In Chapters 11 and 12, Ron Carucci and Toby Tetenbaum provide a diagnostic approach to data collection and project execution. In Chapter 11, they describe the principal research methods that consultants depend on to gather data about the client company from key informants, and about the company's competitors and other aspects of its environment. Carucci and Tetenbaum emphasize that consultants rely heavily on observation, on interviews, and on survey instruments to pull together the necessary diagnostic information from which they can make recommendations. In Chapter 12, the authors address how to design interventions that leverage the appropriate elements of the client system in order to induce change. They explain the four key points of leverage that Mercer-Delta uses in its consulting process: the client company's leadership, its management practices, its organizational context, and employee behaviors. All consultants rely on a mix of these elements as they seek to drive their clients to change.

In Chapter 13, Robert Neiman examines closely the barriers to change that they face when they work with clients. Bob frequently teaches the art of consulting, and in a recent lecture at the Stern School of New York University he offered the case study of "the closet consultant"—a consultant whose job involves helping people reorganize their often disorganized closets. As he pointed out, many such consultants fail: They build beautiful shelves and elegant hanging spaces, and leave the client with a seemingly organized closet—only to return six months later and find the new closets again in disarray. The reason? The consultant failed to change the behaviors of the client which led to having messy closets in the first place. Bob's chapter identifies common blocks to successful implementation, and argues that having a "results orientation" from the start is the approach most likely to produce positive change.

If you're lucky enough to have survived the conceptual and diagnostic phases of a consulting project, at some point you'll be ready to make recommendations and will have to find a way to tell your client what they are. That means communicating, often by means of formal or informal presentations. In Chapter 14, Bob Lillien and Copie Harris tackle head on the often terrifying prospect of giving presentations. They share valuable advice on how to package a set of consulting recommendations and deliver them via a persuasive presentation that will lead to change. Most recommendations get presented: sometimes to individual clients and sponsors of a project, often to small groups of managers, and other times to larger forums with many of the client's employees in attendance. A good consultant will *not* make the same presentation to each group. In each case, careful thought must be given to the audience, the setting, and the visual support. Presenting is no easy skill—it takes tons of practice, if it's ever really mastered at all. There are elements of both careful rehearsal and theatrical improvisation—what Lillien and Harris call "passion"—in all good consulting presentations.

As all the chapters in Part III contend, the "endgame" for every consultant is generating change in ways that enhance the client's performance. Having clear and agreed upon measures of success from the start is essential for ensuring the success of any engagement. Gathering data, managing change processes, and giving presentations are all simply means to the desired end: positive results and demonstrable improvement.

CHAPTER 11

Gathering Data
and Diagnosing Situations

Toby J. Tetenbaum and Ron Carucci

Data collection may well be the most important phase of the consulting process. When conducted well, data gathering reveals the core issues plaguing the organization and hints at the interventions that will be required to successfully address these issues. The quality of the consultant's data—based on questions asked, listening skills, and analytic ability to make sense of what was heard—impacts the success of all that follows.

The topic of data collection is broad. In this chapter, we provide an overview of key methods and issues. We look at the context surrounding data collection and at variables that influence the quality of the data obtained. We explore differences between four primary methods for collecting data; namely, interviews, observations, documents, and questionnaires/surveys. Finally, we end with a discussion of how data analysis can lead to strategies for intervention. Readers are encouraged to pursue more detailed discussions provided in the books referenced in the bibliography.

THE CONTEXT OF DATA COLLECTION

Data collection takes place in an organization that has a unique history and culture. Data are gathered from people whose attitudes and behaviors reflect that history and culture. Sometimes a consultant's efforts are welcome; often, they are not. As a consultant, expect to face *resistance* and allocate time to building the *rapport* you will need to get rich and accurate data.

Resistance   Despite having a client who has asked for your help in dealing with a problem, don't be surprised to meet resistance when you ask permission to collect data. Clients generally believe that they understand their problems and, therefore, may view your desire to collect data as redundant or, worse, if you are an external consultant, as a way to pad your bill. A good consultant tries to convey the sense that,

Toby J. Tetenbaum is President of Toby Tetenbaum Associates, a consulting firm specializing in organizational behavior. A licensed psychologist, she is a professor at Fordham University, where she directs the Human Resource Education Master's Degree Program.

Ron Carucci is a Partner with Mercer-Delta Consulting, a management consulting firm that provides services related to the management of strategic organizational change to major corporations. He is a faculty member at Fordham University Graduate School, serving as an associate professor of organizational behavior in the Human Resource Education Program.

while you appreciate that the client may have a good handle on the situation, everyone has blind spots and it is extraordinarily difficult to be objective and observant in one's own arena. It is important to push back on the sponsor, since rarely is the presented problem the real one and even more rarely is the leader's role in the problem explored. It is up to the consultant to plumb the depths for the real problem and to identify its root causes.

Expect resistance also from the individuals from whom you seek information. Employees are increasingly bombarded with surveys, interviews, and focus groups as companies seek to obtain information for due diligence in mergers and acquisitions, to understand worsening retention issues, and to monitor morale. Rarely do these employees get to see the results or to experience any significant changes as a consequence of these results, leading them to feel exploited when asked to provide information to employers. As a consultant, remember that you are probably just one more person in a long line of individuals seeking information from them, so do not be surprised if they are reluctant to provide it. In addition, recognize that individuals may be loath to disclose their true feelings or to surface issues for fear of reprisal should the promised confidentiality and anonymity not be maintained. This is particularly true in highly political systems in which untouchables and undiscussables are well-established, and collusive silence is the norm.

Rapport To obtain cooperation, to elicit open and honest responses, and to gain meaningful data leading to problem identification and solution, you will have to build rapport with the client. Whether you are asking people to complete a questionnaire or to engage in a one-hour interview, you will need to connect with them and build trust. The best way to do this is through respect and through the ability to convey understanding without judgment. You are asking people for their help. However they present themselves and however they respond, you owe them respect. Be up front with them. Tell them why you are there, what information you will be seeking, who will see the data, and how it will be used. Keep it simple and be straightforward. Do not promise anything you cannot deliver. Maintain a professional attitude throughout the process. You are not a friend, you are a consultant, which means you should maintain a certain distance, professionalism, and objectivity at all times.

Choosing the Right Approach

There are two basic approaches to data collection:

1. *Deductive:* The deductive approach begins with a hypothesis and seeks evidence to support or refute that hypothesis. It relies heavily on quantitative data. A major advantage of the deductive approach is that the resultant data are easily aggregated for analysis. A major drawback is that the design lens emanates from the consultant and may not capture the reality of the situation as perceived by the people experiencing it.

2. *Naturalistic:* The naturalistic approach is inductive. Here the consultant tries to make sense of the situation from the participants' point of view, without imposing preexisting expectations. The approach is fluid and subject to modification as the process moves along and as new information is obtained. Patterns, categories, and dimensions emerge throughout the data gathering process and are not presumed in advance. The naturalistic approach relies more on qualitative methods of data collection, and so typically obtains more rich, open-ended, and detailed information from respondents. Often, however, voluminous data are

CHAPTER 11   Gathering Data and Diagnosing Situations   **181**

obtained, and the nonsystematic, nonstandardized approach makes data analysis more difficult.

Each approach has advantages and disadvantages. Understanding the trade-offs means a consultant must move carefully in planning and implementing a project, thoughtfully weighing different data collection strategies in light of the consulting objective. Often, clients favor a more deductive approach because they believe they understand the nature of the problem and merely want consultants to confirm their suspicions. In general, however, consultants should be more open-minded about what is occurring in the client's world, and so should take a more naturalistic approach to data collection.

MAJOR DATA COLLECTION TECHNIQUES

Table 11–1 describes five major techniques consultants use to gather data in the client organization: interviews, focus groups, observation, documentation, and questionnaires. Each technique has its own strengths and weaknesses. Using multiple methods increases the reliability and validity of the data the consultant obtains, and provides a fuller understanding of the client's situation.

THE INTERVIEW

The interview is the consultant's most commonly used technique for data collection. An interview is a purposeful conversation, usually conducted between two people face to face, in which an interviewer poses a series of questions to gather information from a respondent in his or her own words. Interviews can be more or less structured.

Unstructured interviews are used primarily when there is a single interviewer and little need to standardize questions across different interviewers. It is also used when an interviewer wants to understand the meanings of events and interactions from the client's point of view and does not presume to know what things mean to the people being questioned. Questions cannot be predetermined since doing so would force the consultant's lens onto the situation. In unstructured settings, the interviewer has considerable latitude to pursue a range of topics and to follow the respondent's lead. The consultant often creates new questions as new themes arise. The content, sequence, and wording of questions therefore evolve as the interview evolves.

Note that unstructured interviews are not aimless conversations. Considerable investigative skill is required of the interviewer to unearth a client's personal understanding of events and situations. Think of it as a funnel: The consultant initially casts a wide net to elicit clues from the client about how to proceed. As the conversation unfolds, the consultant constantly reviews what the client is saying and decides how to proceed. As time goes by, a skillful interviewer's questions become more targeted and specific.

The advantage of the unstructured interview is that it reveals the actual meaning of the situation to the participant untainted by the interviewer's biases, assumptions, and interpretations. The disadvantage is that interviews are time consuming and produce massive amounts of data that are not easily digested and require skillful interpretation.

In contrast, the *structured or standardized* interview is typically used when several interviewers are collecting data at different sites, and data have to be pooled and

TABLE 11–1 Advantages and Disadvantages of Data Collection Techniques

Interviews	Focus Groups	Observations	Documentation	Questionnaires
Advantages				
• Can motivate the respondent and enlist cooperation.	• Can obtain many points of view from a variety of individuals in a small amount of time.	• Can gain an understanding of the context and of how people operate in the system.	• Can provide good, objective evidence.	• Economical means of collecting a lot of information from a large number of people in a short time.
• Can address large range of subjects and issues.	• Can produce rich data when members stimulate one another into a good discussion.	• Can learn things participants may be unwilling to talk about in an interview.	• Gets "behind the scenes" to understand how things came into being.	• Can cover a wide range of topics.
• Allows free expression. Can produce rich data.	• May itself be a useful intervention. Has the potential for increasing motivation to make changes since participation in the interviews establishes a readiness to utilize the data provided.	• Can help confirm or disconfirm what has been learned through interviews.	• Provides an unobtrusive measure so there is no reactivity.	• Affords anonymity so people who are likely to disclose "undiscussables."
• Flexible. Can pursue new avenues of inquiry as needed.		• Can capture events in real time rather than as retrospective.	• Is an inexpensive approach to obtaining data that may have been expensive to collect.	• Easily quantifiable; easily summarized.
• Can clarify if respondent does not understand the question or interviewer is not clear on the response.		• Can access things that escape the conscious awareness of those who work at the site.	• Enables tracking of changes over time.	• Useful in making comparisons across groups.
• Can probe deeper and for more information.	• Economical. Saves time and money.	• Can witness interpersonal dynamics.	• Doesn't demand the time of others.	• Can be self-administered by mail or on-line. Can also be administered by telephone.
• Can observe nonverbal behavior.				• Requires little skill to administer.
• Can surface sensitive information.				• People can work at their own speed.
• Can access inner states: intentions, feelings, meanings.				• Can produce timely feedback.

Disadvantages

• Dependent upon interviewer's skill developing rapport and listening. • Takes time, money, and effort. • Typically reaches few people. • Can get unwanted interviewer effects (physical characteristics like race and gender or personality traits like attitudes and opinions). • Can get unwanted respondent effects (social desirability and acquiescence). • Can get unwanted effects from the questions (wording, sequencing). • Can be difficult to code and interpret. • Cannot be anonymous.	• Individuals may dominate air time or have strong influence over group members, constraining the discussion in the direction they choose. • Individuals may not trust others in the room to maintain confidentiality; therefore, may not join in discussion or may carefully monitor their contribution.	• Only gets at external behavior, not internal (e.g., what the person thinks, feels, etc.). • Potential sampling bias owing to selective perception by the observer. • Potential reactivity to the presence of observer. • Access to some situations may be difficult to obtain. • Requires skill to follow what's happening in a group, especially where past history and hidden agendas may provide misleading data. • Data can prove difficult to code and interpret. • Expensive	• Limited by what is available and public. Can present a problem in locating and gaining access to the material. • Materials not always comparable for comparison purposes. Past data collections don't always match exactly what you'd like to ask, wording may be wrong for your purposes, or people in the study may not be a good comparison group. • Can be incomplete, inaccurate, and selective.	• Often fails to gather rich data as questions get paired down for clarity and readability. • Limited opportunity for free expression by respondent. • Respondent may misinterpret the question and provide unusable data. • Poor vehicle to get at behavior. • Relies heavily on retrospection. • No opportunity for follow-up. • Requires some psychometric and statistical knowledge to develop and analyze correctly. • Can have low response rate, introducing bias. • Don't always have respondents' commitment. • Don't always know who filled it out. • Time consuming to develop.

compared. It relies on a prepared protocol in which questions, sequencing, and wording are fixed. Structured interviews reduce interviewer effects and ensure that the same information is gathered from lots of people. A major disadvantage is that interviewers cannot pursue topics or issues that were not anticipated.

What Questions to Ask?

There are many organizational topics that consultants may want information about from clients. Most interviews typically ask questions about some of the following:

Vision, mission, objectives	Structures, policies	Leadership
Issues facing the group	Traditions, values, history	Decision making
Problems and concerns	Assumptions about the future	Problem solving
Strategies	Scenarios of desired futures	Authority and power
Interpersonal relationships	Organization/group culture	Communication
Relations among subgroups	Conflict management	Work norms
Status, gender differences	Behavioral norms	Work processes

Asking good questions is perhaps the most arduous part of the interview process. Good open-ended questions are simply difficult to write. It may look easy when you see someone else do it, but proves extremely challenging when you try it yourself. The primary piece of advice in writing good interview questions is to try to keep them as open-ended as possible to encourage the full and open expression of the respondent. A sample interview schedule can be found in Table 11–2. It contrasts the questions that inexperienced and experienced interviewers might ask. Note that the questions posed by the inexperienced interviewer are more likely to get one-word responses such as "Yes," "No," "Sometimes," or "Somewhat" that provide little information. Those posed by the more experienced interviewer call for respondents to articulate opinions.

In developing questions, the first consideration is the content area to be explored. These could include the following:

- Experiences, interactions, behaviors. *If I followed you on a typical day, what would I observe?*
- Knowledge. *What does value proposition mean? How do you create value in your business?*
- Opinion. *What do you _think_ about . . . how the U.S. government handled the Elian Gonzales case?*
- Feelings. *How do you _feel_ about . . . how the U.S. government handled the Elian Gonzales case?*
- Value. *What is the most meaningful aspect of your work?*
- Sensory. *What would I see when I enter the lobby of your company's corporate headquarters?*
- Demographics or background characteristics of the respondent. *What is your position in the organization? How long have you held that position?*

Although it is difficult to generalize, good interviewers generally observe the following prescriptions:

1. **Make questions value-neutral to avoid cueing the respondent's opinion.** For example, ask "What do you think about the new policy on work–family?" rather than "How does the new policy on work–family simplify your life?"

TABLE 11–2 A Sample Interview Schedule

Background

You are a consultant to a business unit whose leader has recently established a new strategy for growth that relies heavily on innovation. She asks you to interview a random group of people throughout her organization to learn what you can about their readiness for the changes. Try to keep your questions broad and open-ended to get the respondent's perceptions.

Inexperienced Interviewer	Experienced Interviewer
1. Does your business unit have a strategy for growth?	1. What is your business unit's strategy for growth?
2. Were you involved in setting the strategy?	2. What was your role in setting the unit's strategy?
3. Did your involvement make you more committed?	3. How do you feel about this?
4. Are you receiving training in methods of creativity and innovation?	4. What do you personally do to be more innovative?
5. Are diverse types of people put on the team?	5. How is the composition of your team determined?
6. Is your team conflict averse?	6. Describe a conflict that arose on your team and how it got resolved.
7. Are people who have different ideas accepted by the group?	7. How does your business unit view mavericks?
8. Do you have the time and people you need for the project?	8. What resources do you need to accomplish your objectives?
9. List three good things about your new strategy.	9. How will the new strategy lead to greater innovation?
10. List three bad things about your new strategy.	10. What might prevent the new strategy from producing greater innovation?
11. Do you think this project will succeed?	11. What will it take for this project to succeed?
12. Does your leader model innovative behavior?	12. What are some of the innovative things your leader has done?

2. **Avoid closed-ended, particularly dichotomous, questions.** Asking a stream of questions such as "Do you . . .," "Did you . . .," or "Have you . . ." not only fails to elicit rich data, it also can begin to feel like an interrogation.

3. **Make assumptions.** Instead of asking "Have you used the new policy?," assume the respondent has used it and ask, "What are some of the ways you've used the new policy?"

4. **Develop one idea at a time.** Make sure your question contains only one idea so the respondent doesn't get confused about what you're asking and you don't get confused about what the client is answering. For example, separate the three questions asked in this single question: "What telecommuting regulations work for you, which have been obstacles, and what would you recommend doing about them?"

5. **Avoid jargon.** When you want to get at the meaning of a situation from the respondent's point of view, avoid expressions like *continuous improvement* or *empowerment*. Find out what terms the respondents use in describing their work and the organization, then try to use their language in the interview.

Once written, questions have to be organized in ways that make sense to the respondent, are easy to follow, keep the level of motivation and cooperation high, and do not threaten the respondent. Avoid collecting demographic information up front: Those questions are too trivial and responses to them too brief, and it sets a bad model for the rest of the interview. At the same time, avoid starting with questions that put the respondent on the defensive. Asking "How often have you lied to your boss about something?" could shut down the respondent completely. Begin with noncontroversial behaviors, activities, and events. These require minimal recall and interpretation. Then move on to questions dealing with interpretations, opinion, and feelings. Keep demographic questions to a minimum and place them at the end of the interview. It is probably best to order the time frame as present, past, future. Questions about the present are easiest and most reliable. Questions about the past are subject to recall problems. Questions about the future require speculation.

The Interview Process

Skillful interviewing involves establishing rapport with the respondent, asking difficult questions, probing for answers, recording responses, and exiting.

Establishing Rapport   The respondents are typically unpaid for the interview—if they are clients, they're generally the ones who are paying! To engage the respondent, consultants typically spend time on the front end to establish a bond and build trust. They take the time to explain what the study is about, how respondents were selected, what the interview will involve, who will receive the data, how it will be used, and how confidentiality will be maintained. In telling respondents the purpose of the study, it is wise to speak in broad terms so as not to predispose them to what you want to find. To generate full and honest responses in an interview, interest, cooperation, and rapport must be sustained throughout the interview, and renewed with each question.

Questioning   Once rapport is established, you can ease in with important but nonthreatening questions. Start with a broad question and progressively narrow to specific points. Throughout the questioning, maintain respect for the respondent. You are asking for his perspective and he is giving it to you, so never judge the respondent's comments, whatever you might think of them. Keep all verbal and nonverbal behavior value neutral.

Probing   Not all respondents will be articulate. Some will have difficulty putting their thoughts into words; others will be unclear or give incomplete answers. Sometimes a respondent will misunderstand the question and other times you will not understand the answer. There will also be times when respondents are reluctant to "tell all" either because they fear not looking good or don't trust your promise of confidentiality and fear organizational repercussions. In all cases, you will need to follow up the question with probes. Good probing can generate additional information, deepen the response to the question, and encourage the respondent to keep talking. They include the following:

- Nod your head or say "uh-huh." This can be the best encouragement.
- Ask neutral questions:
  Could you tell me more about that?
  Are there any other reasons?
  Could you give me more detail?

- Make neutral comments:

  I'm beginning to get the picture.

  I see. I think I'm beginning to understand.

- Pause. Use this when you feel the respondent has more to say. Remaining silent allows respondents to gather their thoughts.

Probing for additional information, particularly early in an interview session, cues the respondent that more complete responses are expected. Other probes are designed to clarify responses, particularly when they are ambiguous or appear to be non sequiturs. Clarifying questions include:

What do you mean? Could you explain that?

Could you give me an example?

I'm not sure I understand. Could you elaborate?

What you're saying is important and I want to be sure I get exactly what you mean, so could you repeat what you said?

Recording Responses   When you analyze and present the data, people's exact words are highly persuasive in validating your findings, so you will want to use the respondent's exact words, grammar, and colloquialisms—so long as they do not uniquely identify the respondent. Try not to merely summarize or paraphrase the respondent's words, as this can distort the response. The best way to ensure accuracy is by recording verbatim comments. It is important, however, to ask the respondent's permission to make a permanent record of an interview.

A pragmatic note: If a respondent permits the use of a taping device, make sure to have enough batteries, an electric cord, and prelabeled cassettes. Even if you use a tape recorder, however, take complete notes. The one time you don't will be the time the device didn't work. Recognize too that eventually tapes will have to be transcribed—an onerous job. One cassette can take four hours to transcribe and equate to 20 to 40 typewritten pages.

Generally, notes taken during an interview are incomplete. It is always helpful to fill in the gaps immediately after the interview before the freshness of the experience escapes you. Skilled interviewers know that memory is notoriously vulnerable to interceding events, and never put off the task. Take the opportunity to also add in your own impressions, making sure to keep them separate from the respondent's actual words.

Exiting   When you are done, thank them for their time, and make sure they leave feeling good about the interview.

Factors Affecting the Validity of Interviews

Various social factors can influence the validity of the data a consultant can obtain from interviews. They include:

Social Desirability   Most people want to be perceived in a favorable light and so they tend to respond to interview questions in ways that will win them approval. This is particularly true when the questions pertain to beliefs and values. For example, in the American culture, loving children and working hard are "good," whereas admitting to not voting in a presidential election or to harboring a prejudice toward a particular group are "bad." A skilled interviewer will work to word questions in such a manner that social desirability is minimized.

Interviewer Bias   Two forms of interviewer bias can seep into the process. First, it is probable that you will have an expectation of what you will learn and what the research will produce. Second, after a short period of time, you are likely to form an impression of the respondent that leads to unconsciously anticipating and filling in the blanks. The most difficult part of good interviewing is to keep your own expectations and impressions at bay so the words, intentions, and tone of the respondent can truly be heard. What is wanted is an understanding of the problem from the respondent's point of view, unfiltered by you, the interviewer.

Focusing on Asking Questions Rather Than Listening to Answers   There is a tendency for neophyte interviewers to rush through the questions to ensure that all of the questions on the prepared interview schedule get asked. Try to keep focused on listening because that is the only way to know what questions to move on to, to determine whether you understand the response or need to clarify it, and to know if the answer is complete or needs to be probed. Sometimes the respondent will provide an answer that covers considerable territory. When you don't listen carefully, you can end up asking questions that have already been answered.

Assuming an Understanding   It is very easy to assume an understanding of a respondent's vocabulary or intention. For example, it's easy to believe we know what someone means when they talk about "empowerment" or "feedback." But any time a respondent uses a term or concept, they should be asked to clarify what they mean and, even more clarifying, to provide an example.

Lapsing into Closed Questions   The richest data is obtained through open-ended questions but this is easier to understand than it is to do. It takes considerable preparation and practice to maintain a high level of open-ended questioning. Neophytes typically dissolve into closed-ended questions rapidly. The problem with this is that closed-ended questions elicit one-word responses. This leads to the need for probing, which, if the probe is closed-ended, calls for another probe and an undesirable pattern is established. Practice questions beginning with How and What and focus on eliminating those that begin with Did, Is, or Would.

Filling Silence   Many people are uncomfortable with silence during a conversation and therefore jump in to fill the void. This is particularly detrimental during an interview. Understand that respondents need time to think about their answers. Not everyone responds immediately, so allow people time to think. Also, leaving pauses conveys that you are looking for thoughtful, rich, complete responses.

Losing Professional Distance   It is difficult to maintain the balance between professional objectivity and personal warmth that gains rapport and supports good disclosure by the respondent, but this balance is essential. Some respondents view the interviewer as a vehicle to bring a message back to the boss or merely to vent about things that displease them. At these times, you should remain neutral, treating the discussion as just more data. Never participate or collude with the comments.

Losing Control of the Interview   Sometimes the venting goes on and on. First, try returning the conversation to the topic. If this is not effective, turn off the tape recorder or stop taking notes. This signals the respondent that the venting will not be part of the official interview. Sometimes this stops the outpouring, and other times it does not.

When it doesn't, it is sometimes necessary to let the respondent get it all out or the interview can't proceed. When you think the venting has run its course, turn the tape back on or pick up your pen and pad and move to the next question.

Another way you might lose control of the interview is with a highly verbal respondent who gets off track. At these times, stop nodding, stop taking notes, interject a new question when the respondent pauses for breath, or, if necessary, interrupt and say, "Let me stop you for a moment. I hear you saying . . ." Then succinctly sum up what the respondent has said and move onto the next question.

Improving Interviewing Skills

Given the importance of interviewing to consultants, it's useful to build skill in this area. There are two excellent ways to improve your interviewing skills. First, listen closely to people who conduct interviews for a living on television: Barbara Walters, Larry King, Bryant Gumbel, the staff at *60 Minutes*, Geraldo Rivera, any of the Sunday morning public interest interviews. Compare and contrast interview styles. Listen to how they word questions, when they use probes, what they pick up on. Second, interviewing is both art and skill, so practice is essential. Interview your family regarding their history. Interview your friends about topics of interest to them and to you. Then move out to people you know less well and get to know them, working to develop your rapport-building skills. No one is an effective interviewer his or her first time out.

Focus Groups—A Special Instance of Interviews

The focus group generally involves simultaneous interviewing of 7 to 10 people. Group members interact with one another as well as with the interviewer. Lots of information gets elicited from focus groups because people build upon one another's comments, ideas, and feelings.

As the leader of a focus group discussion, a consultant's job is to raise broad questions, guide the discussion, ensure all participants have the opportunity to respond, invite quieter members into the discussion, and record all responses on a flipchart or on a computer with overhead projection that is visible to the group as a whole. This serves as a record of the conversation and keeps the group focused on the question.

Focus groups are used in many different ways. In most cases, the idea is to bring together a group of people that represent a larger population of interest. It may be a group of customers or suppliers. It may also be a mix of employees. In general, it is best to avoid bringing together focus groups of employees in which managers are also expected to participate.

OBSERVATION

Interviews do not always provide complete and accurate information. Fallible memories, selective perceptions, social desirability, political considerations, and simply being too close to the situation are but a few reasons participants, even with good intentions, do not always contribute the best data. To validate what you have been told and to flesh out your picture of what is going on, it is wise to collect data from another source. An effective second source of data comes from observations of the participants in their setting.

Observations involve looking at the actual behavior of an organization's members as they go about accomplishing their tasks and noting how they work together. Examples might include: observing a team involved in problem solving, shadowing a manager throughout her day, attending a stockholder's meeting. As Yogi Berra once noted, "You can observe a lot just by watching." The purpose of observational data is to describe the setting, the activities that took place in that setting, the people who participated in those activities, and the meanings of the setting, the activities, and their participation to those people.

The seemingly simple act of observing is actually a highly complex act comprised of myriad decisions: What should be observed? How should it be observed? Who should be observed? When should the observation take place and how long should the observation last? How and what should be recorded?

Observational techniques range on a continuum. At one extreme, the consultant notes any and all behaviors which are open-ended, unspecified. At the other extreme, the consultant decides on a set of specific behaviors to observe and they are narrowly defined.

Systematic Observation   When observation is used to answer a specific question, it must be systematic—the approach must be deliberate, planned, organized, and methodical. The observer seeks out only that which addresses the key question and engages in active interpretation of what he or she observes.

Nonsystematic Observation   Here the observer tries to determine the meaning of the situation and events to the participants. Thus, anything can constitute data until a specific focus develops.

Observers can also play one of two roles:

1. *Participant observer.* A participant observer participates in the life and activities of the group in order to develop an insider's view of what is happening. Although many consultants take a highly active role in their client's activities, and are often on-site on a regular basis, most consultants prefer to maintain a separate role and to take an objective stance.

2. *Nonparticipant observer.* The nonparticipant observer strives to be unobtrusive, that is, to alter as little as possible the ongoing life of the group, department, or company under observation in order to understand it on the participants' own terms.

Sampling Observations: What and When to Observe

Most companies are too complex to be able to observe or record everything people do. Therefore, one of the first tasks a consultant must decide is to develop a sampling plan with two components: event sampling (what to observe) and time sampling (when to observe and for how long).

Event Sampling   There are many decisions the consultant must make, including what locations to sample (cafeteria, entry lobby, elevator, conference room), who to observe at that location (an intact work team, regional sales managers), and what activities to focus on (interactions between bosses and their subordinates, learning opportunities in the workplace). Events are natural and lifelike and can be observed as a complete entity. Time sampling might not capture the entire event and, if the event is a rare occurrence, might miss it altogether.

Time Sampling   Behaviors can be observed at different points in time and for different duration. They can be selected in systematic units (three 5-minute observations at specified times say, every two hours) or randomly (five 5-minute observation periods selected at random from a specified universe of 5-minute periods). While behaviors that occur infrequently might not be captured when time sampling is used, the technique has the advantage of increasing the probability of obtaining representative samples of behavior.

As Table 11-3 shows, event and time sampling can be combined. For example, if you have hypothesized that this is a very bureaucratic company and that bureaucracy is stifling initiative, you might want to observe managers' behaviors in departmental meetings. You can draw a random sample of all meetings being held throughout the company at different times and observe all interactions that take place during those meetings. The objective of these observations is to collect sufficient evidence to ensure the final description is as accurate as possible, and the conclusion is justified.

Recording Observations

The data obtained from observations can be recorded as either narratives or as categories.

Narratives   The purpose of a narrative is to obtain a detailed description of an event or behavior in order to understand it from the actors' points of view. Consultants who rely on narratives cast a wide lens in both what they observe and what they record. Principles or patterns of behavior are derived from analysis of the data after the observations are made and recorded, not during data collection.

In the narrative approach, consultants themselves are the primary instruments of observation. This means that the data will only be as good as the consultant's perceptual skills. The consultant typically takes "field notes"—written records that capture in everyday language actions, behaviors, and events. Typically, the consultant records those observations in descriptive terms only (e.g., "the manager asked team members to suggest next steps, then had them rank order their listing into priorities."). They are not interpreted (e.g., "the manager empowered his employees"). Interpreting behavior is difficult and can produce disagreement among observers. Rigor depends on separating description from interpretation, although you can work back and forth between them to generate insight and direction for your next set of observations.

Skillful consultants construct narratives by recording their observations as completely as possible, including direct quotes from the actors. They don't rely on their ability to recall things later; instead, they reserve time to reflect on their observations, fill in the gaps in their note-taking while their memory is still fresh, and jot down additional thoughts, feelings, reactions, and interpretations about what they observed.

Categories   Consultants also frequently classify their observations using a finite set of predefined categories. There are usually fewer than 10 categories, each limited in scope and explicitly listing the relevant behaviors so that observers can classify them promptly and with relative ease. In this case, the consultant is only trying to identify and record those behaviors that fall into the predefined categories; no new categories are added.

Reactivity as a Factor Affecting the Validity of Observations

One serious limitation to observations as a methodology lies in the fact that the mere presence of the observer can change the nature of what occurs. This is called *reactivity,* and it affects the validity of what you are studying. People may behave quite differ-

TABLE 11-3 Observation Checklist

Time and Event Sampling of a Leader's Communications

Directions: Observe the leader at the meeting in 5-minute intervals with 3 minutes between observations for a total of 21 minutes altogether (5 on, 3 off, 5 on, 3 off, 5 on). Place a check each time the behavior listed under Item is observed.

Item	Meeting 1			Meeting 2			Meeting 3		
1. Makes a declarative statement.									
2. Asks a question									
3. Elaborates									
4. Rephrases (own statement)						.			
5. Rephrases (other's statement)									
6. Clarifies (own statement)									
7. Clarifies (other's statement)									
8. Issues an order									
9. Interrupts									

ently when they know they are being observed compared with how they behave if they are not aware of being observed. At the very least, reactivity suggests that the observer should attempt to be unobtrusive so that people in the setting aren't overly aware of being observed or, worse, of being judged.

When possible, unobtrusive measures are desirable means for collecting data since they are non-reactive. For example, a funded program to improve sanitary behavior of immigrant pre-school children measured the consumption of toilet paper over time. In another example, a company observed the wear and tear on hallway carpet to determine the use of particular facilities. The disadvantage of using unobtrusive measures is that you might find it difficult to identify a good measure of what you're looking for and, when you find it, it might be difficult to understand what's indicated.

ARTIFACTS/DOCUMENTS/ARCHIVES

A third rich source of information frequently overlooked is the abundance of preexisting printed materials generally available in any organization. Documents can provide information about the organization and lead to clues about the present problem. Some of these documents are designed for external consumption and to demonstrate the organization's official posture—its face to the world. These include:

Annual reports	Legal documents	Shareholder reports
Formal charters	Official correspondence	Public facts and figures
Press releases	Profit and loss data	Productivity rates

Other documents are designed for internal use, aimed at employees, and represent the formal organization. These include:

Strategic plans	Vision/mission statements	Rules and procedures
Organizational charts	Organizational newsletters	Policy documents
Transcripts of meetings	News/media reports	Codes of ethics
Formal job descriptions	Previous reports	Market data

In addition to these official documents, there are day-to-day materials which provide insight about the informal organization. These include:

People's calendars	Personal documents (e.g.,	Minutes of meetings
Personal letters	diaries kept by participants)	
Meeting agenda memos		

Documents can be compared with data obtained through interviews and observations for confirmation, disconfirmation, and as additional information. They tell you what the organization is doing, what its values are, or what top managers deem important (e.g., what it sets as priorities, what it devotes time to) about the company's chain of command, rules and regulations, and leadership. For example, let's say that in the course of conducting interviews, you learn that the managers believe creativity is important to the future of the company, yet your observations fail to reveal the creative behaviors you expect. Similarly, the vision/mission statement that appears in the annual report speaks to the need for creativity and innovation for sustainable growth, but the informal documents you acquire (e.g., people's calendars, memos, and meeting agendas) indicate that time is spent in very traditional ways which are antithetical to what is required for a creative organization. You might begin to suspect that the notion of being a creative organization is merely an espoused value rather than one that is actually practiced.

QUESTIONNAIRES

A questionnaire is a fully structured method of collecting information directly from the people involved about such things as behaviors, ideas, feelings, motivations, attitudes, values, habits, plans, beliefs, and background (age, education, income). When used in the workplace, questionnaires typically focus on aspects of the job, the organization, management initiatives, employee morale, or specific topics such as incentives or work–family. A carefully developed set of questions is administered in exactly the same format using paper and pencil format or e-mail to a selected group of people (a sample) chosen to represent a larger group of people (a population). An example of questionnaire items can be seen in Table 11–4.

TABLE 11-4 Assessing an MBA Program's Effectiveness—A Sample Questionnaire

For each of the items below, circle the appropriate number.

1. Is your participation in the MBA program sponsored by your company?
     1. Yes
     2. No (Skip to Q. 7)

2. If yes, is your tuition reimbursement dependent upon your grade in the course?
     1. Yes
     2. No

3. What led you to choose ABC University for your MBA?
     1. Reputation of the school
     2. Faculty
     3. Curriculum
     4. Convenience
     5. Price
     6. Other: _____ (please specify)

4. How would you describe the quality of the program?
     1. Excellent
     2. Good
     3. Fair
     4. Poor

5. How satisfied are you with the instructional quality of the faculty?
     1. Very satisfied
     2. Satisfied
     3. Neutral
     4. Dissatisfied
     5. Very dissatisfied

6. Which of the following courses have you completed? (Circle 1 or 2 for each course)

Course	Yes	No
Microeconomics	1	2
Project Management	1	2
Global Affairs	1	2
Entrepreneurship	1	2

In the scales below, rate the degree to which you agree or disagree with each of the following statements by circling the appropriate number.

	Strongly Agree 5	Agree 4	Neither Agree Nor Disagree 3	Disagree 2	Strongly Disagree 1
7. The material taught in class is relevant to my work.	5	4	3	2	1
8. There is a good balance of theory and practice.	5	4	3	2	1
9. The readings are current.	5	4	3	2	1

Designing and Implementing a Questionnaire

There are eight steps to designing and implementing a questionnaire: (1) defining the question domain; (2) determining the type of information sought; (3) writing questions and responses; (4) sequencing questions; (5) designing the cover letter; (6) identifying the sample; (7) piloting and revising the questionnaire; and (8) administering the questionnaire. Each of these steps is described below.

Step 1: What Questions to Ask?

Good questionnaires consist of a well-thought-out arrangement of questions whose domain is clearly defined and organized. Since every concept has a wide range of possible definitions, it's important to carefully define the instrument's boundaries. Only when content and boundaries are set are you ready to write the questions.

Items should be selected from the research literature in the field and from past surveys and questionnaires. To know what's important to a specific organization at any given point in time, most consultants begin by conducting interviews and focus groups, and use the language and data identified in those interviews to write appropriate survey questions.

Step 2: What Kind of Information?

Once the domain is known, the next step in designing the instrument is to determine what information within that domain is sought. Typically this information falls into four areas:

1. **Attitudes.** Attitudes describe people's evaluations, positive or negative, about a particular person, object, or event referred to as the attitude referent. The choices indicate the direction of the respondent's feelings (e.g., good versus bad, desirable versus undesirable).
2. **Beliefs.** Beliefs are assessments of what a person thinks is true or false, or what he or she thinks exists or does not exist. Questions can be used to elicit people's perceptions of past, present, or future reality. It isn't always easy to distinguish between beliefs and attitudes, but then, making the distinction isn't always useful.
3. **Behaviors.** Behavioral questions ask people to describe their own behavior—what they have done in the past, what they are currently doing or what they plan to do in the future. Strictly speaking, questions about behavior are more accurately questions about respondents' *perceptions* of their behavior.
4. **Attributes.** Attributes are personal or demographic characteristics that a person possesses, rather than something he or she does. These include age, education, occupation, income, sex, marital status, family composition, home ownership, race, politics, and religion. Most questionnaires include demographic questions for the purpose of exploring how the other kinds of information (beliefs, attitudes, behaviors) differ for people with different attributes.

Attitude questions tend to be more sensitive to wording variations than questions about behavior and attributes. Slightly different wordings of attitude questions can elicit very different responses. In contrast, people can usually state quite unequivocally whether they have or haven't done something.

It is not necessary to include all four types of questions. It depends on the objectives of the study and the type of information desired.

Step 3: Writing Questions

Writing the items requires decisions as to the question structure (open-ended or closed-ended) and response format (forced choice, checklist, rating scale), sequencing of questions, and knowing how to write good questions.

Structure: Open-Ended Versus Closed-Ended.   Questions can be written in two different formats depending on the nature of response behavior asked of the respondent. With *open-ended questions* respondents must create and articulate their own answers and state them in their own words. For example, questions such as "What is the advantage of permitting causal dress in the workplace?" or "What is the best way to stimulate innovation on the team?" leave the answer up to the respondent. There are no answers provided from which respondents can select their response.

The advantages of open-ended questions include:

1. They allow respondents to express themselves freely.
2. They elicit rich data when measuring complex behaviors.
3. They acknowledge there can be more than one right answer.
4. They are the least threatening type of question.

The disadvantages of open-ended questions include:

1. They are demanding of the respondent who is asked to recall past experiences, reorganize them, and find the words with which to express them.
2. They may prove difficult for people who don't express themselves well in writing.
3. They may result in incomplete, uninterpretable, irrelevant answers or no answer at all.
4. They are difficult to code and analyze.
5. They create difficulty in data analysis since there may not be sufficient mention of any one topic across respondents to do a statistical analysis.

The open-ended format is typically used in exploratory studies when the researcher can't anticipate the various ways in which people are likely to respond to a question. The researcher's main purpose in this instance is to find the most salient aspects of a topic in preparation for developing close-ended questions for a later survey.

Closed-ended questions consist of a stem, which presents either a problem, a statement, question, or situation followed by several alternative choices or solutions. The answers can be offered in one of two formats: ordered choices or unordered choices. In the ordered choice format, each answer is a gradation of a single dimension of some thought or behavior. The respondent's task is to find the most appropriate place on an implied continuum for her response. For example, Question: "How do you feel about the statement: 'Parents should be able to choose the school their children attend.'?" Answer: Choose either Strongly Agree, Mildly Agree, Neither Agree nor Disagree, Mildly Disagree, or Strongly Disagree. The ordered-choice format is well suited to determining such things as intensity of feeling, degree of involvement, and frequency of participation. It is also appropriate where there is a series of attitude or belief questions the researcher plans to combine to form a multiple-item scale and to use for sophisticated statistical analysis.

In the unordered choice format, each choice of answer is an independent alternative. For example, the question: "Which of the following reasons led you to select USC for your graduate degree?" Answer: Choose from: Quality of the faculty, reputation of the school, nature of the curriculum, cost, ease of transportation. It is possible in this format to add the choice of "Other" to include responses not specifically cited.

The advantages of closed-ended questions are:

1. They force the respondent to choose from pre-selected independent alternatives and are, therefore, easier to score than open-ended short-answer questions.
2. They are more reliable in that everyone responds in terms of the same options, providing uniform data.

The disadvantages of closed-ended questions are:

1. They may miss an important answer.
2. They don't give respondents an opportunity to express themselves in their own words.

Writing Good Questions   Writing clear questionnaire items that ask for the exact information the researcher seeks is difficult. Each item takes time and effort along with considerable patience to write and rewrite. Recommendations for writing questionnaire items include:

1. Make questions meaningful to respondents. Keep them concrete and close to the respondent's experiences.
2. Keep the writing as simple as possible. Don't use unnecessarily complex words. This helps keep motivation up and confusion and guessing down.
3. Use standard English. Avoid buzzwords, abbreviations, slang, or jargon. While every occupational group shares a particular vocabulary, don't overestimate the vocabulary of respondents. Jointly design the questionnaire with its sponsors so terminology (as well as key issues and practices) are relevant to the client system. Then, too, pretest with a sample of actual respondents to find the commonly shared vocabulary.
4. Check all questions for clarity. When questions are vague, people interpret the intent in different ways. Vagueness can be in the question (e.g., "Have you ever been ill?"—Does a cold or stomach ache qualify as "ill"?) or the answer (e.g., How often is "regularly"—is it monthly? weekly? daily?).
5. Don't seek overly precise data. For instance, people can't always remember exactly how many times they did something (e.g., borrowed books from the library, attended church).
6. Avoid biased questions that influence the respondent to answer in a manner that doesn't accurately reflect his or her position on the issue under investigation. People don't like to answer questions that appear to them to be slanted in a particular direction (e.g., "Do you think managers will continue to hoard information?").
7. Avoid "loaded" words, some of which are strongly positive (e.g., equality, justice, honesty) and others negative (e.g., bureaucrat, boss). It is not always easy to eliminate affective terminology.
8. Check whether questions are objectionable in being either too personal (e.g., about family income) or self-incriminating (e.g., "Have you ever stolen anything?" "Gotten drunk?" "Engaged in a homosexual act?" "Smoked marijuana?"). Objectionable questions can cause the respondent to refuse to answer the questionnaire. If these are areas you must question, ask people to respond in broad categories as opposed to providing precise information. An indirect approach to obtaining these data is to ask: "How do you feel about people who do it?" versus "Do you do it?" Still another approach to dealing with potentially objectionable questions is to establish a context that softens the impact (e.g., "There are many points of view about capital punishment, both positive and negative. We'd like to know whether you agree or disagree with each." Then present one argument for capital punishment and one against).

9. Avoid merging two questions into one (e.g., "Rate the degree to which you are curious and innovative."). The respondent in this situation is asked to give a single answer to what are actually two questions combined into one. Write separate questions for curious and for innovative.

10. Avoid double negatives (e.g., "Do you agree that people who don't vote are not good citizens?")

11. Check that answer choices are mutually exclusive (e.g., "Check the category that represents your age. Answer options: 15–25, 25–35, 35–45." Categories are not mutually exclusive since ages 25 and 35 appear twice).

12. Don't assume too much knowledge because respondents may become embarrassed at not knowing something that the researcher seems to feel he should know (like the name of the state's senators or the model of the car they own). Rather than admit they don't know, they just check any answer. One solution is to add: "I don't know" to the response options. Only pre-testing can provide a basis for knowing how much knowledge can safely be assumed.

Determining the Best Response Format   There are several alternatives to picking a response format. One approach is forced choice in which the respondent is asked to choose one of two alternatives, for example, Yes–No, Agree–Disagree, True–False. Another format is a checklist, which is similar to multiple choice. For example, asked "Which of the following pharmaceutical companies do you view as most innovative?," response alternatives might include: Bristol Myers Squibb, Merck, Johnson & Johnson, Pfizer, Other. Checklists help remind respondents of some things they might have forgotten; however, the problem is that they might think a choice is familiar when it isn't.

A third common alternative for a response format is the rating scale. Numerical rating scales are the easiest to use. For example, an item might read: How supportive is the manager about a department's new ideas? The responses from which the consultant might choose include: "Extremely Supportive," "Very Supportive," "Supportive," "Somewhat Supportive," "Not at All Supportive." These options can then be converted to numbers: 5, 4, 3, 2, and 1, respectively.

Rating scales are fairly ubiquitous, largely because they are easy to construct and administer, and because they gauge any topic the researcher thinks up. The seeming ease associated with rating scales conceals potential problems that can impact the reliability and validity of the instrument:

- *Absence of definition for both referents and rating categories.* One premise of valid instruments is that items mean the same thing to all raters. Therefore, it is important to define the referents to be rated, or raters will resort to their own definitions. In the earlier example, the referent is a "supportive manager." "Supportive" can mean different things to different people so it should be defined carefully. Similarly, the rating categories are not necessarily interpreted in the same way. For instance, 'frequently,' 'often,' 'occasionally,' and 'sometimes' can not only be interpreted differently by different raters, but can also have different meanings for the same rater in different settings.

- *Lack of empirical tests and psychometric analyses.* A common form of rating scale is the Likert summated-rating scale in which the rater's item scores are summed into a total score. The presumption here is that the items measure the same thing so the addition of multiple items into a single score is justified. This premise should be empirically tested with a pilot sample comprised of subjects similar to those for whom the scale is intended. Their responses should be statistically analyzed using factor analysis, which ensures the unidimensionality (or multidimensionality if that's what's desired) of the instrument. Factor analysis can be used to determine the dimensions underlying relations among a set of items.

Consultants should be aware of a variety of well-documented rater biases when using rating scales and try to avoid them.

- *The halo effect.* A tendency of the observer to rate in a constant direction consistent with his general impressions. If an early impression is positive, the ratings thereafter tend to be positive and, conversely, if the early impression is negative, the ratings thereafter tend to be negative. It's also a human tendency to allow the influence of one characteristic on other characteristics.
- *Leniency/severity.* A tendency by some raters to give ratings that are consistently too high (a leniency effect) or too low (a severity effect).
- *Central tendency.* A tendency by some raters to avoid extreme judgments that leads them to use ratings only in the middle of the scale.

Step 4: Sequencing Questions

The order in which questions are asked is important. The first questions should immediately get right into the topic. A cover letter has indicated the significance of the study and of the respondent's opinions, so it is important not to diminish this sense of urgency by asking for demographic information first. On the other hand, the first questions should be easy to understand and answer. They should also be totally neutral, not leaning toward any position.

After that, questions should be ordered logically and minimize the chances of the answer to one question affecting the content of another. They should also be ordered along a descending gradient of importance from those that the respondent is likely to see as most important to those that would be viewed as least important. Logical order helps respondents think through what they're being asked.

Questions that are similar in content should be grouped together and, within content areas, the same format questions (e.g., all Yes or No, all rating scales) should be grouped together. This makes it easier for the respondent mentally; he or she doesn't need to keep switching from one kind of question to another. Then, logically sequence the groupings.

Since there is no interviewer to motivate the respondent, the order of the questions is important in maintaining the respondent's motivation and avoiding confusion. Certain questions need to be asked either before or after certain others. For instance, put sensitive questions toward the end and position questions that are most objectionable to respondents after ones that are less objectionable. Put relatively easy questions at the end, especially if it's a long survey, when participants may be tired. And, in general, put objective questions before subjective ones, familiar questions before those that might be unfamiliar.

Throughout the questionnaire, there may be items which screen respondents on a particular view or behavior. If the respondent holds that view or has behaved in the defined way, he or she answers the next set of questions. If not, he or she is directed to proceed further along in the questionnaire to another set of questions. The benefit of screen questions is that the respondent is asked to respond only to relevant items. The disadvantage is that the presence of more questions than the respondent is actually expected to answer contributes to the perception of a formidably long questionnaire that may discourage the individual from attempting to complete it. For this reason, if many items are to be skipped, then it is better to design different questionnaires for different categories of respondents.

Step 5: Designing a Cover Letter

Since most questionnaires are completed on a voluntary basis, it is necessary to motivate people to participate. This occurs primarily by means of the appeal presented in the cover letter. Since it precedes the questionnaire, it needs to create a positive first impression. It is the only opportunity the investigator has to tell what the survey is about, to convince the potential respondent the study is useful, and to anticipate and counter any questions the letter's recipient might have.

In attempting to motivate the individual, the investigator should describe the results of the questionnaire as useful to some group with whom the respondent identifies. It should be clear that the respondent isn't doing the investigator a favor; she is helping to solve a problem. There's an assumption that doing something beneficial for a group with which the respondent identifies will be rewarding to the respondent.

It is also possible to include a token incentive as a motivator—a silver dollar, a lottery ticket, a personalized pen. One investigator seeking to learn about her company's technology needs included a screen wipe with the letter.

Along with motivating the individual by providing a description of the purpose of the questionnaire, the cover letter should also include information pertaining to whether the questionnaires will be treated confidentially, whether the respondent will receive a summary of the findings, and how and when the questionnaires should be returned. It should conclude with an expression of appreciation. And all of this should be conveyed in a single page.

Step 6: Identifying the Sample

If information is being sought about a small group, then selecting a sample is not necessary. The consultant surveys the entire population, and thereby eliminates sampling error. However, if the population is large, it will be necessary to draw a sample from that population.

There are two methods of sampling: *probability sampling* and *convenience sampling*. In probability sampling, each person in the population has an equal chance of being selected into the sample. People are selected using a table of random numbers and the resulting sample is said to be representative of the population. In contrast, in convenience sampling, people are chosen serendipitously (the first 10 people to pass the news reporter in the street) or purposively (the top 10 Westinghouse science winners or parents of triplets).

In organizations, convenience samples are often used to develop tentative hypotheses. To paint a complete picture, however, and actually test those hypotheses, random sampling is necessary. So, when accurate information about the opinions of particular subgroups in the company (e.g., senior executives, managers, supervisors, non-exempts, exempts), then stratified random samples should be pulled. Here, the subgroups are identified and a number proportional to their representation in the population randomly selected *within each strata*.

The size of the sample depends on the use to which the data will be put, the time and resources available, and the degree of credibility desired. Sampling always results in some degree of error so the amount of confidence required in the findings determines the sample size; the more critical the issue and the greater the degree of confidence required, the larger the sample.

Step 7: Piloting and Revising the Questionnaire

Once a questionnaire is complete, wise consultants invite others with deep knowledge of the topic and about test construction to take a close look at it. Revisions should be made based on their feedback. It's important then to pretest the revised questionnaire with a pilot sample to identify construction defects and inadequacies. The purpose of a pilot test is to help produce a meaningful questionnaire that will gather the necessary data. It is costly and time consuming to print up and administer a questionnaire with unclear items, confusing sequencing, bad content, and other errors. Since there is no interviewer sitting alongside the respondent to hear problems, the pilot test should invite respondents to provide feedback on items or directions they don't understand. Revise the questionnaire once again, based on what you learn from the pilot test.

Step 8: Administering the Questionnaire

A first step in administering the questionnaire is to notify people in the sample with a letter or e-mail that a questionnaire is coming. The cover letter and questionnaire should then be delivered to these individuals about three days later. The cover letter contains the date respondents are expected to return their questionnaire. One week after the return date, a reminder postcard should be sent which thanks to those who have returned the questionnaire and a courteous reminder to those who have not. Most people who answer questionnaires do so almost immediately after they receive them. Some will put it aside thinking they will complete it at a later time. The follow-up postcard reminds them to do so. Typically, some laggards will respond; few, if any, will respond after that.

Formatting Questionnaires

The appearance of the questionnaire is a critical motivating factor in whether the potential respondent elects to become involved. If the questionnaire appears too long, hard to read, difficult to respond to, boring, or disorganized and confusing, there is little to compel them to participate. The presentation must be aesthetically pleasing and professional right down to quality printing.

The questionnaire should begin with a carefully designed cover letter printed on appropriate letterhead. It should define the purpose of the study, and describe all necessary directions for completing and returning the questionnaire. All sections of the questionnaire should have clear directions as to how to respond. All questions should fit on the page. Turning pages in the middle of a question creates confusion and invites errors. Switch questions around if it doesn't disturb continuity or, if it does, manipulate the spacing until the entire question fits.

Leave space at the end of the questionnaire for the respondent to make additional comments. This addresses one of the weaknesses of questionnaires; namely, that the respondent cannot provide unsolicited comments. Being able to express themselves freely makes respondents feel better and provides information to the investigator that can be used for interpretation.

The last page should include an expression of appreciation and the promise of a summary of results to anyone who requests it, but only if you are certain you can and will send it out to them.

Additional Considerations When Using Questionnaires

Response Rate   One of the biggest concerns in using questionnaires is the *response rate*. Obviously, you want everyone to respond, but that rarely happens, particularly when respondents remain anonymous and so feel no pressure to respond. The credibility of the results rests heavily on the response rate and on the ability of the researcher to demonstrate that those who have returned the questionnaires do not differ substantially from those who did not; that is, that there is no bias operating. When the respondents are anonymous, this is difficult to demonstrate. One approach is to compare the demographics of the group who returned the questionnaire to the demographics of the group (unit, organization) as a whole. If there are no significant differences, you can conclude that there is no reason to suspect bias among the group who responded.

Validity and Reliability   As with all instruments, validity and reliability are important. This is particularly true when items from the questionnaire are combined into a scale whose ratings are then tallied, assuming unidimensionality. Psychometric issues frequently get overlooked. It is certainly easier to use an existing, predesigned questionnaire, which already has reliability and validity established. However, most organizations have unique problems and ways of referring to their problems, so ready-made instruments usually need some modification prior to use. This dilutes the usefulness of preexisting psychometric data.

Social Desirability   As with interviews, questionnaires can suffer social desirability effects. Subconsciously, people prefer to answer in ways that present them in a favorable way.

A NOTE ON DATA ANALYSIS

The purpose of data analysis is to bring order to the gobs of data a consultant has amassed during data collection. It involves organizing the data, synthesizing it, searching for patterns and relationships, discovering what's important, and deciding what should be told to others. Data analysis techniques differ; however, they all involve putting the data into a form that makes sense and can be presented to others.

Consultants who take a more naturalistic, qualitative approach to data collection will have carried out extensive data analysis on an ongoing basis based on interviews and observations. By the time consultants reach saturation in data collection, they will have a strong sense of the findings, but will still need to go through a rigorous content analysis of all of the transcripts, field notes, anecdotes, and documents obtained. Many consultants like to work through the data by hand, believing that close readings provide a better sense of the material. Themes can be teased out and counted. They can be sorted by themes that are cited most often, by those that are most germane to solving the problem, or by those that are clearly actionable. An increasing number of consultants rely on computer software for content analysis and to assist with thematic analysis. "Ethnograph" and "Nudist" are among the more popular programs. All content programs have limitations and require a solid understanding of the underlying text.

Raw data should be looked at in relation to the questions raised and the problems identified at the outset. The consultant must attach meaning and significance to the data, to explain patterns and relationships he or she finds. One caution is to be careful not to distort the data in the act of compressing and condensing it.

There is no best way to organize, analyze, and interpret the abundant amounts of qualitative data that consultants generally collect. One way is to use a theoretical model and to organize the data report around that model. The caution in using a model, however, is to be careful not to collect only the data that meet the model's categories or to backfit the data obtained in order to fit the model. When themes are presented to the client, they should be supported with illustrative quotes that come directly from the participants in the study. Unsupported themes lack credibility.

Data gathered from a more traditional, quantitative approach require separate analysis. Typically, two different types of statistical analyses are carried out: *descriptive* and *inferential.*

Descriptive statistics include tallies (frequencies and percentages), measures of central tendency (mean, median, and mode), measures of variability (range, interquartile range, and standard deviation), and correlations, which are measures of relationships. These describe the data obtained on the sample, addressing what the sample "looks like" on average.

Inferential statistics are typically tests of hypotheses and include t-tests, various analysis of variance tests, chi square tests, multiple regression, and other tests. These test the significance of the data obtained; that is, they determine the probability that the results obtained on the sample can be generalized to the population from which the sample was drawn. Statistics can be easily calculated using SPSS (Statistical Package for the Social Sciences).

When data analysis of both qualitative and quantitative data are complete, the results should be presented to the client with identifiable themes. Concrete examples and direct quotes should be used wherever possible to support those themes. If the data have uncovered a diagnosis of the problems and their root causes, the consultant and client can move confidently into the next phase of the consulting process — the design of interventions.

CHAPTER 12

Interventions: Getting the Client to Change

Ron Carucci and Toby J. Tetenbaum

You have collected data. You have drawn some preliminary conclusions from those data. You have selected the key themes to present to your client. You are now ready to incorporate those themes into a diagnosis and intervention plan. A diagnosis helps when a consultant has to answer the client's inevitable question: "So what?" Your diagnostic response has to bridge what you learned from your data collection with the actions you determine the organization should take. For example, your data analysis may have led you to conclude that the company's current technology initiatives will not work well in the current structure, that top managers are sponsoring far too many disparate initiatives, and that the territorial nature of the functional silos in the company will ultimately undermine the return on investments made to streamline the work processes and make them more efficient. Your diagnosis, based on these conclusions, might be that:

- The organization should consider a more integrated approach to change implementation. Current resources and energy are being wasted and results are likely to be suboptimal.
- The technology processes should be examined in the context of the culture and structure in which it must perform.
- The leaders of the organization should be more rigorous in how they determine priorities and allocate resources so that a frenzy of disconnected activities doesn't replace the pursuit of a shared set of objectives.

Assuming you were able to help the client see the data as credible and as supporting your diagnosis, you are now in a position to help the client determine the actions to take. Recognize that even good consultants who are able to collect data, translate that data into meaningful knowledge and into an insightful diagnosis, can miss connecting the dots. In working with your client, do not assume that there is an "obvious" line of

Ron Carucci is a Partner with Mercer-Delta Consulting, a management consulting firm that provides services related to the management of strategic organizational change to major corporations. He is a faculty member at Fordham University Graduate School, serving as an associate professor of organizational behavior in the Human Resource Education Program.

Toby J. Tetenbaum is President of Toby Tetenbaum Associates, a consulting firm specializing in organizational behavior. A licensed psychologist, she is a professor at Fordham University, where she directs the Human Resource Education Master's Degree Program.

sight between diagnosis and the interventions that will best address the issues. There are several reasons for this.

- *The consultant's "expertise bias."* The old expression, "Give me a hammer, and all I see are nails," is very true in consulting. If someone is an expert in leadership development, they are likely to see all issues as problems of leadership. If they are experts in strategy, they will quickly migrate to issues of strategic direction, mission, or focus.
- *The consultant's limited expertise.* No consultant, however broad a "generalist," will have the necessary repertoire to address all issues that were surfaced in a diagnosis. Because many consultants have trouble accepting their limitations, they often overly rely on their limited breadth of expertise to tackle the issues raised, and so issues that fall outside their scope usually go unaddressed.
- *The client's preimposed boundaries around "politically charged" issues.* Clients are not blameless when diagnoses don't translate into effective interventions. If there are "undiscussables" or "untouchables" embedded in political land mines that the client is committed to avoiding, then the consultant's impact will inevitably be limited. As such, when these issues are surfaced in the data, they get reburied as though they had never been uncovered.
- *The client's inability to grasp ramifications.* Clients can often have lofty ambitions for change when beginning a diagnostic effort, but may get cold feet when they realize the ramifications of what has been uncovered. This is especially true when the client begins to realize the level of personal change that will be needed to effect broader organizational change. Often the client experiences cold feet and the urgency of the change effort begins to take a back seat to more comfortable initiatives already under way.

If you are skillful at linking data collection, data analysis, and diagnosis without imposing your own biases, and if you are able to navigate the client's political agenda and personal resistance, you are now in a position to design the interventions best suited to address the issues raised in your diagnosis.

This chapter addresses the following questions: What is an intervention? How can a consultant build a company's commitment to change? What should be the scope and depth of the interventions that a consultant proposes? How should a consultant approach the design process and test design assumptions? How should the consultant work with the client to implement interventions?

WHAT IS AN INTERVENTION?

Intervention is a loaded word, a lightning rod that often elicits rolling eyes from clients who are suspicious of being the targets of "interventions." Nonetheless, it is an accurate term for what consultants do: They help create actions that lead to change. We define an intervention as *an action or series of actions aimed at individuals, groups, or entire organizations with the intent of changing current behavior or direction and, ultimately, improving some aspect(s) of performance.*

In our work, we assume that the design of any action aimed at changing behavior and/or the direction of a company should always be preceded by a diagnosis that combines the insights and perspectives of those who will have to live with the change and those who will lead and/or design the change. A credible diagnosis that clearly reflects the issues most relevant to the client company is essential and builds commitment to change.

Unfortunately, consultants often enter organizations as experts—those charged with "finding the answer"—and not as facilitators—people who can help the organization become more self-sufficient. Often, they embark on massive data collection efforts and produce lofty recommendations—served up in multivolume binders—that seldom get further than the sponsoring executive's office. Why? Because those who are the target of their recommendations have no vested stake in the solution being proposed and no reason to believe that it credibly reflects their most important concerns.

Diagnosis as an Intervention

Diagnosis is an intervention in two ways: First, the act of data collection in a client setting itself changes the dynamics of the situation. When employees are asked to complete a survey assessing morale, for example, the questions raised may lead them to think about issues they hadn't previously considered. If an item on a survey asks me to rate my manager on the degree to which he appreciates the work I do, I may realize for the first time that he has never actually thanked me, recognized me, or rewarded me for the late nights I put in on a project he's spearheading. Although I had never thought about it before, now that I have been forced to think about it, I feel put out! Known as *reactivity,* the individual reacts to the instrument and is not the same person, so to speak, as he was prior to completing the instrument.

Reactivity can sometimes be used to advantage, particularly when it provokes people to produce data that may not have been completely conscious to them. Issues and concerns that lay beneath the surface as frustrations or vague anxieties are now disclosed and opened to exploration. The interviewee has an opportunity to view his or her circumstances in a new light, and the interviewer has an opportunity to intervene in a way that encourages the interviewee to see the circumstances differently, and, as a result, to consider alternative actions.

Second, diagnosis is an intervention in the client setting because asking questions raises expectations that top managers intend to act on what they hear. Companies that regularly implement faddish technologies sometimes get seen as part of the "Change du Jour Club" and stimulate cynicism among employees. As a result, when leaders in these organizations need to pursue real change, they lack credibility.

The process of determining what data to gather and from whom to gather it should take into consideration what will be done once the data are analyzed. At the end of the day, it's the client (top managers and employees), and *not* the consultants, who will have to embrace, digest, and take full ownership of the diagnosis and the actions required to remedy the identified problems. Done well, the diagnostic process can actually help prepare the organization for change by "normalizing" the pent-up emotions and frustrations that surface in conjunction with the issues, helping the organization learn from the data, and identifying those individuals who are most likely to set a positive example of commitment to change. Once identified, these individuals can be used to lead specific initiatives, research alternative solutions, and communicate to the broader organization the importance and direction of change.

THE SCOPE OF INTERVENTION: WHO AND WHAT ARE THE TARGETS?

Choosing an appropriate intervention requires a framework or model that defines the context for thinking about the client organization as a whole. The Congruence Model depicted in Figure 12–1 is a very useful model for viewing organizations as complex systems with interrelated components, and we can use it as a context for building interventions.

Viewing a client organization as a system implies that a change made to any one part of the organization automatically induces changes in the other parts. This key principle of complex systems is vital to consider when designing interventions where the objective is to generate fundamental and sustainable change in the organization. The model suggests that it will do little good, for instance, to train all of middle management in the skills and knowledge of leading teams and implementing effective change if changes are not also made in the organization's structure, reward system, work design, and management processes that are "congruent" with the changes being sought through training.

Unfortunately, many companies invest significant resources and energy in introducing massive interventions that make significant impact on only one or two elements of the organization without effectively considering the complete system. Over time, these interventions frequently fail to achieve or sustain the intended changes because of the system's strong allegiance to the "fit" of its current configuration of elements. Current fit overpowers the intervention, causing it to migrate progressively back to the comfort of the status quo.

Take the short client example we introduced earlier. Let's consider now the process of choosing and designing interventions that might effectively achieve sustainable change. The initial diagnosis of the client concluded that:

- The organization should consider a more integrated approach to change implementation. Currently resources and energy are being wasted and results are suboptimal.

FIGURE 12–1   Mercer-Delta's Congruence Model

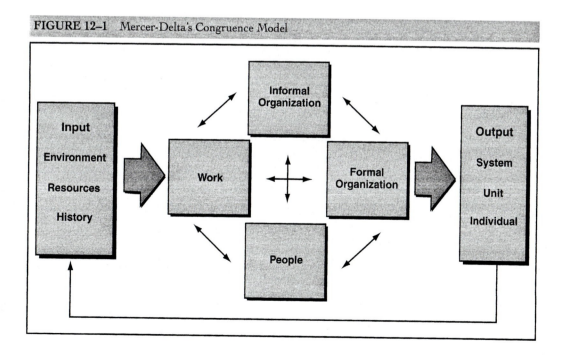

- The technology process work must be undertaken in the context of the culture and structure in which it must perform.
- Top managers should be more rigorous in how they determine priorities and allocate resources so that a frenzy of disconnected activities doesn't replace the pursuit of a shared set of agreed upon outcomes.

Additional conclusions we came to from data collection also suggested the following conclusions:

- The technology processes being developed are expected to increase the speed and innovation of the product development processes in order to increase the organization's speed to market.
- The current research and development (R&D) processes are highly fragmented and don't allow for maximum innovation because the engineers and scientists are always so far behind their development schedules.
- Marketing and Sales are continuously putting pressure on R&D to get the products finished because advertising and promotion began five months before the projected launch, sales people have already made early sales to customers, and finance has made revenue projections based on the published launch date on which the analysts based their assessments.
- Because the organization has operated this way for so long, the culture has become one of "tell 'em what they want to hear" and "accountability equals blame." People do not share information about project delays because the tendency of leaders to "shoot the messenger" is high, and there is lots of folklore about people who were honest disappearing.
- The sales compensation system pays out commissions monthly based on signed deals and is not linked to revenue capture. The policy states that cancelled deals or modified agreements will result in commission adjustments, but, in reality, this varies by region—some do it, many do not.
- The manufacturing and distribution systems are not designed to handle a significant increase in capacity, nor are they designed flexibly enough to move products quickly through wholesale and retail channels. This has never been a major problem, however, because R&D's delays have always allowed time to "catch up."
- Design flaws that have often led to quality issues and the subsequent waste of product that had to be scrapped and remanufactured, provided yet another opportunity to point the finger at R&D for shoddy engineering.
- Although there has not been significant pressure to do so, the manufacturing, distribution, and warehousing organizations have recently completed the installation of an enterprise resource planning system (ERP) that still has many bugs to work out. As a result, orders are still being filled wrong, stock-keeping units (SKUs) have not all been properly accounted for, customers have cancelled orders because of repeated delays and mistakes. But these problems feel manageable in comparison to the R&D issues because those have been chronic for so long, and the sales force can simply redouble their efforts to replace the orders that are cancelled. The technology people are working aggressively to get the new system performing at an optimal level.

Given this sobering picture of the client system, it's not hard to predict the kinds of problems that are likely to ensue should the organization continue down the path of overhauling R&D technologies without making the requisite changes in the rest of the organization.

At Mercer-Delta, consultants leverage four primary areas when considering intervention choices designed to generate sustainable performance improvements. Figure 12–2 illustrates the primary leverage points for considering types of interventions.

FIGURE 12–2   Primary Levers for Intervention

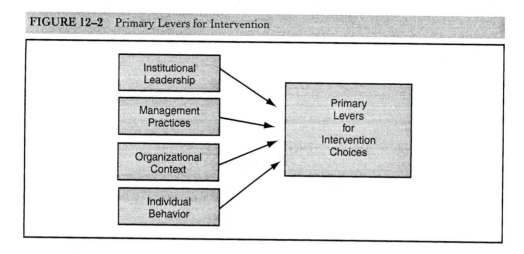

Institutional Leadership   One of the most substantial points for leveraging the change comes from the actions and behaviors of the CEO, senior team, and senior line managers. How effective the change is and how sustainable it will be is largely a function of the degree to which these individuals:

- Articulate a vision for the proposed changes that inspires passion in the followers.
- Set expectations so that each person understands his or her role in effecting the vision.
- Model the desired behavior and embody the desired changes.
- Recognize or reward people for behavior consistent with change objectives and impose sanctions for behaviors inconsistent with those objectives.
- Engage in symbolic acts designed to support the change.

Management Practices   Employees typically learn the messages of their organization by watching the behaviors of their managers. More than anything else, managers' behaviors tell people what's important. Therefore, during any large-scale change effort, how managers interact with one another, their subordinates, and their own management are critically important. Their job is vital; they are the ones who can directly promote behavior consistent with the desired change on the part of hundreds, even thousands, of people.

Organizational Context   The best managers in business will fail in their efforts to transform the organization unless they are supported by changes in the organization's structures, systems, and processes. These include: the appraisal and reward systems, staffing and selection practices, and business processes.

Individual Behavior   Just as people watch their managers for clues as to how to behave, so too do they watch their colleagues. People keep close tabs on who is up and who is down, who is in and who is out. They learn what behaviors are desired by watching who is publicly recognized and rewarded. This alerts them to the behaviors and attributes that are desired as a result of the intervention(s) underway. While people also learn by negative example, it is more difficult to impose sanctions on influential employees who resist required changes.

With these four leverage points in mind, we can now consider how to target specific interventions to bring about sustainable change for our under-performing client. These interventions can be behavioral, procedural, structural, or educational in nature. In Figure 12–3, Mercer-Delta identifies 12 intervention choices which, if employed in a coordinated, integrated fashion, can lead to successful, sustainable change. Associated with each intervention are principles, tools, and specific techniques.

The list in Figure 12–3 is a starting point rather than an ultimate destination. Each organization is different and has unique characteristics and circumstances—there's no "one-size-fits-all" solution. Simply unloading a few silver bullets as though there could be a "panacea intervention" is a prescription for failure. Designing interventions that lead to sustainable change requires careful diagnosis of what is currently working or not working in the client system. Those interventions must be coordinated, sequenced, and aimed at the right target audiences in order to build momentum and create the necessary conditions for achieving desired change.

MAKING DESIGN CHOICES

Given the many systemic issues identified in our simple example, picking and choosing which battles to fight is an important part of the joint client–consultant design process. Although the presenting issues in the client system centered primarily around the R&D organization's challenges, the problems actually stem beyond the boundaries of any single function. Here, different compensation models, marketing and advertising processes, old and new manufacturing and order fulfillment processes, and emerging R&D processes, to name a few, are colliding with each other, with conflicting designs and objectives. For example, new R&D technologies aimed at increasing the speed of product development are likely to wreck havoc in the manufacturing and distribution organization, whose new ERP system and engineering designs are not prepared to accommodate a faster throughput of products, a higher volume of products, or an increase in SKUs. "Success" in one set of changes could therefore create disaster in another part of the client system. The challenge then is how to design a set of interventions that can optimize performance *across* the organization while ensuring short-term performance doesn't suffer.

Drawing on the description of intervention options in Figure 12–3, one possible scenario for change in this client setting would involve the following sequence:

1. *Collaborative direction setting.* Assemble a group of leaders from across the R&D, Manufacturing, Distribution, Marketing, and Sales organizations for a two-day session. The group should include the functional heads of each department and some of their key leaders. The objectives for this session should be to:
   - Review the data and diagnosis to develop a set of agreed upon conclusions and issues to be worked across the organization.
   - Build an "inventory" of current initiatives underway and establish a shared understanding across the organization of what each of these major initiatives is intended to accomplish.
   - Identify potential "collisions," conflicts, and interdependencies among these initiatives, and solutions for how these "seams" will be managed effectively.
   - Identify those issues of organizational performance that need to be addressed, which are not currently being addressed by initiatives underway (e.g., marketing, sales, and distri-

FIGURE 12–3 Types of Intervention

Intervention	Description	Outcomes
Collaborative Definition of the Desired Outcomes	Definition of the desired improvements in performance, and the requisite behaviors required for these improvements to be achieved	Shared agreement, understanding, and commitment to pursue the changes required to improve performance
Measurement and Gap Analysis	Assessment of the gap between the current and desired organization	Shared understanding of priority gaps along with specific action plans to address them
Stakeholder Analysis and Engagement	Analyzing key internal and external stakeholders to understand their position relative to the change	Commitment by key stakeholders to the proposed changes. Resistance to change kept to a healthy minimum
Senior Management Behavior	Leader feedback process implemented with all senior managers	Senior managers model desired new behaviors
Structural Change	Redesign of systems, structures, and processes to reinforce change and new behaviors	New systems reinforce and institutionalize the changes
Management Process Redesign	Redesign of management structures, processes, and metrics	Management processes that support and reinforce the required changes
Recognition and Reward	Redesign of compensation and reward systems to reinforce desired behavioral changes	Desired new behaviors reinforced through focused compensation programs
Formal Feedback Processes	Development and implementation of management feedback process linked to the changes and desired new behaviors	Desired new behaviors reinforced through ongoing, formal feedback process
Large Group Engagement Process	Events and conferences designed to focus and reinforce desired changes in the organization	Concrete changes in the way people work together to accomplish business objectives
Educational Interventions	Development of education and training programs which facilitate the rapid development of the desired new behaviors and knowledge required to sustain the change	Acquisition of desired new behaviors by managers and employees throughout the business
Communications	Development of communication strategies integrated into a coherent change management message	Broad understanding and buy-in of the need for and direction of change
In-Depth Individual Interventions	Constructive coaching and performance feedback for senior leaders	Senior managers "walk the talk" or leave the company

bution will likely need to redefine how products go to market given the increase in SKUs and volume, and determine if there are other channels to be explored in order to achieve growth). Prioritize these issues, choose only the most critical, and assign leaders to develop solutions for them in the context of the larger set of initiatives.

- Establish a "transition team" of cross-organizational leaders who will work together on an intensified basis to lead the implementation of current and new initiatives as an *integrated set* of solutions clearly linked to one another, and to the strategic goals of the organization.

2. *Structural change and management process.* The current configuration of functions and arrangement of departments is likely to be insufficient to maximize the investment and impact of new technologies, process designs, and products. A *design team,* clearly linked to the work of the transition team above, should be created to explore alternative organization designs better aligned with the emerging processes and more suited to the strategic goals of the organization. The work of this team is also to consider the necessary changes in critical *management processes* such as budgeting and resource allocation, governance, talent strategy, and strategy implementation. Whatever processes now exist in these areas are probably incompatible with the changes being pursued, and will also have to be modified to fit the new organization design.

3. *Large-group engagement.* Large-group methods are powerful interventions when used appropriately. In this case, because so much of the work spans numerous organizational boundaries, gathering a large group of people from across the functions currently pursuing change, could be very helpful. This might include 150 to 200 middle management and professional staff coming together in a highly choreographed meeting to:

- Build shared understanding about how the existing and new change initiatives "fit" together.
- Participate in designing the changes since they are the ones who will ultimately implement and "live with" them.
- Provide critical input to the transition team on operational and tactical issues to be considered in implementing the changes.
- Test the assumptions and conclusions reached by top managers at the initial meeting to see if they hold water with the rest of the organization.

4. *Human resource processes.* A subteam of the transition team should be formed (to include people from within the Human Resources function as well as the line organization) to consider training and development implications of the massive changes, as well as modifications to performance planning, evaluation, and rewards. The current process probably reinforces behaviors that are incongruent with the new organization, and therefore should be redesigned to drive new behavior and results from individuals and teams across the organization.

In no way is this meant to be an exhaustive set of interventions for the challenges facing this client organization, but it is certainly a robust "starter set" that will ensure the organization embarks on a trajectory that has some chance of success. As implementation occurs, there will be changes to intervention plans, as well as emerging issues that require new interventions.

Experienced consultants recognize that flexibility in both design and implementation is essential. Developing an intervention design that is cast in stone is a fast track to doom. Many consultants find it difficult to let go of their proposed intervention design because they believe passionately in the efficacy of their suggestions. But if the degree of ownership on the consultant's part is so strong, it has probably diluted ownership and passion from the client organization, and made them too dependent on the consultant—a prescription for failure. The client will simply not be able to sustain its investment or attention long enough to get anything done, and the consultants will eventually feel like they are pushing large boulders uphill.

IMPLEMENTATION: WHERE THE RUBBER MEETS THE ROAD

Intervention plans can be made to look logical and compelling on paper, and to sound energizing and inspiring when presented by top managers trying to mobilize a company to carry out change. The intersections and complexities of the chosen initiatives, however, generally go well beyond the intervention "blueprint"—that's when reality sets in. The starter's pistol is fired, and a windstorm of activity blusters forth.

Keeping large-scale, complex interventions on track toward their intended objectives is probably the most difficult and un-teachable part of the art of consulting. For one thing, the organization still has its daily activities to carry out. There are customers who want products, employees coming and going from the organization, bills to be paid, revenues to collect, shareholders to appease, analysts to inform, competitors making moves, not to mention regulatory, technological, environmental, and global maelstroms, all fiercely competing for the client system's attention—the same people who are simultaneously working on the implementation of the interventions they so passionately helped design.

To help make sure interventions stay on track, *communications*, *measurement*, and *leadership behavior* play pivotal roles in keeping interventions in motion once launched.

Communications   It's crucial to keep informing everyone in the organization, and keeping them informed, about the objectives, rationale, and progress of the initiatives. Communication often eludes organizations, especially those leaders and managers steeped in the work. They forget that huge numbers of people have not participated in the immediate creation and implementation of the interventions, and have little or no clue about what's going on, except from rumors heard around in hallways or at lunch, or a short paragraph they may have read in the company newsletter. A well-conceived, multiple-media communication strategy that spans the entire life of the intervention process (not just the fanfare of the launch) is needed to maintain the attention and commitment of the entire company. Graphics that depict the process and progress of change are helpful, as well as publishing plans and goals of the transition team for all to see. Consultants should help key leaders make use of existing forums where groups of employees gather (staff meetings, quarterly reviews, training and orientation programs, luncheons, etc.) to promote the changes and their benefits, keep people posted on progress and setbacks, mid-course corrections, and continually *reinforcing and repeating* the fundamental business case behind the set of interventions. The establishment of milestones along the route to completion should be broadcast to the organization, and when these milestones are reached, they should be widely celebrated and rewarded.

Measurement   The expression "you don't get what you don't measure" also applies to the implementation of complex interventions. If you don't know whether or not the interventions are on course toward the intended goals at any given time, they probably aren't. A few key metrics should be put in place to track the progress of the interventions, ensure they are on time and on budget, and have their intended impact on performance. Progress against these measures should be made public for the client organization to track progress, to prioritize their work, and to keep pace with the interventions.

Measurement of manager and employee participation in the interventions is also desirable. Those with critical assignments should be assessed and rewarded for their participation, and those blatantly resisting or undermining progress should experience consequences for doing so.

Leadership Behavior Nothing stalls interventions faster than for the client organization to conclude that its leaders aren't serious about the changes they've launched. They watch for the glitz and hype of the "kick off" of major interventions, and many expect the flash in the pan to fade almost as quickly as it is ignited. Leaders must constantly attend to the messages and signals they are sending to the organization about the urgency of the implementation in the decisions they make, the statements they make, how they spend their time, how they give direction, how they staff key assignments, who they promote, and how excessively they beat the drums of their passionate commitment to seeing interventions fully through to completion. Feedback mechanisms should be put in place to monitor stakeholder perceptions of leader behavior. Multirater assessments can be used to help guide leaders in their behavioral choices, and help them make changes when the organizational mirror suggests there is a gap between what they believe they are conveying to the organization, and what is actually being heard and seen. It can be hard for leaders to subject themselves to this type of individual intervention, but those that do often reap great benefits, and are likely to be more successful in carrying out the large interventions they sponsor.

SUMMARY

A key contribution that consultants make to clients is to translate data collected from the organization into a credible diagnosis, and subsequently into a set of integrated interventions designed to solve the problems and achieve the goals the organization has set out to pursue. There are no universal panaceas to designing interventions. Every client company and leader are different. The context of their challenges, their level of capability and commitment, and the severity of the issues they face must all be considered. If consultants ignore these requirements, and only attempt the off-the-shelf, prepackaged interventions that match their core expertise, the failure rate of interventions will grow.

Consultants should continually stretch their capability to diagnose and design interventions across a broad spectrum of challenges, recognizing they will never be able to be a "one-stop shopping" source of solutions for any organizational problem that exists. Having a broad repertoire of capabilities allows a consultant not only to recognize complex problems in the diagnostic phase, but to more effectively design interventions to address those problems.

CHAPTER

Facilitating Change: Implementing a Results Orientation

Robert A. Neiman

Dean Baxter is president of ABC Manufacturing Company, a large manufacturer of mechanical devices located in southeastern United States. When we were ushered into his office for a preliminary meeting, we were struck by the Spartan neatness and evident calm of the scene. No magazine clutter. No piles of reports. No pictures of management team events. No samples of product. No charts on the wall. This was a manager, and probably a company, in tight control, we thought.

Unexpectedly, Dean's story revealed turmoil under the surface. "We've had a successful company here for 25 years. We have 5,000 people in four plants, two in the Southeast and two in the Midwest. Our southeastern plants make metal products for the home furnishings markets. Our midwestern plants make mechanical devices for the auto and automatic control industries. We've been moderately profitable. We have a loyal workforce and managers who have been on the job for decades.

"Two years ago we sold out to the MNO Corporation, and life has been tough since. They want us to grow and grow fast. We thought the Corporation would provide us with capital and new marketing and R&D support. But their income has dropped. So they have not been much help. I didn't know how we could grow outside the Corporation, so they recommended several consultants.

"I hired a series of consultants to do a thorough review of the company. A strategy firm pointed out that we were too focused on the low-priced end of our market, and that we should re-orient the company to the high end—with new special products. An organizational firm recommended dismantling our functional structure and organizing into 'strategic business units' to manage business in different market segments. A third group, industrial engineers, recommended installation of a standard cost system so that we could better understand our true costs and ultimately reduce them. A human resources firm pointed out that we had poor communication in our workforce, and that we should train our supervisors and foremen in total quality management and human relations skills. But we haven't implemented any of their recommendations."

Robert A. Neiman is a principal in the firm of Robert H. Schaffer & Associates. He has led performance improvement and strategic change efforts in electronics, chemicals, public utilities and financial services industries, hospitals, education institutions, and government agencies, as well as working with both consulting firms and internal consultants.

Hearing this, we asked why none of the consulting recommendations were implemented. Dean replied: "To them, it was all or nothing. And I didn't think these were the most important things for us to work on right away. Our auto customers are squeezing suppliers, forcing down margins in our midwestern plant. They insist that we start a total quality program, at our expense, if we want to remain suppliers after this year. The MNO is pressing us for an immediate 20 percent increase in net income. We don't have the time or resources for the growth efforts.

"The consultants' projects also have risks. I'm not sure my vice president of operations is up to the job ahead. He's been effective here for many years. But he doesn't go after the job as vigorously as I think he has to now. I don't want to fire him. I'm not sure what else to do. And the consultants weren't able to help on that score. I got interested in talking to you because I've been told that your approach to consulting is different. You help get results. You help do it quickly. And I think that's what we need."

Pleased at the welcome, we outlined our firm's practice and how it might be helpful in this situation. As our lead consultant put it: "Typically, consulting firms bring in expertise, tools, and methods which are not present in the organization. Thus, new strategic plans, new structures, new systems, and new quality practices are provided by outside experts, hopefully absorbed and used by the clients. Our firm provides a different kind of input. We help organizations make better use of the resources they already have—the skills, know-how, and energy, which exist under the surface—but have not been tapped. Typically, organizations have much more of this 'hidden potential' than they realize. We help organizations get moving quickly toward urgent and important goals by utilizing this hidden potential. Successes can come quickly—sometimes in weeks or two or three months. By making these changes successfully—we call them 'breakthroughs'—the organization is energized to make still greater progress and build, step by step, toward larger-scale strategic changes. Since you have to get more profit now to deal with the challenges to the business, we might start there."

Dean was listening, but not yet understanding what we would do and how it would help. "Would you give me a formal proposal?" he asked. We resisted and suggested instead that we work up some examples to illustrate what might be done. "Where do you believe there are immediate opportunities to get cost down and profit up? Who would be involved? What steps would be needed? What obstacles would have to be overcome?"

In another hour and a half of discussion, we were able to sketch out together the rough design for three possible profit improvement breakthroughs that could put some money in the bank relatively easily. Dean became more intrigued as he saw the possibilities for doing something workable. We suggested, as a next step, meeting with him and some of the key people who would be involved in these initial projects. If there were further agreement, we would then help shape assignments and work with the people to create work plans and get moving. Dean agreed to these next steps and the meeting was scheduled for the following week. We'd meet with Dean; Sam Sandler, the vice president of operations; Denise Bartlett, head of Human Resources; Axel Swenson, chief engineer; and Charles Brown, manager of the largest eastern plant.

Back at our own office, we prepared notes summarizing the discussion and an agenda for the meeting with Dean's direct reports. We also reflected on his past experiences with consultants. Why had none of the others been able to stay with the situation? Here was a manager who needed and wanted help. The firms he had hired were all highly regarded and skillful consultants. They had made recommendations that seemed to make sense. They responded to what the client had asked. Why had they not connected with the client more closely and been more directly helpful? Would we be caught in the same syndrome? Would "consultant fatigue" be an obstacle?

At Schaffer & Associates, we believe that three issues affect the success of a consulting engagement:

1. *Tuning in to a client's readiness to carry out change.* Consultants, like most experts, see situations in ways that are comfortable and familiar to them. The strategy consultants that Dean met with saw strategic issues. The organization consultants saw organizational structure issues and so forth. They may not have understood the pressures the client faced. They may not have appraised his real capacity to act on a new initiative. As we had learned, while Dean wanted to grow the business, there were more urgent pressures to generate profit. It was not surprising that he didn't feel he could "afford the new investments."

2. *Designing projects which clients can implement successfully with quick results.* Many consulting projects tend to require considerable up-front investment—forcing the client to assume more risk than may be feasible. Or they may require the client to wait too long to learn whether the effort really will pay off. Consulting proposals tend to have this speculative feeling to them.

3. *Carrying out work in ways that boost a client's capability and know-how.* It is not uncommon for consultants to conceive brilliant plans that are handed over on the assumption that the client will act on them successfully, but without regard to helping the client learn what it takes to gain the necessary skills and capabilities. Dean might not have said so, but he probably didn't have confidence that he had the right people to go after the high-end market, or to lead new SBUs, or to manage the workforce better. And he probably had trouble visualizing what he would have to do to lead a growth effort.

In our view, a good management consultant helps clients achieve better results. It is therefore vital to understand the client's real capacity to produce results and to help enhance that capability, no matter what the original assignment intended. Doing so requires the consultant to think about engagements in terms of three key sets of skills:

1. *Conducting a readiness assessment.* Consulting involves discovering the inherent capacity in the organization to achieve a new result: the skill, insight, motivation, and energy to produce change. The consultant must ask: Who is the client? What does the client want to accomplish? What does the client know how to accomplish? What forces are in play that would drive the client organization to tackle the change? What forces would impede change? The consultant must be expert in asking and answering these questions.

2. *Designing projects for success.* A consulting project must always be focused on a specific and measurable goal. The size and scope of the project must be within reach of the client's capacity for achievement yet sufficient to produce the result. The people and resources needed for execution need to be identified and lined up. The organization must be educated about the rationale for the change. The work program needs to be defined as well as the measures of success. Counterforces need to be identified and strategies for dealing with them created.

3. *Providing implementation support.* Consultants must be able to play dual roles: On one hand, they are investigators, analysts, and strategists; on the other, they are supporters of implementation. There are many aspects to the role of implementation support. Sometimes it means acting as an advocate of the need for change. At other times, it means acting as helper in defining assignments, as organizer of meetings, as coach and counselor to the action team. Good consultants often advise on ways to overcome obstacles and help coordi-

nate different strands of activity. They can stimulate motivation when energy flags or when diversions intrude. And, of course, they provide "expert" input as needed.

If these capabilities are not part of your repertoire or are underdeveloped, you are not likely to be successful as a consultant in helping clients achieve results.

In the rest of this chapter, we explore these basic skills in more detail and suggest some tools that can help you to apply them.

SKILL SET 1: ASSESSING READINESS

The consultant can ask analytical questions in order to gain an understanding of the business and the key issues to be addressed. The dialogue then gets into the facts about the business: its market position, its competitive status, its strategic issues and problems. All of this is valuable information, but this line of thinking leaves out what the client may be willing and able to do, and the capacity to act successfully. It leaves out the political realities the client faces getting agreement to a course of action. It avoids the process for generating understanding, acceptance, and commitment to a program. Failure to address these issues is a fundamental cause of consulting failures. These factors are vital to success.

To get "under the surface" and bring out these issues of implementation, the consultant needs to ask different questions: "What are you trying to accomplish?" "What is most important for you to accomplish now?" "Who needs to be involved?" "How do others see this issue?" "How would you get started on this?" "What obstacles would need to be overcome?" By means of such questions, a different cycle of thinking is set in motion.

Immediately, the consultant gets insight into the readiness of the client for change. One learns the specific pressures to be dealt with. One learns whether the client's aspiration is clear and specific or vague and slippery. Is there a sense of priority, or is the client unfocused? Is the aspiration realistic, backed up with reasoned thought and data, or simply a dream? Is there evidence of energy and will to make something happen, or is the attitude more passive? Is there acceptance and interest on the part of others whose support is needed? Or do basic differences need to be reconciled? How does the client envision the undertaking unfolding? What would be happening in a month or two? In a year or so? How does the project fit in the priority scheme of the organization? How does the client view his or her own role in the undertaking? How much time and energy can the client invest?

By exploring questions like these—at the beginning of the project, not at the end—the consultant generates several ingredients for success:

- An expectation that action and the pursuit of results is part of the job
- A sense of the capacity and readiness of the client for action
- A grasp of the context in which the project will unfold and the issues that will affect successful implementation

Note that these questions are different from the analytical questions that are designed to elicit the objective business facts involved. But if the consultant ignores the organizational readiness factors, then only a partial picture of the situation is developed, and the consultant is unarmed to help the client deal with the essence of any project—implementation success and achieving results.

Two tools can help in the readiness assessment task. First, a map of the players involved. A simple diagram of the key players in the organization, noting their interests, can help illuminate who has to be involved and the roles they may play. In the ABC case, we first mapped out the different views of senior management. The controller was pressing for profit improvement through cost reduction and efficiency improvement. The group head and strategic planner were more interested in growth and development of new products and markets. Dean was caught in the cross-currents, but agreed that cost reduction was the most urgent matter, because this was most important to some of his major customers.

Later, as we worked with next level managers in the plants, we mapped out their views. This helped us see how different ideas and motivation already present in the organization could come together to produce new results (Figure 13–1).

A second tool is an action-oriented question guide to contrast with analytical questions. Analytical questions are focused on eliciting facts, relationships, and inferences, which are valuable, but which tend to lead to debate, not necessarily action. Action questions elicit what can be done, when, how, and by whom, and with what result. For example, analytical questions probe the nature of the business, its performance, its competitive status, its strategic issues such as market position, pricing, distribution channels, and technology.

Action questions probe the ideas and motivation of the people involved. What do they want to accomplish? How well do they think they are progressing? Where would they like to see greater progress? How would they get started? Consultants should be skilled in asking both analytical and action questions. Figure 13–2 presents a basic question guide.

The funnel in Figure 13–3 illustrates how this kind of thinking can be applied to the situation at ABC Manufacturing to draw down from the broad goal of "growth" to the next level of "profit improvement," all the way down to the far more specific objectives

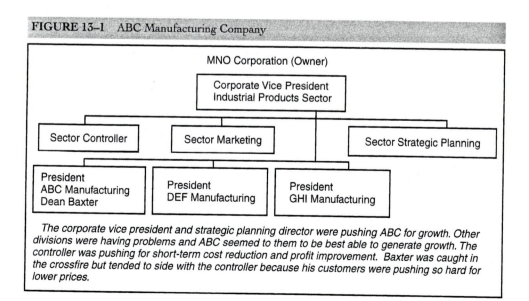

FIGURE 13–1   ABC Manufacturing Company

The corporate vice president and strategic planning director were pushing ABC for growth. Other divisions were having problems and ABC seemed to them to be best able to generate growth. The controller was pushing for short-term cost reduction and profit improvement. Baxter was caught in the crossfire but tended to side with the controller because his customers were pushing so hard for lower prices.

FIGURE 13-1   (continued)

Map of the Players in the initial ABC Manufacturing Company "Breakthrough Projects"

****

Waste and cost reduction—Plant 1

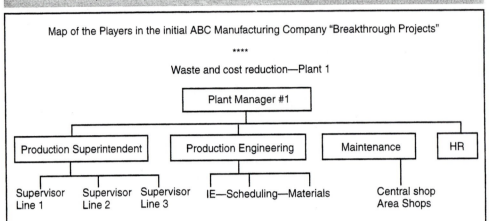

Line 1 supervisor had just completed the annual overhaul of the production line, and was in the best position to deal with waste. He and his people were concerned about it. They had ideas about simply collecting spilled product and other waste in a large bin and challenging their people to drive down the amount of material collected each week. They believed that careful attention and peer pressure would get the job done. The rest of the team supported the idea and it was selected as a profit improvement project. The payoff: $100K was saved in the first two months.

****

New Product Introduction—Plant 2

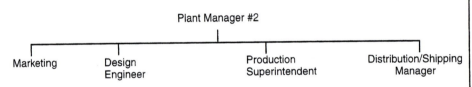

Marketing had an opportunity for a special product with good margin and high volume, if the plant could get it into production and shipping in six weeks—without defects. The group agreed to make a special effort, and formed a cross-functional team to do the job—the first time this approach would be tried in this plant. The payoff: $2 million per year profit stream started within two months.

****

Special Order Processing—Plant 3

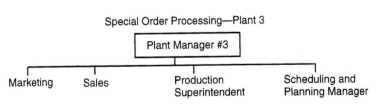

Special short orders were constantly interrupting the orderly flow of work through the plant. Sales people were outraged when the plant failed to meet commitments and shipped late. The team agreed to try a "test week" in which special orders would be shipped 100% on time for the test period. A special team would take the next six weeks to set up the trial run. The "special orders" were processed 100% on time in the test week, and this performance was sustained at above 95%. This opened up an additional $1 million per year profit stream.

FIGURE 13–2   Key Consulting Questions

Consultants must ask action-oriented questions as well as analytical questions, so that projects can be designed for implementation and results.

Analytical Questions	Action Questions
What is the business?	What are you trying to accomplish?
Who are the cusomers?	Where are you in the process of achieving these goals?
What do they buy? What do they value?	
How well are you performing?	How satisfied are you with the progress that has been made?
How do you match up to competitors?	If you were to make greater progress, what would be happening?
What is the fit between your strategy, your structure, and your organizational culture?	What would it take to generate better results?
What do you consider to be your key problems? What have you done to solve them?	Who would be involved in making this happen?
	What would it take to get started?

described by "reduce waste on a production line," "speed up introduction of a new product," and "improve delivery of 'special orders' in order to generate funds for investment."

SKILL SET 2: DESIGNING PROJECTS FOR SUCCESS

Here the consultant is concerned with the specific purpose, plan, and pace of the project to be undertaken. First, what is the goal? Is it to produce a plan, an action program, a specific end result? Is this to be a one-week, one-month, or one-year effort? Is it to focus on one subject and one part of the organization, or several units? How will success be measured? By whom? How will the project be structured? Who will lead? What teams are needed? How will this effort fit with the ongoing organization and its normal ways of working?

There are several prescriptions from the literature on project management that can help. Figure 13–4 summarizes these key elements of work discipline.

- *Define a workable and specific goal.* To design projects for success, the goal should be clear, specific, and measurable. It is useful to work down from the broad and perhaps risky big goal, to something quite specific, measurable, and achievable. Managers and consultants alike often mistake their "vision" of what they want to accomplish for what they are actually capable of accomplishing. While the project size and scope must obviously be calibrated to the size and scope of the job to be done, too often the project is cast in terms that are too

FIGURE 13-3 The Consulting Funnel

Narrow down the "big goal" into more specific smaller goals that are achievable. Immediate progress on an urgent goal (PROFIT IMPROVEMENT) can pave the way for bigger, more strategic goals later.

Grow the Business
Launch High-End New Products
New Market SBUs
Cost Control System

To Get Started . . .
Reduce costs/**increase profit**
with current products to generate
funds for investment.

• • • •

**Specific "Breakthrough"
Projects**

Reduce waste in one
production line in three
months.

Launch one new product with
less rework and cost in six
weeks.

Improve delivery reliability
and income from special
orders in a "trial week."

grandiose, too far reaching, and too complex to be achievable. Especially in rapidly changing businesses and environments, long-cycle projects are hazardous at best. It is better to break the job down into short-cycle, easily implemented pieces. A three-month project, a 100-day plan, even a plan to try something new for a single week.

- *Create clear project assignments.* Use of good work disciplines are crucial to project success. This means a clear "project assignment" is needed to spell out the charge to the project leader and team. Spelling this out in writing helps clarify and build common understanding of what is to be done.

- *Adopt a formal project structure.* Having a formal project structure can help people see how the work is to be organized and the role they are to play.

- *Design a written work plan.* The written work plan is a device, developed by and with the people to be involved in the undertaking, to spell out who is to do what, and when, and how. Hidden assumptions and misconceptions are thus brought to the surface early. Roles are clarified. The "mystery" surrounding the change project is dispelled. People become engaged. The plan is used to track progress. It is a good communication vehicle to tell people what is intended in a project.

- *Develop clear measures*. Finally, clear measures of success are necessary, and a process to feed back results as the project moves forward. Written charts, regular progress reviews, and team planning sessions are devices to measure success.

The Consultant Helps Build Project Management Discipline

The consultant helps to design the project for success by applying these disciplines in the development of the project. The consultant can work with the sponsor to help draft clear assignments. The consultant can sketch out a tentative plan for discussion with the key people. The consultant can propose a project structure. The consultant may organize a planning workshop to bring together the key players and conduct working sessions to develop goals, project structure, work plans, measurements, and reporting processes with the client teams.

In this way, we believe good consultants involve their clients in creating their own success. The consultant advises on the scope, size, and pace of the project to be sure it is realistic and achievable. The consultant asks questions to assure that all key factors have been considered, to assure that the goal is crystal clear and sharply defined, to see that all key parties have been heard and have made their inputs effectively. The consultant reinforces the use of good project disciplines.

Consultants are often retained to be project leaders, and to do all this work. We prefer that clients lead and carry out their own projects, with consultant support. In this

---

FIGURE 13–4   Elements of Project Management

Project Assignment

A project assignment is a written charge to an action team leader and team specifying the goal to be achieved, the rationale for tackling the goal, the main elements to be considered, the help available, and requesting a work plan within a specified time, and results by a specified time.

A clear assignment communicates to everyone what is expected—a key factor in project implementation success.

Project Management Structure

A clear project structure helps people see how they can work to tackle a tough new goal.

Sponsor
(senior manager issues the assignment)

Prime Project Manager
(clear accountability for producing the result and managing the project)

Core Team
(shares the leadership job, members lead specific parts of the project)

Support People
(provide expert inputs and help as required)

FIGURE 13–4 (continued)

Project Work Plan

The work plan is a device to sort out the steps to be taken in a project, by whom, and when. The action team develops this together, so there is solid mutual understanding. Several iterations are often needed to come up with a good plan. The process of developing the plan is highly useful. It brings out different views to be reconciled, makes sure all critical actions are taken, and translates a complex undertaking into understandable terms. It is also used to communicate to people what is being done. It is used as a tool to track progress. The discipline of work planning often makes the difference between success and failure in a change undertaking.

SAMPLE WORK PLAN

Date Prepared:
Revised:

Goal: _____

(Include *what* will be achieved; *how* it will be *measured*; and the *target date*.)

Prime responsibility of: _____

	STEPS (START EACH WITH ACTION VERB)	PERSON RESPONSIBLE*	TARGET DATES		STATUS AS OF:
			BEGIN	END	

*If more than one person is responsible, circle who has prime responsibility.

FIGURE 13–4   (continued)

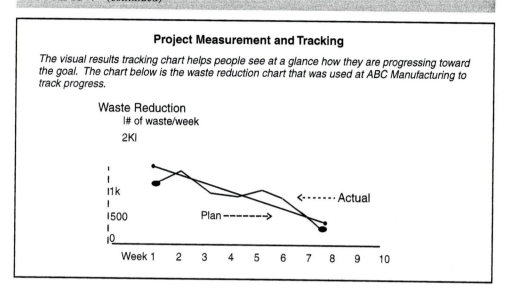

Project Measurement and Tracking

The visual results tracking chart helps people see at a glance how they are progressing toward the goal. The chart below is the waste reduction chart that was used at ABC Manufacturing to track progress.

Waste Reduction

way, the clients get the benefit of the real experience. They get credit for success. They learn how to mobilize more of their resources to accomplish goals. The client organization is strengthened. And the capability does not disappear when the project is over and the consultant leaves.

SKILL SET 3: IMPLEMENTATION SUPPORT

Is the consultant's job finished when the recommendations have been made, the project for improvement planned and launched? Perhaps, but more likely not. There is plenty of slip between the intent and the result.

Most organizations have plenty of projects underway—usually far too many. Energy can easily be diverted from one project to the next. Emergencies and crisis issues arise to distract attention and energy. Hidden factors emerge. Assumptions about the way a process works may turn out to be erroneous. People who thought deadlines could easily be attained are disappointed when suppliers don't deliver on time or other departments slip their schedule. New facts crop up, and the basic concept of the plan is challenged. The organization structure is changed and new people come on to the scene with different ideas about what's to be done.

The consultant who leaves when a project is launched, seemingly successfully, may be disappointed when, a few months or a year later, the project has dissipated, gone off in a wayward direction, or simply evaporated. So, staying with the project to see it through to successful completion is often crucial to achieving results.

To do this, the consultant participates in regular team planning and progress review sessions. The consultant helps to deal with new exigencies to keep the effort on track. The consultant helps people get over and around obstacles. The consultant helps mobilize other groups to keep up their side of the plan.

Most important, the consultant asks the team to take time out to assess what it is accomplishing and what is being learned about how best to achieve the result. What are they learning about how best to mobilize action in their organization? What are they learning about how they can best work together as a team? What are they learning as individuals about their own role, their contribution, and their effectiveness? This learning becomes a permanent part of the organization's capability, and can be tapped for use on future projects.

ABC COMPANY: WORKING THROUGH THE PROCESS

At ABC Manufacturing, we did not suggest another study about change, or a training course in managing change. These would have been just more consulting projects without successful implementation.

Instead, we suggested that the president, the vice president of operations, and their key people get together with us to talk through what could and should be done about costs and profit. We would share some of what we have learned about how organizations create breakthroughs. Then we could formulate an assignment and a project to reduce the costs and improve profit right now.

The meeting with the team was difficult, but ultimately productive. Yes, there was suspicion about yet another consulting project. People had the image of a team coming in to gather data, to take up their time in meetings, and then present a plan no one would implement. No one wanted that to happen again.

We tried to dispel this concern by getting right into the urgent challenge to improve profit. Dean posed the profit issue and the possibility of tackling the three projects we had discussed the previous week. Some people objected. Some felt they should not concern themselves with the short-term profit but go after the high-end product. Others pointed to operating problems and some employee relations problems that had to be solved. Dean persevered, and came back to the need for more profit now. He called for further discussion of specifics of the three projects, what could and could not be done. Soon, an animated work session was underway about how to tackle three cost-reduction projects in the next three months. By the end of the meeting, it was agreed that the vice president of operations and his team would lead. The consultant would help. The reaction in the organization was interesting. "At last we're getting going on something we've needed for a long time, not another consulting study."

We followed up this initial meeting by interviewing people in manufacturing, engineering, sales, and finance to get their views of what needed to be done and how it might best be done. We assembled some of the basic cost data and comparisons to competitors. Then, working with the vice president of operations, we organized a planning workshop with the manufacturing management team, representatives from sales, finance, and engineering. The data was presented, and then work sessions focused on what could be done about the profit situation. People agreed with the concept of the three projects, but each function tended to see the solutions in something *another* function should do. Manufacturing thought sales needed to give longer lead time notice for special orders. Plant managers thought engineering should finish their designs before sending the product into the factory and stop making so many changes afterward. Engineering wanted better defined specs from the marketing and sales people up front before the new product design got too far along.

Figure 13–5 summarizes these common "psychological barriers" that are invariably exhibited when people are uncomfortable or anxious about a new challenge. As we pointed out to ABC, no progress could be made by "blaming others." We suggested instead creating three cross-functional teams to tackle the issues directly. A joint project team could work on productivity and waste reduction in one production line. A second project team could aim to get one new product into manufacturing and shipping with less delay and far less rework. A third project team of sales and manufacturing people could tackle a "trial week" for getting special orders placed with one-week lead time and better performance meeting promised ship dates. The next two days of the workshop were dedicated to organizing the actual work plans for these projects. As the project plans were defined, people became more comfortable that the projects could work and even enthusiastic as they saw the profit impact they could produce. The pall of skepticism was lifting. The "hidden potential" was becoming visible.

Work got underway soon afterward and we worked with each of the teams to help them get their projects underway. Twice-monthly progress reviews were held for all the teams. The president sat in to hear the teams report and made inputs to help overcome obstacles that were encountered. Within six weeks, results were clearly happening and measurable. Within four months, enough gain had been produced that the president was ready to dedicate a small engineering and marketing team to designing one new "high-end" product and get it into production and the market later in the year.

The situation at ABC Manufacturing illustrates the results-focused consulting process:

1. *Assessing readiness.* The initial work sessions and interviews enabled us to select the goal that was seen as urgent and important. We found the ideas and steps that could work. We found the people who were motivated to make some progress.

2. *Design projects for success.* In the planning workshop, we helped the teams design three specific improvement projects and build commitment to carry them out. These were limited in scope and seen as achievable. Project management disciplines were used.

FIGURE 13–5 Typical Psychological Barriers

The following are indicators of anxiety exhibited when people are confronted with a challenge they don't think they can tackle successfully. The concerns are overcome by tackling things people feel they **can** do. Success experiences tend to reduce the anxieties and these kinds of psychological barriers.

Not enough time

Not enough resources

Not enough skill

Others have to do something first

That's different from the way we do things here

Others won't help

3. *Implementation support.* After the workshop, we helped the teams carry their projects to success. We helped strengthen the work plans when changes were needed in them. We helped plan follow-up meetings to review progress and decide how to deal with obstacles. We helped see that new people were brought on board to help when needed.

The success of these projects produced enough confidence (and money) to enable the company to take a next step: get started in the high-end market.

LESSONS LEARNED

The days are long gone when a consulting assignment could be considered successful when the consultant provided a good report, a good system, or a reorganization plan and the client found it helpful and paid the bill.

Now, *results* count. Did the client actually get tangible, beneficial results? That means actual change for the better in earnings, costs, or some other clear bottom-line payoff. While a great deal of consulting work is dedicated to studies, research, and design of new programs or systems, the aim ultimately should be to help the client achieve better results. We stress *achieve* and *results* as the key words. Too often, consulting assignments do not succeed on these dimensions.

We believe that consultants who equip themselves with the skills of implementation—as well as their skills in analysis and strategy—become the truly valuable consultants who are known for their ability to get results as well as their insight as experts in whatever field they may choose. And getting results is what clients value most.

CHAPTER

Delivering Effective Presentations

14

Robert D. Lilien and A. Cowpland Harris

Y ou've completed the fieldwork, the interviews have been analyzed, the survey data tabulated. You and your team have had a dozen client and internal meetings. After an all-nighter, your "Findings and Recommendations" are spiralbound. The big day is arriving: the Client Presentation.

Will that presentation capitalize on all the good work that preceded it, or have you left the preparation to the last minute, with hastily produced visuals and poorly rehearsed presenters? As we show in the matrix in Figure 14–1, knowledge plus professional delivery equals success. A poorly prepared presentation delivered without skill is doomed to failure. A knowledgeable and well-organized presentation delivered skillfully will almost always succeed.

Fortunately, making effective and persuasive presentations is not a difficult skill to develop. Using a few basic principles and with a modest amount of practice, you can be as professional on your feet as you are in using the other skills and techniques of consulting.

But first, a word about fear—fear that makes many people avoid the very practice that would help control it. Know that you are not alone! In fact, according to a survey published years ago in the *Sunday Times* of London and replicated many times since, making presentations leads the list of the 14 worst human fears (Figure 14–2).

Two factors combine to produce nervousness:

- **The fight-or-flight syndrome.** When standing in front of a group of people, pure animal instinct stimulates an increased output of adrenaline to enable us to react to the superior force.

- **Fear of failure.** This is the intellectual component of nervousness. It can build up for days or weeks before the presentation itself.

Robert D. Lilien is the founder of Lilien Communications. A graduate of Andover and Princeton, he holds an AB in English literature.

A. Cowpland Harris is a partner in Lilien Communications. Her particular areas of expertise include the consulting, biotech, and high-tech industries.

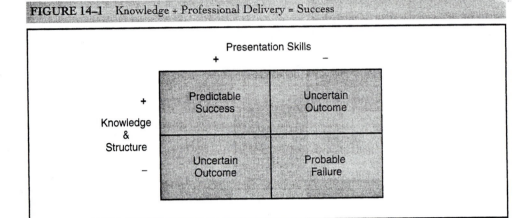

FIGURE 14–1 Knowledge + Professional Delivery = Success

Most presenters don't have the skills to control their nervousness, and this can detract from their effectiveness. The techniques that we describe here will enable you to put your adrenal energy to work positively. Nervous energy is important to good presentations. Without it, we would be dull and uninteresting.

THE TOOLS OF AN EFFECTIVE PRESENTER

Here are the six tools you need to master to be successful when you present:

1. *Audience analysis* to guide your selection of the information you will present
2. *Structure*—ordering the material clearly to help your audience follow your thoughts more easily and absorb the information better
3. *Visuals* to make information understandable to the audience and manageable by you, the presenter
4. *Equipment* to match your audience's orientation, audience size, room configuration, and budget and time constraints
5. *Physical skills* that channel energy and help you display confidence, sincerity, and enthusiasm
6. *Q&A control* to deal effectively with challenging and often interruptive questions that can be as important as the presentation itself

The remainder of this chapter deals with each of the six tools in turn.

TOOL 1: AUDIENCE ANALYSIS

It's almost intuitive to imagine what your audience may be like. But rather than rely on a general sense of whom you're going to face, you should take the time for a more formal analysis. The result of that analysis will be a better fix on what information will be most persuasive, what kinds of evidence will elicit the best response, what equipment to choose, and how to set up the room.

FIGURE 14–2   Making Presentations Leads the List of 14 Worst Human Fears

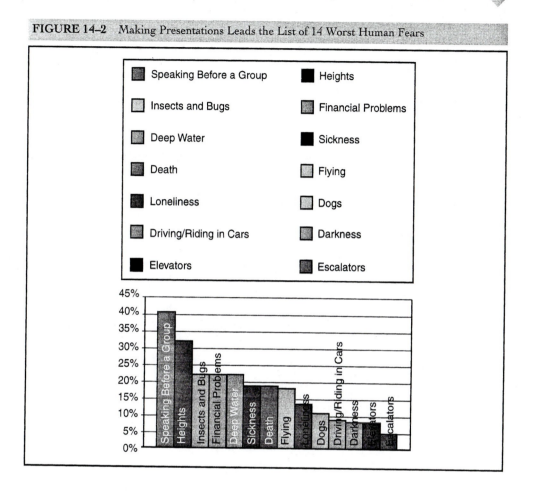

Key Analysis Points

Who are they? This means not only the size of the group, but more importantly, their composition:

- What are their disciplines?
- Are they all familiar with you and your firm?
- Are they more, or less, expert than you?
- Are they decision makers?

Will they listen to you? In a multinational culture, it is critical to ask yourself: Will there be any difficulty in understanding you because of language ability or accent? Will industry or trade jargon help or hurt? Will acronyms baffle? Based on what you know about them, is there a danger of giving them more information than they want to hear? Will your age, sex, or background affect your credibility? Do you have business or professional experience in their field that will interest them?

How will they respond? What's the best guess on how your recommendations will be received? What benefits can you cite that will be most important to the decision makers? What negatives can you anticipate? What challenging questions are you likely to receive?

Once again, if you build an audience checklist that incorporates this kind of analysis, you'll find that what you present will be more effectively targeted—and therefore more likely to be better received.

TOOL 2: STRUCTURE

Most people are not skilled listeners. It is therefore incumbent on the presenter to make his or her report as "listener friendly" as possible.

The process starts with the structure of the presentation. It should follow a logical train so that the listener can easily track where the presenter has been and where he or she is going.

Figure 14–3 illustrates what has proven to be a very successful organization plan for almost any presentation calling for action at its conclusion. (The classic structure for a talk that is purely informational remains: "Tell them what you're going to tell them, tell them, then tell them what you've told them.")

Let's briefly examine each of the elements:

Situation. Is there a problem? Is there an opportunity? Why are you addressing the audience? Is there any background you need to share at this point?

FIGURE 14-3   The Logic Train

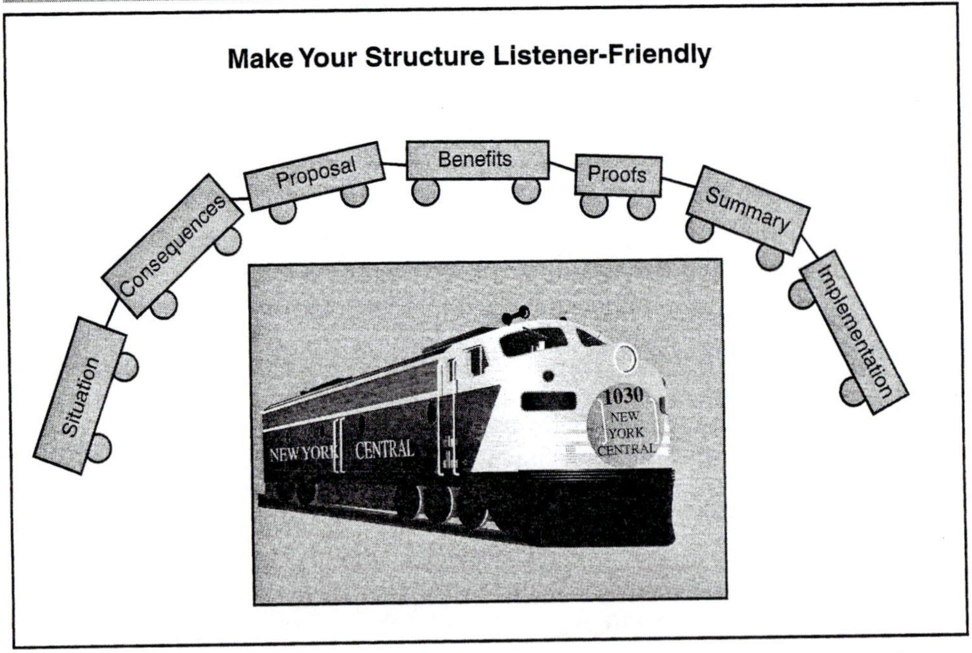

Make Your Structure Listener-Friendly

Consequences. What is the impact of the situation? Are there adverse effects (money loss, employee turnover, lost opportunity) that will impress the audience?

Proposal. What is your idea to address the situation? (It is often risky to examine a range of possible solutions, ending with your recommendation. It can seem like a device; worse, it can raise the possibility that a solution you rejected will be preferred by some of your listeners. Generally, you should save alternative ideas for an appendix.)

Benefits. The benefits of your proposal to your audience.

Proofs. What evidence do you have that your idea is a good one? Probably the most powerful forms of evidence are:

- Examples of how your idea has worked in other situations (departments of the same company, in other companies, in other industries).
- Statistics.
- Although not a form of hard evidence, a well-chosen analogy can be both convincing and memorable.

Summary. This should be a brief recap of the situation, the proposal, and the benefits.

Implementation. How can your audience put your idea into action? The summary should include *who does what*, and *when it should be done*.

If you are going to use a schematic for the action plan, try to make it seem as simple as possible.

TOOL 3: VISUALS

How to create good visuals could be a book in itself and in fact is the subject of many. A classic in the field is *The Visual Display of Quantitative Information*.[1] The American Association of Petroleum Geologists published a manual for technical presentations in 1978 that is remarkably applicable today. And equipment manufacturers weigh in with their own advice, which they will happily share with anyone who requests it.

Accordingly, this section is necessarily a brief overview of a critical part of the presentation process.

To state it briefly, make your visuals:

- Simple
- Bold (easy to read with the room lights up)
- Colorful

These guidelines should underlie the many choices you have to aid your talks:

- Words
- Graphs
- Flow and organization charts
- Schematics
- Other (photographs, maps, cartoons, clip art)

---

[1]Edward R. Tufte, *The Visual Display of Quantitative Information* (Graphics Press, 1983).

Words

Probably the most used and frequently overused visual type consists of words. Presenting with nothing but words will be predictably dull and boring; notwithstanding, word visuals are integral to presentations, so when you use them:

- Create brief headlines, preferably on one line.
- Use bullet points.
- Use dash points sparingly.
- Strive for 4 by 4.

That last point simply means trying to limit your visual to four bullets with no more than four words per line.

Graphs

Whether line, bar, column, pie, or scatterpoint, try to make your graphs uncluttered. Don't overlabel or overdetail the scales. If you can stick to single coordinate graphs (with a vertical Y axis and a horizontal X axis) do so. If you've analyzed your audience properly, you'll draw back from showing complicated graphs that might confuse a significant number of listeners or require what would be tedious explanations for the more sophisticated.

The same admonitions apply to flowcharts and schematics such as matrixes.

Finally, mix up your visuals to stimulate audience interest and remember: be *simple, bold*, and *colorful*.

TOOL 4: EQUIPMENT

If this section had been written in 1990, the standard list of equipment options would have been:

- Flip charts
- Overheads
- Slides

Today, the fourth option is the laptop presentation (most frequently made using Microsoft's PowerPoint software). Tomorrow, overheads and slides may be truly a thing of the past. A few words on each:

Flip charts are the least formal presentation option, excellent for round table or horseshoe seating and interactive meetings. Normally you would hand letter them.

Overheads (transparencies) are still the most widely used equipment option, excellent for all but very large audiences. They are inexpensive, quickly produced, universally available, and have relatively few disadvantages.

Slides (or 35 mm) are no longer produced very frequently. While they are expensive and relatively slow to produce, their quality can be excellent if the producers keep them simple, bold, and colorful.

Laptop presentations have all the advantages of slides and overheads and few drawbacks. Consultants must be cautious not to get caught up in the technology with too much animation and too many fades, builds, and whistles and bells. You—not the light show—should be the center of attention.

TOOL 5: PHYSICAL SKILLS

This brings us to what *you* bring to the presentation—which in one word should be passion. If you aren't committed to your talk, or can't muster up excitement and energy, send an e-mail. Assuming the adrenal energy is there, how do you harness it?

Linkage is the key physical skill. When you make a presentation, create a series of short dialogues with members of your audience, using extended eye contact. This concept of linkage, talking with, not at, people, creates personal engagement. It has immense benefit to the speaker for several reasons:

- In talking to one person, the impact of the group, the "superior force," is reduced.
- **You diminish visual distraction.** Remember that the brain must process all the information the eyes bring in. When a speaker scans an audience, as is often taught in public speaking programs, the speaker overloads his or her brain. Conversing with one person at a time happily supplies the optimum amount of information for the brain to deal with.
- **You can "read" your audience.** One to one, you can see by the facial expression of the person you are talking to whether he or she is "buying in." This is essential to success. (If you are addressing a very large audience, generally over 100 people, you may not be able to make true eye contact at the back of the room. Nevertheless, you should address yourself to a person in the back, rather than a pair of eyes, to create the impact we discuss next.)

Let's examine the effect that linkage has on your audience. As Figure 14–4 shows, it is eventually an incremental relationship builder, the foundation of good business. Credibility, trust, and integrity are just a few elements that contribute to sound relationships.

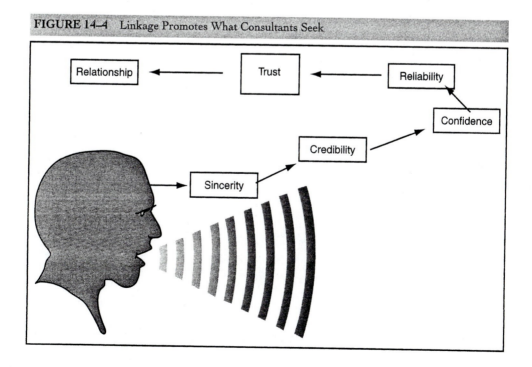

FIGURE 14–4   Linkage Promotes What Consultants Seek

The physical skill that communicates sincerity best is sustained eye contact. Lack of it, even if it is the rapid eye movement caused by nervousness, can undermine faith in the message. (Think of the expression "shifty-eyed" and make sure it doesn't apply to you!)

Linkage not only helps the speaker think better on his or her feet, it engenders trust, the cornerstone of client relationships.

Descriptive gesture is the next key physical skill. One reaction to the adrenal surge that occurs when we face an audience is the tendency to suppress it. This often results in clenched fists, clasped hands, hands in pockets, or other actions that don't contribute to the message and often detract from it.

Sometimes speakers will pace back and forth to release their nervous energy, which can also be distracting. The solution—which comes naturally with linkage—is to allow yourself to gesture as you do in one-to-one conversation. Descriptive gesture, in particular, enhances understanding; simultaneously, it holds listener attention. And when you describe, keep your arms above your waist and away from your body.

It should be emphasized that gesture isn't aimless hand waving or talking with your hands. It is simply allowing the body to do what it does naturally: be a part of the verbal communications process.

What you do with your hands and arms determines your vocal inflection. Rigidity creates monotone; motion creates change in pitch, emphasis, and pace. This, in turn, stimulates your audience to listen better.

Volume

The next skill is simply to *speak up!* One effect of nervousness can be the suppression of volume, which will communicate timidity and lack of confidence in the message.

By initially establishing linkage with individuals toward the back of the room, you will naturally raise your volume to accommodate the greater distance. Remember that the sound that you make when you speak sounds louder to you than it does to your audience. Your voice resounds within your skull; it's at its source. By the time the energy is dissipated by distance, what you feel is adequate volume may sound weak to your listeners.

Work to keep your volume strong. It's almost impossible for most of us to overdo our vocal energy.

Physical Skills with Visual Aids

Now let's look at the actions you should take to ensure that your visual aids really do contribute to your presentation rather than get in your way.

What happens the instant new information is flashed on the screen? Your audience's eyes immediately go to the screen, instinctively responding to the stimulus of new information. Until your audience has absorbed the visual impact of what appears on the screen, your words will go unheeded.

It's therefore important to quench this visual thirst before you get deeply into the meaning of whatever you're showing on the screen.

You can accomplish this by describing to the audience what it is that they are looking at, so that you orient them:

- Read the headline aloud, word for word.
- Touch on the principal elements in the visual.

Phrases such as, "What you see here . . . ," "Here we have . . . ," "The vertical axis of this graph shows . . . , the horizontal shows . . ." are extremely useful. (Always tell your audience what the axes are on graphs; if the next visual shows a graph with the same axes as the preceding one, simply say so.)

How do you get that information onto the screen? Use the overhead projector (OHP) or laptop as your transition center:

1. Stand with the projector on your left, feet at shoulder width. (Unless there is a compelling reason to the contrary, the overhead projector and the screen should always be positioned to the speaker's left. In this way, the audience's attention will naturally swing back to the presenter.)
2. With the visual you are about to describe unexposed, give a brief lead-in to build anticipation for your words (e.g., "So what are the benefits of our proposal?").
3. Place the visual on the OHP without speaking.
4. Move back to the screen before beginning to talk.

When using a laptop with PowerPoint, the same rules apply, except that in most cases you can't preview your next visual. Stay silent as you click forward on your keyboard or mouse.

Once you are back at the screen, remember a primary rule: Talk only when you are in linkage with a member of the audience. (Expressed another way, never talk to the screen!)

Try to follow these steps:

- Look at the visual to orient yourself and give yourself thinking time. Do this in silence.
- With your left hand, direct your audience to where you want them to look—again in silence.
- Pick out a member of your audience and, with your left hand remaining as a pointer, describe/explain, using your right hand to gesture and give a third dimension to the two-dimensional image on the screen.
- Once your audience is properly focused, you can then use both hands to amplify your words.

This can all be summarized in the P-cubed formula:

- **Point**—Direct silently with your left hand.
- **Pick**—Link eyes with an audience member.
- **Present**—Give your first thought to an audience member; continue with a series of linkages; repeat P-cubed as required.

And remember that your left hand, with open palm, is the best of all pointers. Avoid collapsible pointers that often lead speakers into acting like amateur Toscaninis. Even worse is the laser pointer where the palsied red dot almost always misses its target, to the consternation of the speaker and the confusion of the audience.

TOOL 6: Q&A CONTROL

How you handle challenging questions can impact the success of your presentation enormously. If you fail to handle the tough questions well, you may wipe out what you've done well previously. If you respond with intelligence and equanimity, you'll reinforce your status and gain client approval. Here's how you do it:

Always follow the steps shown in Figure 14–5 with a large, unfamiliar audience. You can relax or sometimes omit these guidelines in small groups whose members know each other.

1. Elicit questions with a raised hand (in a large group, hold your hand high; in a boardroom, you can be more casual).

2. Designate the person you've selected with an open palm (pointing can look accusatory).

3. Absorb the question as it comes in—with eye contact and total attention to the content. Even if the question is hostile, you can nod to show that you're listening (not agreeing).

4. Rephrase or repeat the question away from the questioner, to show the audience that the answer belongs to the group.

5. Start your answer with the person who asked the question, but always finish with someone else unless:
   - You truly want approval, a comment, or a follow-up question.
   - The questioner's position in the hierarchy demands it.

6. Raise your hand again to elicit the next question.

When you rephrase a question, avoid saying, "The question was . . . ," "John's question is . . . ," "I have been asked . . . ," or any other lead-in. Simply say, as appropriate:

Who . . .	Where . . .	How . . .
What . . .	When . . .	Which . . .
Does/do . . .	Can/could . . .	
What about . . .	Are/is . . .	
How many/much . . .	Will/would . . .	
Why . . .		

It pays to prepare for Q&A by working with your colleagues to anticipate the tough questions and practice how you'll answer them.

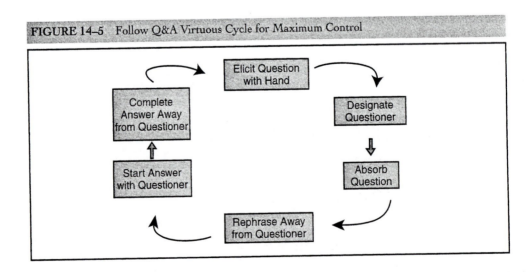

FIGURE 14–5 Follow Q&A Virtuous Cycle for Maximum Control

SUMMARY

How well you deliver your intellectual input will determine how successful you will be. This chapter has described the six tools that shape the quality of professional presentations, each requiring thought and preparation.

Here are some final thoughts that frequently come up when we discuss presenting:

Rehearsal. Certainly run through your presentation at least once, by yourself, or, better, in front of colleagues. But don't overdo it; you don't want to get stale.

Memorization. Don't try to memorize your lines. Unless you're a professional actor, they're likely to sound wooden. Worse, under the pressure we all feel on our feet, you're liable to draw a blank—with no prompter behind the curtain to bail you out. Presenting **isn't** acting, after all, it's **you** in high gear, sharing your ideas with passion.

Humor. Great when impromptu, but no jokes, please! They're a minefield, often falling flat and always in danger of somehow offending someone in your audience.

Standing or sitting. Even if you're in a boardroom, stand if you can. If that's definitely not appropriate, lean forward in your chair, both feet on the floor, and follow the same guidelines of linkage, gesture, and vocal energy.

Disasters. When the unexpected occurs during a presentation, it's easy to get thrown off track. You can prevent some disasters by preparing well: Always bring backup hard copy of your presentation. If everything fails (the room has gone completely dark, for instance) call a break.

Professional help. You can learn tennis without lessons, but you'll probably never be better than a good playground player. The same is true with presenting: It pays to get professional help. Your college, university, or employer almost always offers training.

PART

IV

Learning from Consultants

Although all consultants agree that their job is to help improve a client company's performance, in practice consultants differ markedly in how they approach that task. Some specialize in strategic positioning and examine the competitive setting in which companies operate. Others focus on the development of systems that can increase efficiency. Some look to improve revenues through marketing and reputation building, and still others work on restructuring financial assets to improve profitability.

Part 4 of this book asks a handful of consultants to discuss in specific terms what they do and how they do it—"real life" cases from "the real world." We invited consultants from different companies whose strengths involve working with clients in specific areas to try their hand to writing about their experiences. The assignment we posed was (a) to describe a problem that a real client came to them with, and then to walk us through (b) how they conceptualized the problem, (c) how they structured the engagement, (d) how the engagement unfolded, and (e) what they learned from it. Wherever possible, we also asked that they retain the real client's name. Most authors succeeded in doing so by obtaining client authorization to discuss the situation; some were not able to do so, and in those cases names were disguised to protect client confidentiality.

Among the firms best known for consulting on strategic issues very few names stand out, but McKinsey & Company and Booz Allen Hamilton are always among them. For Chapter 15, McKinsey gave permission to republish an article written by two of their managing directors, Kevin Coyne and Somu Subramaniam. The article illustrates how McKinsey adds value by raising important questions about strategic positioning, and thereby develops a company's ability to think through its current and future competitiveness.

Strategic positioning is ultimately about effective resource utilization. In Chapter 16, Tim Laseter of Booz Allen & Hamilton describes "strategic sourcing" as a key factor in value creation. He revisits an engagement he led in the early 1990s to improve materials management at ARCO's oil production facilities in Alaska, and in doing so shows us in detail how a preliminary pilot project shaped thinking about the situation and led to a broader engagement to implement recommendations.

In Chapter 17, Elise Walton and Peter Thies of Mercer-Delta introduce us to the "strategic enterprise"—a concept developed by their consulting firm to address what they see as the necessity of close and loose coupling between a corporate parent and its subsidiaries. Their case explores an engagement with AT&T's Business Services division in which Mercer-Delta helped the company generate large-scale change. In this chapter, we get to see from the inside the architecture of a change process used to carry out the transformation, the "imperatives" it addresses, and how such an engagement unfolds—political warts and all.

As technology continues to sweep across industry, Chuck Durrant and Deborah Baxley show us how IBM consults to clients to align information technology with business strategy. In Chapter 18, they describe in detail the frameworks they relied on to examine the way a client company uses information technology, and how it might make more strategic use of the technology. We are invited to see how IBM Consulting applied these frameworks in an engagement with First Trust Bancorp.

Often, consulting firms are thought to have an "arm's-length" relationship with their clients. That relationship is often attributed to payment structures based on fixed fees or time-based fees, which can encourage cost escalation and discourage close work between consultant and client. Chapter 19 describes how consulting firms can actually "partner" with their clients. The case concerns the consulting firm PHB Hagler-Bailly (acquired by the fast-growing London-based consulting firm PA Consulting in October 1999) and a client "EdisonOnline," a pseudonym for a large U.S. electric utility company. Consultants Craig Hart, Gloria Moon, and Soam Goel describe how firms like PA Consulting have sought to overcome the limitations of traditional fee structures by accepting equity in lieu of cash payment.

Speaking of financial risks, Chapter 20 takes us into the heady arena of risk management by sharing a case from the careers of Jose Molina and Pedro Masetto when they were with Arthur Andersen. Jose and Pedro worked with "Oilco" (a pseudonym for one of Latin America's largest oil companies) to improve its risk-handling capabilities. Financial risk management is not only about money—it's also about creating an organizational infrastructure and processes, as well as a corporate culture that facilitates communication across departments and units. This case details an engagement that began with identifying critical sources of risk the company faced, and then deducing appropriate hypotheses that, if verified, could drive up profitability and reduce risk. The chapter also shows us how these consultants helped Oilco create an internal "strategic risk management unit" that would identify risk exposures and train managers about them. The subsequent demise of Arthur Andersen itself in 2002 is ironic, to say the least. It resulted from the firm's own inability to fully anticipate and control the risks it faced in getting too close to audit clients such as Enron.

Financial risks develop from uncertainties in input costs and in product revenues. Companies may also face reputational risks that derive from uncertainties that are not only investor motivated, but that derive from loss of support from other constituents such as customers, the surrounding community, government, and even employees. In Chapter 21, Scott Meyer and Charles Fombrun discuss the concept of "reputational risk," and show how it can be embraced through a systematic process of reputation management whose purpose is to reduce the reputation risk exposure a client company faces.

In Chapter 22, Michelle Calhoun, Charles Fombrun, and Robert Laud take us front and center into the buoyant world of venture consulting. As they show us, the consulting world is constantly innovating. The creation of spinoff firms is one of the ways incubator groups like the Stanford Research Institute launch new practice areas. AtomicTangerine was one such company whose beginnings were fraught with promise. The collapse of the Internet bubble that its future was predicated upon shows the challenge of new business creation and reputation building in a turbulent world.

Above all, the chapters of Part 4 show us how consultants *really* work. They illustrate how *conceptual skills* have to combine inextricably with *technical skills* and *execution skills* in real-world situations. When they are able to do so, both consultants and the clients they are serving derive real benefit.

CHAPTER 15

Bringing Discipline to Strategy

Kevin P. Coyne and Somu Subramaniam

Although strategy today is a demanding, complex, and subtle discipline, you would never know it from reading the management journals and business best sellers of the past five years. Each season brings a new crop of experts proclaiming that their frameworks—core competencies, customer retention, management ecosystems, strategic intent, time-based competition, total quality management, "white spaces," managing chaos, value migration—are definitive. These solutions sometimes prove an exquisite fit, but just as often they offer only a mediocre approximation.

Nonetheless, managers reach out to these new theories because the classical microeconomics-based model of strategy is inadequate in a growing number of situations. Consider some recent examples:

- A telco executive must make a $1 billion "yes or no" decision on whether to invest in a new network technology to provide new services to customers. One best-practice market research survey predicts a return on investment of 25 percent; a second, equally valid, forecasts minus 25 percent. What should that executive do?

- How should executives at a software firm deal with a large customer that is also the firm's chief competitor—and one of its biggest suppliers?

- How should the chief executive officer of a credit card company think strategically about positioning when segments and value propositions come and go every six months?

- A large regional bank recognizes that to succeed on the retail level, the bank must take the lead by discovering huge but as yet unrecognized customer needs. How can it embark on such a strategy?

All of these cases lie outside the conditions for which the traditional model of strategy was designed. In fact, our work suggests that up to 50 percent of the strategic problems faced by large companies lie outside those conditions. Equally, no single new framework can address them all.

Therefore, it is time for a new approach to strategy. The past 20 years have seen a wider range of business environments emerge than ever before. No single strategy prescription can be appropriate in each of them. What is needed is a more robust business model that can handle a much broader set of circumstances and suggest when and how specific theories should be used.

Kevin Coyne is a director in McKinsey's Atlanta office.

Somu Subramaniam is a director in McKinsey's New York office.

An earlier version of this article was originally published in *The McKinsey Quarterly,* 1996, number 4.

THE SHORTCOMINGS OF THE TRADITIONAL APPROACH

At the heart of the traditional strategy framework lies a microeconomic model of industry. Figure 15–1 illustrates the model's popularized form, the Porter model, which combines exogenous forces (such as technology and regulation) that act on an industry with endogenous forces.

More important, it makes three tacit but crucial assumptions. First, an industry consists of a set of unrelated buyers, sellers, substitutes, and competitors that interact at arm's length. Second, wealth will accrue to companies that can erect barriers against competitors and potential entrants; in other words, structural advantage is the source of value. Third, uncertainty is low enough to permit you to make accurate predictions about the participants' behavior and to choose a strategy accordingly. Even if any one of these assumptions were correct, the likelihood of all three being so would be low. Let us examine their validity.

Industry Structure

The traditional microeconomic model is based on a "rational" industrial structure in which each player competes at arm's length, not only with its rivals but also with its customers and suppliers for control of economic rents. However, at least two other industry structures are commonly found: codependent systems and privileged relationships. In both of these structures, conduct differs from the sort prescribed by the traditional model—and anyone blindly applying the standard microeconomic rules will get into trouble.

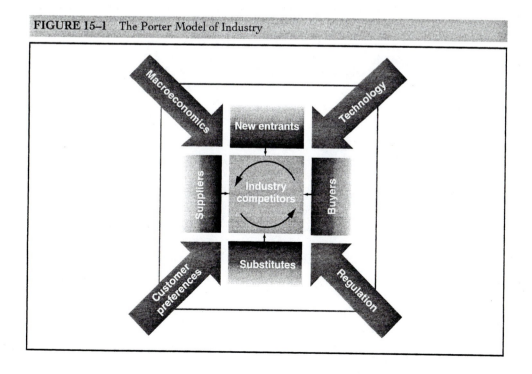

FIGURE 15–1   The Porter Model of Industry

Codependent systems are cross-industry structures such as alliances, networks, and economic webs. The most novel but increasingly widespread of these is the economic web: a set of companies using a common architecture to deliver independent elements of an overall value proposition that grows stronger as more companies join the set (for example, the "Wintel" and Apple webs in the computer industry). The fortunes of any player in a web depend both on the success of the web as a whole and on how well that player uses its own position of influence within the web. The strategic challenge is to strike the right balance between the prosperity of the web and that of individual participants; greedy players can harm themselves as well as wreck the web.

High-tech industries such as computers, telecommunications, software, and multimedia are moving toward web structures, but evidence of webs can also be seen in older sectors such as automobiles, health care, forest products, and financial services.

Privileged relationships are structures within which firms single out other firms in the same market for special treatment because of a financial interest (Korean chaebols, Mexican grupos, and Japanese keiretsus), friendship, trust, or ethnic loyalty. Governments create similar business relationships in the name of national defense or pride.

Consider also the Indians and overseas Chinese, who have networks of family-owned corporations in which relationships among members are clearly privileged. In such situations, the actions of network members must be understood in the light not only of their own strategies but also of the strategy of the whole network and of the individual members' positions in the family hierarchy.

Source of Advantage

The traditional microeconomic model assumes that wealth will accrue to businesses that have a structural advantage over competitors and potential industry entrants. In major sectors of the economy—telecommunications, basic materials, transportation—this is still true. But competitive advantage can also be built on two other foundations.

Frontline Execution   Companies in some industries win by consistently outperforming competitors in the execution of day-to-day tasks. In commercial lines property-and-casualty insurance, for instance, a few players have demonstrated that superior underwriting and claims handling can overwhelm any structural advantage a competitor may have.

Insight and Foresight   Some firms create wealth by possessing knowledge or having insights that others lack. The knowledge may lie in scientific or technical expertise (Hewlett-Packard's continuing superiority in printers), pattern recognition (the ability of some banks to make consistent profits by taking short-term positions in foreign exchange), or sheer creativity (Disney's unmatched success in animated films).

If the three (that is, one old and two new) sources of competitive advantage are brought together with the three (again, one old and two new) industry structures mentioned earlier, the result is a new model that better reflects the rich strategic possibilities of today's industrial landscape (Figure 15–2).

Levels of Uncertainty

The traditional model assumes that uncertainty in an industry is low enough for executives to make reasonably accurate predictions on which to base strategy. In reality, the future is usually harder to judge. When faced with uncertainty, executives tend to leap

FIGURE 15–2   A New Industry Model

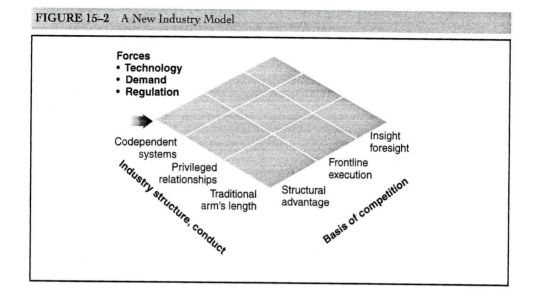

to extremes. Some simply pretend that uncertainty does not exist; others see it, but it paralyzes them.

What should strategists do when the result (at least in part) of their situation analysis is "I don't know, and no amount of good analysis will tell me"? Certainly, they should not just resort to scenario planning and recommend options. The secret of devising successful strategies lies in ascertaining just how uncertain the environment is. Four levels of uncertainty can be identified. At level one, the traditional microeconomic model still holds, and strategists can develop a single useful prediction of the future. This means not that there is no uncertainty, but rather that analysis will be sufficiently robust to allow a clear strategic direction to emerge. Appropriate sensitivity analysis can be performed after a course of action has been determined. Consider the fast-food industry, in which change over the past decade has been evolutionary, allowing companies to base their strategies on predictions.

At level two, analysis shows that the future will follow one of a few discrete scenarios, though it cannot predict which one. In late 1995, for example, the outline of the pending U.S. telecommunications legislation was clear; what was not clear was whether it would pass Congress. In this case, strategy could be built around two possible scenarios. Generally speaking, since the number of scenarios is usually small at this level of uncertainty, strategy can be determined analytically.

At level three, continuous uncertainty prevails. Though there are only a few dimensions of uncertainty, analysis can't reduce the future to a limited number of discrete scenarios. Instead, the reality might lie anywhere along a continuum for each dimension. Many new technologies, for instance, face uncertainty over the rate of market acceptance.

At level four, there is true ambiguity: a number of dimensions of continuous uncertainty. Consider the case of a multinational deciding whether to invest in Russia in 1992. In addition to an unusual degree of uncertainty over demand, the company would have faced uncertainty about the laws that would govern contracts, about who

FIGURE 15-3   Situation Analysis

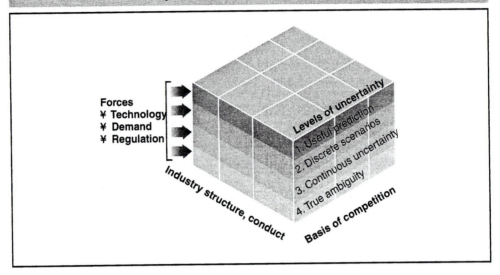

would have the power to enter into them, and even about whether current suppliers and distributors would remain in business.

These graduated levels of uncertainty govern the type of situation analysis needed. At level one, traditional frameworks are entirely appropriate. At level two, scenario planning, quantitative game theory, and options-pricing frameworks will be needed to help determine strategy. At levels three and four, qualitative game theory, latent demand analysis, and evolutionary models will be required.

When this concept of uncertainty is combined with the new industry model illustrated in Figure 15-2, the result is a new approach to situation analysis (Figure 15-3). This new approach takes account of the varying levels of uncertainty about the external forces acting on an industry, their effect on it, and its interactions with itself. It also shows that the level of uncertainty can rise and fall over time.

A NEW DEFINITION OF STRATEGY

Traditionally, strategy was defined as an integrated set of actions leading to a sustainable competitive advantage. This definition continues to work well in traditional industry structures characterized by a low degree of uncertainty. Beyond this limited context, however, we believe that a broader definition is needed. For example, in situations of high uncertainty, strategy is likely to call for more than a single integrated set of actions; it will probably require investment in a variety of options, small bets, and so on. The new definition: Strategy is a handful of decisions that drive or shape most of a company's subsequent actions, are not easily changed once made, and have the greatest impact on whether a company meets its strategic objectives.

To be specific, this handful of decisions consists of selecting the company's strategic posture, identifying the source or sources of competitive advantage, developing the business concept, and constructing tailored value delivery systems.

Let us look at each of these decisions in detail.

Strategic Posture

Depending on the extent of its ambition, a company can adopt one of three strategic postures: adapting, shaping, or reserving the right to play. Adapting is the most common choice. A company analyzes its environment and then commits itself to a set of actions that conform to that environment. Although different levels of uncertainty might require different actions, the mindset is always one of seizing known opportunities and responding to known threats.

Shaping means attempting to change the environment to benefit the firm. Shapers invent entirely new products for which demand is only latent, alter the basic structure of their industry, or develop entirely new ways to compete. They believe they can influence the commercial world so profoundly that a detailed analysis of their current environment is scarcely relevant. This belief may rest on the power of an idea or on consistently superior capabilities. Either way, shapers depend on their own ability to change their external circumstances.

Shaping turns out to be attractive in some pretty counterintuitive cases. In highly uncertain environments, for instance, one would normally be tempted to hedge and avoid commitment. Yet for some strong players, this might be the best time for a bold move. Imagine a group of frightened children lost in a forest. The best strategy might be for the biggest kid to shout, "I know the way. Follow me!" Even if that kid didn't really know the way and it took hours to get out of the forest, the group would stay together. Similarly, if there is uncertainty about the direction of an industry, a bold shaping posture may be the best option.

That said, shaping isn't always advisable. Of the three postures, it offers the highest reward but also the highest risk. It is difficult to create massive wealth without being a shaper; think of the steel and railroad barons of the nineteenth century, Thomas Edison, Microsoft, and Netscape. But think too of Zap Mail, Microsoft Network, Betamax, and the English Channel Tunnel. Reserving the right to play, the final posture, is a noncommittal one that consists of doing the minimum required to keep open the possibility of becoming a strong player later. It is not the same thing as taking no action at all; rather, it is an investment in learning.

Underlying these three postures are fundamental differences in mindset. However, it would be wrong to oversimplify; companies like Microsoft seem able to blend elements of all three, and a company's choice of posture may change as conditions do. In general, though, most companies should aim to develop a single dominant posture.

Competitive Advantage

Earlier, we noted three different bases of competitive advantage: structural advantage, frontline execution, and insight coupled with foresight. Each, of course, has many subvariants, such as core competencies, time-based competition, and hustle. And new sources of competitive advantage may well emerge in the future. Although companies have many tools for selecting a source of advantage, they seldom realize how this choice can "lock them in" in unexpected ways.

A structural advantage comes about when, for structural reasons, competitors cannot copy a company's value proposition. The company is then necessarily locked into a particular set of customers or needs. If these change, the strategy may become obsolete.

Front-line execution strategies are usually even more locked in, committing an entire organization to adhere to a set pattern of performance. One company's program to build execution skills incorporated 65 separate subprograms to change its organization structure and its hiring and pay practices and to introduce new information systems, policies, and procedures. Not surprisingly, the company had little flexibility to adjust its strategy if conditions changed.

Insight and foresight might appear to be a more flexible basis for competitive advantage, since they do not entail locking a company into a single value proposition in terms of its products or markets. However, there is often lock-in at the input level: A company that is dependent on one source of insight can be vulnerable if it becomes less valuable. Moreover, companies can create wealth only if enough customers buy their goods or services, so insight and foresight must usually be combined with structural advantage or frontline execution if they are to create value.

Business Concept

Translating postures and sources of advantage into specific strategic decisions involves more than simply choosing your positioning. Any complex business concept will probably be constructed from four types of building blocks: big bets, real and financial options, no-regrets moves, and safety nets.

Big bets are major commitments to a course of action that may pay off handsomely in some situations but produce dismal results in others. Real and financial options give a company flexibility, either financially or operationally. Financial options are well understood. Real options are investments, in tangible capital goods or operating expenses, that are made to learn more or to create flexibility (e.g., installing machinery that can work on a variety of raw materials). No-regrets moves make sense no matter what eventually happens. And safety nets are options specifically designed to protect a company against a big bet going bad.

Consider the case of a large specialty chemical company that faced uncertainty over which of two new technologies its industry would accept. If the company had decided to make a major investment in one of the two, it might have been able to convince other players that its choice was superior and so shape the industry's technology base. This constituted a big bet: If the company failed to convince the others, its plant would be stranded. It could have complemented the bet with no-regrets initiatives, such as reduced costs and programs to improve sales, and added a safety net provision by planning to retrofit the second technology if the bet proved wrong.

The management at this company actually chose a strategy consisting of several real options: It formed an alliance with a new entrant using one of the new technologies while retrofitting several of its own small plants with the other. It took several no-regrets measures but didn't need a safety net.

Tailored Value Delivery Systems

Big bets, real options, and so on are the building blocks from which new strategies are assembled. For each of these building blocks, companies need to construct separate value delivery systems. Imagine that a company facing a choice between two technologies elects to buy real options to cover both of them. Real options, unlike financial options, are investments in organizations and people. When these options turn out to be poor, a significant human and organizational cost is attached to unwinding them. Thus, strategies capable of dealing with the complexities of today's business environment are likely to call for the ability to create, grow, and manage multiple value delivery systems simultaneously.

EVOLVING STRATEGY

Besides making the four strategic decisions outlined above, managers must learn to recognize the dynamics inherent in every situation and manage the building blocks of strategy effectively over time.

Traditionally, strategic management has meant little more than staying the course. Today, however, it means actively managing the way strategy unfolds month after month, year after year. That might entail drawing up contingent road maps in which the attainment of specific milestones clarifies the right strategy; it might equally mean recognizing that strategy will have to evolve as industry conditions do.

Just as the new framework changes what is required of strategy, it changes the strategy development process—especially who actually develops strategy and when they do it. Where there is little uncertainty, and structural advantage is critical (for instance, capacity decisions in the chemical industry), a traditional strategy development process, led by senior line management and conducted annually, can work well. In industries with low levels of uncertainty where front-line execution is the source of differentiation, bottom-up processes could be the right choice.

By contrast, where uncertainty is high, web-like structures are in the ascendant, or a company aspires to be a shaper, the strategy development process will probably need to be totally revamped. In fact, strategy development might not be a separate process at all. Instead, direction setting by the CEO or business leader would be combined with extremely short communication lines to the workers in the marketplace and with real-time rather than periodic adjustment of the strategy.

How does this new approach to strategy relate to concepts that have been proposed by others? We believe that, like the traditional model, most of these concepts are appropriate only in specific situations within the broader picture (Figure 15–4). The customer retention framework, for example, is really valid only in front-line execution industries with limited uncertainty. Other companies that base their strategy on customer retention will be focusing on minute improvements to a value proposition that competitors could blow away if the environment changed.

We have examined more than 25 separate strategy concepts proposed over the past few years. Close examination of any of these strategies reveals how their underlying assumptions limit the circumstances in which they can be used. Consequently, strategists should be familiar with all of these concepts but not biased toward any of them. The focus should be narrowed to a specific submodel only after it has been determined which strategy is most appropriate to the situation. In today's diverse business world, strategists must take into account a wider range of industry structures and bases of competitive advantage, as well as a higher degree of uncertainty. Admittedly, this is more complex than looking for keys under a guru's lamppost. But if any area of business deserves the extra effort, surely it is strategy.

FIGURE 15-4   Comparison with Other Strategy Concepts

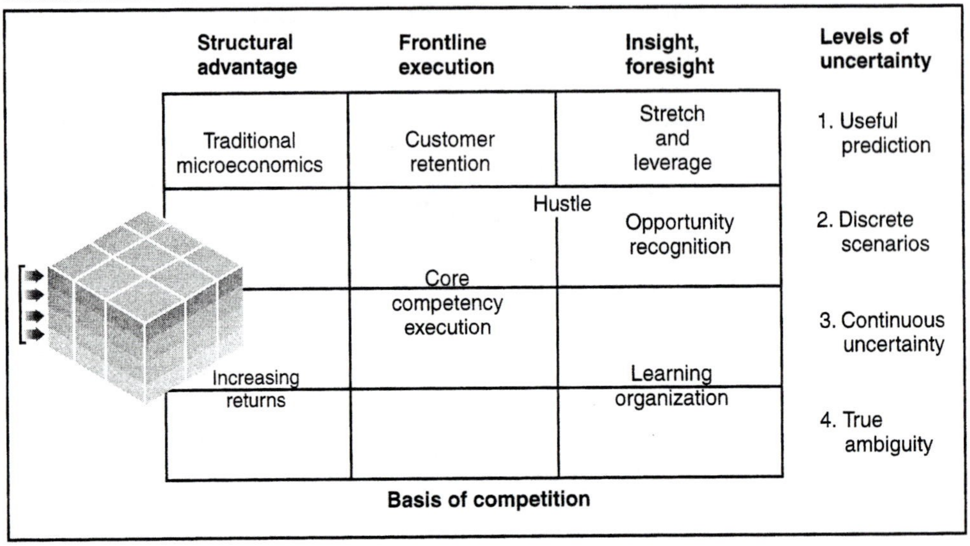

	Structural advantage	Frontline execution	Insight, foresight	Levels of uncertainty
	Traditional microeconomics	Customer retention	Stretch and leverage	1. Useful prediction
		Hustle	Opportunity recognition	2. Discrete scenarios
		Core competency execution		3. Continuous uncertainty
	Increasing returns		Learning organization	4. True ambiguity

Basis of competition

An earlier version of this article was originally published in *The McKinsey Quarterly,* 1996, number 4.

CHAPTER

Strategic Sourcing

Timothy M. Laseter

In responding to the invitation to describe a "typical" Booz Allen engagement for this book, we found ourselves in a quandary. On one hand, given our focus on help-ing senior management solve complex problems, no two client engagements address identical problems or apply identical methodologies. At the same time, given the confidential nature of our work, we cannot share our most current cases without exposing proprietary advantages gained for our clients. As a result, we rarely publicize our engagements and choose to remain in the background—leaving our clients in the forefront. On the other hand, since Booz Allen Hamilton, founded in 1914, pioneered the business of management consulting, we found it inconceivable that a text on man-agement consulting might not include a case study from our firm.

To solve the dilemma, we selected a client engagement that is already in the public domain and that describes one of our more traditional service offerings: strategic sourcing. The case features ARCO Alaska and provides a perspective on our early thinking in an area that was relatively new at the time. With additional retrospective commentary, it reinforces some of our enduring beliefs about management consulting as well as the emerging challenges companies face in the new millennium.

THE INQUIRY

In the winter of 1991, ARCO Alaska, Inc. (AAI) ranked among the largest producers of crude oil on Alaska's North Slope. With operations well north of the Arctic Circle, AAI produced nearly a half million barrels per day—representing almost two thirds of the worldwide production of its parent company ARCO, and accordingly representing a significant factor in the company's overall financial performance.

A hostile environment by any definition, the North Slope places incredible demands not only on the people who work there, but also on the equipment and sup-plies they depend on to drill the wells, produce the oil, and prepare it for the 2,000-mile journey through the Alaskan pipeline, on to tankers and eventually to refineries on the West Coast of the United States.

The frigid physical environment, however, was not the only challenge facing AAI. After more than 20 years of drilling on the North Slope, new operating, economic, and environmental factors posed serious challenges as well:

- Depressed oil prices and the natural depletion in existing oil reservoirs were leading to steadily declining AAI revenues over the near term.
- The North Slope oil fields were maturing, and materials usage began to increase for a variety of reasons: Extracting the less accessible oil was more difficult, equipment had aged, and the regulatory pressures (especially environmental regulation) had become more stringent.
- Acquiring materials represents a significant percentage of the total lifting cost, and was naturally driving an increase on a cost-per-barrel basis as well.

Recognizing these challenges, AAI responded with an internal screening in 1991 to determine best practices within AAI. According to Stewart McCorkle, AAI's Manager of Materials, Purchasing and Contracts at the time:

> We found that there weren't many "best practices" regarding materials management. Our expertise was in oil and gas exploration and production. Materials management had always been perceived as a lower-tier support function, not a value-added one like drilling or maintenance. We knew there was a lot of room for improvement, but we felt we didn't have the capabilities inside to make the needed improvements on the scale and at the speed we wanted.

AAI issued a request for proposal (RFP) to a number of management consulting firms. Booz Allen responded by sending the author of this chapter, a member of the Operations Management Group, and an emerging leader of our nascent network of sourcing practitioners to Anchorage to better understand AAI's requirements. By investing a significant effort to understand the company's unique needs—and avoid suggesting simplistic application of "best practices" from manufacturing industries—Booz Allen ultimately reinforced our competitive positioning as creative thinkers capable of addressing ARCO's issues and developing a truly customized solution.

Once selected, Booz Allen assembled a consulting team with a complementary blend of experiences. The author provided the day-to-day leadership of the effort with two other full-time consultants: one from our Oil & Gas industry practice and one from our Operations practice. Two partners, again one from Oil & Gas and one from Operations, provided senior guidance and quality control through part-time involvement.

PHASE 1: MATERIALS PROCESS STUDY

With Booz Allen's help, AAI launched a comprehensive study of all the processes involved in its materials acquisition and management functions. More than 100 interviews were conducted with representatives of key internal functions (e.g., engineering, drilling, maintenance, purchasing) at both the Anchorage offices and the North Slope, as well as with a representative sample of AAI's suppliers.

The study included a global survey of best practices and benchmarking across industries including oil and gas, utilities, and manufacturing. Inventory and transaction databases for the past 10 years were compiled and analyzed. And pilot "commodity" teams built around various categories of purchased materials reviewed and assessed existing purchasing and inventory practices.

The interviews with suppliers and AAI's internal customers revealed much about the problems and consequences associated with the company's historic sourcing practices:

- Materials management was viewed as a relatively low priority in the overall company mission, unlike high-leverage areas such as drilling and operations. The driving philosophy was to keep the oil flowing with less regard for the cost.
- The company's materials management and purchasing functions were working with a very traditional style of administrative support and control. They sent out bids, controlled purchase transactions, and maintained inventories.
- The organization as a whole, however, did not have faith in the purchasing functions' ability either to control or to deliver the right goods and services at the right time. This "crisis of confidence" was severely inhibiting the company's ability to achieve world-class sourcing performance.

The symptoms and inherent inefficiencies revealed by the study supported these attitudes within the user community:

- Constant reshuffling or "churn" of the supplier base, which limited efforts to develop sustained, mutually beneficial supplier relationships.
- A "bid mentality" for all acquisitions that resulted in excessive use of purchase orders and small order quantities.
- Excessive safety stock as a result of both the field operations' lack of confidence in the existing purchasing function and an incomplete understanding of the true cost of downtime and inventory holding costs.
- Further exacerbation of inventory excesses due to a lack of appropriate inventory modeling tools and inconsistent repair-versus-replace policies.
- Breakdown in communication between North Slope operations and the centralized materials management and purchasing functions in Anchorage and the consequent rise of an adversarial mindset.
- Incomplete understanding of supply economics and the concept of the extended enterprise.
- Lack of knowledge by design and engineering groups of how their decisions affected material costs (e.g., engineers would "try" new piping, leading to new suppliers, excess stocks, and a new learning curve on North Slope construction).

Implementation Efforts

With the diagnostic results of the Materials Process Study in hand, Booz Allen helped frame the following five recommendations to address the broad problems, the inherent inefficiencies, and their symptoms:

1. Create a new "culture" by involving senior management in setting policies and performance targets for the field.
2. Focus the organization on common goals by reorganizing the materials function to dismantle the existing geographic and functional chimneys.
3. Empower staff to execute the executive mandate by modifying tactical planning systems to increase rigor and discipline, both in procedures and systems.
4. Drive results by launching formal teams to develop supply strategies and to capture purchasing, materials, and inventory opportunities.
5. Set the baseline for target stock levels and clean up excess materials.

To implement these recommendations, AAI created a multidisciplinary core team composed of senior managers from the key organizational areas: the business units (field operations on the North Slope), central materials management, purchasing, and materials analysis. They were charged with leading the materials process redesign efforts, specifically creating the structure, systems, and processes that would allow AAI to implement the five recommendations.

One of the first actions of the core team was to break down a lot of the functional chimneys that had built up by decentralizing materials management and realigning the responsibilities, accountability, and authority of operations and purchasing. This helped both areas gain greater appreciation for each other's abilities.

The smaller central materials function began to focus on three key tasks:

1. Working with executive management to set critical policy parameters for the materials processes
2. Expanding the range of forecasting and target setting models used to manage inventory and deploying these tools, through education, into the field (instead of running them from Anchorage and constantly being asked to defend decisions.
3. Shifting the existing purchasing mentality (get out the bids, process the paper) to a more strategic approach to sourcing and the extended enterprise model.

The core team also added a very necessary dimension to the entire initiative. By staffing the team with key managers, executive management signaled its total commitment to the success of the initiative to the entire organization. Such top-level support provided an essential element in any organization's evolution toward a true strategic sourcing capability.

As the core team began to seriously address Booz Allen's five broad recommendations, they recognized the enormous magnitude of the challenge of shifting from traditional purchasing to strategic sourcing. At this point they reengaged Booz Allen to help structure that process and guide them through its implementation. Again, Booz Allen assembled a team of three full-time staff to support AAI in implementing two strategic sourcing pilot teams.

PHASE 2: STRATEGIC SOURCING PILOT

To assist AAI in realizing its strategic sourcing goal, the core team chose to apply Booz Allen's Strategic Sourcing Process (Figure 16–1).

- Research the economics and dynamics of the industry value chain
- Evaluate sourcing strategies and supplier's capabilities
- Structure supply relationships jointly with suppliers

In order to apply the model first in a pilot program, the AAI core team created two commodity teams charged with taking their assigned commodity families through the entire strategic sourcing process and for leading the roll-out of the new approach into their respective company units. AAI used the term *commodity families* to categorize the materials and equipment it purchases.

The initial pilot efforts focused on valves (used in controlling the flow of oil and other fluids in the processing operations) and drilling commodities (primarily the piping and casing that go down the well, but also "down-hole-jewelry" and well-head fit-

FIGURE 16-1   Booz Allen's Strategic Sourcing Process

❶ Research	❷ Evaluate	❸ Structure
Develop an in-depth knowledge of the dyamics of the industry value chain.	Identify and assess various sourcing strategies. Evaluate selected suppliers' capabilities to deliver against them.	Develop supply relationships and action plans to build the relationship infrastructure.
Tasks	***Tasks***	***Tasks***
¥ Document current and future buy. ¥ Build a total acquisition cost model. ¥ Analyze industry structure and trends. ¥ Understand total cost drivers. ¥ Refine hypotheses for the next step.	¥ Examine process and product technology trade-offs. ¥ Develop the extended enterprise model. ¥ Screen selected suppliers. ¥ Identify and quantify key business process opportunities. ¥ Create implementation action plans.	¥ Develop target cost models. ¥ Prepare business proposition and present to target suppliers. ¥ Select sourcing partners (suppliers) and define commercial agreements. ¥ Develop supplier action plans. ¥ Prepare final action plans for developing infrastructure.

tings that control the well flow). AAI chose these commodities for two primary reasons:

1. Both ranked high in terms of their criticality to sustaining operations and both represented significant portions of the total materials spent (Figure 16–2).
2. Distinct differences existed between the two in terms of purchasing and materials management, that would challenge and test the applicability of the strategic sourcing process—and preventing a "one size fits all" mentality in strategy development.

The teams created to carry out the strategic sourcing pilot program included members representing the complete range of functions involved in the full sourcing process from initial design, to the acquisition of commodities and their installation, use, and maintenance. For example, the drilling commodities team included individuals from drilling operations, drilling engineering, purchasing, and materials management. The valve commodities team had similar representation.

Each function selected representatives based on their knowledge, experience, and demonstrated leadership abilities. This gave the process credibility. And a clearly defined mandate from top-level corporate "sponsors" empowered the teams to conduct their tasks with complete cooperation from all functional areas. The sponsors formed the core of a steering committee that provided counsel and support to the teams throughout the strategy development process.

FIGURE 16–2   AAI's Commodity Segmentation Model

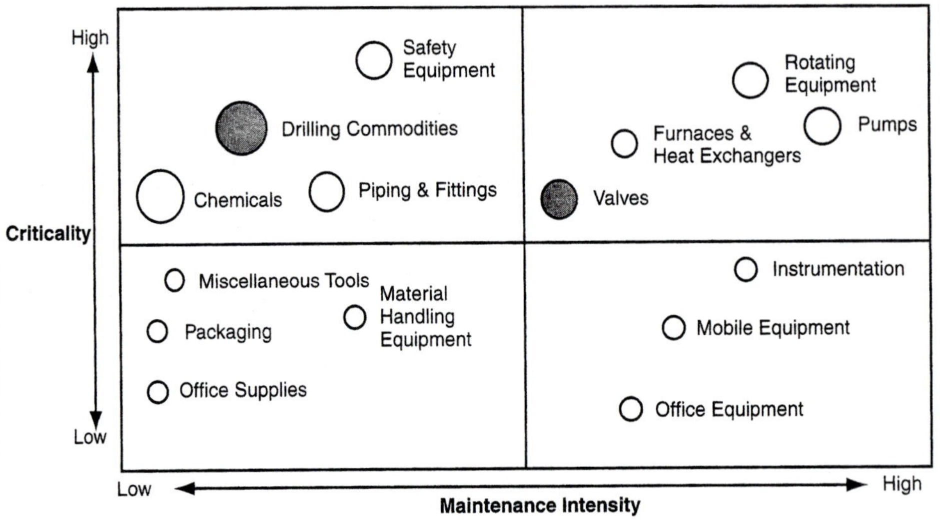

Note: Size of circle indicates relative proportion of the annual materials spent.

The value of the multifunctional nature of these teams cannot be underestimated. They offer the key to the success of strategic sourcing implementation by:

- Providing a broad knowledge base and multiple perspectives in strategy development
- Ensuring smoother implementation because all functions have input into the process
- Serving as information links to their respective functional areas to foster the cultural change necessary to support success

USING A HYPOTHESIS-BASED APPROACH

The teams applied Booz Allen's standard scientific methodology for problem solving: the hypothesis-based approach. Hypotheses generated at the initial formation of the team quickly focused their efforts on the most critical areas and defined unique priorities for each commodity family. Through highly structured analysis, the teams attempted to prove or disprove each hypothesis, adding and dropping hypotheses as the work progressed.

For example, the valve commodities team stated as one of its hypotheses the following:

Working Hypothesis: Increased standardization among the valves AAI uses could drive down prices by consolidating purchases and increasing order volumes, reducing inventory stocking requirements by pooling demand, and improving demand and usage forecasting.

To test this hypothesis, the team chose to look at one family of four-inch, 150-pound valves. Inventory analysis revealed 17 different part numbers for valves with essentially the same basic functionality, but with purchase prices ranging from $750 to $2,200 each (Figure 16–3). They also found that of the 17 different part numbers maintained in inventory, 4 had no demand in the previous year—indicating truly slow-moving stock.

After further research, the team recommended establishing a standard for this type of valve by using the lowest-cost valve that met the needs of all of the users. They determined that such selective standardization would yield annual cost savings of between 5 and 10 percent—even though a higher-priced valve would now be used in some applications. In this case, the hypothesis proved true.

Booz Allen believes that this hypothesis-based approach offers many benefits because it

- Forces teams to make assumptions explicitly and directly in order to test their validity
- Establishes priorities to focus the team's data collection on the key opportunity areas
- Challenges the team to directly address preconceived notions, right or wrong
- Avoids the potential problems of assuming the right answer, since hypotheses can be stated positively or negatively, with the object to either prove or disprove

FIGURE 16–3   Analysis of One-Year Demand/Price Comparison for Four-Inch, 150-Pound Ball Valve

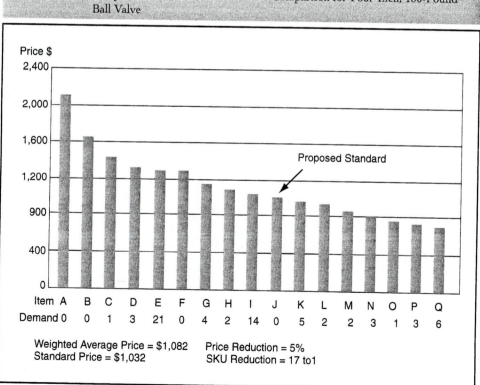

Weighted Average Price = $1,082   Price Reduction = 5%
Standard Price = $1,032   SKU Reduction = 17 to1

APPLYING THE STRATEGIC SOURCING PROCESS

Though hypotheses drove the team's work, Booz Allen's strategic sourcing process provided an overarching structure to ensure that the team fully documented key facts before proceeding to conclusions.

Stage 1 — Research: Develop an In-depth Knowledge of the Dynamics of the Industry Value Chain

Document the Buy   For this task the team developed a detailed understanding of the current spend, and projected the likely future requirements.

For example, AAI's drilling commodities team documented the five-year buying history of "down-hole" tubulars (Figure 16–4). Their research showed that over that time period, AAI had bought from 17 different suppliers and that annual purchases from each fluctuated significantly from year to year. They concluded that this churning of the supply base greatly inhibited the company's ability to sustain improved relationships with suppliers, resulted in excessive inventories, and left suppliers unable to forecast demand and often unable or unwilling to meet it.

Build a Total Acquisition Cost Model   In this task, the teams quantified all the life-cycle costs (some often unrecorded) of materials acquisition and ownership, not just the invoice price. These included the costs of quality rejections, carrying inventory, transportation, material acquisition and handling costs, and internal down-time due to unavailable material. Figure 16–5 shows the total cost of acquisition model developed by the valve team. In this case, the initial purchase price represented only 37 percent of the total life-cycle costs of valves.

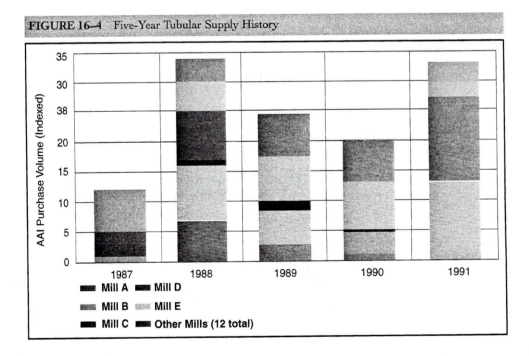

FIGURE 16–4   Five-Year Tubular Supply History

FIGURE 16–5   Total Cost Acquisition Model

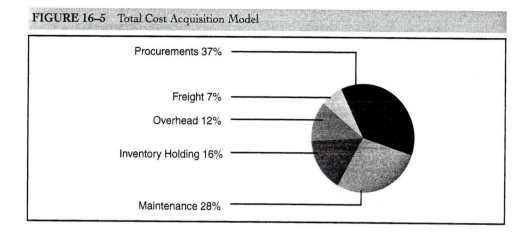

Procurements 37%

Freight 7%

Overhead 12%

Inventory Holding 16%

Maintenance 28%

Analyze Industry Structure and Trends   For this task, the team developed a clear understanding of the supply industry characteristics (e.g., industry size and structure, growth rates, and technology) as well as the players' characteristics (e.g., product range, capacity, niches, profitability). This involved studying secondary information sources, and also conducting interviews with supplier representatives.

One of the drilling commodities team's particular concerns was the potential advantages of buying directly from the manufacturer as opposed to buying through distributors. They wanted to determine which types of suppliers would be the right fit, given AAI's purchase volume and supply requirements. The industry structure model they developed (Figure 16–6) helped them eventually zero in on the distributor segment, where they determined they could create the strongest relationships and achieve better long-term pricing, as much as 5 percent lower.

Understand Total Cost Drivers   This task challenged the team to develop deep insight into each of the individual factors contributing to acquisition costs and to explore cost savings options. For example, in AAI's case, the drilling commodities team hypothesized that freight costs for tubulars could be lowered by reducing expediting. They identified the factors contributing to freight premiums paid in the preceding year (Figure 16–7) and analyzed the reasons for expediting shipments. They projected that 3 to 5 percent of total freight costs could be saved by better materials requirement planning and stronger distributor partnerships.

Refine Hypotheses for Stage 2: Evaluate   The last task of the research stage forced a refinement of the hypotheses based on the research findings. These hypotheses provided the content for the final chapter in a steering committee report. This initial report provided insight into the buy, background on the supply industry, a total acquisition and life-cycle cost model that served as the baseline for improvement, and finally, the hypotheses for the next step. Accordingly, the steering committee received the baseline knowledge to eventually assess the validity of the recommendations presented at the end of Stage 2: Evaluate. In the case of the ARCO teams, the senior management steering committee was impressed with the depth of understanding the team was able to document in a mere five weeks.

FIGURE 16–6   Model of Tubular Goods Industry

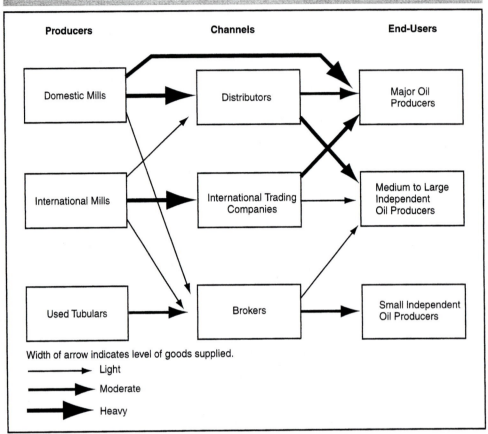

Stage 2 – Evaluate: Identify and Assess the Various Sourcing Strategies and Evaluate Selected Suppliers' Capabilities to Deliver Against Them

Examine Product and Process Technology Trade-Offs   For this task the team considered opportunities to reduce costs or enhance value by changing materials specifications or designs or by seeking alternate process technologies.

When AAI began drilling in the Arctic, the industry possessed limited previous experience in operating in such a hostile environment. Subsequently, initial materials specifications tended toward the conservative. Experience, however, suggested that some initial specifications exceeded true requirements.

The drilling commodities team examined such a specification for certain casings for extended-reach wells. Because of the multidisciplinary nature of the team, which included both drilling operations and engineering representatives, they were able to determine that one of the current casing specifications could be overkill and that a lighter grade would be sufficient. Further investigation revealed that 2 percent of the price of these casings could be saved by changing the specification (see Figure 16–8).

FIGURE 16–7   Reasons for Paying Freight Premiums

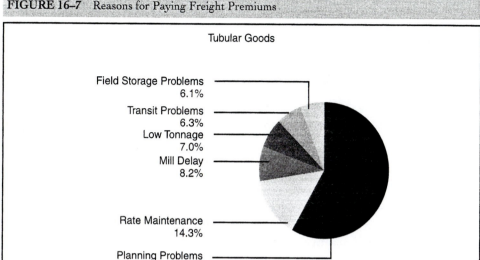

Develop the Extended Enterprise Model   In this task, the teams identified opportunities for improving sourcing practices as well as opportunities for leveraging supplier capabilities—in short, a sourcing strategy.

The valve team began by analyzing its sourcing practices for the three main types of valves AAI purchased. They found that AAI purchased from quite a large number of suppliers and expended minimal effort in building value-added relationships with

FIGURE 16–8   Projected Cost Savings from Changing Specs for 9⅝″ Casings

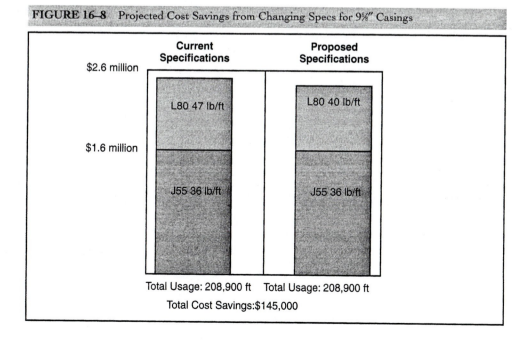

them. From this analysis, the team defined an extended enterprise model that addressed the supply base, the structure of AAI's relationship with suppliers, each type of suppliers' value-added potential, and opportunities for integrating their own functional areas with those of suppliers (Figure 16–9).

Screen Prospective Suppliers   In this task, the teams screened prospective suppliers for the roles required in the extended enterprise using preestablished criteria centering around cost and performance factors. This enabled them to narrow the field for detailed examination of a smaller number of qualified prospects and to ultimately select appropriate strategic suppliers.

The drilling commodities team constructed a detailed matrix of potential suppliers for tubular goods. They analyzed each supplier's product range, capacity and utilization, business strategy and performance, technical and process capabilities, and manufacturing cost structure. Figure 16–10 shows a simplified excerpt from that matrix. This exhaustive analysis gave the team a detailed picture of each potential supplier using the same criteria and provided a sound basis for eventual final supplier selection in the structure stage of the strategic sourcing process.

Identify and Quantify Key Business Process Opportunities   In this evaluation step, the teams sought ways to reduce total acquisition costs by modifying and/or integrating key business processes to more fully leverage the strategic supply base.

Planning and scheduling were priority issues addressed by AAI. Figure 16–11 charts a planned drilling schedule versus actual performance. It compares the magnitude of impact that various factors have on scheduling and AAI's potential for controlling them through improved planning and scheduling practices. The team concluded that AAI had the ability to effect substantial change and thus drive down the costs associated with scheduling disparities.

Create Initial Action Plan   The action plan created in this step identified critical paths and potential bottlenecks in implementing team recommendations. It set the foundation for the next stage in the strategic sourcing cycle, the actual structuring of supply relationships and building the infrastructure required to leverage them most effectively.

Figure 16–12 shows a sample control chart from the valve team's master action plan. It includes defined progress measures, results measures, and milestones. In all, the team developed 17 separate, detailed action plans specifying tasks, time frames, responsibility, and deliverables.

Stage 3–Structure: Develop Supply Relationships and Action Plans to Build the Strategic Sourcing Infrastructure

In Stage 3 of Booz Allen's strategic sourcing process, the teams take the leadership in actually structuring the optimal supplier relationships and building the infrastructure to support them and take maximum advantage of the value-added opportunities they offer. The tasks they must accomplish include:

- Developing target cost models
- Preparing business propositions and presenting them to the identified supplier targets
- Making final supplier selections and defining commercial arrangements

FIGURE 16–9 Extended Enterprise Model—Valve Commodities Team

Extended Enterprise Element	Type of Valve		
	Ball/Plug	**Choke**	**Forged Steel**
Supply Base	✳ Reduce from twenty suppliers to three or four ✳ Use local distributor to provide repair parts for plug ✳ Develop Anchorage repair shop	✳ Reduce from four manufacturers to one or two ✳ Develop new source for repair parts by moving upstream in supply chain	✳ Reduce from four distributors to one ✳ Leverage available only at distributor level
Relationship Structure	✳ Extended relationship with target suppliers ✳ Dedicated suppliers relationship with repair shop	✳ Work toward true comaker relationship with core supplier ✳ Apply lifetime agreement with formula-based pricing long term	✳ Try to develop full-service distributor relationship ✳ Quote annual or multiyear quantities and direct business accordingly
Value-Added Services	✳ Advanced metallurgical support ✳ Hold all hard goods inventory ✳ Maintain documentation files for ready access	✳ Continued engineering support of new designs ✳ Stock all hard goods ✳ Maintain documentation files for ready access	✳ Improved coverage of stocked items ✳ Convert threaded ends to sockets as required
Supplier Integration	✳ Facility engineering to drive specification changes ✳ Supplier engineering with slope maintenance for preventative maintenance ✳ Purchasing with manufacturing engineering to drive down electroless nickel plating cost ✳ Contractors and suppliers to control specifying	✳ Corrosion group to work with supplier designers to improve durability ✳ Material specialists to drive planning ✳ Quality assurance to eliminate source inspection ✳ Contractors and suppliers to control specifying	✳ Maternal specialists to drive planning ✳ Facility engineering to drive specification changes ✳ Contractors and suppliers to control specifying

	Large U.S. Mill	Small Independent Mill	Far Eastern Mill	Large European Mill
Product Range				
Size range	⋇ 4 1/2" to 9 5/8"	⋇ 1.9" to 8.5/8"	⋇ 1.9" to 24"	⋇ 2 3/8" to 26"
Production process	⋇ Seamless	⋇ Electric resistance weld	⋇ Electric resistance weld & seamless	⋇ Seamless
Grade range	⋇ Limited	⋇ Limited	⋇ Limited	⋇ Full
Capacity and Utilization				
Capacity	⋇ 600 thousand tons/year	⋇ 300 thousand tons/year	⋇ 1.2 million tons/year	⋇ 1.5 million tons/year
Capacity utilized	⋇ 30%	⋇ 60%	⋇ 60%	⋇ 30%
Process yield	⋇ 89%	⋇ 93%	⋇ 92%	⋇ Not available
Business Strategy and Performance				
Market focus	⋇ Broad	⋇ Small independent producers	⋇ High end	⋇ High end
Market range	⋇ International	⋇ Market range?	⋇ International	⋇ International
Management style	⋇ Traditional	⋇ Progressive	⋇ Traditional	⋇ Typical European
Order size	⋇ Large	⋇ Small	⋇ Large	⋇ Large
Financial issues	⋇ Trying to cover variable costs	⋇ Financially sound	⋇ Financially sound	⋇ Financially sound
Technical and Process Capabilities				
Scope	⋇ Fully integrated	⋇ Buys coils outside	⋇ Fully integrated	⋇ Fully integrated
Heat treatment	⋇ Full range	⋇ Limited to 95 grades	⋇ Full range	⋇ Full range
Threading	⋇ American Petroleum Institute	⋇ American Petroleum Institute	⋇ American Petroleum Institute	⋇ American Petroleum Institute
Manufacturing Cost Position				
Labor cost	⋇ High	⋇ Moderate	⋇ Comparable to high U.S.	⋇ High
Process flexibility	⋇ Designed for the large runs	⋇ Small runs, quick size change	⋇ Large quantity runs	⋇ Large quantity runs
Inventory management	⋇ Large in-process	⋇ Large, finished-goods	⋇ Low in-progress	⋇ Not available
Other issues	⋇ None	⋇ None	⋇ High energy, raw materials costs	⋇ High energy, raw materials costs

FIGURE 16–11   Impact of Various Factors on the Planned Drilling Schedule

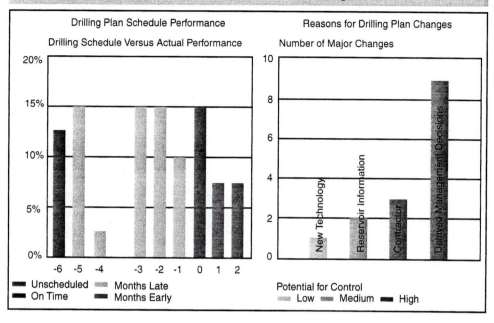

- Developing supplier action plans
- Creating final action plans for developing the necessary infrastructure

The actual implementation of the structuring stage typically takes from three to nine months, but sometimes longer, to put systems and supplier agreements into place.

At this point in Booz Allen's engagement with AAI, we provided training for the team members who would lead the structuring effort. As the two pilot project teams entered this stage, AAI was already forming new teams to apply the strategic sourcing process to other commodities.

SUMMARY

Thanks to the joint approach we took and to Booz Allen's capability-building focus, strategic sourcing became a part of the ARCO Alaska corporate culture. At the same time, the engagement delivered tangible benefits for AAI:

- The valve and drilling commodities teams documented over $5 million in cost savings in the first 18 months of implementation.
- In the rollout of the second wave of strategic sourcing teams, a chemicals commodities team had projected an estimated $7 million in cost savings.
- Previously excessive inventories of drilling supplies dropped from $12 million down to $4 million.
- Many supplies and parts have been standardized, further contributing to efficiency.

Creating a strategic sourcing capability also delivered intangible benefits that went well beyond the bottom line. For instance:

FIGURE 16–12 Sample Control Chart from Valve Team's Master Action Plan

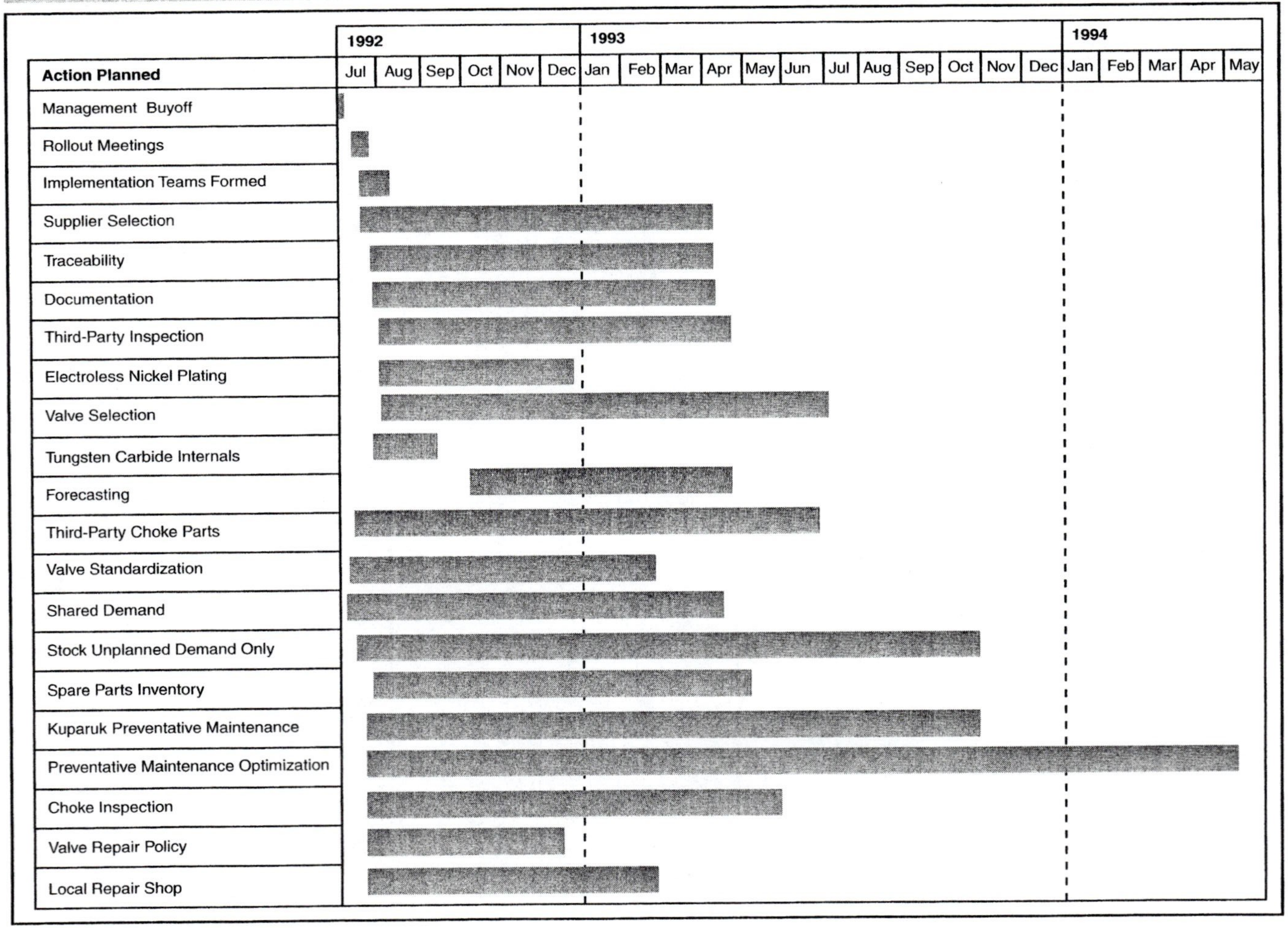

- ARCO Alaska has been able to transfer the knowledge gained from the pilot commodities team project to other commodities areas, and has created a climate of cooperation, communication, and dedication to common goals across its functional areas.
- AAI executives view their experience with strategic sourcing as a model that can be extended far beyond their defined operational area to other ARCO corporate entities.

ARCO Alaska's experience in strategic sourcing, like those of many other Booz Allen clients, was clearly a success. AAI's Vice President for Financial Planning and Control at the time, Joe McCoy, expressed it well, "In an environment where costs are growing, saving 20 percent is very powerful. It's much more than our expectations ever were."

AAI offers strong evidence that methodically applying and effectively implementing strategic sourcing produces real, sizable, and fairly immediate benefits. Though some companies consider consulting an overly expensive option, this engagement demonstrates that in the right context, outside consultants prove relatively inexpensive measured against the results.

By bringing independent outside expertise, Booz Allen helped AAI drive significant changes in organizational behavior, business processes, and corporate structure:

- Changed the behavior of top executives in how they view managing the supply base
- Modified the role, the skills, and even some of the personnel in the purchasing function
- Forced integration across strongly constructed functional "chimneys" that were resistant to change
- Accepted the risk of a more open supplier relationship mode and ultimately relying more heavily on suppliers

Change of this magnitude causes considerable corporate discomfort. Organizations need powerful leadership from the very top—and sometimes an outside catalyst—to accomplish it.

The ARCO Alaska strategic sourcing case demonstrates Booz Allen's early approach to strategic sourcing—well before such a concept became an overused buzzword. Interestingly, Booz Allen's approach to strategic sourcing reflects a consulting philosophy that holds true regardless of the client issue at hand:

- Start with recognition from top-level management of the importance of the issue followed by continuing commitment to the needed change.
- A multifunctional approach acknowledges the needs, experience, and unique expertise of individuals from every area of the organization.
- A broad perspective—in this case, an understanding of the entire supply chain from the suppliers of materials to the ultimate end user.
- Build on a fundamental understanding of microeconomics—in this case, the full life-cycle costs including operating, maintenance, inventory, and disposal.
- Use our institutional understanding of best practices and world-class standards and intelligently apply them to each client situation—not blindly tout them as "ultimate truth."
- Apply a hypothesis-driven approach to efficiently focus analysis efforts on the highest-value opportunities at all times.
- Most importantly, build client capabilities through hands-on pilot efforts and custom training while simultaneously delivering near-term results.

CHAPTER

Large-Scale Change in the Strategic Enterprise

Elise Walton and Peter Thies

Tremendous competitive and technological forces in today's business environment are driving companies to reconfigure their operations. They introduce
unprecedented change in the ways that large and complex organizations are
designed and managed. These changes are not limited to asset restructurings, but
involve governing and financing business activity, as well as different ways of leading
people through change and establishing new ways of working together. At Mercer-
Delta, our clients are finding that to keep up with the rapid pace of change, they need
to move faster, make quicker decisions, redesign their organizations more frequently,
and work together more effectively than ever before.

As they make these changes, companies are also learning that it's not simply a case
of having the right business strategy, the right organizational model, or doing better
teamwork at the top. To change effectively, our clients no longer feel that they have the
luxury of choosing one or the other—they have to do it all: achieve both speed and rigor,
both local autonomy and cross-unit synergy, both consensus and quick decision making.

As large and complex organizations make these changes, we are seeing the development of a new form of organizational architecture we call the "strategic enterprise."
It is a complex organizational form that includes both tight and loose structural linkages between the corporate center and the various business units. By design, a strategic
enterprise attempts to achieve both focus and leverage simultaneously. Within this
architecture, discrete businesses have enough autonomy to execute differentiated
strategies, bringing new technologies to targeted market segments. At the same time, a
strategic enterprise creates structures and processes for leveraging the opportunities
provided by core capabilities, pooled resources, and economies of scale.

Peter Thies is a Partner with Mercer Delta Consulting, a management consulting firm offering strategic
change services to CEOs and senior executives in major corporations. He holds a PhD and an MBA in
Organizational Behavior from Rensselaer Polytechnic Institute, an MS in Educational Psychology from the
University of Pennsylvania, and a BA in Psychology from SUNY Albany.

Elise Walton is a partner at the Mercer Delta Consulting Group, specializing in the practice areas of change
management, executive teams, global strategy, organization design, and quality. She holds a BA from
Bowdoin College, an MA from Columbia University, and a PhD from Harvard Business School.

Many of our clients find the concept of the strategic enterprise useful as they go about aligning their organizations. The basic concept provides a framework for envisioning the type of organization they want to become. Lessons we've learned from our experience with other companies also prove extremely useful in helping them understand what to expect and to put their problems in perspective. In particular, we know that in most companies, sub-businesses have different processes, compensation models, investment models, and cycle times. So unresolved conflicts often develop within a company about opportunities and fairness. Even with experience and perspective, however, leading large-scale change in a strategic enterprise still proves difficult and always a unique and custom event as each company develops its own formula for success.

In this chapter we share lessons learned about both the content and process of leading large-scale change within a strategic enterprise. Our approach is to mix theory and application—to simultaneously point out lessons learned across client situations and describe in greater depth a success story involving a specific client.

THE CLIENT: AT&T BUSINESS SERVICES

The client organization is AT&T Business Services (ABS), then headed by CEO Michael Keith. Within AT&T, ABS is responsible for telecom product management and sales across business markets. ABS's business portfolio includes voice products, data networking services, IP (Internet Protocol) offerings, and emerging markets such as Web hosting. ABS is the primary sales channel to businesses, from pizza parlors to General Motors. ABS is also responsible for selling AT&T business wireless services, although the wireless products had previously been managed (and revenues counted) in a separate organization. With approximately $26 billion in revenues to collect, ABS is a large company within the broader AT&T portfolio, faced with a complex matrix of products and markets to manage.

In recent years, AT&T's competition has intensified dramatically. MCI, making a big bet on the Internet, had developed a growing business in the growth markets. UUNET, MCI's Internet play, had the AOL account. AOL accounted for a substantial amount of the IP traffic. MCI was also the price leader, cutting prices to five cents a minute in the core voice business and weakening AT&T's position in this key segment.

As competitors struggled to connect to the consumers' homes, different technologies were vying for dominance. Many consumers connected via simple analog phone lines, but increasingly there were other options—DSL, cable, and fixed wireless. In a move to access numerous consumers, AT&T made an expensive bet on cable, purchasing MediaOne, one of the largest cable providers in the United States. However, the interest expense on the costly purchase strained AT&T's income statement.

As Figure 17–1 illustrates, perhaps the most challenging development of all was the delayering of the telecom industry. The telecom industry for the last 20 years had consisted of long distance carriers, local carriers, and providers who offered specific solutions. Now the industry seemed to be breaking into entirely different groupings— businesses that offered solutions or outsourcing, businesses that offered specific features (ASPs), and those that offered connectivity. In some regards, AT&T was simply a connectivity offering, and that was the most commoditized of all the offerings. AT&T needed to reshape its businesses or it would vanish.

FIGURE 17–1   The Evolution of the Telecom Industry

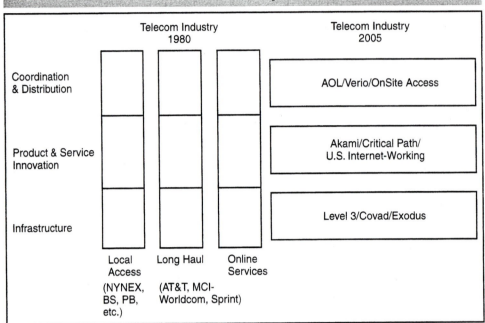

Although facing competition, AT&T still enjoys competitive advantages. The brand has remained strong, with its promise of reliability, service, and continued concern for customers. The company maintains strong relationships with major U.S. companies and has strong technology delivery and go-to-market capability. In addition, AT&T still has the largest network infrastructure anywhere in the world.

As a business service provider, AT&T was organized around products and markets. Among its product lines, the major share of business historically came from voice services and products. Data networking and IP were small but growing businesses, much admired by analysts and customers. However, AT&T's strong image and reputation as a telecom provider sometimes eclipsed its presence in emerging markets such as Data and IP.

When we began this engagement in 1999, ABS was a matrix of product development units and sales segments. In general, the customer segments were designed to be the business leaders, driving the revenues, forecasts, and product development requirements based on specific customer segment needs. Each individual segment looked very different. Three customer segments relied on the products being developed in the product development units (Voice, Data, and IP) and shared a common factory/customer care resource. These segments addressed high-end, *Fortune* 500 customers (the Global Segment), mid-sized customers (the Growth Segment), and small/metropolitan customers (the Metro Segment). Two segments—Wholesale and Government—were relatively self-contained, doing their own provisioning and product development. One product house managed channel relationships, thereby splitting the distribution portfolio between segments and product development houses.

The ABS leadership team had been through some turmoil. Dramatic change in the industry and in AT&T had led to high churn at the top. In 10 years, AT&T had hired over 15 outside executives—some stayed, some departed. The loss of talent throughout the organization was intensified by the wealth of opportunities for telecommunications executives. All told, ABS had five different leaders in four years, including the appointment and later exit of Bob Annunziata, a high-profile executive who left ABS to start his own business, Level 3 Communications. Many of those who left went on to make millions in start-up companies. This environment led to constant internal restlessness among the senior team about the personal economics of staying versus leaving. To make matters worse, AT&T's "Brain Drain" had not gone unnoticed by the press and analysts, making the problem public and embarrassing.

The challenges faced by ABS in early 1999 illustrate the scenario of a company in transition to a strategic enterprise. The organization was clearly in the midst of a rapidly changing industry. ABS's business strategy did not line up with current marketplace demands. Furthermore, despite repeated attempts, it appeared that the ABS organization model still wasn't delivering the performance required for success. The value added from common leadership of product development and the synergy around customers was not realized. Furthermore, the revolving door dynamic was making it difficult, if not impossible, to build a high-performing leadership team.

Mercer-Delta has had a long-standing relationship with AT&T since the mid-1980s. We have worked with AT&T's senior executives on issues involving organizational architecture, leadership change, coaching, team development, and major culture change efforts. In early 1999, the HR vice president of ABS contacted a Mercer-Delta consultant she had worked with several years earlier. She openly shared her concerns that the senior team was not working together. She felt there were multiple reasons for this—unclear roles and responsibilities, an in-group/out-group phenomenon driven by very different backgrounds and tenures, a lack of communication and trust, and the role of a relatively new leader. She felt that "the kind of thing Mercer-Delta did" might be helpful.

After conversations with the HR vice president, the Mercer-Delta team met with the CEO of the business. He had spoken with the HR vice president and shared the same sense of issues. His perspective was somewhat different. He saw issues with morale, but felt that there was a culture of whining and dissatisfaction. Moreover, each of his direct reports could readily see problems with someone else's business, but felt their business was in perfect order. After a few cycles of conversation, the CEO agreed to a series of diagnostic interviews and a team offsite.

Mercer-Delta Point of View

This leads to our first point of view on consulting to CEOs and executive teams on leading change in the strategic enterprise. The initial step in any strategic change effort is to employ a data-driven process that surfaces important organizational issues, develops shared understanding of these issues among top leadership, and builds their commitment to developing and implementing an action plan. Without a shared view of issues and ownership among the CEO and executive team for resolution, there is no basis or platform for true strategic change—it is a necessary (but by no means sufficient) condition for success.

Having said this, building shared understanding of strategic issues and the plan for resolution is no easy task. Clients often state during initial meetings that the problems are known and it is only fast action that is required. In fact there may be a handful of people who agree on a similar set of issues. Yet we often find that as we speak with other key leaders in the company, there are as many different views of the problems and root causes as there are people. Each person has his or her own view of what's needed to fix the problem. Such was the situation at ABS.

PHASE 1: THE PRELIMINARY ENGAGEMENT

The initial agreement with the client was to conduct a short-term diagnostic set of interviews and facilitate a team offsite to understand and chart a course of action around the issues identified. Mercer-Delta has a formal process for conducting interviews and recording comments. A set of 13 executives were interviewed in depth. These interview comments were then entered into a proprietary content analysis software package. The comments were sorted into themes and issues. These themes were analyzed for generality (the degree to which the opinion was shared among the interviewees) and strength (the energy with which the views were held). Themes were also clustered into "viewpoints." This formed the basis of the Mercer-Delta diagnostic report.

The CEO received a report that outlined, in detail, the comments of the extended team. The report was provided first to the CEO and followed by a private meeting between the consultants and the CEO. The head of HR also saw the report early, sharing her reactions and offering her perspective on likely reactions in the team. The results confirmed many of the issues identified by the CEO and the HR VP—issues around the organization and effectiveness of the business, an insider/outsider schism, concerns about specific roles being played by individuals, and a general sense that meetings were ineffective and governance nonexistent. The interviews indicated support for the AT&T CEO's direction, but concern that ABS was funding the CEO's foray into cable (at an unsustainable level). The interviews also highlighted concerns not identified by the ABS CEO and HR VP—that there were some positive relationships in the team, that the ABS CEO might need to be more decisive, and that the organization had redundant activity (specifically, marketing was occurring in the segments, the product houses, and in an independent corporate group). Most importantly, the diagnosis highlighted an agenda for action, which included developing a bold new vision, rationalizing the structure, and building a winning culture.

The consultants, the ABS CEO, and the HR VP then designed an offsite meeting structured around discussing the data with the senior team and creating an agenda for action. The offsite was the first major intervention with the team. To start the session off with a different feel, the team members were put in pairs, and individuals in the pair were to share an accomplishment they felt proud of, as well as identify a characteristic they admired in their partner. This start-up is patterned after work on "appreciative inquiry" (see Pasmore and Purser, 1993) and is a very different type of interaction than executives typically experience. Many found the interaction positive and informative. All found it very different than what they were used to.

The offsite meeting focused a great deal on culture and led to the identification of seven things the group needed to do. One immediate benefit was clarification of the meeting structure. Meetings were often overattended, with as many as 10 people sitting in on the operations meetings, swelling attendance to well over 25. Clarification of what the senior team met to do, and who was to be included and excluded from those sessions, was an important step forward.

There were related small wins. For instance, a senior product house executive had been calling meetings that included the direct reports of the Sales Segment vice presidents. People attending the meeting did not know why they were being called or if they should go. Often, their managers, the meeting chairperson's peers, did not know their direct reports were attending their peers' meetings. When they found out, they were miffed. The simple intervention—sharing information and intent—helped resolve the issue of who was where and why, and the process was blessed. This was a definite process improvement for the direct reports of the senior team.

The team generally believed that the offsite was a success, though, as always, felt follow-through was important. The ABS team began implementing some of the agreed actions from the original offsite meetings. Things seemed to be improving, and the consultants continued to have conversations with the leader. For a while, formal consulting work stopped. Goodwill and teamwork improved from the offsite. However, there remained a lingering sense that the governance issue had not been resolved. Despite improved teamwork, there was a lingering sense that more needed to be done.

Sitting down with the CEO and the HR VP, the consultants reviewed key themes from the interviews, as well as observations they had collected in working with the group over several months. The themes and observations pointed to organizational architecture as a root cause of the problem. The confused structure made it impossible for those individuals with the best intentions to work effectively. Even improved meeting and governance processes were insufficient to create a fundamentally more efficient business.

PHASE 2: BUILDING A STRATEGIC ENTERPRISE AT ABS

ABS was coping with classic issues of the strategic enterprise—how to build an organizational architecture that would provide focus within specific business, provide leverage (such as marketing competence and customer relationships) across businesses, and manage the inherent conflict that occurs among top leadership.

Mercer-Delta Point of View

This leads to our next point of view on consulting to CEOs and executive teams on leading change in the strategic enterprise: *Fundamental strategic change frequently involves rethinking the basic architecture of the company.* In this particular case, one or two interventions alone won't create fundamental change. What is needed is a customized, integrated plan that addresses the fundamental drivers of organizational behavior. In short, we refer to this as working on organizational architecture—changing the ways the various components of an organization (strategy, work processes, structures, culture, and people) fit together.

The need to rearchitect ABS was driven by both internal and external factors. A first internal driver was the incomplete implementation of earlier restructurings. For instance, the case for customer segments was premised on the idea that segments close to customer needs should drive product development processes. In most cases the segments, which were supposed to be managing revenue and earnings, were actually managing revenue only. This left a confusing organization and confused people. No one could be clear on who was doing what and why.

A second driver was the frequent restructurings and turnover that had led to a kind of horse-trading mentality around responsibilities. As described earlier, not all segments looked alike (some included their own product development and "factory," others relied on shared resources). These inconsistencies were amplified by after-the-fact negotiations among direct reports to the CEO. For instance, the Metro Segment sales manager was developing products for his marketplace, though technically that effort should have occurred in the shared resource of the voice product house. The Voice executive, swamped with demands from the Growth, Global, and Emerging Segments, had little time to focus on the Metro Small Business Segment. The Metro Segment president was sure he could shorten the product development cycle if it were done within his segment. A high level of trust existed between the Voice Product president and the Metro Segment president, and therefore the product development activity was farmed out to the segment. There was some fit between the product he was developing and the Metro market, but overall, people were confused about what was done where and why. In the end, the well-known Digital One Rate product developed for the Metro Segment resembled, at least on the face of it, an all-in-one offer being developed in the Voice Product house. (There were in fact differences, but these were not obvious to most observers.) So there were probably missed opportunities for leverage.

The fundamental internal drivers—frequent change, incomplete implementation, and confused roles and responsibilities—were amplified by problems of industry-wide change. The marketplaces demanded different things. For instance, the telecom operating model assumes a market dominated by commodity services focused on basic connectivity, while Data Networking is more likely to focus on solutions; telecom assumes long life cycles for capitalized network equipment and slower technology development, while bandwidth-hungry data solutions drive rapid technology development and assimilation; telecom looks at a market from a wholesale/retail perspective, while IP and Data Networking tend to cut offerings into very different groups of customers and competitors.

Changes in the marketplace indicated that the sources of leverage were likely to change, so not only were there differences in existing business models, but those models themselves were changing. The IP business was growing in part because of joint product development with its channel partners. Voice was successful because of its established relationships with internal buyers and its infrastructure. At an AT&T level, the core strategic advantages were reputation, infrastructure, and customer relationships. However, in certain areas of the company, these might be liabilities. For instance, in terms of building an identity in the emerging IP space, AT&T's reputation as a telecom company was often a liability, overshadowing any media attention they might get for Internet products or Data Networking.

This situation describes the classic problems of the strategic enterprise—where to find focus and where to find leverage. Though there were clearly multiple business models at work—a new start-up IP-type organization that demanded high-velocity action, media attention, and young talent, versus an established voice business selling to

Fortune 500 corporations—there were no clear answers to the structural challenges. New initiatives needed some element of the core network to deliver their offer. This meant that the core business was the host of most new initiatives. Data networking, a new offering being sold to new customers (different buyers within the existing clientele), was housed in the voice business. The logic for keeping Data Networking with the Voice Product house was that they were on the same platform and there were overlapping skills required. At the same time, the IP product development house was arguing that Data Networking was integral to many of its offers and its customers and that Data Networking should rightfully be grouped with IP products. Both arguments were true.

In a specific example of the general challenge of strategic enterprise design, ABS faced the core/newco conflict. In this scenario, the firm has a core business (Voice in the case of AT&T). The core business is the dominant, established, and maturing business, and generates most of the revenue and earnings. However, as the company moves into new businesses, the core business finds itself competing for resources with the new businesses that generate little revenue or even negative earnings. The core business often argues that those funds would be better spent in the core, protecting the revenue stream and the dividend. It is a common dilemma, with no right answer, and the dilemma generates conflict that gets fought out every day.

Needless to say, the strategic differences play out in interpersonal conflicts, border skirmishes, competition, and negative attribution. There was a tendency to assume the worst—that a request for resources was a power grab, that an unreturned phone call meant noncooperation, and so forth. More generally, depending on which organization one sat in (Voice or IP), it was easy to make the case for including the Data Networking products with that organization. It was a less intuitively obvious case for moving it. Thus, the handy explanation for conflict was that the other organization must simply want more control, more power, and the like. So, the consequence of multiple, incomplete changes and senior executive horse-trading was a high degree of conflict—personalized conflict at that—in the organization.

This situation was consistent with our views on organization. Problems are overdetermined, deriving from multiple causes. In the ABS case, numerous factors were at play: market change, leadership turnover, cultural baggage, complex organizational structure, and so on. Our approach to thinking about change at ABS is described in Figure 17–2. It examines corporate performance in terms of a social systems model involving an interrelated set of four components—the work, the people, the formal organization, and the informal organization, all of which interact to translate strategy into performance. Research and practice in the field of organizational behavior show that organizations are effective to the extent that they achieve fit among the primary elements (within the context of strategy).

Change that addresses only one element is less likely to be successful, as the other drivers will act to reestablish the status quo. Therefore, change meant not only looking at the structure, but also the culture. Changing the structure alone will not fundamentally affect organizational behavior. In fact, the informal system will actually strengthen in response to the structural change; during times of change, people rely on established relationships and informal processes in order to circumvent the new formal structure. The increasing strength of the informal system, if left untouched, can negate the impact of structural change if there is nothing else to support the change in direction, such as a change in reward systems and leader behavior.

FIGURE 17-2   Mercer-Delta Organization/Congruence Model

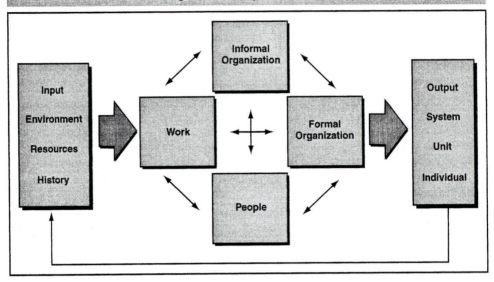

As such, Mercer-Delta's approach to rearchitecting the organization was to examine culture and leadership behavior as well as structure. It would be impossible to exhort the 20,000 ABS employees to be nimble if the leadership team was wrapped up in internecine warfare. Much of change has to do with perception—even a clear, efficient organization design would not resolve problems if it were seen in the context of the old team behavior.

PHASE 3: ORGANIZATIONAL ARCHITECTURE PROJECT

After several discussions with the CEO of Business Services, Mercer-Delta undertook an organization architecture project. The work process was discussed and agreed on up front (see Figure 17-3). Particularly important to agree on was the role of the CEO as sponsor, and the implications for his involvement. Due to budget and timing pressure, the head of Human Resources put a great deal of pressure on Mercer-Delta to come up with a fast-cycle work plan. A nine-month work process was compressed into three months of work. One of the challenges for the consultants was how to deliver sufficiently robust understanding and solid choices in the shorter time frame.

In addition to the CEO's role as sponsor, three other decisions were critical to project success—the selection of the leader, the selection of the team, and the start-up process of the team. Having worked with many transition teams, Mercer-Delta puts a premium on these initial steps. Because the client team actually does the work, it is vital that these people have drive, objectivity, and collaborative skills. This as much as anything else sets the stage for whether the effort will be successful, whether the work process will be followed, and whether results will be delivered.

First, through discussions with Mercer-Delta and the head of HR, the CEO selected Barbara Peda, a respected officer, to lead the team. Peda had delivered good business results in the Wholesale Segment, had strong strategic thinking capability, and

FIGURE 17–3 A Design Process

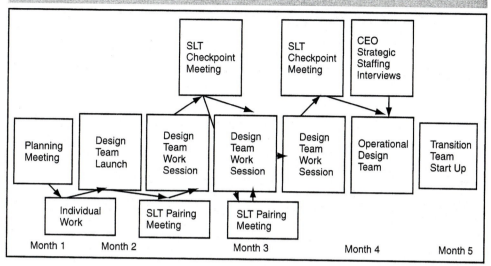

was capable of working across organizations. The selection of an officer signaled real commitment to the effort.

Second, key directors from different parts of the organization were recruited to work on the team. These people had contact with the day-to-day work and challenges facing the business and proved vital to the information scanning required to resolve some of the dilemmas the team dealt with. Peda picked a team to support her from across the organization. There was a product manager from IP, a product manager from Voice, sales executives from the two largest segments, a Finance executive, and most important, two colleagues from the leadership team. Each of these directors served as a link back to their home organization and often became the diplomat and translator.

Three other officers from the senior team joined the architecture design work. This was particularly important during the decision-making meetings of the senior team. This proved very helpful when the time came to represent reasons for decisions—four people could describe the decision process logic versus only Barbara. At times when Peda could not advocate a position without being parochial, the other members were able to explain thinking behind a decision in a more objective way. If Barbara found herself going one on one with a resistant colleague, another executive was able to intervene and try another tactic.

Third, the start-up process had three critical components—a pre-read/soak cycle in which team members got oriented to organization transformation, an explicit start-up process, and a high-engagement work plan. In a preliminary meeting with Peda, Mercer-Delta outlined a work plan for reaching a decision on organization architecture. Peda's role began immediately. She distributed key readings—those proposed by Mercer-Delta, Keith, and her own materials—and set up meeting logistics. The pre-work assignment set the stage for the start-up and immediately made clear that this team would be doing the work of driving for a decision. It also made clear that existing knowledge sources, internal and external, would be used to generate information necessary for informed choice.

While the meeting had a strong logistics element (managing dates and deliverables), Peda also used the meeting to set the stage for the working of the team. Specifically, she set down a few rules:

- Information stays in the room until we decide otherwise.
- No parochialism—explain host organization view then focus on what is best for the business.
- Work should be results driven—no long hours for the sake of long hours.
- Minimal presentations.
- Have fun.

These rules reinforced a different approach from more traditional task force work at AT&T and immediately built rapport between Barbara and the team. Building rapport proved particularly valuable as the team moved on to face difficult political choices. The loyalty and respect for Barbara was visible, reinforcing the sense that she had been the "right pick" as a leader.

The first session began with introductions—a helpful process particularly for those newer to the organization. Of course, each member had a variant of the joke that they were being punished for something by getting this assignment. After a review of the work plan, the team started divvying up assignments. Finally, the team participated in a self-naming exercise that produced the acronym SMART. Following the meeting, everyone remembered the name, but none could recall the root words.

Another element of the start-up process was the background material. While internal experts have day-to-day knowledge of the business and customers, they often lack cross-industry information or exposure to other companies' efforts. An initial contribution made by Mercer-Delta was to share change management approaches used at other similar companies. This approach presents the team with possible models to copy and customize and avoids prescribing a formulaic approach. For instance, one change management effort included a from–to exercise in which the current state was diagnosed using the congruence model, and the future state was articulated, again using the congruence model. The SMART team joked that they would just take the current state described by the other company and use it for ABS's future. It led them to an exercise around clarifying and consolidating the desired future state and its attributes. This was an early, relatively low-risk foray into problem solving as a group and offered a preliminary diagnosis of the organization.

Finally, the start-up process raised awareness about the organizational context in which change was taking place. At the same time that this effort began, corporate launched a "fact-finding" cost-reduction effort and sponsored another consulting firm. The project, called Track II, was designed to discover why AT&T's financials were so weak, and in particular, if all possible cost had been wrung out of the budgets. Peda eventually worked in tandem with that effort to ensure that short-term cost-cutting actions were synched up with the ultimate organization design. Peda was well aware that formulaic cost cutting could lead to strategy-destroying choices. That is, emerging markets typically look bad to cost cutters, but are far more important strategically.

Further, there were several moving parts in the business. AT&T had just completed a joint venture with British Telecom, and this was going to affect ABS's book of business, particularly its global accounts. AT&T had also bought a Data Networking business from IBM which would have to be integrated into ABS. All these efforts needed to be incorporated into the SMART team project.

PHASE 4: BUILDING STRATEGIC IMPERATIVES

Early on, the group realized that the changes were not only about organization structure, but that they involved fundamental questions of strategy. Which combination would lead to greater market success? Which organization did AT&T want to stack up for success? Which organization would have to cut resources (or, in the company's internal vernacular, "have more risk in the plan")? Although AT&T had articulated a strategy that served as an input to the imperatives, it was too high level to provide useful guidance for structuring an organization such as ABS.

We find that in architecture efforts, it is important to identify the basis for evaluating different design choices before any organizational options and models are developed. This avoids having superficial discussions in which the merits of one alternative over another appear to be driven more by personal preferences or political motivations rather than objective criteria.

Mercer-Delta Point of View

This leads to our third point of view on consulting to CEOs and executive teams on leading change in the strategic enterprise: A design effort needs sufficiently operationalized strategic imperatives (sometimes called design criteria) to direct subsequent choice of architecture. Without this, design choice is little more than a random process.

To create a preliminary list of strategic imperatives, the SMART team reviewed strategy documents, analyst reports, and general press material. They brainstormed a long list of imperatives and culled the list down to a short list of 11 high-level imperatives and 40 specific initiatives (grouped under the imperatives). This became the survey they brought around to their interviews. The interviews followed a set of steps including sharing a to–from diagnosis and working through an administered survey on the strategic imperatives.

The selection of interviewees was an important, conscious effort. Besides the CEO's direct reports, who should be interviewed? There was a concern that outsiders would criticize the process and decisions, but at the same time their support and input would be needed to successfully implement any of the desired changes. There was a view expressed that input from only the senior leadership team might be skewed or too high level. The decision was made to interview key outsiders—the factory provider (network manager), the corporate strategist, and various others.

After the sessions, the team debriefed about each interview. The interviewee shared the specific ratings, and also more broadly the interviewee's orientation to the business, to change in the business, to the design team process, and other elements that were relevant to change readiness. This allowed the team to build a holistic sense of leadership uptake around the process (see Figure 17–4).

The one-on-one interviews allowed some quiet time between a key decision maker/implementer and the content expert from the team. It was a perfect forum for building understanding, asking dumb questions, challenging viewpoints, and asking awkward political questions. It facilitated subsequent understanding and involvement. The interviews also served to build relationships between the team members and the leadership team.

Team members did not interview their own organization's leaders, but reached across into less familiar organization space. As such, they learned about the interview-

FIGURE 17-4   Mercer-Delta's Process for Building Strategic Imperatives and Initiatives

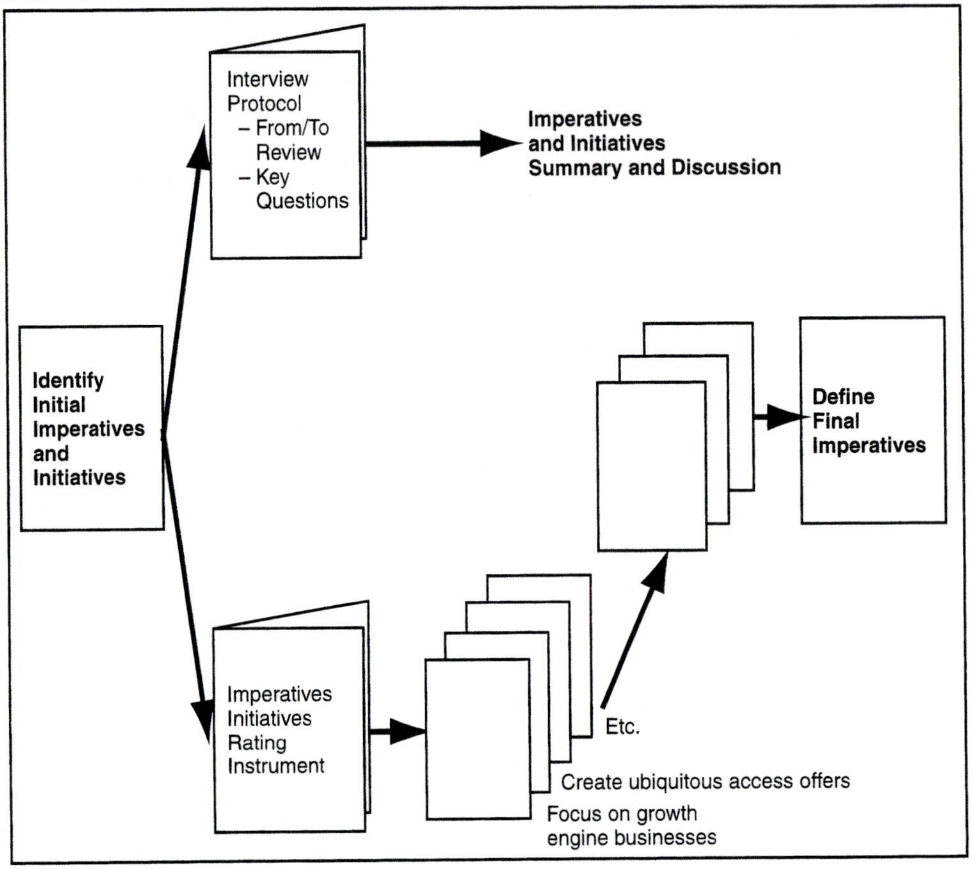

ee's organization and were able to educate the interviewee about other areas of the business. The interviews were between people across organizations, so it gave leadership and design team members a chance to see and hear across the organization in a direct, personal manner. One interviewer pointed out that, from what he had heard, this particular executive was going to be inflexible and bullying. His experience was the opposite. This kind of positive interpersonal interaction led to further success.

The process culminated in identification of a long list of strategic imperatives—things ABS had to do to survive. They ranged from specific cost-containment initiatives to a more general "focus on growth" imperative. The SMART team finalized the list in preparation for a Senior Leadership Team checkpoint meeting.

While the final imperatives seem relatively straightforward, their simplicity belies an important point—it takes a long time to write a short story. It is easy for a group to generate a long list of activities. It is easy for a group to endorse a short set of high-level directives. It is hard for a group to prioritize on a limited set of specific objectives.

Mercer-Delta Point of View

This leads to our fourth point of view on consulting to CEOs and executive teams on leading change in the strategic enterprise: *Achieving buy-in to the design choice crite-*

ria facilitates a group's ability to subsequently make choices. These imperatives, with the associated initiatives, provided the basis for subsequent decisions and assignments.

PHASE 5: BUILDING THE ARCHITECTURE OPTIONS

The next cycle of activity involved sharing the strategic imperatives with the senior leadership team as a group, and getting leadership's endorsement. As this cycle got underway, with Barbara Peda taking the lead, the SMART team began attacking the development of design alternatives. A few group members already had strong ideas about design proposals. A pro-forma design was presented by the consultants, modified by the team, and subteams began fleshing out specific proposals. The roles naturally fell to specific team members as the team coalesced around three different models—first, an enhanced segment model (essentially clarifying and improving the existing model); second, a modified product model that created leverage in the direct sales force and focus in the product lines; and, finally, a market model that essentially created three distinct businesses.

As the subteams worked, they shared ideas and progress regularly. Good ideas moved organically from one proposal to another. At the same time, the groups worked to create distinctions between their models. For instance, one strategic issue that had been identified was the need to focus on access strategies. AT&T paid $9 billion in access costs to local telecom providers. Regulation now permitted AT&T to enter the local markets, which would enable them to avoid these charges entirely. However, gaining local customers and building local infrastructure was a monumental challenge. This put a premium on a strategy for managing access costs—called the "Last Mile" by one team member.

The groups also modified and enhanced the pro-forma designs (see Figure 17–5). One member came up with the idea of "headline news"—a cover sheet that would announce the organization, the basic story of why this change was being made, and why it made sense. Each group was tasked with identifying the pros and cons of the organization. Finally, there was a fairly detailed operational picture of who went with what organization and who was doing what.

This was then incorporated into a flip book and the team again went out into pairing sessions, in which the team member took the leader through the strategic imperatives (again), described each option, and got a reaction from each member on the option. After reviewing each option, the option was rated against the strategic imperative. At the end of the session, the options were rated and ranked. Ranking was important for prioritization.

Debriefings from these interviews led to an interesting observation: Everyone clearly favored the market option—structuring each business for maximum independence. Yet, the process finally recommended (verbally) the moderate option. That is, their personal favorite was a more radical option than what they were willing to recommend. There were multiple reasons for this, but the group moved into operationalizing roles and responsibilities for the modified product model.

One product of the process was an opinion analysis—a document that described the ranges and clusters of opinions. This document helped the CEO build a sense of the group as a whole—where energy was directed, what kind of tensions he might expect,

FIGURE 17-5   A Pro-Forma Design

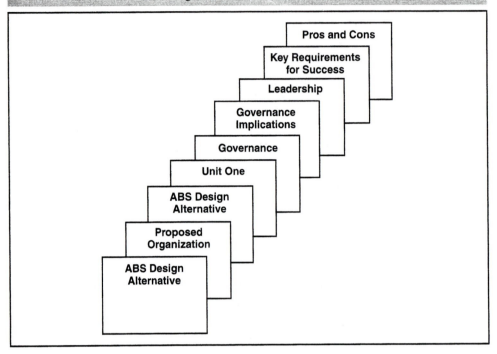

and where agreement might be easily achieved. Further, each interviewee had something to add about the pros and cons of the design options. That, too, was incorporated into the final analysis.

In an important offsite meeting, the leadership team finalized their architectural choice. The session had presenters and included the data analysis and opinion analysis from the one-on-one pairing sessions. Several pre-offsite meetings were also held. Since everyone knew that a decision about organization structure was going to be made at the offsite, as one person put it, "We want to know if this can work before we get to the meeting where we're supposed to decide." This behavior was most salient among the old horse traders. Though it was often negatively labeled as political, it served a very useful function—people were oriented to the choices and the implications by the time they got to the meeting. They had thought through the implications, how implementation would affect existing processes, and so could have an in-depth conversation about how it would work.

Although the design was not everything everyone hoped for, some of the strategic big ideas made it through the process. For instance, the idea of aggregating work on access technologies (the so-called "Last Mile") had come up in one of the design subteams. Eager to copy the good idea, the other teams incorporated the concept in their designs in different ways.

The Last Mile received its final endorsement in the meeting itself. It was predictable in that people's points of view were relatively fixed; however, there were interesting cases of noninterested parties speaking to a specific decision. For instance, there was a great deal of discussion about the Last Mile organization. The

Last Mile organization—a clear need from a design point of view—now had to pass the incumbents challenge. In past practice, connectivity options and negotiations had been the purview of independent organizations. The network people negotiated rates with CLECs and the Voice product managers determined preferred technologies for their products, as did the Data Networking product managers and the IP product managers. The integration of these decisions into a single forum represented some loss of autonomy, presumably with a large increase in market leverage. Still, the change needed to be negotiated.

This created some awkwardness, but ironically, one of the product heads was articulate about the benefits the integration offered her unit. Further, several members from the design team were able to articulate the logic for the decision. The multiple voices were able to carry the day and the Last Mile concept was endorsed. The apparent objectivity of the advocates was immensely helpful.

Another strategic big idea also stuck. As we described earlier, there was considerable debate as to the location of the Data Networking Group. During the sessions, several people came to talk to the design team. One of these was from technical marketing, the part of AT&T that provides the technical support to the customer proposals. The technical marketing director came with a simple sheet of paper—the last 20 requests he had received for technical support for proposals. Of these, 15 were for joint Data and IP services. As one design team member described it, this was an "intellectual wedgie"—that is, a very simple piece of information that strongly supported one point of view over another. This, too, became one of the bigger organizational changes.

PHASE 6: IMPLEMENTATION

About this time, change was heating up at the corporate level. Michael Keith was distracted by constant conversations with CEO Michael Armstrong. Change was afoot, but the ABS team had little involvement with it. Rumors were everywhere, but none were identical, which led to further confusion. The group plunged forward with an "as-if-this-will-work" feeling.

Eventually, it was announced that Michael Keith (the current ABS leader) was moving to Wireless, and Rick Roscitt (CEO of AT&T Solutions) was coming in to run a combined organization of ABS and Solutions. There was some initial trepidation. Relations between Roscitt's group (AT&T Solutions) and ABS had been competitive, and there was a fair amount of jealousy by ABS of the Solutions unit. Solutions was growing and meeting its targets. Those within ABS believed Solutions had a disproportionate share of the most highly compensated staff. At the same time there was a lot of hope because Roscitt was viewed as aggressive, influential, and good for the business. Executives also thought that bringing together the Solutions business and ABS into one organization would improve effectiveness.

Roscitt undertook some initial fact finding and found, at the time, that the SMART team and Track II had a good, though not perfect, reputation. There were some complaints about process (decisions made unilaterally by Keith versus in consultation mode with the affected VP) and errors (program managers inadvertently counted as product managers). Overall, the leadership team had good things to say about the work and the discussions. To Roscitt's credit, he decided to build on the efforts underway, rather than demolish the work begun by his predecessor.

Roscitt accepted the structure the team had decided on, and prepared for a team start-up meeting that focused on roles and responsibilities. An in-depth governance design was developed for the meeting. The governance design included specific forums through which initiatives would be achieved. For instance, a Revenue Council monitored efforts to double the Data Networking revenue, and "catapult" IP revenue. An Operational Excellence Council oversaw e-enabling efforts and cost-reduction initiatives. The Councils acted as centers of responsibility and accountability for achieving objectives.

The meeting went well with high-level teamwork as the group adjusted to the new leader. The sharing of roles and responsibilities gave everyone a chance to get to know each other in greater depth than before, which was particularly beneficial for a merged team. Equally important, the roles and responsibilities discussion provided a forum for some tough discussions and decisions. One individual, for instance, was able to clarify that his organization felt handicapped because it had to rely on scarce project management skills housed in another organization and that it was last on the service list. In other instances, team members naturally noticed where efforts needed to be shared and synchronized.

The offsite meeting provided closure to the architecture process. Much of the strategy would be subsequently reviewed and initiatives reassigned. However, the core elements remained the same and the specific forums became champions for specific goals.

THE CONSULTANTS' ROLE — MERCER-DELTA POINT OF VIEW

At Mercer-Delta, we believe in leveraging the skills and knowledge of the organization. Our objective is to develop and unleash talent already owned by the company. To realize this strategy, *the consultants were clearly in the background throughout work.* No documents had the Mercer-Delta Consulting name on them. The consultants did neither interviews nor presentations, though they helped with questions, suggestions, materials preparation, and coaching. The value of this was manifold.

First, it minimized decision responsibility displacement or "consultant backlash" — the phenomenon in which the client (or specific executives within the client) blame decisions on misinformed, wrongheaded, self-interested, and pillaging consultants. Although there were cases of back-pedaling and responsibility avoidance, there were sufficient internal historians who were able to trace the decision logic and call out the responsibility avoiders.

More importantly, our strategy builds competence, credibility, and connections among the existing members of the organization. It is an irrefutable fact that the people working in the organization know the most about the organization's problems. Analysts and scholars may have a long-term or big-picture view, but they don't have the day-to-day context. External experts aren't the ones testing solutions nor resolving technical breakdowns — they don't live the work. The irony is that, in organizations, people seldom listen to their peers and seldom take the effort to mine the knowledge the organization's members have. Executives hire outside experts and they bypass a wealth of internal knowledge and value — their internal colleagues. The value of the process we follow lies in unlocking organizational knowledge and capacity that otherwise gets missed in the press of activity, deliverables, and conflicting points of view.

Finally, having the consultants in the background affirms the problem-solving capability within the organization and builds capacity. In this model, it is important to recognize and authorize progress and accomplishments. Executives are quick to ignore what they have accomplished as they search for new problems to solve. In the search for what has not yet been done, they overlook their own learning and the organization's development.

At the same time, a temporary team, chartered with a monumental task, is glad to receive support and guidance from experienced professionals, as long as those professionals' motivations seem pure. Consultants can add perspective, break frame, bring new solutions, and bring the long-term and outside view. In particular, we were able to provide real-life examples and experience around major change efforts in other *Fortune* 500s.

Finally, Mercer-Delta was able, at appropriate moments, to act as an impartial third party. In some cases, this meant taking on the CEO when he was failing to make tough decisions. Occasionally, Mercer-Delta had to be sure that design team members were not being shot at in their home organizations. At other times, Mercer-Delta was involved in coaching a senior team member around leadership and teamwork. Finally, we also worked directly in the room and behind the scenes to maintain good relationships among design team members. All this work, however, was in concert with the design team leader and the head of HR.

SUMMARY

The process we described here is a fast-cycle organization architecture client engagement. In order to achieve change, several change strategies were: work with the executive team, a high-engagement process, and an excellent design team. The contribution of the design team was in both the process and content.

As with many change efforts, unanticipated events occurred. On this engagement, change of leadership at a critical time had not been anticipated in the work plan. Fortunately, as the process unfolded, we had built substantial support throughout the organization. When the new leader took charge, this made it easy for him to adopt the work that had been done thus far. It reflects Mercer-Delta's perspective on change and lessons learned from 20 years of change management and organization design. Some key learnings include:

- The initial step in a strategic change effort is to employ a data-driven process that surfaces important organizational issues, develops shared understanding of these issues among top leadership, and builds their commitment to developing and implementing an action plan.
- Fundamental strategic change frequently involves rethinking the basic architecture of the company.
- A design effort needs sufficiently operationalized strategic imperatives (sometimes called design criteria) to direct subsequent choice of architecture.
- Achieving buy-in to the design choice criteria facilitates a group's ability to subsequently make choices.
- The consulting support stays in the background throughout work.

AT&T faces one of the toughest industry environments in business. The company's markets are rapidly changing. Old sources of competitive advantage are eroding and are being replaced by new ones. The revenue value of the core business market—long distance calls made by business customers—is dropping dramatically. In such a situation, the organization has little choice but to utilize the best tactics and strategies of organization architecture. In this case, AT&T leveraged its strengths—the factory, the large portfolio of customer relationships, and its leading technology to gain a foothold in new markets.

CHAPTER

Aligning Business and Technology Strategy

Charles Durrant and Deborah Baxley

Jamie Varvoglis reclined in his chair and reflected on the meeting that was about to take place in his office. He had agreed to this meeting because, as vice chairman of First Trust Bancorp and president and chief executive officer of First Trust Bank (FTB), he wanted to make sure the latest IBM Consulting team that had been brought in worked on the "right things." There had been plenty of other IBM consultants working on projects at FTB, but this one was special: He wanted it to take a long hard look at the strategic role that technology played throughout the company.

IBM had put a new principal on the job—Sandy Saunders—who seemed pretty competent. That much Jamie had heard from Angela Henderson, FTB's newly appointed senior vice president of Information Services (IS) and chief information officer. Jamie knew that Sandy and Angela had already spent some time talking about FTB's long-term planning processes and about potential organizational issues the bank would have to address.

A related issue Jamie wanted to bring up was the status of the bank's key initiative in Internet banking. He knew that Rob Berin, FTB's executive vice president of Marketing and Alternative Channels, was unhappy with the slow progress being made in adding new functions to the Web site. Jamie wondered why rollout had been so slow and costs so high? Now Rob's business plan was at risk and he had been complaining about it to anyone who would listen.

Rob wasn't the only one complaining. Jamie had been getting an earful from the heads of FTB's other lines of business and from several members of the board. They all expressed concern about FTB's investments in information technology (IT) and groaned about the pitiful returns the bank was getting from those investments. But despite meeting with Angela about it a few times, Jamie wasn't convinced they had figured out any of the real underlying issues or developed a plan to attack them. This wasn't going to be easy.

Angela was also worried about the meeting. As a relative newcomer to FTB, Angela felt under tremendous pressure from Jamie and the other senior officers to deliver results. She had spoken extensively with Sandy Saunders about it, and was relieved to see that Sandy seemed to appreciate the pressure she was under. Sandy had talked about IBM's experiences with other banks and had pleased Angela with her

Charles Durant is a Principal in strategy and change in the Practice of IBM Global Services.
Deborah Baxley is a Managing Principal in the Banking Strategy and Change Practice of IBM Business Innovation Services.

insights. Angela and Sandy had jointly planned the one-hour meeting with Jamie that was scheduled for Tuesday morning.

Following her discussions with Angela on Friday, Sandy Saunders had pulled together a small team of IBMers to do some background work. They had spent most of Saturday working on the agenda, with another round of refinements on Monday. Over the weekend, the team had reviewed work IBM had done with other banks in similar situations, and Sandy had talked with two other IBM principals about their work with similar financial services firms. The team had also looked over a recent IBM Best Practices study and summarized the relevant portions for her.

To facilitate the meeting, Sandy had prepared a presentation to use as a discussion guide. While she knew much of the meeting would involve listening to Jamie, she also knew she'd have to move things along to get to where she wanted to go. Sandy was feeling pleased with herself and had high hopes for the project as she joined Angela for the short ride up to Jamie's office on Tuesday morning, laptop in hand.

THE INITIAL MEETING

Jamie welcomed Angela and Sandy. To break the ice, they spent a few minutes talking about a recent bank merger and about Alan Greenspan's latest press conference on the economy. They then got to work.

Sandy proposed that they use her Discussion Guide as an agenda and they agreed. Nonetheless, Jamie, who had also prepared for the meeting, spent the first 20 minutes or so discussing the bank's strategy, the importance of enabling IT to achieve FTB's objectives in the market, and the issues he thought the bank was facing.

Specifically, Jamie began by pointing to the rapid changes that were occurring in the financial services industry—consolidation, disaggregation, decreasing customer loyalty, and the resulting pressures on efficiencies and net interest margins. He described FTB's business objectives in terms of net earnings, return on investment (ROI), return on equity (ROE), and market share. He explained that FTB's key strategies involved enhanced products and services, targeting high-net-worth individuals and small businesses, market expansion into a neighboring region, and leveraging alternative channels. Sandy asked several questions to clarify FTB's objectives and strategies. At one point, there was a lively interchange about how much agreement there really was among senior bank officials about FTB's strategies. Jamie felt certain the senior team knew what needed to be done, but conceded that the team might not always be making the necessary trade-offs.

Jamie then turned to technology issues. As he put it: "Although IT issues are a significant portion of FTB's noninterest expense, I'm less certain about the overall investment level—whether it's too much or too little, or even focused on the right initiatives." Angela pointed out that there was significant IT spend in the lines of business that she didn't control. Sandy added that experience showed that there could be as much as 100 percent additional IT spend outside the IS budget. Jamie agreed that there was probably IT spend in the lines of business but was skeptical that it could be that high at FTB. More importantly, Jamie felt unsure that IT projects planned and underway were the "right" projects. After some discussion, they agreed that the "right" projects might be best defined as those projects necessary to meet strategic business objectives.

Jamie then stressed the recent trends that had made hiring Angela necessary, namely, the bank's rapid growth in size, product diversity, and sophistication. As he indicated, "the requirement for rapid cycle time—between business needs and IS—was going to increase rather than decrease." He described the constant complaints line of business executives made about the IS department's inability to meet their needs on a timely basis and the lack of clarity about the department's priorities. Jamie recited Rob Berin's litany of complaints. Jamie made a point of saying that the IS team was viewed by everyone as working very hard and getting lots done with the skills and resources at hand, but that much improvement was needed to meet the market test.

As Jamie appeared to be winding down, Sandy took the opportunity to recapitulate the key issues they had discussed. Sandy next called attention to various charts she had prepared that addressed some of those themes and the different courses of action IBM consulting teams had taken with previous clients to address those issues.

Sandy then proposed a near-term course of action to help clarify and address the issues. Specifically, she recommended that FTB engage a small team to conduct three fact-finding interviews with business and IS leadership. The information gathered would be summarized and added to the information discussed during the meeting to arrive at a clearly defined issue statement and a detailed course of action. Sandy recommended that her team interview the IS vice president of Development Services, Terry McGuire, as well as Rob Berin and Pat Fogerty, FTB's chief financial officer and the person to whom Angela reported. Angela and Jamie agreed with Sandy's recommendation for the three one-hour interviews. Jamie said he would to talk with Rob and Pat, and Angela agreed to arrange the IS meeting, as well as a follow-up meeting for next week. Jamie then excused himself for another meeting in the boardroom across the hall.

Framing the Issues

The issues discussed in this meeting are common across industries and companies. The importance of information technology to a company's successful operations means that key technology issues have to be recognized, framed, and addressed. Framing the issues means organizing them around an analytic structure or model that is compelling, straightforward, and relevant to the client context. Correctly framing the issues invariably requires a solid understanding of the fundamentals of the client's business. Correctly framing the issues also improves the consultant's ability to arrive at solutions that not only address the fundamental issues, but also have the requisite buy-in from the client that will be necessary for successful implementation and assimilation of any technology-based solutions.

In their initial analysis, Sandy and the IBM team had classified the issues into four categories:

1. **Business and IS strategies:**
   - Completeness and clarity of vision, strategy, and strategic plans of FTB and lines of business
   - Completeness, clarity, and alignment of the IS vision, strategy, and strategic plans
   - Effectiveness of strategic planning and its linkage to the budgeting processes

2. **Communication and governance:**
   - Effectiveness in establishing, maintaining, and leveraging relationships with corporate and line-of-business executive management
   - Effectiveness of communications of priorities, project status, value delivered, and the like

- Clarity of IS and lines of business's roles and responsibilities
- Effectiveness and governance structures and processes

3. Investment decision making and monitoring:
- Agreement and effectiveness of investment decision processes and criteria
- Investment levels and return on investment on IT resources

4. IS effectiveness
- IS operational efficiency and effectiveness

The IBM Team's Initial Response

By the end of the meeting, Sandy felt confident that the issues Jamie and Angela had raised were well within the practice area's competencies in technology, strategy, and organization. The client was also a significant player in the industry, and the practice should be able to develop a strong value proposition for both FTB and IBM. As a result, Sandy initiated a set of actions.

Her first step was to document the key points made during the call using a standard "Call Summary" form. Sandy also began thinking about the necessary combination of skills and expertise she would want her team to have. To build the team, Sandy contacted the Practice's Resource Development Manager (RDM) to discuss the requirements and consultants available for the interviews, also establishing the consideration that if the team was successful, they should be available to continue to work with the FTB team. A critical step in the process was to carefully consider and select the Engagement Leader (EL), a senior consultant who would help develop the initial statement of work for the interviews, and lead the team through the interviews, analysis, and presentation of findings. Further, the EL would be available to develop the follow-on Project Proposal and lead the team through the project.

Sandy and the RDM picked the EL and the team, and they then jointly developed the Team Kickoff Package. The purpose of the Kickoff Package is always to provide information about the client and describe the project's key objectives, approach, team roles, deliverables, and schedule to get the team prepared to work effectively with the client. An associate consultant—and future team member—completed additional research about FTB. The EL scheduled a half-day team meeting, developed the Statement of Work (SOW) for the client and completed an initial pricing worksheet for the fact-finding interviews.

Angela called Sandy with the schedule for the fact-finding interviews. Sandy then met with Angela, introduced the EL, discussed the SOW and price, and asked that Angela distribute the interview guides to the appropriate client participants. The next day, the SOW was signed, and Sandy and the EL contacted each interviewee to confirm the interviews and discuss their objectives and feedback process.

The following week, the interviews were conducted and documented, feedback collected from the interviewees, and a summary and conclusions presentation assembled that included input from Sandy's initial meeting with Jamie. Additional material from IBM's intellectual capital was also included to emphasize key findings and recommendations.

Sandy, Angela, and the engagement leader then met with Jamie to discuss the findings and recommendations. As a result, Jamie agreed that IBM should rapidly put together an experienced team to work with Angela, members of her team, and key

FTB business leadership to address the issues raised. Jamie emphasized that he wanted to be included in all milestone presentations and to review the Project Report prior to its finalization. Sandy and the engagement leader then developed a detailed proposal, secured the client's signature, and the project was under way.

THE BUSINESS AND IT ALIGNMENT MODEL

The underpinnings of an IT strategy is the Business and IT Alignment Model, first proposed by J. C. Henderson and N. Venkatraman in 1993, and diagrammed in Figure 18–1. It cautions that there are several ways in which business strategy and operations can link up to IT strategy and operations. A careful analysis of the client situation, using this framework, makes these linkages explicit.

Most companies operate primarily in an operational alignment mode (see Figure 18–2). Business strategy is generally the starting point from which both organizational and IS infrastructure is derived. Operationally aligned firms tend to think of internal business units as their customers. Focusing on the needs of these units, they strive to develop a world-class internal service organization. IT strategy in these firms creates the capacity to meet customer needs.

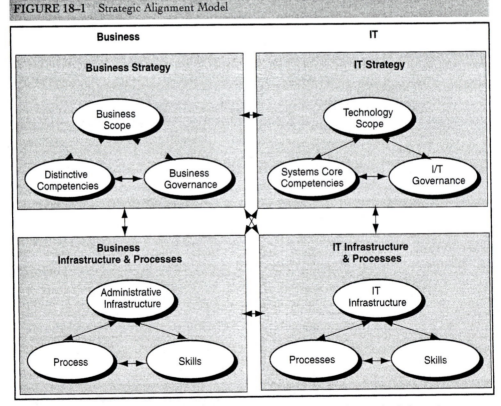

FIGURE 18–1 Strategic Alignment Model

Adapted from J. C. Henderson and N. Venkatraman, "Strategic alignment: Leveraging information technology for transforming organizations," *IBM Systems Journal*, 1993, 32(1): 4–15.

FIGURE 18–2   Creating Operational Alignment

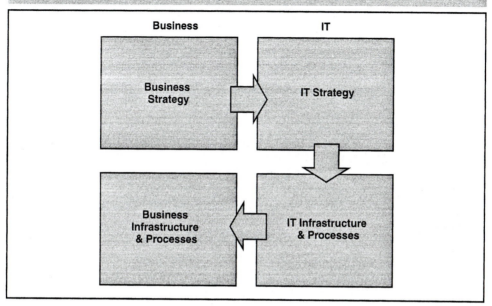

Strategic alignment is achieved by having a linked business strategy and IT strategy, which are then executed at the operational levels of the firm (see Figure 18–3). Strategically aligned firms tend to view IT as a key collaborator, leading to revised business strategy. Successful strategic alignment hinges on sound execution at the operational level. Either business or IT senior management may provide the technology vision that best supports the business strategy.

FIGURE 18–3   Creating Strategic Alignment

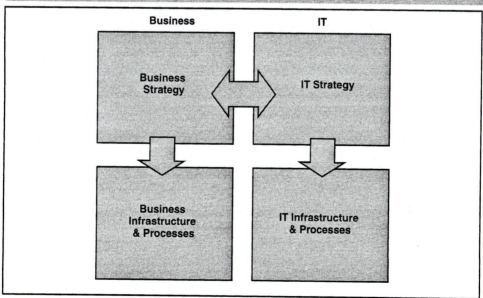

Various internal and external factors determine the way in which alignment is approached. A company facing a stable market with a "most efficient player" strategy is likely to favor achieving operational alignment. A company facing rapid market change is more likely to benefit from strategic alignment. Successful alignment builds the IT capabilities to meet business strategy and needs. As Figure 18–4 indicates, strategic and operationally aligned companies adopt a different IT focus and take different approaches to planning, funding, coordination, and communication of IT.

Developing an IT Strategy

The purpose of an IT strategy is to achieve an ongoing, permanent alignment between business strategy, required business and IT capabilities, and the company's strategic initiatives. Figure 18–5 describes the process through which consultants can help client companies build IT strategies.

The overall goal of an IT strategy project is to ensure that technology investments support business strategies and directives, ensuring strategic alignment. The successful IT strategy refreshes the business strategy with competitive potential based on technology, reflects the new business strategy, identifies the needed changes to capabilities, processes, and structure, and, finally, identifies the needed changes to functionality, architecture, governance, IT processes, and sourcing. It therefore requires an understanding of:

- Industry drivers, business aspirations, and required time frames
- Required business capabilities (people, process, and technology) to support the business aspiration
- Current technology capabilities
- Gap between current and required technology capabilities
- Feasible implementation and investment time frames to fill the gap

There are several clear benefits that ensue from developing close alignment between IT and the business planning process. They include:

- Understanding the impact of technology on the business
- Fostering alignment with business objectives and technology initiatives
- Ensuring that investment decisions are consistent with long-term business and technology decisions
- Providing a vehicle for IT to ensure it is providing maximum value to the business

The Strategic Planning Process

Alignment is a fusion of business and IT plans, funding, and communications that induces focused action toward key business objectives. Some of the key characteristics of the planning process include:

- Strategic business and IT plans are generally reviewed annually at senior management levels. There is a relationship between business and IT plans as well as between strategic and operational plans. Plan measures of success are determined based on business strategy.
- Both senior business management and senior IT management are involved in the creation and review of these plans. Business managers are involved in the creation of IT plans and vice versa.

FIGURE 18–4 Comparison of Operationally Versus Strategically Aligned Companies

Characteristic	Strategic Alignment	Operational Alignment
Roles: • Role of senior business management	• **Visionary:** understanding of the business demands on IT and what emerging IT can mean for the business strategy.	• **Executive leadership:** strategy formulation and prioritization.
• Role of senior IT management	• **Catalyst:** giving business management an understanding of the role IT can play and translating business strategy into IT strategy. The CIO participates in executive steering committees.	• **Executive leadership of IT:** strategy implementation. The CIO understands the service level demands of the business and advises business counterparts.
Focus: • Performance criteria	• Focus on **technology leadership** (e.g., benchmarking position of firm in technology marketplace) or product leadership (e.g., growth, new product introduction).	• Focus on being the **low cost producer.** Focus on customer satisfaction using qualitative and quantitative measures.
• Business view of IT	• IT provides technology for **new competitive positions.** IT sometimes drives business strategy.	• IS is seen as a **top class service** organization responsive to business needs. IS may be seen as a business within a business. IT enables the business plan.
Planning: • Planning horizons	• Business emphasizes **long-term strategic planning;** both business and IT develop annual and long-term plans.	• **Tactical focus** with emphasis on results. IT plans are based on business priorities. Shorter-term planning.
• Degree of plan synchronization	• IT and business units are involved in creating each other's plans, resulting in a **single integrated business plan** with a strong IT component.	• IT and business units create **separate plans.** Business requirements feed IT plans.
• IT plan ownership	• There is **shared ownership** and accountability for success of IT plan or combined plan.	• IT **is responsible** for the success of the IT plan.
Funding: • Funding	• **Business and IT plans provide multiyear funding** for critical initiatives. Senior business and IT management are involved in cross business unit resource allocations.	• IT **is viewed as a cost/service center.** Funding levels are based on business outlook with business units involved in initiative funding and prioritization.
• Infrastructure funding	• **Infrastructure investments are treated as critical** to firm's competitive position, evaluated and approved as part of multiyear initiative plans.	• **Infrastructure is typically funded as a component of a business unit project** as part of a business case.
Coordination: • Plan linkage to goals	• **Strategic plans are shared across business and IT,** and translated into operational goals. IS and business units jointly review plans and goals.	• **IS goals are derived from business unit goals.** There are some shared goals.
Communication: • Communication of strategies and plans.	• **Strategic plans are used as a communication vehicle** across the firm. Employees are aware of their role in firm strategy.	• **IS service level is communicated to business units.** Employees are aware of IS contribution to the business.

SOURCE: IBM IT Transformation Consortium, 1996.

FIGURE 18–5 The Process of Developing an IT Strategy

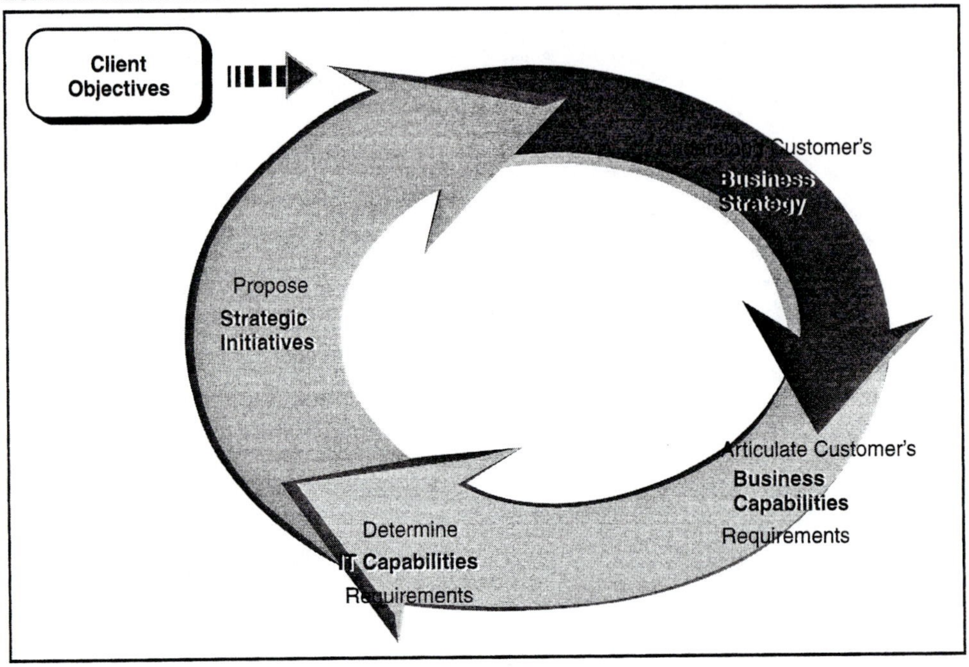

- Large strategic projects are managed and reviewed at a senior management level by business and IT management and are viewed in the light of their impact on the whole business.
- Long-term projects are approved only once and reevaluated annually (budgets are protected). Such projects are structured to produce regular (at least annual) deliverables (see Figure 18–6).

A visionary executive may, in certain circumstances, be prepared to make an investment in IT, which is strategically necessary for the company, even though it is not possible to prepare a business case in advance. This is often the case with infrastructure projects (e.g., e-mail) or experimental e-commerce projects (e.g., trying a new business model).

Organization Alignment — How IT Supports the Business

Companies have three basic organizational levers they can use to improve organizational performance:

1. **Organization structure**, including formal designs and linkages, roles and accountability definitions, policies and operating practices, cost structure, and resource allocation
2. **Organizational behavior**, including values, behaviors, communication patterns, learning practices, attitudes, and leadership models
3. **Structural and behavioral enablers**, such as performance management systems, competency design and management, HR planning, management development and training, communication, and information-sharing programs

IT organizations invariably wrestle with the decision either to centralize or to decentralize IT service/process ownership. While a centralized design allows for easier implementation of cross-business applications and architectures, ability to drive

FIGURE 18–6 The Strategic Planning Process

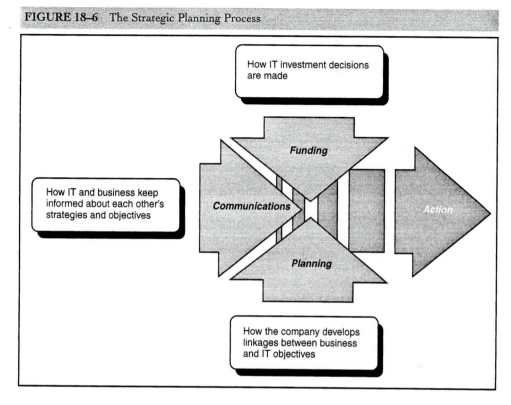

economies of scale, deeper specialization through critical mass and technical career mobility, the need for business unit autonomy and rapid decision making often drives toward decentralization. In a vicious circle, this trend toward decentralization decreases the organization's ability to implement common architectures, leading to fragmented efforts and higher cost bases.

The **coordinated hybrid model** leverages the strengths of the centralized and decentralized models by maintaining operational services, development services, and infrastructure services as central functions, while distributing into "business unit IT" groups such responsibilities as marketing, consulting, education, planning, relationship management, and business analysis. This model can be successful if roles and responsibilities are clearly defined, reward systems encourage teamwork, formal communications networks are maintained, there is a governing body to iron out disputes, and there are joint architecture and service level agreements.

The **shared services model** is another hybrid option that allows a business unit to choose its own applications and standards, yet to purchase services centrally. In this model, centralized IT owns leveraged services (e.g., server operations, wide area networking services) while distributed units maintain responsibility for IT policies, IT standards, and applications. In its purest form, this model operates with the central IT unit competing in the open market against other infrastructure providers—the business units are free to buy from the internal IT group or from an external outsourcing firm. This added dimension ensures that the central IT unit remains competitive in pricing and quality.

Among leading IT organizations, three guiding principles are generally evident:

1. **Business units "own" the applications:** Most computing is done outside the typical IT organization. By 2000, less than 30 percent of computing expenditures was in the IT budget. Even enterprise-wide applications may be owned by functional organizations.
2. **Central IT "owns" the architecture:** As resources become increasingly distributed and heterogeneous, the "glue" that enables applications and data to talk across organizational boundaries is the architecture.
3. **Shared resources are managed centrally:** Shared resources and functions and cross-organizational boundaries should be managed centrally, although at the lowest level of sharing (which may be either at the enterprise or business unit level). Examples include utility services, applications, databases, and competency centers.

Roles and Responsibilities

To be successful, roles and responsibilities of IT organizations and their business unit counterparts have to be clearly defined, understood, and agreed to (see Figure 18–7).

Relationship Leaders

Relationship leaders are middle managers with decision-making authority and responsibility for overall relationship management with specific business units, in addition to their traditional IT management responsibilities. Business units help select people into these liaison roles. Relationship leaders play a primary role in assisting business units in building business justification cases for proposed IT projects. Business units provide input to relationship leaders' performance evaluations. Successful relationship leaders have the following characteristics:

- Strong interpersonal relationships with their assigned business units
- Broad understanding of business operations and current IT projects that may impact operations across functions
- Knowledge of business strategy and objectives to provide a context for decision making
- Performance measurements primarily based on client feedback
- Decision-making authority for incremental resource allocation to resolve client issues

Some basic organizational tenets associated with the function include:

- Relationship leaders have reporting lines to both the IT organization and the lines of business. They have direct reporting to the IT organization, and "dotted line" reporting to the line of business they serve.
- Relationship leader performance measurements are developed and agreed upon by both the IT organization and the lines of business.
- Each line of business and IT group has at least one defined point of contact. Dependent on the breadth of the line of business, there may be multiple points of contact.
- The relationship leader "owns" the relationship for an individual line of business or other entity (e.g., corporate offices) that use/impact IT resources.

As the job description puts it: a relationship leader ". . . will identify, pursue, and influence opportunities to use technology to help the client reduce costs, improve service, or gain competitive advantage/product differentiation." The role statement assumes that relationship leaders have a broad understanding of the line of business

FIGURE 18-7 Characteristic Roles and Responsibilities

	IT Responsibilities	Shared Responsibilities	Corporate and Line of Business Responsibilities
IT Strategy & Plan	• Vision, direction • IT strategy and strategic plan • Architecture/ standards • Advanced technology		• Business strategy and plan • Requirements and business IT strategic plan • Participation in architecture review board
Relationship	• Relationship management	• Jointly establish metrics and measures	• Relationship managers • IT contact points
Infrastructure	• Plan, procure, operate, manage, support hardware and operating systems		
Applications	• Enterprise, shared and most lines of business applications, e-mail		• Limited line of business-specific applications
Data	• Data definition and storage • Data warehouse, mining tools		• Entry, accuracy and maintenance processes • Lines of business-specific aligned
Processes	• Development systems development life cycle • Ownership of processes (e.g., change and problem management)	• Governance process and structure	
Management	• Participate on management committee • Input to investment strategy • IT project leadership • Strategic vendor relationships • IT training • Efficiency and synergy identification • Risk management • Performance reporting, balanced scorecard	• Project ownership and accountability • Service level agreements	• Management committee • Investment strategy • Project priority • Business case development • Project funding • Limited job-specific vendor management • Preparation required to successfully implement projects • Project results • Report user satisfaction

they serve. It requires that they "live" with the client, and spend their time focusing on business needs and actively proposing potential technology solutions originating from within and from outside IT. In essence, they serve as an advocate for the client, helping to develop line of business IT plans and translating business requirements to IT. Conversely, they must translate IT policies, standards, and IT architecture requirements to the lines of business and facilitate the governance process when business requirements argue to move outside these parameters.

Clearly the role requires a broad skill set. Relationship leaders must not only be well versed in the business they support, but must also have a high level understanding of technologies, both existing and emerging, and how those technologies might be applied to business issues and opportunities.

Finally, relationship leaders must also have a solid understanding of competitive developments, and what rivals are doing with technology, processes, and channels in order to help a company establish and maintain competitive differentiation.

The IT Investment Decision-Making Process

Companies optimize the value of their IT investments through an effective investment governance process, which involves selecting the right projects, tracking progress, and measuring and communicating overall results on a continuous basis. The challenge of project selection is in creating a process that balances rigorous business justification with the need for quick action to compete in transforming marketplaces. Many companies have "fast path" mechanisms for approval of smaller requests, which delegate decisions to more appropriate levels of the organization. Most project selection processes are designed around "when to say yes" but lack a clear-cut communication of "no" to projects with weaker business cases.

Effective project monitoring begins before the project development phase. Most companies track schedule and budget during project development and implementation, while few track postimplementation benefits focused on cost (e.g., headcount) reduction and have not yet identified ways to track and measure additive benefits (e.g., increased revenue, competitive advantage, etc.).

A typical investment governance process uses the following steps:

1. Projects are divided into categories of discretionary and nondiscretionary requests. Nondiscretionary projects have a fast path to update the list of available resources. These include projects for regulatory compliance.
2. Discretionary projects require business unit, finance, technology, and training department sign-off to ensure that business cases reflect all true costs.
3. Using a standard, company-wide format, project business cases are developed by business unit with IT assistance.
4. Senior management approves and rejects newly proposed projects on a monthly or quarterly basis. Approval should be followed by immediate funding. Larger projects are sometimes given initial approval to further flesh out the business opportunity.

Some key concepts to keep in mind include:

- The basis for funding is the company strategic plan or the revenue/expense plan of the business unit.
- The funding process makes allowance during the plan period for the funding of projects exceeding the original or not in plan.
- Business and IT executives are actively involved in cross-firm allocation of resources.
- Funding of underlying IT infrastructure is viewed as a key to competitiveness and is pursued by both IT and the business. The funding process facilitates the funding of infrastructure and of projects that impact multiple business units (e.g., at a level above the business unit).

- Overall initiative prioritization and budget approval take place simultaneously with plan approval.
- Benchmarks are done to compare internal costs against industry costs or market prices.
- The funding process provides an incentive to the business unit to migrate from high cost or aging platforms.

Aligning Performance Measures and Incentives

Finally, achieving IT strategic alignment requires developing a set of performance metrics and incentives with which to measure success. Once the IT organizational structure is defined, a set of success measures can be picked that reflect a "balanced scorecard" of value drivers and performance (see Figure 18–8).

CLIENT ENGAGEMENT: FIRST TRUST BANK

The First Trust Bancorp is one of the nation's most progressive and competitive bank holding companies in the United States, with assets of just over $70 billion. Its banking subsidiary, First Trust Bank (FTB), offers a full line of financial services for consumers and leading regional businesses. FTB has the privilege of serving just under 2.6 million customer households in a prestigious marketing region with 775 branches, a rapidly growing number of in-store convenient branch locations, 1,330 automated teller machines (ATMs), and 42 Easy Banking kiosks to more effectively serve the near-rural customers. FTB is very proud to be an emerging leader in Internet banking with the new Anytime Banking Connection (ABC), augmented by a highly trained telephone banking staff. FTB achieves extraordinary service levels with a personable, professional staff backed by comprehensive technology tools to best serve the clientele.

In addition to deposit, credit, trust, and investment services, other subsidiaries provide mortgage banking, commercial and consumer auto leasing, credit-related insurance, asset management, and the new and rapidly growing Discount with Service Brokerage (DSB) services. As of 2001, FTB had total trust assets of $70 billion, including more than $50 billion in assets under management (see Figure 18–9).

Operating Model

FTB is going through a change in its operating and its organization models. The former operational model placed broad powers in state banking executives, including product design, marketing campaign design and implementation, and selling responsibilities. The primary changes in the operating model are:

- Unifying state banks under a single banking charter
- Centralizing marketing power into a headquarters function
- Providing consistent products and services across the bank's marketing footprint
- Centralizing IT resources and the acquisition of those resources into the IS department
- Establishing IT architecture standards

The objectives of these changes are to provide improved and consistent customer service, gain operating efficiency, and reduce new product delivery cycle time. Additionally, the state banking teams are freed to spend their energy on selling products and services.

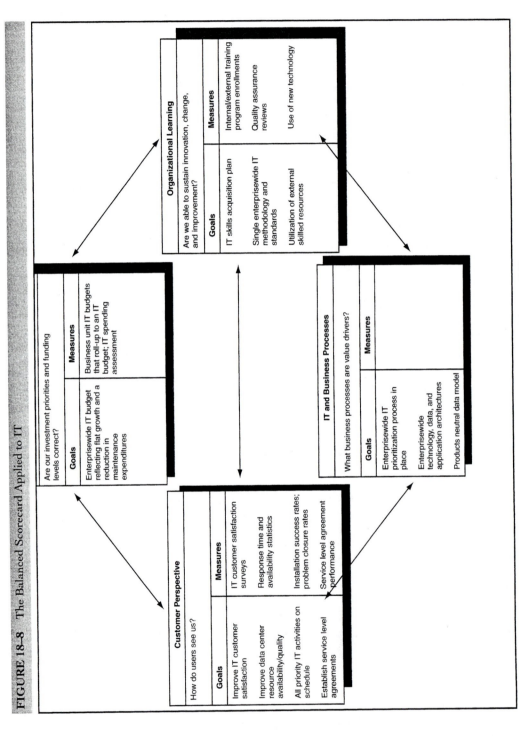

FIGURE 18–8 The Balanced Scorecard Applied to IT

Organizational Learning

Are we able to sustain innovation, change, and improvement?

Goals	Measures
IT skills acquisition plan	Internal/external training program enrollments
Single enterprisewide IT methodology and standards	Quality assurance reviews
Utilization of external skilled resources	Use of new technology

Are our investment priorities and funding levels correct?

Goals	Measures
Enterprisewide IT budget reflecting flat growth and a reduction in maintenance expenditures	Business unit IT budgets that roll-up to an IT budget; IT spending assessment

IT and Business Processes

What business processes are value drivers?

Goals	Measures
Enterprisewide IT prioritization process in place	
Enterprisewide technology, data, and application architectures	
Products neutral data model	

Customer Perspective

How do users see us?

Goals	Measures
Improve IT customer satisfaction	IT customer satisfaction surveys
Improve data center resource availability/quality	Response time and availability statistics
All priority IT activities on schedule	Installation success rates; problem closure rates
Establish service level agreements	Service level agreement performance

SOURCE: HBR: R. Kaplan, D. Norton, IBM Best Practices Benchmark, January–February 1992.

302

FIGURE 18–9   First Trust Bank—Financial Highlights

For the Year	1999	1998	1997
Net Interest Income	$2,201.9	$2,050.4	$1,949.3
Net Income	$1,000.5	$732.3	$736.0
Common Dividends Paid	$308.4	$246.7	$228.4
Net Income (diluted) Per Common Scare	$2.89	$2.13	$2.13
Total Assets	$70,001.8	$64,508.4	$57,329.1
Loans	$47,323.2	$43,432.0	$39,056.4
Deposits	$43,091.3	$41,662.5	$38.425.9
Return on Average Assets (ROA)	1.48%	1.18%	1.34
Return on Average Realized Shareholders' Equity (ROE)	20.83	17.21	19.07
Net Interest Margin	3.88	3.97	4.23
Noninterest Expense	$2,057	$2,052	$1,691
IS Budget	$496	$395	$337
Efficiency Ratio	60.63	62.53	57.68

As Figure 18–10 shows, FTB is primarily organized around its customer segments, with additional departments that focus on specialized markets and products. This structure is fairly consistent with other banks of its size and makeup.

At FTB, the operating model for IS is somewhat different than other IT organizations in banks of similar size and makeup. The IS department is responsible for the shared IT infrastructure and major IT resource acquisitions of greater than $500,000. Several lines of business have created their own IS organizations with CIOs and their own hardware and software. Examples include First Card and trading systems in Wealth Management. Further, Wealth Management and First Card have arranged and manage outsourcing contracts for portions of their needs. IS is responsible for overall IT risk management—security, disaster recovery, and continuity of service delivery.

IS is also organized around specific IT functions and services, much as it is in similar-sized banks and most other industries. Operations claims just over half the people in the department and is one of the largest customers of IS, even though it is part of the department (see Figure 18–11).

Nonetheless, there are some differences between FTB's IS organization and other banks of similar size and position:

- IS is governed by a board of directors made up of several state bank heads, the executive vice president of marketing, the CFO, and one or two other key stakeholders.
- The vice president of development services has responsibility for relationship management with business partners of IS.
- The CIO has a direct responsibility for much of the day-to-day running of the department.

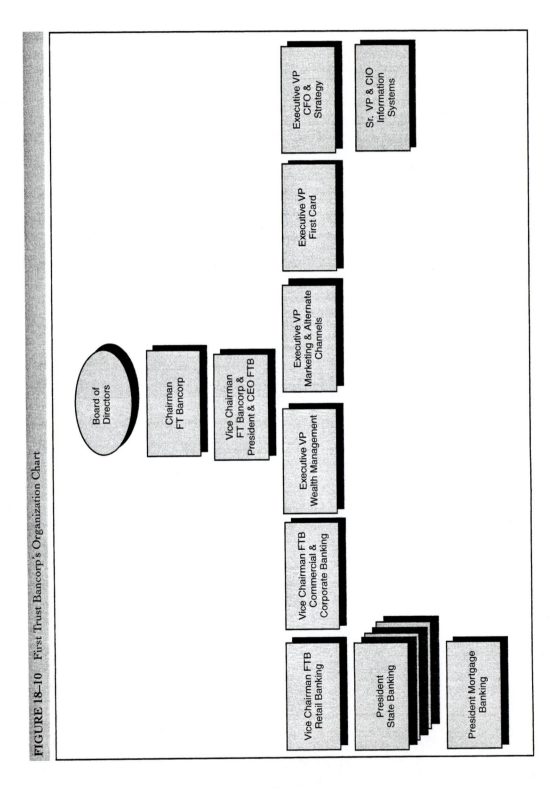

FIGURE 18–10   First Trust Bancorp's Organization Chart

Board of Directors

Chairman FT Bancorp

Vice Chairman FT Bancorp & President & CEO FTB

Vice Chairman FTB Retail Banking

Vice Chairman FTB Commercial & Corporate Banking

Executive VP Wealth Management

Executive VP Marketing & Alternate Channels

Executive VP First Card

Executive VP CFO & Strategy

Sr. VP & CIO Information Systems

President State Banking

President Mortgage Banking

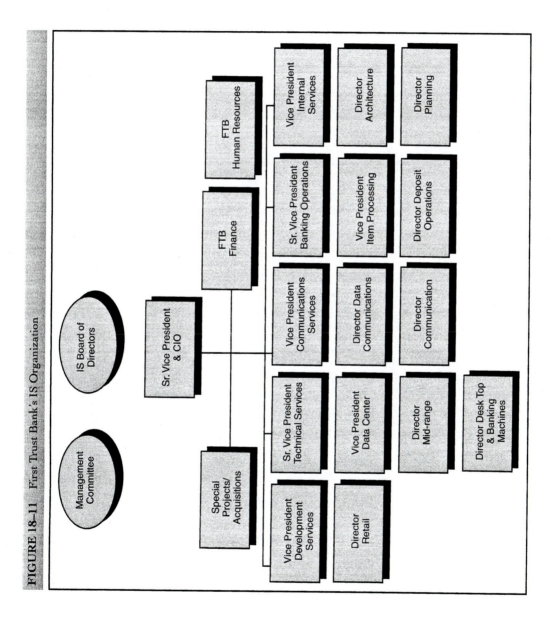

FIGURE 18-11 First Trust Bank's IS Organization

Planning Processes at FTB

FTB has a long established and fairly effective Annual Budget Planning Process. In the spring, the holding company makes business assumptions and sets overall revenue, profit, key business ratio, and investment targets. The FTB Management Committee then allocates the targets to the various operating units including initial overall investment levels for IS. The business units, with some input from the CIO and the solution delivery team, develop a list of business initiatives needed to achieve the objectives. These initiatives are translated into a business unit budget including the impact on and requirements for IS. IS develops its own view of its annual budget including infrastructure investments and the rollup of the input from the business units. The IS board of directors reviews and approves the Round I IS Annual Budget Plan in the late summer. In the fall, the business units have a series of meetings with the Management Committee to complete their Phase II Annual Budget Plan, with the CEO and CFO making final decisions on the initiatives and associated investments. IS presents their Phase II Annual Budget Plan at the end of the meetings. Any overages/underages are resolved, and the Phase II Annual Budget Plan is completed and prepared for review by the board of directors. The board of directors and Management Committee finalize the Annual Budget Plan for the business units by mid-January of the new year. At this point resources are allocated, and the development and tracking systems are initiated.

In the last few years, a number of key issues have been raised with the Annual Budget Plan Process:

- *Budget.* The magnitude of the IT infrastructure investments that have been requested. These requests were not tied to specific business initiatives, rather were sold as needed to position FTB for the future. Many times they were not approved.
- *Synergy.* Little consideration given to cross-business unit synergy opportunities. Each business unit, more or less, developed their budget without considering the impact on IS, or many times each other.
- *Short-term outlook.* Business issues tended to be one-year views rather than more strategic in nature. It was difficult for the business leaders to gain investment approval for fundamental, strategic shifts in the business. Rob Berin constantly raised this issue.
- *Closed door process.* The budgeting process was conducted to a great degree behind closed "country club" doors. Business leaders negotiated in private for their budgets, with little input from their colleagues. The result was investment levels for some business units that did not seem to be aligned with the FTB's overall strategy.

IS Governance Structures, Processes, and Key Measurements

There were several IS governance structures and processes at FTB depending on the level of complexity and size of potential impact. At the highest level was the IS board of directors. As previously mentioned, the board reviewed and approved the IS Annual Budget Plan. It also meets quarterly to review progress against major projects, and address any significant service delivery challenges and any major requested changes to the Annual Budget Plan. The board of directors also set the key measures for IS. The key measures were fairly straightforward and easy to measure. They included attaining or underrunning the Annual Budget Plan, major project completion against target, and a service delivery target measured by system up time. These measurements were typically allocated to each of the senior IS managers as appropriate.

At the business unit level various committees are chaired by a senior business unit executive with representation by a member of the Solution Delivery team. The objectives of these committees were to discuss project progress, resolve operational level issues, and discuss new requests for and changes to projects. The outcome of these monthly committee meetings was changes to project list and reallocation of resources as might be needed. The Solution Delivery team might then be forced to elongate or even cancel previously approved projects, many times impacting other business units. They were loath to have to tell the other business units and at times avoided it completely.

The Engagement

Objectives and Scope

The client and consulting firm always have to be in agreement on three critical factors: project objectives, scope of work, and deliverables. As a result of the three top management interviews and the initial meeting with Jamie Varvoglis, the IBM Consulting Principal and engagement leader developed and gained agreement on the FTB project's objectives and scope.

Specifically, there were four key objectives for the FTB project:

1. Develop a three-year IS Strategic Plan aligned with the business objectives, strategies, and initiatives capable of guiding the investment of IS resources over the period.
2. Develop an IS organization, roles and responsibilities, and recommendations that result in a more effective working relationship with IS's business partners from the perspective of senior business leadership.
3. Develop a balanced scorecard to measure IS effectiveness and use the balanced scorecard to establish IS incentives.
4. Document the IS Strategic Planning Process and transfer planning process skills to members of the IS team resulting in their capability to successfully reinitiate the Planning Process with limited assistance and keep the IS Strategic Plan evergreen.

The scope of the project was also agreed upon and documented, in terms of both what was included and what was not included. The scope was defined as:

Included in the Engagement:
- All FTB business units, including headquarters functions
- All central IS resources
- All IT resources located and managed in the business units

Excluded from the Engagement:
- Holding company business units that were not part of FTB including an international subsidiary
- The outsourced transaction processing agreement that First Card had recently renegotiated. The deal was so newly created it was accepted as a given.

Initial Planning

The IBM Consulting Principal and engagement leader selected the consulting team as they had clear agreement on the objectives and scope. They worked with the client to establish the FTB and IS team members. Both organizations signed a standard Confidentiality Agreement. The Agreement outlined how confidential information would be handled and who would own the final reports. Next they asked the client for existing documentation to help prepare the team. The request included:

- Current business and IS organization charts
- Business objectives, strategies, and strategic initiatives
- IS skills and capabilities documents
- IS logical infrastructure documents

The engagement leader worked with the client to prepare an announcement of the project for both IS and business audiences. Finally, the engagement leader worked with the client to complete administrative details such as work areas, security badges, and so on. The team was ready to begin.

Approach and Analysis

The general approach used by the team to design the consulting project at FTB is described in Figure 18–12 and is generally tailored to the unique needs of a client. It involves six basic steps.

1. **Project Initiation.** It is easy to misunderstand how important this step is. The key activities are to form a joint client and consulting team, prepare a detailed work plan, and very importantly have a Project Kickoff Meeting. The results of the step are a detailed work plan, a team that is committed to the project, and stakeholders who are willing to participate and anxious to see the results.

Two steps then can begin in parallel.

2. **Business Strategy Clarification.** In this step the consulting team interviews senior business leadership to understand their objectives, strategies, strategic initiatives, and required capabilities. These are recorded, and feedback is given to the interviewee for confirmation and finalization. Two other actions occur in this step. The first is that a knowledgeable consulting team will help guide the business leaders if the strategies and forward-looking initiatives are not documented. The second action is that a knowledgeable team will provide input into the business strategic plan, such as knowledge about what others are doing in the market and knowledge of advanced technology and how it might be leveraged by the business. The results are a clarified and validated set of required capabilities linked to strategies, and most importantly, to quantifiable business objectives.

3. **IS Baseline Assessment and Advanced Technology.** In this step the application portfolio, processes, skills, and organizational effectiveness of the IS team are analyzed. The analysis begins with gathering of both quantitative and qualitative data. The data is then compared with Best of Breed databases in the context of the client environment and requirements. Further, both advanced technology and competitor uses of technology scans are being performed. This information is used during the business leader interviews and helps establish a more thorough understanding of the "realm of the possible." The result of the step is a baseline of the capabilities of the IS organization and resources.

4. **Gap Analysis.** This is where the magic occurs. A simple but powerful technique can be used to determine the relevant and significant gaps in IS capabilities. The key is to construct a linkage from quantifiable *strategic* business objectives, through required business capabilities to both existing and missing IS capabilities. The linkage of gaps in IS capabilities to strategic business objectives allows quantifiable business cases. The result is a list of potential IS strategic initiatives that can be linked to business strategic objectives.

5. **IS Strategic Plan.** In this step the team takes the potential initiatives and turns them into initiatives that can be analyzed and evaluated against each other. Business and IS team members create initiative descriptions and business cases. One portion of the analysis determines cross-enterprise benefit and impact. The result is a set of both strategic and tactical initiatives that are linked to and aligned with the strategic business objectives and strategy of the company.

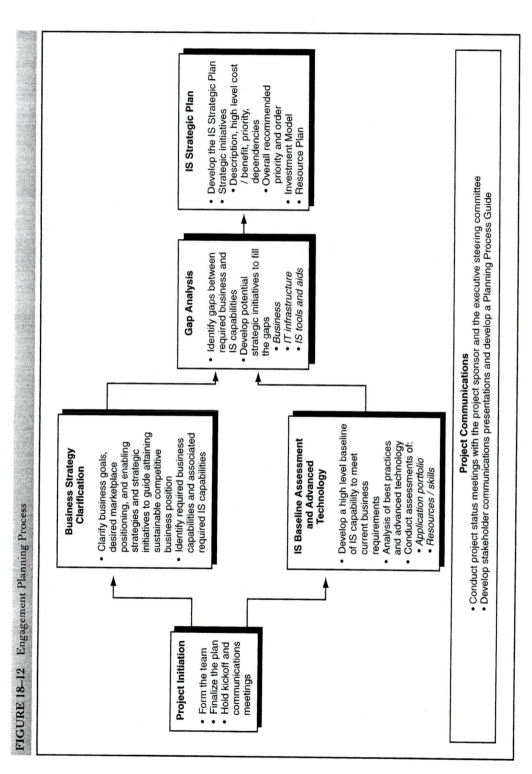

FIGURE 18–12 Engagement Planning Process

Project Initiation
- Form the team
- Finalize the plan
- Hold kickoff and communications meetings

Business Strategy Clarification
- Clarify business goals, desired marketplace positioning, and enabling strategies and strategic initiatives to guide attaining sustainable competitive business position
- Identify required business capabilities and associated required IS capabilities

IS Baseline Assessment and Advanced Technology
- Develop a high level baseline of IS capability to meet current business requirements
- Analysis of best practices and advanced technology
- Conduct assessments of:
  - *Application portfolio*
  - *Resources / skills*

Gap Analysis
- Identify gaps between required business and IS capabilities
- Develop potential strategic initiatives to fill the gaps
  - *Business*
  - *IT infrastructure*
  - *IS tools and aids*

IS Strategic Plan
- Develop the IS Strategic Plan
- Strategic initiatives
- Description, high level cost / benefit, priority, dependencies
- Overall recommended priority and order
- Investment Model
- Resource Plan

Project Communications
- Conduct project status meetings with the project sponsor and the executive steering committee
- Develop stakeholder communications presentations and develop a Planning Process Guide

309

6. **Project Communications.** This step is, like the first, very important but so easy to downplay. Actually, it is ongoing throughout the project. It includes the normal project status reporting and issue resolution. It also includes two critical success factors. The first is to provide communications throughout the project to key stakeholders about the project, its findings, and recommendations. This communication creates an environment where input is gathered and stakeholders become committed to the recommendations. The second is to develop a Strategic Planning Process Guide and transfer planning process skills to the client. The result of this action is acceptance and implementation of the recommendations and the ability for the client to keep the Strategic Plan "evergreen."

Team and Responsibilities

The keys to good team performance involve developing:

- A clear understanding of roles and responsibilities
- A joint client and consulting team
- Capable and committed leadership
- The skills and knowledge on the team to achieve the project's objectives

Below we list a sample set of roles and responsibilities that were used on the FTB project:

Executive Sponsor	Provides input and guidance concerning IS's vision and strategies, reviews Project progress and key deliverables and supports the adoption of the Project's recommendations.
Steering Committee	Provides guidance and confirmation of Project objectives and scope and access to key personnel and documentation. Resolves issues concerning conflicting requirements and priorities, reviews Project progress and deliverables, and provides executive approval against objectives. Supports adoption of the Project's recommendations.
Project Leader	Works hand-in-hand with the IBM Consulting Group Project Leader and is an active participant in all key activities. Should have a broad understanding of IS, and be perceived as a positive change leader. Also ensures that appropriate skills transfer occurs.
Participants	Represent key business and technical constituencies in discussing and analyzing key issues.
Principal	Accountable for IBM's conduct on the Project. Responsible for the Project's success and for ensuring work products meet IBM's standards of quality. Actively participates in thought leadership and maintains regular communications to understand and address client satisfaction.
Project Leader	Provides hands-on Project leadership and directs team activities. Supervises quality of analysis and deliverables. Directs and schedules team activities. Identifies resources and resolves Project issues. Guides development of Project deliverables.
Consultants	Responsible for structuring the Project, running day-to-day Project activities, and execution of assigned tasks. Provide experience and skills in business transformation, workshop facilitation, and specialized areas of knowledge.

The key to successful implementation is to recognize that it is a joint, collaborative unit. Figure 18–13 diagrams a typical team structure that was used on the FTB engagement.

FIGURE 18–13 A Typical Engagement Team Structure

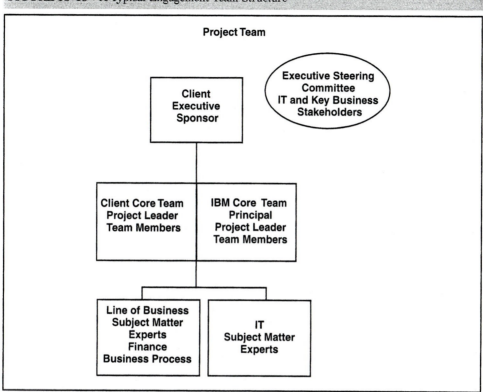

Keys to successful project management include:

- Having a committed executive steering committee that is made up of both champions and adversaries. The combination helps bring to light and resolve key issues. The result is buy-in for project recommendations.
- A collaborative working relationship between the client and consulting team members.

Time Line

Overall time lines for IT Strategic Planning projects have a number of dependencies. Key dependencies include:

- Availability of client senior management
- Quality of existing strategy and its documentation
- Scope and complexity of the company

Figure 18–14 shows a sample time line that is a good proxy for fairly large and complex engagements such as the one we worked on for FTB. The relative times are a reasonable approximation of what we accomplished.

Results

The results at FTB were immediate, dramatic, and longlasting. A turning point was reached when the senior business and IS leaders met to review the cross-enterprise impact of the initiatives in the IS Strategic Plan. They immediately realized the opportunities for creating attractive synergies and the need to prioritize investments for the

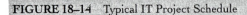
FIGURE 18–14 Typical IT Project Schedule

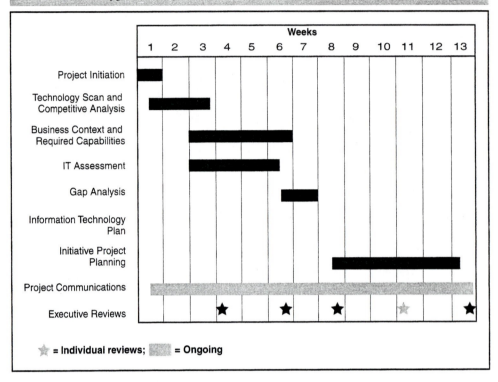

whole enterprise. Most importantly, the leadership team and the IS team both had a clearly delineated and prioritized strategic plan. Later, both teams could revisit the linkages in the Strategic Plan to determine the impact of replacing a previously approved initiative with a new initiative.

A second major outcome was recognition of the need to reorganize IS and change its reporting structure. Figure 18–15 shows the new organization chart. Several key changes are evident. The first is to whom the CIO reports. This results in the CIO's being an integral part of FTB's planning activities. Secondly, the CIO has more time to focus on strategic opportunities, rather than day-to-day issues. Finally, the organization now leverages a new team of highly skilled relationship managers, who interface with business partners of IS.

A final component consists of the changes made in the IS measurement and incentive system. The IS team is now measured on a balanced scorecard, jointly created with their business partners. They have produced mutually reinforcing behavior consistent with FTB's strategic realignment.

Project Challenges

In our experience, there are two challenges consulting teams regularly face with IS Strategic Alignment projects. Addressing these challenges is crucial to successful project completion.

- **Lack of clear business objectives, strategies, and strategic initiatives.** While many firms have clear financial objectives, most do not have clear, documented strategies and strategic initia-

FIGURE 18-15   FTB's Revised Organization Chart

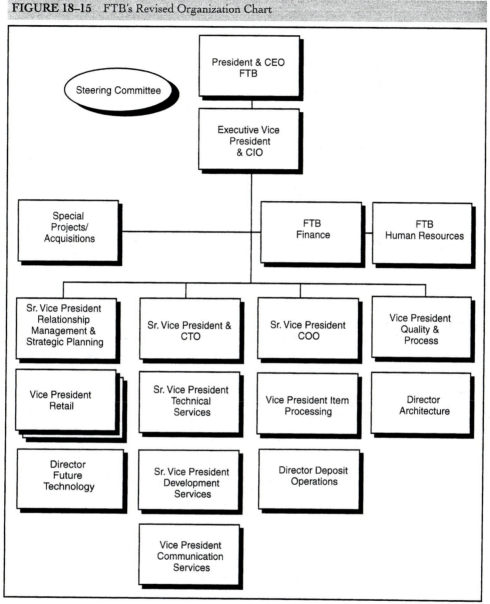

tives. In many instances it falls upon an organization like IT to facilitate the development of the business strategic initiatives.

- **Scope of the project.** The client perceives the value of a highly skilled consulting team. Many clients will then try to expand the role of the consulting team into areas that were not part of the original statement of work. Two potential issues arise. The consulting team takes its eye off the original target and the client does not receive the best value. The second issue is that the client tries to accomplish a set of change that is too broad resulting in suboptimal results. In both cases, the client and the consulting team have not done their best work.

19
Consultant/Client Partnerships

Craig Hart, Gloria Moon, and Soam Goel

Consulting firms have traditionally charged their clients a fixed sum for an assignment or have based their fees on the hours worked. Such arrangements can have limitations for both the consultant and the client, particularly in a start-up situation. The consultant who plays a vital role in launching a start-up that later benefits from an initial public offering (IPO), for example, may end up leaving considerable value on the table. The client for such a venture may not yet have the cash flow to afford expensive consulting services and may not feel that the consultants have sufficient incentive or are sharing enough risk to ensure their full commitment to the client's success.

To overcome the limitations of the traditional fee structure, many consulting firms have begun to accept equity in lieu of cash payment. Some have gone a step further and combined an equity-stake payment structure with equity investment to create true consultant/client partnerships. This case study describes the partnership formed between the consulting firm of PA Consulting Group (formerly PHB Hagler Bailly) and its e-commerce client, EdisonOnline.[1]

THE UTILITY INDUSTRY AND THE INTERNET

In late 1999 and early 2000, the Internet industry was red hot. New players sprung up daily to challenge industry incumbents with new business models. Value dynamics in industries were shifting as technology helped move and reshape boundaries that had existed for years. In some cases, e-commerce ventures enhanced new players' ability to compete. In others, existing players reacted to the challenge and realized their own ability to harness the power of the Internet to add value to their processes and solidify their market positions.

Craig Hart is a consultant in PA Consulting Group's Energy Practice. He received an MBA from the Yale School of Management and an MES from the Yale School of Forestry and Environmental Studies.

Gloria Moon is a specialist in the energy industry. She holds a bachelor's degree in economics and government from Cornell University and a master's degree in public administration from the Cornell Institute of Public Affairs.

Soam Goel is a member of the PA Consulting Management Group. He has a BS in chemical engineering and an MBA from the University of Texas at Austin.

[1]PHB Hagler Bailly was acquired by PA Consulting Group in October 2000; EdisonOnline is a pseudonym.

Within the utility industry, the story was no different. E-commerce was flourishing and the utility industry ranked third in terms of online business trade in 1999.[2] A wide range of e-commerce applications had proven successful, including digitized customer service functions, online bill presentment, wholesale energy trading and retail marketing. The first two applications were yielding tremendous cost savings for utilities. Internet-based wholesale energy trading was helping lower transaction costs and connect markets for new players and incumbents alike. In the area of retail marketing, the Internet was giving small start-ups the ability to offer new services to retail customers and compete with utilities in deregulated markets.

As these applications continued to thrive, attention turned to the next opportunity for e-commerce innovation in the industry. At the time, Internet purchasing solutions were the flavor of the day: industries ranging from automobiles to steel to chemicals were host to nascent e-procurement ventures. These ventures touted such benefits as lower product prices, lower procurement processing costs, and shorter order and fulfillment cycles. What could work for automobile manufacturers, steel factories, and chemical plants could surely work for utilities.

In fact, with its large size and rapidly deregulating markets, the utility industry looked like it could be a particularly rich ground for an e-procurement solution. Foremost, the utility industry has an extremely high purchasing volume. In 1999, this market represented $130 billion in annual expenditures in North America alone. Annual material and supply procurement (excluding fuel purchases) at a typical utility with three million customers may run as high as $1 billion. E-procurement offered the opportunity to provide large processing and administrative cost savings for all transactions.

In addition, the market consisted of a large number of fragmented suppliers and buyers. At the end of the 1990s, there were upwards of 400 utilities and power cooperatives across the country. A typical mid-size utility was served by hundreds and even thousands of vendors. This highly fragmented market made an ideal landscape for an e-commerce solution that would help aggregate buyers and sellers and perhaps lower prices and transaction costs significantly.

Furthermore, the utility industry was in the process of deregulating, which had increased the pressure on competitive procurement. Historically, utility inventory management has not been strong: inventory was part of the rate base, and rather than being a cost, was a source of revenue. Deregulation ushered in performance-based ratemaking mechanisms that reward a utility for managing its costs more effectively. Consequently, utilities now have greater incentive to obtain lower material and service pricing, cut administrative costs, minimize inventory levels, and better manage their working capital.

EdisonOnline Strategy

SCM Holdings,[3] an e-business development holding company, saw the opportunity to be the first to bring an e-procurement solution to the utility industry, and began developing EdisonOnline in mid-1999. SCM Holdings was in the process of building an e-commerce technology platform from which it planned to launch several vertical por-

---

[2]Forrester Research, 1999.

[3]SCM Holdings is a pseudonym.

tals. One of these portals would be designed specifically for the utility industry; it would link buyers and sellers and offer the ability to buy or sell everything from highly engineered goods to off-the-shelf products.

At the heart of the EdisonOnline Web site, and what SCM hoped would differentiate the site in the market, was the ability to automate the utility industry's purchasing of highly engineered products, which typically require a complex procurement process—the request for proposals (RFP). The idea was to create an RFP Manager package that would facilitate the electronic creation, broadcast, evaluation, and award of RFPs. By being fast and easy to use, RFP Manager would lower the transaction costs associated with the RFP process. In addition to purchasing, EdisonOnline users would be able to manage every link in their supply chain with features that included post-sale tracking, vendor benchmarking, and up-to-the-minute market information. Taken as a whole, this package would offer utility users a complete "digital supply chain management solution."

By the spring of 2000, EdisonOnline's team had been working for six months to develop what promised to be the most sophisticated digital supply chain management solution available to date. The EdisonOnline organization consisted of 15 full-time employees, plus contractors, operating in temporary office space. They were well funded, had a core management team, and were hiring additional people as fast as possible in the booming New York City technology market. Like many dot-com start-ups, EdisonOnline was characterized by rapid growth, chaotic operations, high hopes, and many holes that needed to be filled.

PA Consulting Strategy

The opportunity to develop an Internet-based procurement solution for the utility industry had not gone unnoticed by PA Consulting, a management and economic consulting firm. Several of the firm's senior consultants had developed a business plan for a vertical business-to-business (B2B) portal for utilities and their equipment and service vendors. The team was excited about the plan and had begun to look for funding from both internal and external sources.

For PA Consulting, a utility industry B2B e-procurement portal was an exciting proposition. The firm was in the business of providing services to utility clients. It was also exploring opportunities to strengthen its technology expertise and enhance its energy industry e-commerce practice.

But like most of its peer consulting firms, PA Consulting was vulnerable to the turmoil that had engulfed the management consulting industry in recent years. With the phenomenal growth of the Internet and e-commerce, the opportunity to join an Internet start-up had proven extremely attractive to both consultants and consulting recruits. This attraction has led to a migration of talent away from consulting. For the consultants who developed the e-procurement business concept, this was an opportunity they did not want to pass up. Whether in or out of the firm, it was likely that they would pursue the idea. By launching such an effort in-house, PA Consulting could satisfy the desires of their senior consultants and provide other employees with the chance to see firsthand the benefits and drawbacks of life in an Internet start-up.

THE GENESIS OF A PARTNERSHIP

First Meeting

While the PA Consulting team was seeking financing, EdisonOnline retained another senior PA Consulting consultant to help them develop their Web site. Given the progress of the internal team and the potential conflict of interest posed by the EdisonOnline engagement, it seemed most advisable to bring the relevant participants together. Their discussion revealed important synergies between the two efforts, and led to a meeting between EdisonOnline and the PA Consulting team. The options they faced were reasonably straightforward—continue independently as competitors, have one team drop the idea, or work together.

EdisonOnline Perspective

For EdisonOnline, a partnership with PA Consulting seemed an attractive way to complement its strengths and augment its weaknesses. As a partner, PA Consulting brought a well-developed business plan, a rigorous evaluation of the market opportunity, and a team of seasoned consultants with deep process knowledge, strong industry insight, and long-term relationships with key industry participants. As consultants, the firm could provide valuable assistance with product development, operations, content management, and strategic vision.

In the rapidly evolving and increasingly competitive world of B2B e-commerce, industry knowledge and reputation were critical. The few EdisonOnline employees with strong utility industry expertise were overworked; it needed additional people with in-depth knowledge of the Web site's future users. PA Consulting's industry expertise could prove vital in helping shape the site experience and the product's functionality. Its reputation in the industry could also help to brand the product and provide the legitimacy needed to differentiate the site from those of its competitors.

PA Consulting could provide access to many potential customers as well. Several of the firm's consultants were former utility employees and others had contacts throughout utility organizations that would provide a valuable marketing channel. These individuals might prove beneficial in making initial contacts and scheduling meetings with potential customers, both vendors and buyers.

A final asset PA Consulting could provide was industry-relevant content for the Web site. EdisonOnline's goal was to create a customized site that would offer utility purchasing employees all of the information and news they would need in a given day. By creating a community site, EdisonOnline hoped to distinguish its offering from other e-procurement portals and increase the length of time a user stayed on the site. To this end, PA Consulting might be able to use its industry knowledge to select the news, industry information, and tools this specific user group would find interesting. The firm would also be able to provide unique content and research in the form of studies and technical papers. Finally, there was the possibility that PA Consulting consultants could host online discussion forums on topics of interest to EdisonOnline users.

PA Consulting Perspective

An engagement with EdisonOnline was appealing to PA Consulting as well. EdisonOnline had assembled the beginnings of a good team with both technical and industry experience. Its CEO had worked in utility equipment sales and brought numerous industry contacts and a marketing background that would be beneficial in the sales process. It also hired several industry veterans from a well-known utility to be in charge of product development and customer integration, as well as a content manager with significant media experience.

In addition, EdisonOnline had fought an uphill battle to find a chief technology officer (CTO) in the crazed employment market. The CTO had, in turn, assembled a solid team that looked like it could develop the product in a relatively short time frame. The team had already completed a large portion of the design for the technology platform, which put them ahead of the possible competition.

SCM Holdings had raised enough first-round financing to carry EdisonOnline through the initial Web site launch, which was scheduled for August 2000. Through their association with a communications and utility infrastructure private equity fund, SCM Holdings had access to sufficient capital resources. The private equity fund and SCM Holdings also offered start-up experience, an action-oriented culture, and the ability to help with strategic vision and management challenges.

Deal Structure

Given the obvious synergies, EdisonOnline and PA Consulting decided to join forces. The teams entered a brief negotiation period that produced a "win–win" agreement designed to align the incentives of the two parties and enhance the venture's probability of success. The agreement included a cash investment from PA Consulting in exchange for equity, and a consulting contract to be paid in a combination of fees and additional equity. As part of the consulting assignment, PA Consulting would provide support in project management, strategy and business plan development, sales and marketing, industry-related content, and product development.

For PA Consulting, an equity position provided ownership in the venture that, if successful, could supplement its consulting revenues. Similar to the experience of other firms, the inequity between compensation and contribution had become increasingly apparent to PA Consulting. By taking an equity position in EdisonOnline, PA Consulting could narrow the gap between effort and compensation.

The consulting contract had numerous other benefits for PA Consulting. First and foremost, it allowed the firm to play an active role in managing its investment. Consultants would be involved at all levels of the start-up and their participation would greatly enhance the venture's chance of success, thereby increasing the potential value of the investment. The contract also gave the firm the opportunity for hands-on e-commerce experience that would enhance its credibility for future assignments. Finally, the engagement might expand over time as the organization matured and other skills were needed.

For EdisonOnline, the client/consultant partnership was also attractive. PA Consulting's equity position ensured that they would be committed to the overall sustainability and profitability of the venture. Like most start-ups, EdisonOnline was long on opportunity and short on cash. By partially compensating PA Consulting with additional equity, they were able to utilize the consulting services that they needed but had a difficult time affording.

Competitive Landscape

SCM Holdings and PA Consulting were not the only firms to take notice of this opportunity. Taking advantage of low barriers to entry, numerous other utility-focused e-procurement portals were announced during the spring and summer of 2000. What had looked to be a unique idea that would surely benefit from a first-mover position was demoted to one of a series of announcements that were becoming difficult to distinguish.

Web Site Development

Potential competitors followed two very different development strategies. One camp adopted strategies similar to EdisonOnline's, which involved independent product development followed by the recruitment of industry participants. The other camp, and the one that would produce the most formidable competition, was following a consortium approach. This involved end users (utilities) joining together to develop a product. Typically, the participants were equity investors in the project and pooled their knowledge in an effort to develop a site of interest to all.

Other consulting firms were behind two of the consortium ventures. Both PricewaterhouseCoopers and Ernst & Young had organized consortiums focused on developing similar e-procurement portals. The former consortium, entitled Pantellos, formed around a group of the largest investor-owned utilities in the industry. Enporium, the group organized by Ernst & Young, focused on medium-sized investor-owned utilities. The third major consortium that emerged in this period, Utility Frontier, was built around a group of public (federal, state, or municipal) utilities.

The consortium ventures had the advantage of starting with a significant market share commitment. They were also able to benefit from the collective knowledge of the group of participants. The downside of the consortium approach is that its members are prone to the typical group planning problems that center on making collective decisions. This had the potential to retard the development of the site and could also result in a compromised solution that works for everyone instead of developing the best option.

Within the independent camp, Bex.com, Industry Networks and Power Co-op were some of the companies that announced their intent to develop e-procurement platforms for the utility industry. In contrast to consortiums, the independent Web sites had the benefit of speed and efficiency since the key decisions are made by one entity. The hope was that this benefit would help the independents bring their product to market earlier than was possible with a consortium process, a potentially critical advantage in the rapidly evolving e-commerce industry.

Given the number of announcements and the buzz in the industry, the marketplace was looking crowded. But by early fall of 2000, none of these initiatives had actually produced working Web sites. Certainly, some were hollow announcements designed to buy time and to stop others from entering the market, and would likely never materialize as real ventures. Nevertheless, there was formidable competition in the utility vertical portal space.

Business Models

In addition to the differences in approach to Web site development, the business models that they adopted also differentiated EdisonOnline competitors. Direct competitors to EdisonOnline utilized two business models: vertical portals and technology providers. As Figure 19–1 indicates, these two approaches offered very distinct value propositions and relied on entirely different revenue models.

In many ways, these two models represent two ends of a spectrum of options as depicted in the figure below. While some pursued a pure version of a model, others adopted a strategy that incorporated both concepts.

Vertical portals are designed to serve specific industries and operate by offering a wide variety of services used by the target industry. They usually concentrate on raw materials and components that go directly into a product or a process, and that usually require specialized logistics and delivery mechanisms. Vertical portals frequently rely on specific knowledge of the supply chain within the industry and an understanding of the relationships between the key buyers and suppliers. With this knowledge, they can digitize the vertical supply chain and enhance liquidity throughout the supply chain, and can also provide relevant industry news and analysis.

Revenues in vertical portal business models are usually derived from a mixture of advertising, membership fees, and transaction fees. Their portal customers are individual buyers and sellers of products and services within an industry. The success of vertical portals depends on aggregating large groups of customers, holding their attention, and facilitating large volume of transactions. Industry expertise and knowledge are critical to ensuring that users feel a sense of community and that a portal becomes a true destination, thereby increasing the amount of time spent and transactions con-

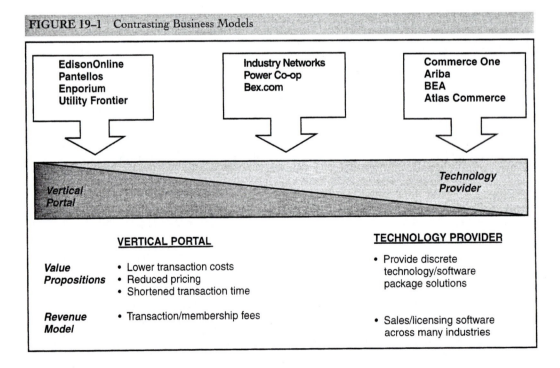

FIGURE 19–1   Contrasting Business Models

ducted on the site. EdisonOnline, as well as Pantellos, Enporium, and Utility Frontier, were all initially pursuing this strategy.

Instead of developing net markets for end-users in one industry, technology providers concentrate on creating discrete software/technology solutions that can be used in many industries. In contrast to vertical portals that sell to end users, customers are typically other companies that are building net markets. Revenues are dependent on large sales and licensing fees instead of transaction fees, and little value is associated with specific industry expertise.

Technology providers build technology platforms that can be adopted and customized by individual companies for use in their industry. The technology platforms usually include the ability to host fixed-price catalogs, auctions, exchanges, and bulletin boards. Ariba and Commerce One are two of the best-known technology providers for this type of e-commerce platform. Platforms can also include more customized supply chain and RFP management capabilities. Companies like Atlas Commerce and BEA are concentrating on developing solutions that fully automate the RFP process and can be used in a variety of solutions.

Industry Networks, Bex.com, and Power Co-op were pursuing a mixed strategy of vertical portal developer and technology provider. These companies developed supply chain management technology that they planned to use to develop their own vertical portals as well as sell the platform to others for use in developing net markets. Most of these companies have targeted the utility industry as one of the many industries they selected for a vertical portal solution. While the mixed strategy tends to increase market size, it also introduces the risk of cannibalization of revenues in the portal by providing the technology to potential competitors.

THE ENGAGEMENT

When PA Consulting joined the project in the spring of 2000, EdisonOnline had secured initial funding and hired key staff. Senior management was in the process of solidifying the corporate vision and refining the business plan, while employee teams were formed around various tasks. Everyone had their eye on the "go live" date and knew that speed to market was critical for success. Any delay in the site's launch meant the potential loss of first-to-market competitive advantage, customer attrition, and, of course, revenues.

As Figure 19-2 indicates, consultants from PA Consulting worked closely with EdisonOnline staff through the spring and summer. The firm was instrumental in the sales and marketing effort, which was aggressively seeking buyers and vendors as test participants for the Web site, and in introducing EdisonOnline to utility procurement executives. In addition, PA Consulting consultants drafted a white paper outlining the reasons why the utility industry should embrace digital supply chain management solutions. This paper was distributed at industry conferences and published in industry journals, which helped to publicize EdisonOnline.

By early summer, the effort was showing signs of success: several utilities had agreed to join EdisonOnline as test participants. A customer integration team was formed to conduct kick-off meetings to prepare the test participants for site deployment. To help this team better understand the specific needs of the test participants, PA Consulting provided insights on characteristics of utility supply chain processes. A

FIGURE 19–2 The Engagement Work Plan

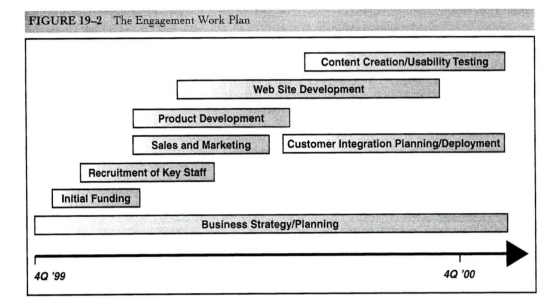

product development team focused on defining the product and business requirements for the Web site. Here, PA Consulting helped incorporate feedback from the test participants and modify the product accordingly.

A content team was formed to design the user experience on the Web site and to provide relevant information that would give the site a feeling of community. PA Consulting provided much of the industry-relevant content for the site in the form of technical papers, research reports, moderated discussion forums, and advice on other information industry that users would find interesting. An agreement was reached with another Internet firm to provide industry-related news and conference announcements for the site. Figure 19–3 describes the different ways in which the client–consultant partnership worked in practice.

At the center of the operation, the technology team was busy building the technology platform for the site. All of the individual teams fed information to the technology team, which was responsible for incorporating all the findings from the field. It also modified the supporting software as the sales team gathered feedback from customers, the integration team discovered the nuances of each participant's processes, and the content team developed the look and feel of the site. PA Consulting was also involved with the technology team and provided valuable business analysis, functionality prioritization, and overall program management support.

Transition Management

By late August, as EdisonOnline was in the middle of building the technology platform, trends in the Internet industry and internal resource constraints caused SCM Holdings to reconsider the company's strategy. As EdisonOnline went further into the detailed planning needed to build the comprehensive set of functionalities, it became clearer that the effort, time, and cash that it would take to develop the product and the market for such a product would be significantly beyond the initial estimates.

FIGURE 19-3 The Client–Consultant Partnership in Action

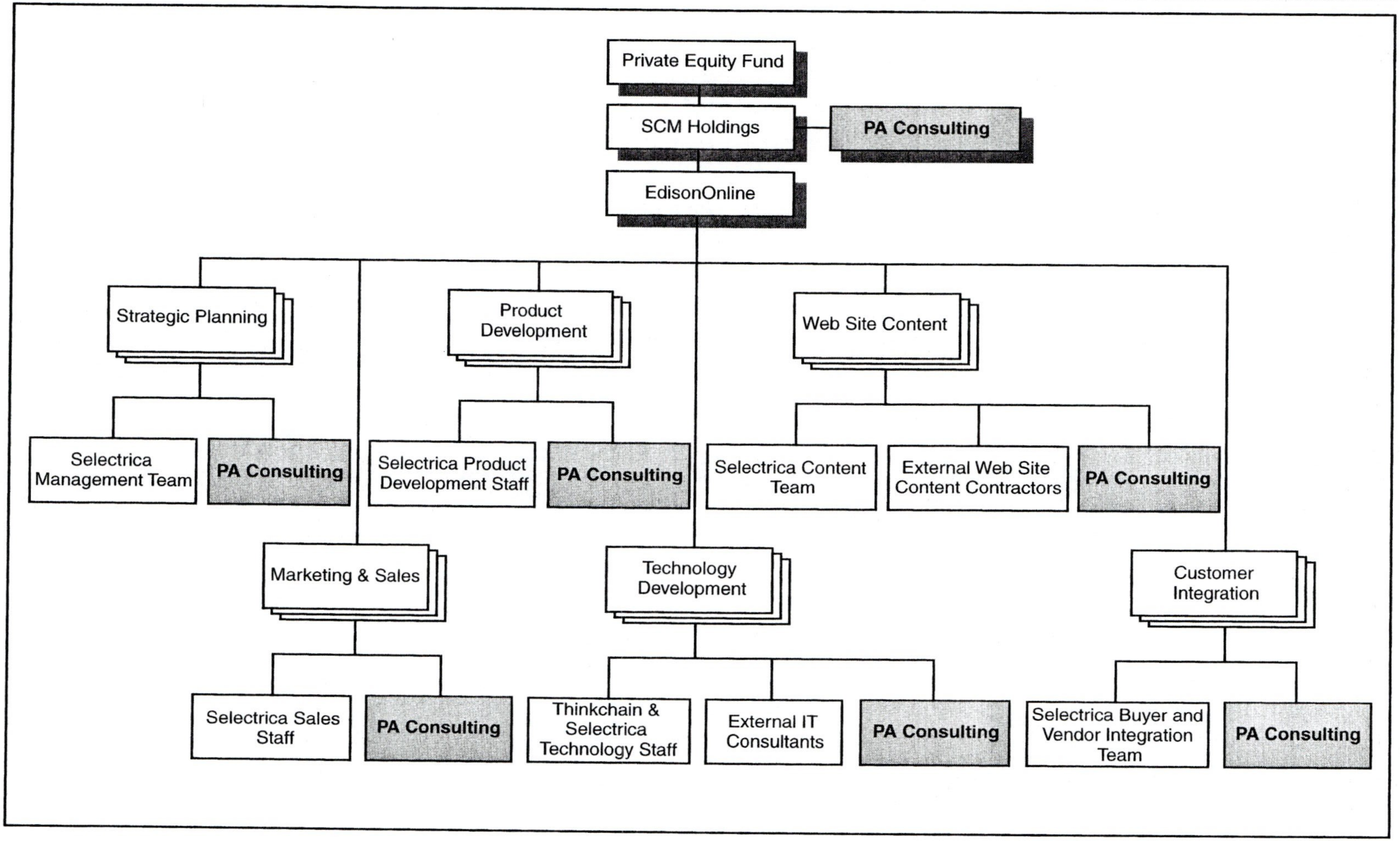

At the time, Wall Street's unconditional love affair with B2B portals was coming to an end. As Wall Street increased the pressure to produce earnings and became more concerned about the cash flows required to sustain some of these ventures, many of the new business models were increasingly scrutinized. Several portals that had not been able to achieve profitability found it impossible to raise more capital and, as a result, were forced to close their doors.

The shake-out in the industry and the tightening capital markets brought increased attention to EdisonOnline's business model. EdisonOnline had set out to develop a comprehensive vertical portal for the electric utility industry that would provide all of the functionality needed by a typical utility procurement employee. Part of this offering was the ability to purchase highly complex, engineered goods using its RFP Manager package. As with many Internet start-ups, EdisonOnline realized that the unique nature of the product being developed brought a host of difficulties along with its obvious strengths. A complex product would likely be more desirable to a potential user and would also prove more difficult for a competitor to replicate. But complexity also meant difficulty in product development, which had resulted in delays and revised estimates of the cost and time necessary to bring the product to market.

In addition, the consortium development strategy utilized by Pantellos and Enporium appeared to be working. These groups had targeted and successfully engaged many of the larger utilities, which controlled a considerable amount of the overall purchasing volume in the industry. Whether the consortium sites would be able to build efficient e-procurement solutions remained to be seen, but their strategy allowed them to at least capture a significant amount of the market up front.

With the demise of several other vertical portals that relied on transaction fees as their primary source of revenue, EdisonOnline's revenue model also seemed less viable. Management was becoming increasingly concerned that the site would never be able to generate sufficient revenues from transactions alone to be profitable, especially with the loss of potential market share to Pantellos and Enporium. With the delays in product development and the questioning of the basic revenue model, PA Consulting and SCM Holdings paused to reconsider the future of EdisonOnline. Both parties needed to ensure a strategy that would allow them to maximize their return on investment.

EdisonOnline's Future Direction

EdisonOnline faced three options. By staying on its current course, it could pursue the pure-play vertical portal strategy, push to finish the technology platform, and hopefully beat the competition to market. Another path involved modifying the strategy and becoming a technology provider that sold tools and services to other portal developers. Finally, they could pursue a combination of the two, using the EdisonOnline portal as the test case for their technology platform.

PA Consulting continued to provide support to the EdisonOnline team through this strategy reconsideration and played an active part in assessing the possible approaches. As the group evaluated the new strategy, PA Consulting considered how the different options would affect their consulting engagement. Whereas the vertical portal strategy played to the energy industry strengths of PA Consulting, the additional focus on technology required support from the technology side of the firm.

Coincidentally, PA Consulting was in the process of being acquired by PA Consulting Group. PA Consulting brought to the table a large information technology (IT) practice and was well positioned to provide support in the technology development arena.

SUMMARY

Although the future of the venture is still uncertain, several preliminary conclusions can be drawn about the consultant–client partnership between PA Consulting and EdisonOnline. Overall, each party has benefited from the complementary strengths of the other and created a whole that is greater than the sum of the parts.

For PA Consulting, the partnership with EdisonOnline provided the desired access to the Internet start-up world that it would have found more otherwise difficult to obtain. The energy and momentum that EdisonOnline had as a hungry, early-stage venture would have been difficult to replicate for a consulting firm engaging in its first start-up experience. In this way, the partnership allowed the firm to gain experience as an equity partner without shouldering all of the risk.

The partnership also benefited the consulting firm in the sense that its continued presence as a partner allowed it to modify the engagement as conditions shifted. If PA Consulting had been retained for a discrete project, it is unlikely that the consultants would have been involved in so many aspects of the business and through so many different stages.

The consulting engagement was also critical to ensuring the success of the partnership for PA Consulting. As consultants, members of the firm were able to play an active role in managing the equity investment. Without the ability to participate actively and contribute to the success of the venture, PA Consulting would probably not have been willing to invest at all.

For EdisonOnline, the partnership had many benefits as well. If the start-up had been able to afford PA Consulting's fees and had hired the firm solely for consulting services, it would not have benefited to the same degree from the latter's industry expertise. The firm would still have provided project management, strategy, and business and product development support. But EdisonOnline would not have been able to use PA Consulting's brand recognition in the industry, sales contacts, or content. As a result, the partnership has left EdisonOnline in a better position to compete than it would have been had either party pursued the concept on their own.

As partners and consultants, PA Consulting was also able to provide added continuity through the different stages, which was important with staff departures and turnover of other consultants. The equity-stake fee structure also allowed EdisonOnline to use more of PA Consulting services than they otherwise would have been able to afford.

The client/consultant partnership developed by EdisonOnline and PA Consulting proved to be a good way to combine complementary assets with the goal of bringing a product to market quickly in a rapidly evolving industry. The equity-stake fee structure aligned the incentives of both parties and provided a way for EdisonOnline to afford needed consulting services. It also gave PA Consulting a way of closing the gap between contribution and compensation and provided consultants with a first-hand glimpse of life within an Internet start-up.

CHAPTER
Handling Financial Risk: An Application to the Oil and Gas Industry

José E. Molina and Pedro Masetto

"Managing risk" has different meanings to different people. Some think of it as protecting personal wealth or safeguarding public health; others think of it as paying insurance premiums or wearing seatbelts. More technically, "risk management" involves maximizing areas over which we can exercise control over outcomes, while minimizing areas over which we can exercise little or no control over outcomes. Risk management is an educated effort to manage the unknown.

Risks are everywhere, and companies, industries, and countries must therefore manage risk. Some companies choose to manage their risk internally, others prefer to let others do it for them. New approaches are constantly being developed—some will succeed, others may fail.

The oil and gas industry is no stranger to questions of risk. Some oil companies are differentiating themselves from the rest by making an asset out of their ability to manage risk. Whether a company has been long established or is a new player, they ask themselves what are their current value-added businesses and how does risk affect where they want to go.

This chapter illustrates how one of Latin America's largest oil and gas companies (OilCo) did precisely that. It's a particularly interesting situation to examine because of the multiple intricacies that its consulting firm at the time, Arthur Andersen (AA), had to deal with: a government organization moved by political interests, an organization reluctant to change, and an organization lacking a basic infrastructure for carrying out risk management.

The chapter is divided into three sections. The first section describes OilCo's situation before they asked AA for assistance. The second section describes the model and concepts AA relied on to help OilCo address the situation. The third details how the engagement actually unfolded.

José E. Molina is a partner with Ernst & Young; formerly he was Arthur Andersen's Financial and Commodity Risk Consulting Managing Partner for Latin America. He holds a master's degree in business and economics from the University of Sevilla (Spain).

Pedro Masetto is a consultant with Ernst & Young; formerly he was a risk-consulting manager with Arthur Andersen's Financial and Commodity Risk Consulting Practice in Chicago. He obtained his MPP in finance and regulation from the University of Chicago and his BS in management from El Colegio de Mexico.

THE CLIENT PROBLEM

Arthur Andersen's Financial and Commodity Risk Consulting (FCRC) practice was approached by the Vice President of Finance of OilCo to assist them in three areas:

1. To identify and analyze the spectrum of financial risks impacting the company.
2. To design an implementation plan to create a strategic risk management unit, based on best practices.
3. To design a virtual trading exercise with derivatives to consider managing financial risks more actively and dynamically.

When OilCo approached AA, it had recently begun a major restructuring of the organization. As a government-owned entity, any initiative introducing change within OilCo's organization was not easy. Other management consultants had previously recommended aligning OilCo's corporate strategy and reorganizing core business units in order to centralize management. Furthermore, risk management was identified as a key function requiring implementation.

Due to extremely volatile market conditions, OilCo was under governmental pressure to begin trading financial instruments to protect the bottom line of the company. Political pressure and public interest had prevented the company from managing its financial risks earlier in time. A financial disaster using derivatives at another government company had made the use of derivatives nondesirable at OilCo. This time, other alternative mechanisms—such as price transferring to final consumers—were discarded. To use derivatives as an effective and reasonable management tool, OilCo needed to be properly equipped. From our initial contacts with the client, we concluded that OilCo lacked an adequate risk management infrastructure. There were no strategies, policies, limits, or consistent procedures in place to do so. Organizational design and personnel functions were not mapped in a manner that could allow for optimization of business goals and risk management strategies. Valuation and risk measurement methodologies, key elements to manage financial risks, were nonexistent. The same could be said about reporting, information for decision making, and systems. Risk management decision making was dispersed and fragmented across the company, and no periodic reviews to test its efficiency and performance had ever been carried out.

We suggested that senior management focus, first, on understanding the basic risks and market drivers impacting OilCo's business, and then assess specific risk management alternatives (e.g., trading derivatives). A key issue was to identify and communicate consistently what exposures were relevant across different levels and units. Senior management recognized exposures related to market risk: "crack spread," foreign exchange and interest rate. However, management was unable to quantify their respective size or magnitude, and consequently manage them. Similarly, we realized that OilCo's corporate culture was defined by a strong vertical hierarchy that discouraged communication across levels and functions, making it difficult to implement an integrated approach to risk management. OilCo's executives had a strong predisposition against creating areas with cross-functional responsibilities, key feature of an effective risk management unit, for fear of power struggles and undesired accountability.

OUR CONCEPTUAL APPROACH

After a brief period of on-site diagnosis, we came to the conclusion that the best way to improve OilCo's situation would be to apply risk management on an enterprise-wide basis. Enterprise-wide risk management (EWRM) means being positive and proactive about managing business risks. Rather than targeting ways to eliminate isolated risks, the goal is to openly acknowledge them and focus on their upside, as well as downside, potential. Furthermore, an EWRM approach emphasized an integrated business-portfolio view that elevates the risk management function to a strategic level.

After years of practicing risk management consulting, we have come to realize that organizations that prosper do so by managing and embracing risks with confidence and proactivity. Traditional risk management tends to focus on minimizing risk by looking at individual transactions and processes and seek to reduce the cost of risk. By contrast enterprise-wide risk management takes a broader business view, and examines risks in terms of potential outcomes and their strategic value to the business.

In process terms, mastering risk on an enterprise-wide basis means making everyone in the organization risk-aware and equipping them to thrive on uncertainty. For OilCo, it would mean redefining risk management from something that is reactive and piece-meal, to something that sits at the heart of the company's business strategy and among its most differentiating assets. It meant changing people's views of "risk" as something negative that should be avoided or controlled, to something positive that should be valued and turned to wealth. This implies identifying accountability or risk/exposure "owners" who are independent from risk "takers" within all business units—again, a significant change for OilCo's management culture.

As risk management consultants, we have been closely involved in helping financial institutions, commodity and energy companies, and corporate treasury departments adapt to rapidly changing conditions in the marketplace. From the work we've done with clients in these settings, we have gained a deep understanding of the challenges involved in implementing EWRM. Our approach is to provide companies with customized solutions to improve business performance and achieve competitive advantage. Creative insights and innovative problem-solving capabilities to improve decision making, increase profitability and productivity, lower the cost of capital, and decrease business risk are the premises of our services.

From our experience helping organizations manage risks, we have developed a business risk management process (BRMP). As Figure 20–1 shows, it identifies seven elements that must be present for effective enterprise-wide risk management. The BRMP provides a general blueprint that we necessarily customize to a company's specific circumstances and organizational culture.

The first step in implementing BMRP is to establish the fundamental rights: Stating goals and objectives clearly aligned with the organization's business models, clarifying what risk means for the company, and making sure everyone knows about it, and setting up a structure to oversee responsibility for business risk management throughout the organization. Accordingly, to establish the process at OilCo, we helped the company to:

FIGURE 20–1   Arthur Andersen's Business Risk Management Process

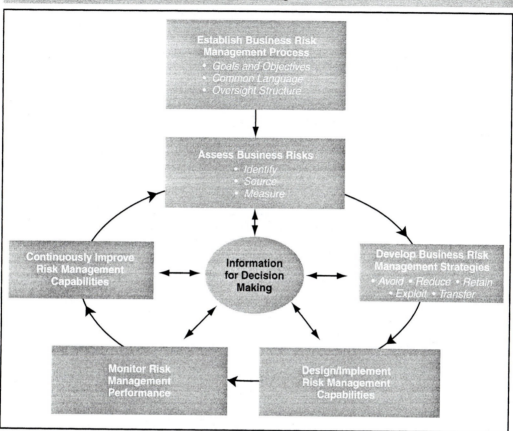

- Link its goals to the risk and exposures inherent in achieving them.
- Develop a common "risk" language to include all relevant business exposures.
- Form a risk management executive committee reporting to the board and CEO.
- Commit senior management to developing EWRM capabilities (key success factor for any future implementation).

At this stage, senior management was aware of the importance of "seeing the big picture" from a risk perspective. Actually achieving it was another matter. On one hand, we had to gather everyone's opinion about risk management and generate consensus on how to link it to business goals. The transition was not evident to all executives as they saw their individual performances subject to a more generalized objective, typically pegged to financial (non–risk adjusted) performance indicators. On the other hand, we had to create a common language understood by everyone. This proved to be even more challenging since individual perceptions on risk were diametrically different. Once we reached a compromise definition, we were ready for the second step: assessing business risks.

The process of assessing business risks enabled managers to develop a thorough knowledge of the uncertainties that affect their business. Where do they come from and how much do they affect the company? It involved identifying (by means of risk mapping), sourcing, and measuring. To do so, we relied on our wealth of best practices that included:

- Identifying risks for intangible assets crucial to value creation
- Identifying a "top 10" list of risks and communicating it widely
- Quantifying the likelihood and significance of risks
- Considering explicit time horizons when developing risk maps
- Performing root cause analysis to identify the real sources of risk
- Integrating risk assessment with business planning

Graphically, Figure 20–2 shows how we visualize the risk assessment phase – as an organized exercise to grasp and categorize some key dimensions of risk.

The assessment phase helped OilCo to understand how to take risks with their eyes open. Reaction among the company executives ranged from great optimism to simple doubt and certain skepticism. This had to change. The idea that the company was subject to a greater set of risks than had ever been thought of created a sense of urgency among top OilCo's executives. They were about to begin a journey with a sin-

FIGURE 20–2   Visualization of Risk Assessment: Key Dimensions

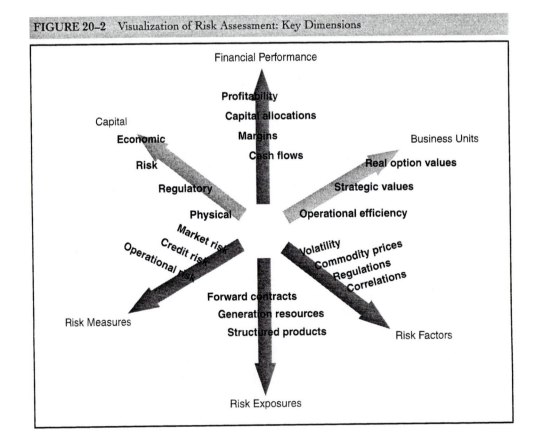

gle destination—value creation. What to do differently and how to do it would be addressed in the next steps of the risk management process.

We then turned to the development of risk management strategies. It was coming clear to senior managers that they could avoid, retain, reduce, transfer, or exploit OilCo's risks. The right strategy depended on the type of risks involved, on their significance and likelihood, and finally on the company's capabilities and appetite for risk. Strategies had to be measurable, manageable, and aligned with overall goals and objectives. They had to provide actionable solutions that allowed the company to take appropriate risks. To develop the right strategies we identified:

- Criteria to offset similar risks on an enterprise-wide basis
- An alignment of risk management strategies with core competencies
- Redesigned processes to control risks at their source

Graphically, Figure 20–3 shows how our initiative aligned OilCo's business models with consistent risk management strategies. The main idea was that strategies would be supported by an appropriate integrated infrastructure that would generate tactical actions aimed at managing risks on an EWRM basis.

Most people assume that senior management has the capacity for strategic action. That is, on the basis of accurate perceptions and adequate information, an executive is able to respond to the risks and opportunities by selecting the strategies that will maximize the company's expected total utility. However, there are multiple cases and examples of executives not choosing the apparently optimal alternative. Without oversimplifying the situation, most such choices can be explained—in many instances—by contextual or institutional factors. That is why we believe in understanding, not only the ultimate drivers of a company, but the environment by which it is surrounded.

FIGURE 20–3   Aligning a Business Model with Risk Management Strategies

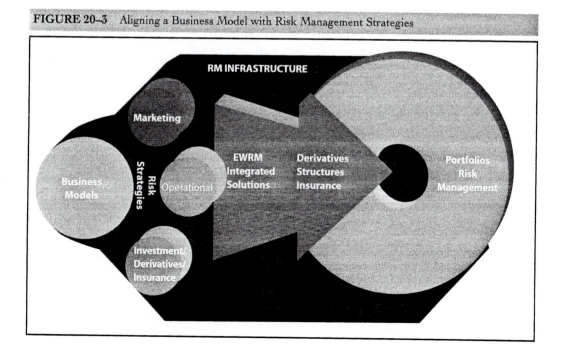

The results at this point were overwhelming. We had already dramatically changed senior management perceptions of risk management. We had aligned OilCo's goals and objectives with business models, and the latter with consistent risk management strategies. For the first time, they felt that the company was able to reconsider not only the validity of its business models, but some critical operational processes as well. At the center of the story was a new willingness to assume risks, which inherently carried the possibility of failure (or success). Obviously, the company could not have known for certain which of the strategies to target. But the series of decisions made also required OilCo to master process risk, and began with the creation of a risk management infrastructure.

When implementing the company's strategies, it was necessary to build the right infrastructure. The company needed policies, processes, people, reports, methodologies and systems. To bridge the gap between what the company wanted to achieve and what the company was capable of achieving, we helped them:

- Adopt a framework for building risk management capabilities
- Make risk an integral part of every job description and performance appraisal
- Establish common management processes for key risks

Processes and structures helped us to ensure specific risks were not overlooked by systematically dealing with risks across all business units and functions. We strongly believe that a company is in the best position to achieve its goal of enterprise-wide risk management when the entire organization is lined up to meet its business risk management purpose. The six key elements that need to work together to build up capabilities within an organization are shown in Figure 20–4.

The different elements of the risk management infrastructure must be linked, all flowing logically from the business strategies and policies. The effects of any deficiency are cumulative. For example, if systems do not capture relevant and reliable data, even the best methodologies to measure risk would be worthless. Inappropriate methodologies will compromise reports. Poor reports will hinder effective management risk owners who suffer from blind spots because of inadequate reports and will not be able to perform the processes that execute business strategies.

This step in the process was complex and long. There were multiple obstacles to overcome. The main one was that business management was handicapped by misperceptions as to the basic elements of the organization, the appropriate relationship among those elements, and the organization's connection to its market in terms of what creates and destroys value. Few managers fully understand that companies are built from essential building blocks of assets, the processes used, and the mea-

FIGURE 20–4 Risk Management Infrastructure

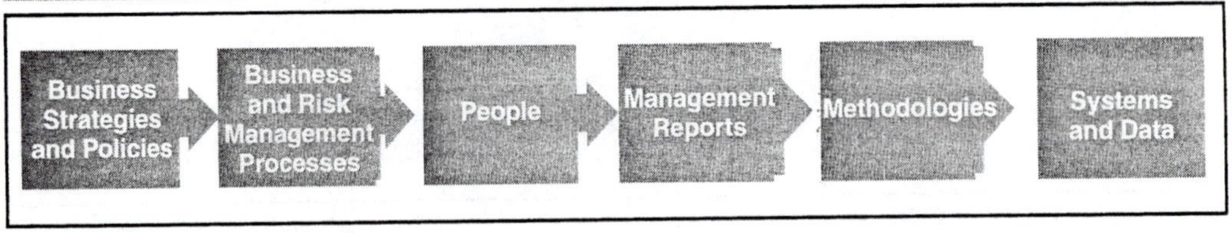

Business Strategies and Policies → Business and Risk Management Processes → People → Management Reports → Methodologies → Systems and Data

surement systems that record success. It is important to see how assets relate to processes, how processes connect to outcomes, and how measurements relate to market results. Otherwise, companies can become unrelated collections of assets and processes.

This was the situation. Senior managers at OilCo did not see immediately the value the company was creating by putting together a strong risk management infrastructure. Different parts of OilCo managed risks with different levels of sophistication and expertise. Companies go through different stages to get from least sophisticated, wherein risks are managed individually and reactively, to most sophisticated, wherein risks are managed on an enterprise-wide basis. These stages are described in the Risk Management Capability Maturity Continuum shown in Figure 20–5.

In the initial stage, risk management activities are ad hoc and depend on the activities of specific individuals. Efforts are often reactive and may be confined to the iden-

FIGURE 20–5   Risk Management Capability Maturity Continuum

Continuum	Capability Attributes	Method of Achievement
Optimizing	(Continuous Feedback) Risk management a source of competitive advantage	• EW strategy—emphasis on taking and exploiting risk • World-class processes • Knowledge accumulated and shared
Managed	(Quantitative) Risks measured / managed quantitatively and aggregated enterprise-wide	• Rigorous measurement methodologies/analysis • Intensive debate on risk/ reward trade-off issues
Defined	(Qualitative / Quantitative) Policies, process, and standards defined and institutionalized	• Process uniformly applied across the firm • Remaining components of infrastructure • Rigorous methodologies
Repeatable	(Intuitive) Process established and repeating; reliance on people reduced	• Common language • Quality people assigned • Defined tasks • Initial infrastructure components
Initial	(Ad Hoc/Chaotic) Dependent on heroics; institutional capability lacking	• Undefined tasks • Relies on initiative • "Just do it" • Reliance on key people

Process Evolution →

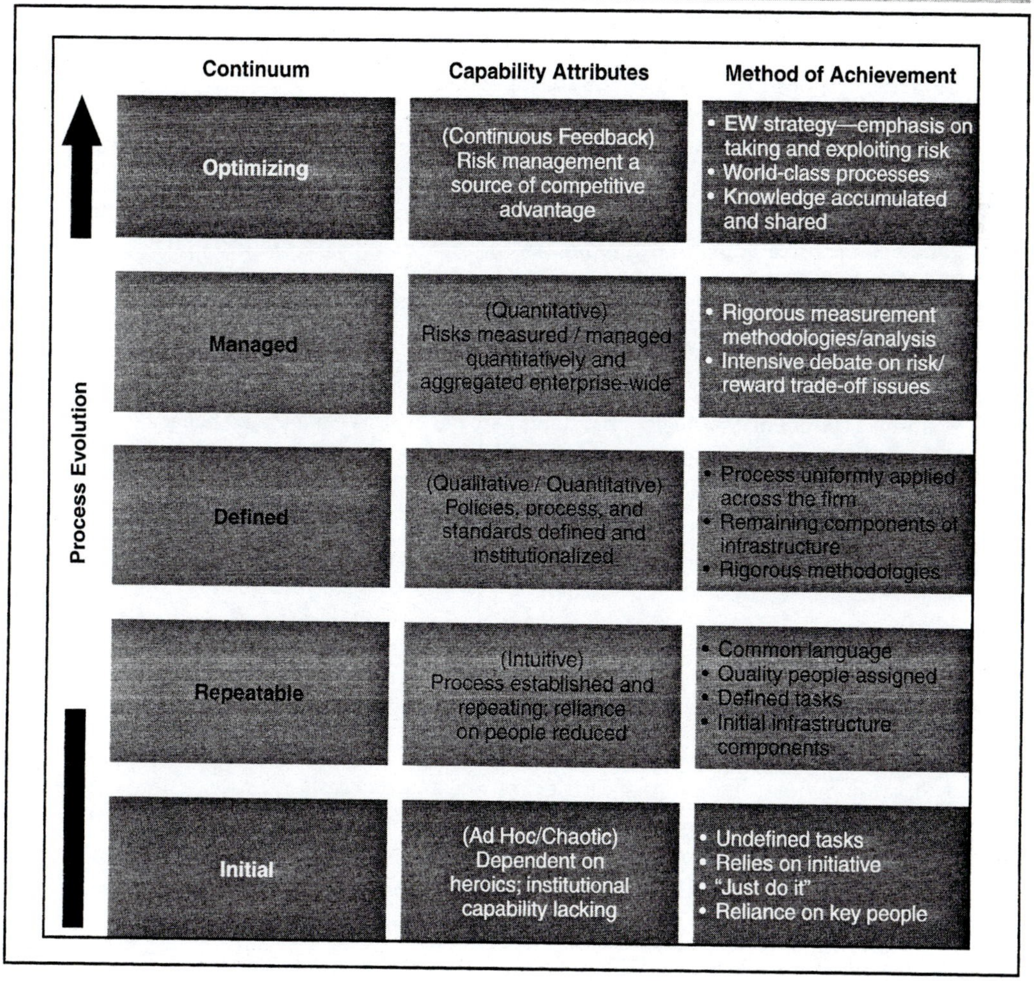

tification of risks. For example, a company may have vague or nonexistent policies, limited risk reporting, and only a few rough measures of risk. When personnel leaves or changes, so do risk management capabilities.

Moving upward in maturity to the repeatable stage, risk management becomes more formally defined within business units and a common language for talking about risk is established. A company is less dependent on individuals. At the defined stage, a company has uniform processes throughout. Standard policies are in place and there is consistent risk measurement and reporting.

The highest degree of sophistication is achieved as firms advance to the managed and optimizing stages. At the managed stage, risks are managed on an aggregated or portfolio basis, enabling them to be offset and diversified. At the optimizing stage, business risk management becomes a sustainable source of competitive advantage. But even here, the focus is on continuous improvement, implying that the optimizing organization never rests on its laurels. In our experience, very few organizations are at the managed or optimizing stages.

We wanted to help OilCo rise above the initial level. Our aim was to define risk management across all business units so reliance on individuals was minimal. We aimed at creating processes that were repeatable and institutionalized. Rigorous measurement methodologies and adequate reporting was to be in place. Systems were key in achieving this. But most important, senior managers had to become conscious of the importance of keeping track of the organization's performance. No process would ever be complete without adequate monitoring.

We instilled the idea that OilCo had to compare actual to expected performance. It needed to perform benchmarking and even take feedback from the market. This was only going to be achievable once the culture of the organization had been transformed. Our aim was to promote a culture of continuous improvement, so risk management was perceived once and for all as a strategic asset that could increase the value of the company. To support this concept we helped OilCo to:

- Instill a culture that challenges the status quo and expects continuous change.
- Make sure that agreed-upon changes happen and ensure they are SMART (specific, measurable, agreed, realistic, and timed).
- Simplify risk management processes and remove redundant controls and condition change.
- Generate ideas for improvement by encouraging "What if?" questions and rewarding new thinking.
- Develop relevant and reliable information. We aimed at elevating information for decision making to the highest possible level.

To make sure the change would happen, we agreed to help OilCo:

- Design measures for all key risks
- Track opportunity costs of risk decisions as well as actual costs
- Ensure information flows four ways (the big picture flows from the top, best practices and benchmarks flow among all units and functions, and reality checks flow upwards)
- Give risk owners online access to the information they need
- Integrate risk management information with other business information
- Quantify the impact of investment choices on overall risk and the cost of capital

THE CLIENT ENGAGEMENT

The first step we took to identify and analyze the spectrum of financial risks within the company was to evaluate OilCo's three main exposures: crude oil price, foreign exchange rate, and interest rates.

Our preliminary conclusions were that:

- OilCo was very concerned with business and financial risks; however, a corporate belief was that volatility of key markets was adequately passed on to refined product prices. Therefore, it is not necessary to undertake a proactive RM.

- Persistent price downtrends and certain slowness in updating refined product prices had impacted OilCo's margins and market share lately. OilCo's view on RM should be reconsidered.

- The three selected exposures (crude oil price, U.S. dollar exchange rate, and labor rate) significantly impacted OilCo's product spreads, operating margins, and net income.

While the analysis of interest rate and foreign exchange risk were relatively straightforward, the analysis of crude oil risk was not:

- Interest rate risk arose as a consequence of OilCo's financing agreements and was evident from examination of its balance sheet.

- Foreign exchange risk originated as a consequence of crude oil purchases and U.S. dollar borrowing.

- To assess crude oil price exposures we would analyze OilCo's operating margin in more detail.

As Figure 20–6 shows, we observed that the operating margin had been fluctuating and declining over time. When contrasting the operating margin to OilCo's net profit, we observed a strong correlation between the two, but not a perfect one.

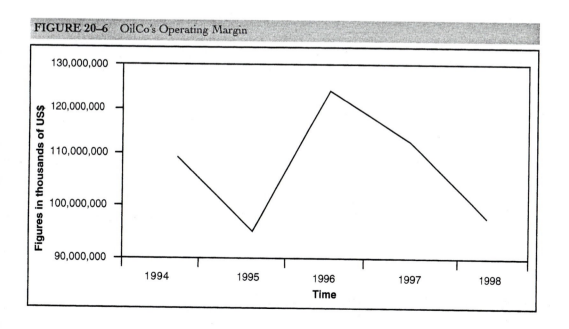

FIGURE 20–6 OilCo's Operating Margin

Figure 20-7 shows further that variations in OilCo's operating margin were mainly explained by time delays arising out of price differences between the time of purchase of crude oil and the time of sale of refined products (crack spread), and fluctuations in the currency exchange rate. It was clear that the time-delay impact on the operating margin merited a more detailed analysis to properly assess if dynamic management was necessary.

The hypothetical operating margin represented as the price of a barrel of a refined product minus the price of a barrel of crude oil, can be decomposed as shown in Figure 20-8.

When examining in more detail the "time" factor in the core business of the company, we identified a "critical time lag," shown in Figure 20-9. The time lag had two main implications. There was significant exposure to price differentials between inputs and outputs (crack spread implications), and corresponding foreign exchange exposure. It was obvious to everyone that market fundamentals were not the only variables directly impacting the bottom line of the company; OilCo had multiple reasons to be concerned.

The daily volatility of its country's currency had increased rapidly in the past 12 months previous to our analysis. Statistical analysis of daily returns was revealing mind and positive skewness, reflecting the frequency of the currency depreciation and excessive kurtosis. We could anticipate that extreme events would occur more frequently than might be expected if we assumed that returns were normally distributed.

When further analyzing OilCo instant margin, we would continue observing a significant variation between what was expected and what was actually occurring. Senior management were aware that OilCo's exposures (crack spread exposure both to gasoline and heating oil) could have a significant and major impact on the bottom line of the company if adequate measures were not taken immediately. As

FIGURE 20-7   Operational Margin Versus Net Profit

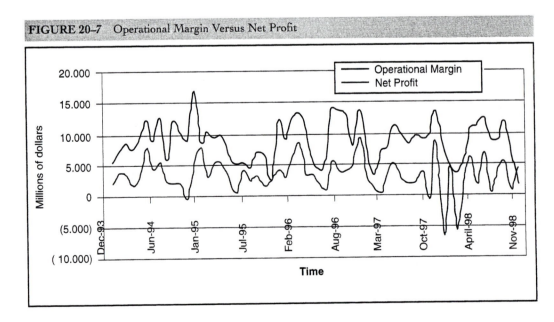

FIGURE 20-8 OilCo's Refining Differentials

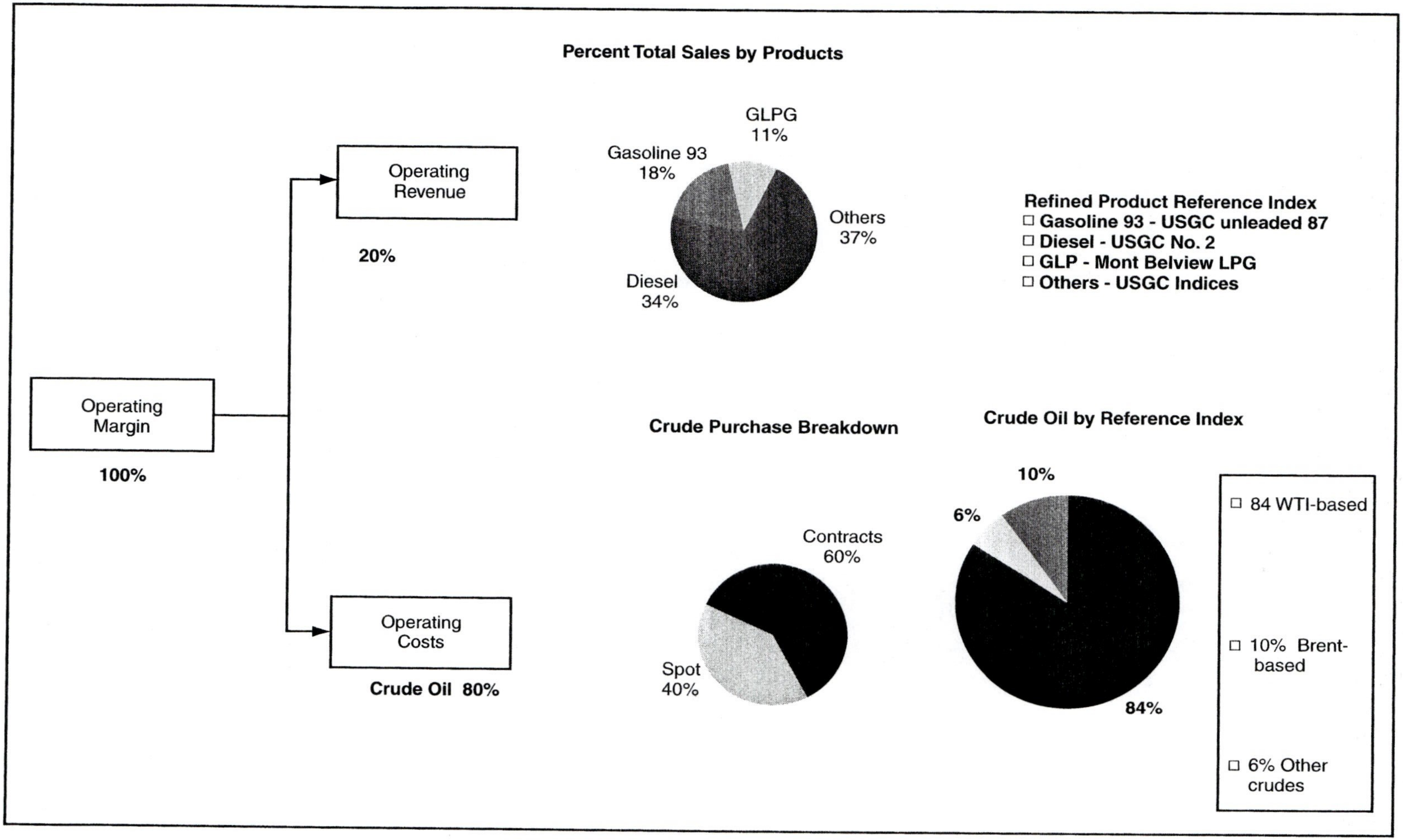

Percent Total Sales by Products

Gasoline 93
18%

GLPG
11%

Others
37%

Diesel
34%

Refined Product Reference Index
☐ Gasoline 93 - USGC unleaded 87
☐ Diesel - USGC No. 2
☐ GLP - Mont Belview LPG
☐ Others - USGC Indices

Crude Purchase Breakdown

Contracts
60%

Spot
40%

Crude Oil by Reference Index

10%

6%

84%

☐ 84 WTI-based

☐ 10% Brent-based

☐ 6% Other crudes

Operating
Revenue

20%

Operating
Costs

Crude Oil 80%

Operating
Margin

100%

FIGURE 20-9   OilCo's Time Lag Due to Refining

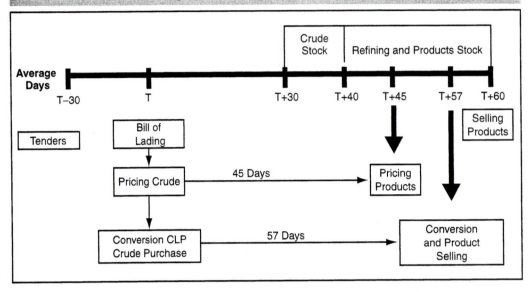

Figure 20–10 shows, OilCo had missed the opportunity to cash in on the differential between the instant and their margins. This was a critical moment for everyone.

We continued our scheduled analysis and showed how the company had a net short position in crude oil created by refinery run requirements (the long position from domestic and international production only partially offset that short position). We documented in our correlation report how OilCo's crude prices were linked to Brent

FIGURE 20-10   OilCo's Margin Against Instant Margin

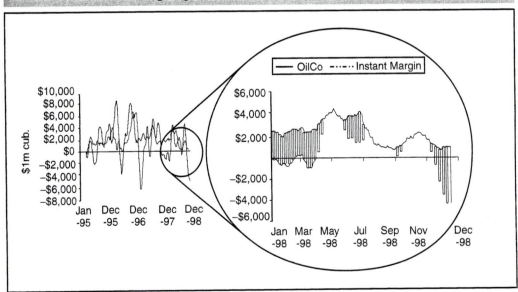

and West Texas Intermediate (in some cases prices were explicit, in others they were implicit), and demonstrated how most components of the crack spread could be controlled.

It was clear for OilCo that a hedging program could be a tool to manage its price risk. The company needed to decide whether it was acceptable to have some residual risk, or whether to hedge as much of the price risk as possible. To exemplify the situation, Figure 20–11 shows how we documented the different hedging alternatives in the market place.

For the specific case of the family of gasolines, to hedge time and quality basis exposures properly, we helped OilCo calculate exposure by month and grade (see Figure 20–12).

At this point, it was clear to OilCo that there were very good alternatives to hedge their main exposures. However, we were concerned about OilCo's not having an acceptable risk management infrastructure in place. OilCo and AA were aware, nevertheless, that even with the information we had provided on the financial exposures, it needed to create the adequate infrastructure to support its risk management operations. The objectives of creating a strategic risk management unit were obvious:

- Attain awareness of OilCo's financial risk exposures.
- Educate about tools and markets available to manage price risk exposure.
- Incorporate market views into hedging and business decisions.
- Formulate and centralize hedging and business decisions.
- Create accountability of senior management in hedging and business decisions.
- Train front, middle, and back offices on risk management processes.

FIGURE 20–11   Examples of Hedging Alternatives for OilCo's Family of Gasolines

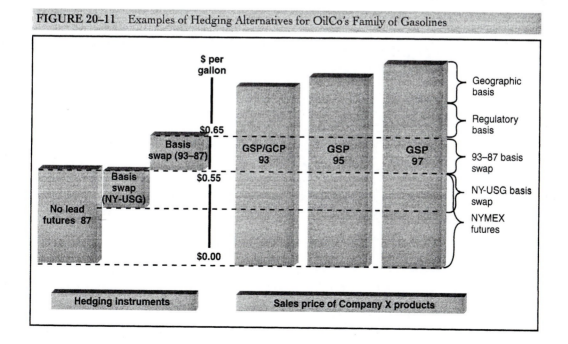

FIGURE 20–12   Examples of Basis Exposures for OilCo's Family of Gasolines

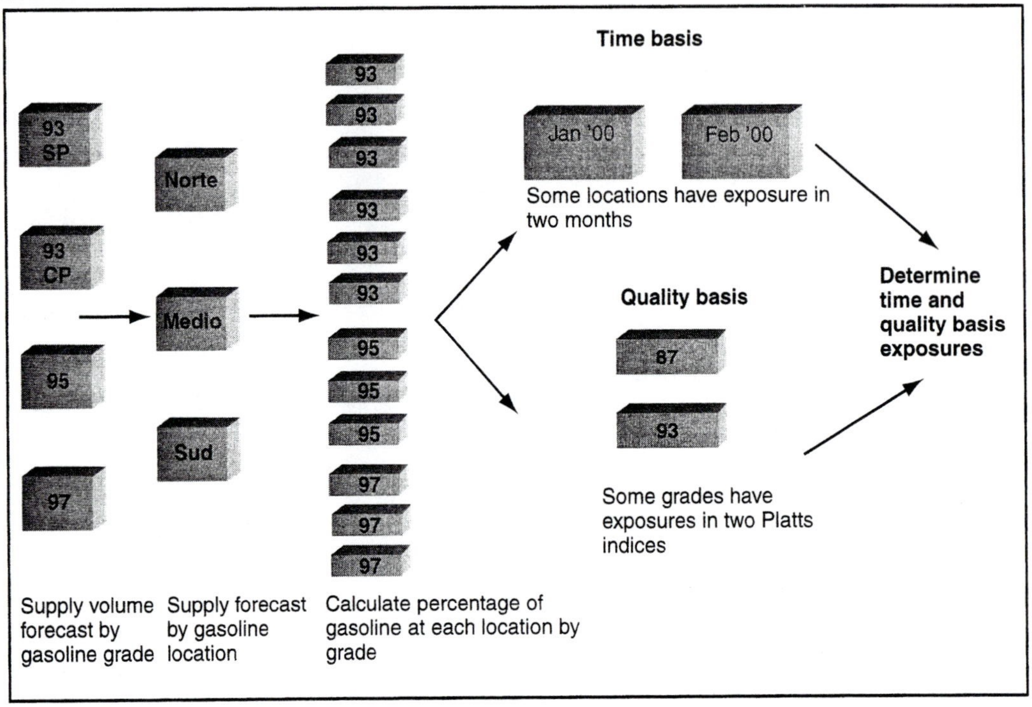

The fundamental idea was straightforward: Create a framework to identify key elements, clarify relationships, understand the complex risk management process with explicit knowledge of every piece, and visualize how each fits into the overall picture. As stated earlier, it was important to look at the entire risk management process and take into account key issues and business opportunities. This framework would enable OilCo to visualize the big picture. It would provide a common conceptual frame of reference. The dilemma was that given the pressure on OilCo's time and resources, trade-offs would be necessary between reaching a merely adequate structure and the desire to implement a best-practice structure.

Time was running out and OilCo's project team needed to prepare and deal with several cultural obstacles to implement a new risk management program. In particular, five concerns had to be addressed:

1. *Lack of commitment.* Senior management must continue to demonstrate a visible commitment to the initiative.
2. *Lack of awareness.* Many personnel do not understand the need or perceive any problems with the status quo. Line personnel must participate actively in implementation and resolution of the issues.
3. *Education.* It will be difficult to realize benefits if concepts are not understood. Given current risk management skills, ENAP will need to improve its competencies.

4. *Fear of negatives.* Some businesses may look less attractive when the underlying risks are made transparent. The planning process must anticipate situations in which personnel may be sensitive.

5. *Distractions/lack of focus.* Other responsibilities can create conflicting priorities, confusion, and frustration. Careful planning and communication processes must be followed.

In addition to the cultural considerations of changing a vertically structured organization, it was important to create all necessary elements to support an adequate risk management infrastructure. Efforts were directed towards the six of them: policies and procedures; business processes; organizational structures; reporting; methodologies and systems.

A company's risk/return profile provides a course for managing its risk and return preferences. Defining risk management policies and procedures allows the company to evaluate its current practices and requirements; to define its goals and strategies by relevant business units; and to monitor its performance against a practical benchmark. Regarding **policies and procedures,** it was necessary to help OilCo to:

- Create an internal policy that would authorize hedging and the use of derivatives.
- Determine corporate objectives and strategies.
- Form criteria on how to identify, measure, and manage crack spread risk on a repeatable and ongoing basis.
- Generate, document, and approve hedging instruments and limits.
- Organizationally define a structure that could replicate the front/middle/back offices paradigm to identify, measure, manage, and monitor risk on an ongoing basis.
- Determine basis risk originating from regulatory price distortions.

Business processes describe "how" an organization manages the risk inherent in its business. Without well-defined processes an organization will manage its risk on an ad hoc basis and will encounter difficulty in achieving its overall strategy. Business processes must also be aligned with the other elements of an effective risk management infrastructure. Business processes can be divided into two categories: "life cycle of a transaction" and supporting processes. The "life cycle of a transaction" processes represent the actions that take a transaction from inception to settlement. The "life cycle of a transaction" processes should include:

- Marketing products and services
- Originating transactions
- Capturing transactions
- Maintaining the portfolio
- Managing the market risk of the portfolio
- Settling retail transactions

Supporting processes represent the actions that must be taken to manage the underlying business of an organization. Supporting processes are often viewed as cost centers within an organization, although they are critical to managing the organization. The supporting processes include:

- Measuring and monitoring portfolio market risk
- Managing credit risk

- Managing financial resources
- Measuring organizational performance
- Performing quantitative research
- Managing and administering contracts

Regarding support processes, it was fundamental to help OilCo to:

- Design a trading process for virtual hedging incorporating best-practice controls
- Design processes and controls for the supporting areas, specifically the front, middle, and back offices
- Implement the newly designed business processes into everyday operations
- Document via flow charts current refinery and optimization planning process

The nature of the business processes will also determine **management's responsibilities** and the **organizational structure.** To effectively manage in accordance with responsibilities, information and reporting had to be determined for OilCo. If the links of integration are deficient, there could be a breakdown in the alignment between infrastructure elements. For instance, if management reports do not provide information for effective management, then personnel cannot perform business processes efficiently. Hence, determining the organization and management structure is one of the key elements that is best performed early in the planning process. Regarding the **organization and management structure,** it was critical to:

- Design an organizational structure that allowed management to identify sources of price risk, utilize tools to reduce exposures, and effectively report and monitor risk
- Define the specific roles and responsibilities of personnel regarding deal origination, deal capture, deal pricing, market-to-market risk aggregation, and hedging
- Promote a strong culture that allowed risk management practices to flow from the top downward reaching all sectors of the company
- Train front, middle, and back offices about risk management processes
- Train finance and refining personnel in basic hedging instruments and techniques
- Document all existing linkages between refined product sales and hedging prior to starting the hedging program

Management reports serve as the primary tool for the communication of risk throughout an organization. The management reports are produced as part of the business processes. Risk management reports typically convey the organization's position, profit and loss, and risk. Reports typically have different levels of detail for different levels of management. For example, a manager responsible for the day-to-day operations will require more detail than a manager with risk oversight responsibilities. Well-designed risk management reports have the following characteristics:

- Timely and meaningful information
- Clearly communicated message
- Design for the intended audience's knowledge
- Appropriate level of detail
- Provides insight into the overall risk position
- Provides insight into the current state of the market

Well-designed management reports allow managers to make better and more timely decisions regarding the level of risk to take and changes that must be made to the overall strategy. Good risk management reports also prevent unnecessary management "surprises." Regarding **management reporting,** it was vital to help OilCo to:

- Create management reports to accurately measure OilCo's risks and key indicators:
  - Wet barrel position
  - Futures hedge book
  - Broker deal log
  - Margin call
  - Broker statement
  - Profit and loss for futures
  - Transaction/cash edit log
  - Price curves
  - Risk profiles
  - Risk sensitivities
- Design a communication strategy to declare management accountable for the decision-making process.

Before any model, assumption, or methodology gets implemented, it is critical that a company searches for a better understanding of the market place and its products. A company, along with experts, usually creates a framework to share knowledge and define the valuation expectations. With that in mind, it is possible to create a sound methodology that clearly reflects on the company's goals. Regarding **models, assumptions,** and **methodologies,** it was a priority to:

- Document, verify, and approve the trading strategies
- Develop a model to simulates the impact of potential hedges on OilCo's exposure as a decision-making tool, that included all relevant parameters
- Develop a portfolio-tracking tool that integrates customer deals and internal transactions to accurately evaluate the entire position of the retail portfolio
- Develop an analytical tool that integrates wet barrel and futures hedges to reflect oil-related commodity price risk exposure
- Develop a correlation tool to simulate the impact of potential hedges against different crude oil hedging instruments
- Develop a value center "Earnings at Risk" (EAR) model describing the retail portfolio risk to feed into the corporate planning process.

Finally, because each area of the industry develops at a different rate, effective and **efficient system solutions** are typically the last area of a new industry to develop. For instance, the number of risk management software applications available for the retail power market is limited. As a result, OilCo was forced into developing its own temporary system solutions. The development of system solutions in a market where the rules are changing day by day can result in the development of inappropriate long-term solutions.

For OilCo, it was necessary to develop and implement an **electronic risk management tool** to meet immediate requirements of trading, including:

- Futures transaction entering and editing
- Cash transaction entering and editing
- Market-to-market value transactions
- Report printing
- Price curve depositories
- Futures and cash transaction edit logs
- Simulated margin call
- Implement system for trade capture of hedges and wet position
- Create tools to analyze basis risk

SUMMARY

We summarize here the results achieved by OilCo during and after the implementation of the solutions it requested of AA. To begin with, OilCo began defining systematic criteria to evaluate and prioritize investment projects, due to enhancements in the optimization and risk management procedures:

- Risk–benefit of key risk processes
- Allocation of capital and resources
- Improved bottom line via systematic hedging

Second, but equally important, OilCo earned significant benefits from the dynamic analysis of gaps between operations and optimization:

- Grades and qualities of inputs
- Exploitation margin and net profit

Third, OilCo experienced significant improvement in its control mechanisms and the means to identify, measure, monitor, and manage risks:

- Integration of a reliable and unique book of physicals
- Reduction in the planning variation of supply and demand
- Market-to-market valuation of its position and tangibles

OilCo learned to use risk management as a strategic weapon. To beat its competition, it was necessary for OilCo to analyze and redefine its strategy, its processes, and the information it could gather throughout the organization to put together a winning combination of value-creating assets. Its imperative was to differentiate itself by improving its risk management process.

OilCo allowed risk management to take its place at the heart of its strategic decision making, business planning, operational processes, and information systems. It allowed it to grow into its planning process. OilCo taught and allowed its managers to see the bigger picture. We feel confident that OilCo is making better decisions today, inspiring greater confidence, and, ultimately, achieving better business outcomes.

CHAPTER 21

Reputation Consulting

Charles J. Fombrun and Scott D. Meyer

All organizations own both tangible and intangible assets. Intangibles are of two types: "knowledge assets" that are *internal* to a company and derive from corporate practices like research and development (R&D), and "reputational assets" like brands that derive from favorable *external perceptions* of the company produced through corporate communications and community relations. In recent years, many consulting firms have developed practice areas devoted to helping companies define, measure, and exploit their "intellectual capital." The focus is typically internal and involves advising companies on how to grow their stock of know-how and develop computer-based applications and systems to facilitate knowledge-sharing among employees.

Consulting to companies about their "reputational capital," however, has taken longer to develop. In part, it's because reputational assets are fundamentally different—unlike knowledge assets, which are rooted in a company's employees and practices, they are not under the *direct* control of a company's managers, but depend on the favorable perceptions held by *external stakeholders* like customers, investors, general publics, media reporters, and financial analysts. Expertise in reputation building is therefore in short supply: It draws on cross-functional knowledge from marketing (focused on customers), finance (focused on analysts and investors), public relations (focused on the public and the media), and from strategy (focused on competitive positioning). An understanding of organizations is also helpful: Academic research shows that companies with strong reputations typically have powerful internal cultures and identities.

Agencies involved in counseling companies on their public and corporate communications have shown the greatest interest in developing a practice area in "reputation consulting." After all, they consider that they have the highest credibility in counseling businesses about how to build favorable impressions. Prime candidates for reputation consulting are therefore major advertising agencies like McCann-Ericsson or Young & Rubicam, and public relations agencies like Burson-Marsteller or Weber-Shandwick. They regularly help client companies build brands and images through ad campaigns, press releases, and special events.

Charles J. Fombrun is Executive Director of the Reputation Institute and Professor Emeritus of Management at the Stern School of Business of New York University. He is widely published in leading research and professional journals.

Scott D. Meyer is former Chief Strategic Officer of Weber Shandwick Worldwide. He is a journalism graduate of the University of Minnesota.

This chapter describes some of the efforts that the world's largest public relations (PR) agency, Weber-Shandwick, made to identify and develop a practice area in reputation management, with the assistance of the Reputation Institute, Inc. We describe the model through which Weber-Shandwick helps clients conceptualize reputation building. We also summarize the way the firm's Shandwick subsidiary applied the model to itself in the late 1990s in an effort to build its own reputation.

BUILDING A REPUTATION CONSULTING PRACTICE

Shandwick is a public relations network that was founded by Lord Chadlington, a.k.a. Peter Gummer, a British entrepreneur who was ennobled in the early 1990s for his active role in assisting the Tory government win parliamentary seats. Lord Chadlington built Shandwick by acquiring small but prominent local PR agencies around the world and, in less than 10 years, leapfrogged the agency into the top five in global revenues. In 1998, the PR agency was itself gobbled up by communications conglomerate The Interpublic Group, whose crown jewel remains the McCann-Ericsson advertising agency network. In 2000, IPG merged Shandwick with the Weber Group, a high-tech public relations agency to form Weber-Shandwick.

In 1998, Shandwick's newly appointed CEO, Scott Meyer, sought to build a reputation consulting practice, and the firm retained Charles Fombrun as an advisor (thus beginning a working relationship between the two authors of this chapter). We jointly defined "reputation management" as a systematic process to help organizations measure, enhance, and protect the value of their reputations. We then developed a process for practicing "reputation management" that became Shandwick's Reputation Management Model (see Figure 21–1).

Shandwick's RM model involves five phases of work with a corporate client. In the *Assess Phase,* the agency conducts internal and external audits of the corporation's reputation. Audits are framed around the Reputation Quotient^{SM}, a measure of corporate

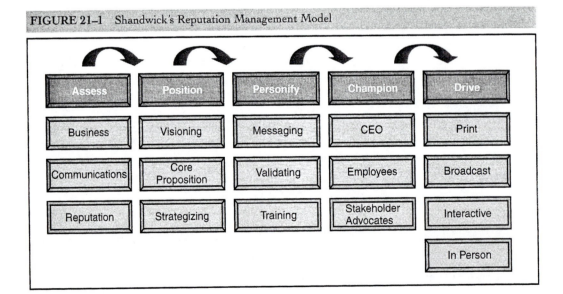

FIGURE 21–1 Shandwick's Reputation Management Model

reputation that was developed by Charles Fombrun with Harris Interactive®, a market research firm. The audits rely on systematic research and data analysis to identify perceptions of the company by stakeholder segments, and to elicit the key "reputation drivers" for each of those audiences. Shandwick also examines the existing portfolio of communications the company makes to its audiences and how it projects its identity.

In the *Position Phase,* the agency conducts senior management interviews and executive/employee workshops to identify the company's existing "core purpose" and "core values" and develops recommendations to close the gap between what the company "is" and what the company "wants to be." Internal gaps are closed by focusing on the four elements of identity building: stories, slogans, symbols, and signs. External gaps are closed through the development of a "core proposition" and appropriate communications strategies, rooted in the company's core purpose that positions the company in the market place.

In the *Personify Phase,* Shandwick helps a client to build its identity around a set of key messages that support the core proposition, core purpose, and core values of the organization. The messages are validated with relevant stakeholder groups, and corporate emissaries are trained to deliver those messages.

In the *Champion Phase*, advocates inside and outside the organization are assigned specific roles to accelerate understanding and appreciation of the organization's core values (which are linked to the six reputation drivers). These assignments are orchestrated through a Reputation Champion Grid.

In the *Drive Phase*, communications are coordinated globally to carry out the reputation-building strategy. Integrated communications are achieved through Shandwick's Global Management Process.

Finally, the model is rooted in measurement: Continual progress in reputation-building for the client is assessed through annual Reputation Quotient℠ surveys that detect changes in perceptions of the company by a representative sample of stakeholders. We describe these five phases in more detail, and then show how Shandwick applied the model to itself.

Phase 1: Assess

The purpose of the Assess Phase is to arrive at a sophisticated and comprehensive understanding of stakeholder perceptions in the marketplace and to identify key drivers of reputation that the company can leverage to build reputation with specific stakeholders. Key questions to explore are:

* What is the client company's current reputation in the marketplace?
* What industry-wide and company-specific reputational issues does the client face?
* How do different stakeholders perceive the company compared to its key rivals?
* What are the key factors that *drive* those perceptions and put the company at a reputational advantage or disadvantage?

To do so, Shandwick relies on the Harris-Fombrun Reputation Quotient℠ to measure corporate reputations. The RQ is based on original research by Fombrun, Harris Interactive, and Shandwick that began with focus groups in the United States and asked people to name companies they liked and respected, as well as companies they didn't like or respect—and why they felt this way. The research extended to large sample polls from different stakeholder groups and industries, and demonstrated that people justify their feelings about companies on one of 20 attributes that were then grouped into six dimensions (see Figure 21–2):

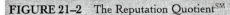

FIGURE 21–2   The Reputation Quotient^{SM}

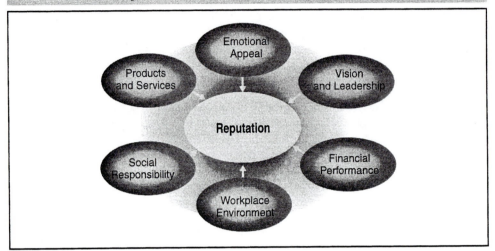

1. *Emotional Appeal:* How much the company is liked, admired, and respected.
2. *Products and Services:* Perceptions of the quality, innovation, value, and reliability of the company's products and services.
3. *Financial Performance:* Perceptions of the company's profitability, prospects, and risk.
4. *Vision and Leadership:* How much the company demonstrates a clear vision and strong leadership.
5. *Workplace Environment:* Perceptions of how well the company is managed, how it is to work for, and the quality of its employees.
6. *Social Responsibility:* Perceptions of the company as a good citizen in its dealings with communities, employees, and the environment.

The Reputation Quotient^{SM} is an index that sums up people's perceptions of a company on these 20 attributes. Various empirical studies were then conducted by the Reputation Institute (an organization founded by Fombrun to advance knowledge about corporate reputations) to benchmark the reputations of companies as seen by different stakeholder segments. The results indicate that the RQ is a valid instrument for measuring corporate reputations and can be used to benchmark companies across industries. Global extensions of the project are under way that confirm the validity of the model in other countries.

The Assess Phase also examines how the company is portrayed in the media using the Media Reputation Index (MRi), a methodology developed by Fombrun with market analysts Delahaye-Medialink that relies on content analysis of all electronically available media about a company and its key reputational rivals. The MRi provides a diagnostic understanding of how reporters describe the company in terms of the six pillars and 20 attributes of the RQ and so how the media currently help or hinder the company's reputation-building efforts.

Finally, the Assess Phase also requires compiling and screening all of the company's communications and examining them for consistency and message content. Juxtaposition of those communications against those of key rivals suggests in what ways the company currently conveys distinctiveness in the marketplace.

Phase 2: Position

Armed with the systematic research gathered in the Assess Phase, Shandwick helps a client to identify its ideal reputational positioning in the marketplace. What are the features of the company that make it unique? What are the company's "core values"? How do those core values relate to the reputation drivers? Through employee workshops and interviews, the company's core purpose is identified and used to provide coherence to the company's internal identity.

Externally, Shandwick then guides the client in developing a "core proposition"—the root image that the company wants to project to build visibility and distinctiveness vis-à-vis rivals. Research suggests that the core proposition should be rooted in the company's core purpose and values. For instance, the athletic supplier Nike values "aggressiveness," "quality," and "competitiveness." Its core purpose is often stated as "crushing the competition." For many years, Nike expressed its values and core purpose through the core proposition "Just Do It."

The three elements of values, purpose, and proposition are the heart and soul of a company's reputation-building strategy. The Position Phase concludes with recommended initiatives for introducing the core values, core purpose, and core proposition into the company's administrative practices:

- *Appraisal Systems:* Reputation-building should be part of every job. The client must make understanding and living the core values a key component of all internal performance appraisals. How does every employee demonstrate support for the company's reputation elements and strategy?
- *Reward Systems:* Ultimately, you get what you pay for. How should a client reward its employees for behaviors consistent with core reputation elements?

Phase 3: Personify

Research shows that companies with strong reputations are more likely to be personified—that is, identified as having attractive "personality traits." The third phase involves personifying the company to its different stakeholders. What traits is the company projecting? What key messages are consistent with those traits, and derive from the company's core values, core purpose, and core proposition? How different should they be across audiences? Which ones are likely to differentiate the company from rivals?

In this phase, alternative messages are compiled and validated with focus groups that represent the company's key audiences. The most effective messages are selected. Shandwick then builds training programs designed to help company managers and employees understand the "message platform" and use it in all of their communications.

Phase 4: Champion

Although every employee should act as an ambassador for the company in communicating the company's reputation strategy, some have more influence than others. Phase 4 focuses on identifying the specific individuals who can act as champions for the company and can help magnify the key reputation-building messages it seeks to construct to the right audiences.

Central to the championing process is the corporate CEO and top management team. They have to be trained to convey the reputation elements in all their official, symbolic, and informal communications, internally and externally. This generally requires significant training to ensure consistency.

At the same time, Shandwick also helps clients identify a diagonal slice of key influentials internally and externally who can be persuaded to act as reputational advocates. Advocacy is the end product of familiarity, understanding, and appreciation of the company's activities. Converting key influentials (both internally and externally) into advocates is at the heart of Shandwick's reputation-building strategy.

Phase 5: Execute

Ultimately, clients must communicate their activities to all of their stakeholders. The final phase of Shandwick's RM Model involves selecting from the portfolio of available media those that are most appropriate to reach specific stakeholder segments and imbue them with the company's key reputational elements. As part of The Interpublic Group, Shandwick can call on a comprehensive array of media, including public relations, media relations, advertising, special events, sports marketing, and the like, to deliver print, broadcast, interactive, or personal communications to relevant stakeholder groups.

Finally, Shandwick's RM Model ends where it began—by conducting repeated reputation measurement and media impact analysis and thereby assessing the company's success at influencing stakeholder perceptions and media communications about its activities.

CLIENT CASE: MIRROR, MIRROR, ON THE WALL . . .

Giving truth to the old edict "doctor heal thyself," in early summer 1999 Shandwick decided to apply the RM Model to its own reputation, using internal staff to carry out most of the research. Most of the attention was placed on the company's U.S. operations, although some efforts were made to involve offices in other parts of the world. Figure 21–3 shows the top PR brands in terms of total 1998 revenues and parent company.

FIGURE 21–3   The Top PR Brands (1999)

		$ Revenues (MM)	Parent Company
1	Burson Marsteller	$258	Y&R
2	Hill & Knowlton	206	WPP
3	Porter Novelli	183	Omnicom
4	Shandwick	170	IPG
5	Fleishman-Hillard	161	Omnicom
6	Edelman	158	....
7	Ketchum	125	Omnicom
8	BSMG	119	True North
9	Weber	83	IPG
10	GCI	80	Grey
11	Ogilvy PR	78	WPP
12	Manning, Selvage & Lee	76	MacManus
13	Golin/Harris	53	IPG

NOTE: *Shandwick, Weber, and Golin-Harris are PR brands owned by The Interpublic Group.*

Phase 1: Assessing Shandwick

Environmental Scan.   The process began with a scan of articles on the PR industry and about Shandwick's key rivals, drawn from the Lexis-Nexis database. Figure 21–4 summarizes some of the trends that were identified. They confirmed rising competition, consolidation, and growth in the industry.

The business scan also showed that during 1998, Shandwick ranked #5 out of the 7 brands in total print media visibility. Figure 21–5 shows the relative visibility of Shandwick in terms of the number of media articles in which it was mentioned. When Shandwick was mentioned in an article, it was generally in the context of either client work or internal personnel changes, but not on capabilities or expert involvement. Nonetheless, Shandwick was among the few PR brands that avoided negative coverage during 1998. Previous media emphasis on Shandwick's own global takeover spree was lower in 1998 than in previous years.

Executive Interviews.   Over 43 personal interviews were then conducted with a cross-section of Shandwick's leadership. The interviews focused on Shandwick's internal operations, its identity, and corporate culture. Specific questions included:

- Who are Shandwick's key competitors? Do you have a clear sense about Shandwick's strategy for competing against them?
- Is there such a thing as a "Shandwick employee"?
- What skills do you need to have in order to do well at Shandwick?
- Do you always have the support you need to get the work done? What have you lacked in the past? What could you get more of?
- Are there some things that Shandwick does particularly well with clients? What are the things we don't do so well with clients?
- Is Shandwick well organized? What works and what doesn't?
- Are the "rules of the game" clearly spelled out at Shandwick?
- What gets you ahead around here? What gets rewarded?
- Does Shandwick treat people well? Describe.
- Is there a "Shandwick Way" of doing things? Can you describe it?
- Is Shandwick better than our competitors at some things? What are we getting known for?

Figure 21–6 (on page 354) captures some of the key diagnostic responses made by the agency's leadership. It paints a picture of an agency that has grown rapidly through acquisitions and so has considerable local strengths but lacks a shared agency-wide identity.

Media Interviews.   Ten prominent media analysts who cover the public relations industry were interviewed. They were asked their opinions of Shandwick, its operations, strengths and weaknesses, and reputation. The findings showed that Shandwick had relatively low visibility for its size and reach. They indicated a need for increased communication to the media about Shandwick itself. Figure 21–7 (on page 255) summarizes the results of these interviews.

Shandwick's Internal Communications. In the spring of 1999, Shandwick authorized a doctoral dissertation by NYU Stern School PhD candidate Bill Newbury that proposed to examine the cross-national and cross-office pattern of e-mail exchanges

FIGURE 21–4   Key Trends in the PR Industry (May 1999)

1. Technology/Internet: As relates to keeping up with what client companies are doing, communicating with media and other constituents (related to the boom of communication systems). IT finally genuinely infiltrating and changing the way we need to market companies. Creating phenomenon of the "audience of one," which is perfectly suited to PR; creating the need to protect reputation from cyber-crises and instantaneous information/disinformation; opportunities to support the growth of a whole new and exploding economy.
2. A healthy and developed all-around economy, requiring companies to look for the competitive edge/added value for their brands that marketing tools can give them. More firms than ever before allocating marketing budget for PR. This is benefiting the small and medium firms as well as the large firms.
3. Advertising having to fight harder for its share of marketing budget due to fragmentation of media, phenomenon of the "audience of one."
4. Globalized economy. Causing demand for a coherent communications policy/company reputation on a global basis. Effecting larger PR firms in particular.
5. M&A activity. 1998/9 have broken all records in terms of volume of M&A activity. Creating demand for internal/reputation communications skills.
6. The realization that PR can build brands, as seen with Starbucks, Body Shop, Furby, Harley Davidson, iMac, VW Beetle, Gillette Mach 3, and Gillette Dazzlers.
7. A new wave of CEOs. The old breed are giving way to a number of young CEOs who see the importance of being more than just a profit-center. They are increasingly interested in how their companies look to the outside world.
8. Changing demographics of America. More Hispanic and Black buying power.
9. Hot economy creating real shortage of skilled labor.
10. Interest of management consultants, accountants, lawyers in the communications function.
11. The PR field itself is getting bullied by advertising types that are moving more into the PR area.
12. A lot of corporations are looking at PR companies for integrated solutions, not just media relations— from external to internal strategies. The alignment of key messages.
13. Clients are getting more scrupulous about billing. Don't want hourly rates, only retainers. And they want to know what they are getting for their money. Asking for measurement results.

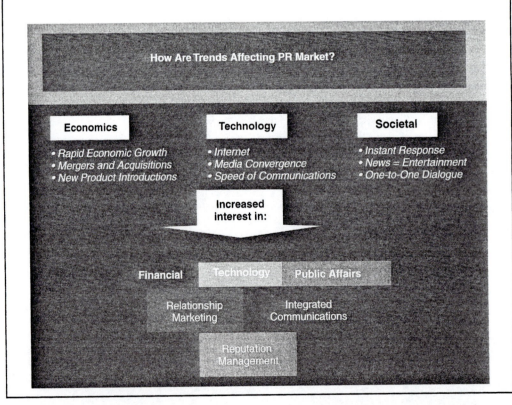

FIGURE 21–5   Media Visibility of Leading PR Agencies (1997–May 1999)

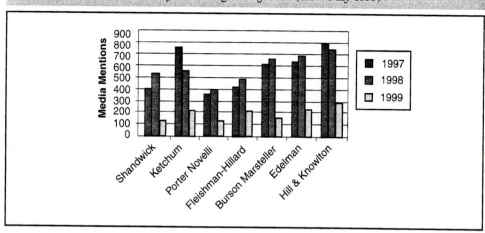

within the agency. Employee surveys confirmed that the e-mail system was the number 1 means of communicating across the agency. We therefore selected a representative sample of over 114,000 e-mails sent and received via the central Shandwick server located in Minneapolis in January 1999. Shandwick was careful to protect the confidentiality of all e-mail content and no content was ever visible, and we examined only the pattern of exchanges. The results are shown in Figure 21–8 (on page 356).

Reputation Surveys.   Finally, to replace commissioning an RQ[SM] for the PR industry itself, various industry surveys (particularly the 1999 Harris Impulse Survey of communications officers) were used to provide input about client perceptions of Shandwick and its key rivals. The surveys confirmed some of the weaknesses identified through the executive and media interviews, particularly the lack of a shared culture or seamless processes with which to serve clients. Figure 21–9(a) (page 357) shows the results of the Harris Impulse survey on the awareness and reputation of the major PR agencies. Figure 21–9(b) plots awareness and reputation on a two-dimensional space. The results confirm the lack of both familiarity and reputation from which Shandwick suffers in the eyes of corporate communications officers of major companies.

Phase 2: Shandwick's Positioning

To explore their perceptual positioning in the industry, Shandwick relied on Fombrun's conceptual model of reputation-building, which assumes that reputations are the outcome of a process through which a company:

- Builds an understanding of who it is and what it stands for (its "identity")
- Expresses its identity through its actions and communications (its "projections")

and

- From which interpretations are made by stakeholders (its "images")
- From which overall judgments and evaluations are made that aggregate into a "reputation"

The purpose of this phase was to examine Shandwick's identity, the images it holds of itself and that others have of the agency, from which to distill the agency's core values, core purpose, and core proposition.

FIGURE 21–6   Key Results of Shandwick Management Interviews (January–March 1999)

	FAVORABLE/STRENGTHS	UNFAVORABLE/WEAKNESSES
VISION AND STRATEGY	Reputation management Having fewer and larger clients State-of-the-art business pitches Strategic thinking	No clear sense of Shandwick's strategy. Not clear how we are unique or tangible If we do, I don't know it Seems like we should know better what competitors are doing
LEADERSHIP AND MANAGEMENT	Diversity Flexibility Creativity I have access to lots of expertise in the Shandwick network Support has gotten a lot better	Often Shandwick just puts bodies into assignments versus putting those with the right capabilities into a job We tend to over-promise in order to please I'm more worried about those in other offices—I would only refer business to 50% of them. They don't know what we do.
EMPLOYEE AND WORK ACTIVITIES	Like people I work with and the laid- back atmosphere Quality of work and the pride people take in it Creative problem solving Opportunity to succeed or fail based on one's own merits Trusting environment Not overly administrative Trusted by clients	Silos and geographic boundaries Idea of Shandwick with "no boundaries" is just not there yet. You're forced to make decisions based on what's best for your office rather than what's best for the client.
STRUCTURE/SYSTEMS INTERNAL STRENGTHS		Too much talk about vision and too little execution. Too little substance in communications. Too much dreaming with little action. Accounting and administrative work. Budget constraints. IPG parent will drain Shandwick for revenues. Lack of clarity on global accounts.
CULTURE	Newsletter is helping Collaboration is growing	Feel very local—no global glue holds us together.
FINANCIAL PERFORMANCE	Good growth and financials Better, but still behind others	We look and act 2nd tier. No equity in our name.
FUTURE PROSPECTS		
MORALE	Good, but weakened by IPG buyout Good when we work together on pitches and with clients.	A lot of résumés are circulating.
REPUTATION	No real negatives—that's a plus.	Not much is known about Shandwick out there. We're seen as expensive.

Personal interviews were conducted by an external consultant with some 20 senior corporate communications officers in major firms. The interviews focused on descriptions of the relative positions of the key firms in the industry. Figure 21–10 (on page 358) shows a perceptual map of the industry that we developed based on the ratings they provided of the major PR firms. The results suggest that Shandwick competes most closely with a strategic group that includes Ketchum, Fleishman-Hillard,

FIGURE 21–7   Results of Media Interviews about Shandwick (January–February 1999)

	FAVORABLE/STRENGTHS	UNFAVORABLE/WEAKNESSES
VISION AND STRATEGY		No clear sense of Shandwick's strategy, mostly due to Shandwick's newness to the industry in the United States and the lack of a unified structure.
LEADERSHIP AND MANAGEMENT		Because of the many changes Shandwick has had in the past couple of years and lack of media relations, top leaders are unknown.
EMPLOYEE AND WORK ACTIVITIES	Little knowledge about the quality of Shandwick's work, however, the number of awards and long-term clients speak for itself.	
STRUCTURE/SYSTEMS INTERNAL STRENGTHS	Shandwick's global ability and network is most commonly known.	
CULTURE		Have no idea of Shandwick's culture or values.
FINANCIAL PERFORMANCE	Shandwick's growth in Washington and New York offices is most known.	
FUTURE PROSPECTS	Shandwick is in a good position to compete with other large firms. As the M&A activity continues, it will come down to 2 or 3 big firms. Also, big agencies must position themselves as an integrated solutions firm and a contender in technology.	It remains to be seen if Shandwick will offer integrated solutions and position itself as a leader in technology.
MORALE		Have no idea
REPUTATION	Shandwick is best known as a large, global firm.	Shandwick has a branding identity crisis (i.e., Shandwick USA, Shandwick Int'l, Miller, R&C, etc.).
VALUE OF BECOMING A SUBSIDIARY OF INTERPUBLIC GROUP	The possibility of creating synergies and offering our clients more services is appealing.	Most of the editors were not sure of the benefit.

Edelman, and Porter-Novelli and should therefore develop its competitive positioning principally against these direct rivals.

We then examined the core propositions of the leading PR agencies, which are listed in Figure 21–11 (on page 358). A close look suggests that there is considerable overlap in the way the major PR brands position themselves against each other. When

FIGURE 21–8   E-mail Communications Between Shandwick Offices and Other IPG Brands (January 1999)

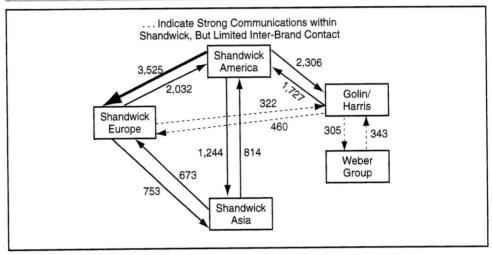

NOTE: *Numbers indicate the number of e-mail messages between brands in January 1999.*

firms adopt similar perceptual positioning, they make client differentiation difficult at best, and therefore fail to capitalize on an important source of competitive advantage.

To examine Shandwick's own core values and to identify the agency's views of its core purpose, various workshops were conducted with groups of 10 to 15 Shandwick employees in multiple offices around the world. The one-hour workshops involved structured exercises designed to explore how employees think about the agency and what they identify as its key attributes, personality traits, and core values. Ultimately, each moderated group was encouraged to produce a single statement that would capture Shandwick's "core purpose." Numerous such core purpose statements were developed in the different offices. The principal candidates were:

Build relationships to tell our clients' story and increase their bottom line

To partner with clients to help solve problems with strategic, creative solutions

To tell our clients' story and fulfill their vision

To protect and enhance our clients' reputation

To enhance the credibility, profitability, and longevity of our clients

Connecting people to connect clients

Making connections and crossing boundaries

Counseling clients on how to communicate with all their audiences

Making clients look better and succeed

Delivering what we promise to clients and employees

The pooled set of statements developed by employees were reviewed by Shandwick leadership at an offsite retreat in Banff, Canada, in May 1999. The assembled senior team weighed pros and cons of each statement, with general support for:

FIGURE 21–9   Awareness and Reputation of PR Brands by Nonclient Corporate Communications Officers in Major Companies

(a) Shandwick, Weber, and Golin-Harris are the principal PR brands of the Interpublic Group (1999). Though larger, Shandwick has weaker awareness and reputation than Golin-Harris.

		$ Revenues (MM)	Awareness (%)	R
1	Burson Marsteller	$258	59	
2	Hill & Knowlton	206	59	
3	Porter Novelli	183	42	
4	**Shandwick**	**170**	**25**	
5	Fleishman-Hillard	161	50	
6	Edelman	158	52	
7	Ketchum	125	55	
8	BSMG	119	20	
9	**Weber**	83	9	
10	GCI	80	15	
11	Ogilvy PR	78	43	
12	Manning, Selvage & Lee	76	33	
13	**Golin/Harris**	53	30	

(b) Awareness and reputation are highly correlated. Shandwick suffers.

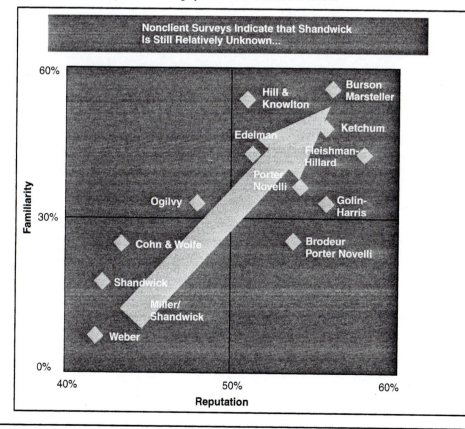

SOURCE: Harris Impulse Survey.

FIGURE 21-10 Perceptual Map of the PR Industry

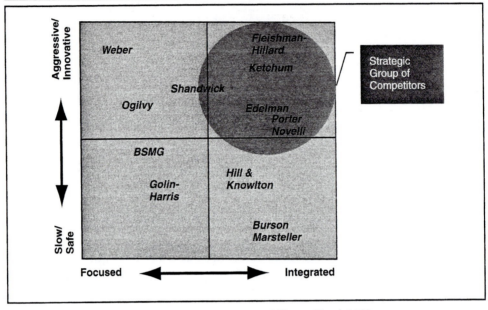

SOURCE: Survey of 20 Senior PR/Communications Officers, March 1999.

Core Values: Small agency personality and service; big agency network
Core Purpose: Connecting People to Connect Clients
Core Proposition: We build the best reputations in the world.

The latter had already been in place as Shandwick's motto, and leadership agreed to devote more resources to communicating the core proposition externally.

FIGURE 21-11 Core Propositions of Major PR Agencies

Top Tier	
Burson-Marsteller	Managing Perceptions, Building Informed Opinions
Hill & Knowlton	Harnessing Knowledge
Edelman	Delivering Outstanding Knowledge
Shandwick	Building the Best Reputations in the World
Ketchum	Delivering Extraordinary Value to Clients
Fleischman-Hillard	Make Ourselves as Valuable to Client as They Are to Us

2nd Tier	
Porter Novelli	Managing Reputations, Building and Protecting Brands
Weber	Premier PR Agency for the Information Age
Ogilvy PR	To Be Valued as an Essential Partner/Brand Stewardship
Golin-Harris	Building Trust Worldwide/Enhancing Client Reputations
Manning, Selvage & Lee	Creating Preference

Phases 3, 4, and 5: Shandwick Personifies, Champions, and Executes

Shandwick CEO Scott Meyer was chosen to embody the core proposition. In speeches at different Shandwick offices in the network, he reiterated the agency's core proposition and reaffirmed the values that underpin it. At a global leadership reunion assembled in Lucerne, Switzerland, Scott addressed a cross-section of over 200 Shandwick senior employees from around the world at which he also expressed the core proposition and related values and core purpose.

Video interviews were conducted with members of the leadership team and with the agency's outside consultants. The content reaffirmed the company's strategic direction, and indicated how Shandwick leadership would be positioning the agency against rivals in the months to come.

The result was a consistent set of internal projections rooted in an integration of core values, core purpose, and core proposition. Missing from this process, however, was a systematic pretest of whether the core proposition and core purpose would be useful in providing *external stakeholders* with a sense of the uniqueness of Shandwick and its strategic direction.

The company's Web site *(www.shandwick.com)* was used to affirm the core proposition by featuring "Reputation Management" as both a key strategic positioning for Shandwick and the armor behind the agency's various integrated offerings. Additional communications were targeted.

Advertisements were placed in leading industry publications, including *PR Week, Reputation Management*, and the *Corporate Reputation Review*. Local stories featuring Shandwick clients involved in reputation management were also placed in local newspapers. Among them, Shandwick advisor Charles Fombrun co-authored articles with local Shandwick Managing Directors that were used to convey the agency as ideally placed to help clients "build the best reputations."

To signal its commitment to "reputation management" as a discipline, Shandwick supported founding of the Reputation Institute (RI) with PricewaterhouseCoopers in Fall 1999. Seed funding enabled the RI to finance the first public surveys of corporate reputation to use the Harris-Fombrun Reputation Quotient^{SM}. Surveys of the "best companies in the U.S.A.," of "the best companies in high-technology," and of the "best airlines" were published and featured in the *Wall Street Journal*. These surveys lay the groundwork for Shandwick's current clients to examine in greater detail the drivers of their reputations and to develop strategic programs to enhance their reputations. It also set the stage for Shandwick to act as strategic counsel to potential clients interested in building stronger reputations or in defending their reputational capital from erosion.

Today, Shandwick is among the few PR agencies to have systematically built a rigorous methodology for reputation-management, and to rely on it for strategic positioning in the highly competitive PR marketplace. Shandwick's merger with the Weber Group in 2001 and its embeddedness in The Interpublic Group increase the agency's ability to harness a wide range of communications in support of a company's reputation-management activities. It remains for the consolidated agency to fulfill its potential in this area and to defend its first-mover advantage from the threat of aggressive rivals both in the United States and in other parts of the world.

CHAPTER

Quickly, Into the Breach: Building a Venture Consulting Firm

Mikelle Calhoun, Charles J. Fombrun, and Robert L. Laud

In May 2000, some 15 months before the September 11 terrorist attacks on the United States that paralyzed the nation, an Internet security meeting was held in Menlo Park, California. At the time, few of those in attendance understood the kind of devastating impact that security breaches could have, the kind of impact the United States would recover only slowly from in the years to come. Although that Internet security meeting had a relatively limited agenda, in hindsight it was a fore-warning of how unprepared companies were to deal with both operational and reputational risks.

The security summit of May 2000 was held at SRI International (SRI) in Silicon Valley, on the heels of what had been one of the most devastating global Internet crises caused by a computer virus ironically called the "I Love You" virus. More than 100 technology industry leaders attended, along with politicians and law enforcement representatives. The purpose of the meeting was to discuss worldwide computer-based crime. Raymond Kendall, Secretary General of Interpol, addressed the group via satellite and warned of the serious threat by cyber criminals who left governments behind with their speed and flexibility. He commented that the very recent "Love Bug" virus had made people realize how serious the issue was: "Especially since the Love Bug was so simple and did so much damage." The coincidence of the recent global Internet security breach was probably the reason for the large attendance at the conference, prompting many to attend who would not normally take the time.

The summit was an opportunity for those with an interest in cyber crime and security issues to share ideas, set agendas, and bring attention to the growing threat and vulnerability of businesses, universities, governments, and individuals around the world. In addition to the Secretary General of Interpol, other prominent attendees included

Mikelle Calhoun is an assistant professor at Valparaiso University. She received a BA in communications studies from Pennsylvania State University and an MA in speech communications from the University of Minnesota. She later received a joint JD/MBA degree from the University of North Carolina.

Charles J. Fombrun is Executive Director of the Reputation Institute and Professor Emeritus of Management at the Stern School of Business of New York University. He is widely published in leading research and professional journals.

Robert L. Laud is currently affiliated with Deloitte Consulting. Bob received his PhD from Columbia University, MBA from Adelphi University, and BA from Colgate University.

Senator Fred Thompson, R-Tennessee, a leading advocate of U. S. computer security; Peter Watkins, President and COO of Network Associates; Gary White, security manager of BP Amoco; Lawrence Brown, with Edison Electric Institute; Dave Allison, director of software innovation at IBM; Jim Maloney, then VP in the Security Practice at SRI Consulting and currently CEO at SecurityPortal.com; Rhonda MacLean, a senior vice president at Bank of America; Beth Dickinson, a chief in the Los Angeles County Sheriff's Department; Chris Vargas, president of Finland-based F-Secure; Glenn Tenney, director of Pilot Network Services; Selwyn Gerber, managing partner of PrimeGlobal; and representatives of Microsoft, Oracle, AT&T, and the British Department of Trade and Industry.

At the summit, SRI, formerly known as the Stanford Research Institute, also announced the release of hacker detection software entitled "Emerald" and invited other companies to present and discuss their security products and security needs. In response to current Internet security concerns, SRI also divulged plans to create an Internet site where cyber security information could be shared. Creation of the site met the concerns of many of the corporate security managers present at the conference who commented that a better system for exchanging security information between companies and law enforcement was needed.

The new Web site, *www.atomictangerine.com/summit*, corresponded with the name of an SRI spin-off, AtomicTangerine, a co-sponsor of the Summit. SRI and AtomicTangerine took advantage of the Summit pulpit to publicize AtomicTangerine's new name. AtomicTangerine was introduced as a first-of-its-kind venture consulting firm that would marry advanced information technology (IT) with management consulting and the features of an incubator. As chief executive officer Jonathan Fornaci explained: "AtomicTangerine is redefining e-services as a venture consulting firm that combines emerging technologies with an organic services delivery model and a business strategy that ties our compensation to the value we deliver to clients."

BACKGROUND

The Stanford Research Institute was founded in 1946. It is credited with being Silicon Valley's soul—the foundation for the Valley's explosion of innovation. It received the first message sent on Arpanet, the predecessor of the modern Internet. It created the modem, the mouse, on-screen windows, handheld computers, and the software for point-and-click surfing. SRI made significant contributions to speech recognition, human–computer interfaces, and information security systems. Stanford University spun off the Institute in 1972 because the think tank had become a military brain for command and control software, which Stanford students opposed and actively resisted. The name was changed to SRI International and the Institute went on to produce a constant stream of next-generation technologies in engineering, systems, medicine, chemistry, molecular physics, pharmacology, and energy, to name a few. SRI would then spin off companies and license its technology to them. As with many think tanks, SRI would face a constant struggle to manage and create margins despite a number of very successful spin-offs, such as the prestigious Sarnoff Laboratory in Princeton, New Jersey.

In the mid-1990s SRI set up a subsidiary—SRI Consulting (SRIC)—as a means to commercialize the technologies coming out of SRI. Approximately 400 SRI personnel became part of this group and tried to compete with the well-established consulting firms. By the late 1990s it became clear that SRIC's research mindset was no match for the business of professional consulting. In 1999, SRI reassigned approximately 320 of these people back to the think tank, wrote a new business plan, and established a new consulting entity that for a short time would be called Adario.

The new entity, Adario, which eventually was renamed AtomicTangerine, would be different by design. SRI's intent was to retain strong ties with AtomicTangerine and to provide significant financial support to the fledgling enterprise with the clear intent of taking it out as an initial public offering (IPO). In return, SRI would own approximately 40% of AtomicTangerine stock and would partner with AtomicTangerine to develop and market new technologies. Additionally, new management blood would be recruited from top-tier consulting firms who could help lead the practice into the future.

The SRI connection and heritage provided immediate reputational capital to the spin-off organization. The spin-off could gain attention and access to resources based on the name recognition of its founding parent organization. Perhaps the greatest advantage would be access to the nearby venture capital community on Sand Hill Road where SRI was well known. However, the spin-off would eventually need to be recognized on its own. That recognition would depend on the spin-off's ability to develop a brand and on the firm's delivering what was promised to clients. Initially, the brand would be determined by such things as the image associated with its chosen name, its logo, its mission statement, and its efforts to create a shared meaning internally and externally of the value proposition of the firm, its sources of uniqueness, and its culture. Much of the story of the spin-off relates to early decisions about its name and positioning—as the first of a new breed of venture consulting firms.

BIRTH OF ADARIO VENTURE CONSULTING

In early 2000, e-business was expected to generate as much as $900 billion in online sales and $125 billion in cost savings worldwide by 2002. According to Hambrecht & Quist, businesses would spend $50 billion a year on Internet strategies by 2005. Correspondingly, International Data Corporation predicted at the time that worldwide revenues for Internet consulting services would grow from $7.8 billion in 1998 to $78.5 billion in 2003, a 10-fold increase. Although hard to assess, these revenue predictions appear to have proven true.

In 2000, many industries felt a sense of urgency due to perceived destabilization of existing industry structures brought on by the Internet. Firms felt pressured to reexamine their most fundamental tenets and to redefine their competitive strategies and business models and implement appropriate technology solutions. Solutions spanned all elements of strategy, process redesign, infrastructure development, and, importantly, quantum leap technologies. In addition, clients were also feeling pressured to develop innovative insights, often based on quantum leap technologies, and therefore needed solutions that provided at least some temporary source of competitive advantage.

SRI's experience suggested that even the most sophisticated organizations could not resolve these strategic issues and develop solutions independently. They needed the services of e-business integrators due to the rapid pace of technological change and to shortages of both technically skilled and e-business–savvy professionals. The market for such e-business professional services was already nearly $10 billion and growing at nearly 60 percent per year. Into the breach came Adario, a company formed on the belief that "companies that want to take full advantage of the global digital economy must embrace new ways of thinking and the innovative technologies that provide first-mover advantages."

According to Dr. Robert Laud, chief performance officer and vice president at Adario, "Venture consulting . . . involves all four disciplines of incubation, emerging technology, venture capital, and traditional e-business combined." Adario wanted a brand that would position it to be the first to take on the challenge of being the full-service, e-business integrator. Diane Kegley, chief marketing officer for the new company, noted that the goal was to "help companies innovate themselves and create new category killers by leveraging SRI's deep technologies." Key to achieving this goal was recruiting top SRI technology talent such as Dr. Yadu Zambre, who became Adario's chief technology officer. Adario's venture consulting approach intended to go beyond the offerings of the competition. Instead of doing business with clients, Adario would go into business with clients and become their partners on a new level. As the company put it in its marketing materials:

> Like a venture capital company, we invest in you.
>
> Like an incubation lab, we work with you to get your new venture off the ground.
>
> Like a business consultant, we help you develop the strategies to take your business to an ultra-competitive model.
>
> And like a technology integrator, we help you take advantage of the most advanced technology possible.
>
> In short, we'll bet on our ability to deliver value.

Despite a rapid influx of new firms, many of which were outperforming the Standard & Poor's (S&P) 500, the competitive environment still welcomed niche exploitation and e-business integrators were positioned for sustained value creation as business architects of the new economy, a highly attractive offshoot of traditional IT integration services. E-business—or the linking of value chain members through electronic transactions—expected to fundamentally transform both industry structures and business processes.

THE COMPETITIVE ENVIRONMENT

To understand Adario's business, it is helpful to consider the competitors who then defined the different disciplines. Most competed on only one or two of the multiple components of venture consulting.

Scient was then the market leader in the Internet consulting business and had the highest market capitalization and fastest growth. The three-year-old company went public in May 1999. Scient claimed strong ties to telecommunications giant AT&T and to IBM. Scient's revenues per employee ($303K) were impressive, and it had well established relationships with its clients. However, most of Scient's growth had been internal, and there is some compartmentalization in its approach. For example, Scient

Capital is the venture capital arm of the organization and there an Affiliate Fund allows employees to invest in promising clients.

Founded in 1991, **Sapient** was one of the first Internet Professional Service (IPS) firms and had doubled its revenue every year since its founding. Originally, the company focused on being a client/server consulting firm and later changed to working on enterprise management systems. Eventually, Sapient became a leader in offering end-to-end solutions using the Internet. Sapient's growth had also been almost entirely internal with four acquisitions. It had a low employee turnover rate and an organizational structure with vertical industry groups. It used a fixed-price, fixed-time-frame approach and had a strong information technology system to handle project management. As an older company, it suffered from a continual identity problem as new firms entered and changed the landscape. In addition, it was not given the leeway of the start-ups and had more pressure imposed by investors to be profitable.

Founded in 1996, **Viant** was a strong competitor in the general IPS market with extremely high internally driven growth. It had positioned itself as the leader able to quickly and cheaply deliver Web-centric solutions to clients. Viant's brand was a replicable project approach of "envision, experience, and launch." Viant had benefited from blue-chip client relationships and large contract sizes that have driven high per employee revenues ($324K). However, Viant had suffered from a fairly high turnover rate at times. It also was distinguishable from Adario in its approach of providing client-sought solutions without providing extra reasoned advice about the client's position in their industry space.

Razorfish had traditionally focused on Internet-based technologies, but planned to address wireless, satellite, and broadband solutions. Razorfish targeted financial services, media and entertainment, retail and technology/telecommunications industries, but without a matching structure. It also ventured into the European wireless community. Razorfish's strongest assets were its creative image and ability to attract top talent. It had been faced with integration problems following its recent acquisition of I-Cube. However, in November 2000, Razorfish was ranked by Deloitte & Touche as one of the fastest-growing technology companies—number four overall, number two in New York.

Proxicom was a fast-growing rival driven by three acquisitions and a focus on four vertical industries. Proxicom used fixed-price, fixed-time-frame, and time-and-materials pricing approaches. It was somewhat dependent on a few large contracts. One such contract involved Intel and was entered into in September 1999. The following year, in November 2000, Proxicom announced that, building on this existing relationship, it had entered into a new agreement with Intel to develop and deploy e-commerce solutions utilizing Intel architecture-based hardware and software.

iXL was formed through a process of acquisitions and over time had developed a large list of blue-chip clients in a large number of industries. It was in the process of changing from a fixed-price billing system to a time-and-materials billing system, and had been able to acquire the skills necessary to deliver end-to-end Internet strategies and solutions. Due to mergers and affiliations, with one merger occurring in December 1999, iXL had faced the challenge of assimilating various companies and cultures. By the end of 2000, iXL positioned itself as being involved in creating "e-transformation" and claimed to offer a comprehensive set of strategic services designed to generate success for clients.

AppNet, like most competitors, had grown rapidly through acquisitions and lacked a strong infrastructure to integrate its activities. The acquired companies had been a rich source of skills related to application development, systems integration, Web development, interactive community building, and strategic and technical consulting services.

Agency.com was a smaller IPS that differentiated itself by providing strategy services. The backgrounds of certain key employees had promoted an image of the firm as a creative leader with strength in creative design/branding and Web development. Agency.com relied on a comprehensive system termed *interactive relationship management*, which focused on creating a fluid dialogue between the company and the customer to encourage long-term purchasing relationships.

Zefer, a company that began as a Harvard Business School assignment, was a very unique firm. It was proud of not having discrete service lines as it provided clients with truly integrated solutions. Zefer added program management to the usual array of competencies—strategy, design, and technology. Zefer also ran a six-week workshop for senior executives to help them envision an e-business strategy. To implement its programs, Zefer had been able to attract leaders from competing e-business firms.

Xpedior was a subsidiary of Metamore Worldwide and just completed its IPO in December 1999. Having been created from seven different companies, Xpedior was somewhat fragmented but had all the pieces of an end-to-end e-business. Continuing to integrate the members of the firm was Xpedior's major challenge.

US Interactive developed the e-roadmap, a brand that integrates a range of services. Over time, the company had developed a 360° approach that allowed companies to construct their e-business and complete it with a single solution. Two recent acquisitions and an August IPO had also allowed the company to obtain and pursue new specialties. Most of US Interactive's work was billed on a fixed-fee basis, but the company had the unique policy of allowing clients to terminate projects at any point without penalty.

In addition, the major consulting firms were already well entrenched in e-Consulting. They had the advantage of being well known for conducting deep technology and industry-based consulting, with large, blue-chip client bases, and a global presence. Among the giants at that time were Accenture (the former Andersen Consulting), Deloitte Consulting (now Braxton), Ernst & Young (now CGE&Y), IBM, KPMG (now BearingPoint), and PricewaterhouseCoopers (now IBM Global Solutions).

Finally, consider **Devine InterVentures.** This was an example of an Internet "incubator" that had struggled with its identity following its IPO efforts. It acted as a holding company, owning stakes in and helping to foster 52 business-to-business online commerce companies. Devine has been described as an Internet venture capital company with investors including Microsoft Corporation, Dell Computer Corporation, CMGI, Inc., and Michael Jordan, former NBA player for the Chicago Bulls. Devine claimed to offer "a single platform that provided the vertical application functionality with which a company can grow." Devine executives explain that Devine was providing start-ups and corporate spin-offs with capital, strategic guidance, operational support, and business services needed to be successful, creating a network of partner companies.

Devine had a tough time going public. After two delays and a significant reduction in the offer price, Devine saw its price drop on the first day after the IPO finally occurred. Randall Roth, a senior research analyst of Renaissance Capital's IPO fund, remarked, "It's a very ambiguous kind of company, precisely the kind of company that doesn't do well when people are worried." Much of the ambiguity has stemmed from the fact that many of the companies in Devine's portfolio are little known. Roth claimed: "People don't want to hear stories now, they want concrete examples of progress in their business world."

Lisa Leiter of CNN/FN's *Moneyline* program tied Devine's problems to those of its founder: "This man, Andrew Filipowski, wants to put Chicago on the Internet map. But in just seven months, his company, Devine InterVentures, has gone from the Windy City's hottest dot-com to its biggest potential flop. Devine InterVentures has delayed its initial public offering seven times since filing last December." Only 30 of the 52 companies in Devine's portfolio have revenue. However, Devine has been backed by the entire city of Chicago and received $14 million in tax breaks to build a new head-quarters.

The Devine IPO was described by the media as "confusing." With investments in very small companies, a complicated director structure, and outside investments concurrent with the IPO, the company raised questions about how it would perform going forward. Commentators remarked about the IPO problems that "[I]nvestors are not going to dive into something just because it has a dot-com" and further explained that so far Devine had not "proven anything to anybody other than that they can create a whole lot of hype."

Although the competitors appeared formidable, the market remained highly fragmented, with the acknowledged value creation leader (Scient) claiming less than 1 percent of the market.

ADARIO'S HERITAGE

With over 50 years of technology innovation heritage and the promise of new leapfrog technologies to come, Adario was spun off and launched as a company on December 26, 1999. Adario was a new kind of e-business consulting company born out of a strong technology innovation lineage. Adario chose to become an integrator and to provide end-to-end consulting solutions. Adario positioned itself between incubator companies and consulting companies. Adario has a comprehensive service offering, which includes e-business strategy, supply chain management, collaborative product development, architecture and planning of e-business systems, network design and engineering, information security policy and implementation, custom Web-enabled application development, and the implementation of quantum leap technologies such as speech recognition. Adario's work in custom application development and the application of quantum leap technologies uniquely differentiated the company based on the complexity of the client problems solved and the integrating abilities of the company to bundle the services offered.

Adario's value proposition was embodied in its approach of rapidly developing integrated solutions that could leverage quantum leap technologies in an industry. Particular details of Adario's value proposition and sources of uniqueness included:

- *100-Day implementations or customized solutions*—quick implementation of off-the-shelf e-business technologies such as Ariba, Vignette, Broadvision, and the like or development of custom proof-of-concept prototypes that can then be quickly implemented to provide first-mover advantage. This approach later became known as *Spectrum 20/20 Methodology* as Adario determined that in most cases it could create the initial strategy and business plan in 20 days and implement it in 20 weeks or less. Quickly developed e-business solutions later included products for CommerceOne and Oracle.

- *An incubation lab* where technology is identified, cultivated, and commercialized to ensure it moves quickly out of the labs and into the business world. Adario can offer an advantage over other e-business providers who focus solely on commercially available technologies.

- *A spin-off mentality*—a commitment to identifying cutting-edge ideas within Adario and, if appropriate, launching spin-offs to ensure that the ideas have a chance to flourish, obtain funding, and gain market presence.

- *A variety of pricing options*—offering traditional and nontraditional pricing options designed to ensure maximum value for clients and upside for Adario shareholders alike and which allows Adario to work with companies at all stages of evolution, whether a *Fortune* 500 company or two people in a garage who don't know how to make their idea a reality.

From the start, Adario enjoyed four significant advantages: experienced and highly talented employees, a strong management team, established clients, and a unique experience profile.

Expert Staff.   Almost overnight, Adario opened offices in Menlo Park; San Francisco; Alameda; Seattle; Boston; Washington, D.C.; London; and Tokyo and quickly amassed a staff of 150 highly motivated technology and business professionals. Adario's employees have relevant industry expertise and strong capabilities in scenario planning, e-business strategy formulation, process design, change management, and e-business technology planning and development. Adario has very deep and highly differentiated technical expertise in custom, near-real-time Java application development, speech recognition, information security, and network planning. Adario's technology experts are recognized throughout the world as futurists who can take businesses to the next level. In addition, Adario employees, many coming from SRI, have been known throughout the world for their expertise in computer and information security and intrusion detection.

Management Team.   When building the organization, the management team was a primary concern for Adario. The management team was selected from other major consulting firms and has backgrounds in high-tech, Internet, management consulting, and research sectors. Experienced people with a track record for leadership were prime candidates. Employees and management combined, Adario offers world-class strategists who have been operating at a boardroom level, literally dealing with the day-to-day decisions affecting their company's livelihood. Adario relies on its industry experts to offer an in-depth understanding of the issues affecting a wide variety of sectors, enabling the company to offer a level of insight and expertise unrivaled in the e-services market.

Top-Tier Clients.   As a spin-off, Adario had an existing base of top-tier clients, including such heavyweights as Deutsche Bank, DuPont, McDonalds, Charles Schwab, Visa, Royal Caribbean Cruise Lines, Mitsubishi, Oki-Electric, Sprint Communications, Bank of America, NTT Data Corporation, Dentsu Inc., Motorola, and the New York Stock Exchange. In addition, included in the company's client base were the members of its International Information Integrity Institute (I-4), a 75-member multiclient information security program with a *Fortune* 500 client base. The I-4 program was a source of subscription revenues and unique sales channels to e-business professionals who are involved in the planning and implementation of information security within their organizations. Adario's client base demanded the highest level of business management consulting and industry expertise.

Unique Experience.   Adario's unique experience in emerging or quantum leap technologies from its prior association with SRI has been further augmented by its strong alliances with the world's top research labs and e-business technology innovators. The purpose of these alliances was to allow Adario to strengthen its resources, capabilities, and reputation. Early alliances include not only the involvement with SRI International (access to quantum leap technologies under development at SRI), but also alliances with Nuance Communications (joint efforts to develop voice-enabled Web applications), Blaze Software (data-mining capabilities are used to add value to larger systems), Diverse Networks (platform and contract operations support are obtained for Palm wireless network applications), David Sarnoff Research Center (access to innovative electronic, biomedical, and information technologies), Oracle, and CommerceOne.

In addition, Adario's existing relationships allowed it to apply quantum leap technologies that were not yet commercially available. The company had not stopped with its innovation capabilities, but had coupled them with proven experience in implementing proof-of-concept applications for first-mover advantage, thus offering clients a compelling mix of services that no other e-services firm could offer. Adario therefore redefined e-services as a venture consulting firm that combined access to emerging technologies from SRI—including speech recognition, information security, broadband, and wireless—with a business model that took a bet that these technologies would achieve the next quantum leap for clients' businesses. Even alternative e-business integrators could not offer the breadth of service nor the depth of expertise. Adario had a holistic approach with end-to-end renewal-focused solutions.

A Flat Organization.   Adario went to market as a flat organizational structure common to many start-up firms. Recognizing that what works in one industry might not work in another, the company operated in a matrix fashion by overlaying six market units with 10 centers of excellence. The six original market units were:

1. *Communications*. Clients were assisted in their efforts to execute competitive programs involving online proactive customer care, rational bill presentment, efficient information exchange, and value-based marketing.

2. *Digital enterprises*. Teams of experts could be mobilized to assist with obtaining funding, recruiting and hiring, going to market, building the dot.com business, and dealing with special needs such as security, wireless, voice recognition, proof-of-concepts, and greater user interfaces.

3. *Financial services*. Financial services firms could be positioned to offer customers cyber access and solutions, having been involved with digital and electronic data management product innovations for many years.

4. *Information security*. E-business security assistance was provided by published professionals who could perform security assessments, architecture, design, policies, procedures, and education.

5. *Manufacturing*. Adario would enable manufacturers and retailers to have Web agility and provide expertise in electronics, robotics, process systems, business-to-business (B2B) transactions, and e-commerce Web development.

6. *Asia/Pacific.* Adario's Tokyo office offered expertise to multinational companies and Japanese government agencies on matters concerning telecommunications, Internet and intranet design, and wireless communications.

The 10 centers of excellence allowed Adario to provide "end-to-end" solutions covering every potential aspect of a client's e-business needs—assessing, designing, creating, providing, and securing needed e-business services and applications. The company's methodology for providing end-to-end solutions involved four phases of activity: visualize, focus, actualize/architect, and commercialize. Adario envisioned its client's digital future and then took steps to cause the future vision to become reality through application or innovation of technologies to make quantum leaps over the competition. Focus allowed Adario to select the most promising opportunities and coordinate the appropriate resources and elements. The architect phase involved creating and testing with prototypes, marketing mock-ups, and exposure testing. The final step, commercialize, was the capitalization on the opportunity through marketing programs and development of ongoing implementation procedures for the company.

RETHINKING THE BRAND

"Adario," the original name of the SRI spin-off, was selected through an internal brainstorming session with a general preference for a name that started with an "A" and would not mean anything. No marketing group was involved in the name-selection process. When the "Adario" name was selected, the firm was still in the process of determining its identity and niche. The value position, venture consulting, also had not been fully identified or even defined internally. As a result, senior officer Laud explained that after the company had been launched "we began our own brand search process to see whether or not that name would be appropriate moving into the niche that we were defining as we were still forming the company."

Eventually, there was a general sense that "Adario" did not work well as a name. Laud characterizes it as ". . . a general malaise around the name. It didn't capture anything. It wasn't negative, but it certainty wasn't a powerful statement in the market place. It didn't lend to any image of who we were. It was bland." Eventually, the name was empirically tested for memorability, credibility, uniqueness, and personality; it rated poorly. Adario was about to be reborn.

Top management at Adario decided to invest in building a more thoroughly conceived brand, changing the name, creating a new logo, and redefining the company to fit the venture capital, "business *un*usual" approach. Diane Kegley, who had been hired away from CNET where she had been Vice President of Industry Marketing, was to lead Adario's marketing efforts. In general, management wanted to position the company as the logical choice for e-business consulting services when compared to the competition and sought to build awareness at the corporate level that Adario was a company that offered a clear customer benefit and was different from other competitors.

Personify the Brand

The strategy applied for building the brand involved three considerations: definition, communication, and consistency. Adario sought to clarify how the firm defined itself—

its desired brand image. The effort was matched by carefully planned communications internally (through employee meetings) and externally (through media and marketing campaigns). Finally, all communications and actions by the firm had to be consistent with the brand. In particular, the name and logo of the company had to embody the image Adario wanted to portray.

The company turned its goal into a mission statement: "To combine and apply disciplines of venture capital, technology innovation and strategic consulting to create category killers and incubate new industries." It also promoted its aggressive "bet-taking" compensation model. As explained by CEO Fornaci, "Everyone will be paid based on the value we bring to the customer, instead of on the older basis of hourly billing. With our customers, we tie our value to revenue or profits, or some other measure of success, and we base our compensation on that. The goal of the company is to help clients stay ahead of the curve." Thus, the use of terminology such as "quantum leap" and "over-the-horizon" is included in most explanations of what the company is about.

In addition to finding a niche and seeking to consistently communicate an understanding of that niche to others internally and externally, the company sought to proactively build a company culture instead of just letting it evolve. Patty Hsiao, VP of Human Resources, initiated a culture-building process by interviewing others in the firm to identify what would be important to them about the organization and what kinds of things would make them want to get out of bed each morning and come to work. Management hoped to determine attributes that would get people excited, were sustainable, and could be looked for in other people who would be joining the organization. A conscious decision was then made to form the culture around the ideal values that everyone had expressed.

Naming

The second time around, management decided to approach the naming issue more formally and aggressively. Adario hired Wow.com, which handles naming and branding for firms in Silicon Valley. A second consulting firm, Landor Associates, also was retained to assist with bringing the new name to market. Landor provided further guidance in addressing potential cultural issues for the soon-to-be-renamed global firm. Naming involved considering impressions of the various name possibilities in terms of the messages each gave concerning credibility, memorability, ownership, and positioning.

Extensive work and testing was involved in selecting possible names, which included: epicLab, Magnity, epciFusion, SRI Action Team, Epitomic, giantIDEAS, Sitrus, StanfordFusion, Ferent Technology, Cobalt Box, Stanford Tool Shed, Fuselabs, Odes, SRI Fusion, The Juice Hut, Esrion, Nuclea, Stanford Tech. Rangers, Sraio!, Espri Labs, SRI Tech Rebels, SuperFeron, Credos, Espiron, The Juice Factor, and AtomicTangerine.

Eventually, the field of prospects was narrowed to one proposed name: AtomicTangerine. AtomicTangerine embodied many of the more unique and salient aspects of the firm's image and presented them with positive connotations. The name itself is a juxtaposition of the company's heritage of technological innovation from SRI labs and the organic side of any business.

Atomic embodies the SRI lineage. It connotes the DNA or origins of the company to its research and technology-oriented predecessors, Stanford Research Institute and SRI. *Tangerine* is intended to suggest the reseeding, growing, incubation, and spin-off sequence a new venture goes through as well as the human component that helps the technology come alive in a company and which is instrumental in implementing the technology. Finally, *Tangerine* is an icon for the ecosystem of "business *unusual*" wherein people, process, and technology interact in unison around seeds of innovation.

After review and some final testing of the proposed new name, AtomicTangerine was selected and a logo was developed. Amusingly, the company had to decide that the existence of a rock band and a Crayola crayon both with the same name would not pose any conflict or problem.

On April 12, 2000, the new name, AtomicTangerine, was made public. A special launch Web site was released. Between April 12 and April 30, 2000, a series of press and analysts meetings, advertisements, and direct marketing efforts to existing and targeted potential clients were conducted together with a strategic announcement with SRI.

A New Identity

AtomicTangerine staked a claim in the new business territory of venture consulting. SRI CEO Curt Carlson, PhD, claimed:

> AtomicTangerine is a messenger for advanced technological solutions and an innovator in strategic planning and implementation. The company leverages both theoretical scenarios and practical applications to devise comprehensive, high-value, and secure e-business solutions.

AtomicTangerine began promoting its experience in combining emerging technologies with real-world business consulting to give clients a quantum leap in their business. AtomicTangerine developed a plan to publicize its unique features, its brand and its name. A logo was created and tested for the firm. The logo selected for the company was intended to correspond with the juxtaposition of the name and reflect a dynamic and revolutionary image. A logo should become a recognizable symbol that immediately calls to mind the company and its image. The meaning of the logo as it relates to and embodies the spirit of the firm can become clear to the viewer only through constant and consistent repetition. Figure 22–1 shows the final logo that was selected.

The primary colors of the logo, orange and green, relate to the words in the company's name, *atomic* and *tangerine*, and reflect the central elements of AtomicTangerine as dynamic, revolutionary, atomic, and futuristic (green), and organic, warm, and retro (orange).

As Carlson stated, "One of SRI's business goals is to innovate and commercialize new technologies and services that will have major impact for business. AtomicTangerine has created a new business model that will shape the consulting and customer relationship models of the future." Sam Armacost, Chairman of the Board and SRI Chairman, added: "Never before has technology been as critical to creating a competitive edge as it is today. In light of that business environment, AtomicTangerine has developed an unprecedented channel for the delivery of precommercialized technologies to the private sector."

FIGURE 22–1   The AtomicTangerine Logo

Generating a Shared Understanding of AtomicTangerine

The success of AtomicTangerine's brand-building efforts required developing a shared understanding of what it stood for among both internal and external audiences.

Mobilizing Internal Support

To successfully promote the new brand, management needed to be supportive of the plan and employees needed convincing. Management buy-in to the plan was aided by the company's compensation that is tied directly to the performance of the project and which affects employee income through AtomicTangerine's reliance on a 100 percent employee ownership plan. The overall compensation plan has been designed to assist the company in achieving its financial and strategic objectives. AtomicTangerine hopes to promote an energized, cooperative, and performance-driven culture that backs management decisions and embraces the new name and *un*usual business concept.

In an effort to provoke a strong, positive, internal response, Fornaci and Kegley went on a "world tour" to meet with employees at all the various firm locations to discuss the change in the name of the firm and the redefining of the firm's brand image to more accurately reflect the nature of the firm. The intent was not to make employees feel good; in fact, they should squirm because of the level of commitment to providing exceptional quality that covers every aspect of the e-business. They were not presenting a guide for how business should be done, but were explaining to employees what the business was becoming. The meetings were a send-off and transition from business-as-usual at SRI to business *un*usual at AtomicTangerine. Employees were also given examples of attributes that apply to AtomicTangerine and attributes that do not apply. AtomicTangerine was described in these ways:

What AtomicTangerine is:	What AtomicTangerine is not:
• Real, down to earth	• Processors, circuit boards
• Informative	• Institutional
• Organic, natural, and personable	• Cold, digital, nonhuman
• Warm and fuzzy, edgy and gritty	• Intimidating or heavy in process
• Future thinking	• Futuristic
• Current	• Stuffy
• Retro from the 1960s until now	• Retro from the 1950s and earlier
• A source for new innovations	• Boxed software solutions
• People	• A drink
• Easy to recall	• Full of jargon-speak
• Venture consulting	• E-business consulting
• Physics, atomic theory, quantum leap	• *Star Trek, Star Wars*, outer space

Generating External Support

AtomicTangerine's prescription for "business *un*usual" involved: (1) speed to market; (2) greater value to the customer, partners, vendors, and employees of their clients; (3) access to over-the-horizon technologies; and (4) being a partner with, not a vendor to, the client. The company decided to use a marketing strategy of "layered messages" and related programs to build the corporate brand over the following 6 to 12 months. The foremost intent of the campaign was to make AtomicTangerine synonymous with *venture consulting*. The campaign was to include a wide variety of marketing approaches, involving marketing, client and partner communications with existing clients, promotions, and recruiting efforts.

The marketing plan also involved raising funds. On April 26, 2000, Atomic-Tangerine closed its second round of funding, securing $15 million through the issuance of series B convertible preferred stock. Fornaci explained: "The capital raised will enable us to present our model on a global stage, where we fully expect a variety of companies will recognize our ability to provide first-mover advantage by leveraging quantum leap technologies from SRI International and other innovative labs and partners."

LAUNCHING THE BRAND

AtomicTangerine was launched under its new name as a spin-off of SRI, but one with strong continuing connections with SRI. On April 19, one week after the new name was announced, Business Wire announced the event as involving a spin-off from SRI with no mention of the interim "Adario" name or company. As a result, AtomicTangerine was positioned immediately at the forefront of growing e-business and e-services through its close relationship with SRI International. Dr. Zambre described AtomicTangerine as offering "deep expertise with over-the-horizon technologies such as information security, speech recognition, agent technology and broadband/wireless" technologies for "communications, financial services, product supply chain and digital enterprise markets."

And along came the I Love You virus (see sidebar). AtomicTangerine used the opportunity to come out blazing, announcing its new name, while at the same time entering into a strategic alliance with Diverse Networks to provide a variety of network operations and management services. The alliance was viewed as supportive of AtomicTangerine's efforts in design, deployment, and operation of communication networks and of hosting and supporting data centers for other AtomicTangerine clients.

I Love You—A Viral Opportunity

The former SRI staff now working with AtomicTangerine had developed, among other things, experience with a variety of network and Internet security issues, products, and services. AtomicTangerine provides confidential information to and runs the world's best-known information security multiclient program—the International Information Integrity Institute (1–4)—whose limited membership boasts 75 Global 2000 companies. The company has also conducted more than 500 information security reviews worldwide—on land and online. It led over

3,500 cases in computer crime, incorporated into a proprietary database believed to be the most comprehensive security database in the world. In addition, AtomicTangerine has developed an automated tool for companies to use to protect their infrastructure called NetRadar. This substantial experience positioned AtomicTangerine well to take advantage of the heightened concern over Internet security that followed a global gridlock of love in the form of a virus.

On the morning of May 4, 2000, an insidious and devastating virus began circulating the world, growing in its coverage exponentially as unsuspecting computer users opened up seemingly innocent e-mail messages with the re: line "ILOVEYOU." E-mail systems around the world were overloaded as the virus went into every computer it reached, found address books, and sent itself to everyone on the person's e-mail list. Entire systems crashed from the overload, and individual computers lost files, had files corrupted, and sometimes were wiped out completely. Damage estimates from the virus ran into the billions of dollars, sending companies scrambling to find some way to make their computer systems more secure. The virus crippled corporate and government networks around the globe.

As Fornaci explained, the virus was "a wake-up call for people. This virus moved around the whole world in just 36 hours." He also warned, "What if, instead of just changing .jpg files, the virus had deleted .doc (text) files? Think of the damage that would have caused." As for future threats, Fornaci believes that based on how quickly the I Love You virus spread, the situation is going to accelerate. As Dave Nagy of Global Media Corp. agrees, "It seems like about twice a year now, everyone gets a big scare. The world is really changing from a few years ago when the Internet was free and fun-loving."

The I Love You virus appeared less than a week before the scheduled Internet Defense Summit. SRI and AtomicTangerine were sponsoring the summit. Suddenly, it was getting much more attention. SRI and AtomicTangerine recognized that this presented an opportunity with respect to the newly redefined and renamed fledgling organization (the spin-off) and they acted to take advantage of the virus-created attention and opportunity. SRI was given an opportunity to essentially launch the newly renamed AtomicTangerine for a second time.

At the summit, AtomicTangerine discussed some of its recent activities, including its recent security product development called NetRadar. AtomicTangerine made NetRadar available for free to allow companies to analyze publicly available security information. During his presentation at the summit, Fornaci explained that NetRadar uses artificial intelligence engines to warn organizations of impending attacks in time to allow for offensive security positions to be taken. In addition to NetRadar, AtomicTangerine also announced its recent spin-off, the first since completion of its own spin-off process from SRI. Security/Portal was presented as evidence of AtomicTangerine's mission to create, claim, and own the category of venture consulting. Security/Portal was fully operational with 30 security professions and service offerings of security audits and benchmarks, custom surveys and security alerts, incident response, security forums, and a brand new Internet Security University.

Receiving a significant amount of media attention, the summit was a success and AtomicTangerine's send-off was an exceptionally positive branding experience. As Diane Kegley, AtomicTangerine's director of marketing, noted about the event: "We more or less weaved ourselves into the entire event from the advertisements that were placed in the *Wall Street Journal*, that featured Jonathan's signature next to Sam Armacost and next to Mike Velone, the editor of Forbes, to strategically placed branding throughout the conference, to having Jonathan be one of the lead MCs and really host the day, positioning him as a leader and as the young, up-and-coming CEO of a hot, new company. We used the opportunity to establish our brand and credibility within the context of SRI."

EPILOGUE

As international cyber crime laws were being drafted, a record numbers of IPOs were occurring each month involving mainly dot-com companies, with everyone agreeing that business would never be the same. AtomicTangerine sought to capitalize on these changes by advertising its newly created niche capabilities as a venture consultant. The I Love You "wake-up call" was fortuitously timed for AtomicTangerine. The new name and message had been launched less than a month before and AtomicTangerine sponsored the security summit less than one week after the virus brought companies and governments to a virtual standstill around the world. These coincidences gave AtomicTangerine considerable attention at a critical time.

Media coverage following the summit touted AtomicTangerine as being at the forefront of the growing e-services market, due in part to its close relationship with SRI and joint ventures with many *Fortune* 500 companies. By June 30, 2000, the company had grown to 225 employees in line with year 2000 plans of doubling the number of employees, adding offices in New York and Frankfurt, and reaching revenues of $25 million.

By September 2000, AtomicTangerine seemed to be reaping the success of a very successful launch. Its image firmly entrenched internally and gaining recognition externally, AtomicTangerine could provide testimonials of its successes. Its global business plan was glowing and optimistic. AtomicTangerine outlined a 3- to 5-year vision that involved building "an AtomicTangerine kei-retsu of 100–150 companies" adding "20–30 customers and 3–5 spin-offs per year." The company had expanded its market units and envisioned launching, by the end of 2000, an Integrated Marketing Group market unit in addition to the then existing seven units. Much of AtomicTangerine's confidence was based on its strong alliances at the time, including associations with SRI International, Interpol, Kent Ridge Laboratories, Nuance Communications, Ariba, Oracle, Exodus Communications, Autonomy, Edify, David Sarnoff Research Center, Mitsubishi Electric Company, Oki Electric Industry, NTT Data, Nippon Systems Development, Blaze Software, Skyva International, Diverse Networks and Viacore. Employees were being allowed a $5,000 annual training budget and significant expansion was projected.

Initially, there were no direct competitors that could provide the full range of venture consulting. Quickly, however, AtomicTangerine was joined in the Internet venture consulting field by new competitors, including: marchFirst (claiming to transform businesses, helping them build visionary business models, brands, systems, and processes), Agency.com (committed to inventing new ways to do business online), Chinadotcom (providing a full range of Internet services around the Asia Pacific region), C-quential (focusing on the needs of telecommunications, information technology, media and electronics, and time-enabled industries), Diamond Technology Partners (assisting clients with the development and implementation of digital strategies and business strategies for the digital age), eLoyalty (focusing on the sole goal of providing customer loyalty), Luminant (claiming to "stretch the net" by delivering measurable business results in the form of increased revenues, productivity, and customer loyalty), and Xpedior (claiming to use its proprietary systems to deliver a broad range of services for clients to succeed in the emerging networked economy). In addition, Andersen Consulting had already entered the field with an investment of over a billion dollars, and was quickly joined by other Big 5 firms including Ernst & Young and Deloitte Consulting. In addition, the leading industry periodical, *Consulting News*, which AtomicTangerine's awareness campaign oddly never included, began coverage of activity in the venture consulting field, thus encouraging more entrants.

Notwithstanding the continuing increase in e-business activity, by the end of 2000, many companies had suffered significant declines in their stock value. The average decline by November 2000, was averaging approximately 83 percent. Public and private companies were being forced to lay off employees. Media commentators claimed simply that many companies had not been nimble enough. In the third quarter, many competitors, including US Interactive, Viant, iXL, and Xpedior, announced that they would miss numbers—a foreshadowing of a much more dismal scenario to follow. Speculation began concerning who the survivors would be. Digitrends claimed that dot-coms were closing at a rate of one a day and an Internet site of the failures was born.

By September 2000 the glow for many dot-coms, including AtomicTangerine, was gone. Retrenching, downsizing, restructuring, and blood financing were now issues in the forefront. The sobering effect of the free market was taking its toll on those firms that for whatever reason had not applied the soundest business judgment, or were simply a victim of bad luck and timing. AtomicTangerine delayed its IPO and began to refocus on its deepest strength, its core capability, that is, security consulting. All market units were eliminated and the management team and 100 staff were streamlined and refocused, nonessential offices were closed, and the marketing/branding budgets slashed to reflect a new bottom-line orientation.

There were many lessons to be learned from AtomicTangerine's early months, and small bits of crucial information made monumental differences in the outcome. We outline here some of these lessons and raise questions heavily enlightened by hindsight. We challenge all newcomers in this space to be sure to have in-depth answers to each of the following questions. If you don't, you'll most likely never sustain profitable operations, not too mention make it to a successful IPO.

KEY ELEMENTS FOR VENTURE SUCCESS (See Figure 22–2)

1. Stick to Your Knitting

Almost all new ventures cited in this chapter refocused their energies somewhere along the way. Some refocused very quickly, while others had to be brought to the

FIGURE 22–2   Five Key Elements for Venture Success

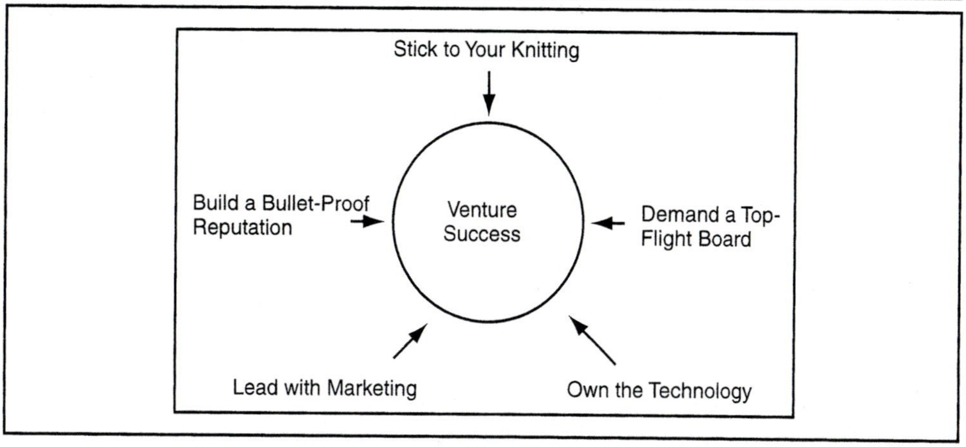

brink of extinction before they would listen. Start-ups need to ask: What are we really good at? Where can we compete best regardless of how "sexy" it is? How do we leverage what we know to new heights? How do we avoid being lured into "new frontiers" where others have played successfully for years?

2. Demand a Top-Flight Board

Expect that many boards will have sound and reasonable intentions, but often little relevant or current experience. Board formation may be required by law, but that does not constitute business acumen. Dissecting board qualifications may reveal a deep knowledge of finances, but little industry experience. Conversely, deep industry experience from years ago may reveal little understanding of today's level of competition. Boards derived from successful parent organizations can be especially hard to work with as they may apply models they've used before, but have little to do with a different type of business. New ventures need to ask: Does the parent board or start-up board really understand the spin-off operations? Have they been in it recently and are they current? Have they succeeded or failed before? What will they do differently? What specific experience do they have? How current is it? Is the board qualified to pick senior officers? How will the spin-off or start-up be affected by CEO turnover, which is fairly frequent? Could the board defend the strategy, the operations, the structure, the culture? How hands-on will they be? Will they be hands-on when they should be? Who will have access to them?

3. Own the Technology

New ventures need to be crystal clear regarding how they are unique and how they will sustain their advantage. This is something many start-ups struggle with as the marketplace is rife with the ashes of "also rans" and "out-of-gas" firms who couldn't sustain advantage. Exclusivity to software or a proprietary methodology is a strategic advantage. Simply having "access to technology" only puts you in the sights of your entire group of competitors. This can be worse than no visibility at all. New ventures need to ask: What does the firm really own and have exclusive rights to? Is the technology truly unique? Tested? Usable? Can our firm implement it or do we need alliances? What is our core strength, and is it renewable? Who else can deliver similar software, and could they be better positioned to regularly upgrade it? Is our focus on the software, the technology, or the implementation?

4. Lead with Marketing (i.e., Sales-Oriented Marketing)

Early-stage organizations are dependent on marketing to drive sales. There should be no mistake about this. Marketing, in turn, must be linked to the sales function, which, in turn, must be driven by the line organization. Well-funded start-ups are often lulled into a false sense of security with significant venture capital money providing a cushion to float, with no discernible end in sight. Top executives from start-ups may place too much emphasis on their roles as business visionaries, spokespersons, or branding gurus, and forget that running a successful new business requires exemplary financial and operational management. Media relations are also critical, but can't take the place of solid bottom-line results. Marketing events are extremely important but need to be orchestrated at the right time by the right team of experts. If too much attention is placed too early on "building the hype," it will only lead to uncomfortable exposure. Instead, the emphasis early on should be on the critical business success factors, especially marketing (by which we mean sales, the right sales, and quality delivery). New ventures should ask: Do we have distinct budgets for marketing, branding, media relations, and the like? Is marketing driving sales? Can we track sales against marketing costs? For every dollar of marketing, what is the return on sales?

5. Build a Bulletproof Reputation

Building reputational capital may well be the greatest challenge faced by the senior executive team. Most start-ups, and any firm looking for an IPO, will come under the microscope of a multitude of stakeholders including the board, the equity investors, industry analysts, financial analysts, customers, suppliers, alliances, media, employees, and government regulators.

Every conceivable metric will be evaluated—and frequently so. Aside from the hard financial data, consulting firms will be very susceptible to additional evaluations for their intangibles such as thought leadership, knowledge management, repeatable methodologies, and management team experience and cohesiveness. Knowledge is a key asset in consulting and can walk out the door very quickly. New ventures need to ask: Are we absolutely sure we are focused on the right things, at the right time, with the right people? Are we spending our money correctly? Is the management team functioning as a unit and setting a good example for the employees? Is the culture stimulating, energetic, open, and motivating? Are all the stakeholders on board with our direction and progress?

No firm will be able to excel on all five critical success factors. Further, we should also add luck as a key success factor that can't be controlled, encompassing new entrants, stock market fluctuations, and government changes. However, firms like Atomic Tangerine and the others noted here, deserve immeasurable credit as true pioneers exploring new business models and taking bold risks. Companies like these are the unsung heroes who dared to take a chance. Clearly, some stumbled along the way, but much can be learned from them that can help the next wave of start-ups as they too leap into the breach of opportunity.

PART V

Being a Consultant

A tidal wave of layoffs took place in the late 1980s, when many large U.S. companies radically restructured and downsized their operations as they struggled to cope with global competition, changing technologies, and deregulation. A surprised workforce made up of middle managers in midlife, most of them with years of industry expertise, found themselves looking for work. Some started businesses and joined the bandwagon of new technology mavens; many more, however, hung out their shingles and started life anew as, you guessed it, "management consultants."

The results were uneven. Most of these people were "content experts" with technical or administrative backgrounds, and few had ever worked as "advisors" to others. The differences between managing and consulting quickly became apparent.

The chapters in Part 5 address the major issues faced when crossing the boundary that separates the managerial world from the consulting world. We begin with a chapter by David Maister who sets the tone by asking: "What is the consultant's role?" This question necessarily causes him to raise questions of professionalism and trust. Maister forces us to confront our own cares and concerns when we work with professionals who ask for our trust.

Dan Idzik and Mark Nevins build on Maister's insights by arguing that strong ethics are the cornerstone of the consulting business. Clients have to trust in their consultants, and consultants must be beyond reproach. In turn, a consulting firm cannot maintain its reputation for objectivity and institutional integrity for long without having in place processes and procedures that are well understood and adhered to by all of its consultants. The authors point to common problems that consultants and consulting firms confront when dealing with confidential client information, with record keeping, with conflicts of interest, with personal relationships, and with cross-cultural considerations. However, codes of conduct go only so far. Ultimately, only professionalism and an institutionalized, firm-wide culture of ethics can ensure against the downside risks of consulting—and in recent years the newspapers have been too full of examples of the perils of *not* adhering to strict ethics.

Given all these vagaries, who then really wants to be a consultant? Mark Nevins and Kristina Alterson pick up that question in Chapter 25. They take a close look at what might motivate smart young professionals to build careers in consulting. Questions of pay, travel, and lifestyle invariably suffuse discussions of consulting as a job choice or career—and this chapter forces personalized thinking about the tradeoffs between what I like to do, what I'm good at doing, and what others are willing to pay me to do. Ultimately, consulting is about problem solving, about working with people, and about client service. It's as simple as that—but not everyone is suited to the demands of the profession.

Of course, being a consultant is also about selling, networking, business building, and managing your contact base, your exposure, and your time. In Chapter 26, Deon Binneman looks at the nitty-gritty of consulting: the need continually to replenish your client base to ensure revenues. Opportunism is key, and capitalizing on past relationships is crucial to the success of every consultant. Like all service professions, consulting is about establishing credibility, and then marketing the heck out of it—systematically.

Consulting is also competitive: it's about putting together winning proposals, getting assignments, persuading clients, and putting yourself on the line. In many ways, it's about being better than anybody else at doing the work. Getting a job in a consulting firm is often the biggest stumbling block: as consulting careers have become more attractive to MBA students, so have jobs become more difficult to get. To identify the "best of the best," consulting firms have developed sophisticated screening mechanisms, not least of which is the "case interview." In Chapter 27, Daniel Oriesek and Charles Fombrun describe typical case interviews, and how they create stressful situations for consulting candidates as a way to replicate the conditions consultants experience in working with clients. In business schools around the world, consulting clubs gather regularly to put their students through grueling exercises intended to simulate the unsettling process that many consulting firms use to recruit the best graduates. These exercises help prevent the otherwise embarrassing responses uninformed candidates make to the kinds of brain-teasers and problem situations they are exposed to during typical consulting interviews.

Chapter 29 gets personal, as it reports results of a survey of MBA students who worked as summer interns in a consulting firm, and compares their responses to those of consultants with over three years' work experience in a consulting firm. The respondents make revealing comments about their interviewing experiences, the mentoring process, what they've learned, and how well they've adapted to life in the fast lane of the consulting world. They offer responses to the probing question that Mark Nevins and Kristina Alterson asked earlier in Part 5: So, you want to be a consultant? Judge for yourselves.

CHAPTER 23

The Consultant's Role

David H. Maister

Early in my career, the management team of a large professional firm asked my opinion about how they were conducting their affairs. I responded with an honest, direct, and candid answer. "Here are the things you are messing up, and this is what you should have been doing." To my surprise, I was fired for being a disruptive influence. This was hard to understand since I knew (and I knew that *they* knew) that I was correct in my diagnosis and prescriptions.

Eventually, I learned the obvious lesson. It is not enough for a consultant to be *right*: An advisor's job is to be *helpful*. I had to "earn the right" to be critical. Critiquing one's clients is, *by definition*, a part of every consultant's job, since suggestions on how to improve things *always* imply that all is not being done well at the moment. We must not only be smart, we must be diplomatic, sensitive, gentle, and behave in such a way that we are trusted!

Many consultants approach the task of giving advice as if it were an objective, rational exercise based on their technical knowledge and expertise. However, consulting is almost never an exclusively logical process. Rather, it is almost always an emotional "duet," played between the consultant and the client. If you can't learn to recognize, deal with, and respond to client emotions (and client politics), you will never be an effective consultant.

To see how the success of your career depends on these things, consider your own purchases of professional services. Whether you are hiring someone to look after your legal affairs, your taxes, your child, or your car, the act of retaining a professional requires you to put your affairs in someone else's hands. You are forced into an act of faith, and you can only hope that the person you choose will deal with you appropriately. When the final decision on whom to hire comes, you must ultimately decide to trust someone with your "baby," which is never a comfortable thing to do.

Here are some other common emotions you and your clients might feel when selecting and working with an outside advisor:

David Maister has been a consultant to prominent firms in a broad spectrum of professions for two decades. He holds degrees from the University of Birmingham, the London School of Economics, and the Harvard Business School.

1. I'm feeling <u>insecure</u>. I'm not sure I know how to detect which of the finalists is the genius, and which is just good. I've exhausted my abilities to make technical distinctions.

2. I'm feeling <u>threatened</u>. This is my area of responsibility, and even though intellectually I know I need outside expertise, emotionally it's not comfortable to put my affairs in the hands of others.

3. I'm taking a <u>personal risk</u>. By putting my affairs in the hands of someone else, I risk losing control.

4. I'm <u>impatient</u>. I didn't call in someone at the first sign of symptoms (or opportunity). I've been thinking about this for a while.

5. I'm <u>worried</u>. By the very fact of suggesting improvements or changes, these people are going to be implying that I haven't been doing it right up till now. Are these people going to be on my side?

6. I'm <u>exposed.</u> Whomever I hire, I'm going to have to reveal some proprietary secrets, not all of which are flattering.

7. I'm feeling <u>ignorant</u>, and don't like the feeling. I don't know if I've got a simple problem or a complex one. I'm not sure I can trust them to be honest about that: It's in their interest to convince me it is complex.

8. I'm <u>skeptical</u>. I've been burned before by these kinds of people. You get a lot of promises. How do I know whose promise I should buy?

9. I'm <u>concerned</u> that they either can't or won't take the time to understand what makes my situation special. They'll try to sell me what they've got rather than what I need.

10. I'm <u>suspicious</u>. Will they be those typical consultants who are hard to get hold of, who are patronizing, who leave you out of the loop, who befuddle you with jargon, who don't explain what they're doing or why? In short, will these people deal with me in the way I want to be dealt with?

What all this shows is that when retaining and working with a consultant, what you want is someone who understands your interests, and will not put their interests ahead of yours while working for you. You want someone you can trust to do the right thing. You want someone who will *care*.

Have you ever had a trusted advisor? Someone you turned to in order to help you solve your problems? What made them so helpful to you? Here is a listing of traits that great trusted advisors have in common. They:

1. Seem to understand us, effortlessly, and like us
2. Are consistent: We can depend on them
3. Always help us see things from fresh perspectives
4. Don't try to force things on us
5. Help us think things through (though ultimately it's our decision)
6. Don't substitute their judgment for ours
7. Don't panic or get overemotional: they stay calm
8. Help us *think* and separate our logic from our emotion
9. Criticize and correct us gently, lovingly
10. Don't pull their punches: we can rely on them to tell us the truth
11. Are in it for the long haul (the relationship is more important than the current issue)
12. Give us reasoning (to help us think) not just their conclusions
13. Give us options, increase our understanding of those options, give us their recommendation, and let us choose

14. Challenge our assumptions: help us uncover the false assumptions we've been working under

15. Make us feel comfortable and casual personally (but they take the issues seriously)

16. Act like a person, not someone in a role

17. Are reliably on our side, and always seem to have our interests at heart

18. Remember everything we ever said (without notes)

19. Are always honorable: they don't gossip about others (we trust their values)

20. Help us put our issues in context, often through the use of metaphors, stories, and anecdotes (few problems are completely unique)

21. Have a sense of humor to diffuse (our) tension in tough situations

22. Are smart (sometimes in ways we're not)

What is significant about this list is that it is only in small part about intellectual skills. Equally critical are the items we are rarely taught: social skills, interpersonal skills, and, above all, emotional skills. All are critical to being a successful consultant.

FOCUS ON THE OTHER PERSON

There is an old saying: "You'll have more fun and success by focusing on helping other people achieve their goals than you will by focusing on your own goals." For some this sounds like an idealistic, spiritual, or religious principle. Others may think of it as communism: a cry to place others before yourself. However, a moment's reflection will reveal that the aphorism is the very definition of what a capitalist exchange economy is about. To get what you want from someone, you must first focus on giving them what they want!

This is harder than it looks. In the midst of a conversation with a client, we are likely to find ourselves thinking things like, "How will I solve this problem?" "How will I get the client to buy this idea?" "What am I going to say when the client finishes talking?" "How can I appear expert?" We're not thinking about them. We're thinking about our reactions to them. We're thinking about *ourselves*.

If we strip down all these distractions to the core, we are likely to find fear at the root: fear of embarrassment, of failure, of appearing ignorant or incompetent, or fear of loss of reputation or security. Ironically, the service professions attract people who are prone to these fears.

More often than not, consultants are high achievers who have consistently overcome our fears through constant application of skill and hard work in the pursuit of technical mastery. And, up to a point, these things are rewarded. In the early levels of consulting life, we are often asked to focus on little else.

Then comes that crucial career transition, from technician to full professional, from content expert to advisor. As technicians, our task is to provide information, analyses, research, content and even recommendations. All of these are basically tasks performed out of the clients' presence. In contrast, our task as advisors is an "in-person," "in-contact" challenge to help the client see things anew or to make a decision. This requires a complete change of skills and mindsets.

It can be unsettling to find that the client is primarily interested in having his or her problem understood, in all its emotional and political complexity, as a precondition to having the problem diagnosed and solved. Some of us never make it over this hurdle. The key to prior career success (technical excellence) can actually become an impediment at this level.

The types of people who typically succeed in consultant service firms are often driven, rational, and meritocratic, with a high need to achieve. It is the natural thing for such people to stay focused on their own individual performance, (something that is reinforced by many firm cultures), and to look for confirmation that what *they* are doing is all right. This is not a situation conducive to building skills in developing trust. It is in some sense a wonder that so many do so well.

Another prime obstacle to focusing successfully on the other person is the apparently common belief that mastery of technical content is sufficient to serve clients well. It is ironic that a business in which the serving of clients depends so heavily on interpersonal psychology should be peopled with those who believe in the *exclusive* power of technical mastery.

The professions are havens of rationality for those less comfortable with a more direct, emotional approach to life. Good social skills and an excellent mind, in the professions, can generally compensate for a very large degree of emotional avoidance. Combined with an ethos that worships the mind, it is not surprising that some advisors feel that working on consulting skills such as intimacy is risky and uncomfortable.

AN EXAMPLE

I once had to hire a lawyer to probate a relative's will. The first few lawyers I spoke with tried to win my business by telling me when their firm was founded (really!), how many offices they had, and how much they would charge. None of this inspired much confidence. In fact, the more they talked about themselves and their firms, the less interested they appeared to be in me and my problems.

Finally, I encountered a lawyer who, in the initial phone call, asked how much I knew about probating a will. My reply was "Nothing!" The lawyer then offered to fax to me a comprehensive outline of the steps involved, what I needed to rush to do, and what I should forget about for a while because it was not urgent. The fax also provided the phone numbers of all the governmental bodies I needed to notify, even though this had nothing to do with the legal work (or the lawyer's fees).

All of this (immensely helpful) information was provided freely (and for free) before the lawyer had been retained. Naturally, he got the business. He had built confidence by demonstrating that he knew what information was most relevant to me, even though some of it had nothing to with the practice of estate law. He had earned trust by being generous with his knowledge, and proving that he was willing to earn the potential client's business. He wasn't focused on himself: He was focused on me, and it was irresistible!

PROFESSIONAL OR PROSTITUTE?

Whenever a consultant is trying to sell something, there is only one question on the client's mind: "Why are you trying to sell me something?" There are two possible conclusions the client could come to. First, he or she might believe that the consultant is trying to sell something just to get more revenues. Or the client might believe that the consultant is trying to sell something because he or she is interested in the client, truly cares, and is sincerely trying to help.

Under what conditions is the sale made? It should be clear that new business will be won only to the extent that the client believes that the consultant is interested, cares, and is trying to help. The noble path wins. One *could* argue that the consultant's task is to make the client *think* that the consultant cares, i.e., consultants must learn how to fake sincerity. (Indeed, many sales training courses are filled with such tips and tactics.) However, faking sincerity is a prostitute's tactic, not a professional's. It may work occasionally, but not as often as real sincerity.

Is this moral counsel or business advice? Either way, the conclusion is the same. You will get hired, rehired, obtain referrals, and have lessened fee sensitivity to the extent that you care passionately, both about your work and your clients. Believe passionately in what you do, and never knowingly compromise your standards and values. Act like a true professional, aiming for true excellence and the money will follow. Act like a prostitute, with an attitude of "I'll do it for the money, but don't expect me to care," and you'll lose the premium that excellence earns. True professionalism wins!

HOW MUCH DO YOU CARE?

Very few consultants become known by their clients as "great" purely as a result of their intellectual or technical abilities. The opposite of the word *professional* is not "unprofessional"—the opposite of professional is "technician." Professionalism is predominantly an attitude, not a set of competencies. A real professional is a technician who cares. (You may recall the old slogan "People don't care how much you know until they know how much you care.")

One of my favorite discussion questions is to ask people "Why do you do what you do?" Too many consultants don't do what they do because they want to help their clients: They're in it only for the money or the personal prestige. Such consultants may become good—and even earn good incomes—but they will never be considered great. The reason is simple: The clients can tell! (If you're not sure you believe this, draw on your own experiences as a buyer. Can you tell if your doctor really cares, showing an interest in you as an individual? Does it matter to you? Can you tell if your accountant is just sticking to the technical tasks, or thinking ahead on your behalf? Does it matter? Does it affect your buying behavior?)

Being a professional is neither about making money nor about your professional fulfillment. Both of these are consequences of an unqualified dedication to excellence in serving clients and their needs.

Perhaps it is time for our schools, and our consultant firms, to stop teaching students that they are the best and the brightest, the special elite in the noblest profession of all (whatever that profession happens to be). Maybe schools and firms should find ways to teach more about what it is to *serve* a client, and about how to work with *people* (not just business problems). When I talk with business school alumni about their careers and what they would do differently, the most common reply is "I wish I had paid more attention to the courses about dealing with people."

Consulting success requires more than talent. Among other things, it requires drive, initiative, commitment, involvement and, above all, enthusiasm. Yet these things are often missing from consultants' lives. Consider the following quiz.

Think back on all the work you have done in the past year or so, and divide it into one of three categories. The first category is "God, I love this! *This* is why I do what I do!" The second category is "It's okay, I can tolerate it—it's what I do for a living." The last category is "I hate this part—I wish I could get rid of this junk!" Before reading on, estimate your answers to this question.

Figured it out? Then let me report the results of putting this question to top consultants in prestige firms around the world. The typical answers I am given are 20 to 25 percent for "God, I love this!"; 60 to 70 percent for "I can tolerate it"; and 5 to 20 percent for "I hate this part." In other words, the typical consultant in a top firm is (I am told) positively enjoying his or her work about one day a week.

Now, a second question: Think about all the clients you have served in the past year and, again, divide them into one of three categories. Category one is: "I like these people, and their industry fascinates me." (Yes, I know I'm combining two things.) Category two is: "I can tolerate these people and their business is okay—neither fascinating nor boring." Category three is: "I'm professional enough that I would never say this to them, and I'll still do my best for them, but the truth is these are not my kind of people and I have no interest in their industry."

Ready to compare results? Typical answers from top consultants around the world are 30 to 35 percent for "I like these people," 50 to 60 percent for "I can tolerate them," and 15 to 20 percent for "I really don't care for them." (I must stress that these are *not* my opinions about professional life, but what individuals in top-drawer firms tell me about their work lives.)

These estimates provide the single biggest reason to reintroduce some energy into your professional life, and into the process of client development. Why spend the majority of your professional life working on *tolerable* stuff for *acceptable* clients when, with some effort in (for example) client relations, marketing and selling, you can spend your days working on exciting things for interesting people? Do you really want to have your tombstone say "He (or she) spent his life doing tolerable stuff for people he could tolerate, because they paid him?"

A consultant should build skills necessary for practice development (generating business) for one main reason: The better you are at getting hired, the better the chance you will have to work on fun stuff for people you can care about, and the less you will be forced to take on work and clients you don't truly enjoy, simply to "feed the baby."

As my probate lawyer, described above, illustrated, getting hired has no magic to it. If you really *are* interested in a client, and can clearly demonstrate both your ability and willingness to help them, you can earn their trust. The biggest trouble for many consultants is that they haven't taken the time to figure out who they do like. You don't have to like every client—indeed, that's the whole point, you can't. You need to figure it out. Now!

When one reviews who is successful (and happy) among consultants, it quickly emerges that it has nothing to do with IQ, where you went to school, or what training you received. Those who succeed are those who can sustain the magic and excitement they felt when they were first setting out to build a career, and were willing to work to "make it happen." All it takes to find the fun is a little energy, excitement, ambition, drive, enthusiasm—and passion! However, so scarce are these characteristics today, they have turned out to be the dominant competitive advantage for both individual consultants and firms.

The good news is that professionalism and marketing are not in conflict with each other at all: They are the same thing. Both are defined by a dedication to being of service and helping people.

BUILDING BUSINESS RELATIONSHIPS

In our ordinary lives, when we want to build a strong relationship, we try to be understanding, thoughtful, considerate, sensitive to feelings, and supportive. All of these adjectives apply equally well to what is needed to build a strong business relationship.

To earn a relationship, you must go first. The client must visibly perceive that you are willing to be the first to make an investment in the relationship, in order to earn and deserve it. You want to get hired by someone, someday? Find a way to be helpful to them now. Even if it's only a small gesture, give something.

Small gestures can count as much as big ones, as long as they don't become too rote. Take the issue of proving or demonstrating that you care about the relationship and value it. On a random day, of no particular significance, call your client and say, "I've been thinking about you, and ran across some information that made me start thinking, and I have an idea for you. I don't think it involves us, I just wanted to contribute the idea to you."

What are you demonstrating by this action? That you care, that you're thinking about the client in the client's terms, not yours, that you are a source of ideas (some good, some not so good) and that you are someone they will want to stay in touch with. Not a bad set of outcomes for such a simple action.

To make anyone believe something about you, you must demonstrate, not assert. For example, your questions can reveal that you have done your homework: "I know by the research we've done on your firm that you merged with ABC nine years ago to become third largest in the world. What I would like to learn more about is how you cope with the integration challenges of employees from so many cultures and backgrounds."

Such questions give evidence that you are thorough, that you respect the client's time enough to be prepared, and that you are ready to get right to the issues.

At the core of building a relationship with someone is convincing them that you are dealing with them as a human being, and not as a member of a group or class or subset. Accordingly, as you listen to a client talk, the question on your mind should be: "What makes this person different from any other client I've served? What does that mean for what I should say and how I should behave?"

Unfortunately, this is hard work. The natural tendency of most of us is to do the exact opposite: We listen for the things we recognize and have met before, so that we can draw upon past experience to use the words, approaches and tools that we already know well. It's the way most of us work, but it doesn't always serve us well.

Before you can help people, you need to understand what's on *their* mind. You must create situations in which they will tell you more about their issues, concerns, and needs.

WHAT ROLE ARE YOU PLAYING?

Also essential to being an effective consultant is having a good understanding of one's role. This is illustrated by a friend of ours, who once said: "Sometimes I feel like I'm explaining things to a child. My client can't seem to grasp even the basic logic of what I'm trying to convey. I feel like saying, 'Shut up, just accept what I'm telling you! I'm the expert here!'"

What makes this friend's comments so understandable is that, in many advisory relationships, the client may be untrained in the consultant's specialty, while the consultant may have seen the client's problem (or variants of it) many times before. There is thus an almost constant threat of coming across to the client as patronizing, pompous, and arrogant.

It is understandable why advisors can feel this way, and it is equally clear why clients resent it. After all, when I'm the client, I'm the one in charge. If I don't understand what you are saying, then maybe the problem is you, not me. Maybe you don't know how to convey what you know and understand to a lay person. *Of course* I don't know your field, that's why I hired you! *Explain* it to me in language I can understand. Help me get it! Your job is not just to assert conclusions, but to help me *understand* why your recommended course of action makes sense. Give me reasons, not just instructions!

Excellence in advice giving requires not only the right attitude, but also a careful attention to language. There are always a number of ways of expressing the same thought, each of which differs in how it is received by the listener. Saying "You've got to do X," even when correct, is very likely to evoke emotional resistance. No one likes to be told that they *must* do anything (even when they do).

It is usually better to say something like:

Let's go through the options together. These are the ones I see. Can you think of anything else that we should consider? Now let's go through the pros and cons of each course of action. Based on those pros and cons, action X seems the most likely to work, doesn't it? Or can you think of a better solution?

If the client doesn't want to do X, the conversation is still alive. If you've said "you've got to do X" and the client says "No, I don't," you've got nowhere to go. Your effectiveness as an advisor has just been lost, and you have placed yourself and the client on opposite sides. The odds are that what will follow will be an argument, not a discussion.

In many ways consulting skills are similar to those of great teaching. A teacher's task is to help a student get from point A (what they know, understand, and believe now) to point B (an advanced state of deeper understanding and knowledge). It is poor teaching for the professor to stand at the front of the class and say: "B is the right answer!" (As the old joke says, a lecture is the fastest means known for getting ideas from the notes of the teacher into the notes of the student without passing through the minds of either.)

A teacher needs two skills to be really effective. First, the teacher must have a good understanding of point A: Where is the student (or client) starting from? What does he or she understand now? What do they believe and why do they believe it? For what messages are they ready? What are they doing now and why are they doing it that way?

The second required skill is to develop a step-by-step reasoning process that takes the student/client on a journey of discovery. The goal here is to influence the student/client's understanding so that, eventually, the student/client says: "You know, on reflection, I think B is a better answer," to which the teacher/advisor can respond "Okay, that's what we'll do!"

Among other things, effective advice giving requires an ability to suppress one's own ego and emotional needs. It is immensely tempting once a client describes an issue to jump in, even before the client has finished talking, and say "Oh, I know the answer to that one, that's easy!" There is no surer way to give offense than to be too overeager to show off one's expertise!

DO YOU HAVE THE COURAGE?

The single biggest barrier to success in consulting is courage. Many consultants (and consulting firms) lack the guts to stick with the plans and goals they have set for themselves.

I first learned this lesson some time ago, when I set for myself the goal of trying to become a strategic advisor to international professional firms. Shortly thereafter, a firm asked me to accept a project conducting sales and marketing training courses for their people.

The assignment was very attractive: a large volume of familiar, comfortable, enjoyable work, which would provide a significant portion of my revenue target for the year. However, it was obvious that spending most of my year doing sales skills training would do nothing to help me achieve my strategic goal. Rather than becoming a strategic advisor, I would, by the end of that year, be a sales trainer.

Taking the expedient path would not have been immoral, but it would have meant that I would not have obtained the benefits of my declared strategy. Obviously, resisting the expedient path is hard. You have to really bet on yourself and believe your own vision. You have to have the courage of your own convictions. Believing in the benefits of your goals is one thing; living by the diets that are necessary to achieve those goals is another.

So which did I want? Easy cash (and it was *a lot!*) or an ambitious strategy that would require hard work to create? Did I want a comfortable, well-paid year or one in which I had to accept the burden of generating an equivalent number of days of "real" work that would move me toward my strategic goal as well as generate income? I decided to stick with my strategy and pass on the "easy money" opportunity. I arranged for a friend to look after my client, and worked hard (and successfully) to bring in the kind of work that was "on strategy."

All strategies, at some time or the other, involve a trade-off between short-term cash (doing what's expedient) and executing the strategy (living the vision of excellence you have set for yourself). If you're going to pursue a strategy, you must be willing to make hard choices and act as if you truly believe in your own strategy. In short, having a strategy takes courage.

Business life is filled with daily temptations, short-term expediencies, and wonderful excuses why we can't afford to execute our strategy today. Accordingly, that new article never gets written, work is delegated only when it must be (not when it can be), the junior staff remains only "adequately" supervised, and the marketing principle is "We never met a dollar of revenue we didn't like!"

The importance of courage is not meant to be an inspirational point, but simple logic. In business and professional life, you reap the benefits of what you actually do, not what you hope to get around to doing someday if it is convenient and you're not too busy. If you want to be known as excellent at something then you have to *be* reliably, consistently, excellent at that thing.

If you don't feel passionate about it, if you can't *care*, don't become a consultant!

CHAPTER

Strong Ethics: The Cornerstone of Professionalism in Consulting

Daniel R. Idzik and Mark D. Nevins

" What do ethics have to do with growing the bottom line?" It seems that question arises in senior executives' discussions less frequently today than in years past. However, it is not difficult to imagine that "business ethics" was regarded as a quaint oxymoron by, for example, the most senior executives of Archer Daniels Midland—who created a corporate environment that resulted in the company's pleading guilty in 1996 to price-fixing conspiracies, paying a $100 million fine, and having its reputation sullied, perhaps for good. Archer Daniels Midland is not a unique story: The last few years have seen an alarming number of headlines related to corporate malfeasance and a lack of ethics and principles: Enron, WorldCom, and how many more before this chapter sees print? A sizable list could easily be drawn up of companies who have suffered financial losses or damage to their brand because of missteps and infractions, and the cases that have received public exposure undoubtedly represent only a fraction of the actual losses suffered annually by corporations due to a failure to adhere to a strong set of ethics, values, and principles.

Fortunately, more corporations are now recognizing that ethical behavior is important to their success. The enlightened view requires a shift in perception—from an attitude that ethical behavior should be encouraged in order to avoid punishment to a more positive affirmation that a strong culture of values can in fact drive performance and profitability; that is, that ethics are not just "nice," but that they make compelling business sense. A 1999 study conducted by DePaul University found that "companies committed to ethical business practices do better financially and have significantly greater representation among the top 100 financial performers than companies that do not make ethics a key component of management."[1] And there are few better case illustrations of the power of values than the manner in which Johnson & Johnson han-

---

Daniel R. Idzik joined the firm of Booz Allen Hamilton, Inc., in 1967. He has lectured extensively and conducted seminars related to corporate and professional ethics and responsibilities. He is a graduate of Harvard Law School.

Mark D. Nevins is President of Nevins Consulting, and a moderator for The Aspen Institute's Executive Seminar on values-based leadership. Dr. Nevins has been global head of organizational development and training for both Booz Allen Hamilton and Korn/Ferry International. He received a PhD in English Literature from Harvard University.

[1]Curtis C. Verschoor, *Management Accounting*, October 1999; referenced in *The New York Times*, October 18, 2000.

dled the Tylenol cyanide poisoning scare in the 1980s: immediately addressing the problem, being open and honest with shareholders and the general public, and taking a short-term loss (by recalling millions of bottles, destroying stock, and instituting additional safety measures) that has resulted in long-term profitability. Remarkably, and probably to the dismay of their competitors, following that incident the company's image and profitability actually *improved* because of the way the matter was handled.

Given today's headlines, there should be little, if any, room for doubt that good ethics make good business, particularly in professional service firms. Successful professional service firms, employing "the best and the brightest" graduates and offering high-quality services to prestigious clients, cannot grow and prosper if they do not aggressively protect their reputations for objectivity and integrity. Consulting firms do not sell products—they sell services, and the foundation for their reputation is trust, honesty, and principles of the highest order. Endangering in any way, even "trivially," the faith that a client places in a consultant undermines the entire relationship between client and consulting firm: the trust, brand, and reputation that can take years, or decades, to build across an entire firm can be weakened or destroyed by the irresponsibility or misbehavior of a single consultant. A precarious balance indeed, and a matter that is of extreme importance to professional services firms, as former employees of the once lauded Arthur Andersen can certainly attest.

Adhering to ethical behavior, however, is not always easy—not since the Garden of Eden, and certainly not in the complex world of multinational business. Our global economy raises additional complications, because values sometimes prove not to be universal. In different situations, different "rules of the game" may come into play. For example, an American consultant working in a non-U.S. environment may come into contact with ethical gray areas, or behaviors that seem problematic but are not specifically legislated against or policed—and these situations may be referred to euphemistically as "cultural differences." Above and beyond the fact that a U.S.-based company can be accountable to American law in its foreign offices or subsidiaries, it is worth considering an example that points out the wisdom (and profitability) of taking the ethical high road in any case.

Several years ago a major management consulting firm submitted a competitive proposal for a large assignment to a governmental agency in a Middle Eastern country. In a month or so, the consultants were informed by a well-known "commission" firm headquartered in that country that their proposal was judged to be superior, but that if awarded the contract the consultants would have to agree to a 10 percent "commission," and that the commission could be built into the final contract price. The discussion between the consulting firm's senior executives was brief and unanimous: They advised the governmental agency that the proposal was being withdrawn. Within 48 hours the consulting firm's offices in more than a half-dozen countries were called by representatives of the "commission" firm and told that "your American executives don't know how to do business in this part of the world." A year later, that same consulting firm was invited to submit a proposal to another governmental agency in the same country. Through an intermediary, the firm was able to determine that it was highly likely that another successful proposal would result in the same unwelcome "commission" request. The consulting firm declined to bid, and the governmental agency was advised informally of the reason for the decision.

Two years later, proposals were requested for one of the largest nonconstruction projects that country's government had ever undertaken. Considering whether or not to bid, the consulting firm in question once again inquired about the business practices surrounding the project, and this time the executives were assured that they would not face the "commission" request if the proposal were accepted. The proposal was accepted. When negotiating the contract, the firm's legal counsel was asked, "Do you know why you're going to get this contract, and get it at the price you quoted?" The counsel replied that he assumed the proposal was more responsive than others were, and that the fees quoted were reasonable. The response was, "Yes, but over and above that, the government said that it wants no question to be raised about this contract being 'clean'—and you people have a reputation for being clean." That contract led to enduring relationships in that country for the consulting firm, which resulted in fees totaling tens of millions of dollars, with no further requests for "commissions."

The moral of the story? Good business ethics lead to good business; a commitment to sticking to values and principles—to "who we are"—creates a "virtuous cycle" that raises perception and profitability. Conversely, succumbing to the "everybody does it" argument to justify shoddy professional practices, whether in the United States or in other countries, inevitably leads to unpredictable and potentially (legally) hazardous activities that are difficult to monitor and that will drive out quality professionals. Like a chain, a consulting firm is only as strong as its weakest link—its foundation is only as firm as the behavior of each of its professionals.

WHY ETHICS?

Building an ethical foundation, creating and nurturing a set of values that all of the professionals in the firm live by—these efforts are "fuzzy" and "soft" and seemingly unrelated to the business of solving client problems and getting work done. Why expend the effort?

A consulting firm's reputation is fundamentally grounded in the professional excellence with which it serves its clients and the uncompromising integrity of each member of its staff. A consulting firm cannot maintain a reputation for objectivity and institutional integrity without having in place supportive processes and procedures that are well understood and adhered to by its employees at all levels in the organization. A consulting firm's only real and enduring assets are its people—well-educated and well-trained professionals who have explicitly chosen to work for that firm in large part because of its reputation. Quality professionals are a strategic differentiator and are critical to maintaining the strong brand and reputation, and quality professionals relate best to companies and colleagues who believe in and maintain high ethical and professional standards:

- These professionals want a sense of pride in their firm and in its accomplishments. (They want to be able to look into the mirror in the morning and feel good about the firm that employs them.)

- They want their firm to have a reputation for professional competence, excellence, and integrity—above and beyond compensation and opportunity for growth, the firm's reputation is one of the keys to attraction and retention. (They want to be able to feel proud of their employer when they talk with friends and acquaintances.)

- They want to believe that they are a special group of people who, because of their competence and promise, deserve to be associated with the firm. (Again, here is the basis for that "virtuous cycle"—good ethics lead to a strong ethical culture, which reinforces good ethics.)
- They would want their mothers to be proud of them if their mothers knew what they were doing, how they were doing it, and who they were associating with professionally!

Fundamentally, "the best" want to be associated with "the best." Professionals are most satisfied and productive working in organizations they believe to be ethical. In a time when it is increasingly difficult to attract and retain highly talented individuals, a strong ethical culture and practices offer a powerful reason for a consulting firm to ensure that it is respected not only for the quality of its services but as an employer who really is committed to "doing the right thing."

Values also have a great deal to do with how a consulting firm is perceived by its clients and potential clients. "Branding" is a result not of the efforts of the marketing department so much as it is an outcome of the cumulative actions of each consultant each day, over time. A firm's brand and reputation are the aggregate of every single consultant's behaviors, activities, and decisions. It is of paramount importance for the firm to be made up of high-quality professionals with a strong ethical bent, who will in turn create and maintain a culture that attracts like-minded professionals—the "virtuous cycle" that over time embodies the essence of the firm for current and potential clients and employees.

SNARES AND PITFALLS: THE MOST COMMON ETHICAL CONSIDERATIONS FOR MANAGEMENT CONSULTANTS

The lifeblood of consulting is the application of professional experience and rigorous analysis in order to develop recommendations for clients. Since information and data are critical to quality results, it is imperative that all consultants be trained to ensure the integrity of the data on which they rely. Objectivity and integrity demand that data are collected from reliable sources and that strict intellectual rigor is applied in analyzing data and framing recommendations. In serving their clients, consultants must maintain their objectivity at all times—they have a duty to their clients to ensure that they do not obscure, distort, or omit significant findings or recommendations even if the client may not welcome them. It may be politic to present findings and recommendations in a manner that will gain client acceptance, but a professional consultant must, in the end, "tell it like it is." The best consulting firms ensure that their internal culture and training programs establish integrity in serving clients and the primacy of the clients' interests as cornerstones of its value system. Many of the more complex or sophisticated points of ethics derive from this basic and unwavering commitment to integrity and intellectual honesty.

The task of codifying policies and procedures to address adequately all areas that raise ethical concerns for consulting firms may not be an easy one. Codes of ethics, or values statements, are complicated documents to draft, and moreover they are useless if they are not followed. In fact, it can be more damaging to the firm and its professionals if the "values in action" do not align with the "espoused values." Furthermore, as analytical and often highly independent creatures, consultants tend to accept little at face value—therefore, most strong ethical cultures are based not on *rules* but on *values*. If I give you a rule book, you may question specific rules, argue about their applicability in this situation versus that one, or simply fail to have the rule book in hand when it comes time to make a critical decision. However, if I provide you with a set of values or principles, and am confident that you agree with these values, I can be more assured that you will behave in an appropriate manner or make the right decision even in circumstances that I might not be able to imagine at this time.

The power of values will be discussed further; for now, there are a handful of common and frequent problem areas and potential "hot spots" that should be addressed in training programs as well as in policies and procedures.

Safeguarding Client Confidential Information

Clear rules have to be in place to ensure that the identity of clients and the nature of the consulting services being rendered to specific clients are kept completely confidential. As a rule, information should not be shared within a consulting organization except on a strict "need-to-know basis." Staff members should be made sensitive to the potential damage to clients' interests that can result from unguarded conversations in elevators, restaurants, and over cell phones.

Documents and computers containing client confidential information must be securely maintained at all times. While it is not unusual for consultants to work on airplanes, writing or reviewing reports, common sense dictates that you should make sure nothing is visible that would disclose client information. You might also make an effort to ensure the person seated next to you is someone who would not be interested in what you are doing. (Why not ask?—if the person sitting next to you is not another consultant or a competitor of your client, he or she might be a potential future client, and worth getting to know!)

One of the obligations of any officer or project manager is to establish what is "client confidential information" and under what circumstances, if any, client information or information gathered in providing services to one client can be utilized in serving another client. And in the absence of such clear stipulations, good consultants will err on the conservative side.

Record Retention

Without question, concerns related to protecting client confidential information and record retention have multiplied substantially in recent years. Laptops and the Internet are marvelous for facilitating the dissemination of information, but they can be dangerous technology for losing control of sensitive information. Most worrisome are those "packrat" consultants who hoard and preserve interview notes, client-furnished data, draft sections of client reports, and similar materials—sometimes long after the project has come to a close. The potential for such materials to do damage is generally much greater than any benefit they may have.

Concerns in the area of retaining materials are not only related to control of client confidential information. In a highly litigious environment such as the United States, consultants and their records are frequently subpoenaed in litigation involving their clients. Observations drawn from interviews, which frequently are tentative or speculative, or drafts of reports and internal communications among consulting team members, may contain comments or other notes that can be detrimental to a client's interests (or the consulting firm's interests) when reviewed by litigation lawyers years later. As a general guideline, upon the completion of a client assignment, all working papers, interview notes, and drafts of reports should be reviewed. Unless there are good reasons to retain specific information, all such documentation (including related materials on computers) should be destroyed or, as appropriate, returned to the client. "Scrubbed" information and intellectual capital, devoid of client-specific or client-proprietary information, may be stored on knowledge systems or data warehouses, but care must be taken to ensure that such materials really are generic.

Conflicts of Interest

Most large consulting firms provide services to clients with competing interests. Firms may differ in how they identify, deal with, and resolve potential conflicts of interest; however, clear rules, established with the guidance of the firm's experience, have to be in place. Conflicts cannot be dealt with on an *ad-hoc*, one-off basis. Resolving conflicts by comparing the revenue of one assignment against another, or on the basis of which consulting partner or officer has more clout, place the reputation of a consulting firm at risk. A consulting firm has to establish a conflict resolution mechanism that, as objectively as possible, gathers the facts, hears the arguments, carefully considers the clients' interests, and makes a decision on behalf of the firm. The senior partners/officers charged with such responsibility must be widely respected within the firm for their integrity and judgment.

Providing consulting services to a client with fees determined in whole or in part on a contingency basis potentially gives rise to a thicket of serious conflicts of interest and ethical concerns. It is difficult to avoid questions concerning the objectivity of your recommendations and their strategic or tactical consequences if a significant portion of your fees is, as is often the case in such situations, determined by near-term savings or profits. Nonetheless, many companies are now asking their consultants to enter into such arrangements. Consulting firms and their clients should understand fully the potential conflicts inherent in many such arrangements, discuss them openly, provide for mutually agreed-upon safeguards, and document their understandings. A more recent trend of consulting firms taking equity interests in start-up company clients in lieu of professional fees has already raised difficult conflict-of-interest issues.

A consulting firm's conflict of interest policies should be made known to and understood by all members of its professional staff. Staff members should also understand that they have a personal responsibility to identify and avoid conflicts of interest. Consulting firms must ensure that separate consulting teams conduct assignments involving similar issues for competing clients and that procedures are in place to ensure that client information is never shared. Individual staff members have a responsibility to voice their concerns if they believe they cannot serve on a client consulting team because, in the process of serving another client, they acquired confidential or competitive information that they cannot share or that might bias them or make objectivity difficult. And, finally, staff members should understand clearly that their responsibility to preserve client confidential information does not end with the termination of their employment—and employees should be required to sign a statement to that effect.

Individual Consultant Relations with Clients

Employees should be required to disclose any ownership interest they or members of their immediate families may have in any client company. As a general rule, a professional staff member should not be assigned to a client consulting team serving a client in which the staff member has an economic interest. Accounting firms often have much stricter rules, barring ownership interests in any company served by the firm. Since accounting firms have significant fiduciary responsibilities to their clients, their clients' shareholders, and, in many cases, regulatory bodies, they would seem to be accountable in ways that consulting firms might not be; but where consulting firms may not have a practical need for such detailed rules, they should nevertheless strive for the same level of discretion.

Quite frequently, consultants are wooed by and accept employment offers from client companies they have served. Good consultants acquire considerable insight into client companies and establish good personal and professional relationships with the client executives they work with. It is understandable that a good job offer can be tempting—especially if it means you will be traveling less and having more personal time. There are, however, some important guidelines for such cases: to avoid actual or perceived conflicts of interest, individual consultants—particularly senior consultants—should not engage in discussions concerning possible employment by client organizations while engaged in performing assignments on their behalf. Policies should also stipulate that, in the event a client initiates discussion of possible employment opportunities with a consultant, the consultant is required to advise an appropriate superior in the consulting firm. While such an occurrence does not necessarily mean that the consultant should be removed from the consulting team, this is an area in which prudence and transparency can help avoid perceived conflicts and misunderstandings.

Insider Information

No effective orientation session for new consultants would be complete without a section dealing with issues related to trading in the securities of client companies. Staff members must understand that they absolutely may not engage in such activity when they have information that is not publicly available and that could affect an individual's decision to buy or sell a security. Such activity endangers them, their consulting firm, and their client. Consultants must also be made sensitive to the personal legal risks involved in sharing insider information with third parties who might make buy or sell decisions based on that information. A quick Web search will yield plenty of illustrations of penalties paid by professionals in insider trading cases. Years ago, insider trading was viewed as almost exclusively an American issue; that is no longer the case, since most developed nations have begun to enact and enforce laws against insider trading. A firm's policies to prevent insider trading should apply on a worldwide basis.

"Internal" Issues

There are a host of ethical issues that relate principally to the relationships between individual consultants and the consulting firms by which they are employed.

A consulting firm must be committed to providing personally and professionally satisfying careers for all of its employees. To do so it must continuously nurture and strengthen an institutional commitment to "doing the right thing"—not only in serving its clients but also in recruiting, training, developing, and respecting its employees. The firm's practices and track record must demonstrate to employees that it is truly devoted to their professional development. Training sessions, sharing best practices and expertise, and providing opportunities and time to develop new skills are important. Procedures and practices, known to all employees, must be in place to ensure that appraisals are completed on a timely basis, that they are conducted with objectivity, and that they provide sound bases for decisions dealing with professional development as well as promotions and salary increases.

In a growing number of countries, laws forbid employers from discriminating in their hiring, compensation, and promotion practices on the basis of race, sex, or religion (and in the United States several additional prohibitions apply). Enforcement of such laws is sometimes uneven. A consulting firm—particularly a global consulting firm—has to maintain an environment in which all employees are treated, and treat each other, fairly and with respect. Ensuring that the workplace—no matter what part of the world it's located in—is free from subtle or overt sexual harassment is another area that requires continuous attention.

Firms that work globally should not accept arguments that sensitivity to issues related to sexual harassment are illustrations of "American political correctness." The core question is not what the laws are—it is what a firm perceives itself to be and what it wants to stand for in terms of its own integrity and in the eyes of its employees. Years ago, many consulting firms reimbursed club membership dues for its officers. In one such firm, the suggestion was made that dues should not be reimbursed if a club discriminated on the basis of race, sex, or religion. Officers in several countries outside the United States argued that this concern was an American issue that had no application in their cultures. After thoughtful consideration at a board of directors meeting, the chairman summarized the conclusion by stating that ultimately it did not matter what the laws might be in various countries: If an officer of the firm could not invite another officer or a staff member to lunch, dinner, or a meeting at a certain club because of the person's sex, race, or religion, then the firm would not reimburse the membership dues for that club. That decision sent a powerful message to the entire firm.

Time and Expense Reports

Requirements of compliance with expense report policies are not unique to consulting firms. Policies have to be clearly articulated with respect to what expenses are reimbursable and what documentation is required to support expenses. Consultants know that they are not to consider their expense reports as a means of supplementing their salaries, but anyone who has worked in the human resources, finance, or law department of a consulting firm has heard accounts of many creative interpretations for the appropriateness of certain claimed expenses. Expenses are usually included in billing statements to clients, and consultants must understand that since they are spending the client's money they have a responsibility to the client as well as to the consulting firm to be responsible in spending and honest in reporting.

Similarly, consulting firms have a responsibility to their clients and to their employees to bill their clients with integrity. In the early 1990s there was a good deal of embarrassment among prominent New York City law firms when newspaper articles documented their practices of significantly "writing up" their expenses. Consulting firms who tolerate "writing up" professional time charges or expenses send clear and wrong messages to their employees.

A CULTURE OF ETHICS: DEVELOPING, DISSEMINATING, AND GAINING ACCEPTANCE OF ETHICAL STANDARDS

An organization's institutional culture is enhanced if its employees share, accept, and adhere to the same fundamental principles. Written ethics policies, or codes of ethics, are important: They can be disseminated easily; they serve as a reference point for discussions; they help in determining the appropriate course to be followed in situations that give rise to ethical concerns; and, when necessary, they furnish bases for corrective action. Employees want to have guidance for determining what "the right thing" is in given situations, and the most powerful yardstick for behavior is a strong set of values and principles that are codified but are also supported and endorsed by the visible behaviors of senior management. It is only through the alignment of "espoused values" and "values-in-action" that a strong ethical culture is created.

The most effective codes of ethics are usually set forth in broad, "this we believe" statements of principle that are applicable throughout the organization, regardless of geography. They are not manuals. They deal with matters that the firm and its employees consider to be important to the firm's business, professional reputation, clients, and employees. In a consulting firm they should address, at a minimum, the various ethical issues and dimensions that have been discussed above. If codes of ethics are to be broadly accepted and relevant, they must be grounded in principles that employees can embrace and that reflect their own beliefs concerning proper behavior and values—the "virtuous cycle." Broad idealistic statements fashioned in the abstract will not be taken seriously by employees, and they seldom provide appropriate guidance.

It is not unusual for a professional services firm to share its code of ethics with its clients in order to illustrate policies that it has adopted to protect clients' interests. Published codes of ethics are also very useful in recruiting programs, where they can furnish a framework for explaining the firm's policies and practices to individuals and organizations outside the company. Doing so ensures that the right people are attracted to the firm, and that those people then accept and reinforce the values, making the culture even stronger. Of course, there is a critical need, day to day, for guidance by the more senior consultants in how to translate values into actions in specific situations. And if the actions and behaviors of the senior consultants are not aligned with the code of ethics, it will fail to have any impact on the firm's true culture and practices: Junior consultants learn more quickly by watching what their seniors do.

The process of developing an ethics code for any business, and particularly for a consulting firm, is important in itself. It can and should be a valuable exercise and, done properly, serves to enhance acceptance of and adherence to the code. How a code comes into being sends a message on how important the firm believes its commitment to ethical standards to be. A code of ethics prepared by the public relations department, the general counsel's office, or a business school professor, and then neatly packaged and nicely posted, does not pass muster.

To be credible, the code of ethics should be created by the firm and for the firm— it cannot be distinct from the core of the firm's business. The reasons why a firm adopts a code of ethics and the process by which the code is developed should be communicated to all employees. Senior management, including the CEO and the most senior line managers, should be visibly involved; after all, they have to buy into the process and the final product. As leaders of the firm they have to be evangelists and true believers if they are expected to be, and are seen to be, people who really "walk the talk." The most senior human resources managers (and, in a global firm, HR managers from representative geographies), the general counsel (or outside legal advisers), the chief financial officer, and communications staff for "packaging the message" should be involved in working through the draft statement of principles to be reflected in the code of ethics—but they cannot drive it. After sufficient progress has been made and initial review by senior management, it is helpful if the proposed code of ethics is presented for comment to representative cross-sections of all employees. The final draft must be carefully reviewed by the most senior management team and should be approved formally by the firm's highest governing or policy body.

"WALKING THE TALK": NOW THAT YOU HAVE A CODE OF ETHICS, WHAT DO YOU DO WITH IT?

A values statement or code of ethics that is posted in the boardroom but not read, understood, and lived by the firm's members is useless. The best values statements will be part of each staff member's vocabulary, and will drive that person's actions and decisions. The firm's values should influence its business processes, the way it manages performance, and the grounds on which it appraises and rewards its employees. Each employee should receive a copy of the code of ethics with a letter from the firm's most senior executive; the accompanying memo should explain how and why the code was developed and emphasize its importance to the firm, its employees, and their service to clients. In the best cases, all employees will sign and return to senior managers a statement that the code of ethics has been read and understood and that the provisions of the code will be respected and upheld. It would also be powerful if all consultants were periodically asked to sign a "renewal of vows" statement to reaffirm their commitment, perhaps during times of organizational restructuring, the implementation of a new strategy, or upon renewal of employment contracts.

Orientation sessions for new employees should include a section dealing with the company's code of ethics, and someone who is clearly recognized by new employees as being senior in the organization should lead the session. Case studies can be used to illustrate how various provisions of the code are applied or interpreted. While it should be recognized that there are many situations that do not lend themselves to easy categorization or resolution, the most important thing is to involve the employees in discussing and debating how a provision of the code should be applied in a given situation. In this way, the members of the firm can learn to apply the values and make the right kinds of decisions; employees should also be encouraged to reach out to their managers, the HR professionals, or the legal department if they are having trouble determining the right course of action. Codes of ethics cannot influence behavior and decision making, and cannot be made meaningful to employees, if they come across as compendiums of abstract principles. The code of ethics should be referred to with some frequency when detailed policy communications are sent to employees; it should be seen as a constitution of the firm's collective conscience; and all policies should be consistent with the code.

In order to ensure that the code of ethics continues to shape the firm's culture and practices, it should be made clear to all employees that they have a right and, indeed, a responsibility to report to management any violations of the firm's code. Employees must believe that they can do so without fear of retribution. Processes for the reporting and the investigation of alleged breaches of the firm's code of ethics should be developed and communicated to all employees. Violations should be reported to individuals who can be expected to merit the trust and confidence of employees (generally the firm's law department or outside legal counsel). Employees should know and feel confident that their actions will not result in any reprisals.

Management has to proceed on the very valid assumption that employees talk with each other about things that bother them. If employees conclude that reported violations have been buried or investigated in a cursory manner, or if a person who reported a violation is passed over for promotion or otherwise held back in professional development, the word gets out quickly and management loses credibility. Every professional firm faces the tough issue of dealing with situations in which a senior member of the firm, a "rainmaker," clearly and in many cases somewhat openly violates the firm's policies in areas such as, for example, cheating on expense accounts or engaging in sexual harassment. The failure of a firm to take appropriate action is a clear signal to employees that violations of the firm's code of ethics, no matter how serious, are viewed differently depending on where you rank in the firm's hierarchy. Sending memos to employees periodically after someone has been dismissed for violations of the firm's code of ethics can have a long-lasting therapeutic effect. Details do not have to be mentioned, nor does the individual have to be identified. Chances are that many employees will be able to fill in the blanks.

Even more important than "public hangings" are positive affirmations of the core values of the organization. While noncompliance should be disciplined appropriately, it is just as important—perhaps even more important—to find ways to visibly support the actions of the best proponents and advocates of the firm's values. More firms should realize the power of affirming and rewarding positive behavior. The creation of a vital culture of values and ethics requires an ongoing process that monitors the "threshold" below which no consultant's behavior may drop, and constantly works to raise the level of that threshold for the good of the clients, the firm, and each of the individual employees.

SUMMARY

The challenges of maintaining high standards of professionalism, meeting obligations to provide high-quality client services, fulfilling the aspirations of bright consultants who demand and merit meaningful careers and professional advancement, and protecting institutional integrity make the management of a professional service firm a difficult proposition. Managing within a culture in which hard-driving dedicated entrepreneurs are expected to share a commitment to a set of fundamental values is not an easy task—in fact, managing a professional services firm has been likened to the challenge of "herding cats." Senior consulting firm executives are constantly trying to balance, compromise, and reconcile the short term versus the long term, while being responsive to the needs and expectations of various stakeholders. The dynamics of the larger organization are uniquely bound to and determined by the individual actions of each consultant: Professionals who learn to make proper ethical decisions as junior consultants will be better trained to deal with bigger and more important ethical decisions as managers of client service teams and of the firm.

Most critically, senior managers must lead by example: They must provide values-based leadership. The best consulting firms, as all the best professional organizations, are not run by rules or manuals of prescriptions and proscriptions but by clearly understood and widely held values. Firms that have clearly communicated codes of ethics that are consistently promulgated and respected within the organization have a clearer sense of mission. They articulate what they and their employees expect of each other, in contrast with other firms that, for whatever reason, choose to deal with troublesome issues and situations on a one-off basis without developing consistent frameworks of guidance. Firms that adhere to ethical constructs that are broadly understood and shared within the organization are likely to avoid crises that may result in professional embarrassment or serious legal problems. The same prognosis cannot be made for firms that appear to assume that "people know what is the right thing to do" but do not consider it important to articulate their views and expectations of what *is* the right thing to do.

At the end of the day, "Do the right thing" may well be the consultant's best motto. For management consultants, the motto has a double meaning, which suggests just how important the idea is: "Right" can mean both "intellectually correct" and "ethically correct." Both are critical aims for consultants, and as we suggested at the beginning of this chapter, they are inextricably intertwined for professionals who serve their clients by analyzing data and making recommendations. Strategies and value propositions aside, for the best consulting firms it is their ethical codes—and the cultures created and fostered by their core values—that are their strongest strategic differentiators. A strong sense of ethics and mission attract the best people, and the best people reaffirm the values that determine the culture. As the former leader of one world-class consulting firm was fond of saying, "We believe that if we attract the best and teach them the right way to do things, everything else takes care of itself." A strong code of ethics is the custodian of the culture for any professional services firm, and good ethics *is* good business.

CHAPTER

So You Want to Be a Consultant?

Mark D. Nevins and Kristina Alterson

For the last generation, management consulting has run neck-and-neck with investment banking for the top spot as recruiter of graduating business school students. Before the heady days of the late 1990s, some pundits even based predictions about the state of the economy on whether McKinsey or Goldman-Sachs was the most desired MBA employer in a given year. While MBA programs have traditionally been the leading supplier of junior consultants, many of the top consulting firms have in recent years begun to look elsewhere for talent as well: to industry, to other professional schools (medicine and law), and even to PhD programs in fields as seemingly unrelated to business as Physics or Literature. With reports of glamorous lifestyles, high pay, and the mysterious prestige of being "business doctors," many people are interested in pursuing careers in management consulting; even when the economy is depressed and consulting firms slow their hiring or lay off staff, management consulting retains its status as one of the elite professional occupations.

If you are reading this chapter, you are probably asking yourself: "Is consulting the right career for me?" First, an observation: Articles and books about management consulting tend to dwell on the extremes of the profession. They either overemphasize the glamour and the money associated with being a consultant, or they demonize the dreaded work/life balance issues that consultants often face. Ditto the reports from consultants themselves: Expect consultants to expound on their impact on major companies as well as the Herculean travails of the profession itself. (The listener is never quite sure if the long hours and accrued air mileage are things the consultant laments or takes perverse pride in.) Finally, the firms themselves have mastered the art of content-free propaganda: They promise prospective employees and prospective clients the same levels of Nirvana, but are very coy about disclosing much about their own inner workings.

Of course, all consulting firms are not the same—in terms of the kinds of work they do (this includes both the kinds of work they *claim* to do and the kinds of work they are actually *good* at), their industry and functional areas of focus, their cultures, their approaches and methodologies, their compensation levels, and their lifestyle norms and expectations. If you are curious about a career in consulting, the best recommen-

---

Mark D. Nevins is President of Nevins Consulting. Dr. Nevins has been global head of organizational development and training for both Booz Allen Hamilton and Korn/Ferry International. He received a PhD in English Literature from Harvard University.

Kristina Alterson is Manager of Organizational Development for DoubleClick, based in New York. She holds a BS in Human Development and Family Studies from Cornell University.

dation is to treat the career search itself like a consulting engagement: gather extensive information on firms, analyze your own fit, do informational interviews, and test your own hypotheses about which firms might be best for you. There are many excellent and extremely detailed sources of information and up-to-date references, often including "insider tips," that overview each of the consulting firms. These guides are readily available to anyone interested in a career in consulting, and include the Wet Feet Guides, the Vault, MBA Jungle, various publications published internally by business schools, and online sites too numerous to mention.

Three questions are inevitably asked by people interested in consulting careers:

QUESTION #1: "WHY DO — AND HOW CAN — CONSULTING FIRMS PAY SO MUCH?"

Don't necessarily confuse high compensation with high value — those who understand the dynamics of consulting know that the high starting salaries may be less a reflection of the value-add, and more an indicator of the kind of incentive needed to justify what can be a very tough tour of duty indeed. The first years in any consulting career will be a struggle for most: perhaps not as grueling as being a Wall Street analyst in terms of sheer hours worked, but perhaps more challenging because of the steep learning curve and necessity of adapting to what appear to be frequently changing rules of engagement. The work can often be tedious — and less lucrative than may initially appear, if calculated on a per-hour basis and weighing in the "opportunity costs" of all that free time sacrificed.

While most firms are ultimately meritocracies, where the smartest will survive and prosper (provided they are dedicated as well as smart), there is also a real sense that junior staff have to "pay their dues." Marketplace dynamics at times force consulting firms to modify the traditional aspects of the working arrangement, but often (especially in the top-flight partnership firms) a sense of "hazing" remains; of course, it's a very genteel and intellectually austere form of initiation. The most cynical critics might suggest that consulting firms are really a sort of "pyramid scheme" — and indeed, they are profitable if and when they efficiently employ leverage to do work in a cost-effective manner and fund the senior consultants' handsome salaries and bonuses. But some of the better firms have begun to realize — and many firms are learning even more painfully in today's "war for talent" environment — that treating their people like "units of capacity" is not a long-term success strategy in an environment of intense competition among employers and when the supply of bright young professionals no longer seems unlimited.

QUESTION #2: "IS THE LIFESTYLE AS BAD AS PEOPLE SAY IT IS?"

Every job has its ups and downs. Consulting is a wonderful job for you if (to make use of a business metaphor) the "cost–benefit analysis" works out in your benefit, especially if you enjoy intellectual challenge and don't like routine. But make sure you gather the data and employ proper objectivity to do the cost–benefit analysis properly. And remember, more than one lifelong consultant has observed that "there are much easier ways to make money than management consulting."

Pay less attention to the myths and legends of consulting, and more attention to what your own strengths, interests, and style are. One of the especially painful ironies of the consulting career path is that many of the people who might make the best senior consultants (partners, vice presidents, officers, senior client service professionals—the terminology is different from firm to firm) will not find it possible or acceptable to "jump through the hoops" required to advance beyond associate (or whatever the entry level position is called). Management consulting is often an "up-or-out" career, with the final goal being partnership or the seniormost tier focused on business development or client management, and there are several phases to pass through on that journey and prove oneself in: from basic data-gathering and analysis through project and team management.

Many consulting firms still have a "one-size-fits-all" approach to career development—a Darwinistic approach that says the best will survive—and in this single-minded pursuit of "efficiency" in career development and selection they lose some of their better and more creative people. The very best and most savvy consultants will figure out that their success depends on mastering the core craft skills of analysis, while not abandoning the people- and process-related skills that will become of paramount importance when they are promoted to project manager.

QUESTION #3: "IS IT POSSIBLE TO SUCCEED IN CONSULTING AS A LONG-TERM CAREER?"

As suggested by the above—yes, it is possible to succeed, in terms of remuneration as well as happiness and fulfillment. Even with the good luck to have a senior member of your firm take interest in your career and "pull" you through the ranks, you have to be smart, savvy, tenacious, and able to learn the game.

It's also worth pointing out that the decision does not have to be an all-or-nothing one. A wonderful aspect of management consulting is that it can be a discrete and very beneficial stage in a career—and may be thought of as the equivalent of a "postdoctoral internship for MBAs." Whatever their plans when they joined their firms, many people decide to stay with consulting only for a few years before moving on to do something else, and consulting can be a superb choice for a smart young person just out of college or an MBA program. It can also be a beneficial experience for some people who are trying to transition from a nontypical background (law, engineering, academics) into the traditional business world. Consulting prepares one for a variety of follow-on careers, and builds essential business and management skills: discipline, analytical ability, client handling skills, problem-solving, project management, writing and presentation skills, and business development.

But in considering a long-term career in consulting, in some strange self-reflexive way, the people who will make the best consultants may well be those who are able to learn how to succeed in the profession. That is, the test for consulting competency is in fact survival and prosperity in the career itself. Much of the basis for success lies not in skill but in attitude, and in making a clear and accurate assessment of whether the career is the right one for you. It may be that the only way to know is to try, but we can offer some insight to those who are contemplating the plunge.

IS CONSULTING RIGHT FOR YOU?

Know thyself.
—SOCRATES, QUOTING THE ORACLE AT DELPHI

We are living in an age when work is more *personal* than ever. While the media has delighted in telling stories about superstar employees who insist on having a ping-pong table in the office or bringing their parrots to work, such sensationalism obscures the point that, at the beginning of the twenty-first century, the essence of professional work has changed fundamentally—perhaps more than it ever has since the birth of modern management following the Industrial Revolution. Part of that change is a result of the dynamics of a society in which knowledge workers have shifted to the forefront; but along with those changes comes a deeper shift in what might be called the "social contract" between employer and employee. (See Drucker and Nevins/Stumpf.) For the first time in the modern world, the more elite classes of employees seem to be as concerned about *who they are* as *what they do*. It is this shift in values—perhaps not thought permissible or valid in past generations—that has created the new dynamics of the workplace. In-demand employees are requiring that, above and beyond compensation, work provide a deeper source of personal satisfaction than ever before. Employers who do not understand this fact—or who do not change to recognize it—are in many cases losing their best people.

This repositioning of "who I am" in the context of employment is a good and necessary one if we believe our career counselors or the philosophers. Career advisors have long noted that the people who are happiest and most successful are the ones for whom "who I am" has the greatest overlap with "what I do." Or, as one popular book puts it, "Do what you love, and the money will follow." In the consideration of any professional career—be it management consulting, interior decoration, or trial law—significant effort should be expended on a thoughtful consideration of *self* as well as a hard analysis of the potential career. Most aspiring professionals are reasonably good at the latter and devote almost no time to the former. Plato tells us that his teacher Socrates claimed "An unexamined life is not worth living," yet modern society and culture encourage us to spend time on most anything other than self-reflection, and unfortunately business schools and the custodians of professional education do little to counteract that momentum.

To succeed as a consultant you need to understand yourself. Self-awareness is not easy—it's the work of a lifetime, and better minds than most currently practicing management consulting have devoted their lives to that very pursuit. The title of a recent business best seller asked, "What If Aristotle Ran General Motors?"; perhaps a better prerequisite question would have been, "What if Plato or Immanuel Kant had considered the necessary attributes of a good leader, and helped to choose the CEO of General Motors?" Business school curricula, of course, do not have required courses in philosophy, but some time spent on self-reflection—alien though the experience might be—will prove very beneficial. Spend the time now in reflecting, or spend it later to correct and control the damage of poor career decisions: The choice is yours.

Examination of one's own values, skills, and aspirations can and should be done both alone and with others. Create a framework for self-analysis: There are many, and you can find them through career counselors, on the Internet, or in your local bookshop. One classic is *What Color Is Your Parachute?*; most would-be consultants, given their typical empirical backgrounds, will find the methodology espoused by this book strange and frustrating—but if you bear with a program such as it recommends, the resultant process of self-discovery will serve you well beyond your decision on which consulting firms to apply to. There are many books and resources of this type. A full self-reflection will not be complete without the input of others—people close to us often have a much clearer and less biased picture than we ourselves do of our own strengths, skills, and even interests. You might consider seeking a professional career coach, who can administer instruments that gauge your aptitude and interest, and predict best-fit careers. Such coaches can often be expensive, however, and much of this kind of instrumentation can now be self-administered via books or tools found on the Internet. But do engage the input of other people to complete your feedback loop. Mentors can give you useful insight and advice—and a mentor experienced in consulting, if you can develop a relationship with one, would be especially invaluable. Finally, be sure to seek input from your spouse or significant other: Not only can he or she provide you with a useful image of yourself, he or she has the right to understand the pros and cons of consulting, and should be fully aware of the implications of the decision you may be making.

Many books have been written to advise would-be professionals on career development. We would like to close this section by offering one simple model that provides some obvious but often-forgotten wisdom on the process of choosing a career (see Figure 25–1).

As you assess yourself in terms of your future career, don't forget to take into account what you *like to do* as well as what you are good at. (How do young would-be professionals know what they are good at? One of the reasons to enter consulting is to find out!) Remember that just because you are good at something doesn't mean that you will enjoy and succeed in a career in that area: There are many mathematical geniuses enjoying careers as novelists or social workers. Don't forget, too, that you need

FIGURE 25–1   Criteria for Choosing a Career

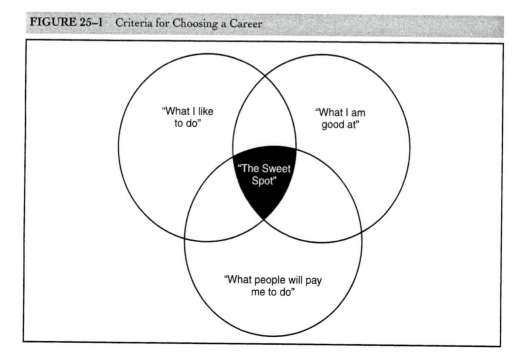

to be good at something (and get demonstrable experience in doing that something) or it's unlikely someone will pay you to do it. The simple secret to success for the employer as well as the employee is finding the overlap between what you like doing, what you are good at, and what people will actually engage you to do in return for compensation. Take all of these aspects into account as you consider a career in management consulting—and don't fail to give them the same weight in your decision making as you give to specific details about this firm's business practices or that firm's compensation profiles.

Socrates, the father of philosophy, is alleged to have endorsed the inscription on the temple of the Oracle of Apollo at Delphi: "Know thyself." What this statement may have meant in fifth-century B.C. Greece, long before the advent of modern psychology, is still being debated by scholars, but we can take the inscription as a simple touchstone for the process of considering a career in consulting. Adopt the motto by doing the following:

- Make an honest self-assessment: Set aside dedicated time for serious introspection and creation of an inventory of your skills and interests.
- Articulate career goals and reassess them regularly.
- Honestly consider the costs and benefits of the profession both now and longer term (global travel is great until you have a baby and your spouse wants you at home to share the burden).

Do these things now, and make a habit of doing them regularly over the course of your professional career. (Difficult as it may be to believe, three years into your career in consulting, you will look back on the time now as a period of comparative repose and tranquility—and yet three years into your consulting career will probably be an even more critical time for asking yourself "Who am I?" and "What am I doing in this career?") With a commitment to self-understanding as your foundation, you can now ask where you might fit into the consulting industry—and, of course, whether you *want* to fit in. Let's start by exploring the attributes of a successful consultant and what competencies are in demand from consulting firms.

GURUS, GEEKS, AND WITCH DOCTORS—WHO WANTS TO BE A CONSULTANT, ANYWAY?

What is a consultant? A guy who, when you ask him what time it is, borrows your watch, tells you
the time, then charges you for the service and doesn't return your watch.
—OLD JOKE

Consulting firms come in all shapes and sizes. From the "Big 5" to the "elite firms" to the "boutiques," each consulting firm has its own business, strengths, methodology, style, and stereotypes and clichés (some of the stereotypes are fair and accurate; most are not). If you are interested in pursuing a career in consulting, you can (and *must!*) do intensive research on every firm you are considering. Make sure to research those firms you're *not* considering as well—to make sure you're not dismissing a firm that might be a great fit for you based on nothing more than hearsay or fashionability.

Since there are numerous sources that provide an overview of the firms themselves, we will focus here instead on understanding what kinds of people may be best suited to a career in consulting. The following observations are intended to lay out the skills and proclivities that a smart, disciplined, and driven person needs to make a go of consulting. Having these competencies does not guarantee that one will *succeed* as a consultant—but someone who is lacking one or more of the characteristics described in the paragraphs following will probably not find consulting a satisfying job in the long run. Remembering Socrates's and Plato's advice, there is no magic answer: the key to solving this equation correctly is *for you* to marry an understanding of the profession of consulting with a clear and honest assessment of what you are good at and what you truly enjoy doing.

However dissimilar they may be in other ways, the better consultants have the following traits in common:

A Thirst for New Ideas and Finding Answers

"Ideas are the real currency of the economy." "Our people are our only assets." You may have heard these words uttered literally dozens of times by corporate executives, or read them in all of the business publications. Perhaps better than any other profession, consulting embodies these two concepts. The main assets of a consulting firm truly do go home every evening (except when they're on the road for work). While most consulting firms sell their methodologies as their products or services, the real value they have to offer consists of insights, expertise, intellectual capital, the ability to create change, and, of course, ideas.

Ultimately, consulting firms are little more than reservoirs of human capital. For this reason, successful consultants have a passion for ideas and are able to deal comfortably in the theoretical and intangible. They have the ability to conceptualize in the abstract (sometimes more than their clients would like), tolerate ambiguity, and generate relevant ideas based on careful research and rigorous brainstorming. The intellectual focus of consulting is a critical factor in deciding whether you would do well. Many consultants were people who enjoyed their time in school and think of themselves as lifelong learners.

Of course, as with anything, too much of a good thing can be detrimental. There are consultants who seem to be more interested in the problem than the solution. Since clients ultimately hire consulting firms for results, not ideas, successful consultants will have to balance the conceptual with the practical—take the good ideas and turn them into tangible improvements. Consultants who deal so much in the abstract that they underestimate the complexity of moving from identifying the answer to actually fixing the problem will not succeed. Some consultants do not understand (or care) what it means to "do it"—and, increasingly, clients will not tolerate a consultant who cannot or will not roll up his or her sleeves and "implement."

An Interest in People

Ideas notwithstanding, consulting is a "people business." Many consultants are introverted by nature (this observation is not intended to perpetuate the erroneous association of introvertedness with a quantitative bent), but good consultants need to learn to exhibit behaviors more similar to extraverts—at least some of the time. The ability to build long-term mutually beneficial relationships with clients and colleagues may be the master key to success. The much-vaunted quality of "being a team player" really is important. Networking within one's own industry, practice, and office is, especially in larger firms, the fastest way to be recognized and staffed on consulting engagements that are interesting to you and that match your skill set. Consultants do not need to be flamboyantly outgoing (though some of the more well-known ones are), but they must be good listeners and clear and concise communicators who can really connect, on a personal and professional level, with their teammates and their clients.

Good consultants also have a "partnership mentality." They realize that working in teams (with peers, colleagues, and their clients) is truly the most effective way to leverage the talents of everyone involved on the consulting project (consultants as well as clients), and to attain the best and most lasting results. Besides building relationships with clients to help them achieve success, great consultants also find ways to build relationships within their own organizations to help them grow and develop as professionals. Good consultants will have many mentors over the course of their careers. They will also serve as coaches and mentors to others within their firm and sometimes even within the client company—not out of obligation, but because they realize the importance of relationships. There was a time when the joke was that the best consultants were "brains on sticks": that sheer intellect and analytical skill was what mattered most, and anything else got in the way. Thankfully, for the good of both the profession and its clients, most firms have now learned that "brains on sticks" may be useful in some capacities, but will rarely drive productive change.

A Commitment to Client Service

In his book *True Professionalism*, David Maister asserts that "being a professional is neither about money nor about professional fulfillment. Both of these are consequences of an unqualified dedication to excellence in serving clients and their needs." Successful consultants have a personal commitment to excel and a strong desire to provide quality and value far in excess of their fees. Understanding and enjoying the fact that you are there to help your clients is vital for success and also happiness in the consulting profession. (Some arrogant consultants act as if "we are smarter than the client," but such an attitude rarely leads to success in the long term.) It is when you perform well for your clients and *with* your clients, by meeting and exceeding their expectations, that consulting becomes more than just a means to an end—when it becomes a profession rather than simply a job.

What most newly minted MBAs do not realize is that if they are fully committed to serving their clients to the best of their abilities, then the dollar signs will follow, rather than the reverse. A number of critics have made the unpopular proposal that business schools stop teaching students that they are "the best and brightest" and that consulting firms stop throwing top talent huge sums of cash up front for joining their ranks, but instead that both sides work to teach new consultants about what it really means to serve a client and about how to work with people. Consulting firms have made money in the past by teaching their youngest members that in order to be promoted and rewarded they needed to sell, sell, sell, and therefore consultants spend their time thinking about what they are going to sell the client next, rather than how to solve the problems at hand. Some consultants get so focused on their own growth and profitability that they forget to serve their clients.

If you believe the preceding traits describe you, and you are interested in pursuing consulting as a profession, it's probably worth taking some time to appreciate what consulting firms themselves are looking for. In screening candidates, the best consulting recruiters will be looking for the following competencies. (*Note*: It's worth pointing out that not all consulting firms are renowned for their skill at interviewing, so don't assume that the person interviewing you has a clear idea of success factors such as the following, or how to assess candidates against them!)

Intellectual Profile

- Good at problem identification, analysis, and resolution
- Has an interest in improving things and giving advice on how to improve things
- Is capable of "multitasking"—juggling many ideas and operations simultaneously, and not losing priorities
- Has solid written and verbal communications skills and presentations skills
- Is able to tolerate ambiguity—and work effectively in spite of it

Experience/Knowledge

- Has a strong academic pedigree (usually)
- Has a basic understanding of fundamental business issues (though, increasingly, consulting firms are realizing that business knowledge, historically thought to be a *sine qua non*, is actually one of the easiest on this list to teach)
- Has specific industry/functional expertise (ditto above)

"Personality"

- Likes discrete projects—ones that have clear beginnings and ends—and is results oriented
- Has flexibility—of intellect as well as interpersonal style
- Shows tenacity, stubbornness, and a streak of perfectionism
- Is not averse to frequent travel or to being away from home for significant amounts of time
- Can stand occasional (and sometimes more than occasional) long hours
- Can work well both independently and in a team environment (these two abilities do not often coexist comfortably)
- Is not uncomfortable working alone and/or being "an outsider"
- Can handle the "ups and downs" (in terms of workload as well as emotional intensity) of consulting projects

"REALITY BITES": THE DAY-TO-DAY LIFE OF THE MANAGEMENT CONSULTANT

Success in consulting increasingly requires the schizoid mix of an artist's imagination, and a dullard's tolerance, a maniac's energy, and a triathlete's stamina, and at times a killer's aggression, coupled with a monk's humble compliance.
—LEWIS PINAULT, *CONSULTING DEMONS*

Management consulting is a wonderful occupation for anyone who knows he or she would be bored doing the same thing month after month at a big company. In fact, there are many consultants who leave their firms for "industry" jobs (with the promise of 9-to-5 and the novelty of sleeping at home more than away), only to return to consulting after a few years because they were ultimately unsatisfied with a "regular" job. Those bitten by the consulting bug are often bitten for life—they will find that no other profession has the "ups" of consulting, if one can manage and deal with the "downs."

While it's true that there may be a greater chance of being exposed to dynamic, fast-paced environments working in consulting, such is not always the case, especially for junior consultants. In fact, some engagements may seem never-ending and excruciatingly boring, because the fact is that those massive restructuring or implementing jobs that require large teams of experienced junior staff dedicated for months (or even years) are the most profitable engagements for the consulting firms themselves. But these kinds of assignments are in most cases not what junior consultants expected when they chose consulting. ("Please get me off this job! Look, if I wanted to work for this client company full time, I would have joined them directly out of business school, and then I'd be working reasonable hours, too!")

New consultants need to remember that—in spite of what the firms say during the on-campus "wooing" process, or even in spite of the best intentions of staffing managers—there are times when junior consultants will have no exposure to senior corporate executives, and will spend all of their time in a "team room" rolling up their sleeves, creating spreadsheets and databases, and digging into a mass of numbers that need to be "crunched." At the other end of the spectrum, most consultants have also been faced with a project that is *too* dynamic, too unstructured, and/or too ambitious, and hence extremely demanding of time and energy. Clients may impose next-to-impossible goals and deadlines, and in response project managers will be unwavering in their insistence on 5 full days on-site at the client and 14+-hour workdays. Worse, many inexperienced or ineffective project managers or handling officers are not good at managing the client or the engagement: They over-promise or lose track of the scope and focus, and the result can be those legendary "death marches" that result in a deliverable that is rarely of a quality that any team can feel proud of. Consultants who work with good project managers experience how wonderful and gratifying the job can be; those who work with poor project managers can describe in detail the true hell that management consulting can be.

Finally, remember that, no matter how bad it may get in any given project, one of the realities is that there is always light at the end of the consulting tunnel. First, consulting engagements, in general, have a definite end date. Additionally, consultants themselves usually have "roll off" dates—a by-product of the need for the project manager to allocate resources in a cost-effective and profitable manner. Fixed end dates mean you will not be stuck on that boring assignment forever—and if you bite the bullet, do high-quality work, and network with your colleagues and clients, the chances are good that you will have better opportunities (and maybe even a say) in your next assignment. Hard end dates also mean that, if you manage well, you can plan true vacations and, since you are "between jobs," you can really leave your work at the office. The dynamics of staffing—the process of matching available consultants to engagements to maximize utilization of resources—sometimes mean that you will occasionally be "on the beach" (or unstaffed) for a period of time, which will allow you to work on proposals, develop intellectual capital, practice marketing skills, or learn something new. You should also remember that the consulting business tends to have peaks and valleys in terms of stress and productivity. Excessively demanding projects will, in time, give way to ones that are less arduous and all-consuming, and in the course of a given engagement you will balance "crunch" times with less stressful time. (One of the keys to success, in fact, is to avoid the highs and lows in an engagement by working proactively early to minimize "crunch time" later.) Cleverness, patience, perseverance, and the ability to balance one's personal and professional lives are the keys to surviving the rough spots in the consulting industry.

THE THREE HALLMARKS OF A GREAT CONSULTANT

> *If you give a man a fish, he will be hungry again tomorrow.*
> *If you teach him to fish, he'll never be hungry again.*
> —ANCIENT PROVERB

It is an ironic reality that management consultants often attempt to describe their profession and what they do by asserting what they are *not* in terms of other professions. Creating a sort of social continuum, they argue that they are not like investment bankers (who, after all, "are only in it for the money") but, at the other end, that they are not like academics (who are "too theoretical and have no impact"). Consultants and consulting firms certainly enjoy and perpetuate the mystique of their profession. Perhaps, in addition to pride, insecurity is one of the drivers of this guardedness: Consultants don't want outsiders to know what they do and how they do it because potential clients might be underwhelmed, which could threaten the high fees!

We'd like to conclude with some thoughts that are more prescriptive than descriptive. Earlier we discussed the basic attributes of a successful consultant. We would like now to suggest that the great consultant—no matter what his or her firm, area of expertise, or style—shares in three key hallmarks. Rare is the consultant who truly embodies these three hallmarks—and many consultants who do embody them might not realize the preeminent value of these hallmarks—but consultants with these qualities are the ones firms will benefit most from hiring, and junior (not to mention more experienced) consultants could do worse than to craft and develop themselves along these lines.

Hallmark 1: The Great Consultant Asks the Right Questions and Is Truly Eager to Find Out the Answers, or Answers Better Than the Ones That Other People Might Take for Granted

Inherent in this attribute is a powerful natural curiosity—the desire to understand why things are the way they are—as well as a strong organizing principle for assembling the answers to the questions into a coherent whole. Consultants are natural organizers—they cannot stand intellectual messiness, and are not comfortable unless things are put into their "proper piles." Heuristics come naturally to great consultants—they see underlying patterns and use questions as scalpels to cut to the core of problems. The entire "hypothesis-driven methodology" discussed in an earlier chapter is based on the ability to ask good questions, and to be dogged about following them up with the right next question until the answer is elucidated.

Many consultants focus on tools and techniques: Tools and techniques are useless, or even dangerous, if the user doesn't know how and where to use them. An ability to perform a regression analysis or create a spreadsheet is useless if you don't understand *why* you are doing that analysis or building that spreadsheet, and knowing why depends first and foremost on asking the right questions. The ability to ask good questions is crucial to any great consultant, and you can often recognize the great consultants early on by the kinds of questions they ask. It's worth adding that this questioning applies, too, to the consultant's *own* development: constantly asking "how can I be better?" and being able to listen to and learn from feedback and experience.

Hallmark 2: The Great Consultant Is Able to Manage Multiple Points of View Simultaneously

This ability is deployed in many important ways: to see the strategic as well as the tactical details of an engagement; to take a "big picture" view of the whole scope while not losing sight of the individual tasks, in order to keep them on track; to see the world from the job manager's point of view (if you are the associate) as well as the associate's point of view (if you are the job manager); to understand the situation and issues from the point of view of the consultant as well as the point of view of the client; and to realize that "the client" is not a monolith, and in fact different members of the client organization will have very different motivations, needs, and fears—and that the best solution will address all of them.

The ability to manage multiple points of view has sometimes been called "business empathy" or "EQ," and that certainly is an important skill, but there's also more to it. Being able to consider and work from different frames of reference is critical for the "content" of the consulting work, but it's even more critical for the "process." The very best consultant does not work *for* his or her clients but works *with* them. The best consulting is *collaborative*: The client is not merely the taskmaster or the purchaser, he or she is a colleague and a co-worker. This key difference has not been described well or often enough; one articulate proponent of the idea is Robert Schaeffer, whose elegant book *High-Impact Consulting* argues that the relationship between consultant and client is rarely a true partnership, though it should be. Consultants will have more impact driving change *and* selling more work if they treat their clients like collaborators—and being able to see the world from the client's point of view as well as your own is necessary to do so.

Hallmark 3: The Great Consultant Truly Derives Pleasure and Satisfaction from Seeing Others Find Successful Resolutions for Their Problems

If you don't get a thrill from seeing positive change effected in an organization, from seeing your clients do their jobs better than they did before, then consulting will not be the best career for you in the long run. To be a great consultant takes a very peculiar kind of ego. On the one hand, you need to believe you are smart enough and can learn quickly enough to tell a group of businesspeople how to fix their problems or how to improve something some of them have been doing for many years. On the other hand, you have to take satisfaction from success even when you can't claim it as your own. Many times, getting the right solution implemented (rather than just identified) requires allowing the client to claim responsibility, and enjoy the limelight. Every day, the business periodicals report on innovations and changes in companies: Many of these projects are driven by consultants, but rarely do the consulting firms get any credit in the press. Often, consultants take on the most visible risk in an engagement but don't get the most visible rewards. Sometimes, the reward is simply knowing that a company is better because of your efforts.

A senior executive once provided a crucial piece of advice, speaking in general of management consultants: "You guys are great—you're really smart, and you give me all kinds of ideas and industry experience, but you're missing one higher-level opportunity. When you leave, I don't feel like my people are better as a result of your having been here." That comment points to the essence of great consulting: The best consultants are not just thinkers and doers, they are coaches and teachers; *and* they are willing themselves to be coached and taught—by their peers, their subordinates, and their clients.

To some extent, the first two hallmarks can be taught: Much of the training in the better firms focuses on developing the ability to ask the right questions and to see the problem from more than one viewpoint. The third hallmark, however, may be harder to teach: The best consultancies will look for it when recruiting, and the best consultants will determine early on if in fact it is a hallmark that matches their own values and style. It's the third hallmark that really makes the difference, and if you don't have that one, you will probably never be a great consultant.

SUMMARY

In conclusion, there is no simple answer to the question: "Should I pursue a career in consulting?" It's not possible to deliver a recommendation—a diagram or a model of the perfect consultant. It is ironic that a profession aimed at creating simple, direct, tangible solutions does not have a direct and tangible solution for identifying its own best professionals.

However, if we have been something like consultants to you in this chapter—helping to frame better the question of what it means to be a consultant—then, like the best consultants, we have to put the question (clarified and supported with data and insight) back to you. Are you right for consulting, and is consulting right for you? Look at the data; assess it in the context of your own situation; be realistic about the most important levers and drivers; and make the decision for yourself. In the end, if you think being a consultant will work for you, then go for it. If you are one of the lucky ones, you have a tremendous, constantly fulfilling career in front of you. But if it doesn't work out, don't despair. To use the jargon of the profession itself, you've tested a hypothesis ("I would make a good consultant") and it proved to be incorrect. You now know something that you didn't before you began the experiment. Don't consider yourself a failure: Knowledge is power, and you now have a new insight into yourself, not to mention a tremendous platform of experience, a powerful set of tools, and a great line on your résumé. Learn from the experience—some of the best business leaders are former consultants—and then choose the best *next* step.

CHAPTER

Consultancy Marketing: Developing the Right Mindset

Deon Binneman

What makes a consultant successful is — CLIENTS.
—MARVIN WEISBORD

In his book *Unlimited Power*, the popular Tony Robbins speaks of the concept of modeling—that is, "To become successful, you need to model yourself on the knowledge, skills, and attitudes of successful people. By role modeling them, you can shorten the very expensive learning curve and become successful far quicker yourself." In comparable ways, researchers in systems thinking speak about leverage points—those small, well-focused actions that can, when used at the right time and in the right place, produce significant, lasting benefits exponentially beyond the effort required to take the action step itself.

This chapter focuses on the practices and problems that consultants face in marketing consultant practices and the leverage points that can be used to build a reputation and grow your practice. We also examine some pragmatic tools, formal and informal methods, offline and online.

THE BUSINESS CASE FOR MARKETING

"We all live by selling something." "It's the second oldest profession in the world. . . ." So go the adages. But in these words resides considerable wisdom, whether for consultants already working in private practice or who find themselves suddenly self-employed, as well as consultants working in large practices.

Many consultants resist marketing. Their resistance develops largely from a disdain for commercialism (the interests of clients are placed above self-interest), the tendency of technically trained and oriented consultants to consider themselves experts in all disciplines, the lack of time, and the sales-pitch mentality to which so many consultants have been subjected to. Another problem is that consultants often have a misconception of marketing because they equate it with advertising or traditional hard-selling.

Deon Binneman is Managing Partner of Repucomm, based in Johannesburg, South Africa. His electronic newsletter, *Powerlines*, is read by readers from Canada to India.

Compounding the problem is the fact that buyers of manufactured goods don't need to think about who produced the goods they buy, whereas buyers of consultants' services must do so. Unable to try out the service before buying it, the buyer does the next best thing and relies on the judgments of others to assess what it would be like to work with the consultant who will deliver. This means that, sooner or later, all consultants must market and build their reputations if they want to advance their careers and grow their firms.

A paradigm is a mental model that describes a particular view of the world: a set of rules and regulations that define boundaries and provide a means for being successful within those boundaries. A paradigm shift is a big change—an abrupt, unprecedented, revolutionary, rules-altering change. When a business paradigm shifts, the success of the past becomes less relevant, because the criteria for success have changed and new standards have been developed.

In business this has surely happened. The advent of the Internet has changed traditional rules for marketing. Today writers talk about the Unit of One: marketing to one customer at a time. With the Internet, a consultant can undertake contracts in other countries without leaving home. The Internet and increases in technology have also had their effects on the work landscape.

Change in the world of work has meant many people finding themselves suddenly self-employed. It's happened in consulting, too, with many consultants outsourced from larger practices starting their own consultancies. Faced with stiffer competition, consultants must approach marketing in an innovative frame of mind, with a broader and long-term vision. Here are a few points to keep in mind from a marketing perspective:

- *Have the qualifications, and clients will come.* Many consultants think about what they do in terms of their own past experience or vocational point of view. The essence of marketing is to redefine your mission or the fundamental purpose of your business from the point of view of the customer.

- *Think: I am a consultant, not an entrepreneur.* Many consultants fall into the trap of forgetting that they are first and foremost businesspeople. Whether you work for a large consultancy or run your own, you have to be profit driven, and that essentially means developing a marketing and business mindset that makes growing the practice your highest priority. After all, without clients you won't be in business. It is even easier to fall into this trap if you are working for a large consulting practice that has a separate marketing department.

- *Market yourself to sell your firm.* This is true of accountants, architects, consultants, engineers, and lawyers. It is certainly true for economists, executive recruiters, PR specialists, human resources consultants, estate agents, and increasingly the medical profession. Historically, development of consultants towards winning new clients has been haphazard. Law, accounting, engineering, medical, and HR schools teach virtually nothing about marketing when you are an independent consultant or running a SOHO (Small Office Home Office). Yet, for any consultant, the learning of specific marketing and selling skills could mean the difference between survival and success.

- *Big company marketing tactics do not work.* The sales methods that stand big companies in good stead may not always work for a consultant in private practice. First, you may not have the budget, and second you do not have the resources or time. This means that you need to use different methods and processes to get your messages across.

- *I am not a marketer.* Many successful consultants make the transition to marketing, while others never make it at all, at great cost to their careers and future. The bottom line is that having consultant skills and training just isn't enough to advance in running your own practice. To succeed you must learn to market and sell.

- *Every consulting business needs new clients to thrive and grow.* Building a business is an activity that should never stop. The trick lies in dividing your time between doing the actual work and marketing constantly. Keeping one eye on your current client and another on the horizon for future clients is a difficult juggling act. Just as many different roads will get you from one place to another, there are many different ways to bring new clients into your business. You can place ads and hope that your customers may see it, or you can cold-call, hoping that you will get an appointment for an interview. The trick lies in developing the most cost-effective way to reach clients and to build your business. Effective ways could range from obtaining referrals to building a reputation through writing articles in the media.

- *If I bat, I will lose.* Marketing is like a game of cricket. The only way to increase your batting averages is to go and bat. If you go and bat there is a good chance you will be caught out. But the more times you go to bat, the better your chances for striking it rich. Thus, the better your marketing planning and execution, the higher your probability of success. The bottom line is that successful consultants market. Remind yourself daily that you should be working on something.

- *Imprecise cash flow and objectives.* "Having an imprecise cash flow is normal for a consulting practice. It is normal for my consulting income to be like the flows of the tides—up one month, down the next." The point is lost that perhaps this is due to a matter of wishful thinking rather than goals based on realistic and solid marketing data and plans.

- *Time spent on marketing is not billable.* Unfortunately, time spent on marketing is not billable. To someone with a cost-saving mindset, returning ten phone calls may seem a waste; to someone with a marketing mindset, it is an investment.

- *Unforeseeable costs.* Marketing costs are high and I don't have the funds to market. I also have never investigated low- or no-cost marketing opportunities.

- *Lack of time.* You are so busy consulting that you forget about or cannot make the time for marketing. To make a success of consulting, you need a radical rethink in your attitude. You need to develop a marketing mindset. David Freemantle writes in his book *The Profit Boss* about having a profit attitude that translates itself well to a marketing mindset: "The eyes of a profit boss focus only on profit. It is an obsession with him; he sees profit in every business situation. He seeks a profitable opportunity every second of the working day: A profit boss sees no profit in breaking the law. Nor bending it. The profit boss sees no profit in treating his people badly. Nor suppliers. The profit boss sees no profit in neglecting his customers. The profit boss sees profit in every business contact he makes."

Part of the problem is that as a consultant you get so wrapped up in consulting that you forget all about marketing. To market consulting services successfully, a consultant will need to master the following:

DEVELOP A STRATEGIC MARKETING MINDSET AND APPROACH

Being extremely good at what you do is useless unless customers know about you. Consultants have to learn how to market themselves, with style, passion, good taste, and a low-key honesty that is shame-free and comfortable for everyone around them.

To do this, they need to develop a marketing mindset. A marketing mindset is ideally an opportunity-filled abundance mindset—one that says: "I am a valuable person. People value my services. It's fun sharing about what I do and the results I produce for my clients. Marketing is about getting out there and presenting an authentic message that represents my business. I am going to provide a service that is so great that people will want to pass my name along. When you do what you love and share that passion, business is effortless."

A marketing mindset goes beyond that of only looking for ways to sell what you know; that's the classic product-looking-for a-market approach. Instead, it means looking for opportunities to help your clients solve problems and to spread your name and reputation.

Therefore, to be successful in consulting you will need to, first of all, begin to think like a marketer and an opportunist. You will need to become familiar with marketing terms and use them. Some consultants, especially, tend to reject marketing ideas as having no relevance to them.

Many consultants miss opportunities to market themselves because they are not open to opportunities. A marketing mindset implies that you have to know your marketplace and know the needs, perceptions, and attitudes of clients, but also the strengths and weaknesses of internal and external competitors. It means understanding general business and social trends. It means reading widely and getting involved in the environment.

Some consultants believe that you should plan the marketing and promotional activity of your consultancy as though no one knows what you do, but before you can do that you need to be clear about what you are marketing and the image you want to portray.

It is no longer enough to be a good generalist. You cannot be "all things to all people." Consultants tend to want to be so, but it will eventually only lead to problems since what the client actually "buys" is the consultant. How you position yourself is part of this strategic mindset. Let's take a look at finding your niche or, as some call it, positioning:

Positioning: Finding Your Niche

Positioning involves adopting a particular image or positioning to differentiate the consultancy from competitors in the minds of current and potential clients. It must be realized that the emphasis is on the perception (in the mind) by the client, and not necessarily what the consultant may think he or she is projecting.

Clear positioning is of central importance to the marketing of any consultant service because it guides all subsequent marketing actions, which are aimed at establishing a competitive advantage. Because each consultant is an individual, different from all others, it follows that one particularly effective positioning strategy would be for the consultant to project a specific individuality.

This strategy of "manufacturing" an image/personality/positioning is known as The Pygmalion Principle and is an approach propounded for the marketing of the individual. The "Principle" follows from George Bernard Shaw's *Pygmalion,* a play made memorable by the musical adaptation of *My Fair Lady,* in which Henry Higgins succeeded in transforming a coarse Cockney girl, Eliza Doolittle, into a well-spoken fixture of high society.

Positioning strategy amounts to choosing, developing, and managing a distinctive image or positioning for the consultancy (particularly the consultant him/herself) that can differentiate it from other firms.

The following exercise is useful in assisting consultants in finding their positioning or niche in the marketplace:

- Redefine your business from the customer's point of view.
- Define the business in the 30-second elevator speech/soundbite format.
- Use 35 words or less.
- Ask yourself: What is my USP (unique selling point)? This is what differentiates you from the competition—the essence of your business. It's your unique value that the customer is willing to pay for.
- Ask yourself: What do I do that is uniquely different and better than anyone else?
- Remember the line: "What does Goodyear sell?" What do you sell? What do you really provide? Minolta had this on a billboard: "We understand offices."

As someone once said: "A potential client could not care less as to whether a firm thinks it has the best professionals or the most sophisticated approach or that they have previously obtained outstanding results. The client wants to know what you can do for MY problems."

Position Yourself as an Expert

Your reputation is your stock in trade. The danger is to rely on your current reputation. Howard Shenson says that "a reputation does not take care of itself, and you must water it as if it is a plant." He writes that reputations can become outdated, distorted, or spread haphazardly if not planned properly.

Building your reputation is a planned process that is influenced by day-to-day activities. A useful technique is to position yourself as an expert, and to build your reputation accordingly. Here are some ideas and tips on how to go about it:

- Invent something new: a product, service, idea, or solution.
- Get quoted by the media; this will give you instant credibility, and one good story leads to another.
- Get a book published.
- Develop some fans and followers. They will act as referrals; their feelings are contagious.
- Get other credentialed people to endorse you.

MAKE TIME FOR MARKETING

Faith Popcorn, described by *Fortune* magazine as "the Nostradamus of marketing," writes in her worldwide best-seller *The Popcorn Report* about the need for streamlining—sorting out your life, getting rid of "garbage," spending more time on those activities you regard as important. Time management, in essence, is self-management. This section will provide you with ways and strategies to give you more quality time for marketing.

You are the biggest KEY to effective management of your time. There is a saying, "Time waits for no one." On the other hand, "Time is the only equal opportunity we have."

How do we make the most of the time that we have? Simply: We plan and organize our lives and our work so that we can attain maximum impact. Here are some ideas and hints that you can incorporate into your daily routine which will make you more effective at marketing:

- *Spend time planning and organizing.* Using time to think and plan is time well spent. In fact, if you fail to take time for planning, you are, in effect, planning to fail. You need to organize in a way that makes sense to you and that will aid your marketing efforts. Prepare your next day before going home. Very few people perform at their peak levels around quitting time; before you leave at night, set your objectives for the next day. Scan your files. Prepare for your calls by drafting your opening statements and questions. Think of how much you could increase your production if you were able to simply walk in and sit down at starting time, and knock out about four or five calls before most people even get back from the coffee pot!

- *Set goals.* Goals give your life, and the way you spend your time, direction. When asked the secret to amassing his fortune, one of the famous Hunt brothers from Texas replied: "First you've got to decide what you want." Set goals that are specific, measurable, realistic, and achievable. Establish at least one major objective each day and achieve it.

- *Prioritize.* Use the 80–20 Rule, originally stated by the Italian economist Alfredo Pareto, who noted that 80 percent of the reward comes from 20 percent of the effort. The trick to prioritizing is to isolate and identify that valuable 20 percent. Once identified, prioritize time to concentrate your work on those items with the greatest reward. Marketing should be very high on the priority list.

- *Use a marketing to-do list.* Some people thrive using a daily to-do list, which they construct either the last thing the previous day or first thing in the morning. Such people may combine a to-do list with a calendar or schedule. Others prefer a "running" to-do list, which is continuously being updated. You may prefer a combination of the two previously described to-do lists. Whatever method works is best for you. Don't be afraid to try a new system—you just might find one that works even better than your present one! Alternatively, you could use a PIM: a computerized personal information manager such as Microsoft's Outlook.

- *Be flexible.* Allow time for interruptions and distractions. Time management experts often suggest planning for just 50 percent or less of one's time. With only 50 percent of your time planned, you will have the flexibility to handle interruptions and the unplanned "emergency." When you expect to be interrupted, schedule routine tasks. Save (or make) larger blocks of time for your priorities. When interrupted, ask Alan Lakein's crucial question, "What is the most important thing I can be doing with my time right now?" to help you get back on track fast.

DEVELOP A CONSULTANCY MARKETING PLAN

> *If you don't use your head today, you are going to use your feet a lot tomorrow.*
> —ANONYMOUS

It is often said that *planning* eases a person's task, that it helps you to "work smarter rather than simply harder," and that it saves you time, energy, money, and materials. In the same way a consultancy's marketing plan can be the difference between success and failure.

Would you travel in a foreign country without a road map or build your house without a plan? Probably not, yet many consultants launch their consultancies on the market without having first prepared a marketing plan.

Perhaps the most important aspect of building a business such as a consultancy is developing an effective marketing plan. Being extremely good at what you do is useless if customers don't know about you or can't find you. Too often, especially for small businesses or consultant offices, marketing falls through the cracks because there is no budget for marketing, and people are too busy running the consultancy to market it effectively.

As a businessperson, you probably want to make enough profit to support yourself and your family comfortably. Through research, good planning, and a bit of luck, you can expect to reach this goal. Notice the use of the words *planning* and *research:* the more research and planning you do, the more luck comes your way!

In the past, business owners created a product and then tried to sell it. Today, successful businesspeople are market driven: They provide exactly what the customer wants and needs, throughout the life of the business. Every decision—from research through production, to storage, packaging, distribution, and promotion—should reflect the customer's desires.

Many new businesses fail in their first two or three years of operation for a variety of reasons: insufficient financing, poor location, demands that clash with the owner's personality and lifestyle, or simply a lack of customers. But look closely at those failures and it becomes clear that in most cases the blame should fall on poor planning.

Consulting practices are by definition small. So the same rules apply. This section has been developed to help you improve your chances of success by explaining the most basic steps for creating a marketing plan and adopting a strategic marketing approach.

A consultancy marketing plan is essentially a more structured way of thinking things out in order to act more effectively. It is meant above all as a practical tool for reflection and action. It is also the ideal tool for the consultant who wants to act, not react. Drawing up a marketing plan consists of scheduling, within a specific time frame, the actions that follow from your defined strategy.

What is important is that you do a plan in writing based on the Strategic Marketing Approach. Lee Iacocca, former chairman of Chrysler, says that the discipline of writing things down is the first step toward achieving them.

Strategic Marketing is a conscious and systematic process that involves the following steps:

1. Selecting target market segments using such classification as industry, readiness for consulting, company or division size, function, or issues such as productivity and the like
2. Analyzing the specific needs of those market segments
3. Developing the capabilities to address the target markets' needs with expertise, relevant programs, and assessment and evaluation tools (that includes determining costs and prices and delivering service options)
4. Designing visibility and credibility strategies to increase recognition and reputation in the selected marketplaces
5. Identifying prospects and making presentations to specifically address prospective clients' unique interests

6. Providing the highest quality of consultant services on client projects

7. Managing consultant–client relationships to ensure ongoing mutually beneficial partnerships

This section is intended to create a better understanding of the utility of a structured plan, if only to enable you to visualize more clearly the direction and plan of action of your business.

Utility of a Plan

A marketing plan covering a one-year period is the ideal tool to help a consultant meet the marketing challenges it faces. This tool allows you to:

- Have clearer vision and greater control over activities to be carried out in order to achieve your annual sales objectives
- Establish more clearly the steps to follow when launching a new product or service on the market
- Ensure that the products and services offered by your business correspond exactly to the real needs and expectations of current and potential customers
- Provide a coherent work plan focusing on results to be achieved
- Avoid acting at the last minute and being forced to rush, especially in preparing for marketing activities
- Ensure that your company's strategic plan will be carried out systematically and coherently
- Have greater control over the costs of all marketing activities: product development, market studies, advertising and promotion programs, and sales costs

How to Draw Up a Plan

Many books can guide you on how to draw up a marketing plan. Preparing an annual consulting marketing plan is more time consuming in the first year than in subsequent years because, among other things, questions of methodology and format must be settled the first time around.

In business, information is your greatest tool. As a consultant, you have to identify the type of quantitative and qualitative information essential to managing your business effectively. In practice, I suggest that you summarize your plan in a marketing agenda—a calendar covering the principal actions to be taken over the next 12 months.

As a major component of a consultancy's plan, your marketing plan outlines the steps you will take to match your customers' needs with the best products and services you can provide. It helps you decide how to spend your marketing budget, and it keeps you from making costly mistakes by reminding you what your business really is. There can be no successful business plan without a marketing plan.

The marketing plan is your project management tool. It outlines your basic goals and the things you will do to design each of these marketing mix elements:

- The product and services you will offer for sale
- The product's or services' prices
- Your customers and the distribution network (place) or path your product will travel to get to them
- The promotional methods you will use to let potential buyers find out that your product exists

In addition, a good plan will make sure that your product and services match the image you want to create. In summary, your marketing plan will need to cover the following three steps:

1. Decide who you are. Create a clear description of what your business has to offer.
2. Decide who you want as clients.
3. Devise a plan to attract those clients and determine the best way to reach clients without wasting money.

DEVELOP AND IMPLEMENT COST-EFFECTIVE STRATEGIES, TOOLS, AND TACTICS

Howard Shenson, in his book *The Complete Guide to Consulting Success*, writes that the marketing strategies consultants use have a profound effect on their chances for success. He advocates the use of low-cost and no-cost strategies for consultants, as his research showed that the use of indirect, more public relations–like activities are far more effective than direct, hard-sell techniques that so many consultants use.

Tom Lambert echoes this advice in his book *High-Income Consulting*. In Europe, Lambert conducts the world's leading seminars on building and sustaining a consulting practice, which have been attended by more than 200,000 attendees worldwide. Lambert says that your overall marketing strategy should be aimed at becoming well known in your field, and that indirect methods of marketing bring clients to you. He also emphasizes that the tactics you select must be consistent with the reputation and image you want to create.

In *Zen and the Art of Making a Living*, Laurence G. Boldt writes that the name of the game in marketing is circulation—getting into circulation, and staying in circulation. Getting out and meeting people is circulating. Circulating flyers and making speeches is circulation. I liken it to name recognition. Whatever technique or tactic you use must be designed to increase your name recognition and build your reputation. Above all, you need imagination and effort to try and see what works and what doesn't work.

This section suggests a smorgasbord of tactics to use. What's important is to realize that you need a mix of tactics that suits your budget, time, and stage of development of your practice. This list is not exhaustive and is just designed to get you started. Never forget that time, energy, and imagination is your most powerful marketing tools. Here then are some key tips:

- *Referrals.* Referrals top the list of most effective marketing methods. Good news does travel fast, but always remember that bad news travels faster. So be sure your consultancy always stays in integrity and does its best to stay on the leading edge. To do that, you'll need to know who and what influences the buyers of consulting services in your target markets. Then look for developing strategic alliances and a referral network in the marketplace (the organization).
- *Communicate.* Establish a program of ongoing communications and building relationships with your contacts. Drop notes and comments about trends you see, experiences and events, any observations of interest. Do the same with other writers, academics, researchers, and the like. Remember, once you have been quoted, you are more likely to be quoted again. When you are quoted a few times, you become known as an expert.

- *Stay in touch.* As demonstrated by Saatchi and Saatchi over a 20-year test period, 90 days is the maximum cycle for building relationships. Think what it's like to get a call from someone you met two years ago. They invite you to lunch and you know three things absolutely: They are in trouble, they want your help, and you will end up paying for lunch. This is not the reaction you want people to have to you. Staying in touch regularly, within 90 days, takes away the sense of "this is going to hurt." Go back to the companies you have worked for, seek updates on how they are doing, and keep the door open for ongoing assignments.

- *Human contact.* Mingle at conventions, consultant organizations, and seminars in your field where prospects might be open to learning about your services. Remember that nothing beats meeting face to face with a client.

- *Get published.* You may get lots of inquiries after prospects read about you in trade publications, magazine articles, or even from participating in e-discussions on the Internet.

- *Use the Internet.* Some of our business comes from prospects surfing the Internet. Companies should be sure they have effective meta tags on their Web site so they will come up first or near the top in a search engine. It also helps to be listed on others' Web sites, which increases your chances of being seen, and increases a sense of credibility. Participating in Web Forums is a good technique.

- *Design your own Web site.* Run Online Marketing programs. Put URLs on stationery. Ensure signature file on e-mails and promotional materials.

- *Do charity work.* By participating in high-profile community charity projects, you can connect with some movers and shakers that can hire you and/or refer you. Give to get. Do volunteer work. Join and become actively involved in consultant organizations. Do some volunteer or community outreach work—let this be a taste for what you can do for pay, and treat this as an audition to get referrals.

- *Create a directory.* Create a directory for businesses or people who fit into your niche. Make the listings be for free, though if you want to be like the yellow pages, you can charge for bigger, more bold, or box-enclosed display advertisements. Include short articles; even highlight a business in each issue. Be sure to include your contact information and your attractive offer. This is a good way to become known, establish expertise, and provide value at relatively little cost to yourself. Ask for your name to be put in databases and directories. Ask to be listed in their bulletins.

- *Scan for opportunities.* Read the local paper daily and look for new businesses, merging businesses, or businesses in trouble. Follow up through phone calls, letters, or contacts.

- *Join local consulting associations and attend their meetings.* These can be a great source of contacts.

- *Give talks.* Meetings give you the opportunity to present your services' features and benefits orally. Prepare carefully for each meeting by scanning the agenda and noting discussion items in which your service should be involved. Don't wait to be invited. Remember all employees are your customers and, therefore, your lifeline within the organization. When making a formal presentation, incorporate features and benefits into your remarks beforehand. In making comments from the floor, focus on those features and benefits the assembled group is most interested in.

- *Publish articles.* Company newsletters are a secondary source for marketing your business. Since the company newsletter has a wider distribution than memos, reports, and presentations, articles allow you to reach a wider audience with your message.

- *Send articles.* Route interesting articles on communication to senior managers. Always read with scissors in your hand. Send your clients copies of articles, and attach a compliment slip that states "Thought you could make use of this. . . ." When you write an article and it appears in print, a useful technique is to arrange for reprints and to send it to your target market with a note. Clip and send articles of interest; doing so shows personal interest on your part. To enhance the personal touch, handwrite a note to send along with the clips.

By sharing articles, information, and facts with your customers, you can begin to pave the way for an increased commitment to communication. Remember, awareness always precedes behavior change, and these methods will help to put your name foremost in the customer's mind. Whichever method you use—remember that it is all in aid of one thing: Name Recognition.

Prepare Media Lists

You may have opportunities to be quoted in the local press, which would have an interest in you as a local expert on almost any subject. Find out who on the local paper covers your subject or area. Nearly all working writers and editors keep a file of experts on whom to call if they want to verify facts, get ideas, and generally deepen their understanding of a subject. Use phone, letters, or some contribution to make the first contact. Describe your qualifications as an expert; offer to be of help any time the writer/editor is covering the subject. Watch the publications you read, especially local ones, for references to people who are involved in your niche specialty. These could be potential clients, sources of new information, or people who can refer you.

Use the Media

- Draft press releases agreeing or disagreeing with statements of opinions by taking a controversial position—you will more likely get coverage.
- Prepare a one-page backgrounder outlining your areas of experience, including news cuttings about you and any broadcast experience you have had. Circulate this to key journalists and TV and radio producers.
- Always have an updated press kit available—updated release, bio, photo (head and shoulders), reprints of articles written by you or about you, testimonials, and business cards.
- Try to land a position as a self-syndicated columnist or commentator for radio, TV, or a magazine.
- Write articles for publication in consultant or trade journals and circulate copies to others who are influential in both your internal and external target markets.
- The media loves an expert, and it is easy to promote yourself as one. Make sure that your options are quoted in press releases and articles. Be prepared to make predictions, voice concerns, or call for changes in your field of expertise. Volunteer your views to the media whenever possible.
- Write opinion pieces and letters to the media. Make sure your name is attached to features and articles on your subject. Become known as an expert in your field. Generate press releases with information. Become a valuable, reliable source for the media. Write columns or articles. Send press releases in live with editorial closing dates.

Direct Mailings

- Do regular mailings to customers, prospects, and target media.
- Identify any high-profile speaking opportunities such as conferences, local inquiries, and public meetings.
- Call your consultant or trade organizations; check trade media for any events that are organized. Consult exhibition organizers and business directories.

- Get involved in local or regional trade organizations such as the Rotary Club and Chamber of Commerce. Offer to act as press officer for them. Put yourself forward for committees and branch duties.

- Offer yourself as speaker to every local group you can find to attract potential clients. Tell people convincingly and pleasantly that you can help them achieve their goals and they will take the trouble to ask you how. Offer to speak at associations. Speak at your local Rotary Club, Lion's Club, and other civic organizations. Speaking at these events, even for free, helps your marketing. If people will not listen to you when your fee is free, they are not likely to pay for consulting. Send your details as a prospective speaker to a number of organizations, councils, committees, associations, and boards. Tell them why you feel what you have to say will be of interest to their needs.

- Always present a giveaway after any speech.

- List in as many directories as possible.

- Start your own networking group.

- Join up with people with similar objectives. Meet with them and explore the idea of associating with and supporting each other. Present yourself as a narrow specialist in the area of greatest immediate need.

- Make a list of all your clients, prospective clients, and sources of referrals. Ensure that as many people as possible who may need your services or refer you to others know about you.

- Compile a newsletter. Circulate it to your database. A newsletter is not perceived as advertising but as information, so it gets past the secretary.

- Run seminars and workshops.

- Run live public seminars in every major city in the country.

- Do speaking tours in other countries with both local people and corporations. Produce tapes (cassettes and videos) and books for selling. Brainstorm topics.

Quick Follow-Up

- Remember the popular "48-hour" and "90-day" cycle rule. The "48-hour" rule holds that all letters, phone calls, and contact should be done within 48 hours after the initial contact is made. Follow up meeting someone new with a "nice to meet you" letter. Include with it a small recap of what you have done.

- People are warm when you are not trying to sell them anything. Congratulate others on their accomplishments, including people known to you or those you have targeted to meet.

The Value of a Good Name

- The most effective advertisement is word-of-mouth. Your most important asset is your good name. Establish a good reputation and build your contacts and references.

- Make time for marketing.

- Spend time marketing every week.

- Build strategic alliances.

- Look for ways in which you can align yourself to what others do to start networking. Look for ways to build future business together. The best way to get subcontracting work is to network with local consultants, preferably those with complementary, not competitive, talents or specialties. Let other consultants know you are available for work, but do not ask for it directly.

Image

- Remember the impact of a logo and color in name recognition. Get letterheads, stationery, cards, and labels.
- Make contact with CEOs.
- Many people may not want to speak to you, but when you tell them that you are an editor of a publication, and are willing to write a piece on their industry or are seeking to interview the three top opinion leaders in the world, this is likely to get a response. But remember, you must act as a journalist, not an editor. Conduct your interview. Draft your article and send a copy to the chairman for verification that he is happy that you quoted him as indicated. After publication, send 20 copies and a brief "thank you" note. There is every chance that he will circulate those 20 copies.

Leverage Existing Relationships and Clientele

- Manage the client relationship. This stage of the marketing process deserves special attention; it is a critical step in determining whether a particular marketing effort will be deemed a success.
- Repeat or add-on business directly from current clients and the potential for referrals provides marketing with relatively low marketing costs. Because regular customers can be vital to the success of a consulting business, the relationship is critically important in the marketing of consulting services. Unfortunately, it is not usually seen as a direct step in the marketing process.
- The consultant should establish a relationship with a client as early as possible in the marketing cycle. The better the initial relationship, the greater the chance that a project will result. By getting close to a prospective buyer, you can learn about the buyer's specific issues, resistance, personal styles and preferences, purchasing process, and organizational culture.
- Strengthening your relationship with the client—not just delivering on the work proposed—will build an important marketing foundation. That is true throughout the sales cycle and after the project is sold, as well as into the service-delivery phase.
- It is not enough to schedule progress-review meetings only to explain schedules, deliverables, and budgets. As a marketing-oriented consultant, you should assume responsibility for initiating face-to-face informal meetings to discuss such questions as: Are you satisfied with the way our consultants and your staff are working together? Do you have complaints that you haven't discussed with us? Can we provide you with any additional information? What work do you see us doing together in the future? Have I told you how much we appreciate your business?

The bottom-line: In this increasingly fast-moving, complex, and competitive world, the consultants who will be able to leverage their marketing success are those who stay close to their clients; who work with them in business partnerships to anticipate needs and develop demand-driven solutions; who create distinctive advantages in the marketplace; and who use marketing plans to run their consulting businesses.

For those who are willing to commit to the discipline required for a strategic-marketing approach to consulting, the payoffs will show on the bottom line and in increased satisfaction for clients and the business.

In summary, leveraging existing clients is like mining gold in your own backyard as they present a virtual captive market. With these clients a premium should be placed on maintaining and improving quality relationships, particularly also because they constitute the major source of referrals, other sources being nonclient influences such as bankers who might provide leads or mention their clients and others.

It is considered that, among the professions, 80 to 100 percent of all new business obtained comes from the referrals network or word-of-mouth. For this reason, all referrals should be identified and then analyzed by considering questions such as the following: How many referrals per client and nonclient types? Why are they making referrals? Why aren't others making referrals on my behalf? What is the quality of the relationship with key referral sources? How often are these referral sources contacted to thank them for their efforts and such additional referrals? And how frequently does this firm reciprocate by making appropriate referrals to them?

After answering these questions, many consultants find that they have been lax in the cultivation and maintenance of referral sources, a most important market segment.

THE RESULTS OF MARKETING

Marketing will increase your consultancy's credibility and visibility and maintain and extend your own reputation. Remember the secret to any marketing successes is *continuity*. Whatever you decide to do, keep doing it!

CHAPTER 27

Interviewing with Consulting Firms

Charles J. Fombrun and Daniel F. Oriesek

All interviews can be divided into three stages: Pre-interviewing, interviewing, and post-interviewing. You learn something from all three stages. The main focus of the pre-interviewing phase is on generating actual interviews and preparing as best you can for those interviews. The interviewing phase itself addresses the ways you sell yourself during the interview and providing prospective employers with such a good feeling that they want to make you an offer on the spot. The post-interviewing phase provides an opportunity to evaluate what went well and what did not. The lessons learned should have an impact on how you approach your next interview, whether a day later or in the distant future. Figure 27–1 depicts these three stages of the interview process. We will look more closely at each of these phases in this chapter.

STAGE 1: PRE-INTERVIEWING

Suppose you have decided that you want to pursue a career in consulting and that you have done some preparatory reading to familiarize yourself with the different kinds of specialty areas in the consulting industry such as Strategy Consulting, Operations Consulting, Human Resources Consulting, or Technology Consulting. You have decided which one of the areas you have the greatest affinity for and which of these areas you are most likely to seem qualified for. You've used available Web resources to identify the key players of interest in these areas, and have actually studied the company Web pages and all promotional materials you could get your hands on.

Your big job now is to market yourself as best you can to those firms. To do so, you have to recognize that every year thousands of applicants are trying to get into the same firms that appealed to you, and that only a few will ever get on the inter-

Charles J. Fombrun is Executive Director of the Reputation Institute and Professor Emeritus of Management at the Stern School of Business of New York University. He is widely published in leading research and professional journals.

Daniel F. Oriesek is an associate with Booz Allen Hamilton in Zurich, Switzerland. He holds a BS degree in management from City University in Zurich and an MBA from the Stern School of Business at New York University.

We gratefully acknowledge the contribution of Peter Eliopoulos, a Stern School graduate, who contributed to some of the examples and background in this chapter through joint work with Professor Fombrun on the first Interviewing Workshop conducted at the Stern School (NYU).

FIGURE 27-1   The Interview Process

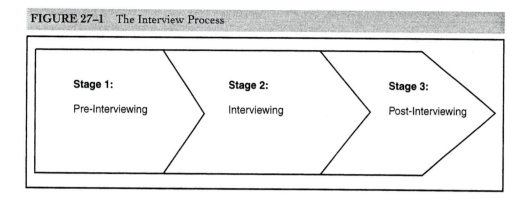

view list, let alone into the firm. Be very aware that you are competing with very bright overachievers from all the best schools in the world, all of whom probably have terrific backgrounds, good grades, and think they are God's gift to consulting. Your challenge is to find a way to cut through the clutter of applications from this large pool of applicants and get noticed. That's no mean feat, and here are some words of advice.

Rule 1: Be Professional

A famous proverb states:" You never get a second chance to make a first impression!" That's true of all high-profile jobs, and will prove just as true in the consulting market-place. Whether you attend a corporate presentation, call in for an information package, or are preparing your résumé, always remember that every interaction you have with the firm—however seemingly remote—is an interaction with someone who, at the end of the day, can prove to be either a supporter or a detractor. That first encounter and first impression can help you or hurt you when it comes time to decide who makes it on to the invite lists.

Consulting firms deal regularly with *Fortune* 500 companies where they themselves are held to high standards of professionalism in dress and style. Consequently the firms' first pass at assessing prospective employees generally involves the most superficial criteria—appearance. Some basic tips here: Always dress for the occasion. If an invitation states "business casual," make sure you know what that means. Do not show up in sneakers and blue jeans, just because you feel more comfortable in them or think you'll stand out. You will indeed, but it will be for the wrong reasons. If you are in doubt, talk to people, and as a last resort check it with the host person listed on your invitation. A good rule of thumb most consultants adopt is that it is always better to be overdressed than underdressed, and it's generally wise to dress one notch above your client.

When you've made contact with company representatives, make sure to thank them for their assistance. Not everyone gets a personal thanks, of course, but try to send a little note or e-mail to the person who sent you information or an invitation—they'll appreciate it and might have a good word to say about you at the right moment. Without a doubt, you want to make contact with the people who took personal time to provide you with an informational interview.

A related issue is to try as best you can to know something about the people you are interfacing with. No ingratiation is necessary in all this, and you don't want to act differently with some people just because they are higher in formal status. Administrative staff can be quite influential and involved in judging potential candidates.

Make no sloppy mistakes in letters and documents you submit. Consulting is a details business, and you should convey care in your handling of communications and materials. Have others read your résumé and incorporate their feedback where it makes sense. Take advantage of any formal advisors or family friends you may have access to—they can help improve your self-presentation. If possible, try to find out from people who worked there what the culture of the firm is like, what they look for, and how to best present yourself. Every little bit can help.

Few résumés are well written, and that's a no-no. After all, it's the first impression you'll make. A few words of advice here: Résumés should be kept as simple as possible. Try very hard to fit your life on *one page*. The idea is to be comprehensive in conveying what you've done, but not to fully describe every last detail of everything you've ever done in your life. Ask yourself: What does it all add up to? Why should they want me to work for them? It won't be in the details of every job you have held or course you have taken. It will be in the *pattern* that they read into the combination of jobs you've held, the trajectory you've been on, the extracurricular work you've done, and how it all fits together to make for someone likely to fit the profile of their kind of consultant.

A few nitty-gritty points: Recruiters go through hundreds of résumés. In doing so, they read left to right, and so tend to focus on the left side of each line of text. It is therefore wise to start each line of your résumé with an active verb (such as *analyzed, managed, presented*, etc.) in order to highlight your skills and the activities you were involved in. Instead of writing: "I put together a spreadsheet in which I compiled the financial data of firms in the entertainment industry in order to rank them according to their profitability . . .," you could simply write "Analyzed companies in the entertainment industry." In doing so, the recruiter instantly gets an idea of what skills you bring to the table, and at the same time you might spark his interest for what exactly it was you analyzed. Do not worry about keeping the résumé at a rather general level, because during the interview, you typically get an opportunity to elaborate on the details. While writing your résumé, you should also be aware that what you state under "additional information" will often be used as an ice breaker to start the interview. So understand that if you write about your hobby being golf, you're likely to be asked about your handicap or whether you are following the PGA tour. It's very dangerous to stretch the truth on a résumé to impress an interviewer—you'll probably get caught. It is best to be genuinely yourself—after all, that's what you will want to be when you're on the job, so what's the point of acting like what you're not.

Figure 27–2 shows a prototypical consulting résumé. There are other ways to do it, but consider this as a workable format. The cover letter that accompanies the résumé you submit is also important: It should describe why you are applying to the firm, and why you think your strengths would be a good fit for the firm. It's okay here to be specific about key skills you bring to the table. Also make it clear here that you are eager for a formal interview. A sample cover letter is provided in Figure 27–3.

FIGURE 27–2   A Prototype of a Consulting Résumé

FIRST NAME, LAST NAME
Street Address
Phone/Fax
E-mail

Education:	**NEW YORK UNIVERSITY**
	Leonard N. Stern School of Business
	Master of Business Administration, May 2003
	Emphasis in Finance and Management
	   Management Consulting Association, Vice President of Public Relations
	   Graduate Finance Association Member
	   Academic Committee Member
		New York, NY

	SYRACUSE UNIVERSITY
	Bachelor of Engineering and Commerce, 1995
	   GPA 3.7
	   Pinnacle Award for Outstanding Public Relations Student
	   London Study Abroad Scholarship
	   Portfolio Manager of Investment Club
		Syracuse, NY

Experience:
1999 - 2001
	ANDERSEN CONSULTING
	Senior Associate, Corporate Practice
	   Led team of 4 managers and subordinates; devised research methodology analyzing
	   perceptions of customers, employees and investors; presented strategic recommendations to
	   director of global communications; resulted in change of corporate communications strategy.
	   Conducted research and worked on team to prepare CEO for pending spin-off announcement.
	   Managed investor relations client relationship, responsible for strategically positioning client to
	   investment community, writing corporate materials, and Web site content.
		Detroit, MI

1997 - 1998	**FORD MOTOR COMPANY**
	Engineering Supervisor
	   Earned outstanding employee award for Corporate Practice; one of youngest worldwide promoted to
	   Senior Associate.
	   Wrote marketing proposals for NYSE listing ceremonies; implemented programs.
	   Developed and presented new business presentations to client prospects.	

1995 - 1997	**Line Engineer**
	   Worked on prototype development team for major car division; coordinated team logistics.
	   Managed new parts ordering system.	

1995 - 1996	**CAPITAL ASSOCIATES** **Finance Intern** Conducted competitive analysis of global automotive sector.	Syracuse, NY

1994 - 1995	**FEINSTEIN PARTNERS**
	Investor Relations Intern
	   Worked on financial analysis of transportation industry.
	   Wrote news releases, quarterly reports.
		Cambridge, MA

Additional:	Member of Executive Board, Neighborhood Community Center Baseball umpire Enjoy golf, politics, bridge, history Expertise in computer graphics, machine language, and Web services	

Rule 2: Be Prepared

Assuming you had good grades, are smart, and followed all the advice above, you should now be receiving invitations to interview. Congratulations, you've passed the first hurdle! The time has come to make sure that you are as prepared as you can be for the actual interview. Consulting interviews are typically case interviews, meaning that a

FIGURE 27–3 A Prototype of a Cover Letter

27 October 2003

MAJOR CONSULTING FIRM
Street Address
New York, NY 10001

Dear Mr. or Ms. _____

I write to you on the advice of _____ regarding joining [MAJOR CONSULTING FIRM]. I have followed the development of [MAJOR CONSULTING FIRM] over the last few years and am particularly interested in the assistance you've provided to clients in the automotive industry. I became familiar with some of that work from reading some of your widely reported studies.

My work with Ford Motor Company over the last few years has provided me with a privileged understanding of the operational and strategic challenges facing the automotive sector. Strength in both engineering and my more recent managerial responsibilities equip me well to join the transportation practice at [MAJOR CONSULTING FIRM].

I look forward to speaking with you directly and to have the opportunity to join the team at [MAJOR CONSULTING FIRM].

Regards,

Signature

Your Name

good portion of the time will be spent working on particular case problems. While the types of cases vary depending on the type of consulting work you want to get into, some things hold true for almost all consulting interviews. First, you are typically given only a few minutes to take the interviewer through your résumé. This is when you get to tell your story, so don't start in kindergarten! Tell them about your adult years and explain key stages of a career that has now brought you to consulting. While you should be ready to answer detailed questions along the way, you should also emphasize how each step was a logical evolution of the previous one. You want to demonstrate how your interest in consulting evolved over time and that it is not just a fad, because you heard that one could make a lot of money.

A question frequently asked by people applying for consulting positions is whether they should mention failures at all. While it depends on the situation, once more, you should be yourself and generally not be afraid to talk about the tough times and how you overcame them. What lessons did you learn and how did you manage to move on. This is especially true if you were in a business of your own (Internet start-up?) and for some reason had to close it down. Rather than just leave a gap in your timeline, you should proactively address what happened during that time and what its effect was on your development. Of course, if this was only a small side business, while you were at school or on a regular job, you probably don't need to mention it unless specifically asked about it.

Most consulting interviews also include some sort of behavioral questions. Here, interviewers ask you how you might behave in a given situation and try to extract information about your character. For example you might be asked: "You are a member of a workgroup and one of the other members is performing below par. What do you do?" There are no right or wrong answers here, and again you should answer in a fashion that is consistent with the real you. However, it helps to bear in mind that consulting firms typically emphasize teamwork but are also very output oriented. When answering this kind of question, you should try to convey two points: One, that you have the necessary interpersonal skills to work with other people, and two, that you keep in mind that you still have to deliver some output by the end of the day. Therefore a possible answer might be: "Well, I would sit down with the individual and try to understand why performance isn't up to par and remind him that it's a drag on the whole team. Based on his comments, I would devise an action plan with him to improve his performance going forward and get him working with the team. However, if performance does not improve, I would have to replace him in order to still meet the deadlines for the deliverables."

Preparing intensely for cases is vital. We will examine some typical consulting cases in the next section describing the Interview Stage. For now, suffice it to say that in the pre-interview stage, take every opportunity to "practice, practice, practice, and then practice some more!" There is no better preparation for live case interviews than to feel comfortable with how they are done and to know that you have aced your prep cases. You can practice on your own, or use practice cases from such online sources as Wet Feet Press, Vault, or your school's consulting club. It always helps to do some sparring sessions with people who have already been through case interviews. You can practice with colleagues who are in the same situation as you, but typically these sessions are less productive and lack the necessary objectivity. Business schools typically offer mock interviews with more senior students, and consulting clubs frequently invite industry experts to coach people through the interview process. Online cases are another resource offered by some of the consulting firms, such as The Boston Consulting Group (*www.bcg.com*) and McKinsey & Company (*www.mckinsey.com*). The nice thing about these cases is that you get immediate feedback and they show you expected approaches for solving the case as well.

A prerequisite for successful case interviewing is familiarity with the most common frameworks. Figure 27–4 summarizes a selection of frameworks that prove most useful in case interviews.

You can find most of these frameworks in the current business literature or in preparatory guides such as those provided by Wet Feet Press or in the publications from the various consulting clubs in business schools.

A final suggestion: Familiarize yourself with some key cultural, demographic, and geographic information involving the region in which you are interviewing. This includes population size, number of households, and a few other useful numbers. While you will not be probed about whether you know the exact number of households with people aged 65 years and older, knowing the approximate number will help you significantly when faced with estimations of market size or other calculations.

After all the intense prepping, a final piece of advice for the pre-interview phase: Relax! All the numbers and frameworks are of little use to you if you are so nervous and stressed out that you fail at simple calculations. We therefore suggest that 48 hours

FIGURE 27–4   Useful Frameworks for Case Interviews

Framework	Application
Internal/External	The firm versus the market/environment
Supply/Demand	Market analysis, strategy, pricing
Cost–Benefit	Evaluating business opportunities, strategy
Marginal Cost Analysis	Profit or operational questions
Fixed Cost/Variable Cost	Profit or operations of new business opportunities
BCG (Growth-Share) Matrix	Evaluating a current product portfolio
Customer–Company–Competition	Strategy, market opportunity
4 P's	Marketing and new product development
Porter's Five Forces	Industry analysis, strategy
Value Chain	Where money is made from supplier to end consumer

prior to the interview, you put away all your cases and do whatever you enjoy most. You might review a few frameworks and numbers before the interview, but the general wisdom holds true that if you don't already know it, you won't learn it in the last two hours before an interview. If it gives you piece of mind, think of it this way. The fact that you have been selected for an interview indicates that the firm sees you as a potential candidate. They believe that you are qualified enough and that you probably have what it takes to be working for them. Just show it!

STAGE 2: INTERVIEWING

It's D-day. You got a good night's sleep and feel comfortable about your knowledge of the frameworks, facts and figures, and the firm. You arrive early for the interview, check your general appearance once more, and are greeted by someone from the firm who takes your name and offers you a coffee or soda. Since you arrived early, you will have a few minutes to collect yourself. Soon you'll be ushered into a room for the interview. Showtime!

The typical consulting interview can be broken down into three phases: The interviewer is there to (1) find out who you are, (2) find out whether you have what it takes, and (3) "case you."

Who Are You?   In the first phase of the interview, interviewers try to discern whether you have an engaging personality, and will fit with the people they know at their firms, and are fun to be around. The interview typically starts with an energetic greeting like: "Hi, my name is Joe Consultant. How are you doing today?" Although this sounds trivial, it serves the purpose of finding out whether you are mentally present and whether you are excited about the opportunity to interview with this particular firm. After the initial greeting, the interviewer might follow up with a question about your interests. So if in your résumé you said that you are into football, you might get a question like: "The Jets are heading for a pretty poor season, wouldn't you agree?" The question is designed to break the ice and make you feel a little more comfortable. No relaxing here—remember what you're there for: It's not to make friends with the interviewers but to impress them. Interviewers have been trained in how to get you to let down your guard, and if you do so, you might act more like a buddy rather than a consultant. While there is nothing wrong with actually getting to like your interviewer, be aware of the pitfall of forgetting the rule about professionalism. In answering such questions, be responsive, but do not get carried away. A good rule of thumb is to let the interviewer decide how deeply they'll get into a subject and leave them in control.

After the introductory chitchat, most interviewers give you a brief rundown on their own background and career at the firm. Listen carefully, for you might pick up clues that can be useful later in the interview. After the introduction, it is up to you to briefly walk the interviewer through your résumé. Now is the time to sell your story! Take about two to three minutes and briefly comment on all major stages of your career after graduating from college. This should be no problem, since you have practiced this part of the interview several times. Stress points you want to drive home, but always keep the overall timing in mind. When you come to the end of your rundown, you may conclude with a sentence like: "And this is why I am sitting here with you today." By using a well-chosen closing sentence, you signal that you are finished and hand the ball back to the interviewer for the second phase.

Do You Have What It Takes?   In the second phase, interviewers want to find out whether you'll make a good consultant. By now, they have a pretty good picture of who you are and why you are here, and they want you to address specific questions about your résumé. In doing so, interviewers typically stick to three kinds of questions. One is to ask you to "explain the gap" questions, aimed at finding out what you did between activities indicated on your résumé. A typical question might be: "So I see that after college, you took a break for six months. What exactly did you do during that time?" While in reality you traveled Europe to try as many brands of beer as possible and party at all the cool places, you might not want to state that in your answer. Try to link what you did to some skill building that the firm might appreciate. For instance, you could stress that you were looking for international exposure, that you liked to travel, or that you were working on your foreign language skills. Just make sure that if you say that you are fluent in Dutch that you are. It can very well happen to you that an interviewer speaks the foreign languages you claim to speak and, just for fun, could choose to conduct that part of the interview in another language.

A second type of question interviewers like to ask are "give me the details" questions: "So tell me about the work you did for XYZ" or "You write that you did several industry analyses at XYZ. What exactly did you look at and what kinds of deliverables did you produce?" When answering these questions you'll want to convey that you have the work experience, that you can work well on teams, that you have an aspiration to lead, and that you have the necessary intellect to do the kind of heavy conceptual and quantitative work often required of consultants.

The third type of questions is behavioral, such as: "How would the people working with you in a group describe you?" Here, be honest, recognize your strengths and weaknesses, and keep your team strengths at the forefront.

At this point, the interviewer will typically tell you that it's now time to do a case. Just as an aside, while interviewers usually indicate when they are giving you the case, some interviewers don't always make the transition apparent. Applicants have told us of instances in which the candidate walked out of the interview and thought to himself: "How come I did not get a case? All I did was answer questions about a project from my previous job." Two days later, after being "dinged," he realized that the questions regarding the project actually were the case and that he had failed to go into enough depth in his answers. In most cases, however, the same person who asked you behavioral questions will also work a case with you.

The Case Interview

A case is generally a problem posed to you by the interviewer to which he or she expects an answer. Most people, when confronted with their first case, show some of the following typical reactions:

- I have no idea . . .
- Good God, what am I doing here?
- Maybe you have got me mixed up with someone else . . .
- I am not a physicist, chemist, or mathematician . . .
- I am way out of my depth on this one . . .
- I am really not sure . . .
- What a crazy question . . .
- Can you give me more information?
- I will have to do some research . . .
- Can I get back to you on this one?

No matter how clever or humorous, these are not good answers. You'll look either nervous, desperate, or worse—at a total loss for what to do. And that's no way to look in front of a client who is challenging you in front of the rest of the company. How, then, should you react in such a situation? A good way to start is by smiling and staying calm. Let the initial horror wear off, take a few seconds to think about the question, and jot down a few preliminary ideas on a piece of paper. The key is to find some way to approach the problem systematically, using what you do know, and make some key assumptions if necessary in order to frame your general approach for the interviewer, forge ahead with estimates if expected, and conclude with an answer.

Why do consulting firms use cases? Not to torture you, but to get around well-known problems of standard behavioral interviews that mostly involve "chemistry" between interviewer and interviewee, are not an accurate test of the skills of the candidate, and are poor predictors of future performance on the job. Since consulting is all about problem solving with clients, consulting firms led by Booz Allen Hamilton developed case interviewing in the 1970s as a more valid tool for assessing candidates than behavioral résumé-based interviews. Cases are designed to help recruiters verify that you have the kinds of skills you'll need to be a good consultant. Specifically, cases are used to assess three types of skills:

1. *Diagnostic skills.* The ability to identify a problem and untangle key issues from peripheral ones. Do you ask pertinent questions and can you prioritize the issues raised?

2. *Analytical skills.* Do you have the ability to select and follow a logical line of reasoning, demonstrate systematic thinking, and make back-of-the-envelope calculations, and appreciate the implications of specific actions.
3. *Communication skills.* Can you express your ideas clearly? Are you a good listener? Can you defend your ideas if necessary, and how do you handle pressure?

Most cases can be described as one of three main types: calculation cases, problem cases, and probing cases. There are very many of each type. McKinsey & Company likes to use "big picture" cases and "technical" cases to probe for specialized knowledge. A.T. Kearney and Deloitte Consulting often use "operational" cases.

Figure 27–5 illustrates a general model for approaching a case. It suggests that you should begin by clarifying the stated problem: Rephrase it, paraphrase it, make sure you understand what's being asked, and demonstrate your listening skills in the process. Your second step should be to structure your approach to the problem by outlining your approach in more detail. In the third phase, you actually make some calculations or propose an answer or a solution. You end by concluding how well your answer addressed the initial question posed in the case.

The clarification phase is crucial. Here you want to explore the problem by asking questions. Say the interviewer raised a question about manufacturing in Spain and asked for an estimate of the potential market for the company. Since Spain is part of the European Union (EU), you might want to clarify whether you should only look at Spain (about 40 million people) or the entire EU (around 300 million people).

Crucial to the structuring phase is demonstrating that you are systematic in your approach and that you use some kind of framework or model to guide your thinking. If you know the perfect framework, use it. If none of the standard frameworks seems to apply, build your own. Try to crystallize a clear road map in your own mind about how you'd like to approach the issue. Doing so not only helps you organize your thoughts, it also makes it easier for the interviewer to follow your thinking. Form causal hypotheses if you can, such as: "Company A could be losing market share because its products are outdated." Based on this hypothesis, look for evidence to accept or reject the hypothesis. For example, if you learn from the interviewer that Company A was selling telex equipment, while the fax machine was introduced, you have a clue about one of the problems. After forming and testing several hypotheses, you should be in the position to summarize your findings and come up with a set of recommendations.

Keep in mind that the final answer to a case does not really matter as much as the thinking process you undergo in reaching your conclusion. Be sure that each time you

FIGURE 27-5   How Should You Think About a Case?

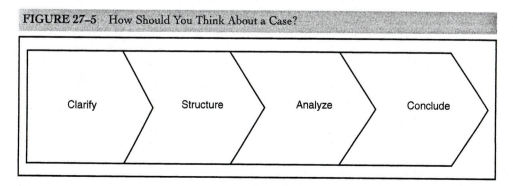

make an assumption or an estimate, you let your interviewer know, so that he or she can follow your line of reasoning. If you've had to make some calculations, try to double-check the validity of your numbers by doing a feasibility check. For example, if the case required that you estimate the total number of grocery stores in the United States and you came up with an estimate of 500 million, you might want to reconsider when you juxtapose it against the 280 million people living in the United States! The feasibility check helps you to be comfortable with your calculations and demonstrates to your interviewer that you pay attention to detail.

We provide below examples of cases of each major case type.

Calculation Cases

In calculation cases, the interviewer expects you to come up with a number. Getting to that number requires some calculations and estimations. Settings can be abstract or very concrete as the two following examples will demonstrate.

Question: How much money would it cost Arnold Schwarzenegger to fill up the Statue of Liberty with Russian vodka?
A possible approach is to estimate the volume of the Statue of Liberty based on an approximation of the standard formula for a cylindrical volume stated as $3r^2h$, where r refers to the radius of the statue and h refers to its height.

You might estimate it as: 30 stories, 8 feet per story, 20 foot radius
Volume of Statue of Liberty would then be about 288,000 cu. ft.
Estimate: 1 gallon of vodka is about 1 cu. ft. and costs about $30.
It would cost approximately $8,400,000 to fill the Statue of Liberty with vodka.

Question: How many gas stations are there in Canada?
A possible approach is to make a preliminary estimate of the demand side, then to estimate the supply side, and to assume that in equilibrium, demand must equal supply. For the demand side:

Assume Canada's population is about 30 million.
Estimate that there are approximately three people per household and one car per household, for a total of about 10 million cars.
Estimate: Every car refuels once a week for a total of 10 million car visits to gas stations per week throughout Canada.

Now look at the supply side of the equation at the gas stations:

Estimate: Cars come to a gas station at the rate of 10 visits/hour, 14 hours per day, seven days a week, for a total of 140 visits/day* 7 days = 980 visits/week

If equilibrium holds in Canada, demand will equal supply and everybody gets the fuel they need:

Total number of gas stations = 10 million visits per week / 980 visits per week per station
= 10,020 stations

Problem Cases

These types of cases are designed in order to observe you solve a specific problem. They can come in many forms and relate to many industries and settings. The questions are typically fairly detailed and indicate that the interviewer is looking for a clear approach to answer the question. To give you an example, imagine the following:

> Your client is a U.S. manufacturer of men's tailored suits. The company sells about half a million suits a year exclusively in the United States through specialty and department store retailers. Currently, wholesalers buy the suits from independent sales reps, who earn a commission of 5 percent or roughly 10 percent per suit. The manufacturer wants your advice on whether or not to establish an in-house sales force.

You can approach this case in many ways, but we would suggest you first peel out the key question: "In-house sales force or not?" Once you focus on this question, you ought to think about what would affect your decision, or, in other words, what are the key decision variables? After some reflection, you might end up with a short list like this one.

- Cost of in-house versus independent agents
- Type of cost (variable vs. fixed) → operational leverage
- Value chain → Is there an opportunity to reshape the way suits are sold to retailers?
- Incentive systems
- Operational challenges (training, administration, equipment, etc.)

You then want to analyze each of your points in order to make a final recommendation. Your first hypothesis could be: "An in-house sales force costs less per year than the current model." In order to accept or reject it, you would do some basic back-of-the-envelope calculations. For example, 500,000 suits times $10 per suit makes a total cost for sales reps of $5 million. Now you probably need some additional information, such as how many independent sales reps the company currently has, whether they are exclusively selling the company's products, whether they have access to clients that we would not have on our own, and so on. You then try to estimate how much it would cost you to build your own sales force, considering things like training, fixed salaries, equipment, and overhead needed. Then you basically try to come up with a cost–benefit analysis, weighing the pros of the two approaches versus the cons. In doing this analysis, you would further try to figure out whether there is a stable demand for suits or not. Given the variable cost character for an independent sales force, this approach could at first seem more expensive, but in times of weak demand prevent you from large cash outflows. After analyzing the two approaches, you could even go as far as drawing the current value chain and then see whether you could integrate not only the sales reps but possibly the wholesalers by going direct. This would allow you to capture more of the margin.

As astute readers will recognize, we consciously avoided providing a single answer here. That's because there are no right or wrong answers to this problem. Depending on the information your interviewer provides and your own judgment, you can argue in favor or against building an in-house sales force. The challenge of this kind of problem case is to make clear to the interviewer why you arrived at your conclusion and demonstrate your ability to back up your line of reasoning with data.

Probing Cases

A third common type of case is the probing case. With these cases the interviewer wants to force you to narrow down a problem. A possible case could go like this:

Your client is an established tire manufacturer in Germany, but over the last three years has constantly been losing market share. What do you think could be causing this problem?

The question is very broad and leaves you with plenty of possibilities. You would typically try to get more information before digging into the case. One possible question could be: "Has the overall market been shrinking, growing, or has it remained stable during that period?" This question has actually been asked during the interview and the slightly puzzled interviewer replied: "Why are you asking this question?" The interviewee then replied: "Because if the overall market is growing and we are not growing as fast as the rest, this could be an indication for a marketing problem or a change of consumer preference. However, if the market is shrinking or stable, this would more likely hint at a problem with our product or our customer base . . ." The interviewer, obviously impressed, stated that the market was stable. Given this additional information the interviewee went about testing his hypothesis with respect to product attributes. He asked the interviewer about product characteristics and quickly realized that the company's tires were as good as any other manufacturer's. So the problem was not with the product. After that, he tested his hypothesis with regard to the customer base. He again asked questions and found out that tire sales shifted away from traditional garages to superstores and discount outlets. He also learned that the people using this new channel were typically of younger age, and after asking about the characteristics of the company's customer base, he realized that they were growing older, while no new customers were coming in. He finally was able to summarize his findings and recommend that the company should look into offering their products in the new distribution channels and attracting younger customers as well.

Again, there is no right or wrong answer, and the way the case interview goes depends largely on whom you are interviewing with and the slant this person has on specific problems. There is nothing to be afraid of: Ask lots of questions and always know why you are asking them.

STAGE THREE: POST-INTERVIEWING

No matter how you did on your interview, you should always conduct a debriefing. Be honest with yourself and think about what went well and what did not. Of the things you believe did not go well, ask yourself why and how you could improve them if facing the same situation again. Did you know your numbers? Were you able to structure your problem? Did you double-check your answers? These are just a few reasons for trouble during the interview. Also be aware that you can always encounter people who actually do not like you and are giving you a hard time. We are not saying you should blame it all on them, but you should also realize that "personal chemistry" plays a big role in an interviewers final decision.

Consulting interviews usually have fast turnaround times and you often know within a day or two whether you passed or not. If you get that dreaded call: "Well Mr. X, we were very impressed by your résumé, but unfortunately cannot offer you a position with our firm . . ."—don't despair. Remain professional and ask the person whether he or she could give you more concrete feedback. Most firms do not, but from those that do, you can learn a lot when preparing for your next interview.

CHAPTER 28

Testimonials from Consultants

Charles J. Fombrun and Daniel F. Oriesek

How do people who have been working at a consulting firm for a few years recall their experience? What do they remember as key experiences along the way? With the wisdom of experience, what would they say to people who are now interested in pursuing jobs and careers in the brave new world of consulting, whether traditional or "extreme"?

To get some perspective on the issue, we decided to survey a stratified sample of Stern School (NYU) students working for five or more years, three to five years, less than three years, and who had only interned for a summer at a consulting firm. By selecting Stern graduates, we eliminated school effects that might have a strong effect on the experience, and thereby enabled a focus on the common issues that they faced across consulting firms.

The survey was conducted in spring 2000 directly on the Web. Participation in the survey was entirely voluntary and anonymous, and no incentives were offered. Figure 28–1 presents the invitation letter that was sent to these alumni. Figure 28–2 shows the questions that were asked of them. A comparable list of questions was also asked of summer interns.

Of 200 or so invitations to participate that were sent in March 2000, we received some 48 responses, a reasonable number for these types of surveys. Although the results are not necessarily representative of all MBA students who went into the consulting world, they provide some indication of the kinds of experiences current and past consulting students make to questions about the interviewing process, the work itself, training, mentoring, and the consulting career.

Figure 28–3 summarizes their average responses to these questions. As the diagram indicates, interns are a generally enthusiastic group, and more experienced consultants are less satisfied than interns, suggesting that the halo of the experience eventually wears off. The greater satisfaction of interns may also stem from the highly individualized attention they receive during internships—after all, the firms are on

Charles J. Fombrun is Executive Director of the Reputation Institute and Professor Emeritus of Management at the Stern School of Business of New York University. He is widely published in leading research and professional journals.

Daniel F. Oriesek is an associate with Booz Allen Hamilton in Zurich, Switzerland. He holds a BS degree in management from City University in Zurich and an MBA from the Stern School of Business at New York University.

FIGURE 28-1   Invitation Letter E-mailed to Stern Alumni

April 2000

Dear Stern Alum:

I am putting together a new book about the consulting industry for Prentice Hall. The book is entitled *Management Consulting: Fundamentals,* and introduces readers to the art, the practice, and the problems that consultants face. The book also sheds light on the complex roles that consultants and consulting firms play in enhancing the effectiveness of their clients.

Aside from more theoretical chapters written by me and by experienced consultants working in the major firms, the book will also address questions about life in consulting firms. To this end we are conducting a survey among Stern alumni who have been working in consulting firms for the last few years.

The survey is divided into two sections. The first section (click here) takes about 30 seconds and asks you to rate different aspects of your experience. The second section (click here) asks you to share some personal insights and advice with others who might be interested in becoming management consultants. Needless to say, we are very interested in both sections. Together, they should take you about 5 to 10 minutes to complete.

Note that your answers are completely anonymous and will be used only in summary form for this book, and not for any other promotional purposes.

On behalf of future readers, I thank you for your support.

Regards,

Charles Fombrun
Professor of Management
Director, Stern Management Consulting Program

their best behavior and eager to persuade them to return. We provide their more detailed responses below to add perspective and possible contrast to the formal presentations that consulting firms themselves make at career fairs.

THE RECRUITMENT PROCESS

Consultants generally say they are drawn to the profession for several reasons. The good salaries, the exciting projects, and the talented people they get to work with. In fact, this shared vision and excitement (also known as the "consulting bug") as well as innovative thinking seem to be among the strongest attractions for both interns and consultants, and make the average 60- to 70-hour workweek fun and exciting.

FIGURE 28–2 Consultant Survey Questions

Year Graduated: _____

Employer: _____

Principal Job (Check One):
_____ **Consultant**
_____ **Associate Consultant/Researcher**
_____ **Team Manager**

Length of Employment with this Firm: _____

Think back when you first joined the firm and your experiences since then.

1.) INTERVIEWING: What do you recall as your most memorable experience (positive or negative) during the recruitment process?

2.) WORKING: What do you recall as your most memorable experience (positive or negative) working with fellow consultants and with clients?

3.) TRAINING: Describe the kind of training the firm has provided you with since coming aboard.

4.) MENTORING: Has the firm provided you with useful career guidance and mentoring?

5.) WORK: How many hours do you work on average per week?

6.) CAREER: Are you contemplating any career changes or do you plan to remain in consulting for the foreseable future? If you're planning a change, describe the most attractive alternatives you would consider.

7.) SUMMARY: In your opinion, what are the key STRENGTHS and WEAKNESSES of this firm?

Overall, how satisfied are you with working in a consulting firm (circle one)?

	Not at all satisfied						Very satisfied
Training/Learning Opportunities	1	2	3	4	5	6	7
Contacts Made/Networking	1	2	3	4	5	6	7
Pay and Benefits	1	2	3	4	5	6	7
On-the-Job Socializing	1	2	3	4	5	6	7
Working Conditions/Scheduling	1	2	3	4	5	6	7
Career Opportunities	1	2	3	4	5	6	7
Travel	1	2	3	4	5	6	7

FIGURE 28-3 Survey Responses: Consultants and Interns

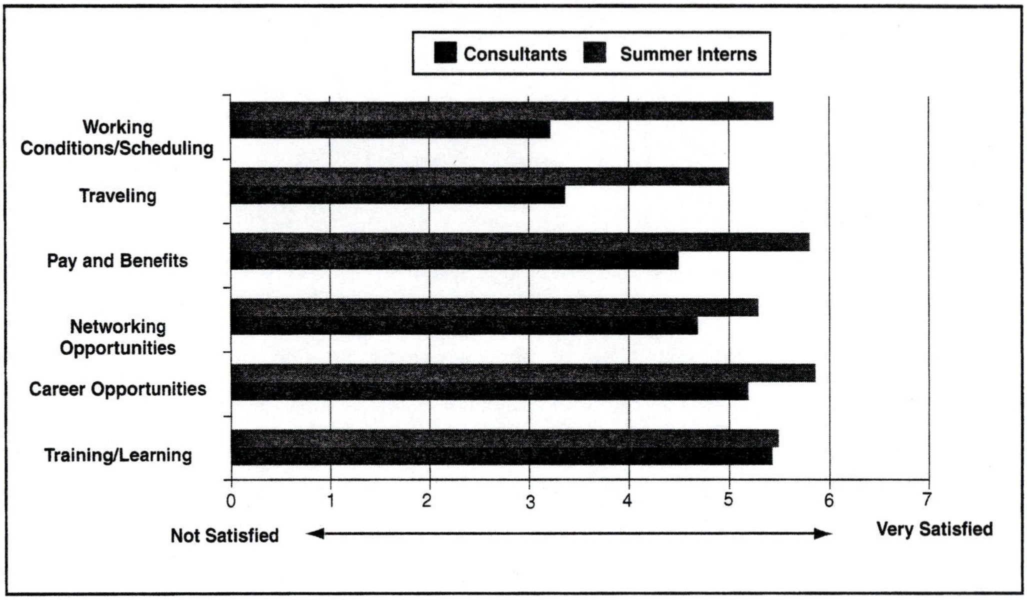

Here are representative quotes about their experiences during the recruitment process from survey respondents:

One of the managing directors with whom I interviewed told me that I might not have the necessary skill sets. Whereas after I was hired, the same managing director told me that I was the most qualified candidate and was best suited for the position. Don't fall for intimidation tactics on the interviews or negotiations.

Four months elapsed from between first interview to offer in hand . . .

The people seemed approachable and friendly. It made me want to work with these people.

You need to participate in lots of case interviews and do the long hours of practicing.

Most memorable for me was having a senior partner fall asleep during my interview with him—and I got the job.

Great fun with the cases. Be excited about solving the cases, don't be afraid to answer questions, and co-opt the interviewer into the problem-solving process. Don't presume that you have to do it all alone. Ask intelligent questions. I really enjoyed all the cases because I approached them as challenges. The interviewers loved this and the sense of fun and success was shared. Experienced interviewers know how to bring out the best in people. I came out feeling both exhilarated and having put together some well considered, well structured solutions!

I found that the key to impressing interviewers during the case was demonstrating logical, structured thinking, sometimes at the expense of intelligence, speed-of-thought, and breadth of knowledge.

I was asked "Why?" at least ten times during the interview to test my reasoning process.

Everyone was very relaxed and nice. There were no "head games" or stress testing.

The consultants were genuinely interested in finding out whether or not they wanted to work with me.

The interviewers at this particular firm were hot and cold. They were also defensive about their "strategy" work. When asked about their work, they launched into a speech about the value of the strategy and how it is not appreciated because it doesn't affect the bottom line immediately. It seemed they had answered this question before.

It's all about the case!

WORK EXPERIENCES WITH COLLEAGUES AND CLIENTS

Respondents were also asked about their work experiences during their internships or in subsequent assignments with the firms. Responses were generally favorable. Some of the more memorable experiences are indicated by the following quotes:

An assignment in Singapore in which the client was very hospitable. The client allowed us time for sightseeing, treated us to a great meal of indigenous cuisine, and client-personnel showed us around. We successfully completed the project in 10 days and had a great time as well.

One of our clients told us that it was the first time that he had worked with a team of consultants that had taught them and guided them (instead of having the consultants learn from them).

A client making unfounded accusations of poor work quality to extort free work. The client had just lost two staffers and did not have the budget to hire our help, so they lied.

Winning an award for "Core Values Champion" at an annual picnic. It is an award voted on by project members to recognize those who follow the core values of the firm.

I truly felt that within my project team, we were all in it together, despite rank, or anything else.

I came to feel over time that the partnership was interested in short-term gains to a fault—particularly when such considerations took precedent over the long-term development of their people.

Positive: Making friends in various countries and of course the work . . . Negative: Getting stuck in the Ho Chi Minh airport overnight because of a missed connection.

I spent six months on a project where three particular assignments were on the Cayman Islands. It was a very rewarding project because it had complete backing of the client (financial, resources, time, etc.).

Presenting to the VP of E-Business at a major corporation to describe to her what her business will look like in 5 years.

Working with a consumer products company and helping them to change the culture of their organization to be a "high performance" culture.

TRAINING AND LEARNING

Overall, respondents seemed satisfied with their consulting careers partly because of the great training and learning opportunities the firms provided. Their replies suggest that by far the most valuable part of training happens on the job. The opportunity to work on real-life problems with a select group of highly talented people was mentioned as the most exciting aspect of training.

Most consulting firms also have formal mentoring programs, in which more junior consultants get advice on job-related questions and career decisions from an experienced member of the organization. Other forms of training are more formal in nature and include professional seminars, conferences, outings, technical training, and managerial and skill-building courses. These training sessions range anywhere from one day up to several weeks and tend to decline as one advances to more senior levels within the organization.

More senior respondents also indicated that a key to their success in consulting was their ability to build a strong network of informal mentors. These people can be colleagues from a project or from one's home office. Mentors are largely self-selected and can be a powerful source of firsthand information about opportunities in the firm and in the industry.

Most summer interns in consulting were sent through an intensive training session at the beginning of the summer. These sessions ranged from one-day orientations up to a week of training, and were typically conducted in comfortable resorts where interns from around the world got to meet each other. More senior respondents to the survey pointed out that this was a great opportunity to network, because of the shared experiences they provide that will subsequently become a natural icebreaker in future meetings with other members of the firm.

CAREER OPPORTUNITIES AND NETWORKING

Respondents seemed pleased with the career opportunities provided to them. As some indicated, advancing to partnership level within a consulting firm is almost like running your own business, with all the entrepreneurial implications it entails. Even if you do not make partner, however, they all emphasized that the skills acquired, the reputation of the profession, and the alumni network you build with other consultants you work with and with clients are an invaluable asset.

Large consulting firms are also known for helping to outplace their own and some people mentioned the opportunities they were given to take positions at client companies. A few respondents mentioned the brain drain of the last few years that has developed as consultants were tantalized into leaving their firms to get involved in Internet start-ups. They all saw this as a direct result of networking with peers and clients.

WORKING CONDITIONS AND TRAVEL

The nature of project work forces consultants to work closely together over extended periods of time, and their satisfaction ultimately depends on the specific individuals you end up working with, as well as the specific projects to which you get assigned. Overall, respondents to this survey indicated they were happy with the degree of socializing they get on the job. Some suggested that the worst thing about their experience was their inability to choose the teams they worked with, but countered that the good thing was that most consulting firms make sure you do not have to work with people twice if you do not get along.

Almost all active consultants said they were satisfied with the degree of compensation they receive, but were less enthusiastic when it came to questions of work scheduling, work–life balance, and travel. Newer consultants appear to enjoy the travel aspect of the job more, but the initial excitement seems to wear off after the first year. Some of the respondents recognized that their firms had been trying to accommodate the geographic preferences of their employees. They also pointed out that most firms now make sure that consultants who are away on long-term engagements return home on weekends. Finally, most respondents indicated that they were happy about their ability to work from their home offices and enjoyed the flexibility it has created for dual-career couples.

Bibliography

Arrow, Kenneth J. *Essays in the Theory of Risk-Bearing*. Chicago: Markham Publishing, 1971.

Asher, Mark, and Eric Chung, *The Vault Guide to the Case Interview*. Vault Reports, 2001.

Barcus, S. W. III, and J. W. Wilkinson. *Handbook of Management Consulting Services*. New York: McGraw-Hill, 1986.

Bellman, G. *The Consultant's Calling: Bringing Who You Are to What You Do*. San Francisco: Jossey Bass, 1990.

Bernstein, Peter L. *Against the Gods: The Remarkable Story of Risk*. New York: John Wiley & Sons, 1996.

Black, Fisher, and Myron Scholes. "The Pricing of Options and Corporate Liabilities." *Journal of Political Economy*, vol. 101, no. 3 (May–June, 1993).

Block, Peter. *Flawless Consulting*. San Francisco, CA: Pfeiffer & Co., 1981.

Bogdan, R. C., and S. K. Biklin. *Qualitative Research for Education: An Introduction to Theory and Method* (2nd Edition). Needham Heights, MA: Allyn & Bacon, 1992.

Boldt, Laurence G. *Zen and the Art of Making a Living*. New York: Penguin, 1993.

Bolles, Richard Nelson. *What Color Is Your Parachute?: A Practical Manual for Job-Hunters and Career Changers*. Berkeley, CA: Ten Speed Press, 2001.

Boulton, Richard E.S., Libert, Barry D., and Samek, Steve M. *Cracking the Value Code*. New York: HarperCollins Publishers, 2000.

Brause, R. S., and J. S. Mayher. *Search and Re-search*. Philadelphia: Falmer Press, 1991.

Carucci, Ron A., and Toby J. Tetenbaum. *The Value-Creating Consultant: How to Build and Sustain Lasting Client Relationships*. New York: Amacom, 1999.

DeLoach, James W., *Enterprise-Wide Risk Management: Strategies for Linking Risk and Opportunity*. New York: Financial Times/Prentice Hall, 2000.

Dillman, D. A. *Mail and Telephone Surveys: The Total Design Method*. New York: John Wiley.

Drucker, Peter F. "The Age Of Social Transformation." *Atlantic Monthly* November 1994, pp. 53–80.

Farrell, John D., and Richard G. Weaver. *The Practical Guide to Facilitation: A Self-Study Resource*. Amherst, MA: HRD Press, 2000.

Fombrun, Charles J. *Reputation: Realizing Value from the Corporate Image*. Cambridge, MA: Harvard Business School Press, 1996.

Freemantle, David. *SuperBoss: The A–Z of Managing People Effectively*. Aldershot, UK: Ashgate Publishing, 1985.

Friedman, Milton, and Leonard J. Savage. "The Utility Analysis of Choices Involving Risk." *Journal of Political Economy*, Vol. 56, no. 4 (July–August), pp. 279–304.

Goetz, J. P., and M. D. LeComptre. *Ethnography and Qualitative Design in Education Research*. Orlando, FL: Academic Press, 1984.

Greiner, L. E., and R. O. Metzger, *Consulting to Management*. Prentice Hall, 1983.

Guba, E. G., and Y. S. Lincoln, "Competing Paradigms in Qualitative Research." In N. K. Denzin & Y. S. Lincoln (Eds.). *Handbook of Qualitative Research*. Thousand Oaks, CA: Sage Publications, 1994.

Harding, Ford. *Rainmaking: The Consultant's Guide to Attracting New Clients*. Avon, MA: Adams Media Corporation, 1994.

JP Morgan Securities Inc., "Equity Research Industry Report Beyond the Internet. The Emergence of Broadband and IP Data Services and the Prime Mover of a Technology Driven Economy," San Francisco, December 7, 1999.

Kubr, Milan (Ed.). *Management Consulting: A Guide to the Profession*. Geneva, IL, 1992.

Lambert, Tom. *High-Income Consulting*. London: Nicholas Brealey Publishing, 1997.

Landsberg, Max. *The Tao of Coaching*. Santa Monica, CA: Knowledge Exchange, 1997.

Lincoln, Y. S., and E. G. Guba. *Naturalistic Inquiry*. Thousand Oaks, CA: Sage Publications, 1985.

Maister, David, Charles Green, and Robert Galford. *The Trusted Advisor*. NY: Free Press, 2000.

Maister, David H. *True Professionalism: The Courage to Care About Your People, Your Clients, and Your Career*. New York: Free Press, 1997.

Maister, David. H. *Managing the Professional Service Firm*. New York: Free Press, 1993.

Mercer Delta Consulting Group. "Reshaping the Enterprise: Understanding the Dimensions of Organizational Change." *Mercer Delta Insights*. New York: Mercer Delta Consulting Group, 1999.

Merriam, S. B. *A Case Study Research in Education: A Qualitative Approach Analysis*. San Francisco: Jossey-Bass, 1988.

Merton, Robert, Myron Scholes, and Mathew Gladstein. "The Returns and Risks of Alternative Call Option Portfolio Investment Strategies," *Journal of Business*, Vol. 51, No. 2, 1978.

Micklethwait, J., & Wooldridge, A. *The Witch Doctors: Making Sense of the Management Gurus*. Random House/Times Business, 1996.

Miles, M. B., and A. M. Huberman, *An Expanded Source Book: Qualitative Data Analysis*. Newbury Park, CA: Sage Publications.

Miller, Merton H. "Behavioral Rationality in Finance," *Midland Corporate Finance Journal* (now *Journal of Applied Corporate Finance*), vol. 4, no. 4 (winter 1987), pp. 6–15.

Millhauser, Steven, *Martin Dressler, The Tale of an American Dreamer*. New York: Vintage Books, 1996.

Moustakas, C. (1990). *Heuristic Research: Design, Methodology, and Applications*. Thousand Oaks, CA: Sage Publications.

Nevins, Mark David, and Stephen A. Stumpf. "21st Century Leadership: Redefining Management Education." *Strategy and Business*, Vol. 4, 1999.

O'Shea, J., and C. Madigan. *Dangerous Company: The Consulting Powerhouses and the Businesses They Save and Ruin*. Random House/Times Business, 1997.

Pasmore, William A., and Ronald E. Purser, "Designing Work Systems for Knowledge Workers." *Journal for Quality & Participation*, Vol. 16, no. 4, 1993, pp. 78–84.

Patton, M. Q. (1990). *Qualitative Evaluation and Research Methods* (2nd Edition). Newbury, Park, CA: Sage Publications.

Pilipovic, Dragana, *Energy Risk: Valuing and Managing Energy Derivatives*. New York: McGraw-Hill, 1998.

Pinault, Lewis. *Consulting Demons: Inside the Unscrupulous World of Global Corporate Consulting*. New York: HarperBusiness, 2000.

Popcorn, Faith. *The Popcorn Report*. New York: HarperBusiness Publishing, 1992.

Raiffa, Howard. *Decision Analysis: Introductory Lectures on Choice Under Uncertainty*. New York: McGraw-Hill, 1968.

Rasiel, Ethan M. *The McKinsey Way*. New York: McGraw-Hill, 1999.

Schaffer, Robert H. *High Impact Consulting*. San Francisco: Jossey-Bass Publishers, 1997.

Shenson, Howard, and Ted Nicholas. *The Complete Guide to Consulting Success*. Denver, CO: UpStart Publishing, 1997.

Stone, Douglas, Bruce Patton, and Sheila Heen. *Difficult Conversations: How to Discuss What Matters Most*. New York: Penguin Books, 1999.

Strauss, A. L. (1987). *Qualitative Analysis for Social Science*. Cambridge, England: Cambridge University Press.

Taylor, S. J., and R. Bogdan. *Introduction to Qualitative Research Methods* (2nd Edition). New York: John Wiley & Sons, 1984.

Thomsett, Michael C. *The Little Black Book of Project Management*. New York: AMACOM, 1990.

Tichy, Noel M. *The Leadership Engine*. HarperBusiness, 2002.

Tufte, Edward. *The Visual Display of Quantitative Information*. Cheshire, CT: Graphic Press, 2001.

Tversky, Amos, and Daniel Kahneman. "The Framing of Decisions and the Psychology of Choice." *Science*, Vol. 211, 1981, pp. 453–458.

Vault.Com: *www.thevault.com*

Wet Feet Press: *www.wetfeet.com*

Wharton MBA Consulting Club. *The Wharton MBA Case Interview Study Guide: Volume I*. Wet Feet Press, 1997.

Yin, R. K. (1984). *Case Study Research: Design and Methods* (2nd Edition) Thousand Oaks, CA: Sage Publications.

Zelazny, Gene. *Say It With Charts: The Executive's Guide to Visual Communication*. New York: McGraw-Hill, 2001.

Index

Page number followed by f indicates figure.